I0822046

KINGDOM in the WEST

The Mormons and the American Frontier

Will Bagley, series editor

VOLUME 14

Dale L. Morgan at 24, from a portrait taken in 1938 or 1939, shortly after joining the staff of the Utah Historical Records Survey.

Dale Morgan on the Mormons

Collected Works
Part 1, 1939–1951

Edited, with introductions, by
Richard L. Saunders

Foreword by
Will Bagley

THE ARTHUR H. CLARK COMPANY
An imprint of the University of Oklahoma Press
Norman, Oklahoma
2012

Library of Congress Cataloging-in-Publication Data
L. (Dale Lowell), 1914–1971.
Dale Morgan on the Mormons : collected works / edited, with introductions, by Richard L. Saunders ; foreword by Will Bagley.
p. cm. — (Kingdom in the West series v. 14)
Includes bibliographical references and index.
ISBN 978-0-87062-416-2 (hardcover : alk. paper) 1. Church of Jesus Christ of Latter-Day Saints—History. 2. Mormon Church—History. 3. Church of Jesus Christ of Latter-Day Saints—Bibliographies. 4. Mormon Church—Bibliographies. I. Saunders, Richard L., 1963– II. Title.
BX8611.M663 2012
289.309—dc23

2012013677

The paper in this book meets the guidelines for permanence and durability of the Committee on Production Guidelines for Book Longevity of the Council on Library Resources, Inc. ∞

Published by the University of Oklahoma Press, Norman, Publishing Division of the University.
Manufactured in the U.S.A.

1 2 3 4 5 6 7 8 9 10

Contents

Illustrations

Foreword

Todd Berens was a Marine Corps veteran of Chosin Reservoir and graduate student at California State College Fullerton who was writing a master's thesis about John C. Frémont's maps. In December 1965, he wrote to his friend Dale L. Morgan to ask how our mutual scholarly hero would answer the philosophical question, "What is history?" Perhaps history was "the missing link that binds the individual to that chain of human experience which transcends time and space to give man his identity," Berens suggested. The question took Morgan "somewhat by surprise. They say that poets are entitled to whatever readers can get out of their poems, and I suppose the same applies to historians. But I have never been much concerned with a philosophy of history as such." Morgan was "more interested in practical questions, straightening out the enormous distortions of the record that I have found on every hand; and beyond that, being continuously interested in the causes that produce certain effects, and the effects that are produced by certain causes." Historians, he felt, had trouble enough with such fundamentals, "to say nothing of wrestling with large abstractions." This philosophically positivistic, empirical, and entirely naturalistic historian, who wrote human history entirely from a human perspective, then waxed as philosophical as his great-grandfather, Mormon apostle Orson Pratt. For Morgan, " 'history' is not limited to human experience as such. Why scrub oaks grow in one place or another, or what became of the Pleistocene fauna, or for that matter, how the universe was put together, is all 'history' to me." He observed, "So far as we know, only human minds concern themselves with these matters, but I am also prepared to accept the possibility of non-human intelligence being found in the universe somewhere, sometime, which would do away with the human referent entirely, and establish history as such independent of the human minds that are now cognizant of it."[1]

Dale Morgan's legacy made him "one of the foundational figures in the historiography of the American West." His work deeply influenced the new perspectives on life in the American borderlands that a new generation would introduce during what historian Gary Topping has called the "reconstruction of western history." To describe Morgan as a prodigious researcher and writer, noted his devoted disciple Harold Schindler, was an understatement. "Stricken as a youngster with meningitis, which robbed him of his hearing, he was fated to live in a silent world, alone with his thoughts and ambitions. His concentration was total; his ability to reason through the most difficult and complex array of data was immense." Morgan spent much of World War II at the National Archives, transcribing virtually every mention of Latter Day Saints, the continental fur trade, and overland trails in federal records and reports. "As a measure of Morgan's astonishing work ethic," Schindler pointed to the "thousands of pages of typescript" from every article about Utah, the Mormons, and the West in the Library of Congress's vast newspapers file, which "permitted him to write on virtually every aspect of western history with authority far and above that of any other scholar." Not everyone might agree with Hal's exalted tribute, but Morgan's contribution to western history can be measured by his appearance in the acknowledgments of dozens, perhaps hundreds, of the most important studies of his time. Morgan "put every researcher and writer on both the Mormons and the Far West since him in his debt because of his wide-ranging industry and his fabled generosity," wrote his friend William Mulder.[2]

Morgan died on 30 March 30, 1971, shortly before his fifty-seventh birthday, far too young. He left behind twenty original books and masterfully edited documentary works, plus nearly fifty articles and other contributions. His body was cremated at his request, and his ashes lie beneath a large tulip poplar overlooking the Potomac. His friend Wallace Stegner mourned the loss of a great scholar and "so fine and decent and generous and long-suffering a man."

---

[1]Dale L. Morgan to Todd I. Berens, 10 December 1965.

[2]Gary Topping, *Utah Historians and the Reconstruction of Western History* (Norman: University of Oklahoma Press, 2003); Roderick Korns and Dale L. Morgan, eds., *West from Fort Bridger: The Pioneering of Immigrant Trails across Utah, 1846–1850*, rev. and updated by Will Bagley and Harold Schindler (Logan: Utah State University Press, 1994), ix; John Phillip Walker, ed., *Dale Morgan on Early Mormonism: Correspondence and a New History* (Salt Lake City: Signature Books, 1986), 1.

Juanita Brooks said, "I have long since ceased trying to figure out the why's of the Universe. I can only accept these tragedies with what grace I can muster."[3]

Richard L. Saunders, editor of *Shoshonean Peoples and the Overland Trail*, a collection of Morgan's articles, and *Eloquence from a Silent World: A Descriptive Bibliography of the Published Writings of Dale L. Morgan*, may know more about the historian and his career than anyone alive. No one is better acquainted with Morgan's literary legacy than Saunders. He has surveyed all 76 boxes and 27 cartons—103 cubic feet of the Dale L. Morgan Papers at the Bancroft Library, which, at Hal Schindler's prompting, Gregory C. Thompson, director of Special Collections at the University of Utah's Marriott Library, helped process and microfilm. I have long wanted to include a "Morgan on the Mormons" volume in the Kingdom in the West series: the title appeared in 1999 on a list of forthcoming volumes, "in hopes it would encourage Richard Saunders to sign up to do it." He seemed to support the idea but he was "all tied up" at the time "and didn't take the bait."[4] So I was delighted when Robert A. Clark suggested incorporating Saunders's two-volume study of Morgan's work on the Mormons in the series.

Morgan considered his documentary histories of the fur trade and the overland trail his masterworks—they established his reputation and made irreplaceable contributions to our understanding of the American West. Two of them, *The West of William Ashley* and *Overland in 1846*, endure as invaluable classic studies. Scholars occasionally deprecate documentary editing as "a lesser and somehow inferior" work, as Brigham D. Madsen observed, "but I have found the research and writing involved to be just as demanding as conceiving and writing an original product."[5] Morgan dramatically influenced the creation of Fawn Brodie's *No Man Knows My History* and Juanita Brooks's *The Mountain Meadows Massacre*, the two most important books written about Mormonism in the first half of the twentieth century, but he never published anything on the Latter Day Saints as remotely significant as these pathbreaking works. The multi-volume study of Mormonism he hoped would be his masterpiece, along with a half-dozen documentary studies and a narrative history of the fur trade, died with him. This gap in his legacy appears puzzling: why did he leave the glory and the peril of writing such

[3]Walker, ed., *Dale Morgan on Early Mormonism*, 21.

[4]Bagley, e-mail to John Needham, 3 January 2001.

[5]Brigham D. Madsen, *The Craft of History: A Personal View* (Salt Lake City: The Utah Westerners, 1995), 15.

controversial books to his two brave friends? Was it a failure of courage that left only manuscripts to challenge the sacred history of his native faith? I came to a different conclusion while reading his correspondence: it was not cowardice but compassion and kindness that diverted him from writing his definitive history of the Mormons. Dale's closest relations remained devout Latter Day Saints, but after his mother's death in 1969, he was hoping "to clean up five or six more books in 1970 to clear the decks for (a) my big fur trade history; and (b) the Mormon history."[6]

I had long thought Morgan's published canon refuted Richard Saunders's conclusion that Morgan wanted to be remembered as the scholar who mastered and encompassed the historical puzzle of Mormonism. My assumption was wrong and Richard is right. No one understands the twists, turns, and box canyons of Morgan's career better than he does. Saunders's study of Morgan and the Mormons incorporates insights about a complicated and difficult career only someone as deeply familiar with the historian's work, immense correspondence, and papers as Richard could propose. Morgan's deeply researched and engagingly written publications, Saunders notes, did not represent the subjects he most wanted to address: his letters to his closest associates reveal that he tried in vain to return to his study of the Mormons throughout his career. "Somehow time keeps squeezing us along the path we must go," Dale complained to Fawn Brodie in 1957.[7]

I take a less worshipful view of Dale Morgan than did Hal Schindler but feel Morgan spent more time wrestling with abstractions and was a better interpretive historian than his critics (or Morgan himself) acknowledged. "Morgan conceived historical writing to be merely establishing an accurate factual record rather than probing for the larger significance of his materials," Gary Topping observed: his answer to the question "What is history?" makes clear that Morgan might agree the criticism was accurate. But a review of Morgan's published correspondence provides countless examples of how intensely and often he sought to grasp the deep meaning in the vast collection of facts he had marshaled in his remarkable mind. Certainly no one has matched his ability to correlate the interconnected stories of the Indian Nations, the fur trade, the Mormon frontier, overland emigration, government explorations and surveys, the gold rush, and California and the West better than Dale Morgan.

[6]Morgan to Fawn Brodie, 24 December 1969, in Walker, ed., *Dale Morgan on Early Mormonism*, 211.

[7]Morgan to Fawn Brodie, 19 September 1957, in ibid., 111.

Morgan recognized and acknowledged his limitations. His interpretive technique was to *show* rather than *tell*—or, heaven forbid, pontificate. Beyond his mastery of historical minutia, Morgan applied his gift for analyzing the implications of all those facts in extraordinary ways. Morgan's primary concern was always with "the gathering of facts, and in particular, facts from the sources. It is my experience that if you gather enough facts, and organize them properly, they provide their own conclusions." He felt "the pattern of fact" he had gathered about the Deseret alphabet, published in this volume for the first time, "was sufficient almost to say everything that needed to be said about the Alphabet."[8]

Four days before the attack on Pearl Harbor, he shared his research on the movement's orthographic reforms from his "tons of miscellaneous notes on the Mormons" with Wallace Stegner. Morgan found "the singularly complete parallels in Mormon autocracy and modern totalitarianism" described in Stegner's draft of *Mormon Country* to be interesting and amusing, but the comparison was dangerous, Morgan advised his former advisor. He must give due weight to the dynamics of the Mormon encounter with "the conditioning influence of the American frontier," Dale warned, "otherwise the parallels become confusing and misleading." Both men were dealing with a movement absorbed on one hand with "the psychology of dispossession; on the other there is a frontal attack by a society upon an environment. The whole Mormon experience with the land must be taken into consideration in any dissection of Mormon society."[9] As his proto-environmental analysis reveals, Morgan's interpretations were subtle: his published works show more concern for writing good prose and establishing a solid factual foundation for his arguments than with reinterpreting historiography. Would formal academic training have helped Morgan address and explain broader issues, or would such a background have had unpredictable effects on his work? Any answer is speculative. "If you'd have gotten a Ph.D.," Martin Ridge advised when I suggested formal advanced studies might have made me a better historian, "they'd have beaten whatever writing talent you have right out of you."

That said, two examples show Morgan could be a formidable and innovative interpreter of the Mormon past. "Dear Wally," as Morgan's addressed his former professor, had already embraced an insight Dale expressed in 1940 in

[8]Morgan to S. A. Burgess, 26 April 1943, in ibid., 45.

[9]Morgan to Dear Wally, 3 December 1941, Wallace Earle Stegner Papers, Ms0676, Special Collections, Marriott Library, University of Utah.

his still-definitive study of the State of Deseret: while individual enterprise reigned everywhere in the West but in Mormon country, the Latter-day Saints came as "a closely integrated group" whose religious mission and varied persecutions gave "them an extraordinary group-consciousness. They came to the Rocky Mountains with a motive nowhere else displayed in the history of the western frontier. They came as a great group in flight from an antagonistic society, a group in search of the peace and social freedom isolation could confer. They came with a remarkable conception of social responsibility and with a full recognition and acceptance of a ruling authority which was at once political and ecclesiastical."[10] This key insight into the central significance of the gathering to Zion unlocks a puzzle that has long confounded historians of Mormonism, including this one.

Over time Morgan refined his view of the role of persecution in Mormon history. He chided Bernard DeVoto for his insistence that Joseph Smith was a "paranoid reaction type," noting DeVoto's definition was broad enough to encompass Babe Ruth, Gypsy Rose Lee, General Eisenhower, Franklin D. Roosevelt, and for good measure Morgan and DeVoto themselves. Morgan granted that persecution was "a constant theme in Mormon history, and some of it is real. But of that which is not real, how much stems from abnormal psychology and how much of it was purposive propaganda?" History did not support the prophet's stories of persecution while translating the Book of Mormon, and Morgan even doubted that Smith himself actually felt persecuted. "A lot of Joseph's history is retrospective; it is an instrument in the furtherance of specifically evolved purposes. When he came to dictate his history, the kind of history he needed to have was the history of a prophet of the living God." Persecution became "not only a name for his troubles but a name of force to his followers."[11]

Such insights came from a historian who in his youth had been president of his Deacons quorum. Morgan felt that having once been a dutiful Latter-day Saint gave him an emotional understanding of Mormonism. His personal beliefs went through a decade-long "period of adjustment" after he lost his hearing. By the time he graduated from the University of Utah, he "could no longer believe the things I had formerly believed, but made the transition without bitterness, as some persons I know have not been so fortunate in accomplishing." Yet his published writings failed to appreciate the animating

[10]Morgan, "The State of Deseret," 68.

[11]Morgan to Bernard DeVoto, 20 December 1945, in Walker, ed., *Morgan on Early Mormonism*, 98.

force of religion and belief in pioneer Utah, and Morgan himself failed to understand was how disorienting and threatening many Mormons, even the faith's scholars, found his naturalistic view of historical events. He did "not expect that the average Mormon will accept in its entirety the evaluation of Mormon history that I shall make, but I do expect that he will acknowledge my integrity within what he regards as the limitations of my understanding, or point of view," he wrote to S. A. Burgess, a Reorganized Latter Day Saint historian. On that basis he expected to "get along very equably, and we may find that my interpretation of Mormon history will not, after all do such violence to Mormon ideas of that history." Morgan's hope reflected a remarkable naiveté about his own culture—as Gary Topping observed, the unfinished fragments of his history of the Mormons "could hardly have elicited anything *but* objection from faithful Mormon readers."[12] "It all boils down finally to that old philosophical conundrum, 'What is Truth?' " Morgan wrote Juanita Brooks. "There is no absolute or final definition of truth. It has emotional values for some people, intellectual values for others." Confusion resulted when "people try to square their emotional truths with the intellect, while their intellectual truths they try to invest with emotional meanings."[13]

This first volume of *Dale Morgan on the Mormons* traces the evolution of a young historian's understanding of the Latter Day Saint experience in the American West. It begins with Morgan's historical overview in *Utah: A Guide to the State* and ends with his intriguing analyses of the papers of Oliver Olney and James Strang for Edward Eberstadt. It presents for the first time Morgan's unpublished manuscripts on the Kingdom of God and Council of Fifty, the Deseret alphabet, and the Missouri origins of the Danite legend. These studies reveal the swift and sweeping expansion of Morgan's historical knowledge and reflect his desperate struggle to patch together an income. Saunders has integrated his own considerable experience as an archivist and teacher to approach his subject in creative ways: consider his innovative description of a bygone (if not very bygone) age when duplicating technology relied on expensive cameras and film or time-consuming manual typewriters and carbon paper. As an experienced bibliographer himself, no one is better qualified to examine Morgan's legacy of pathbreaking Mormon bibliographies. As a dedicated research historian, no one has acquired such a comprehensive and sympathetic understanding of Morgan's difficult career as Richard L. Saunders.

[12]Ibid., 43; Topping, *Utah Historians*, 145.

[13]Morgan to Brooks, January 1945, in Walker, ed., *Dale Morgan on Early Mormonism*, 85–86.

When I began researching and writing a quarter-century ago, the history of the American West still commanded a broad popular audience. The historians who taught me the craft almost universally had the highest regard for Dale Morgan and his legacy—some of them would have elevated him to sainthood if it had been in their power. Scholars such as Chad J. Flake and Brigham D. Madsen built on the foundations that Morgan had laid, with his massive research files and transcriptions to complete his comprehensive bibliography of Mormonism's first century and publish his transcriptions of the journals of Captain Howard Stansbury's topographical expedition to Utah. For several years during the 1990s, reprints of Morgan's classic trail studies were the best-sellers at Nebraska and Utah State university presses. As the New Western History movement becomes the Old Western History, the aging revolution resembles the hidebound and elitist profession it set out to replace. Academic history seems focused (if not obsessed) with narrower and narrower debates about whether its monocular monographs should concentrate on gender or race or post-colonial history with little regard for the facts, which do not exist—let alone matter. Documentary histories have fallen so far out of fashion that the organ of the Western Historical Association no longer reviews them.

Historical trendsetters may have largely forgotten Dale Morgan, but his work can still make a difference—its enduring reliability reflected in its use by scholars as diverse as Howard R. Lamar, Al Hurtado, Susan Lee Johnson, and Candy Moulton reflect his enduring reliability. Years ago a gifted young Western Shoshone scholar working on violence in the early American West asked for advice about where to go to find out what the first Americans to enter the Great Basin knew and thought about its Native peoples. Later, as a professor of history at Yale University and winner of the Frederick Jackson Turner Award and the Robert M. Utley Award, Ned Blackhawk told a class on the borderlands how he had found the answers to his many questions in Morgan's *The West of William Ashley*. Readers of Richard Saunders's study of Morgan on the Mormons might agree that whatever fads or fashions might overtake our attempts to understand the American West and frontier Mormonism, Dale L. Morgan matters after all.

WILL BAGLEY
Salt Lake City

Preface and Acknowledgments

Annually I pass yet another double-digit anniversary of telling people I am at work on a Dale Morgan biography. It was not conceived as a project to be measured in decades. For twenty years I have peered sporadically into film readers, conducted interviews with people who knew or worked with Dale, compiled notes, and drafted chapters. After each day's or week's energetic effort, no matter how I approached the life and work of this noted scholar of the early American West, some element of the topic inevitably circled back to his work involving the Mormons. Following the publication of *Shoshonean Peoples and the Overland Trails: Frontiers of the Utah Superintendency of Indian Affairs, 1849–1869* (Logan: Utah State Univ. Press, 2007), I finally admitted to myself that I was really nowhere near completing my long biography project. As I sifted through notes and files, ready to hew a few more strokes on the project, I suddenly realized a biography would be much stronger if a careful, focused study of Morgan's work with the Latter Day Saints was completed first. After nearly two decades studying Morgan and his work in detail, I feel that his work on the Restoration set the boundaries of Morgan's intellectual approach to history and abilities as a researcher and writer. The Mormons had been the magnet which attracted him to history in the first place, it was the realm in which his approach to history and historical method solidified, and Mormonism was a subject to which he tried vainly to return throughout his career. The thought of a focused study on Morgan's relationship with LDS history was attractive for a biographer. Having a book specifically on the topic would allow me to focus on the defining themes of his early life and nearly half of his writing career. A separate publication would allow defining influences to be teased out and treated with greater detail, which frees the biography—which *will* come at some point, I promise—to address him as a whole person and not become topically lopsided or mis-focused.

In his Foreword, Will Bagley cites Dale's revealing 1965 letter to Todd Berens. Morgan occasionally addressed a correspondent with similar comments about the nature of history and historians, including S. A. Burgess, Leonard Arrington, Fawn Brodie, Juanita Brooks, and a few others. Mostly he wrote about the facts of history and the process and results of research. From his earliest experience in the Historical Records Survey to the end of his life, Dale Morgan remained convinced that facts existed independent of perception; all that was required to uncover *the* story was to order facts correctly, and create a complete picture—to have truth. But determining relevant facts of history is a bit like plotting a child's dot-to-dot sheet with unnumbered points: there is no way to tell if dots were missed, or if there are some that don't belong to the image, or if the picture is upside down. The analogy is imperfect, of course; history remains a much more complex undertaking, but the point (sans pun) remains valid. Morgan unknowingly adopted the perspective of Lord Acton and his fellow nineteenth-century empiricists in seeking a cumulative body of unambiguous evidence that could resolve any dispute. E. H. Carr reminded us that there is a difference between a fact of history and a historical fact. Life's unfolding complexity leaves for us facts of history, but the writing of history creates historical facts. "Status as a historical fact will turn on a question of interpretation. This element of interpretation enters into every fact of history."[1]

A writer must necessarily weigh and include or set aside facts by some standard of relevance—that is, by a standard of value. Writing history necessarily involves meaning and interpretive assumptions and has its philosophers, though perhaps not those with names like Aristotle, Neitzsche, Locke, and the like. History may not involve morals, one may write without a persuasive agenda, but denying that one has a philosophy becomes an act of staking out a point of view—of adopting a philosophy. Like many who decry bias or agenda in others while overlooking their own, and get upset if

[1]Edward Hallett Carr, "The Historian and His Facts," *What Is History?* (New York: Alfred A. Knopf, 1962), 11. Carr's is easily the most accessible book on the subject for readers, but historians of all stripes and variety assert essentially the same conclusion (maybe excepting materialists like Marx and company); I encourage trying a subject search under "History Philosophy" in an academic library catalogue.

tagged about their assumptions, Morgan missed the philosophy that held his work together.

Dale Morgan and others dismiss graduate education as a poor tool for writers of history. That may be, but grad school also helps one identify the unquestioned assumptions in their point of view. My goal for this compilation is not to show that Morgan was somehow wrong about the Mormons or to defend my faith. I expended time and effort on this particular collection specifically to show how Dale Morgan developed his approach to historical sources and point of view—his philosophy of history—and to illustrate the results as they developed through the defining years and in the defining subject of his career. Could that process have unfolded differently? Certainly. However, it did not. I emphasize point of view and philosophy in these pages because Morgan so assiduously denied having either. In terms of Mormonism, Morgan's point of view involved two key elements: an insistence on demonstrable and interconnected evidence (primary source material) taken at face value, and a personal faith in naturalism (that is to say, a supramortal reality did not exist; therefore revelation could not happen). If one aspires to write the social history of a denomination, such a point of view will be tremendously influential about what documentary evidence is accepted as relevant and the way sources will be viewed. It will also largely determine what can be drawn from sources as well.

Dale L. Morgan (1914–1971) is still cited as one of the foundational figures in the historiography of the American West. His factual knowledge of trans-Mississippi exploration and travel was very nearly encyclopedic. Still, no reader should assume that the masterful Dale Morgan was capable of putting a final, definitive explanatory nail into the coffin resolving overland-trail chronology or fur-trade geography. The same observation is equally true of Morgan's work with Mormon history, but the list would include *Book of Mormon* origins, Joseph Smith's character, or even the Emmett company's story. The human story is organic. The field of Mormon studies has grown far beyond what Morgan had been familiar with. Dale Morgan's work was that of a historiographic pioneer. These two volumes collect the scattered shards of Morgan's work on Mormonism's broad cultural and religious tradition. It includes the complete and incomplete, the published and unpublished. As objects of study, a scholar's published works provide polished windows into his thinking and perspective. Book reviews are included because they reveal point of view in ways that focused studies themselves do not. Unpublished and often incomplete manuscripts are presented because they represent new contributions to the field and help illustrate his general approach to history and to the culture he set out to circumscribe.

There are, however, a number of completed writings touching on historical Mormonism that this compilation does not include. One is the chapters of *The Great Salt Lake* (Indianapolis: Bobbs-Merrill, 1947) that deal with the church or its members. In that study the saints are woven so inextricably with the book's larger narrative that there is no meaningful way to extract them. Fortunately the volume has been reprinted repeatedly. *The State of Deseret* (1940) is likewise reluctantly omitted since it is widely available both in its original periodical form and in the 1987 edition by Utah State University Press. This collection likewise does not include his eight or nine varied introductions to county-records inventories for the Utah Historical Records Survey (only five of which were published), nor "The Constitutions of Deseret and Utah, 1849–1887," "The Changing Face of Salt Lake City," or *A History of Ogden* (Ogden, Utah: Ogden City Commission, 1940), all of which are defining early works of general regional history rather than substantively religious studies. It passes over three draft descriptions of Temple Square and the Beehive and Lion houses that were intended for tourism publications. It *does* include the brief introduction but does not include the checklist entries that became *A Mormon Bibliography, 1830–1930* (Salt Lake City: University of Utah Press, 1978) in a later generation and under other hands. It does not include the pensive introduction to *Utah: A Guide to the State* (Hastings House, 1940), or a number of entries authored for the *Encyclopedia Americana* and *Encyclopedia Britannica* in the mid 1960s. Finally, it does not include, except cited occasionally in notes, his voluminous correspondence. A short selection of the same was made in *Dale Morgan on Early Mormonism* (Salt Lake City: Signature Books, 1986), but the sheer scope and breadth of topics among his private writing makes any thematic presentation of Morgan correspondence a badly imperfect collection.

Because this is a volume of collected works by a single author, the introductory essays focus rather more heavily on the biographical setting for his works and on the limits of his approach to history than is often the case in an edited compilation. I feel this is necessary, for in most cases his major published works were affected—constructively or not—by the attention he gave to his other work, and the completion (or incompletion) of each in turn was influenced by larger circumstances. In the process I hope my introductory matter will help illustrate how little purpose or method Dale paid (or was able to pay, perhaps) toward building his scholarly career. It did not unfold so much as it careened between opportunities.

Besides setting boundaries to the topic, the other purpose of a preface is to thank the folks who help an author along the way. Thus, thanks are extended to the generous people who contributed to the compilation or production of this volume, particularly Gary Topping and Daniel Howe (Maurice Howe's oldest son and an emeritus professor of history at the University of California–Los Angeles) for criticism and insight. Bob Clark took a risk on these volumes, and series editor Will Bagley tried strenuously to keep me honest. A cadre of ever-helpful fellow librarians have assisted with running facts or citations to ground and with other research details, including Ann Buttars, Larry Draper, Bill Slaughter, and Russ Taylor. Permission to reissue Morgan's work has come from the respective publishers noted at the beginning of each entry, and from the Bancroft Library, the Yale Collection of Western Americana at the Beinecke Rare Book and Manuscript Library, and the late James S. Morgan for the previously unpublished material. Peter Hanff and Jack Von Euw of the Bancroft Library hosted me in 2009 for a research foray under an exceedingly unusual and generous arrangement.

Some debts are never payable in full. To my much better half, Carrie, belongs the lioness's share of gratitude, and to Nathan, Missy, R. Dan, and Rebecca am I grateful for generous release time from fatherhood. David, Heidi, Stephen, and AnnMarie count too, but they are now excitedly building lives of their own. Thanks to all y'all—the family has always gotten the final drop of recognition in a preface when they deserve the cream off the top.

Editorial Procedures

I intend this work chiefly to present Dale Morgan's texts to a new generation of scholars, rather than as a vehicle to discuss or critique his work. Some contextual criticism is merited, particularly in a collection of this sort, and especially as the documents presented here exist in a wide variety of states, from rough manuscripts to published texts. Rather than attempt to produce textual facsimiles—maintaining the strikethroughs, insertions, and lacunae in print—I have instead collocated and integrated the author's changes to produce clear, readable texts representing his latest stage of thinking, or at least his latest extant revision. Morgan's published works have been reproduced from the typeset copy of the respective publications where possible and been checked against his own corrected copies of the publication. This compilation also provides scholars with the first widely available access to key but unpublished studies predating *The Mormons.* For unpublished work, the typed (and usually corrected) manuscript of each piece in Morgan's papers has provided a basic text. Copyedited corrections, additions, and deletions made by the author are reflected in the printed text without notice, unless a comment on a conflict is necessary for historical or transcriptional clarity. In a few locations, as in the untitled study on the Kingdom of God, the author left citations blank, doubtlessly intending to complete the references during revisions. Citations to quoted source material have been supplied or completed when the origin is clear, although my contribution always appears in brackets. Inserted editorial notes are made in the same way, marked by typographic symbols to preserve Morgan's original note numbering. Very few spelling corrections have been required and have been made without notice, except for names. Texts have remained essentially as Morgan himself saw them into publication or last handled them. Dates in the notes, however, have been converted to meet the publisher's style. All citations to correspondence are to letters in the Dale L. Morgan papers at the Bancroft Library (BANC MSS 71/161c) and are drawn from the microfilm version of his papers, unless a different location is specifically noted.

And now for a few words about the editorial process, curious word usages, and punctuational oddities you will encounter. First and foremost, in editing these various pieces—some previously published and others merely working drafts in varying stages of completion—published texts are preferred over an extant manuscript, and the latest discernible form of a manuscript is preferred over earlier versions, except as noted. Punctuation practices are updated somewhat (pulling commas and periods inside closing quotes, for instance). I have also made some substitutions. An editor traditionally interposes and sets off his insertions in brackets, [ ], so the brackets around Morgan's own editorial insertions in his notes and elsewhere have been uniformly replaced with braces, { }, to maintain editorial clarity. His parentheses, ( ), however, remain parentheses.

Second, the arcane Latin note forms common to his time are standardized to modern conventions, and all of Morgan's original citations (including incomplete ones) are filled out with appropriate detail. For some reason he consistently dropped publisher names from his notes; that valuable element is inserted editorially without indication. Dale was a stickler for up-to-the-minute detail and I feel he would heartily approve the improvement. Unless otherwise noted, his text in the notes themselves have been left as-is, except for date forms as noted above. New notes supplied by the editor are indicated by characters (asterisks, daggers, etc.) to distinguish them from Morgan's numbered ones. This necessitated an editorial imposition in Chapter 7 of *The Mormons* (vol. 2). Occasionally some clearly noted re-numbering was required; and obviously notes in the editor's introductory material clearly are not Dale's, despite being numbered. Since many items included here were unpublished and are often incomplete, I insert a short underscore as a place marker for the "holes" he typically left as blank lines or empty space for later completion. When the source is clear and data can be completed, I have done so, but only by setting off my addition in brackets, as noted above.

Third, until the 1870s it was common to see the name of the church punctuated incorrectly in print—as *Latter Day Saints* rather than *Latter-day Saints*—even in official publications, reflecting the grammatical sophistication of the nineteenth century. The "Utah Mormons" eventually updated and standardized the spelling they used, while many of the other post-1844 sects maintained the initial spelling through their existence. Thus, in the introductions and editorial material I employ the earliest name form of *Latter Day Saints* when discussing Mormonism's broadest religious heritage. The spelling maintained by the Utah branch, punctuated with a hyphen and lower case *d*, is used when discussing that specific branch of the Restoration. Similarly, to describe an individual as an *-ite* or their church as *-ites* and their beliefs as an *-ism* was once commonplace in LDS history, as in "Strangite" or "Josephite" or "Brighamite" (and even earlier, "Mormonite"). This practice was adopted among Restoration groups by speakers and pamphleteers after 1844 as a means of dismissing an opponent's claim to the Restoration's social or sacred authority. "If you suffer the Spirit of the Lord to leave your hearts," said George A. Smith as early as 1853, "and the devil comes along and finds an empty house, he then enters in, and inasmuch as we are under transgression, he lays his hand upon us, saying, 'You shall be my tool for me to work with, you have transgressed the laws of God, and my spirit shall lead you about; you shall go into Gladdenism, to this and that ism.'"[1] Most of the intended barbs had blunted and passed into common usage at the time Morgan wrote, but the practice was beginning to fall out of fashion in the 1980s when I wrote my master's thesis on Francis Gladden Bishop and the religious heritage of the "Gladdenites." Irrespective of personal beliefs, using *-ite* and *-ism* imposes a value judgment that should not be made historically, so in the spirit of the Golden Rule, I drop the *-ite(s)* suffix where an editor can in favor of using name and affiliation directly.

Fourth, in keeping with the public name change accepted by the Reorganized Church of Jesus Christ of Latter Day Saints in 2000, "Community of Christ" is substituted throughout the notes as appropriate, although always in editorial brackets. The name or abbreviation "RLDS" remains in place in when used in Morgan's texts.

Fifth, I have opted to mention more recent scholarship only occasionally. Literally hundreds of works have grown from the soil of Restoration studies since Morgan's time, and the field is annually producing new crops, introducing a new challenge for editing older works. Only occasionally for this anthology do I update his notes with citations to more recent, more

[1]George A. Smith, 16 February 1853, *Journal of Discourses,* 2: 437.

complete, supportive, or contradictory research, and instead direct readers toward bibliographic resources like Steven L. Shields, *The Latter Day Saint Churches: An Annotated Bibliography* (New York: Garland Press, 1987), and James B. Allen, *Studies in Mormon History, 1830–1997: An Indexed Bibliography* (Urbana: University of Illinois Press, c. 2000). For newer material, you are on your own in perusing library holdings and journal articles (which can easily be done electronically these days). Fortunately, institutional libraries with broad and deep Latter Day Saint holdings now exist, as does inter-library-loan capability, as they hardly did in Morgan's time.

Dale Morgan and the Latter Day Saints
An Introduction

The volume(s) you hold, which collect and make widely available for the first time Dale L. Morgan's writings about the Latter Day Saint heritage, also provide a useful key to understanding an important and influential writer and his broader career. Collectively these works are evidence of the reason that the historical studies he did complete took on the physical and stylistic forms he gave them, forms that both freed and shackled his time, attention, and even ability as an historian. After two decades studying Morgan and his work in detail, I feel comfortable asserting that his work on the Restoration set the boundaries of Morgan's broader intellectual approach to history in general. Dale Morgan became a great writer about Western trails and the fur trade in part because he had learned important lessons while working on the history of the Mormons. At the same time, his work on the Mormons exemplifies a broad conflict between differing approaches to history, and to religious history particularly.

Students and book collectors of Western Americana typically express skepticism if I mention that Morgan himself did not think highly about most of his published output. Surely not, they tell me, perhaps wondering quietly to themselves if the self-proclaimed biographer really understands the subject. But the truth is there, buried in his mountainous correspondence: few of Morgan's copiously researched and engagingly written articles, books, and maps represented topics he really *wanted* to work on. While he is rightly remembered as a historian of the overland trail, of the American fur trade, and less often of California, he wanted to be remembered as the writer who circumscribed Mormonism. His writing priorities shifted with the teetering and ever-growing weight of opportunity and demands. He expended thousands of research hours and hundreds of hours writing and editing, but until retiring from the Bancroft Library in 1970 at age 56, work on the Mormons was consistently the single topic for which he mentioned *wanting* to be remembered. Sadly, choices—many of them dictated by the circumstances of a moment—and a drive for absolute inclusivity wrecked his chances to complete any of his centerpiece Mormon studies at all.

Despite his many published works (twenty original books or carefully edited works, nearly fifty articles and contributions), he personally considered only two, *Overland in 1846* and *The West of William H. Ashley,* both published in 1964, to be works of substance on a scale and quality for which he wished to be remembered. Within two years of its publication he was so disgusted with *Jedediah Smith and the Opening of the West*—fifty years later still a standard text in the field—that he refused to authorize reprints and was furious when paperback rights were sold to the University of Nebraska Press, which has kept it in print continuously since 1968. As proud as Dale Morgan was of *Ashley* and *Overland in 1846,* even those works occupied second rank in his estimation. The works which *he* named preeminent among his career projects were three, none of which were ever completed. Had the colorectal cancer which felled him been held off long enough to allow sufficient time to complete his masterworks, I am not sure he would have, anyway. I *am* certain that given his record and work habits, his attention would have remained as distracted by tangential opportunities as it ever was.

What did Morgan regard as his "important" work? One of these top spots he reserved for a massive and never-begun account of the American fur trade between 1742 and 1840, a respectable draft of which he probably could have dictated from memory had he taken the trouble to do so—text, notes, citations, and all. This was the project for which he was preparing in 1970 with the support of an exceedingly uncommon second John Simon Guggenheim Memorial Foundation research fellowship, awarded just before his passing. The other two places at the top of his personal-importance list are, ironically, reflected in this collection. Both concerned the religious tradition founded by Joseph Smith and inherited by the Church of Jesus Christ of Latter-day Saints, among others. As he envisioned it in midlife, this contribution would have been completed separately in two parts: the first and foundational part was to be a consideration of Latter Day Saint printed culture, a historical bibliography of Mormonism between 1830 and 1849 (and which, according to a 1952 letter to Yale University Press's Eugene Davidson, he almost certainly would have expanded to include later years); the second part was to be the perennially put-off cultural study of the Restoration, conceived in at least three volumes. The first volume of the Mormon study itself was to take in Joseph Smith's lifetime (and possibly the Nauvoo exodus); the second was to address the period between Nauvoo and either Brigham Young's passing (1877) or Utah's statehood (1896), and the final volume—to which he hardly devoted thought beyond the most general sort of temporal dates—would carry forward to the then-present. Those three projects—the fur-trade history, the historical bibliography of Mormonism, and the trilogy on LDS history—crowned Morgan's personal list of career goals. How he chose them, how he pursued them, how they affected his career as a writer, and why he never completed the last two of them, are illustrated in these books.

Upon being introduced to historical research in 1938, Morgan's historiographic sense evolved quickly and within a very short time became unwaveringly straightforward: the mastery of historical details became the warp and woof which was woven into story. If he lined up enough of them, he felt, historical reality would be obvious. That was the goal, anyway. At the broadest level, his forays into cultural history became so tangled in detail that he failed to comprehend their place in the context of either American society or of the ineffable realities of faith and belief. But, while either unequipped or disinterested in the broad scope, he succeeded marvelously in the narrative microcosm. It is easy and unjust to look back critically and say Morgan should not have been driven so deeply by details. He had sound reasons to be so driven. Between the 1940s and 1960s he was studying for what seemed like the first time both the crusty rime of "well-known" documents and a seemingly bottomless fountain of new source material bubbling to the surface. Morgan deserves credit for bringing one of the earliest and most rigorous factual approaches to the study of Latter Day Saint history. When a new perspective becomes available, sources must be reexamined—as Morgan would perceive the matter—to clear away bias stemming from cultural assumptions or legends that were responsible for *post hoc* views of history which tended to read the present onto the past. In some ways he succeeded marvelously; in others, he hardly managed to see the forest for the trees.

The pursuit of Latter Day Saint history and perceptions of its collective past have changed dramatically since Dale Morgan studied and wrote these pieces. Mormon history is entering the topical mainstream in non-Mormon institutions. As you use these volumes, recall that many of the foundational sources of primary documentation were unavailable to him or anyone else. He saw virtually none of the manuscript material in the Church Historian's Office belonging to the Church of Jesus Christ of Latter-day Saints (now the Church History Library), other than the transcripts and clippings in the scrapbook "Journal History of the Church." The broad, deep collections now assembled at Brigham Young University or University of Utah had not even been begun; at Utah State University he had access to only the second of the Frederick Pierce book collections. The Community of Christ archives were still reeling and disorganized from the 1907 fire that consumed the *Saints Herald* office and quantities of church records. The vast bulk of scholarship regarding Mormonism postdates him as well. Dale Morgan's work on Mormonism belongs to a different time with different assumptions, but having that work available at all helps us partly understand how and why the present study of Latter Day Saint tradition evolved in the way it has. "Historical knowledge is based on, and limited by, experience and insight," historian Robert Park once observed, "the insight of the man who writes, but also the insight of the man who reads. Therefore . . . history has to be constantly rewritten to make it intelligible to each new generation."[1] This is essentially why Morgan picked up the challenge to write about the Mormons, and a good share of why I have picked up the challenge to write about Morgan writing about the Mormons.

When I began pursuing Dale Morgan as a biographical and historical study, I must admit that I looked over his work and what was said about him with awe, and some trepidation. Morgan's reputation as a researcher still sets him apart from contemporaries. Most historians would count themselves lucky to generate one path-breaking work in their careers; Morgan produced several, in my estimation. The Morgan papers at the Bancroft Library are positively massive. Merely looking down the inventory to the collection gave me the mental picture of a methodical, well-organized mind sitting down

[1]Robert Park, review of Werner Sombart, *Die Drei Nationalökonomien: Geschichte und System der Lehre von der Wirtschaft* (Munich: Duncker & Humblot, 1930), quoted by Janet Abu-Lughod, "The World-System Perspective in the Construction of Economic History," in *World History: Ideologies, Structures, and Identities*, ed. Philip Pomper, Richard H. Elphick, Richard T. Vann (London: Blackwell Publishers, 1998), 71.

regularly to push out another manuscript. The truth is a little messier but no less impressive. Dale Morgan seemed to spend his life chronically stirring around in preliminary research. Only rarely, usually under duress imposed from some quarter, did he ever push a project through to publication.

The Great Basin kingdom produced other observers and critics of Mormonism in his generation, but Morgan is a curious and important transitional character. He was not an apologist like Francis W. Kirkham and Milton R. Hunter; did not stand sniping at the culture from the outside, as did Bernard DeVoto or Charles Kelly; he did not purposefully reject the faith as an apostate in the fashion of his good friend Fawn M. Brodie; nor did he reshape or reinterpret its values to suit himself, as would a heretic like the various polygamy sects that were beginning to emerge in his day. Morgan methodically and self-consciously objectified his historical research, setting himself beyond both cultural dissensions (between Mormon Utahn and non-Mormon Utahn) and sectarian dissensions (Mormons, other Restoration sects, and other Christian churches) by adopting the interpretive stance of a studied agnostic and affirmed philosophical naturalist. Despite that difference, Morgan was ever after exceedingly careful to never allow his dissent from the family's religious tradition to injure their beliefs or their relationships with him—especially his mother, Emily's. That would have been uncharacteristic of his native generosity and a breach of the familial integrity he felt keenly. His, like all of ours, was a complex but somewhat compartmentalized personality. To complicate matters, deafness-imposed isolation also shaped his approach to records and evidence. Early practical experience with Utah's history as it was narrated county by county tied Morgan to a strong sense of geographic reality. From friends Charlie Kelly, Rod Korns, and Will Lund he adopted the perspective of research as an exercise of resolving geographical clues, and by extension, temporal ones as well. But if his trail buddies helped him focus on specific individuals moving across the landscape on a particular vector at a given time, other influences helped shaped his view of society. Whatever the subject, Dale Morgan's work was always grounded in documentary sources concerning the immediate actions of individuals or discrete groups at specific times and in particular places.

On the other hand, Morgan's single-minded pursuit of fact created for him an Achilles heel. He excelled at *chronicle,* a straight telling of the factual past popular with general readers and left to the talented amateurs in local communities. A different type of history was emerging from universities by the 1940s, which involved fact but also a grasp of arguments *about* fact. This history became a formalized discussion, with writers anticipating questions and weaving answers to potential criticism into the work before they were made. Morgan did not care for viewpoint and discussion. The difference between narrative chronicle (often "local" history—not a pejorative) and academic history is similar to the difference between a machinist and a mechanical engineer. Dale Morgan was a uniquely skilled machinist, perhaps the last great amateur historian of the American West in the distinguished tradition of writers like William H. Prescott and Francis Parkman. While he was trying to make a living as a researcher and writer, Western history was being drawn into academia and the discipline was professionalizing rapidly around and beyond him. He carried the discipline of fact-based local history to its apex, but in the form of classical Greek tragedy, relying upon his greatest strength also involved overlooking an inherent weakness in that strength—a work of history invariably reflects the limitations of the writer. Ideologically confident, almost smug in his documentary approach, lacking the capacity to discuss his work with fellow writers in "real time" due to deafness, he was left to develop almost in isolation a peerless domination of the written word. If it was not written somewhere or was not his own literary evocation, an idea was difficult for him to involve in his historical writing. Dale Morgan earned a reputation as a masterful researcher and narrator, yet his Mormon studies, important focal points of Morgan's attention and effort until 1952, all fall well before the works that earned him his reputation. They are the work of a youthful and somewhat naïve exuberance, not products of the seasoned scholar. That raises a personal stake in this volume: as a practicing Latter-day Saint myself, and a believer in the immutability of personality beyond the grave, I fully expect to meet a furious Dale Morgan on the other side of the heavenly veil. He did not suffer ignorant historical fools and will want to know how I had the temerity to publish material he as the author did not feel was at a point of completion, even when he was working on it. For the sake of practice, dear reader, let me set down for you what I expect to tell him.

Morgan's work on the Mormons falls at the cusp of modern Latter Day Saint history. As a writer he has receded somewhat into the historiographical shadows, his work outshone by the first generation of LDS academic historians and the explosion of solid, insightful scholarship that followed.

His position makes Morgan into both a pioneer and a pariah as Mormon history was in transition. "Transitions in history," Gary Topping reminds us in his biography of Morgan contemporary Leonard Arrington, "are never as clean and clearly defined as historians, in their efforts to divide complex historical realities into intellectually comprehensible units, often make them appear."[2] In offering to scholars a collection of Morgan's fifty- and sixty-year-old studies of the Latter Day Saint movement, modern readers bump against the issue of relevance: why is Dale Morgan's work relevant, especially since so much has been done after him, and particularly since he left so much of it incomplete? As someone who has worked with Morgan's papers for years, let me propose several reasons, in no particular order of importance.

The first reason Dale Morgan remains relevant to present and future generations of historians is because even written over half a century ago, his work remains provocative and insightful about the difficulties under which believers must conduct themselves. Jesus Christ could remind his hearers that he had no earthly priorities to accomplish and "was not of this world" (St. John 8:23). His followers did not (and still do not) have that luxury—they must function within the temporal and cultural present, responding to challenges and pressures from all sides while carrying forth the message entrusted them. It is difficult for a group with an other-world mission to function outside present-world social realities. As a result, believers usually suffer for the cause, or as the apostle John put it, "in the world ye shall have tribulation" (St. John 16:33). One of Morgan's chief contributions to Mormon historiography was to point out that some of their legendary trouble was merely the Saints' own doing.

A second point of relevance is that the scholarly study of Mormonism is passing to a new phase with the turn of the twenty-first century. The recent establishment of Mormon-studies chairs at institutions as diverse as Utah State University, Claremont Graduate University, and the University of Durham in England signal that the field is moving into a level of scholarly sophistication that invites a closer look at defining figures and influences. As a field moves forward, it becomes important to have a grip on its historiography. Morgan was a pivotal character and perhaps *the* pivotal character within Latter Day Saint historiography during his generation. It could be claimed without too much exaggeration that Morgan represents a hinge that

---

[2] *Leonard J. Arrington: A Historian's Life* (Norman, Okla.: Arthur H. Clark Co., 2008), 198.

allowed modern LDS history to swing into the present, and these works help illustrate why. Mentor, sounding board, research assistant, and confidant—what he hauled with him from the interpretive past and what he passed forward into the rising generation of historians (chiefly by reputation, as he had no graduate students) is critical. He is given far too little credit for his behind-the-scenes assistance with work upon which others among Utah's "Lost Generation" writers built their careers.[3] A careful study of relationships and influences between him and others in his circle needs to be made. A checklist of Morgan's contributions to his fellows is impressive enough: he provided much of the documentary record underpinning Fawn Brodie's *No Man Knows My History* (New York City: Knopf, 1945) and twice read her drafts, providing the critiques that prevented her study from being written at a level comparable to any title by sensationalist J.H. Beadle. Because of his criticism, irrespective of its flaws, her work became historically relevant. He arranged for the transcription, correction, and donation of the remarkable Hosea Stout journals—the standard source for any second-generation study of the Utah branch of the church—and then allowed Juanita Brooks the credit for editing them. He pooled his documentary discoveries on the Mountain Meadows massacre with Juanita Brooks and served as the sounding board as her famous book of the same name unfolded. In addition, Morgan critiqued the manuscript and proofread and corrected page proofs for Wallace Stegner's *Mormon Country* (New York City: Duell, Sloan & Pearce, 1942), supplied documents and interpretive critiques for Bernard DeVoto as the latter was writing *Year of Decision* (Boston: Little, Brown, 1943), and provided much of the documentary research and criticism for Nels Anderson's *Desert Saints* (Chicago: Univ. of Chicago Press, 1942).

Nineteenth-century detractors had gnawed Mormonism's cultural oddities and personal failings for years, but Morgan's approach to Mormonism as a genuine social construction, apart from its metaphysical ideals, was new and compelling. It reflects the duality behind the divine charge to be *in* the world without being *of* the world. Morgan's take was a much more complex explanation for Mormonism than the generations of earlier polemicists on both sides had advanced. Given what had been written before him, this was

[3]Edward A. Geary, "Mormondom's 'Lost Generation': The Novelists of the 1940s," *BYU Studies* 18, no. 1 (Fall 1977): 89–98. Geary's invocation of a term used for post–World War I American writers is appropriate. His study includes non-fiction writers as well as novelists.

a significant departure from how the Mormon past was viewed. As late as the 1930s only the Latter Day Saints could be said to be interested in their history. Morgan aspired to carry the Mormons to a broader audience, and a third point of relevance is that Morgan was among the first researchers to attempt bridging the divide to make the Mormons interesting in American culture at large. He chose to write both for the cultural insiders (albeit posing a direct challenge to that faith culture), as well as for those looking on from the outside. In doing so he became the critic and the effective standard for research for a group of untrained professional writers who collectively defined "Mormon history" for a generation.

Related to this third point is a fourth: Morgan remains relevant because he pioneered a comparatively new approach in the field, plunging into source material to an extent that no contemporary and few successors have attempted. Though some excellent biographies have been written and the Joseph Smith Papers Project is proving to be a turning point in the LDS approach to its history, two generations ago even the staff of the Church Historian's Office (committed cultural encyclopedists who focused on compiling biographical and organizational summaries) had only an imperfect grasp of the rich archival holdings they cared for. Understanding Morgan as pioneer of documentary research within Mormon studies provides a reckoning point for understanding successive approaches down to the present. As the field changed, Morgan personified the document-driven methodological approach to Latter Day Saint history. The approach he insisted upon is now the footings on which the foundations of modern historical study rests, a dramatic turn in the historiography. In his role as a reviewer and adviser to other writers, he underscored the primacy of contemporary source material when invoking fact and event. Partly because he had such a grip over the source material, partly because he remained a formidable critic, Morgan was a looming personality to the first generation of academic LDS scholars. Whether or not he openly critiqued a given work or author, prior to 1970 the real or imagined fear of Dale Morgan pointing out overlooked relevant sources had the effect of upping the factual ante for many who aspired to study and write LDS history.

More broadly, Morgan's empirical approach to history, grounded in a sort of soft and informal philosophical positivism, represents a fourth measure of relevance to Mormon historiography, albeit an outdated one. As the United States adopted modern educational methods from Europe in the 1880s, humanistic studies like history and the emerging social sciences were influenced strongly by Germanic positivism. Morgan himself lacked historical training but developed a distinctly positivistic view of human motivation from self-directed reading in the early literature of psychology. By the time he began a career in historical research and writing, his approach to epistemology (how one knows) and the intricacies of motivation was already fixed into a soft version of scientific positivism, even as the smug scientism that infected the humanities and social sciences coming out of the 1920s was being challenged on philosophical grounds by Progressive writers like Charles Beard and Carl Becker. Human development cannot be predicted like chemical reactions—history is *not* science. The positivistic perspective of history that Morgan exemplifies, certitude about cause and effect that injected an inflexible empiricism to his writing, has not been precisely discredited in the field, but it has weakened in the withering glare of postmodernism. Though he never studied philosophy and did not consciously adopt an overtly philosophical stance on historical interpretation, Morgan leaned hard on several philosophical *-isms* that strengthened his path-breaking work but also lent their inherent weaknesses. In this way Morgan's work, as it reflects his approach to understanding and relating to the past, represents a cautionary tale for later students about making definitive statements about what happened and why. Admittedly, it is a bit unfair to judge Dale Morgan's capacity as a historian of religion solely by his incomplete drafts, for most never reached a point—even in draft form—where he was required to present to reader the story of a mature Joseph Smith or Brigham Young and their ideas. The closest he comes is with the Kingdom of God manuscript. Even here he still lays out a narrative, built around circumstances, that is inherently teleological—ordering and explaining facts that inevitably toward a specific condition or setting in the past. As a rule, Morgan tended to pose only historical questions which documents could explicitly resolve. He made a few efforts to trace the immutabilities of ideas and motivations, but his deeply documented research and compelling narrative focused on action. He inferred motives or comprehended ideas only within the narrow confines of the record at hand and a commitment to historical explanations that disqualified metaphysics.

Finally, the man and his works remain relevant because in his short career Dale Morgan generated a number of studies that have not yet been superseded either factually or as historical treatments. His study of the political anomaly of Deseret remains a foundational work, updated only in details. No major new sources have been discovered since setting aside his sidelong study of the 1838 "Mormon war" in Missouri, so his incomplete Danite work stands solidly beside the most thorough studies of topic done more than half a century later. The Dispersion bibliographies remain without peer. No one has yet provided a study of the Government of God that goes as deeply into its historical origins. Thus, Dale Morgan did not merely pioneer bibliographic research and a more factually driven approach to LDS history, but much of his work remains unique.

To be sure, even great minds have limits imposed by perspective. One solid historiographic reason to study Morgan's works on the Mormons, particularly when so much remained incomplete and unpublished, is that his published work showcases his remarkable ability to collate and organize primary sources. Yet, only by examining his unpublished work may his limitations—both interpretive and documentary—be fairly seen with its gaps and holes. Interpreting the sweep of large cultural ideas or movements and comparative interpretation was foreign to him. Being a writer with a regionalist bent, lacking any academic training in history yet consumed by work in the primary material of his topic, Dale Morgan seems to have remained completely unaffected by the stirrings in American historiography during the 1940s and 50s. He simply did not read Daniel Boorstin, Henry Steele Commager, Carl Becker, Bernard Bailyn, or other scholars who were beginning to look differently at the American past and in the process were laying the thematic foundations for the social-history revolution of the 1960s. He read Arrington's *Great Basin Kingdom* (Cambridge, Mass.: Harvard, 1959) only as a skeptical critic. Morgan was not one to pursue broad context, either in the primary or secondary material. His one attempt at comprehending a broad American cultural context proceeded no further than a concept and reams of transcriptions. A preliminary volume to *The Mormons,* tentatively titled "This Was America," was a study that he hoped would summarize U.S. culture and the national character between 1800 and the Civil War. It would serve as a background volume for his Mormon studies. His preparation, however, seems to have been limited to reading carefully through Jacksonian newspapers and periodicals. There is no indication that he ever broadened his reading to include the work of other historians, chiefly because that project was abandoned in the early 1950s. It never progressed to the point of drafting, and Morgan did not sketch outlines or make preliminary notes. It is tempting to wonder whether he could have carried off such a study. The result certainly would have been closer in style and substance to his *Humboldt: The Highroad to the West* (New York City: Farrar & Rinehart, 1943) and *Great Salt Lake* (Indianapolis: Bobbs-Merrill, 1947) and the modern popular works of writers like Stephen Ambrose or Shelby Foote than to an academic treatise: his work would have been well informed, but written for a general readership.[4] Among his Latter Day Saint work he made only one nod to broader cultural context, the Castiglioni citation in *The Mormons*. With it he tried vainly to link his detail-driven historical method to larger cultural forces, but he lacked both the training and the interest in secondary literature that would have allowed him to truly contextualize Mormonism within American society.

Another shortcoming as a student of a religious faith is that he had none; because he could not accept faith, he could not account for it in others. He was left to explain the faith and its adherents strictly in terms of his naturalism and their circumstances. He dismisses the metaphysical. His work's insightfulness—and it is insightful—is limited to the mortal plane. I will not argue that non-believers cannot comprehend and write profitably about a religious faith, only that by rejecting the reality of his subjects' faith and doctrine, Morgan did not do so. He was a master at relating *what* happened, but caught up in a ceaseless effort to master details, he struggled to come up with a convincing method for addressing *why* the details mattered to them. As you will read in the following introductory essays, I feel Dale Morgan exhibits an approach to history that it is at its roots philosophically positivistic and empirical, the perfect expression for a personal belief structure that was entirely naturalistic. That approach to history—a quest for what could be measured, plotted, and proven—provided an excellent basis when he stuck to the collocation of facts. His single foray into synthetic history, *The Mormons,* failed partly because he could not find time to write on it, but also because he was simply foundering, out of his stylistic element in trying to explain the "whys" motivating Mormonism, unable to balance convincing explanation based on adequate detail—in short, to interpret a religion by dismissing its claim to the religious concerns of its adherents.

---

[4]DLM to Virginia Sorenson, 29 December 1943; DLM to Stanley Rinehart, 31 March 1943.

However, it was also with the Mormons that Morgan discovered his forte as a documentary editor. He may have been incapable of producing broad historical synthesis like John D. Unruh's *The Plains Across* (Urbana: University of Illinois Press, 1978), but the brilliance of juxtaposed detail in any of his edited works cannot be gainsaid. That virtuosity can be seen in his balanced treatment of William Empey's journal and James Holt's memoir. Morgan was most comfortable and effective when teasing out tangles of primary sources or laying out a neat, concrete chronology. As a result, his work on the West remains foundational. The footings for *that* historiographic foundation is his work—finished, unfinished, published, and unpublished—that involved the Latter Day Saints.

A Biographical Introduction

Dale L. Morgan is known best as a historian of the American fur trade, exploration, and nineteenth-century overland trails. His work stands fundamental to each subject. Curiously, both specializations were somewhat secondary interests. His first passion in historical enterprise began with the local history of Utah's exploration and settlement and the larger world it represented, the Latter-day Saints or Mormons. Biographically, Morgan's work on the Mormons belongs to the period between 1940 (though mostly after 1942) and 1952. He worked for the Office of Price Administration during the Second World War, crossed the country on a Guggenheim Foundation research fellowship, marked time between jobs in Salt Lake City, and then took a second residence in Washington, D.C., until settling into an editorial position with the University of California at the Bancroft Library in 1953.

Morgan must be understood in the temporal and regional world of 1930s Mormonism in the way that novelist William Faulkner must be seen in the context of the American South in the 1920s. Both writers were products of their cultural environment, and their work reflects the tensions they perceived in their native cultures. Until writing *Jedediah Smith and the Opening of the West* in 1952 and becoming an editor and research historian for the Bancroft Library the next year, Morgan's world centered around his bibliography of Latter Day Saint publications and his perennially incomplete history of the church he had consciously shrugged off as a youth. Irrespective of time spent in Washington, D.C., or California, Dale Morgan forever remained a native of

Salt Lake City and the Utah culture that surrounded it, and until late in life he viewed himself primarily as an historian of Utah and of the Mormons.

Morgan's approach to history and his perspective of the knowable past were shaped by influences outside his discipline, perhaps more telling for him than other writers. Born in December 1914, he grew up in a Latter-day Saint family in the post-war, pre-Depression suburban housing developments located just north of 21st South Street in Salt Lake City, the oldest of four children. Emily Holmes Morgan, his mother, was left a widow when Dale was five. Lowell Morgan's lingering death from the infection of a ruptured appendix was an important but not defining event for his four children, who were all too young to recall his passing. Life without father was simply the order of things. Emily never remarried and set about providing for her family as an elementary school teacher. Dale Morgan grew up normally into a responsible, popular, and social teen.

If every life endures a defining event, Dale's defining event happened in the summer of 1929 when he was fourteen, nine years after his father's death. He returned from a summer swimming party dizzy and nauseated. Within hours he was tossing feverishly in bed. For a week he lingered near death, wracked by what was likely a case of bacterial meningitis. He survived and slowly recovered, but the cranial swelling incident to the infection strangled the blood supply of his aural nerves. As he recovered, he was puzzled by an inability to hear anything. Though he would never understand precisely what had happened, his deafness proved absolute and irreversible. The inability to hear was itself not the major blow; rather it was the shift in his social and interpersonal relationships that deafness forced instantly upon him. Being unable to participate in the conversational give and take of peer groups at school, at church, and in impromptu social settings put him beyond the fringe of all his established relationships. It was a crushing change for a once-popular adolescent. After a full year's convalescence, "I could not and would not establish myself socially," he explained later. He continued to socialize as best he could at school and within the family, two circles that accepted him out of duty or familial affection, but casual interaction and acquaintances ended abruptly. He drifted away from participation in his local congregation and eventually from belief in its religious principles but remained and identified himself as a "cultural Mormon," one who felt he understood the social relationships, expectations, and activities of members in the Church of Jesus Christ of Latter-day Saints without believing or participating in them.

Cut off from casual relationships, the young man was left to stumble through adolescence feeling intensely isolated. Emotionally he became an introspective near-recluse, one who observed the interactions and relationships around him and projected himself into what he imagined the intimacies of life were like. Despite tutoring with lip reading, he found its imprecision frustrating and physically taxing. He remained uncomfortable speaking because he had no means of checking vocal tone, volume, or clarity. As time passed, his speech became a flat monotone. He instead turned to a succession of manual typewriters, which, through the mail, became his voice and primary means of professional interaction.

In a day when accommodations for handicaps were nonexistent in higher education, Dale enrolled at the University of Utah as a student in 1933 and graduated in 1937. His course work, chosen to support a career in commercial art (today we would call it graphic design), prepared him not at all for the career path through Western American history that he eventually chose. He completed no more than the three-term history survey required of all students. The classes skipped across the span of Western culture from Classical antiquity to early modern Europe. He did not take a single course under the one historical Ph.D. on campus, Andrew L. Neff. History as a subject was simply irrelevant to either interests or career plans. However he was an active member of the Scribblers club, a writing group, and a member of the *Utah Chronicle* staff, the collegiate newspaper, under its student editor Richard Scowcroft and faculty advisor Wallace Stegner. Decades later, both men would found the influential creative writing program at Stanford University. As a student, Morgan published short stories in the quarterly literary magazine, the *University Pen.* His college work, particularly non-fiction, demonstrates that he had developed a sound familiarity with writing and could analyze literature well.

Besides its historic significance for the country at large, the 1930s held personal significance for Dale as he began looking for work and a suitable place in the world. Morgan's graduation in the late spring of 1937 came just in time for the "Roosevelt Recession." Finding a job in Depression-era Salt Lake City proved difficult, made the more so for his inability to hear. When he chanced to learn that a federal writing program was looking for a competent part-time editor, he leapt at the opportunity. The Historical Records Survey (HRS) was a national resource study, staffed as a New Deal relief project. It was conceived partly to replicate at a state and local level the basic archival descriptive work being done for federal records in Washington, D.C., under the newly established National Archives and Records Service.[5] Morgan was hired as a "non-certified" employee (that is to say, not under a welfare appointment) chiefly on his collegiate newspaper experience and the fact that for over a year he had reviewed books for the *Salt Lake Tribune*. At twenty-three he was already a good structural writer, critic, and careful copyeditor. His desk became the final stop for writing destined for publications issued from the Ogden office. He wrote occasional press releases, but the chief duty was quality control and involved picking out inconsistent verb agreements, misspellings, and the odd discrepancies between stated facts. His memory for and a native ability to correlate details across sources soon proved its worth. Within two months of being hired, project assignments were shuffled and he was reassigned as "Historian"—still in a part-time position—responsible for generating the final form of the twenty-page county historical "sketches" being produced as introductions for records-inventory volumes. Work in the Historical Records Survey and later in the Writers' Project was Dale Morgan's sole preparation for the discipline and profession he ultimately chose to follow.

How Morgan was introduced to history is important. He neither pursued nor even viewed as relevant traditional academic training in history. To use a garden metaphor, Morgan grew up in history as a volunteer plant rather than a set. He was content to draw what strength he needed from his surroundings as a seedling and was content to flower without seeing what else might be gained. While his subject knowledge expanded dramatically, his approach hardly shifted at all throughout his lifetime. The HRS office was an

[5]Luther H. Evans, "The Historical Records Survey," *American Political Science Review* 30, no. 1 (February 1936): 133–135. The HRS succeeded the Public Archives Commission, established in 1899, which surveyed state-held archival holdings between 1900 and 1917 but which did not reach into local records. It succeeded the Historical Manuscripts Commission, an arm of the American Historical Association, which had been created as professional historians began recognizing the differences between public records and private papers. The AHA counted the development of archival standards among its founding purposes in 1884. The National Archives of the United States was established during the Hoover administration, but Franklin Roosevelt created the unit as an independent agency in 1934; it opened officially in 1935. "Development of the U.S. archival profession and timeline for the National Archives" (http://www.archives.gov/about/history/milestones.html, date of access 17 November 2011).

enterprise and setting strongly influenced—*dominated* would not be too strong a word—by a new approach to fact-based writing known as "documentary" style. Documentary had been born and named in the late 1920s and matured quickly in the following decade. The business-led Depression tarnished the paternalistic message of patriotic nationalism and narratives about the country's elite figures. Human "authenticity" was the focus of documentary, and authentic experience was to be found not in the artificial existence of the barons of business and politics but rather in the lives and struggles of common women and men and the forces that drove them. Documentary's great expressions came in the photographs, theater, and guidebooks of the federal relief programs, notably the Farm Security Administration, Writers' Project, and Historical Records Survey, all part of the Works Progress Administration (WPA).[6] And that is where we will begin.

[6]William Stott, *Documentary Expression and Thirties America* (New York: Oxford Univ. Press, 1973).

Chapter 1

Utah
A Guide to the State (1941)

Editor's Introduction

Though not Dale Morgan's earliest writing about the Mormons, the second of his two anonymously written contributions to the 1941 volume *Utah: A Guide to the State* is given the place of precedence in this collection. This essay dates later than *The State of Deseret* and the Kingdom of God manuscript, but his contributions to the *Guide* is a summary work that fits perfectly at the front of this collection.

Morgan himself was very much a child of third-generation Utah and one who had not yet adopted a culturally inclusive viewpoint about the Restoration. That would change. Eventually two volumes of his projected three-volume history of the Mormons—the pin around which turned his career as a writer a decade later—would concern the geography and the period covered by this early essay. Mormon history itself was bounded sharply by the tradition to which a writer belonged. Interaction between perspectives was limited chiefly to apologetic works defending one's church and attacking the beliefs or historical assumptions of another group. In the broad context of history produced and read during the 1930s and 1940s, the story of Utah *was* the story of Mormonism. Salt Lake City's Latter-day Saint culture assumed that point, and because the Utah branch of Joseph Smith's legacy had long had the most attention in the press (much of it negative), many writers outside the state saw the history of Mormonism in the same terms. Such cultural myopia has since been corrected in both directions, and the state's rich ethnic and cultural history has been the subject of writers like Dale's University of Utah classmate Helen Zeese Papanikolas and others.[1]

[1] *Utah: A Guide to the State* (New York: Hastings House, 1941), 46–90. *The Peoples of Utah,* *(continued, next page)*

Even though the *Guide*'s historical essay is heavily overlaid by editing and reviews, the sections provide the only reasonably complete historical framework for Morgan's overall perspective on LDS culture and history. Utah's guidebook was the chief product of the Utah Writers' Project, which was itself a descendant of Depression-era Federal One recovery programs. Early in its existence the Project's national administration hit upon the idea that the branch in each state would compile a general guidebook. Nationally, the project was championed by writers and editors who determined that they would create a body of work as valuable and lasting as any of the Civilian Conservation Corps' improvement projects. This *raison d'être* infused a sense of mission to Project workers across the country. Producing such a guide was labor intensive. Writing and editing was time consuming, of course, but compiling data and resource material from across the state from which to write was the more difficult task. Duplicating technology was limited to two methods: photostats (photographs) and manual typewriters. Copying or replicating notes, data, or quotations required that every page be laboriously retyped by hand, character by character. Carbon paper and a firm keystroke could make as many as four duplicates from a single typed page, which were divided between files or offices. In 1935 Utah's state project director, former Ogden journalist Maurice Howe, scattered his staff among local libraries, county courthouse record vaults, and newspaper research departments to compile the project's own resource files. They also began slowly and painstakingly transcribing original documents that were in family hands, offering a typed copy to any family which allowed an early diary, journal, or reminiscence to be transcribed for the project files.[2]

In Utah, however, the process of compiling a descriptive state guidebook also faced challenges not experienced in most other states. First, source

---

ed. Helen Z. Papanikolas (Salt Lake City: Utah State Historical Society, 1976). See Leslie G. Kellen and Eileen Hallet Stone, *Missing Stories: An Oral History of Ethnic and Minority Groups in Utah* (Logan: Utah State Univ. Press, 2000); Stan J. Layton, *Being Different: Stories of Utah's Minorities* (Salt Lake City: Signature Books, 2001).

[2]This material is now the "WPA Papers" and other files at the Utah State Historical Society. The first or ribbon copy went to the loaning individual or agency, the second and third to the HRS and often Federal Writers' Project master files. A fourth uncommitted carbon ultimately made its way to Dale Morgan's personal collection. "Shortly after joining HRS I thoroughly reorganized the historical files into something usable.... There were a great many duplicates, and when it appeared that these were likely to be thrown away, I asked for and was given the privilege of taking them myself" (DLM to Bernard DeVoto, 1 May 1944). A good treatment of the borrow-and-transcribe process is described in Levi S. Peterson, *Juanita Brooks: Mormon Woman Historian* (Salt Lake City: Univ. of Utah Press, 1987), 100. The importance of the WPA writing as historical literature is addressed in Charles S. Peterson, "Introduction," in Dale L. Morgan, *The State of Deseret* (Logan, Utah: Utah State Univ. Press, 1987), x–xi.

material was limited. No major public research libraries existed in the state, even at the universities, and only one substantial private one existed, the Church Historian's Office. Administrators and staff in the CHO were used to being the authorities on the church and its history and looked warily on a government attempt to tell a story with the church and its history near the center. Second, the state was sharply divided between the Democratic state leadership, which had been elected by mostly mine-labor, rural, and lower-class urban voters, and a staunchly oppositional Republican class of largely business and community leaders. Business leaders wanted the Depression to end, but disapproved vocally with recovery measures that did not involve business and private capital, which they controlled but which they did not wish to risk. The federal project mandated that all writing had to be reviewed and approved by local "experts." Approval for the text of Utah's guide fell into the tension between opposing priorities. As with every guide, there were also practical limits of page counts, within which even the best-told story would be required to fit. No work was ever all-inclusive, but Utah's competing welter of cultural and social heterogeneity complicated matters tremendously.

Howe's workers drew in and produced reams and reams of transcripts, notes, and abstracts from the project's inception. Beginning in 1936, Utah project staff began drafting its guidebook centerpiece, sending dozens of outlines, drafts, and mock-ups to the Washington office. Most were promptly filed and ignored or given an cursory glance and returned as unacceptable—the Federal Writers' Project suffered from its own unique brand of bureaucratic inefficiency.[3] In June 1938, Howe was reassigned from Utah to the national office and moved his young family to Washington, D.C., but continued supervising the state project via correspondence. Two months later, Dale Morgan, a year out of college, was hired by a parallel documentary project, the Historical Records Survey, as a publicity specialist and editor. Within a short time his facility with writing, sound editorial ability, and remarkable memory for facts was garnering attention. Initially he provided final stylistic critiques of HRS county histories; soon he was drafting them.

With supreme irony and utter ignorance of its own culpability, the Federal Writers' Project (FWP) office finally expressed concern that Utah's guidebook

[3]The subject is treated more completely in Richard L. Saunders, "The Utah Writers' Project and Writing *Utah: A Guide to the State*," *Utah Historical Quarterly* 70, no. 1 (Winter 2002): 21–38. Cf. Jerre Mangione, *The Dream and the Deal: The Federal Writers' Project, 1925–1943*, 2nd ed. (Philadelphia: Univ. of Pennsylvania Press, 1983). My summary is very general; the relationships and circumstances were a good deal more complex than can be explained here.

was not progressing, even as draft chapters submitted months earlier were languishing in their own files. In April 1939 the FWP administration asked Idaho director and novelist Vardis Fisher to restart Utah's guidebook. The acerbic Fisher arrived at the project office in Ogden to find that interoffice politics, incompletion, and general disorganization within the drafts and files outweighed office efficiency. By August he had thrown up his hands and returned to Boise. Publicity surrounding his activities in Utah, however, created a curious denouement. HRS workers were threatened with expulsion from the Church Historian's Office following the late-summer publication of Fisher's novel *The Children of God.* The book presented a fictionalized summary of Mormon history and the founding of pioneer Utah. The coincidence of Fisher's activity in Utah, the presence of HRS workers at the Church Historian's Office, and the publication of the novel were strictly circumstantial, but the Historian's Office staff, Morgan wrote Howe, "[w]ent straight up in the air when they read the book, and talked about barring HRS workers from the office, on the grounds that they were supplying people like Fisher with material for their 'anti-Mormon' works."[4] Modern readers of Fisher's largest and most lasting paean to hard work and sacrifice would be hard-pressed to describe *Children of God* as "anti-Mormon," but in the context of the 1930s, with the last of the "Pioneer" generation slowly passing from the scene, Fisher's humanism did not sit well with the church's historical staff. The idea of too-human conflict within its leadership quorums or personality clashes between its leaders—anything short of a smooth, certain, and gracefully heroic flowering in the desert—landed on the institutional keepers of the church's past like a jarring Modernist chord in a lyrical Romantic symphony. Fisher's book generated a relationship crisis. The Writers' Project had no power beyond good will; the guidebook project was a cooperative venture that functioned under a sponsorship by the Utah Institute of Fine Arts, a state agency. It was critical not to lose the limited access to the Church Historian's Office. As the HRS historian/editor and de facto supervisor of its research program, Morgan was called upon to clarify what had and had *not* happened with the HRS workers, Fisher's novel, and the guidebook draft text. The process required several face-to-face meetings with Historian's Office staff, although it is not evident that the Church Historian, apostle Joseph Fielding Smith, was involved. Eventually the CHO staff was mollified, but the federal project staff

[4]DLM to Maurice Howe, 26 September 1939.

were thereafter very careful that research assistants' activities and requests for material were clearly understood and transparently related to current writing projects. "Sometimes," Morgan confided to Maurice Howe in Washington after cooperative arrangements had been restored, "I think enviously about writing history elsewhere than in Utah, some place where the historical truth is the only validity, and you do not have to put up with modern ideas of how old timers, including God, should have acted."[5]

With Fisher gone and the guidebook still stalled, the Writers' Project administration needed help. By December 1939 the capable young editor/historian of the Utah Historical Records Survey became the subject of a tug-of-war between office directors, pursued by the Writers' Project to help rescue the foundering state guidebook even as the Records Survey tried to hang on to his services. The directors finally agreed to allow him to work in both offices (each position was part-time). In retrospect, the appointment represented a critical juncture in Morgan's unfolding career. It kept him firmly engaged in historical and cultural research in Utah for another two and a half years, committed him still more deeply to the study of Latter-day Saint history, and it allowed him to collect thousands of pages of transcripts of early documentary material.[6]

Morgan's chief responsibility in the Writers' Project was to see the Utah guidebook to completion and through publication. As a guide, most of the book's sections were straightforward descriptions. The Project's goal was to provide accurate, interesting, and reasonably detailed look at a state. Each state faced its own tensions over what would and would not be said. For Utah, the challenge would lie in the opening chapters, "The Contemporary Scene" and "History," some version of which were required for the WPA guide in every state. Given the outburst from the Church Historian's Office the previous August, the general contents of those two sections took on increased importance.

In January 1940 Morgan's initial critique of the previously written draft history had run to thirteen single-spaced pages. Overall, he felt "the emphasis

[5]DLM to Howe, 26 September 1939.

[6]DLM to Maurice Howe, 19 February 1940, and Darel McConkey to DLM, 21 June 1940. Besides the detailed county histories produced by the HRS and the state guidebook, with Morgan's participation or under his direction between 1938 and 1942 the HRS and UWP generated dozens of other history-related projects, including inventories of Utah's county archives (not all of which were completed or published), a daily "this day in history" radio spot, the texts for new state historical markers, a dictionary of Utah place names, a history of the Forest Service, the state guidebook, a documentary edition of the state's first book of laws, and the massive and never published manuscript "History of Grazing."

lies too greatly on event, on political history, and too little on the people."[7] Between March and the first week of April, Morgan completed an entirely new draft for the History chapter, turning then to other work as it was put through the slow crush of successive administrative reviews and approvals. Before it returned and six months after agreeing to juggle the demands of both editorial jobs, Dale was selected to head the Utah Writers' Project. In July 1940 he assumed administrative responsibility for the office and its chief charge, the state guidebook.

At its publication in 1941, Morgan was afforded personal praise for the volume as the head of the Writers' Project office. He demurred taking credit he felt was due his staff and predecessor. Responding to Maurice Howe's effusions after the guidebook's publication Dale ticked off a list of his contributions: "I only wrote History, Contemporary Scene, Tour 4, section 1f of Tour 1, and the end-matter, plus stray paragraphs here and there."[8] He need not have been so modest. Though his predecessor's drafts can no longer be found for comparison, Morgan turned out an astute, forthright, and thoughtful prose portrayal of the state and its dominant culture that possesses some lyrical passages and the right balance of perceptiveness, accuracy, and tact. The history is necessarily concise and presents a credible outline to the state's political history. Typical of the 1940s and a view that would characterize the post-war consensus school of U.S. history, it was a mainstream document, lacking insight and even acknowledgement of the ethnic and cultural diversity that characterized the half-century immediately preceding its production but emphasizing the contributions of common people in keeping with the 1930s documentary style. Shaped by accommodation as well as by historical evidence, the essay was intended as a public and semi-official comment about the state rather than a study. As professor Daniel Fox pointed out two decades after the Federal Writers' Project ended, the guides were written for interest rather than analysis. Within a few years, Morgan would have been able to correct a number of factual errors and editing oversights. To note a few, Fort Bridger is 113 rather than 300 miles from the Salt Lake Valley; news of the placer gold discovery in California reached Brigham Young on the trail before it reached the Salt Lake Valley, where he reportedly told Nathan Hawk, "I

[7]DLM to Charles Madsen, 24 January 1940.

[8]DLM to Howe, 10 January 1941. Separate sections addressed "Archaeology and Indians" and "The Mormon Church." Morgan would have reviewed, corrected, and approved these texts within the office but he did not write it. The book's index itself was an intense collective effort.

do not want my people to go digging for their God"; Franklin Pierce did not name the Mormon leader to a second term after Young's appointment as Utah's governor expired in 1854—the territory's organic act simply kept Young in office until his replacement arrived; the Utah Expedition, not the Army of the West, marched to Utah in 1857; the Utah War ended not with negotiations but with the acceptance of a pardon and an ultimatum; and plural marriages involved between 15 and 30 percent of Mormon households in the territory, rather than the 2 or 3 percent stated.[9] But overall, the Utah guide was highly praised within and beyond the state. The book appeared in three reprints during the 1940s and 1950s. Morgan's introduction to the volume, the "Contemporary Scene," was reprinted a decade and a half later in *Among the Mormons* (New York City: Knopf, 1958), a collection of firsthand accounts and impressions of the Latter-day Saints.[10]

Morgan's essay is still bright and readable. It represents a young, energetic, and optimistic writer finding a measure of success while still in his twenties. Beyond its relevance as Morgan's work, this chapter from *Utah: A Guide to the State* remains important to modern readers because it exemplifies the general style and approach to historical writing commonly read during the 1930s. The work of Progressive historians like Carl Becker was falling out of favor in academic circles, and social history was still a generation off. The "consensus school" of history was in ascendancy. This group of historians looked for large narratives that led neatly toward present realities. Interested less in what challenges might have nudged circumstances differently, the consensus writers looked back expecting to find out how the nation arrived at this point in history. Notice that Morgan's focus is on notable figures, political shifts, and large-scale processes leading temporally straight toward the present. There is comparatively little about subjects like water or women or ideas; certainly this reflected limits imposed by space, but it also reflected what was important for then-present readers. The Mormon heartland was, like much of the rest of the country, modernizing still rather slowly. This essay was completed at a time where the nineteenth century was still very visible, and suburbanization had not yet paved and blighted Utah's valleys.

[9]Daniel M. Fox, "The Achievement of the Federal Writers' Project," *American Quarterly* 13, no. 1 (Spring 1961): 3–19; *Sacramento Evening Bee*, 4 January 1906, in Kenneth N. Owens, *Gold Rush Saints: California Mormons and the Great Rush for Riches* (Spokane, Wash.: Arthur H. Clark Company, 2004), 202–203. Thanks to Will Bagley for cataloguing these historical tics.

[10]Reprinted 1945, 1954, 1959; *Among the Mormons*, ed. William Mulder and A. Russell Mortensen (New York: Alfred A. Knopf, 1958; Lincoln: Univ. of Nebraska Press, 1973; Salt Lake City: Western Epics, 1994), 467–474.

Streets still bounded large, semi-rural, ditch-bordered city blocks. The venerable vernacular stone and adobe houses of local grandsires and stolid Victorian homes of their children were only beginning to be replaced with their grandchildren's modern structures collared in mown lawns that climbed the valley benches. People in communities remembered the pioneers from personal acquaintance. They were proud of who they were and what had been accomplished. The guide presented a neighborly face of welcome to visitors. On the other hand, as communities looked into the future and the increasing out-migration of the state's younger generation, they also wanted affirming accounts to reinforce the security of knowing where they had come from. This piece of writing laid out the messy conflicts of Mormon Utah as forthrightly as could be managed diplomatically.

History*

The Mormon Pioneers

The story of the Mormons is also the story of two great leaders. Joseph Smith established the Church and its vital doctrines, and gathered around him an extraordinary body of energetic and able men. Brigham Young was one of the greatest of these proselytes; after the death of the prophet and founder, he held the membership together, successfully carried the Church to Utah, and in an extraordinary struggle with a bitterly adverse environment accomplished the conquest of the desert.

Smith was born in Sharon, Vermont, in 1805. Ten years later his father moved the family to Palmyra, on the New York frontier, and four years later to Manchester, six miles south. That much about Smith is accepted, but practically everything else about him has been for more than a century a subject of fiercest debate. Few men ever had such passionately devoted friends, or such bitterly antagonistic enemies. Between the devotion and the enmity, the true stature of Joseph Smith as a man has been slow to emerge.

Upper New York State at this time was roaring with religious hysteria. The whole Atlantic seaboard from 1790 had been convulsed by the revivals

*[*Utah: A Guide to the State* (New York: Hastings House, 1941), 46–90. Parenthetical in-text references to other guidebook sections are irrelevant in this presentation and have been dropped. Readers will have to seek Morgan's "Contemporary Scene" essay elsewhere, and the long History essay has been shortened by eliminating the concluding division, "Utah as a State," in the interest of space. The extract reproduced here is long enough to provide a view of the approach and method Morgan employed in his bit of official history. —Ed.]

of Methodist exhorters. Congregations went virtually mad; men barked like dogs, drowned out the preacher with their screaming, or spoke ecstatically in tongues; orgiastic camp-meetings lasted for days as men "got religion." Herbert Asbury has observed that "all the congregations were jerking, barking, jumping, hopping, dancing, prancing, screeching, howling, writhing in fits and convulsions, falling in cataleptic trances, and performing many other strange and holy antics." Religious feeling was a consuming flame which ate at the whole frontier, but even the seaboard cities were not immune; Baltimore in 1789 was shaken as by madness. Even where religious excitement did not take these violent forms, men pored over the Bible by day and by night, seeking the ways of grace and salvation, and pondering the imminence of the second coming of Christ. Everywhere new churches were springing up, and were splitting into sects and subsects. From this confusion, this nightmare of religious zeal, the Church of Jesus Christ of Latter-day Saints, the Mormon Church, emerged on April 6, 1830.

The Mormon story of the origin of the Church is that the boy, Joseph Smith, troubled by the welter of religious sects, was led in 1820 to inquire of God concerning the church he should join; in a vision the Father and Son appeared to him and told him that all the churches were wrong, and he must join none of them. Subsequently an angel of the Lord appeared to him several times, informed him that he was to perform a great work, and that his name would be known "for good and evil among all nations," and at last revealed to him golden plates, an ancient record buried in the Hill Cumorah, which he was to translate with the aid of the "Urim and Thummim." In 1827 the plates were delivered to him, and for the next two years he translated. The Book of Mormon was published in March, 1830, and formal organization of the Church in Fayette, New York, occurred soon after.

Ever since, disbelievers have proposed other explanations. It was common at first to term Smith a rogue, charlatan, a shiftless money-digger and a seer in peepstones, who encountered a Campbellite preacher named Sidney Rigdon, and with him plagiarized a manuscript by Solomon Spaulding, which had described ancient peoples in North America. Joseph Smith and his "Gold Bible" were subjects for bitter derision. Later the prevailing non-Mormon view of Smith changed, and he was conceived to have been altogether sincere, but deceived by burning hallucinations; a still later view, advanced by Bernard DeVoto, is that Smith was a paranoiac alternating between periods of sanity and insanity, at the same time a man of great energy and spiritual force. The inability of non-Mormons to reach any settled conclusions about Smith has confirmed the Church membership in its belief in him, for the Church viewpoint from beginning to end has had the advantage of thorough consistency. Here, however, it is not important whether Joseph Smith was or was not a prophet of God; it is important that his followers believed him to be such, and they wrought greatly in consequence of this belief.

In 1831, because of persecution in New York, the prophet moved the Church to Kirtland, Ohio, previously a Campbellite stronghold; whole congregations there came into the fold. The Church grew amazingly. Missionaries "without purse or scrip" spread into the country, preaching and baptizing. Others heard the word, and sought out Joseph Smith; such an one was Parley P. Pratt. The first temple of the Church began to rise in Kirtland. In the summer of 1831 Joseph Smith visited the brethren in Jackson County, Missouri, and felt Missouri was Zion; a revelation directed the faithful to assemble in Zion, "the land of your inheritance, which is in the hands of your enemies."

Alarmed Missourians found the "Saints" settling among them in droves, with the prospect that more would follow. The two groups mixed like fire and gasoline. The Missourians were hard individualists, frontiersmen of slave-soil sympathies. The Mormons settled on the land as solid social groups, announcing themselves as the chosen of God arriving upon God's designated gathering place; they held to themselves, voted as a group, and sometimes talked unwisely of ultimately possessing all Zion—Jackson County—"the earth and the fullness thereof." Additionally, they came from free soil.

In July, 1833, amid scenes of rape and rapine, the Mormons were driven from Jackson County; they settled in Clay County. But the sympathies of Clay citizens soon soured; in 1836 the Mormons were expelled again, into Daviess and Caldwell counties, where they founded the towns of Far West and Adam-ondi-Ahman. "Persecution" and "mobocrat," two burning words in Mormon history, were being graven upon Mormon feeling. The Church in Kirtland likewise encountered difficulties, for Joseph Smith, gathering around him in the Quorum of the Twelve and the higher priesthood the men who later served the Church so ably, was harassed by a lunatic fringe of charlatans, adventurers, and zealots. Disaster for Kirtland came with the panic of 1837; the city was caught in a fever of land speculation, and because of undercapitalization and embezzlement by its cashier, the Mormon bank closed its doors.

Smith, Rigdon, and other Mormon leaders journeyed west, but Missouri, where they arrived in March, was no sanctuary. Embittered people there listened avidly to counsel of resistance. In July, 1838, according to Hubert H. Bancroft, Sidney Rigdon delivered a rousing sermon, in which he declared, "We take God to witness and the holy angels to witness this day, that we warn all men, in the name of Jesus Christ, to come on us no more forever. The man or the set of men who attempt it, do it at the expense of their lives; and that mob that comes on us to disturb us, there shall be between us and them a war of extermination, for we will follow them till the last drop of their blood is spilled, or else they will have to exterminate us; for we will carry the war to their own houses, and their own families, and one party or the other shall be utterly destroyed."

The Missourians took Rigdon at his word. Mormons clashed in August with non-Mormons who sought to prevent them from voting at Gallatin. Minor in itself, this incident was a prelude to open combat. In October the two parties fought at Crooked River, and a week later a mob fell on the Mormons at Hauns Mill and massacred eighteen. The same day a mob-militia of 2,000 appeared before Far West, prepared to execute the order of Governor Lilburn W. Boggs that the Mormons be utterly exterminated or driven from the State. Joseph and Hyrum Smith, Sidney Rigdon, Lyman Wight, Parley P. Pratt, and other Mormon leaders were delivered into the hands of the mob-militia, and the expulsion of the people began on November 1. Smith lay in Missouri prisons until April, while the scattered members of the Church were led into Illinois by Brigham Young, who now began to demonstrate his great capacities for organization and leadership. At length escaping prison and rejoining his people, Joseph Smith designated Commerce, Illinois, as the gathering place for the inconquerable young Church.

The impoverished Mormon people found sympathy and a warm welcome in Illinois. But Illinois sympathy was not altogether altruistic: an increase of population seemed to promise an increase of business and a local remedy for the depression following the 1837 panic, and the numerically equal Whig and Democratic parties hoped to gain the Mormon vote. On the site of Commerce Joseph Smith set about building Nauvoo, "the Beautiful." He obtained a remarkable city charter from the legislature: Nauvoo was permitted to levy, collect and disburse taxes without reference to any authority except the city council; its courts were given exclusive jurisdiction over city affairs; more extraordinarily, the city was granted the right to raise and maintain an independent militia, the Nauvoo Legion; and a charter was granted the University of the City of Nauvoo, said to be the first municipal university in the United States.

Nauvoo rose amazingly; within five years it was the largest town in Illinois. But the causes which had operated to alienate the Missourians still were implicit in Mormon group relations. Again they had come as new settlers into an already occupied land; again they were coherent and powerful as a social group; again they alienated their fellows by their insistence that they were the chosen of God—the "saints" of the latter days. They began to be cordially hated by many, and lost the favor of both political parties by voting consistently for neither. There were new sources of irritation, too. "Mobbing and robbing" at the hands of the gentiles (non-Mormons) in Missouri had led some of the people to feel that reprisal at the expense of any gentile was justified; and the urban growth of Nauvoo attracted unsavory characters, by no means averse to having their misdeeds assigned to the Mormons. Rumors of adultery and polygamy overspread the country. Relations between Mormons and non-Mormons grew steadily worse. Mobs descended on outlying Mormon farms, killing and mutilating Mormons and firing their houses and crops. The legislature began to consider repeal of the Nauvoo charter.

It had now become clear, with a prospect only of increasing violence, that the Mormons would have to find a new land. As early as 1842 Joseph Smith had predicted that one day the Mormons would establish themselves in the Rocky Mountains and become a great and mighty people; in February, 1844, Joseph "instructed the Twelve Apostles to send out a delegation and investigate the locations of California and Oregon, and hunt out a good location, where we can remove to after the Temple is completed, and where we can build a city in a day, and have a government of our own, get up into the mountains, where the Devil cannot dig us out, and live in a healthy climate, where we can live as old as we have mind to."

At the same time he resolved on a bolder step: he announced his candidacy for the Presidency of the United States. If he were successful, "the dominion of the Kingdom of God" would forthwith be established; if unsuccessful, the Mormons might turn westward, to California, Oregon, or Texas, and escape persecution. These plans were shattered in June. Apostates from the Church published, in the *Nauvoo Expositor,* charges about Smith and the leaders which were regarded as libelous. The city council smashed the press as a nuisance, and the countryside was aroused. Imprisoned at Carthage under pledge of protection, on the 27th of June Smith was shot dead with his brother, Hyrum, when a mob stormed the jail.

In August, 1844, Brigham Young, in his capacity as president of the Quorum of the Twelve, was accorded leadership of the Church; it is said that he "spoke with the voice of Joseph," so that the mantle of Joseph demonstrably had fallen upon him. Although not all Church members were disposed to accept this leadership, and special dissenting groups broke off, notably followers of James J. Strang, who later established the "Kingdom of Saint James" in the islands of Lake Michigan, the greater part of the membership followed Young.

Brigham Young, the guiding genius of the Church in Utah, was born in Whitingham, Vermont, in 1801. He joined Joseph Smith in 1832, and was made a charter member of the Quorum of the Twelve in 1835. A man of enormous energy and great vision, he has come to be recognized as one of the major figures in western history. No man could have been found more brilliantly suited to the task of overseeing the removal of the Mormons to a new land. In the autumn of 1845 he announced that the following spring the Mormons would move from Nauvoo. In February, 1846, advance companies crossed the Mississippi.

Mormons on the Iowa plains made their way slowly westward, the advance companies building bridges and houses, and putting in crops for companies that followed. Captain James Allen arrived at Council Bluffs on July 1 with a Government proposal that 500 men be mustered into a Mormon Battalion for service against Mexico. Although in later years Battalion members were fond of referring to themselves as the "Ram in the Thicket," offered in sacrifice to save Israel, and Mormon leaders declared that the Government had "demanded" such a battalion to test Mormon loyalty, it is now thought that the idea was of Mormon origin. Brigham Young and the apostles in Iowa actively aided in the recruiting, and the Battalion departed in July on an epochal 2,000-mile march to California.

Before the Mormons settled into winter quarters in the fall of 1846, the absolute necessity of a "gathering place for Israel" was demonstrated by the final expulsion of the Saints from Nauvoo. Difficulties there had been constant, and the city was definitely abandoned to the anti-Mormons after the pitched "Battle of Nauvoo" in September, when a small band of Mormons and "Jack Mormons" (gentile friends) gallantly fought with a large force of anti-Mormons in defense of the city. From their winter quarters on the west bank of the Missouri River near present Omaha, and pursuant to the "Will and Word of the Lord," vouchsafed Brigham Young as a revelation in January, 1847, the Mormons dispatched an advance company of pioneers to find in the mountains an "abiding place for the Saints." In Mormon tradition, Brigham Young knew from vision, before leaving Nauvoo, that he should locate in Great Salt Lake Valley. Historically, his decision was determined by reading the published reports of [John C.] Frémont and other travelers, and by special considerations affecting the Mormons as a group. In Nauvoo he received letters, sometimes insolent, from other intending migrants, warning him that the Mormons might expect trouble in California and Oregon; these must certainly have confirmed him in his conviction that the Saints must find a place where they would be the first settlers, and where they would be privileged to say to later comers what had been so often said to them: "Get out!"

Oregon, already peopled by many emigrant Missourians, seems to have attracted Young at no time; he gave some consideration to Vancouver Island, more especially for the English emigrants; but it was the Great Basin, so named by Frémont, that seized upon his imagination. As early as 1845 he had specifically mentioned Great Salt Lake Valley, the outstanding topographical feature of the Basin, and all through the early months of 1846 he talked about the Basin. Addressing the Battalion prior to its departure, he informed them that the Saints in all probability would locate in eastern California some 800 miles from the Pacific Coast; and to Colonel Thomas L. Kane he talked specifically of locating in Bear River Valley or Great Salt Lake Valley.

The general place of settlement had been determined sight unseen; accordingly, only the specific locality remained a question mark as the pioneers rolled up the North Platte and thence along the Oregon Trail to the tune of "The Upper California, O, That's the Land For Me." In June the westbound Saints conferred with Jim Bridger and other mountain men, from whom they got discouraging reports, but the party pushed on from Fort Bridger in the tracks of the Donners, and into Salt Lake Valley. Orson Pratt and Erastus Snow, on July 21, 1847, were first to enter; a small body arrived the next day, and the greater part of the company on the 23rd. Young, who had been ill with "mountain fever," entered the valley with the rear companies on July 24, which has since been "Pioneer Day," Utah's outstanding holiday.

Plowing began July 23, the day before Young's arrival, when the waters of City Creek were turned out of their bed to soften the land for plows. It was necessary to hasten if anything was to be grown this year, and a harvest would be important, for Parley P. Pratt and John Taylor were bringing westward more than 1,500 colonists who expected to winter in the valley. The original company, augmented at Fort Laramie by a few immigrant Saints from Mississippi, received further additions on July 29, when the rest of the Mississippi Saints and the sick detachment of the Mormon Battalion, which had wintered at Pueblo, arrived in the valley. Other Battalion members appeared from the west a few months later, having been mustered out in California on July 16, but the greater part of the Battalion stayed in California, and some members, working at Sutters Mill near the site of Sacramento, participated in the discovery of gold the next year. Notwithstanding the need for a harvest, exploring parties were dispatched north to Cache Valley, west to Tooele Valley, and south to Utah Valley. Exploration, however, only served to convince the Mormons that they had already found their place of settlement. In August, Brigham Young and others turned back to their families at Winter Quarters, having, in George A. Smith's words, "broke, watered, planted, and sowed upwards of 100 acres with various kinds of seeds; nearly stockaded with adobies one public square (ten acres)," and built "one line of log cabins in stockade."

The colonists were not permitted to scatter out over the land. Co-operative practices and thinking, which had characterized Mormon life in the Midwest, had led to an emphasis upon the group, and the nature of that group life made possible exploitation of the arid lands and the creation of a desert civilization. As with all Mormon colonies in later years, the 1847 settlers gathered in a fort, not only for protection against Indians but because such a communal settlement allowed for valid social life and religious activities. The settlers lived close together, and went out to a distance to farm their lands. It is one of the great triumphs of the Mormon Church that it not only surmounted the problems of an arid land, which forced settlers to scatter widely over a large area, but made those problems of isolation and tremendous distances contribute to the power and coherence of its social organization.

The first laws in the region, issued as decrees by Brigham Young on July 25, 1847, related to land ownership and conservation of resources. Land, Young said, was neither to be bought nor sold; it was to be apportioned to the settlers, and if they were to hold it, they must take industrious care of it. He also decreed community ownership of water and timber resources. The Mormons, neither then nor thereafter, were much concerned with formal law; in general, broad principles were laid down, and the people were governed to a considerable extent according to the moral codes and social relationships developed within the Church.

Upon Young's departure for Winter Quarters, a president and two counselors, together with a "High Council" of twelve high priests, were nominated to administer the affairs of the "Stake of Zion" in the valley. Major acts of the council were approved by congregational voting. In general, local administration was by the bishops of the several wards, although, during the first year in Great Salt Lake Valley, the High Council served in virtually all capacities, legislative, executive, and judicial. In later years the High Council served more especially as a court of appeal from decisions of the bishops' courts. High Council decisions could be overturned only by the Quorum of the Twelve, the court of last resort. Since Brigham Young's time, the President of the Church has always been the senior apostle, and decisions of the presidency have usually been synonymous with decisions of the Twelve. No attempt was made until 1849 to establish a formal civil government, though civil laws were passed by the High Council in December, 1847, with legislation against vagrancy, disorderliness, theft and arson, adultery, and misconduct in general. There was no need for civil government, since Church government was functioning effectively. The land they occupied still belonged to Mexico, and was not ceded to the United States until after signing of the treaty of Guadaloupe [*sic*] Hidalgo in 1848.

In accordance with instructions given by Young before his departure, the High Council in November bought out [Miles] Goodyear's interests on the Weber River. When Young, who in December, 1847, had become officially designated as President of the Church, returned from Winter Quarters in September, 1848, the Utah region lay ready for systematic colonization. Already, indeed, Goodyear's property had become transformed to "Brownsville," and Peregrine Sessions had located the town of Bountiful.

Because their preoccupation with the desert was the outstanding feature of their civilization for the next quarter of a century, it is important to realize the mood in which the Mormons migrated to Utah. The Church in the early years had a stirring millennial tone; to its members the day of judgment seemed very imminent. In designating Missouri as Zion, Joseph Smith named a place of gathering for the faithful, and although he ridiculed the claims of Millerites, who predicted the Second Advent for 1843 or 1844, and although he said on more than one occasion that many years would elapse before the maturing of this event, yet he anticipated the millennium at a relatively early date, once saying that if he lived to be eighty-five, he should see "the face of the Son of Man."

The power and conviction of this belief, the deeply moving belief of a people, may be heard in the hymns still sung by Mormon congregations:

The Spirit of God like a fire . . . is burning!
The latter day glory begins to come forth;
The visions and blessings of old are returning!
And angels are coming to visit the earth.
We'll sing and we'll shout with the armies of heaven,
Hosanna, hosanna to God and the Lamb!
Let glory to them in the highest be given,
Henceforth and forever; amen, and amen!

Because the Mormons looked to the afterlife more than to this life, colonization of the desert was possible. "Faith through works" was the keynote to Mormon living. Men starved on sego-lily bulbs and thistle greens, on hawks, owls, and crows, while they stayed stubbornly with the land. They were working out their salvation on earth. They clung together because they had to; they succored one another because they could depend only upon themselves. Not all of the Saints were saints; often there were rascals among them; often their suspicion of the gentiles made them socially difficult; often as a people they were unbearably self-righteous. Had the Mormons aimed less high, however, and achieved less greatly, their shortcomings would have been less emphasized.

Brigham Young's efficient colonization of the arid mountain valleys was remarkable for its success and for the social discipline that resulted in success. Church members were "called" as for a mission. Groups were carefully selected to include blacksmiths, tanners, millers, carpenters—perhaps also a doctor, though for the most part the frontier settlements depended upon midwives and amateur doctors. Everyone, actually or potentially, was a farmer. A resident would be named for the group, and on a designated date it would gather its property into wagons and set out, perhaps to the valley of the Sevier, perhaps to "Dixie," perhaps even to Idaho's Salmon River, or

Nevada's Carson Valley. Arriving on the site of settlement, sometimes selected in advance by Brigham Young, as Fillmore was, the colonists would build a fort, then irrigation ditches, fence farm lands, and raise log or adobe houses. Major missions departed in midwinter, and crops were put in as soon as spring opened. Often newly arrived immigrants were incorporated into such colonizing missions, but the backbone was supplied by experienced settlers who had dwelt longer in Utah. A man who had proved himself once might suddenly be called to forsake the few comforts he had wrested from the desert for a new struggle with a barren untilled land. Sometimes he might feel that death was preferable to another uprooting, but almost invariably the "called" man obeyed, for he was contributing to the "upbuilding of the Kingdom"; he was laying up glories in heaven by his work on earth.

The late-sown crops of 1847 were scant, but the colonists planted several thousand acres to wheat and corn. John Steele recorded in his journal in the spring of 1848, "Our wheat, corn, beans and peas are all up and looking grand and grass is 6 inches high. Sunday, June 4th, there is great excitement in camp. There has come a frost which took beans, corn and wheat and nearly every thing, and to help make the disaster complete the crickets came by the thousands of tons, and the cry is now raised, 'we can not live here, away to California,' and the faith of many were shaken, but . . . {the Battalion boys} almost to a unit said God had sent us here, and here we were going to stay, come weal come woe. This seemed to turn the tide of affairs in our favor but times still looked very dark and hunger stared us in the face at every step until about the 15th of July when we began to get some new wheat which relieved us wonderfully, and we then thought of beginning to live once more." The frost was forgotten, but the crickets were remembered, because gulls came in flocks to gorge upon them; the "miracle of the gulls," sent by God to succor the people, has become a cherished part of Mormon folklore.

Crickets and late frosts were only a single feature of the Mormons' environmental adjustment. Their first houses were built, on the advice of Sam Brannan, after the California manner—flat-roofed adobe—but the water gathered on the roofs and reduced some of the houses to mud puddles; then the Mormons built houses to withstand the storms. They lived thousands of miles from manufacturers and supplies; what they did not have, they went without or made themselves. Tanners made shoes, shirts, and breeches along with harness and saddles; expeditions were sent back along the emigrant trails to recover metal from discarded wagons, to be reworked into tools and plowshares; native clays were made into pottery; lumber, laboriously hauled from the canyons, was utilized for a thousand things, from wooden shoes to boats. Parley P. Pratt could write in his journal concerning 1848, "My family and myself, in common with many of the camp, suffered much for food. . . . I had ploughed and subdued land to the amount of near forty acres, and had cultivated the same in grain and vegetables. In this labor every woman and child in my family . . . had joined to help me. . . . Myself and some of them were compelled to go with bare feet for several months, reserving our Indian moccasins for extra occasions. We toiled hard and lived on a few greens and on thistle and other roots. We had sometimes a little flour and some cheese, and sometimes we were able to procure from our neighbors a little sour skimmed milk or buttermilk." But to his brother, Orson, then in England, he could write romantically, "All is quiet—stillness. No elections, no police reports, no murders, no wars, in our little world. . . . It is the dream of the poets actually fulfilled."

In December, 1848, the Mormons wrote a memorial to Congress for creation of a Territorial government. This memorial, bearing 2,270 signatures, and said to have been twenty-two feet long, was sent east the following May, but by that time the Mormons had undertaken to create a provisional government. A constitution was drafted in early March, and officers for the "State of Deseret" were elected in Great Salt Lake City. Brigham Young was named governor, Heber C. Kimball lieutenant-governor and justice of the supreme court, and Willard Richards secretary of State; the Mormons simply installed the First Presidency of the Church in the leading civil offices. The first session of the legislature was held in July, 1849, but no legislation was passed until the second session. The State of Deseret, named for a Book of Mormon word interpreted as meaning "honey bee," included within its proposed boundaries virtually all of what is now Utah and Nevada, the greater part of Arizona, and portions of Idaho, Wyoming, Colorado, Oregon, and New Mexico, as well as a strip of seacoast in Southern California near San Diego. One of the few physical reminders of the State of Deseret, in 1940, was an inscribed stone, donated by the provisional government, and still to be seen inside the Washington Monument in the Nation's capital.

The legislature sent east a delegate, Almon W. Babbitt, with a petition to Congress for admission as a State. Babbitt's application for a seat in the House was refused on the ground that seating him would be a quasi-recognition of Deseret. By July, 1850, a compromise committee headed by Henry Clay had drawn up a plan by which California was to be admitted as a State, and New Mexico and Utah admitted as Territories. Bitter argument between slavery and abolitionist partisans held up disposition of the territory acquired from Mexico and it was not until September, 1850, Congress having become frightened by the necessity of doing something, that proposals of the compromise committee were substantially adopted. The Mormon name of "Deseret" was held to be repulsive, and the territory was named Utah, to the chagrin of those who thought that "Utah" was descriptive only of a "dirty, insect-infested, grasshopper-eating tribe of Indians." The Territory of Utah extended north and south from the Oregon (now the Idaho) line to the New Mexico (now the Arizona) line, and east and west from the summit of the Rockies through what is now central Wyoming and Colorado to the Sierra Nevada Mountains.

The Mormons had fled from civilization, done with its abominations, but they had fled directly in the path of empire. In January, 1848, James W. Marshall picked up the first gold in Sutter's mill races. The first overland gold-seekers arrived in Great Salt Lake Valley in June, 1849. Almost all of them were in need of provisions and fresh horses when they arrived at the Mormon oasis. Many of them had brought stores of merchandise—clothing, tools, manufactured goods—which they sacrificed ruthlessly for fresh livestock and crops. Priceless goods were offered to amazed Mormons at far less than cost. The Lord had provided for His own.

But the Mormons must have agricultural self-sufficiency if they were to survive. Gold was a convenience, but food and livestock, iron and coal, were necessities. Moreover, Mormon isolation must be maintained. Young forbade prospecting for precious metals in Utah, and rebuked those who would have gone to dig gold in California. "Gold," he thundered from the pulpit, "is for paving streets. The business of a Saint is to stay at home and make his fields green." Members of the Church in California left the gold fields without regret. James S. Brown, the first to see Marshall's gold, returned to Zion in 1848 with other members of the Battalion. Just as he was preparing to leave, he located a rich find from which he washed out $49.50 in gold between 11 A.M. and sundown, but the next morning he left, never to see the spot again.

The "kingdom" began to build in Utah. Settlements spread down the mountain valleys south from Great Salt Lake City. Fort Utah was built near the site of Provo in 1849; the walls of Manti arose soon after in Sanpete Valley and by the end of 1850 George A. Smith was en route south to settle the Little Salt Lake Valley. But "building" did not proceed without harassment from without. In the summer of 1851 the officials named to Territorial office by President [Millard] Fillmore appeared from the east. Fillmore had been gracious to the Mormons; he had named Young governor of the new Territory, and all the other officers were Mormon except four. These arrived to find that Young had completed a census of the Territory, apportioned representation for the Territorial legislature, and set a date for elections. The general assembly had formally dissolved the State of Deseret, and Young had assumed office as Territorial governor, upon receiving word of his nomination through eastern newspapers brought from California.

Unfortunately for the hope that the Mormons would get on amicably in their new relation to the United States, the gentile Federal officials were the first in a long line of scoundrels, fanatics, and well-meaning but ineffectual men who thoroughly exasperated the Mormons, who in turn thoroughly exasperated the rest of the nation. Invited to address the general conference of the Church in September, 1851, Associate Justice Perry D. Brocchus exhorted the Mormons to be true to the Government, and then alluded to the as yet officially unadmitted practice of polygamy, strongly admonishing the Mormon women to be virtuous. An uproar ensued. Brigham Young hushed the audience and turned on Brocchus. The United States Government had not, he said, earned the esteem of the Mormons when it stood idly by during the persecutions visited on the Mormons in Missouri and Illinois. It was an insult for such corrupt individuals as Brocchus to come before the Latter-day Saints as authorities on morality and virtue. "I love the constitution and government of the United States, but not the damned rascals that administer the government."

A further source of irritation soon appeared. Broughton D. Harris, secretary of the Territory, was dissatisfied because strict legal forms had not been followed in apportioning representation to the Territorial legislature. A new census should be taken, and everything done over. Brigham Young was not disposed to comply. Having completed a census of Utah's 11,380 inhabitants, he saw no need to do it over. Harris decided to return East with Brocchus. Lemuel G. Brandebury, chief justice of the courts, sided with Brocchus and Harris.

Hastily the Territorial legislature was summoned, and an attempt was made by legal means to restrain Harris from leaving the Territory with its papers and funds. Brocchus and Brandebury, meeting as the supreme court despite the fact that no legal session could be held until the time and place was designated by Governor Young, sustained Harris, and the officials turned their backs on Utah, leaving the Saints to make what shift they could.

The Mormons were not dismayed. They had been getting along by themselves for four years. The legislature dispatched a memorial to Congress strongly protesting the action of the Federal officials, and declared the laws of the Provisional State of Deseret in effect wherever applicable and not in conflict with Federal territorial statutes. Congress was also memorialized for roads, railroads, and a magnetic telegraph. Young named Willard Richards secretary *pro tem,* while the courts were sufficiently served by the Mormon justice, Zerubabbel Snow, who had refused to leave with Brandebury and Brocchus. The story goes that the runaway officers, reporting to Congress, undid themselves by asserting that "polygamy monopolized all the women, which made it very inconvenient" to live in Utah. In itself this first difficulty between Mormons and Federal officeholders was of no significance, but, as the first of a long series of troubles, it was an important indicator.

Before the next group of officeholders arrived, the Mormons had taken the plunge, and formally avowed the practice of polygamy as a fundamental tenet of Church doctrine. Polygamy was the pretext for all the varied dislikes and antagonisms the Saints aroused in the other citizens of the United States. More than any other feature of Mormon culture, polygamy has distinguished Utah and the Mormons in the public mind, and while it is no longer generally believed that the Mormons have horns and are practicing masters of the dark arts of seduction, Utahns are continually seized upon for information about polygamy.

The doctrine of polygamy (more correctly, polygyny, inasmuch as polygamy signifies "many marriages" rather than "many wives") seems first to have been put in written form in the revelation issued by Joseph Smith to Church members at Nauvoo in 1843. It is evident, however, as concluded by B. H. Roberts, distinguished Church historian, that the doctrine had been advanced in some form much earlier, perhaps as far back as 1831, in Kirtland. Persistent rumors of unorthodox marriage ideas and practices accompanied the Mormons throughout their migrations, and while these rumors were denied by Church authorities, there must, as Roberts notes, have been some basis for stories so persistent.

Joseph Smith seems to have lived in plural marriage from about 1841, and other leaders adopted the practice after issuance of the revelation in 1843, but the principle was not proclaimed to the world until 1852, at a special conference of the Church in Great Salt Lake City, when the Saints were solidly established in their mountain home. Many Mormon leaders shrank from it, and took plural wives only after earnest inquiry of God: polygamy was a stern ethic, the very guerdon of morality, not an easy flowering of sensuality. The question of *why* the Saints adopted polygamy, or "plural marriage," in Church terminology, is susceptible of as many explanations as there are viewpoints on Joseph Smith and the Church. The Church doctrine has been that plural marriage was divinely ordained, a higher order of marriage, as much advanced over monogamy as monogamy over celibacy. A man's wives and his children added to his glory in heaven, and they shared in that glory. Acceptance of plural marriage was thus, for Church members, an act of faith and belief, an essential expression of religious conviction.

Although individuals may now and then, in taking a new wife, have found as much encouragement in a pretty face as in religious conviction, it is important to emphasize that polygamy was never, for all the impact it made on American mores, an immoral institution. Moral standards were higher in polygamy than out, and adulterers were harshly dealt with by law. Mormons held that it was the right of every woman to be a wife and mother—indeed, in Mormon society a man could be compelled to marry a woman on her initiative—and a great many social evils were ascribed to the fact that many men refused their responsibilities, and women were reduced to celibacy and prostitution. The Saints inveighed against such social irresponsibles, and as fast as a Mormon could support a wife, he was urged to take one, sometimes to his discomfiture. Nevertheless, the number of polygamists among the Mormons has always been grossly overestimated; Levi Edgar Young, Church authority and Utah historian, places the figure at 3 per cent of marriageable adults, while Bernard DeVoto, critic of the Mormons, estimates it at perhaps 2 per cent.

Polygamy was a gathering storm, but for twenty years the Mormons occupied themselves with more immediate concerns. The dispossession of Indians from their lands inevitably led to embitterment among the aborigines, and though the Mormons endeavored to induce the Indians to settle down along with their white brothers, and were more humane than settlers elsewhere on the western frontier, the Indians were unable to adapt themselves at once to a new manner of living. The lands east of the Wasatch Mountains were at first ignored by the Mormons, and the economy of the Utes was not greatly disturbed, but the best lands of the Paiutes and Gosiutes were soon occupied by Mormon settlements. Indians were reduced to beggary or to intermittent theft and warfare. The important troubles of the white colonists, however, came at the hands of the powerful Utes, more particularly in the Walker War of 1853 and the Black Hawk War of 1865–68. The earliest local difficulties of importance occurred in Utah Valley, in 1850, when a militia force, aided by Captain Howard Stansbury's men, routed Utes under Big Elk at Fort Utah, but until 1853, Indian-white relations on the whole were peaceable.

The essential cause of the Walker War was the prohibition of Indian slave trade by the Mormon government, though the growing dissatisfaction of the Utes at white encroachment was also a factor. The Ute chief Walker (Wakara) had been friendly, and Manti was settled at his request. The Utes had been given to raiding lesser tribes and selling their captives in New Mexico. In 1852, the Territorial legislature passed a law designed to stop all traffic in Indian women and children. Enforcement of the law at the expense of white traders from New Mexico alienated Walker. In July, 1853, a raid on Springville initiated a series of attacks in Utah and Sanpete valleys, the Utes striking swiftly at the smaller settlements and retreating into the mountains after each attack. Previously, Young had advised that all settlements be fortified, and the outbreak of the Walker War led to general fortification throughout the Territory. The hostilities lasted only until spring. Twelve settlers were killed and a number wounded. Several hundred head of cattle and horses were stolen, but the greatest economic loss to the settlers consisted in the time lost in building forts and in the temporary abandonment of settlements. In May, 1854, to close hostilities, Young met Walker in a conclave on the Sevier River. Walker thereafter was friendly, and no more serious troubles were experienced until the Black Hawk outbreak of 1865.

A tragic event that accompanied the Indian difficulties of 1853 was the massacre of Captain John W. Gunnison and seven men, engaged on a Federal railroad survey. The murder of Gunnison near Sevier Lake was to revenge the killing of a Pahvant Indian by non-Mormon emigrants a few days before. The

Pahvants fell on Gunnison's party at dawn; four men escaped and reached the rest of Gunnison's command. Mutilated almost beyond recognition, the bodies were recovered by the Mormons, and conveyed to near-by towns for burial, the body of Gunnison being interred at Fillmore. Despite the fact that Gunnison's *History of the Mormons* (1852), had been criticized as being over-friendly to the Mormons, enemies of the Saints were quick to deduce that Gunnison had been slain by disguised Mormons or by Indians at Mormon instigation. This widely broadcast belief was not exploded for some years, despite explicit disavowals by Gunnison's second-in-command. The constant slow irritations of Mormon-Federal relations, and the continued stream of anti-Mormon stories circulated in the East, determined President Pierce, in 1854, not to nominate Brigham Young as governor of Utah Territory for a second term. Lieutenant Colonel E. J. Steptoe, who wintered at Great Salt Lake City in 1853–54, was chosen. Steptoe, however, declined the honor—the anti-Mormon story was that he had been neatly framed by Young with a variant of the "badger game"—and joined with the Mormons to petition the re-nomination of Young. Pierce acquiesced, and named the Mormon leader for a second term.

Events in Utah during the next three years piled upon one another kaleidoscopically. People continued to pour into the Territory, especially from Great Britain and the Scandinavian countries; in 1856, a census enumerated some 76,000 inhabitants, and while this was perhaps 36,000 too high, colonization of the arid mountain valleys was proceeding amazingly. The problem of raising sufficient food for such a flood of immigration was not light, and there were grasshopper infestations, commencing in 1854. The hoppers of that year laid their eggs by the millions, hatching out in such numbers in 1855 as to threaten famine for the whole Mormon people. Crickets had almost ceased to be a problem; irrigation ditches and other obstacles, with the aid of bird predators, reduced their number. But winged grasshoppers blackened the sun at midday and filled the air with their rasping flight. The winter of 1855–56 was exceptionally severe and increased the suffering consequent upon crop losses.

To some Mormon leaders, the grasshopper infestation appeared in the light of a rebuke from God for the wastefulness of the people. Many Church leaders commenced to feel that the Saints needed a reformation; they were losing sight of God. Additionally, as the Mormons proceeded with their conquest of the desert, non-Mormons were beginning to look on the Utah country with more favor, and were settling down among the Saints. The authorities had forebodings. The Saints should be made into a tighter group. Church leaders reinstituted the idea of "consecration of property," a socialistic plan first experimentally tried in Missouri between 1831 and 1833. Devout Saints "for and in consideration of good will" held toward the Church, deeded to it all their property, real and personal, amounting in some cases to thousands of dollars. While no land titles had yet been granted in the Utah area by the Federal government, it was thought that by acting together through the Church, the Mormons would be in a position to defend themselves against an influx of gentiles.

The idea of "consecration" gained more currency after September, 1856, when the "Reformation," initiated by Jedediah M. Grant in a speech at Kaysville, took fire among the people. Throughout the Territory, the Saints confessed their sins and were rebaptized. The legislature of 1856–57, before being allowed by Heber C. Kimball to proceed with legislation, went to the Endowment House to be baptized for the remission of their sins. The emotions of the people were profoundly wrought upon; in some sections of Utah the emotional tension broke out into religious violence—and the Church ever since has had to reckon, in books of anti-Mormons, with wild stories of blood atonement.

The feelings aroused by the Reformation were worked upon by other happenings of 1856–57. The anxious desire of many poorer English converts to migrate to Zion induced Church authorities, in the autumn of 1855, to issue an epistle to the Saints: "The Lord, through his prophet, says of the poor, 'Let them come on foot, with hand-carts or wheelbarrows; let them gird up their loins, and walk through, and nothing shall hinder them.'" But the thousand-mile trek across the plains, pulling or pushing heavy hand-carts, the women, the aged, and small children alike walking the entire distance, took a tragic toll; many immigrants were buried by the wayside, and the first year of the hand-cart migrations, 1856, was darkened when the Willie and Martin companies were caught by October snows along the Sweetwater River in Wyoming; many of them perished.

Mormon relations with the Federal government thoroughly disintegrated. A new attempt to obtain statehood in 1856 was fruitless. Almon W. Babbitt, Territorial secretary, was killed by Indians in Wyoming, and again Mormon critics were blackly positive that the sinister hand of the Saints was in the deed. The relations with the "foreign" judiciary continued to be cancerous. The Saints thoroughly resented being ruled by outsiders with whom they had nothing in common, and who too often revealed themselves as rascals. Nor were they always on their best behavior; in conflict with a group of Mormon lawyers, Justice George P. Stiles had his office raided and certain of his personal papers burned. Early in 1857 Stiles returned to Washington to report, in effect, that the Mormons were in a state of rebellion. W. W. Drummond, colleague of Stiles, was even more exasperating to the Saints; he refused to recognize the decision of the probate courts, which in Utah had an extraordinarily extended jurisdiction; he bluntly disposed of the whole body of Utah law as having been "founded in ignorance"; his despotic behavior on the bench looked no better to the Saints when it was discovered that he had abandoned his family in the East, and that the woman whom he had brought to Utah as his wife, and whom he was accustomed to seat beside him on the bench, was in fact a harlot. Returning east via California, Drummond reported that the Mormons regarded Brigham Young as sole authority in matters of government, and that they did not consider the laws of Congress binding; that the Church maintained a secret organization which took the lives and properties of those who questioned the authority of the Church; that Mormons had willfully burned the records of the Supreme Court; that Federal officials were daily subjected to public abuse and slander; that Young abused his privilege of pardon and was guilty of instructing juries whom and whom not to indict; that Gunnison had been killed by Indians at the instigation of the Church; and that Babbitt had been killed at the express order of Brigham Young.

In view of the fact that the Republican National Convention, as a part of its 1856 platform, had termed polygamy and slavery "the twin relics of barbarism," that the Democratic Stephen A. Douglas, once a Mormon friend, had denounced Mormonism as "the loathsome ulcer of the body politic," and that the authorities in Washington were anxious to divert public attention to something other than the continuous strife over slavery, such charges could not expect sober consideration and investigation. The Mormons were characterized as being in open rebellion; President Buchanan issued an order terminating Brigham Young's governorship and directed General W. S. Harney to proceed to Utah with the Army of the West and put down the rebellion. The news reached Mormon leaders on July 24, 1857. On the invitation of Brigham Young, many of the people and most of the leaders were gathered at Silver Lake (Brighton) in Big Cottonwood Canyon, for the tenth anniversary of the arrival of the pioneers in Salt Lake Valley. To this gathering the ominous news was brought. In 1847 Brigham Young had declared, "Give us ten years of peace and we will ask no odds of the United States." The ten years were up.

The "Utah War"

Young and the Saints unshrinkingly faced the prospect of conflict. For years they had felt that the forces of Satan would be unleashed upon the Lord's elect. With the crisis upon them they made preparations for defense. Brigham Young declared martial law in the Territory; to the Mormon colonies on the Salmon River, in Carson Valley, and in Southern California, he issued orders to gather in Zion. The Utah militia, the Nauvoo Legion, began drilling, and Lot Smith, with a company of scouts, was ordered to the eastern plains to harass the Government columns. To Captain [Stewart] Van Vliet, who interviewed him in behalf of the army on September 8, 1857, Young said grimly, "We do not want to fight the United States, but if they drive us to it, we shall do the best we can; and I will tell you, as the Lord lives, we shall come off conquerors. . . . We have three years' provisions on hand, which we will cache, and then take to the mountains and bid defiance to all the powers of the government."

He was threatening a permanent guerilla warfare. That the threat was not an idle one is demonstrated by the success of Lot Smith, who had been dispatched to hamstring Government wagon trains. Smith burned almost all available forage between South Pass and Fort Bridger; he cut off the advance army supply trains and burned them; swinging behind the main column of the Utah Expedition, he burned several more supply trains. In his entire campaign less than fifty shots were fired, and not a single man was killed, but his tactics forced the Federal troops into winter quarters near Fort Bridger, 300 miles short of their objective. The precipitous walls of Echo Canyon were fortified by the Mormon troops, but it was lack of provisions and the onset of winter that enforced the decision to winter at Camp Scott on Black's Fork.

During September of this year, before the troops had settled down for the winter, the Mountain Meadows Massacre occurred in southern Utah.

Fear and hatred aroused by the approach of the troops was a major element contributing to the commission of that crime.

General Harney, when ordered to Utah with his troops, had loudly declared, "I will winter in the valley or in hell." He wintered in Kansas, and the command was given to Colonel (brevetted Brigadier General) Albert Sidney Johnston, who later fought brilliantly for the South. Johnston joined his troops in November, and with them eked out a miserable winter near Fort Bridger, waiting for spring. But the tide of affairs had now taken another direction in the East. Captain Van Vliet reached Washington in November with his report of the interview with Brigham Young, and of the Mormon "scorched earth" policy. This, with an outbreak of scandal in connection with army contracts, gave public opinion a new perspective on affairs in Utah. The whole idea of the Utah Expedition began to be sharply criticized in the press, where it was frequently termed "Buchanan's Blunder." Several million dollars had been and were being expended, and more sober consideration was given to just what was being accomplished at all this expense.

With an acute sense of political timing, Colonel Thomas L. Kane, a Philadelphian who time and again had proved himself a staunch Mormon friend, interviewed [President James] Buchanan about a possible solution of the Utah difficulty; Buchanan evidently made no official commitments, but Kane packed his bags and departed for Utah via Panama and southern California. He arrived in Great Salt Lake City in February, 1858, and after conferring with the Mormon authorities, made a difficult journey to Camp Scott, where he arrived March 12. Johnston received him coldly, but Alfred Cumming, named the previous July to succeed Young as governor, gave him a gracious reception, and was so impressed with him and his pacific proposals that he agreed to accompany Kane back to Great Salt Lake City. They arrived in April.

Brigham Young had declared in June, 1853, "'I am and will be governor, and no power can hinder it until the Lord Almighty says, 'Brigham, you need not be governor any longer.'" Acting on that assumption, and over his signature as governor, he had in September, 1857, issued a proclamation forbidding the army to enter the territory, and had advised their commander that the troops might remain only if their arms and accouterments were delivered over to the Mormon quartermaster general for safekeeping. The Lord Almighty, apparently, had spoken to him, for he received Cumming with official deference. But if Cumming was governor in name, Brigham remained governor in fact, and however Federal officials might come and go, to the end of his life Brigham Young's was the word by which the Mormons were guided. Young had, Cumming discovered, no faith in the troops and new officials. Despite his pledges of protection, the dismayed governor found the Mormons busy with preparations to flee the troops, and little disposed to give ear to reassurances. The idea of fighting the army had been given over, but now it had been determined that the people would enter upon a new migration. It was not exactly clear where they would go—rumors of Sonora and the South Sea islands were most current among the people; only Young knew that he had sent out an exploring expedition which he hoped would locate, somewhere in the desert wilds south of Great Salt Lake Valley, new oases where the Mormons might live in peace.

In late April and early May, the people began an active exodus. All the settlements north of Utah Valley, where they gathered, were abandoned; there remained behind only a few men in each settlement, to fire the houses and crops if the exodus should definitely be decided upon. Dismayed, Cumming watched the progress of "The Move." But from Brigham Young he won the assurance that if the troops did not molest the people, nor settle near them, the thirty thousand would return. Cumming went back to Camp Scott in mid-May to report that the Mormons acknowledged his authority, and that many stories circulated about them were false. A few days after his arrival peace commissioners arrived from the East, bearing a proclamation of pardon which President Buchanan, bowing to the change in popular clamor, had issued on April 6. The commissioners and Cumming went to Great Salt Lake City, where they conferred with Young, Heber C. Kimball, and Daniel H. Wells, the first presidency of the Church. The Mormons were offended at being "pardoned" for "rebellion" they declined to admit, but granted that they had burned army supply trains and stampeded army cattle; for these acts they accepted the pardon. They also declared their desire to live in peace under the constitution and laws of the United States. This constituted sufficient compromise, and Johnston was notified of the successful outcome of negotiations. Johnston replied with a proclamation assuring the Mormons that all would be protected in person, rights, and the peaceful pursuit of their vocations. This proclamation was published with a declaration from Cumming that Federal and Territorial laws were to be strictly obeyed. Johnston left Camp Scott with his troops, and late in June marched through the silent, deserted streets of Great Salt Lake City. He crossed the Jordan River, marched south, and located west of Utah Lake in Cedar Valley. The Mormons waited upon events a few days, but since the soldiery showed itself pacific, turned their faces homeward in July.

Establishment of troops at Camp Floyd was, for the Mormons, a mixed evil. The camp-followers of Johnston's army transplanted themselves to Great Salt Lake City, and flourished like the green bay tree. Gambling, theft, drunkenness, and murder signalized the arrival of civilization among the Saints; the principal thoroughfare in the Mormon capital became known as Whisky Street, and the oldest profession took root for the first time. Yet farmers were able to sell surplus foodstuffs and livestock at prices previously undreamed of, while manufactured goods of all kinds fell into their hands at absurdly low prices. Eastern speculators and contractors had licked up the greater part of the rich gravy attending the Utah Expedition, but the scattered drops that fell in Utah amazed the people. The army remained in Utah three years, until the outbreak of the Civil War—it was said that Southerners in Washington had much to do with this disposition of able Union troops—and through most of those years there was imminent possibility of clashes between troops and people, each holding the other in contempt. Establishment of *Valley Tan,* first gentile newspaper in Utah, in 1858, did nothing to cement relations, since frontier editors had vigorous ideas as to how newspapers should be run.

The position of Governor Cumming was wholly unenviable. He was handicapped by his status as the resented successor of Brigham Young, and by the attitude of the judiciary, which thoroughly antagonized the people—a gift the judiciary always seemed to possess. Judge Charles E. Sinclair opened his court at Great Salt Lake City with the announcement to the grand jury that he could not take judicial cognizance of the presidential pardon, and strongly recommending that body to give close attention to the crime of treason; Judge John Cradlebaugh, presiding at Provo, opened his session with 100 troops in attendance "to take care of the prisoners and to preserve the peace." When Provo citizens protested, Cradlebaugh summoned eight more companies. Governor Cumming, to whom appeal was carried, requested Johnston to remove the troops; Johnston refused, and the question of authority was not settled until the U.S. Attorney General formally delegated to the governor power over all ordinary troop dispositions. Like other judges who came to Utah, Cradlebaugh was thoroughly sincere and fanatically devoted to his duty, but also like his fellows, he had little social insight and no social sense of humor, and a talent for putting his worst foot forward. His arrogance completely nullified his usefulness. His grand jury refused to find indictments according to instructions, especially refusing to accept his suggestion that the authorities of the Mormon Church, to whom they looked for temporal and spiritual guidance, be indicted for the Mountain Meadows Massacre. Enraged, Cradlebaugh discharged the jury and proceeded south to look into the massacre. Although he obtained some evidence, and the names of the principal white participants, the guilty fled to the hills and Cradlebaugh accomplished nothing.

The arrival of Johnston's Army was significant of the breakdown of Mormon isolation. However the Saints had kept to themselves with the statement that "we are a peculiar people," their location athwart the highroads of American empire made inevitable constant adjustments to the current of American life. The soldiery was followed by the Pony Express, which began operations through Great Salt Lake City in April, 1860. Two stage lines had preceded the wild-riding horsemen, but neither had succeeded in maintaining anything like a schedule, especially in winter. The Pony Express brought Great Salt Lake City within seven days of the national capital, with semi-weekly service; the riders were hip-hurrahed east and west until completion of the Overland Telegraph in October, 1861.

"The Move" had thoroughly shaken up the people; some remained in the south, while those who returned to their homes in the north sometimes were accompanied by southern settlers. Utah's population was forever in a state of ferment, men migrating or being "called" constantly from one part of the Territory to another, so that they had roots in many places and knew many people; a thoroughly homogeneous culture resulted from this constant intermixing of the settlers, who were further confirmed in their identity with the Church by continual service in its behalf.

Following the "Move," Cache Valley and Provo Valley were settled in part during 1859, and the following year the settlements were more firmly established. Sanpete Valley was more completely settled, and the Church turned its eyes definitely toward Utah's Dixie, emigration pouring into that southern country in 1861–62. In 1863–64 Sevier and Circle valleys were settled, and the towns of Richfield, Salina, Monroe, Marysvale, Circleville, and Panguitch were founded. Almost immediately thereafter, Charles Coulson Rich led a company of settlers north to the Bear Lake Valley. By the end of the Civil War all of the principal valleys west of the Wasatch Mountains had been colonized, and the Church was spreading into Idaho and Arizona. An attempt to settle the Uintah Basin was defeated through an adverse report by scouts and through use of the region as an Indian reservation. The desolate lands east of the Colorado and Green rivers were not attractive to colonists so long as less arid lands were unoccupied.

This intensification of colonization was accompanied by a paring of Utah to its present-day dimensions. In 1861, after years of agitation, citizens of western Utah succeeded in persuading Congress to organize the Territory of Nevada, and all of Utah west of 116 degrees west longitude was lost to the new Territory. By a somewhat disgraceful political deal Nevada was made a State soon after its creation as a Territory; Utah lost two more degrees of longitude to Nevada, in 1862 and 1866. At the same time lands were carved off on the east, the creation of Colorado Territory in 1861 cutting off all the country between the summits of the Rockies and 109 degrees west of Greenwich. The final slice of Utah was taken in 1868, to complete the rectangle created as Wyoming. Though Utah in later years argued for more territory, notably for the "Arizona strip" north of the Grand Canyon of the Colorado, the boundaries of 1868 were not again altered.

The Civil War impacted spectacularly upon Mormon society. Here was fulfillment of the prophecy made by Joseph Smith in 1832, that civil war should break out in South Carolina, and that war should be poured out upon all nations. Surely the day of the Lord was at hand. Hardly three weeks before the attack on Fort Sumter in 1861, Brigham Young declared to a congregation in Great Salt Lake City, "The whole government is gone; it is as weak as water. I heard Joseph Smith say, nearly thirty years ago, 'They shall have mobbings to their heart's content, if they do not redress the wrongs of the Latter-day Saints.' Mobs will not decrease, but will increase until the whole Government becomes a mob and eventually it will be State against State, city against city, neighborhood against neighborhood, Methodist against Methodist, and so on. It will be Christian against Christian and man against man; and those who will not take up the sword against their neighbors, must needs flee to Zion." To the Latter-day Saints, the Mormons were convinced, the world must turn for guidance. All that was good in the government of the United States should live in them and because of them. "We shall never secede from the Constitution of the United States," Heber C. Kimball, Young's first counselor, promised in an address on April 6, 1861. "We shall not stop on the way of progress, but we shall make preparations for future events. The south will secede from the north, and the north will secede from us, and God will make the people free as fast as we are able to bear it."

Those "preparations for future events" took active shape next year. The Saints drew up their third constitution for a "State of Deseret," elected a governor (Brigham Young) and a legislature, and dispatched to Congress a memorial seeking admission to the Union. Congress, instead, passed a new law aimed directly at the practice of polygamy, and the Federal government so far suspected Utah's loyalty as to detail Colonel Patrick Edward Connor, with 300 California-Nevada volunteers, to duty in Utah. Vowing that he should subdue the obstreperous Mormons though all hell yawned, the fire-eating Connor crossed the Jordan River in October, and established his camp on the bench above Great Salt Lake City, his cannon within range of Brigham Young's residence.

The legislature of the "State of Deseret" met in January despite failure of Congress to recognize the Mormon State; the members met this and every succeeding year until 1870, a total of nine sessions, yearly passing, for the State of Deseret, the same legislation they had passed while sitting as the Territorial legislature, so that, in Brigham Young's words, "everything {might} be in readiness when Congress {should} recognize our State organization, and to save confusion and trouble when the transition from a territorial condition to that of a state {should} have been fully accomplished." Privately the legislature and the Mormons generally conceived that they sat as the Kingdom of God. The "ghost government" of Deseret persisted through nine years as an ideal, at once pitiful and inspiring, tragic and ridiculous. The Saints' eyes were fixed on heaven, but during the nine years the government lasted, things were happening on the earth.

Many terrestrial things happened because of the Irishman, Connor, whose military activities were confined to massacring the Shoshones at Bear River in 1863, to fighting the Sioux at Tongue River, Montana, and to minor skirmishes with Indians who harassed the mail and stage routes through western Utah. But Connor was a man of parts, with social and economic ideas. He disliked Mormon authoritarianism, and sought some means of inducing sufficient gentile migration into Utah to equalize or dominate the vote. Agriculture was no solution; the Mormons already held virtually all the land which would offer a living, as well as much that would not. In the mining industry, however, he saw potentialities. The Church had stifled mining initiative except in the development of iron, lead, and coal deposits. Precious metals lay untouched—if they could be found. Connor gave his men leave to prospect the hills, organized the first mining district in the Territory in 1863, and wrote its mining code. Personally he never benefited from his exertions, but he earned his reputation as the father of Utah mining. His efforts to stimulate the mining industry bore no real fruit until the seventies; meanwhile the Mormons spoke sarcastically of the "poor, miserable Diggers" inhabiting the bench above the Mormon capital. But gentile business men took firmer root in Great Salt Lake City.

The Ute Black Hawk War, Utah's last major Indian conflict, broke out in 1865, and until 1868 intermittent, desperate warfare was carried on between marauding Utes and the settlers of central Utah. More than fifty Mormon settlers were slain, and immense quantities of livestock lost, while many of the southern settlements for a time were abandoned. Economic losses of the settlers were estimated in excess of a million dollars, but despite the fact that the militia served for more than two years without pay, Congress declined to reimburse Utah settlers. The Utes finally quieted down, the greater part of the tribe not having participated in the war, and were settled, for the most part, on the reservation in the Uintah Basin.

On May 10, 1869, the transcontinental railroad was completed at Promontory. This railroad had been dreamed about in 1850, and as early as 1852 the Mormons had memorialized Congress for its construction. The United States government for almost a decade kept surveying parties in the field, with the new emphasis on communication with California, but until [the] outbreak of the Civil War there was no active progress. In 1862 Lincoln authorized the construction of a transcontinental railroad, and the following year work was launched by the Union Pacific and Central Pacific companies. The enterprise slowly gathered momentum, and by 1868 the two companies had graded into Utah. The Union Pacific built its grades down Echo and Weber Canyons to Ogden, and thence around the northern end of Great Salt Lake, but Ogden subsequently was made the junction city. When it became apparent that the transcontinental road would miss Great Salt Lake City (renamed Salt Lake City in 1868), Brigham Young organized a company to build a trunk line between the Mormon capital and Ogden, the last rail of the Utah Central being placed at Salt Lake City on January 10, 1870.

The immediate effect of the railroad was to break down once and forever the physical isolation of the Mormons, but the destruction of isolation in space promptly led to a new stress on isolation in spirit. The nature of the Mormon group life gave shape to the economic struggle. The ideal of co-operation, as also of consecration of property for co-operative ends, had become ingrained in Utah life. As the railroad neared Utah in 1868, Mormon leaders, in recognition of the success of co-operative stores, tanneries, and mills, organized a major commercial concern, Zion's Co-operative Mercantile Institution, more familiarly called ZCMI. Pressure was immediate upon gentile entrepreneurs, for the Saints were expected to trade with their own store rather than with outsiders, who were regarded as mere profiteers. Monetary exchange was always scarce in Utah, and barter and scrip were too common to be remarked; Mormon leaders had no desire to see the Saints placed under the economic thumb of gentile merchants. ZCMI virtually drove those merchants to the wall; they were saved only by completion of the railroad, which enabled them to compete on even terms with ZCMI. Although no all-seeing eye of God, or legend "Holiness to the Lord," was engraved over their doors, a bargain is a bargain, and the gentiles survived the lean months until the mining industry awoke at the magic touch of rail transportation.

The Church now had to contend with a revolt in its ranks, of fateful social and political implications. Schisms before 1869 were not new to Brigham Young, though the removal to Utah had stilled many disruptive movements; in 1852 the public announcement of polygamy caused an uninfluential and unfruitful schism led by Gladden Bishop; a more spectacular apostasy was that of the Morrisites in 1861–62. The Godbeite rebellion of 1867–69 was a more formidable development. At the heart of the movement were the wealthy and influential William S. Godbe and Elias L. T. Harrison, who in 1869 were expelled from the Church for advocating, among other things, development of the mining industry. Essentially the conflict was between first and second generations in the Church, a struggle between the philosophy of aloofness and that of fraternization with gentiles; more directly, the established Church authority was challenged in its right to speak solely for the Mormon people—the Godbeites did not question Mormon doctrine, and even declared their course sanctioned by heavenly beings.

In the religious field the "New Movement" amounted to nothing, but a coalition of Godbeites with followers of Colonel (now General) Connor led to organization of the Liberal Party. At its first organization in 1870 at Corinne, the Liberal Party was primarily a reform organization, but extremist elements subsequently gained full control, and when the Godbeites withdrew, the Liberal Party became bitterly anti-Mormon, its voice for many years being the *Salt Lake Tribune*. Previously no political parties had existed in Utah, candidates for public office being named by Church leaders and "sustained" by the populace in periodical plebiscites. The Mormon organization now, however, assumed the name of People's Party and rolled up its sleeves. The political situation was complicated by the fact that the Mormons were under assault from without, and struggles within the Territory echoed thunderously in anti-Mormon activity outside. Except for local Liberal successes in the mining camps, and such freak developments as establishment of the "Free Republic of Tooele," as the Liberals called their 1874–78 Tooele County regime, the People's Party controlled Utah until the catastrophic eighties.

The Issue Over Polygamy

The struggle over polygamy took particular shape after 1870. Previously it had been a moral more than a political issue, and except for the dead-letter Anti-Polygamy Act of 1862, the Saints had been pretty much left to themselves. Moral indignation in the East unquestionably influenced the refusal of Congress to admit Deseret into the Union, the niggardly appropriations by Congress for the Territory, and perhaps the disposal of land, no land titles in Utah being granted by the Federal government until 1869; up to that time the Mormons had the status of squatters. President Ulysses S. Grant gave polygamy its political aspect. With his accession to the presidency in 1869 the battle lines were clearly drawn: polygamy was to be crushed. Two bills to that end were introduced into Congress in 1869–70. In substance they would have abolished trial by jury in cases arising under the 1862 law, transferred appointment of Territorial officers to the governor, made the governor auditor of Church funds and properties, given the judiciary right to seize any building for its needs, and transferred direction of jails and prisons from the legislature to the governor. Both bills were voted down by

Southern legislators, who had tasted carpet-bag rule, but they are significant of the thinking Washington did about Utah during the next two decades. The Federal government was searching for political expedients to get at polygamy and the Mormons.

In Utah the new campaign against polygamy was inaugurated spectacularly in 1870 by a debate between the Reverend J. P. Newman, chaplain of the U.S. Senate, and Orson Pratt, Mormon scientist and philosopher. Held in the Tabernacle, the debate on Biblical sanction of polygamy attracted thousands and was publicized all over the nation: no formal decision was made, except in the national press, which concluded that Newman had been technically bested but was nevertheless right: Bible or no Bible, polygamy was not to be tolerated in American society. The spiritual fire the Saints had carried to the war against the deserts now availed them little. They had been rooted in Utah for more than twenty years. A generation had grown up which "knew not Joseph"; another migration to escape persecution would not be easy. The Church considered removal to Mexico before the conflict was over, but the membership was too firmly rooted for flight. The Mormons had to stand their ground and fight persecution with the spiritless weapons of the law.

The Mormons had troubles with Federal governors, but their desperate struggles were with the judiciary. One of the most formidable Federal judges was James B. McKean, a Grant appointee of 1871. McKean was exemplary in his private life, a fine scholar, and a man of high principles. His principles, however, he was willing to sacrifice for the ends to be attained. He set aside the Territorial law governing selection of jurors by lot from the taxpayers' lists, and transferred selection to the U.S. marshal. With the handpicked grand jury thus obtained, he set about scuttling the Mormons. A Salt Lake City alderman and his officers were arraigned before McKean for destroying the stock of the Engelbrecht Liquor Store, which had violated the city license ordinance. A decision was rendered against the city, with damages in excess of $50,000. By one slender thread the whole Mormon resistance hung: damages above $50,000 could be appealed to the U.S. Supreme Court. Had McKean limited the amount to $49,999.99, the Mormons would have been utterly without recourse before the arbitrary dicta of his court. Carried to the Supreme Court, the decision in the Engelbrecht case was unanimously overturned in 1873, and all indictments made by McKean's juries were ordered quashed.

The Mormons might well be thankful for the Supreme Court, for McKean had shown every intention of making a frontal assault upon Mormon authority. In 1871, his grand jury had indicted Brigham Young for "lewd and lascivious cohabitation," McKean flatly declaring, "The case at the bar is called the people versus Brigham Young, {but} its real title is Federal Authority versus Polygamic Theocracy." This case dragged on but came to nothing; General Connor had by this time so far come to respect Young as to offer bail for him. McKean's willingness to sacrifice strict legality for anti-Mormon ends is evidenced by his decision in 1873 when Ann Eliza Webb Young, who later wrote *Wife No. 19*, sued for divorce and alimony. The Federal government did not acknowledge the validity of polygamic marriage, and there could be no civil divorce where there had been no civil marriage, least of all any alimony; notwithstanding these contradictions, McKean assessed Young with court and lawyer fees and ordered him to pay alimony at the rate of $500 per month. When Young refused to pay and appealed the case, McKean found him in contempt of court, fined him, and imprisoned him for twenty-four hours. The case was, after several years, decided in Young's favor.

McKean was replaced in 1875, but he had given the Mormons a frightening view of their helplessness before autocratically inclined Federal officers. The fourth effort in 1872 to attain statehood was a desperate reaction to oppressive Federal administration. The Saints believed polygamy only an expedient by which they were subjected to a religious crusade; polygamy, they argued, was an exercise of religious worship with which the Federal government could not, under the Constitution, interfere. Moreover, the Mormons contended that "a territorial or colonial system, under which a government is provided by a remote power and without the consent of the governed, is inherently oppressive and anti-republican." Congress thought otherwise. The memorial for State government was ignored, and the Poland Act of 1874 voided the extended jurisdiction of the Mormon probate courts, where polygamists previously had been assured a sympathetic hearing at the hands of fellow religionists. The courts thus were given over completely to the Federal judiciary, and effective prosecution of polygamists was made possible.

This attack from without, together with the success of Mormon cooperatives, and perhaps the depression following the panic of 1873, was influential in the effort of 1874 to reestablish the United Order. Principles of "consecration" and of "stewardship" had characterized Mormon social thinking since 1831. After a series of revelations issued by Joseph Smith, Church members had lived for a time in what was variously known as the "United Firm," "Order of Enoch," or "United Order." The Order, according to Joseph Geddes, was a Mormon attempt to redefine the relation of the individual to property, and was socialistic in nature. The earth was considered the Lord's; the people were stewards only over their possessions, which were to be known as stewardships or inheritances. Those who had surplus property, more than required to provide a frugal living for the family, were to consecrate it by deed to the Church, to benefit the poor. Surplus production beyond family needs was to be turned over to the bishop's storehouse. The bishop was to apportion inheritances among the people on three bases, equal according to their families, circumstances, and wants and needs. Those who left the Church kept the inheritances deeded to them, but did not receive back the surplus. In other respects, business relations were to be carried on in the usual manner, and the virtues of simplicity, frugality, cleanliness, industry, and honesty were stressed.

"The Order of Enoch" was disrupted in Missouri when the Mormons were expelled from Jackson County in 1833 and no direct effort was made to reestablish it until 1874, though co-operative thinking, with the principles of consecration, strongly conditioned Mormon social life through the intervening thirty years. The lesser law of tithing to a considerable extent replaced that of consecration. Church members had always anticipated restoration of the Order, and since conditions in Utah appeared to necessitate reintegration of Mormon society in the face of gentile infiltration and attack, the "United Order of Zion" was established in 1874.

The United Order was an effort by a local group to attain self-sufficiency and a favorable balance of trade. If the Saints lived frugally, bought nothing from without, and produced an exportable surplus, they might, in Brigham Young's view, become a rich people. Moreover, by uniting their individual means, the Saints might evade mortgaging themselves to outside capital. The United Order was also a religious reaffirmation. Applicants for membership frequently were required to renew their covenants by baptism, and religion strongly influenced all that was done, not alone by such famous Orders as that at Orderville but in northern Utah, where little was accomplished temporally. Although there were outstanding local successes, notably at Orderville, Glendale, Richfield, and Brigham City, the United Order as a whole hardly survived its first year. In none of the urban centers was anything at all accomplished. Southern Utah was the field of principal success; previously agricultural communities built tanneries, shoe and hat factories, and cotton and woolen mills, but these enterprises for the most part collapsed with collapse of the Orders. The Church finally terminated the existence of surviving Orders. Social and economic pressure from without and reluctant co-operation from within were probably factors in ending the experiment. Ultimate re-establishment of the United Order is still taught as an essential Church doctrine, but the date is placed in some indefinite future when the people shall have proved themselves worthy.

Brigham Young hardly outlived the United Order—many Church members thought the Order could have succeeded had he lived. On August 29, 1877, in the Lion House in Salt Lake City, he breathed his last. The Saints were stunned and the entire nation took note of the death. For thirty-three years he had been the Mormon colossus, a giant who bestrode the Mormon universe and who symbolized Mormonism for the world. The Lion of the Lord had led the Saints to an empire, built it with them, fought for it with them. By some he had been hated; by more he had been loved. Thousands of his people he knew and called by name. So dominant a figure had he been that many believed Mormonism must collapse with his death.

With Young the Church lost its last great personal leader, but if there was no dominant personality to succeed him, there were able men trained in a hard school of experience, who have led the Church since 1877. Congress periodically rumbling its dissatisfaction over polygamy, Young's death was followed by an "apostolic interregnum" of three years and the accession of John Taylor to the presidency of the Church. The people in Utah were occupied with economic concerns—with dry-farming possibilities, with mining, and with the growth of the livestock industry. Political battles between Liberal and People's parties grew yearly more spectacular.

Struggle in the eighties centered fiercely and conclusively about polygamy, which was in actuality the lever, not the object to be moved. Enemies of the Mormons wanted primarily to shatter the temporal power of the Church, to break down its economic, social, and political domination of Utah. Prelude to the combat was the dispute over the office of delegate to Congress, fought out on the floor of the House between 1880 and 1882 by George Q. Cannon, Mormon incumbent, and Allan G. Campbell, gentile contestant.

Cannon had won the election by an overwhelming majority, but Governor Eli Murray had certified Campbell on the ground that Cannon was not a citizen. Campbell was not admitted, and Cannon was rendered ineligible by passage of the Edmunds Bill in 1882.

This new act was designated to implement the Anti-Polygamy Act of 1862 and the Poland Act of 1874. It defined polygamy as a felony, punishable by fine not exceeding $500, and by imprisonment not exceeding five years. To evade the difficulty of proving Church marriages, it defined polygamous living (unlawful cohabitation, within or without the marriage relation, with more than one woman) as a misdemeanor, punishable by a fine not exceeding $300, by imprisonment not exceeding six months, or both. It excluded all found guilty of either offense from the right to vote and hold office. It declared vacant all elective and registration offices in Utah, providing for a commission of five men to supervise registration of voters, conduct of elections, eligibility of voters, counting of votes, and issuance of certificates to elected candidates. Between 1882 and 1884 the Utah Commission disfranchised some 12,000 voters, utilizing a test oath which required the prospective voter to swear that he was not a polygamist, bigamist, or guilty of unlawful cohabitation, or in sympathy with these practices. The people of Utah made another effort for statehood in 1882, the first under the name of Utah, but the effort was fruitless.

Chief Justice Charles S. Zane, arriving in 1884, convicted Rudger Clawson, subsequently a member of the Quorum of the Twelve, of polygamy under the Edmunds Act, and sentenced him to four years in the penitentiary. The appeal to the Supreme Court was lost. With this case under their belts, Federal authorities began intensive prosecutions. Mormons were peremptorily excused from jury service if they declined to deny the doctrine of polygamy; wives and minors were permitted, even forced, to testify against husbands and fathers. Prosecution centered about the misdemeanor clause of the Edmunds Act. Federal officials devised a system of indictment for separate offenses, so that sentences might be pyramided even to life imprisonment. The Mormons had to give up all they had stood by for forty years, all the sternly held religious beliefs of four decades, their wives and their children to whom they were bound by all the ties of tenderness and love, or take refuge in flight and risk imprisonment if caught.

Six terrible years ensued for the polygamists. Church leaders almost uniformly had embraced polygamy as a test of their faith. The most prominent leaders were forced into hiding. Brandishing warrants, United States deputies broke into homes at the dead of night on "polyg hunts." It went hard with the "cohabs" who were caught. Popular feeling was exemplified in Salt Lake City on July 4, 1885, when flags were flown at half mast until raised by angered gentile mobs; in Provo the *Enquirer* carried a large cut of a coffin inscribed "Independence Day, Died July 4th, 1885." But the true meaning of this period is written in the journals of the humble. "The hounds of hell were laying in wate for me," wrote one hunted polygamist, and again, in despair, "How long will the Lord allow these wicked reches to gain power over us?" Another prayed God to move the heart of the President of the United States. Imprisoned men were considered martyrs, and often were met by the town band upon their release, and parties were held in their honor. Congress put even more savage teeth in the laws against polygamists with the Edmunds-Tucker Act of 1887: the L.D.S. Church was disincorporated and most of its property confiscated; female suffrage was abolished; the Perpetual Emigration Company was abolished; the Utah Commission was continued in office, and a test oath was required of citizens who would vote, hold elective office, or serve on juries. The Church was already in financial stress; this last blow all but bankrupted it. Congress was memorialized again in 1887 for a State government, the proposed constitution expressly prohibiting polygamy, but Congress had no intention of giving up its power over Utah while the struggle over polygamy endured, and the warfare continued until 1890.

By that year the leadership of the Church once again had changed hands, John Taylor having died while in hiding in 1887. Acting for the Church, the new president, Wilford Woodruff, in September, 1890, published in the *Deseret News* a manifesto advising all members of the Church to abstain from the practice of polygamy. In October the manifesto was ratified at a general conference, and the Saints officially abandoned polygamy as an essential Church doctrine. This crucial decision was not taken without bitterness among the Church membership, or skepticism among the gentiles. Many of those who had suffered for polygamy doubted the power of man to set aside the decree of God, and in the ensuing fifty years there have been undercurrents, always diminishing, of polygamic thinking in Church ranks. Many gentiles were unable to conceive that Mormonism in a few decades would become as wholly monogamic as Methodism; in their view the Church had made a shabby deal to save itself from extermination. Chief Justice Zane, however, accepted the pronouncement of Woodruff at face value. Further punitive legislation pending in Congress was abandoned, and the President of the United States, after a period of waiting, pardoned all polygamists, and restored their civil rights.

Developments within the Territory gave promise, between 1887 and 1890, of better days for Utah. Gentile business men began to desert the radical anti-Mormons. The Mormon People's Party, in 1889 offered four places on its Salt Lake City ticket to prominent gentiles in a gesture of reconciliation, and the fusionist party easily carried the election. In Salt Lake City, a Chamber of Commerce was organized which made a point of ignoring creedal differences. The immediate effect of the capitulation to Federal pressure was to deliver populous centers, politically, into gentile hands. The Liberals carried Ogden in 1889, and next year took Salt Lake City. They embarked on a program of spending for municipal improvements. The People's Party officeholders had tended to over-conservatism in expenditures for public improvements; the Liberals had less hesitancy about bonding cities for waterworks, sewers, and other appurtenances of urban civilization. The Liberal ascendancy also bore fruit in the schools, an 1890 act of the Territorial legislature establishing public schools throughout the Territory for the first time. Centralization of education on a non-sectarian basis emphasized the separation of church and State. As though to offer an earnest proof of their continued sincerity, the Mormons abandoned the People's Party, Church leaders advising the people, in 1891, to affiliate with the Democratic and Republican parties. Reluctant to abandon its hard-won victory, and perhaps distrustful of Mormon trickery, the Liberal party maintained its organization two years longer.

Joseph L. Rawlins, elected to Congress in 1892, introduced an enabling act for Utah, and a bill providing for the return of escheated Mormon Church property. Both bills carried; Caleb W. West, governor during the last phase of the polygamy struggle, recommended statehood in his annual report for 1893. The Enabling Act was signed by President [Grover] Cleveland the following July.

[*End of extract; essay continues in the original publication.*]

Chapter 2

The State of Deseret
Editor's Introduction (1939)

Editor's Introduction

Barely three months after beginning work as an editor for the Utah Historical Records Survey, in October 1938 Dale wrote to his close friend and cousin Jerry Bleak, commenting disdainfully on the status of writing about the state and its history that existed at the time. "Practically nothing really worth while touching upon Utah and Mormonism, what they have been, and what they have become, is worth one single damn, and that goes not only for non-Mormon writing but for Mormon writing. There is a golden opportunity," he wrote with what seems to be prophetic irony, "for some gifted writer to produce the first extensive, penetrating work on the whole amazing phenomena of Utah, the West, and the Mormon relation to itself and both."[1] Though the project that became the monographic *State of Deseret* was not his idea, Dale Morgan regarded that study as his down payment on the subject.

"Deseret," the author observes in the opening line to *The State of Deseret,* "is almost a lost word in Utah." The name enjoyed a legacy more distinguished than "Beehive" and "Zion," the region's two other uniquely distinguished word-names. Deseret, however, did not make the leap into popular culture. It was adopted for only the occasional respectable institution rather than as a catchy small-business moniker. While Beehive and Zion were painted across streetscapes on blinking neon signs and panel windows from bakeries to undertakers, Deseret was reserved as an adornment for staid local pillars like financial institutions and (at the time this was written) labels for the

[1]DLM to Jerry Bleak, 5 October 1938, Dale L. Morgan letters to Jerry Bleak, University of Utah Special Collections, Salt Lake City (hereafter "Bleak letters").

Church's new cooperative welfare commodities. Deseret itself was shrouded in myth, but because the myth was largely political, it was rescued from obscurity by the Historical Records Survey.

Dale L. Morgan began working a ninety-hour work month as "historian" in the Ogden office of the Historical Records Survey on 10 August 1938. "My work is somewhat diverse in character," he explained in a letter to Jerry, "but I will handle all the publicity for the Survey in Utah, do general rewriting and editing work on the inventories of all the county records, which the Survey has gathered and is publishing, and in general make myself useful."[2] To produce archival descriptions on a suitable scale using unemployed (and, detractors argue, unemployable) white-collar workers required focus and a managerial and editorial staff capable of ensuring a measure of stylistic consistency and content quality. Morgan's hiring as a professional editor, three years after the Survey office was established in Utah, was a step toward that larger goal.

The Historical Records Survey was conceived only partly as the white-collar public-relief program that it was. Of the five arts and culture projects under the WPA umbrella (Writers, Theatre, Art, American Imprints Inventory, and Historical Records Survey), the mission for the HRS was most directly comparable to the blue-collar Civilian Conservation Corps that built public park facilities, improved recreation areas, and stabilized watersheds and drainages across the country. To WPA administrator Harry Hopkins, the Survey represented a historic opportunity to throw a descriptive net over the nation's public records for the first time. In its five years the project dispatched a succession of 4,400 workers across the lower Forty-eight to catalogue the holdings of county courthouses and federal repositories.[3] The project's overarching goal was to generate descriptive lists of records series for each county and federal repository outside of Washington, D.C., and not under the immediate control of the newly established National Archives. The WPA projects were instituted in Utah in 1935 under the energetic direction of Maurice L. Howe, a journalist from the *Ogden Standard Examiner* who had conducted and reported a lengthy series of interviews with remaining members of the state's pioneer generation during the early 1930s.[4] Howe

---

[2]DLM to Jerry Bleak, 13 August 1938, Bleak letters; Jarvis Thurston interview, 16 June 1994, transcript in author's possession.

[3]Cedric Larson, "The Cultural Programs of the WPA," *Public Opinion Quarterly* 3, no. 3 (July 1939): 491–496.

[4]William T. Ingleheart [Utah WPA personnel director] to Juanita Brooks, 14 October 1935, Brooks papers, Utah State Historical Society. Howe's interview series was published in the *Ogden Standard Examiner* between 1934 and 1938; Howe's volume of clippings is found in carton 27 of the Morgan papers.

was transferred from Utah to the national office in June 1938, shortly before Morgan was hired, but maintained direct consultative involvement through the twice-daily mail deliveries. At his departure, the HRS and Writers' Project were divided under separate heads. The state WPA staff recruited Dee Bramwell, a University of Utah law student, to head the Survey division, and promoted Charles Madsen from the Writers' Project staff to superintend that branch, which moved its offices to Salt Lake City.

Besides describing county records, part of the Survey's mission involved the country's vast organizational history at the state and local level. One practical direction that projects often followed involved the re-publication of rare works relating to state organization and political development. Morgan's private assessment quoted at the opening of the chapter (about the relative value of historical writing in his native culture) was a response to a preliminary assignment to write a short piece about the Provisional State of Deseret.[5] Once it was complete, the small-scale writing project was scratched administratively in favor of something larger and more involved. As a law student, Dee Bramwell was familiar with Utah's earliest constitutional history and felt that a new edition of the laws from the Provisional State of Deseret would be a worthwhile endeavor, provided the straightforward ordinance text could be given appropriate context. Copies of the first book of laws were genuinely rare; in fact, the Church Historian's Office owned the only copy in the state. In June 1939 Bramwell formally proposed that the Survey republish the volume with a suitable introduction. Approval through the state WPA and federal office was quick in coming, and the Survey's new historian and his staff were delegated the task.[6] The resulting study was of seminal importance to his career, less for the doors it opened than for its effect on his approach and expectations of history, how it shaped his research and writing habits, and perspective on Mormon history specifically.

Morgan's extended essay would be the introduction to an edition of the provisional state's constitution and a collection of its laws. Having superintended data collection, Morgan felt he knew the subject well enough to "write the introduction and interpretation within a week of completion of this field work." It was an ambitious claim, and to complete it the hundred

[5]DLM to Jerry Bleak, 1 December 1938, Bleak letters.

[6]Dee Bramwell to Maurice Howe, 18 June 1939; Bramwell to Luther Evans, 17 July 1939; Bramwell to DLM, 7 September 1939. Seventy years after this decision, still only three copies of the *Ordinances* are recorded.

pages of historical introduction in fact eventually required nearly a month of near-constant work between October and November 1939.[7] Morgan's offhanded assertion thus also represents perhaps the first instance of his chronic practice of underestimating the time required for a major writing project, both a degree of personal confidence in his own ability and a shortcoming that would plague him for the rest of his life.

"Deseret," said to refer to a honeybee, is a name drawn from *The Book of Mormon*. After staking a claim to the Salt Lake Valley and surrounding valleys, the Mormons set about seeking political recognition following the Mexican Cession. In 1848, less than a year after arriving, the church leadership (there was no other authority or organization) generated a petition for recognition as a U.S. territory and dispatched it eastward. Evidence of the placer gold discovery in California landed in the valley within weeks, and at almost exactly the same time that Almon Babbitt arrived from Washington, D.C. Babbitt brought news that President Zachary Taylor had naively set congressional sectional factions in an uproar by proposing that California be allowed to file its own petition for statehood without organization as a territory. Admission of a new state delegation to the House and Senate threatened to upset the tenuous balance of power between potential voting blocs of slave-holding and non-slave-holding states. If California could do it, surmised Babbitt just as naively, then certainly the Mormon state should be admitted as well. In less than a month the "proceedings" that had supported the territorial petition had been re-described and the organization of the Provisional State of Deseret was recast as a statehood petition. With it, and with new, hastily printed copies of the *Ordinances of the State of Deseret*, Babbitt raced back eastward. It could not have arrived at a worse time. Utah's petition was named in Henry Clay's omnibus compromise bill that held the country together for another decade, but Deseret's bid for statehood was a casualty of the process. The newly created legislature of Utah Territory simply absorbed the laws into its new territorial system, and Deseret passed into memory.[8]

The State of Deseret was Morgan's first monographic study and seems to be the first major study of Utah state history that drew upon and *cited* primary

[7]DLM to Bramwell, 19 September 1939; DLM to Maurice Howe, 14 October 1939; Bramwell to DLM, 13 November 1939.

[8]Richard L. Saunders, *Printing in Deseret: Mormons, Politics, Economy and Utah's Incunabula* (Salt Lake City: Univ. of Utah Press, 2001), 24–33, 44–50, 56–60, supplements Morgan's internal view of the State of Deseret in terms of external forces. The publication itself is described in Saunders, *Printing in Deseret*, no. 42, along with other imprints from the provisional state.

sources directly. Prior to this point Morgan had produced and directed the equivalent of article-length treatments of settlement for half a dozen Utah counties, each of which involved the dominant social order only tangentially. Assembled from the Survey's growing research files and transcript collection, the introduction was drafted between October 1939 and March 1940. It is the more remarkable to recall that the author had been involved with historical research on a part-time basis for barely a year with no formal training beyond the requirements and expectations of his Survey position. Even this early in his career, Morgan demonstrated not only an admirable commitment to factual accuracy, but also an innate grasp of historical research suited to his sharp memory, which gave him a remarkable ability to collate facts.

Morgan's approach to the study reflects a self-taught empiricism that joined his interest in social psychology with his experience in the HRS: if it was not written down in contemporary records or in a participant's first-hand account, it did not merit consideration. He was unwilling to accept secondhand sources of any type. Readers will notice that there are very few secondary sources named among his notes (precisely four, not counting Bancroft's *History of Utah*, which he regarded as a primary source). The rest are diaries—often published versions—newspapers, and the ever-useful historical scrapbook maintained by the Church Historian's Office known as the Journal History. The atmosphere of Salt Lake City during the Franklin Roosevelt years was politically charged, and the author was acutely aware of the political nature of this production. Relying on primary rather than secondary sources was good historical methodology, but it also avoided the trap of citing the politically "wrong" secondary material in the process. By the first week of February 1940, now deeply involved in revising the draft introduction, Morgan confided to Howe his how aware he was of walking a political tightrope with the project: "I wish I were writing this [study] on my own, with entire liberty of interpretation and phraseology; since I am not, I shall hold to objectivity as far as possible where not sticking my neck out too far."[9] In Dale Morgan's eyes, "objectivity" meant hewing closely to demonstrable facts and statements. No editorial digressions were tolerated, nor were insertions of historical interpretation, no matter how relevant. It was much safer to stick with straightforward facts, which could not be challenged. This position was admittedly good sense. Morgan wrote Howe that he felt

[9]DLM to Maurice Howe, 6 February 1940.

he could "write a documented account that would knock your eye out. But!!! It would also knock HRS out of the eye of the church historian's office."[10]

The concern was not merely an idle one. Besides being the chief research source outside the HRS's own files, Church Historian's Office staff were participants in the Deseret writing project itself. Survey policy stipulated that at least one knowledgeable individual outside the project staff have direct input on any local-history material published. Histories for the county records inventories were usually reviewed by a clerk, judge, or other local figure with an interest in the community's past. Outside vetting was an intended check on interpretation, limiting the possible interpretive power of the essays and tying them to the sensibilities of a community. The Survey could therefore determine what facts on which to accept as valid as a piece was written, but the reviewers held a brake on the interpretive presentation of those facts. Well aware that the major sources for the topic were housed in an institution which regarded the federal project with only a narrow margin of tolerance, Morgan made an effort to solicit input from Church Historian's Office staff. For the "State of Deseret" manuscript, the reviewer was A. William Lund. While apostle Joseph Fielding Smith was the official church historian, he was much more interested in church doctrine than in church history (except as history was unfolding in the present). Assistant Church Historian Lund constituted the entire front-line defense of the official Latter-day Saint view of its own past. Not much of a writer himself, Lund was more of a garrison protocol officer than soldier, with unquestionable allegiances and a sharp but inconsistent eye for the appropriate treatment of the church's past.

The first seventy-two pages of the manuscript were dispatched to Lund for review in January 1940 while the latter half of the "The State of Deseret" manuscript was being drafted. Morgan dropped in to see Lund during the first week of February to review his editing. A few outright errors were picked out, "but most of the conversation revolved around certain of the interpretations," he reported to Howe the next day. "He [Lund] was 'reasonable' enough, not assertive—but quietly insistent on his point of view (I should say more accurately, unconscious of any other point of view.)." Morgan accepted the criticism and churchly concerns graciously and then later confessed he planned to "restate them so as, while still saying the same things, I somewhat meet his objections. I hope I don't wind up with

[10]DLM to Howe [O'Niel?], 27 February 1939.

a Levi Edgar Young opus and an approving pat on the back from Heber J. Grant."[11] A series of other interviews with Lund completed the semi-official external review. Their final visit with Lund concluded with a pleased and uncharacteristic "fatherly slap on the back" for the HRS writer. By 2 March 1940, the manuscript was complete, approved by Lund, and in the hands of the typists to create a fair-copy for the printer. The clean draft was officially handed to director Bramwell on 1 April, and from there to *Utah Historical Quarterly* editor J. Cecil Alter for publication. It appeared in July as a single monographic publication across three unified issues of the 1940 *Quarterly.*[12]

At almost the same time Dee Bramwell formally proposed the new edition of Deseret's laws, Maurice Howe sent Morgan a copy of his and Charles Kelly's book *Miles Goodyear: First Citizen of Utah, Trapper, Trader and California Pioneer* (Salt Lake City: Western Printing Co., 1937). Howe had a proposal. The two of them had commiserated over the dearth of solid data about the annual trading fair held for the American fur trappers of the early nineteenth century. Howe suggested that the two of them cooperate on a book documenting the rendezvous of the fur-trade era. "What is needed is a well documented book, it need not be dry reading, which will give sources, either secondary or primary." Morgan was definitely interested and volunteered to begin the process in the way he knew best at that time: with a bibliographic survey of the topic. The Great Basin valleys had been a crossroads for fur brigades operating out of St. Louis, Vancouver, and Santa Fe. He had already been introduced to elements of the state's pre-Mormon history while compiling county-records-inventory introductions. Despite making a job hunting trip to the West Coast, where Morgan used the opportunity to visit the Bancroft Library, before July was gone he sent Howe a bibliography representing the state of the field and laying out three different approaches they might take in writing the book.[13]

The fur-trade book never progressed past the point of checklisting relevant works due to the pressure of other responsibilities and Maurice Howe's untimely death in 1945, but Howe's encouragement was the tug that initially

[11]DLM to Howe, 6 February 1940. Young was a president of his church's First Quorum of Seventy and author of *The Founding of Utah* (New York City: Charles Scribner's Sons, 1923), an unqualified paean to the state's founding generation and which affirmed Utah readers' sense of triumphant progress.

[12]DLM to Dee Bramwell, 20 February 1940; DLM to Howe, 3 April 1940. The original monograph was reprinted in full in *The State of Deseret*, ed. Charles S. Peterson (Logan: Utah State Univ. Press, 1987).

[13]Howe to DLM, 28 June 1939; DLM to Howe, 30 June 1939; DLM to Howe, 26 July 1939; Howe to DLM, 8 November 1941.

pulled Dale Morgan's focus to the broader field of early Western Americana beyond Utah's borders. In pursuing the fur-trade checklist, he began buying books as he could afford them, building a personal research collection as well as laying the foundation for his later studies. But, he confessed to Howe as their project lagged, "I have been more especially investing in Mormonia."[14] That was where his core interested lay in 1941.

The State of Deseret remains the foundational study of the topic and has not yet been superseded. It is a remarkable accomplishment for someone with merely a year and a half's familiarity with the discipline of history. It stands as a defining point in Morgan's career for several reasons. First, its unimpeachable accuracy and its reception, both in public and private, convinced him that history had to be grounded on an inarguable grasp of primary sources. To miss a relevant document was to allow a hole to remain in one's understanding. Second, it seems to have convinced him that interpretation was an improper undertaking for a historical writer. The church, he felt, often ignored its own factual record, instead asserting a "proper" version of the past based on little more than an agenda and tradition. Far better to let the facts speak, which, if properly approached, required no biased interpretation and stripped motive out of the historical discipline. What Morgan overlooked was that facts, even when ordered properly, still required the historian to choose, weigh, and explain. This created an important blind spot in his approach to the past. Explanation required interpretation, which was shaped by the historian's viewpoint. Third, the short, intense writing schedule set a pattern for the way Morgan would operate for the rest of his life. By the time he began writing history seriously as a vocation, his process was set: expend most of the available time and effort toward collecting every suitable source, and then hammer out the draft in a sustained burst of creativity as necessary. "Except for the nervous tension involved, I rather enjoy it, as there is a novelty and interest to working under pressure and finding out things under pressure," he would confess to Fawn Brodie a couple of years later, before beginning on *The Mormons*.[15] "If I come sane through the next two months, I should be equal to any other strain on my mind during the rest of my life."[16] Fortunately he was equipped for the process, with a

[14]DLM to Howe, 18 November 1941.

[15]DLM to Fawn Brodie, 16 April 1946.

[16]DLM to Jack [Thornley], 6 June 1946.

native ability to collate sources mentally and recall details precisely, which made the high-stakes process workable. Fourth, his success in producing this study and the praise it drew seems to have produced or at least reinforced a mild disdain for the output of Utah's academically trained writers of the time, like Levi Edgar Young. "I could put my time to better use than to involve myself with a lot of schooling I didn't need just for the sake of tacking on a couple of degrees," he wrote Bernard DeVoto in 1941.[17] By the time he departed Utah in 1942, Morgan had convinced himself that through the Survey and Writers' Project, he had already learned the fundamentals of history and had served a practical apprenticeship equivalent to or more valuable than graduate school. Dismissing the importance of graduate education and largely ignorant of the philosophical questions involved in history, he was confident enough in his ability to remain self-directed.

Writing this monograph, with its record-based approach to the past, solidified Dale Morgan's perspective of what historical research was; the praise that it garnered reinforced what he expected that history should be. He settled into a pattern of insatiable and omnivorous research, replicating the processes that he had learned in the WPA programs and which produced the highly praised *State of Deseret*. However, the process also fitted him with a set of blinders as well, since it did nothing to test or expand his historiographic sense or provide a broader contextual view in terms of national culture, politics, economics, or any of the social history topics that now populate history. In retrospect, experience with the WPA program and *The State of Deseret* showed what history he could do best, and also shaped the expectation of what history he would do.

[17]DLM to Bernard DeVoto, 1 October 1941. Cf. DLM to Brodie, 29 September 1945.

Chapter 3

Untitled Kingdom of God Manuscript (1940)

Editor's Introduction

Immediate success writing historical sketches for the county-record inventories and the praise from the national office for *The State of Deseret* understandably lent twenty-five-year-old Dale Morgan confidence in his abilities as a historical researcher and writer. While aware of emotions that the past and its telling engendered, early in his career he came to regard the politics of interpretation as a historical non-issue. Following closely the ideals of the empirical model he was developing as a historian, a narrative was either accurate or inaccurate; either it was true or it was not. The historian's task was to be sure the telling was accurate and descriptive of lived realities. This ideal of context as the goal of historical inquiry put him into a low-grade conflict with the dominant social entity within the state. In Morgan's view, the Latter-day Saints advanced socially constructive and affirming stories about their past, while the historical record was never so clear cut and sometimes suggested contradictory or at least decidedly more complex motivations and factors behind an event. He seems to have partly adopted the dichotomy expressed by early British psychological theorist Havelock Ellis who noted that "'religion' and 'Church,' though often confused, are far from being interchangeable terms. 'Religion' is a natural impulse, 'Church' is a social institution."[1] By the time Morgan began drafting this introductory study of the Kingdom of God, sometime between October and December 1940, he

[1]Havelock Ellis, *The Dance of Life* (Boston: Houghton Mifflin Co., 1929), 211. Morgan read Ellis extensively immediately after college, and his view of historical figures seems to have been shaped strongly by Ellis's stated views on humankind, society, and perception.

had solidly accepted the sentiment expressed in Ellis's position, convinced that the Mormon past should be understood primarily as a socially driven story rather than a religiously motivated one.

Morgan knew as early as February 1940 that he would not be putting into *The State of Deseret* material that predated the Latter-day Saint arrival in the Great Basin, which was just as well. "I am pretty certain that my 'guess' about the origin of the state of Deseret will meet with Lund's disapproval; but I am all prepared for him; if he says a word about it, I am going to tackle him with the proofs and leave him with the impression that it will be better for me, in a friendly work, to deal with the subject, than to have some unfriendly person whose ideas have been stimulated by my publication, present the material from the other viewpoint. In other words, I am going to beard him in his den." "I've found out a hell of a lot about the background to the period since I wrote the first draft [of *The State of Deseret*]," he had written Maurice Howe confidently. "I know why the Mormons were such upholders of the Constitution (it is a consequence of their social background, the period when everything was proved by the Bible and the Constitution), and how they came to conceive themselves as the legitimate heirs of the Constitution, both the North and South being conceived as having seceded from it—this and lots of other stuff. This background won't get into print [with *The State of Deseret*], but it will condition my rewriting."[2] After the *State of Deseret* manuscript was submitted, however, Morgan continued to watch carefully for related documents. Beginning in March he was officially at work on the state history essay for the guidebook that is contained in the first chapter here. Eventually, however, he returned to the ideas that preceded the Provisional State of Deseret. The manuscript reproduced here, very likely the sole draft, was generated after the successful publication of *The State of Deseret* and while he was working busily with his Writers' Project staff to get the Utah guidebook to the printer, with a few emendations tossed in as late as July 1941.

This piece played to the interests of a significant correspondent, Utah expatriate and *American Mercury* editor Bernard DeVoto. To DeVoto in Cambridge, Massachusetts, Dale noted that he had collected every piece of Mormon-related source material he could locate and felt himself prepared to write "a thorough examination of the Kingdom of God among the Mormons—an examination not merely of the idea . . . but of the actual fact itself,

---

[2]DLM to Howe, 6 February 1940.

the 'Kingdom of God' the Mormons actually established." The claim had the intended effect; the older man was impressed. But by the time DeVoto responded, and despite speaking of the project in a present tense, Morgan had already set it aside, incomplete. He pulled the thirty-ninth occasionally typed sheet from his typewriter, a sentence and line incomplete at its base, and simply shelved the project to work on his manuscript for *The Humboldt: Highroad to the West* (Indianapolis: Farrar & Rinehart, 1943). It remained shelved, lacking even a title, for the rest of his career.[3] Why? Only the author could say for sure, but in a comment to Maurice Howe, his closest confidant, made as the newly typed sheets were cooling in February 1940, Dale said that he did not intend the piece for publication. With *The State of Deseret* already in print, there was little need for an introductory chapter. A year and a half later he explained to Bernard DeVoto that the study amounted to "an entire rewriting of Mormon history for the period 1842–1847," and that, pressed for time, he decided to concentrate on readying his *Humboldt* manuscript for submission.[4] But why else? The manuscript was not set aside—it was dropped, incomplete.

The State of Deseret seems to have clinched his resolve to focus time and attention on the Latter Day Saints, but even as he worked on it he felt the Kingdom of God manuscript was not the place to start. He never returned to the Kingdom of God manuscript, but the draft he did complete exists untitled and misfiled among his papers. "The major job I hope to take up," he late wrote DeVoto as a justification for dropping the Kingdom of God study, "is to write a book that will deal with the Mormons as a people." A decade after this exploratory Kingdom of God study was written, he might have been toying with using the draft to conclude his first volume of the three-volume Mormon history, or as a leading chapter in the second, but this is merely speculation.

Morgan may have left the study incomplete and unpublished, but it is as important to understanding his developing sense of historicism as *The State of Deseret* or later writing he would see to fruition. Thematically the piece prefaces *Deseret,* although it was written months later. That he cites the *Millennial Star* rather than the earlier *Times and Seasons* statements may be evidence that it was a private project and not a serious historical study, but despite his

[3]DLM to Bernard DeVoto, 1 October 1941. Klaus Hansen later produced the standard work on the subject with *Quest for Empire: The Political Kingdom of God and the Council of Fifty in Mormon History* (Lansing: Michigan State Univ. Press, 1970).

[4]DLM to DeVoto, 1 October 1941.

intent, here we can see Morgan thinking through historical complexities in a way that later characterizes his work. Morgan seems to come away from the *State of Deseret* exercise having concluded that revisionist social history could be accomplished by straightforwardly marshalling available facts and ordering them in correct relation to each other and to the statements and assumptions made upon them by other writers. In this piece he repeats the pattern of detail and documentation as reinterpretation itself. It was a pattern he had established with the county histories and followed in laying out *The State of Deseret*. Now in the Kingdom of God study he got a view of what narrowly focused facts and chronology could do to broader topics. The result was an amazing thing "which will force a rewriting of one of the most crucial periods of Mormon history." "This is really a major piece of historical detection, and I can document it almost wholly from authorized church sources," he cackled assertively to Howe.[5] Morgan's attitude shines a raking light across his developing vocation. He was beginning to think in terms of historical facts as direct challenges to received Mormon history (at least among his contemporaries). Had Latter-day Saint historians been willing to stick to the facts—even those in the "authorized church sources"—he implies it would be impossible to maintain the hoary tales that passed for inspirational history. Morgan was not setting out to demolish the church's official historicity so much as to call it to factually account for its claims. To be related truthfully, he felt, Mormon history required a methodical, scientific return to the source material. If that happens, he clearly felt, Mormondom's version of its sacred history would be discredited by its own sources. If this reading is accurate, then the Kingdom of God manuscript becomes a private exercise in historical revisionism and a personal validation of an empirical approach—his empirical approach—to writing Latter Day Saint history.

The study on the Kingdom of God, which came so early in his formative experience as a researcher, was shown to no more than one or two people of which there is record. Wallace Stegner was one, though DeVoto never saw the study. Its nature as a private exercise and the fact that it reflects essentially the same documentary process as *Deseret* confirms that it is more stylistically significant than might be expected from an incomplete work. Though he would come to learn well the importance of research in original and not just published primary sources, this work and its antecedent in *The*

[5]DLM to Howe, 2 October 1940.

State of Deseret suggest that by 1941 his concept of historical enterprise had solidified. It had, and in fact would not move (except to sink more deeply into sources) through the rest of his life and in any field he addressed. History, to Dale Morgan, was an exercise in empiricism; accounting for the factual record and correcting what was known from and about historical facts, became fundamental rationales and functions of Latter Day Saint history as he conceived it. Joseph Smith's Kingdom of God was as good a place as any to begin the process.

[Untitled draft manuscript on the Kingdom of God]

The time which saw the founding of the Mormon Church was perhaps the most intensely individualistic American life has known.* The wooded frontiers lay open west of the vigorous young Atlantic seaboard cities, and a people flushed with the pride of locally successful wars against the might of British empire was thrusting into this frontier all along the Alleghany rampart. Every man brought to his daily life the most unbounded belief in his capacity, as an individual and as a citizen of the United States. The frontiersman believed he could do everything, and was willing to try; more often than not he lived up to his opinion of himself. The average frontiersman was perhaps more ignorant than not; this was a factor in the religious frenzy of the Alleghany frontier of which Mormonism was a characteristic offspring, but I will restrict myself to broader social questions; the lack of

*[The draft begins with two introductory paragraphs on Joseph Smith's lynching, which the author marked for deletion on the manuscript and are thus not included in this version of the unfinished work. A few oddities unique to this manuscript have also been smoothed out. The typewriter on which this draft was typed the lacked bracket characters, [ ], typically used to mark editorial insertions. Instead, Morgan signified his additions with an opening or closing paren and underscore at the beginning and end of his text, as (_ _), which saved him keystrokes. These marks are replaced with braces, { }, to be consistent with the balance of the volume. Notes, you will see, are drawn from a limited number of resources, all of them periodicals, making his original citations in the manuscript a litany of *ibid.* and *idems*, in keeping with the style of the times. I have taken the liberty to flesh them out to genuine citations for the ease of modern readers. Finally, toward the end of the manuscript, knowing that he was engaged in merely a self-fulfilling academic exercise, he merely inserted empty parentheses in text where references should stand. These are left as place markers. Readers will notice the use among the materials cited of *ultimo* (often abbreviated ult. or ulto.), *instant* (inst.), and *proximo* (pro.), useful temporal markers for a time when calendars rather than clocks were the basis for setting and keeping appointments. They refer respectively to a date within the preceding month, the present month (whether the date was past or coming), or a coming month. —Ed.]

a deep intellectual life, with its self-doubts and critical hesitancies, emphasized the accomplishing force of action—even ignorant action—so that, on occasion, individuals overmastered difficulties from which rationally they should have shied, although also, as will be seen in the examination of certain Mormon courses of action, individuals occasionally put themselves in absurd and dangerous positions. It is important also that the westward-flooding emigrants carried with them a double scripture, the Bible and the Constitution. Neither of these, perhaps, was held more sacred than the other, for if the Bible was the word of God, the Constitution was inspired of God.

Between 1830 and 1844 American society, briefly dammed in the Mississippi Valley, flooded on out into the Plains. By 1836 Texas was wrested from the hands of Mexico by an insurgent group of American emigrants who wanted, at once, to shelter their new republic under the Constitution; other American emigrants carried to Oregon white-topped wagons that were to doom the uneasy makeshift of joint American and British occupancy of that green land. Frontier America was hot with its youth and its pride, boiling with religious fervor, quick in the consciousness of its lusty strength. Although Mormon society had its own characteristics, it was compounded out of this *zeitgeist*, and its final period on the Midwest frontier rings to the time-spirit.**

Although the church itself was national—even international—in design, its immediate difficulties as an organic group had always been local in character. The Ohio period had been a turbulent one, and the Missouri period was darkly illumined by the mob violence which resulted, in 1838–1839, in the ultimate expulsion of the Mormons from that state. The Kirtland difficulties had been financial, for the most part; but the conflict in Missouri, like that which followed in Illinois, owed much to the political power acquired by the Mormons in moving, as a solidly integrated group, into regions otherwise divided almost evenly between Democrat and Whig. The political adventures of the Mormons had had no national reverberations of any significance. By the fall of 1843, however, their intervention in Illinois's politics had placed the Mormons in so equivocal a political position and so dangerous a social

**[Morgan did not read contemporary historians and was unaffected by the discussion of objectivism and relativism among professionals. His introductory paragraphs are also intentionally literary, but his characterizations reflect the lasting popular influence of Frederick Jackson Turner's environmental determinism and of the residual nationalistic triumphalism of Manifest Destiny and the McKinley-Roosevelt expansionism. However, it is important not to be too precise with historiographic parallels and influences; Morgan aimed at readability and an evocation of the period rather than laying out a school of thought on American expansion. —Ed.]

position that, as a measure of social and political self-defense, they were forced to enlarge their political thinking to a national scale.

On October 1, 1843, the Nauvoo *Times and Seasons* published a political editorial which may be taken as the first step toward an amazing series of adventures. Inquiring, "Who Shall Be Our Next President?" the editor recited the "injustices" experienced in Missouri and the total lack of redress for wrongs experienced at "mobocratic" hands, concluding:

> Still we are American citizens; and as American citizens we claim the privilege of being heard in the councils of our nation. . . . We make these remarks for the purpose of drawing the attention of our brethren to this subject, both at home and abroad, that we may fix upon the man who will be the most likely to render us assistance in obtaining redress for our grievances[—]and not only give our own votes, but use our influence to obtain others; and if the voice of suffering innocence will not sufficiently arouse the rulers of our nation to investigate our case, perhaps a vote of from fifty to one hundred thousand may rouse them from their lethargy.
>
> We shall fix upon the man of our choice, and notify our friends duly.[1]

This editorial may well have fallen into thoughtful hands. The presidential election was to take place [the] next year, and political maneuverings, as the editorial indeed itself is evidence, already were beginning. In all probability it is no coincidence that a Colonel Frierson at Quincy, U.S. surveyor-general for Illinois, shortly afterward approached Joseph L. Heywood, Mormon representative in that city, concerning possible Mormon support for John C. Calhoun. On October 23 Heywood wrote Joseph Smith from Quincy, accounting the conversation. It was intimated that Calhoun was warmly sympathetic to the Mormons, and the suggestion was made that the Hon. B [i.e., Congressman Robert Barnwell] Rhett of South Carolina would be pleased to present to Congress a memorial in behalf of the Mormons. Frierson intimated further that Calhoun, to the Mormons, unquestionably would be much more acceptable as a candidate for the presidency than [Martin] Van Buren, disliked for his refusal, or inability to do anything with respect to the Missouri expulsion when he was so petitioned by the Mormons in 1841. Heywood's letter was received at Nauvoo on November 2, and considered by Joseph Smith in council with his brother, Hyrum, Brigham Young, Heber C. Kimball, Willard Richards, John Taylor, William Law, and William Clayton. After deliberating, the council "agreed to write a letter to the

[1] *Times and Seasons* 4, no. 22 (1 October 1843): 343–344.

five candidates for the Presidency of the U.S., to inquire what their feelings were towards us as a people, and what their course of action would be in relation to the cruelty and oppression that we have suffered from the State of Missouri, if they were elected."[2]

Frierson came to Nauvoo November 25 for a conference with the Church leaders, but events he had set in motion gathered momentum during the interim. On November 4 Smith dispatched to "Gen. Lewis Cass, Hon. Richard M. Johnson, Hon. Henry Clay, and {ex-}President Martin Van Buren" letters soliciting "an immediate, specific, and candid reply to '*What will be your rule of action relative to us as a people,*' should fortune favour your ascension to the chief magistracy?" To Van Buren's letter was added the postscript, "Also whether your views or feelings have changed since the subject matter of this communication was presented you in your then official capacity at Washington, in the year 1841, and by you treated with a coldness, indifference, and neglect, bordering on contempt."[3]

The idea of reaching out for national attention for their wrongs continued so attractive that on November 21 "Elders Richards, Hyde, Taylor, and Phelps," it was decided, should "write a Proclamation to the Kings of the Earth."[4] This decision was never carried out as such, although its importance for a tendency in Mormon thinking will be shown. There soon were written, however, "appeals" more modestly addressed.

Frierson having come to Nauvoo on November 25, a "council" met with him the following morning. In consequence of this meeting, Frierson on the 28th wrote a "Memorial to Congress"[5] of which he took a copy, on leaving next day, to get signers in Quincy.[6] This memorial, made in eleven copies for circulation and signature, recited at great length the Missouri experiences and the failure to obtain redress either in Missouri or Washington, concluding:

> It is true the Constitution of the United States gives to us, in common with all other native or adopted citizens, the right to enter and settle in Missouri;

[2]"History of Joseph Smith," *Millennial Star* 22 (1860): 262, 263 [The citation is an error; it does not appear in the source cited but is found in *History of the Church,* 6: 63. —Ed.].

[3]"History of Joseph Smith," *Millennial Star* 22 (1860): 310. [Unless otherwise noted, all remaining *Millennial Star* references are to this serialized narrative, the title of which is not cited further. —Ed.]

[4]*Millennial Star* 22 (1860): 343. [In his text Morgan cites a number of important publications, brief histories of which may be found individually in Peter Crawley, *A Descriptive Bibliography of the Mormon Church,* vol. 1 (Provo: BYU Religious Studies Center, 1996). —Ed.]

[5]*Millennial Star* 22 (1860): 343, 344.

[6]*Millennial Star* 22 (1860): 357.

> but an executive order has been issued to exterminate us if we enter the State, and a part of the Constitution becomes a nullity, so far as we are concerned.
>
> Had any foreign State or power committed a similar outrage upon us, we cannot for a moment doubt that the strong arm of the General Government would have been stretched out to redress our wrongs; and we flatter ourselves that the same power will either redress our grievances or shield us from harm in our efforts to regain our last property, which we fairly purchased from the General Government.
>
> Finally, your memorialists pray your honorable body to take their wrongs into consideration, receive testimony on the case, and grant such relief as by the Constitution and laws you may have power to give.[7]

On the same day, the 29th, a meeting of citizens was convened in Nauvoo to enlist popular support for the memorial.[8] To this meeting was read Joseph Smith's "Appeal to the Green Mountain Boys,"[9] first of many "appeals" written by Mormon authorities seeking to enlist support in their native states for the effort to obtain "redress" in the Missouri affair. Smith also "read a letter in reply to one he wrote to Henry Clay."[10] Before the meeting closed, it was voted that "every man in the meeting who could wield a pen write an address to his mother country,"[11] and a number followed this injunction. Before closing the meeting, Smith read to the congregation the Memorial, observing, "The State rights doctrines are what feed mobs. They are a dead carcass—a stink, and they shall ascend up as a stink offering in the nose of the Almighty. They shall be oppressed as they have oppressed us, not by 'Mormons,' but by others in power. They shall drink a drink offering, the bitterest dregs, not from the 'Mormons,' but from a meaner source than themselves. God shall curse them."[12]

December drew together more and more of the important threads which so decisively wove into the fabric of Mormon action through the next months. A way of thinking rather than a course of action had been the product of the last few weeks. Now, however, a renewal of anti-Mormon hostility about Nauvoo impelled the Mormons to think seriously about ways in which they might more securely entrench themselves. The legislature at its previous

---

[7]*Millennial Star* 22 (1860): 357–359.

[8]*Millennial Star* 22 (1860): 359, 377.

[9]*Millennial Star* 22 (1860): 375–377; 390–391.

[10]*Millennial Star* 22 (1860): 392.

[11]*Millennial Star* 22 (1860): 392. On 31 January Sidney Rigdon produced an appeal to the legislature of Pennsylvania, and on 2 February Phinehas Richards one to the legislature of Massachusetts.

[12]*Millennial Star* 22 (1860): 392.

session had given attention to the proposed repeal of the extraordinary Nauvoo charter behind which the Mormons had so effectually established themselves; and while the Mormons, in a process of wish-fulfillment, argued that the legislature had no power to repeal the charter, they commenced also to consider whether Nauvoo might not, in some manner, remove itself from under the hand of any possible local enmity. A precipitating agent in this thinking was a rumor of invasion by Missourians which reached Nauvoo in early December. On the 8th the city council notified the marshal of Nauvoo to place the troops in readiness, and Joseph Smith, as Lieutenant-General of the Nauvoo Legion, ordered Major-General Wilson Law, commanding the Legion, to mobilize portions of the Legion in readiness for any call that might be made upon them. At the same time the city council passed an ordinance, unconstitutional but reflecting Mormon reaction to harassment from without, providing that if any person or persons should come to Nauvoo attempting to serve process on Joseph Smith for another of many "vexatious lawsuits," such person or persons would be subject to arrest, and, remarkably, "if found guilty, {be} sentenced to imprisonment in the city prison for life; which convict or convicts can only be pardoned by the Governor, with the consent of the Mayor of said city." Developing logically this same trend of thought, Joseph Smith suggested to the city council the idea "of petitioning Congress to receive the City of Nauvoo under the protection of the United States' Government, to acknowledge the Nauvoo Legion as U.S. troops, and to assist in fortifications and other purposes, and that a messenger be sent to Congress for this purpose, at the expense of the city." John Taylor, Orson Spencer, and Orson Pratt were appointed to draft such a memorial.[13]

It was attractive in prospect if absurd in practice to consider that Congress might carve from Illinois a separate Mormon realm; Joseph Smith also was doubtless attracted, with his love of military trappings, by the idea of transforming his militia into a federal military unit. His own prestige would have been enhanced, and the Mormon position in Illinois immeasurably strengthened.

On December 16 Smith, as mayor, and the alderman and councilors of Nauvoo, officially signed the memorial to Congress for "redress of losses and grievances in Missouri." In discussing the petition, Smith ventured to prophesy "by virtue of the holy Priesthood vested in me, and in the name of

[13] *Millennial Star* 22 (1860): 422 [i.e., 423].

the Lord Jesus Christ, that, if Congress will not hear our petition and grant us protection, they shall be broken up as a government, and God shall damn them, and there shall nothing be left of them—not even a grease spot." He also "informed the Council that it was my wish that they should ask the privilege of calling on Government for the United States' troops to protect us in our privileges, which is not unconstitutional, but lies in the breast of Congress."[14]

Five days later the city council voted that Orson Pratt should present the "Memorial and Ordinance to Congress." The memorial was another long recital of the conflicts of Mormons with Missouri mob law; the ordinance, however, was distinctly out of the ordinary.

> Be it ordained by the Senate and House of Representatives of the United States of America in Congress assembled, that all the rights, powers, privileges, and immunities belonging to Territories, and not repugnant to the Constitution of the United States, are hereby granted and secured to the inhabitants of the city of Nauvoo, in addition to the spirit, letter, meaning, and provisions of the afore-mentioned charter, or act of incorporation from the State of Illinois, until the State of Missouri restores to those exiled citizens the lands, rights, privileges, property, and damage for all losses.
>
> And be it further ordained, in order to effect the object and further intention of this ordinance, and for the peace, security, happiness, convenience, benefit, and prosperity of the said city of Nauvoo, and for the common weal and honour of our country, that the Mayor of Nauvoo be, and he is hereby empowered, by this consent of the President of the United States: whenever the actual assembly of the case and the public safety shall require it, to call to his aid a sufficient number of United States forces, in connection with the Nauvoo Legion, to repel the invasion of mobs, keep the public peace, and protect the innocent from the unhallowed ravages of lawless banditti that escape justice on the western frontier; and also to preserve the power and dignity of the Union.
>
> And be it further ordained that the officers of the United States army are hereby required to obey the requisitions of this ordinance.
>
> And be it further ordained that, for all services rendered in quelling mobs and preserving the public peace, the said Nauvoo Legion shall be under the same regulations, rules and laws of pay as the troops of the Unites States.[15]

While in this frame of mind, on December 27, Smith received letters from "gen. Lewis Cass, of Michigan, and Hon. John C. Calhoun, of S. Carolina,

[14] *Millennial Star* 22 (1860): 455.

[15] *Millennial Star* 22 (1860): 486–488; 502–504. [The quoted text is on p. 504. Morgan transcribes the paragraphs without the section numbers appearing in the text. —Ed.]

in answer to mine of November 4."[16] Nothing more is known concerning the Cass letter, but Smith published on January 2, 1844, Calhoun's letter and his own reply. Under date of December 2, Calhoun observed merely that if he should be elected President, he would "strive to administer the government according to the Constitution and the laws of the Union; and that as they make no distinction between citizens of different religious creeds, I should make none. As far as it depends on the Executive department, all should have the full benefit of both and none should be exempt from their operation." With reference to Missouri, Calhoun said only that, according to his views, "the case does not come within the jurisdiction of the Federal Government, which is one of limited and specific powers."[17]

Calhoun's letter was considered and dignified; Smith's reply was savage and rhetorical, and concerned itself principally with Calhoun's contention that the federal government had no jurisdiction in Missouri and that its powers were limited.

> "I would admonish you," he said in closing, "before you let your *'candour compel'* you again to write upon a subject great as the salvation of man, consequential as the life of the Saviour, broad as the principles of eternal truth, and valuable as the jewels of eternity, to read in the 8th section and 1st article of the Constitution of the United States, the *first, fourteenth,* and *seventeenth* 'specific' and not very 'limited powers' of the Federal Government; what can be done to protect the lives, property, and rights of a virtuous people, when the administrators of the law and law-makers are unbought by bribes, uncorrupted by patronage, untempted by gold, unawed by fear, and uncontaminated tangling alliances—even like Caesar's wife, *only unspotted, but unsuspected!* And God, who cooled the heat of a Nebuchadnezzar's furnace or shut the mouths of lions for the honour of a Daniel, will raise your mind above the narrow notion that the General Government has no power, to the sublime idea that Congress, with the President as Executor, is as almighty in its sphere as Jehovah is in his."[18]

On January 19 Smith "gave a lecture on the Constitution of the United States, and on the candidates for the Presidency:"[19] no details survive concerning this lecture, but Smith's mind now certainly was occupied with new ambitions, if indeed he had not already come to a decision for which he was

[16] *Millennial Star* 22 (1860): 536. [Morgan inserts two notes numbered 15, but misses note 30; this version corrects the numbering in the typed manuscript. —Ed.]

[17] *Millennial Star* 22 (1860): 587.

[18] *Millennial Star* 22 (1860): 587, 602–603.

[19] *Millennial Star* 22 (1860): 648.

preparing a public announcement. In November of this year a president was to be elected. . . . Who was better fitted for that responsibility than Joseph Smith, seer and revelator, the prophet of God? Considering his qualifications, he must have told himself that, as the Constitution was of God, no one was better suited to defend it than he. But also the power inherent in the presidency must have appeared to him an escape from the frustrations the Mormons had consistently encountered in their relations with local governments.

A sermon he had delivered in Nauvoo on October 15 offers explicit insight into the shape of Joseph Smith's thought, especially when it is realized that this thought had been crystallizing between October and January.

> It is one of the first principles of my life, and one that I have cultivated from my childhood, having been taught it by my father, to allow every one the liberty of conscience. I am the greatest advocate of the Constitution of the United States there is on the earth. In my feelings I am always ready to die for the protection of the weak and oppressed in their just rights. The only fault I find with the Constitution is, it is not broad enough to cover the whole ground.
>
> Although it provides that all men shall enjoy religious freedom, yet it does not provide the manner by which that freedom can be preserved, nor for the punishment of Government officers who refuse to protect the people in their religious rights, or punish those mobs, states, or communities who interfere with the rights of the people on account of their religion. Its sentiments are good, but it provides no means of enforcing them. It has but this one fault. Under its provisions a man or a people who are able to protect themselves can get along well enough; but those who have the misfortune to be weak or unpopular are left to the merciless rage of popular fury.
>
> The Constitution should contain a provision that every officer of the Government who should neglect or refuse to extent the protection guaranteed in the Constitution should be subject to capital punishment; and then the President of the United States would not say, '*Your cause is just, but I can do nothing for you,*' {the statement asserted to have been made to the Mormons by Van Buren in 1841} a Governor issue exterminating orders, or judges say, 'The men ought to have the protection of law, but it won't please the mob; the men must die, anyhow, to satisfy the clamour of the rabble; they must be hung, or Missouri be damned to all eternity.' Executive writs could be issued when they ought to be, and not be made instruments of cruelty to oppress the innocent, and persecute men whose religion is unpopular.[20]

It is more than probable, also, that an exchange of letters with James Arlington Bennett of New York, in November, had had some effect in heightening

[20] *Millennial Star* 22 (1860): 262–264.

Smith's sense of his importance. Bennett had suggested on October 24, that he might one day run "for a high office" in Illinois, and that Smith, through whose influence he could anticipate election, could be sure that Bennett would repay the favor. "In short, I expect to be yet, through your influence, Governor of the State of Illinois."[21] In a loquacious reply, under date of November 13, Smith arrived at the following point:

> Shall I, who have witnessed the visions of eternity, and beheld the glorious mansions of bliss, and the regions and the misery of the damned,—shall I turn to be a Judas? Shall I, who have heard the voice of God, and communed with angels, and spake as moved by the Holy Ghost for the renewal of the everlasting covenant, and for the gathering of Israel in the last days,—shall I worm myself into a political hypocrite? Shall I, who hold the keys of the last kingdom, in which is the dispensation of the fullness of all things spoken by the mouths of all the holy Prophets since the world began; under the sealing power of the Melchizedek Priesthood,—shall I stoop from the sublime authority of Almighty God, to be handled as a monkey's cat's-paw and pettify myself into a clown to act the farce of political demagoguery? No—verily no! The whole earth shall bear me witness that I, like the towering rock in the midst of the ocean, which has withstood the mighty surges of the warring waves for centuries, *am impregnable,* and am a faithful friend to virtue, and a fearless foe to vice,—no odds whether the former was sold as a pearl in Asia or hid as a gem in America, and the latter dazzles in palaces or glimmers among the tombs.
>
> I combat the errors of ages; I meet the violence of mobs; I cope with illegal proceedings from executive authority; I cut the gordian knot of powers, and I solve mathematical problems of universities, WITH TRUTH—*diamond truth; and God is my right hand man.*[22]

In all probability; it was President [John] Tyler's Third Annual Message to Congress, which was delivered in December, and fell into Smith's hands about the third week of January, that stimulated him to the final announcement of his candidacy. There was much in that message that reasonably serves as the actuating motive in a great deal that followed. Smith himself records that on January 26 he dictated to his clerk "an article on the situation of the nation, referring to the President's Message, &c."[23] This article almost certainly was a preliminary draft of Smith's political "Views," shortly to be published.

On January 29 Smith met with the Twelve Apostles, Hyrum Smith, and J[ohn]. P. Green, "to take into consideration the proper course for this

[21] *Millennial Star* 22 (1860): 324–325.

[22] *Millennial Star* 22 (1860): 325–327; 342.

[23] *Millennial Star* 22 (1860): 664.

people to pursue in relation to the coming Presidential election." Concerning proceedings, Smith wrote:

> The candidates for the office of President of the United States at present before the people are Martin Van Buren and Henry Clay. It is morally impossible for this people, in justice to themselves, to vote for the re-election of President Van Buren—a man who criminally neglected his duties as chief magistrate in the cold and unblushing manner which he did, when appealed to for aid in the Missouri difficulties. His heartless reply burns like a firebrand in the breast of every true friend of liberty—"*Your cause is just, but I can do nothing for you.*"
>
> As to Mr. Clay, his sentiment and cool contempt of the people's rights are manifested in his reply—"*You had better go to Oregon for redress,*" which would prohibit any true lover of our constitutional privileges from supporting him at the ballot-box.
>
> It was therefore moved by Willard Richards, and voted unanimously—"That we will have an independent electoral ticket, and that Joseph Smith be a candidate for the next Presidency: and that we use all honorable means in our power to secure his election."
>
> I {Joseph Smith} said—
>
> "If you attempt to accomplish this, you must send every man in the city who is able to speak in public throughout the land to electioneer and make stump speeches, advocate the 'Mormon' religion, purity of election, and call upon the people to stand by the law and put down mobocracy. David Yearsly must go,—Parley P. Pratt to New York, Erastus Snow to Vermont, and Sidney Rigdon to Pennsylvania.
>
> After the April Conference we will have General Conference all over the nation, and I will attend as many as convenient. Tell the people we have had Whig and Democratic Presidents long enough: we want a President of the United States. If I ever get into the presidential chair, I will protect the people in their rights and liberties. I will not electioneer for myself. Hyrum, Brigham, Parley and Taylor must go. Clayton must go, or he will apostatize. The Whigs are striving for a king under the garb of Democracy. There is oratory enough in the Church to carry me into the presidential chair the first slide."[24]

On the same day that this meeting was held, Smith dictated to William W. Phelps the heads of his pamphlet, "Views on the Powers and Policy of the Government of the United States."[25] On February 5 he revised these "Views," remarking that he was "the first one who publicly proposed a national bank on the principles set forth in that pamphlet," and on the 7th when he met

[24] *Millennial Star* 22 (1860): 684.

[25] *Millennial Star* 22 (1860): 664.

in the evening with his brother, Hyrum, and the Twelve Apostles, "at their request, to devise means to promote the interests of the General Government," he completed and signed his "Views," which he promptly published in the *Times and Seasons* for [15 May 1844].[26]

After a historical review of the rise of the American civilization until its decline under the "withering touch of Martin Van Buren," he proposed abolition of slavery through Congressional purchase of slaves; abolition of military and naval courts-martial, greater economy in government, and less taxes, establishment of a national bank with branches in each State and Territory, empowering of the President to suppress mobs by Federal troops, and the acquisition of Oregon, the annexation of Texas—and Canada and Mexico also, if those countries so desired.

The "Views" were first read publicly at a political meeting in the Assembly Room in Nauvoo on February 9. Concerning his candidacy, Smith told the gathering:

> I would have not suffered my name to have been used by my friends on anywise as President of the United States, or candidates for that office, if I and my friends could have had the privilege of enjoying our religious and civil rights as American citizens, even those rights which the Constitution guarantees unto all her citizens alike. But this we as a people have been denied from the beginning. Persecution has rolled upon our heads from time to time, from portions of the United States, like peals of thunder, because of our religion: and no portions of the United States and no portion of the Government as yet has stepped forward for our relief. And under view of these things, I feel it to be my right and privilege to obtain what influence and power I can, lawfully, in the United States, for the protection of injured innocence; and if I lose my life in a good cause, I am willing to be sacrificed on the altar of virtue, righteousness, and truth, in maintaining the laws and Constitution of the United States, if need be for the general good of mankind.[27]

Other speeches were made by Orson Hyde and John Taylor, and a unanimous vote taken to support Smith's political views. Another meeting was held the following night. On February 12 the memorial to Congress which had been passed on December 21 was again read and signed by the councilors, aldermen, mayor, recorder, and marshal. Smith instructed Orson Pratt, who had been designated to take the memorial east, "to call all the Illinois Representatives together, and tell them our sufferings have been such that

[26]*Millennial Star* 22 (1860): 712; *Times and Seasons* [5, no. 10 (15 May 1844): 528–533].

[27]*Millennial Star* 22 (1860): 774–775.

we must have that document passed, and we *will* have it. 'You must go in for it. Go to John Quincy Adams and ask him to call the delegation from Massachusetts separate from the Illinois delegation, and demand the same. Go to Henry Clay and other prominent men. Call public meetings in the city of Washington. Take the saloon, publish the admittance so much per ticket, invite the members of both houses to come and hear you, and roar upon them. You may take all my writings you think anything of and read to them &c., and you shall prosper in the name of God. Amen.' "[28]

Still another political meeting was held in Nauvoo on the 14th, and next day the *Times and Seasons* published a long editorial, asking again its question of last October: "WHO SHALL BE OUR NEXT PRESIDENT?" and providing the answer: "GENERAL JOSEPH SMITH." "And if," the editor concluded, "we have to throw away our votes, we had better do so upon a worthy rather than upon an unworthy individual, who might make use of the weapon we put in his hand to destroy us with."[29]

Now, however, events took an entirely new course. Joseph Smith's restless mind found an exciting new thought. On February 20 he "instructed the Twelve Apostles to send out a delegation and investigate the locations of California and Oregon, and hunt out a good location, where we can remove to after the Temple is completed, and where we can build a city in a day, and have a government of our own, get up into the mountains, where the Devil cannot dig us out, and live in a healthy climate, where we can live as old as we have mind to."[30]

In view of the fact that the Oregon venture would seem a complete denial of Smith's belief in his chances for the Presidency, it is interesting to consider what impelled him at this time to advance the idea of this exploring expedition. On August 6, 1842, while visiting across the Mississippi in Iowa, he had predicted in casual conversation that "the saints would continue to suffer much affliction and would be driven to the Rocky Mountains, many would apostatize, others would be put to death by our persecutors, or lose their lives in consequence of exposure or disease, and some of you will live to go and assist in making settlements and build cities, and see the saints become a mighty people in the midst of the Rocky Mountains,"[31] and church

[28] *Millennial Star* 22 (1860): 775.
[29] *Times and Seasons* [5, no. 4] (15 February 1844): [439–441].
[30] *Millennial Star* 22 (1860): 819. [See note 16.]
[31] *Millennial Star* [19, no. 40 (3 October 1857): 630].

historians have seen here the genesis of the plan for western emigration, but there were certainly more immediate stimuli. The increasingly ominous appearance of anti-Mormon agitation in Illinois was not calculated to let Smith view with comfort the immediate Mormon future in that state, and this certainly must have impelled him to settle upon some direct course of action on behalf of the Mormon group. He must also have had frequent reports concerning the Oregon emigration of 1842 and 1843, especially since the main avenue of approach to Nauvoo was up the Mississippi, past St. Louis. That the Oregon question stood sharp in popular awareness is evidenced by Smith's comments on Oregon policy in his various political addresses. But it is more than probable that President Tyler's Third Annual Message gave Joseph Smith his specific idea. Tyler had discussed the Oregon question at considerable length, and his conclusion was especially calculated to arouse the Mormon leader to action:

> . . . Many of our citizens are either established in the Territory or are on their way thither for the purpose of forming permanent settlements, while others are preparing to follow: and in view of these facts I must repeat the recommendations contained in previous messages for the establishment of military posts at such places on the line of travel as will furnish security and protection to our hardy adventurers against hostile tribes of Indians inhabiting these extensive regions. Our laws should also follow them, so modified as the circumstances of the case may seem to require. Under the influence of our free system of government new republics are destined to spring up at no distant day on the shores of the Pacific similar in policy and in feeling to those existing on this side of the Rocky Mountains, and giving a wider and more extensive spread to the principles of civil and religious liberty.[32]

Steps at once were taken in Nauvoo to put into operation Joseph Smith's suggestion. The day after he first broached the idea, a council was convened in the Mayor's office.

> At a meeting of the Twelve . . . B. Young, Parley P. Pratt, O. Pratt, W. Woodruff, J. Taylor, Geo. A. Smith, W. Richards, and four others, being present, called by previous notice, by instruction of President Joseph Smith on the 20th instant, for the purpose of selecting a company to explore Oregon and California, and select a site for a new city for the Saints.
>
> Jonathan Dunham, Phineas H. Young, David D. Yearsley, and David Fullmer volunteered to go: and Alphonzo Young, James Emmet, George D. Watt, and Daniel Spencer were requested to go.

[32]James D. Richardson, *A Compilation of Messages and Papers of the Presidents*, 10v. (Washington, D.C.: GPO, 1897), 4: 258.

> Voted the above persons to be notified to meet with the Council on Friday evening next, at the Assembly Room.[33]

On Friday, February 23, Joseph Smith met with the Twelve, Hyrum Smith, and Sidney Rigdon in the Assembly Room "concerning the Oregon and California Exploring Expedition."

> I told them I wanted an exploration of all that mountain country. Perhaps it would be best to go direct to Santa Fe. "Send twenty-five men: let them preach the Gospel wherever they go. Let that man go that can raise $500, a good horse and mule, a double-barrel gun, one-barrel rifle, and the other smooth bore, a saddle and bridle, a pair of revolving pistols, bowie-knife, and a good sabre. Appoint a leader, and let him beat up for volunteers. I want every man that goes to be a king and a priest. When he gets on the mountains he may want to talk with his God: when with the savage nations have power to govern, &c. If we don't get volunteers, wait till after the election."
>
> George D. Watt said, "Gentlemen, I shall go." Samuel Bent volunteered. Joseph A. Kelting, do.; David Fullmer, do; James Emmett, do; Daniel Spencer, do; Samuel W. Richards do.[34]

Concerning his own enlistment, Samuel W. Richards told B. H. Roberts in 1897, "Early in the year 1844, while employed by day upon the temple then building at Nauvoo, Illinois, and standing guard by night, I was visited by my uncle Willard Richards, (who was then the private secretary of the prophet Joseph Smith) and informed by him that the prophet, with his brethren and council, had determined to send a pioneer company of twenty-five young men westward to find a suitable place for the saints to move to, where they could rest for a time from the constant harassing and persecutions to which they were then being subjected, and which was likely to increase if the mob did not have the life of the prophet placed at their disposal; and wished to know if I would be one of the number, to which I freely and readily gave my consent. Soon after I was notified of what would be required of each one of the party for an outfit for the contemplated journey."[35]

Other enlistments quickly followed, as reflected in Smith's journal. On the 24th "Seth Palmer, Amos Fielding, Charles Shumway, and John S.

---

[33] [Private meeting minutes quoted in] "History of Joseph Smith," *Millennial Star* 22 (1860): 820. See also "History of Brigham Young," *Millennial Star* 26 [(1864)]: 327.

[34] *Millennial Star* 22 (1860): 820.

[35] "A Statement by Elder Samuel W. Richards," in B. H. Roberts, *Succession in the Presidency of the Church of Jesus Christ of Latter-day Saints,* 2nd. ed. (Salt Lake City: George Q. Cannon & Sons, 1900), 118. This was a polemical book, [first published in 1894,] and Roberts gathered the statement primarily with an eye to its effect on Josephite [i.e., Community of Christ] claims that the western migration was the product solely of Brigham Young's mind.

Fulmer [*sic*] volunteered to go to Oregon and California."[36] On Sunday, the 25th Smith "attended prayer-meeting in the Assembly Room. We prayed that 'General Smith's Views of the powers and Police of the United States' might be spread far and wide, and be the means of opening the hearts of the people. I gave some important instructions, and prophesied that within five years we should be out of the power of our old enemies, whether they were apostates or of the world; and told the brethren to record it, that when it comes to pass they need not say they had forgotten the saying."[37] On the 26th, "Ira S. Miles volunteered to join the mountain exploring expedition,"[38] and on the 27th "Almon L. Fullmer and Hosea Stout volunteered to go on the Western Exploring Expedition."[39] Again, on the 28th, "Thomas S. Edwards volunteered to join the Exploring Expedition to the Rocky Mountains."[40] And on the 29th, "Moses Smith and Rufus Beach volunteered to join the Oregon Exploring Expedition."[41]

Nineteen names of the twenty-five designated to go are included above. The other six names have not been recovered, but it is almost certain that the full complement was raised. On March 1 Willard Richards wrote James Arlington Bennett, offering him the vice-presidency on the Joseph Smith ticket, and at the same time observing, "We are now fitting out a noble company to explore Oregon and California. . . ."[42] His nephew, Samuel W. Richards, notes further, "In the months of February and March. . . . I attended meetings, held weekly for the purpose of instructing the company as to necessary preparations, and what would be expected of the company in seeking to accomplish the object of their mission. My personal and familiar acquaintance extended to quit a number of the party selected, among whom were Daniel Spencer, Geo. D. Watt, Charles Shumway, Hosea Stout, David Fullmer, Samuel Bent and others with whom I had frequent association. California and Oregon if deemed necessary, were to be the fields of our exploration; while it was thought lower California would offer the greatest inducement for locating a city for the saints."[43]

36 *Millennial Star* 22 (1860): 820.
37 *Millennial Star* 22 (1860): 820.
38 *Millennial Star* 22 (1860): 821.
39 *Millennial Star* 23 (1861): 4.
40 *Millennial Star* 23 (1861): 5.
41 *Millennial Star* 23 (1861): 5
42 *Millennial Star* 23 (1861): 7.
43 Roberts, *Succession*, 118, 119.

But on March 8, 1844,[44] George Miller arrived in Nauvoo from the north, bringing with him letters which precipitated action of such far-reaching importance that the proposed exploring expedition was indefinitely postponed pending the unfolding of larger plans.

One of the most stalwart of the early leaders of the Church, Miller had been baptized in 1839, and on January 19, 1841, by special revelation, was declared presiding bishop of the Church, with the particular responsibility of erecting a temple. Late that year he established a sawmill in the pineries on "Black River," a tributary of the Mississippi, in Wisconsin Territory. Lyman Wight joined him there in the autumn of 1843. On February 15, 1844, the members of the Church at Black River Falls convened in council to survey the result of their operations, and concluded to write to the authorities in Nauvoo. Two letters were written.

The first, after reviewing conditions generally, continued:

> . . . A few of us here have arrived at this conclusion in our minds . . . that as the Gospel has not been fully opened in all the South and South Western States, as also Texas, Mexico, Brazil, &c., together with the West Indian Islands, having produced lumber enough to build the Temple and Nauvoo house,—also having an influence over the Indians, so as to induce them to sell their lands to the United States, and go to a climate southwest, more congenial (all according to the policy of the U.S. Government),—and having also become convinced that the Church at Nauvoo or in the Eastern States will not build the Nauvoo House according to the commandment, neither the Temple in a reasonable time, and that we have, so far as we have made trials, got means in the south,—we have it in our minds to go to the table lands of Texas, to a point we may find to be the most eligible, there locate, and let it be a place of gathering for all the South (they being incumbered with that unfortunate race of beings, the negroes); and for us to employ our time and talents in gathering together means to build according to the commandments of our God, and spread the Gospel to the nations according to the will of our Heavenly Father. We, therefore, our beloved brethren, send our worthy brother {John} Young, with a few of our thoughts, on paper, that you may take the subject-matter under consideration, and return us such instructions as may be according to the will of the Lord our God. . . .[45]

The second read to much the same effect:

> . . . Your servants, the Committee, have viewed the Colorado river with all its beautiful hills and valleys and fertile soil with deep regret, when viewing

[44] *Millennial Star* 23 (1861): [70].

[45] *Millennial Star* 23 (1861): 103, 104.

> the countless thousands of inhabitants on either side thereof, without the knowledge of God or the doctrine of the Church of Jesus Christ of Latter-day Saints and say in their hearts: Would it be expedient to form a mission of those true and full blooded Ephraimites who from principle and love of the truth have borne the most extreme burdens, fatigue and hunger to prosecute the mission to procure lumber sufficient to build two houses, to open the door to all the regions, which we have named, which regions have never yet had an opportunity to hear the gospel and to be made acquainted with the plan of salvation. . . . Is there not thousands of the rich planters who would embrace the Gospel, and if they have a place to plant their slaves, give all the proceeds of their yearly labor, if rightly taught for building up the kingdom; being directed by the President of the whole Church to make the right application? We answer, yes, we believe they would. Our servants, the Committee, are of the opinion that a concert and reciprocity of action between the North and the South would greatly advance the building up of the kingdom. The Committee is well informed of the Cherokee and the Chocktaw nations, who live between the State of Arkansas and the Colorado river of the Texas, owning large plantations and thousands of slaves, and that they are also very desirous to have an interview with the Elders of this Church upon the principles of the Book of Mormon. . . . We, your servants, . . . will wait patiently the result of your council and submit ourselves to the same with all cheerfulness, our only object being to advance the cause and kingdom of God, stand ready to take hold wherever your wise council may consider it to be of the most advantage. . . .[46]

These letters, borne by Miller rather than by John Young, struck with an extraordinary impact upon the authorities in Nauvoo. Only the day before Miller's arrival, Joseph Smith, in a address in Nauvoo, had given particular attention to Texas:

> As to politics, I care but little about the Presidential chair. I would not give half as much for the office of President of the United States as I would for the one I now hold as Lieutenant-General of the Nauvoo Legion.
>
> We have as good a right to make a political party to gain power to defend ourselves, as for demagogues to make use of our religion to get power to destroy us. In other words, as the world has used the power of Government to oppress and persecute us, it is right for us to use it for the protection of our rights. We will whip the mob by getting up a candidate for President.
>
> When I get hold of the Eastern papers and see how popular I am, I am afraid myself that I shall be elected: but if I should be, I would not say, "*Your cause is just, but I can do nothing for you.*"

---

[46] *Millennial Star* 23 (1861): 117–119.

What I have said in my views in relation to the annexation of Texas is with some unpopular: the people are opposed to it. Some of the Anti-Mormons are good fellows. I say it, however, in anticipation that they will repent. They object to Texas on account of slavery. Why, it is the very reason she ought to be received, so that we may watch over them; for, of the two evils, we should reject the greatest.

Governor [Sam] Houston, of Texas, says—"If you refuse to receive us into the United States, we must go to the British Government for protection."

This would certainly be bad policy for this nation: the British are now throughout that whole country, trying to bribe all they can; and the first thing they would do if they get possession, would be to set the negroes and Indians to fight, and they would use us up. British officers are now running all over Texas to establish British influence in that country.

It will be more honourable for us to receive Texas and set the negroes free, and use the negroes and Indians against our foes. Don't let Texas go, lest our mothers and the daughters of the land should laugh us in the teeth; and if these things are not so, God never spoke by any Prophet since the world began.

How much better it is for the nation to bear a little expense than to have the Indians and British upon us and destroy us all. We should grasp all the Territory we can. I know much that I do not tell. I have had bribes offered me, but I have rejected them.

The Government will not receive any advice or counsel from me; they are self-sufficient. But they must go to hell, and work out their own salvation with fear and trembling.

The South holds the balance of power. By annexing Texas, I can do away this evil. As soon as Texas was annexed, I would liberate the slaves in two or three States, indemnifying their own owners, and send the negroes to Texas, and from Texas to Mexico, where all colours are alike. And if that was not sufficient, I would call upon Canada and annex it.[47]

"Upon my arrival at Nauvoo," Miller wrote, "{I} presented the documents to Joseph Smith and Hyrum Smith, whom I found together in consultation. And after a hasty perusal, Joseph said to me, Brother Miller, I perceive the Spirit of God is in the pineries as well as here, and we will call together some of our wise men and proceed to set up the Kingdom of God by organizing some of its officers."[48]

There was thus so easily initiated one of the most extraordinary and least known chapters in Mormon history.

---

[47]*Millennial Star* 23 (1861): 39.

[48]*Correspondence of Bishop George Miller with the Northern Islander from his First Acquaintance with Mormonism up to Near the Close of His Life, Written by Himself in the Year 1855*, ed. Wingfield Watson [Burlington, Wisc.?: Watson?, 1916], [20].

The concept of "The Kingdom of God" itself for some time had unquestionably been taking shape in the back of Joseph Smith's mind. On January 31 he had recorded in his journal, "there seems to be quite a revival throughout Nauvoo, and a inquiry after the things of God, by all the Quorums and the Church in general."[49] On February 4, perhaps not altogether by coincidence, in attending "prayer meeting with the Quorum in the Assembly Room," he "made some remarks respecting the hundred and forty-four thousand mentioned by John the Revelator[50] showing that the selection of persons to form the number had already commenced.[51] The concept of the Kingdom of God, and even certain of its rites, sprang direct from this passage of the Bible. Indeed, the "Kingdom of God" itself assuredly derived its name from the further passage in St. John (Rev. 11:15), "And the seventh angel sounded; and there were great voices in heaven, saying, The Kingdoms of this world are become the kingdoms of our Lord, and of his Christ; and he shall reign forever and ever." It must not be forgotten that the Mormon Church was essentially a millennial church, that the people were being "gathered" to Nauvoo and that the "signs of the last days" were being continually heralded by church writers and speakers, although Joseph Smith, out of the conflict with the Millerites, who had predicted the Second Advent for 1843, and, later, for 1844, was moved to say that at least another forty years should elapse before the advent of the Son of Man. With the millennium near it was logical that God must have begun the selection of

[49]*Millennial Star* 22 (1860): 694.

[50]St. John's text reads: "And I saw another angel ascending from the east, having the seal of the living God: and he cried with a loud voice to the four angels, to whom it was given to hurt the earth and the sea, Saying Hurt not the earth, neither the sea, nor the trees, till we have sealed the servants of our God in their foreheads. And I heard the number of them which were sealed: and there were sealed an hundred and forty and four thousand of all the tribes of the children of Israel . . . After this I beheld, and lo, a great multitude, which no man could number, of all nations, and kindreds, and people, and tongues, stood before the throne, and before the Lamb, clothed with white robes, and palms in their hands, And cried with a loud voice, saying, Salvation to our God which sitteth upon the throne, and unto the Lamb. And all the angels stood round about the throne, and about the elders and the four beasts, and fell before the throne on their faces, and worshipped God, Saying, Amen: Blessing, and glory, and wisdom, and thanksgiving, and honour, and power, and might, be unto our God for ever and ever. Amen. And one of the elders answered, saying unto me, What are these which are arrayed in whit robes? And whence came they? And I said unto him, Sir, thou knowest. And he said to me, These are they which came out of great tribulation, and have washed their robes, and made them white in the blood of the Lamb. Therefore are they before the throne of God, and serve him day and night in his temple: and he that sitteth on the throne shall dwell among them. They shall hunger no more, neither thirst any more; neither shall the sun light on them, nor any heat. For the Lamb which is in the midst of the throne shall feed them, and shall lead them unto living fountains of waters: and God shall wipe away all tears from their eyes." [KJV] Revelation 7: 2–17.

[51]*Millennial Star* 22 (1860): 711–712.

the hundred and forty-four thousand, that the Prophet of God should have some comprehension of this—and that he should organize, in anticipation, the Kingdom of God on earth.

The form of this organization, crystallized by Miller's arrival, was certainly suggested by an event of February 6. On that date Joseph Smith, Hyrum Smith, Sidney Rigdon, and the Twelve Apostles, with their wives, met at John Taylor's for supper. Brigham Young records that the Twelve "discussed the propriety of establishing a moot Congress for the purpose of investigating and informing ourselves on the rules of national intercourse, domestic policy and political economy. Joseph advised us not to do it, lest we excite the jealousy of our enemies."[52] Now, however, Smith's fertile mind unquestionably saw the suitability of adapting a "moot congress" to the Kingdom of God. He would establish a legislature, composed of Fifty Princes of the Kingdom. This inner council would make an authoritative instrument for advancing the temporal affairs of the Church and the Church membership.

Miller's letters were considered on March 10[53] by a "council"—probably including Smith, the Twelve, and a few others—and the next day, as Brigham Young records, "Joseph commenced the organization of a Council for the purpose of taking into consideration the necessary steps to obtain redress for the wrongs which had been inflicted upon us by our persecutors, and also the best manner to settle our people in some distant and unoccupied territory: where we could enjoy our civil and religious rights, without being subject to constant oppression and mobocracy, under the protection of our own laws, subject to the Constitution. The Council was composed of about fifty-members, several of whom were not members of the Church . . . Joseph Smith was appointed chairman, William Clayton, clerk, and Willard Richards, historian of the Council."[54]

Smith's journal provides further particulars. Present at the first meeting were Joseph Smith, Hyrum Smith, Brigham Young, Heber C. Kimball, Willard Richards, Parley P. Pratt, Orson Pratt, John Taylor, George A. Smith, William W. Phelps, John M. Bernhisel, Lucien Woodworth, George Miller, Alexander Badlam, Peter Haws, Erastus Snow, Reynolds Cahoon, Amos Fielding, Alpheus Cutler, Levi Richards, Newel K. Whitney, Lorenzo D. Watson, and William Clayton, "whom I organized into a special council,

[52]"History of Brigham Young," *Millennial Star* 26 (1864): 327.

[53]*Millennial Star* 23 (1861): [119].

[54]"History of Brigham Young," *Millennial Star* 26 (1864): 328–329.

to take into consideration the subject matter contained in the above letters {brought by Miller} and also the best policy for this people to adopt to obtain their rights from the nation and insure probation for themselves and children; and to secure a resting place in the mountains, or some uninhabited region, where we can enjoy the liberty of conscience guaranteed to us by the constitution of our country, rendered doubly sacred by the precious blood of our fathers, and denied to us by the present authorities, who have smuggled themselves into power in the States and nation."[55]

Smith writes on the 12th that ". . . the brethren who were in council with me yesterday assembled there in the afternoon and evening,"[56] and Brigham Young records that the "Council of Fifty," or "General Council," as it euphemistically came to be called in the church records, met again on the 12th, 13th, and 14th.[57] Neither the Smith nor Young journal offers much direct light on the proceedings within the Council, but from succeeding events and from Miller's writings the course of thought and action can be quite closely followed.

Inevitably the Council was religious in its bias, although there is excellent reason to believe that friendly non-Mormons were admitted to its deliberations. Brigham Young mentions a meeting in April which closed "with shouts of Hosannah,"[58] and from William Clayton's journal, as will be seen, it is evident that either at this time or later, members of the Council donned priestly robes for their sessions.

The letters brought by Miller evoked bold courses of action far beyond anything that might have been anticipated by the church branch at Black River Falls.

The Oregon mission was held in abeyance, although the members of the expedition evidently continued their weekly meetings pending clarification of the other plans.[59] The "princes in the kingdom of God," which Miller numbers at fifty-three, decided, Miller says,

---

[55]*Millennial Star* 23 (1861): [119].

[56]*Millennial Star* 23 (1861): 119.

[57]"History of Brigham Young," *Millennial Star* 26 (1864): 329.

[58]"History of Brigham Young," *Millennial Star* 26 (1864): 330.

[59]Samuel W. Richards remembered, "At those meetings, which I attended, Hyrum Smith and Sidney Rigdon were always present, also those members of the quorum of the Twelve then in Nauvoo. The Prophet Joseph was seldom present, as he was most of the time in hiding from his persecutors. At these meetings much of a prophetic nature was communicated by the two first named, as to what would result from the power of their enemies, and when the remnants of Israel should join them in the great work of the restoration of God's covenant people, preparatory to the reign of Christ upon the earth, in the thousand years of millennial rest promised" (Roberts, *Succession*, 119). Although Richards specifies only February and March, it is more than probable that these meetings continued into April, and possibly in May.

> that we would run Joseph Smith for President of the United States, which we would certainly do, and also Sidney Rigdon for Vice President; and in case they were elected we would at once establish dominion in the United States, and in view of a failure we would send a minister to the . . . Republic of Texas to make a treaty with the Cabinet of Texas for all that country north of a west line from the falls of the Colorado River to the Nueces; thence down the same to the Gulf of Mexico, and along the same to Rio Grande, and up the same to the United States territory and get them to acknowledge us as a nation;[60] and on the part of the church we would help them defend themselves against Mexico, standing as a go-between the belligerent powers. And if successful in this matter we would have dominion in spite of the United States, and we would send the Black River Lumber Company to take possession of the newly acquired territory. Lucien Woodworth was chosen minister to Texas, and I was to return to the pineries to bring down Lyman Wight, and leave matters there that the work could go on without my presence, and be back by the time Woodworth might return from Texas. We severally started the same day, Woodworth for Texas, and I for the pineries.[61]

Woodworth left "on a mission to Texas"[62] on March 14, so presumably Miller departed for the pineries on the same day. Miller returned May 1 and Woodworth next day,[63] but meanwhile events in Nauvoo became ever more complex.

The Council of Fifty met on March 19 and again on March 21. By the latter day Smith's thinking with respect to Oregon had taken a new tack. "In Council in the Assembly Room," he recorded, "discussing the propriety of petitioning Congress for the privilege of raising troops to protect the making of settlements in the uncivilized portions of our continent."[64] In consequence Willard Richards was appointed a committee to write a Memorial to Congress. On Monday March 25, Smith read the product of Richards' labors, "and was pleased with the instrument."[65] The Council convened next day from 9 to 12 in the morning and from 2 to 5 in the afternoon, Richards' memorial being "read, discussed, and approved."[66]

---

[60]This proposed Mormon country was as grandiose in its proportions as the Provisional State of Deseret later established west of the Rockies, embracing roughly three-fifths of modern Texas, the eastern half of New Mexico, the Oklahoma panhandle, approximately a ninth of Kansas, a third of Colorado, and a large rectangle of south-central Wyoming. Of the land claimed by the Republic of Texas in 1836, the Mormon state would have comprised between two-thirds and three-fourths. This area was, however, virtually unoccupied [by settled Euroamericans] at this time. The "falls of the Colorado River" mentioned by Miller is present Marble Falls in Texas.

[61][Miller, *Correspondence*, 20.]

[62]*Millennial Star* 23 (1861): [135].

[63]*Millennial Star* 23 (1861): 407.

[64]*Millennial Star* 23 (1861): 151.

[65]*Millennial Star* 23 (1861): 165.

[66]*Millennial Star* 23 (1861): [165].

The memorial, written in the name of Joseph Smith, "a free-born citizen of these United States," after a remarkable if somewhat florid flight of rhetoric, proposed that, in view of emigration to "Texas, Oregon, and other lands contiguous to this nation," in view of the helplessness of Texas to maintain its independence, and the primary claim of the United States to Oregon, and in view of the desirability of extending the dominion of the United States to the "almost boundless extent of territory on the west and south of these United States, where exists little or no organization of protective Government," that Joseph Smith should be empowered "to extend the arm of deliverance to Texas {and} to protect the inhabitants of Oregon from foreign aggression and domestic boils," through raising "a company of one hundred thousand armed volunteers in the United States and Territories, at such times and places, and in such numbers, as he shall find necessary and convenient for the purposes specified. . . ." He was to be constituted a member of the army of the United States, and authorized to act as such in the United States and Territories and all bordering lands, provided those lands were not within the jurisdiction of my acknowledged national government; moreover, anyone hindering him in his designs was to be punished by a fine not exceeding one thousand dollars, or by hard labor not exceeding two years, or both, at the discretion of the District Court of the United States nearest the place of offense. The army itself was not to be considered as constituting any part of the army of the United States, nor was Smith, as a member of the United States, to "disturb the peace of any nation or government acknowledged as such, break the faith of treaties between the United States and another nation, or violate any known law of nations, thereby endangering the peace of the United States." A final provision was that Smith was to confine his operations to "those principles of action" specified in the preamble, "the perpetuity of which shall be commensurate with the circumstances and specifications which have originated it."[67]

The immediate relationship of this memorial to everything that had happened in preceding months is at once manifest. Smith's liking for military trappings and authority, his proposal that the Nauvoo Legion be constituted a part of the U.S. Army, and Nauvoo virtually a separate Territory, his ideas concerning annexation, his ideas of exploring Oregon and California, his ideas for removal to Texas, and his exasperation at obstructionist enemies all

[67]*Millennial Star* 23 (1861): 165–167.

are united in one extraordinary document. Only his presidential candidacy is not considered, unless he bore in mind the predilection of the American voting public for military heroes.

On March 30 a duplicate memorial was prepared for presentation to President Tyler, and [the] next day, after again hearing and signing the memorial, Smith signed an introductory letter to Orson Hyde, who had been designated to carry the memorials to Washington.[68] On April 4, the Council met all day: "Elder O. Hyde was in the Council, and left immediately for Washington."[69]

He arrived there April 23, and on April 25 wrote a long letter to the Council. Pratt, he said, had been "indefatigueable in the exertions in prosecuting the business entrusted to his charge. His business has been before the Senate and referred to the committee on the judiciary, and the report of said committee is not yet rendered which is the cause of this delay in writing to you." On the 24th he and Pratt had conversed with the Illinois delegation in Congress, whom they found attentive and "deeply interested in the Oregon question," but inclined to be doubtful that anything could be done about the memorial at this time, in view of the fact that Congress had voted down a resolution requesting the president to notify Great Britain of its desire for the abolition of the treaty of joint occupancy. Hyde continued, expressing his doubts that Congress would pass at the current session any bill in relation to Oregon or Texas:

> She is afraid of England, afraid of Mexico and afraid the presidential election will be twisted by it. The members all appear like unskillful player at checkers, afraid to move, for they see not which way to move advantageously. All are figuring and playing around the grand and important questions. . . . A member of congress is in no enviable situation. If he will boldly advocate true principles, he loses his influence, has no power to benefit his constituents, so they all go to figuring and playing around the great points. Mr. {Robert} Semple {senator from Illinois} said that Mr. Smith could not constitutionally be constituted a member of the Army by law, and this if nothing else would prevent its passage. I observed that I would, in that case, strike out that clause. . . . There is already a government established in Oregon to some extent. Magistrates have been chosen by the people, etc. This on the south of the Columbia, north of that river, the Hudson bay company occupy. There is some good country in Oregon, but a great deal of sandy barren desert. I have seen a gentleman who has been there, and also in California.

[68] *Millennial Star* 23 (1861): 184.

[69] *Millennial Star* 23 (1861): [184]

> The most of the settlers in Oregon and Texas are our old enemies, the mobocrats of Mo. If, however, the settlement of Oregon or Texas be determined upon, the sooner the move is made the better, and I would not advice any delay for the action of government for there is such a jealousy of our rising power already, that government will do nothing to favor us. If the saints possess the kingdom, I think they will have to take it, and the sooner it is done, the more easily it is accomplished.
>
> Your superior wisdom must determine whether to go to Oregon, to Texas or to remain within these United States, and send forth the most efficient men to build up churches, and let them remain for the time being. In the mean time, send some wise man among the Indians, and teach them civilization and religion, to cultivate the soil to live in peace with one another and with all men. But whatever you do, don't be deluded with the hope that government will foster us; and thus delay an action, which the present perhaps is the most proper time that ever will be.
>
> Oregon is becoming a popular question. The fever of emigration begins to rage. If the Mormons become the early majority, others will not come, if the Mormons do not become an early majority, the others will not allow us to come. . . .[70]

The following day Hyde wrote again, to relate that he and Pratt, on the previous evening, had had an hour's interview with President Tyler, who had proved friendly. Hyde also related that Stephen A. Douglas, senator from Illinois, was "ripe for Oregon, and the California. He said he would resign his seat in congress, if he could command the force that Mr. Smith could, and would be on the march to that country in a month." Hyde doubted that Texas would be immediately annexed, but if that project were carried through, the northern Whig members, antagonistic both to Texas and to Oregon, certainly would "turn round in favor of Oregon, for if Texas be admitted, slavery is extended to the south; then, free states must be added to the west to keep up a balance of power between the slave and the free states." Douglas, Hyde reported, "says he would equally as soon go to that country {Oregon} without an act of congress as with, 'and that if in 5 years a noble state might be formed, and then if they would not receive us into the Union, we would have a government of our own.' He is decidedly of the opinion that congress will pass no act in favor of any particular man going there, but he says if any may go, and desires that privilege, and has confidence in his own ability to perform it, he already has the right, and

[70] *Millennial Star* 23 (1861): 502–504

the sooner he is off, the better for his scheme. It is the opinion here among politicians, that it will be extremely difficult to have any bill passed in relation to the encouragement of emigration to Oregon; but much more difficult to get a bill passed designating any particular man to go; but all concur in the opinion that we are authorized already.["]

In case the Mormons should remove to Oregon, Hyde continued, Nauvoo would be the place of general rendezvous. They would thence cross Iowa westward to the Missouri, thence westward to the Platte, and up the north fork of that river to the mouth of the Sweetwater, up the Sweetwater to South Pass, and from South Pass to the "Umqua and Clamet [Klamath] valleys in Oregon bordering on California," a distance he estimated at 1700 miles. There was no government established in Oregon, Hyde observed, and when a government should be so established, it might readily embrace California also. "There is much barren country, rocky and mountainy[,] in Oregon, but the valley are very fertile." Frémont, to whom the Mormons were to be so greatly indebted, appears for the first time in Mormon literature in the next paragraph of Hyde's letter.

> Judge Douglas has given us a map of Oregon, and also a report on an exploration of the country lying between the Missouri River and the Rocky Mountains on the line of the Kansas, and great Platte Rivers, by Lieut. J. C. Fremont of the corps of topographical engineers. On receiving it, I expressed a wish that Mr. Smith could see it, Judge Douglas says it is a public document, and I will frank it to him. I accept his offer, and the book will be forth coming to him. The people are so eager for it here, that they have even stole it out of the library. The author is Mr. [Senator Thomas Hart] Benton's son-in-law. Judge Douglas borrowed it of Mr. Benton. I was not to tell any one in this city where I got it. The book is a most valuable document to any on contemplating a journey to Oregon. The directions which I have given may not be exactly correct, but the book will tell correctly. Judge Douglas says he can direct Mr. Smith to several gentlemen in California who will be able to give him any information on the state of affairs in that country, and when he returns to Illinois he will visit Mr. Smith.

Hyde concluded his letter by relating that he and Pratt had drafted a bill, which they had given to the Senate committee on judiciary, asking an appropriation of two million dollars for the relief of Mormon sufferings in Missouri. "We intend to tease them until we either provoke them, or get them to do something for us. I have learned this much, that if we want congress to do any thing for us in drawing up our memorial, we must not ask, what is right in the matter, but we must ask, what kind of a thing will congress pass?" Closing, he promised to write soon again and let the council know "what restriction, if any, are laid upon our citizens in relation to passing through the Indian Territories."[71]

On April 30 Hyde wrote once more to express a positive opinion that Congress would neither annex Texas at this session nor pass the Mormon Oregon bill. He himself displayed somewhat less enthusiasm concerning Oregon. "Oregon is a good way off, and is not a very good country when you arrive there. I have read something of its history since I left, and have also conversed with gentlemen who have been there. The Tax, upon women and children in removing there, would be severe indeed." Accordingly, he made a bold proposition regarding Texas:

> As Texas will not be admitted into our union, how would it do for you to write to prest. Houston and ask him what encouragement he could give us if we could commence an immediate emigration there, and supply him with 1, 2, 3, 4, or 5 thousand soldiers to help fight the battle, and then if Mexico would not acknowledge the independence of Texas, but continue to harass her by small parties, make one tremendous rush upon Mexico, and capture and subdue the whole country. This would secure Texas, Mexico and California. If Mexico should acknowledge the independence of Texas without bloodshed. Then we should have a delightful soil and climate, and an opportunity of extending our settlement into California, and we should not be out of the reach of communication, or the necessaries and comforts of life. Texas would be a central point for emigration; for the coming in and going out of the elders. Or if this would not do, let some man whose mind is well balanced with judgment and discretion go and establish a stake in Texas, and let the converts from the south who have slaves gather there and raise our sugar, and we in Illinois there provisions. But if this is not advisable stick fast in Illinois and hold on. Let the elder go forth in multitudes and raise up churches, then let the Twelve visit those churches and give certificates for all such to gather into Hancock and other counties contiguous as are able to buy farms, and let the poor remain when they are without certificates until we shall have a large territory, heavy and extensive agricultural capital, and an abundance of produce, then let the poor come in and fill up the vacancies. If, with our limited means, we now attempt to establish manufactories, we have strength perhaps to half complete them, then we might as well have an inheritance in the moon "or all the good it would do us, as to have those half finished

[71] *Millennial Star* 23 (1861): 518–519.

> manufactories. The fruits of agricultural labor are sooner realized than any other, and now, would it not be our most political course to strengthen ourselves by agriculture, extend our borders, enlarge the territory in Illinois as I have spoken, and break up the plan of settling so much within the limits of the town. If we were to get Texas, or rather go there under the most favorable circumstances, which we have any reason to hope for. There is an army to support, and also a Navy, and an executive and legislative government. Ministers and consults to all nations. Would not this enormous weight of taxation keep out capitalists and sink the infant government.

Hyde explained that he had thought it well to dwell upon the darker side, because their inexperienced minds would bend to dwell first upon the sunny side, but that if his thoughts were wrong, he knew the council's "superior discernment {would} not only discover, but reduce them to a proper bearing." He concluded by announcing that he was leaving Washington, and that Orson Pratt would take care of the memorial, if any action was to be had upon it, but also that he would return to Washington immediately if his presence there at any time became desirable.[72]

Hyde's letters of April 25 and 26 arrived in Nauvoo on May 13. But between the time of his departure and that of the arrival of his letters, the Mormon plans had ripened amazingly.

Hyde had left Nauvoo April 4, but the sessions of the Council of Fifty continued regularly, with new names now and then being added to the council, including J. W. Coolidge, D. S. Hollister, and Lyman Wight on April 18,[73] and Jedediah M. Grant on May 6.[74] On April 25 the council met in session all day, "appointing a State Convention to meet in Nauvoo on 17th May." Smith notes that the council then dispersed to go abroad in the nations,"[75] but this was a merely temporary disposition of the council, for at once there arose important occasions for further sessions.

Lyman Wight and Miller arrived in Nauvoo from the pineries on May 1, and next day "Lucien Woodworth returned from Texas."[76] On May 3 the General Council convened to hear Woodworth's "account of his mission," the session lasting all day.[77] Neither Smith's nor Young's journal is

---

[72]Letter, Orson Hyde to the Council, in Journal History, 30 April 1844.

[73]*Millennial Star* 23 (1861): 391.

[74]"History of Brigham Young," *Millennial Star* 26 (1864): 343.

[75]*Millennial Star* 23 (1861): 392.

[76]*Millennial Star* 23 (1861): 407.

[77]*Millennial Star* 23 (1861): 420.

communicative concerning this session, though a letter written by Young on May 5 to Reuben Hedlock, president of the British Mission, indicates very clearly its general trend.

> We shall have a State Convention at Nauvoo on the 17th inst,—an election. A great many are believing the doctrine. If any of the brethren wish to go to Texas, we have no particular objection. You may send a hundred thousand there, if you can in eighteen months, though we expect before that you will return to receiver your endowment: and then we will consult your interest, with others who may be going abroad, about taking their families with them.
>
> The kingdom is organized; and although as yet no bigger than a grain of mustard seed, the little plant is in a flourishing condition, and the prospects brighter than ever...[78]

What Young only hints at George Miller explicitly records:

> Some time towards the last of April, 1844, we (Lyman Wight, myself and families) arrived at Nauvoo. Soon after this Woodworth returned from Texas. The council convened to hear this report. It was altogether as we could wish it. On the part of the church there was commissioners appointed to meet the Texas Congress, to sanction or ratify the said treaty, partly entered into by our minister and the Texas Cabinet. A. W. Brown, Lucien Woodworth and myself were the commissioners appointed to meet the Texas Congress, and upon the consummation of the treaty, Wight and myself were to locate the Black River Lumber Company on the newly acquired territory, and do such other things as might be necessary in the premises, and report to the council of the kingdom.
>
> It was further determined in council that all the elders should set out on missions to all the States, get up electoral tickets, and do everything in our power to have Joseph elected President, and if we succeeded in making a majority of the voters converts to our faith and elected Joseph President, in such an event the dominion of the kingdom would be forever established in the United States, and if not successful, we could but fall back on Texas, and be a kingdom notwithstanding.
>
> It was thought and urged by the council that so great an undertaking should require in order to ensure success, the entire united effort of all the official members of the church. And accordingly on the sixth of May I started to Kentucky and Lyman to the eastern States; and at no period since the organization of the church had there been half so many elders in the vineyard, in proportion to the number of members in the church.[79]

---

[78]*Millennial Star* 23 (1861): 420–422.

[79][Miller, *Correspondence*, 20–21.]

The Council of Fifty met again on May 6. Smith records, "Elder J. M. Grant was added to the Council. Voted to send Almon W. Babbitt on a mission to France, and Lucien Woodworth to Texas. Sidney Rigdon was nominated as a candidate for the Vice-Presidency of the United States."[80]

Orson Hyde's letters of April 25 and 26, arriving in Nauvoo on May 13, encountered this feeling of elated accomplishment. A General Council convened to hear the letters, instructing Willard Richards to answer, and Lyman Wight and Heber C. Kimball to carry the answers to Washington. On the 16th Smith went to his office in the morning "and heard read a letter written by Elder Richards, in behalf of the Council, to Elders Orson Hyde and Orson Pratt at Washington."[81]

This letter does not seem to be extant, but its contents can be reasonably conjectured from its effect on Hyde, to be noted. Wight and Kimball remained in Nauvoo a short while longer, to attend the State Convention, held in Nauvoo on the 17th. This convention officially declared Joseph Smith its presidential candidate,[82] and provided for the holding of a national convention in Baltimore on July 13.

On May 20 there was held a meeting at the stand for the purpose of collecting means to enable Elder Lyman Wight to go to Washington"[83] And the funds were evidently raised, for next day Wight, Brigham Young, Heber C. Kimball, "and about a hundred Elders left for St. Louis."[84]

Kimball writes concerning his journey with Wight:

> {We} took passage on a steamer . . . to St. Louis, and from thence took steamer to Pittsburg, where Elder Wight and myself parted with President Young and proceeded to Washington city and presented to the rulers of the nation the petition for redress of grievances.
>
> We put up at the National Hotel, which cost us $2 dollars per day. We had an interview with General [David R.] Atcheson and Mr. [Stephen A.] Douglas, members of Congress, they treated us very politely Mr. Douglas came to our room to see us.

---

[80]*Millennial Star* 23 (1861): 423. The Vice-Presidency had originally been offered to James Arlington Bennett, but it was discovered that he was ineligible because [he had been born] an Irishman. It was then offered to Colonel Solomon Copeland of Paris, Tennessee, but he evidently showed no interest, so that Rigdon finally was named for the office.

[81]*Millennial Star* 23 (1861): 860.

[82]*Millennial Star* 23 (1861): 591–594; 607–610; 623–624.

[83]*Millennial Star* 23 (1861): 825.

[84]*Millennial Star* 23 (1861): 825.

> We went up to the White House to see President Tyler, but he was absent.
>
> I went into the galleries of the Senate and House of Representatives and witnessed the confusion which reigns there.
>
> We visited General Semple, Senator from Illinois; he seemed very friendly presented our memorials which were referred to the Senate committee on public lands.
>
> Lyman Wight occasionally steamed so freely that I had to lock him up in our room in the hotel, and attend to our business alone.
>
> * * * * *
>
> June 6th. A full band of music played in the Capital grounds, which attracted thousands who promenaded through the walks, displayed their finery, and perhaps secured customers for the next twelve hours. I recorded "the Lord is with us and the Devil all about."
>
> I inquired of the Lord what we should do and he revealed to me that Congress had not got it in their hearts to do anything for us and we were at liberty to go away.
>
> We visited a few Saints who were in Washington and ordained one Elder: the Saints were cold and stupid.
>
> 11th. We went to Wilmington, Del. And preached to the Church. . . .[85]

Kimball is incommunicative concerning Orson Hyde, but he quite evidently brought a message so blistering as to induce Hyde to write on June 9 an almost abject letter to the council in Nauvoo.

Before taking up that letter, however, the reaction will be noted to Hyde's letter of April 20, received in Nauvoo on May 25. To that letter Smith instructed Willard Richards to write the following reply:

> Yours of April 30th is received. The Council convened this afternoon, and after investigation, directed an answer, which must be brief, to correspond with a press of business.
>
> All the items you refer to had previously received the deliberation of the Council.
>
> Messrs. Lyman Wight and Heber C. Kimball will doubtless be in Washington before you receive this, from whom you will learn all things relative to Texas, &c. Our great success at present depends upon our faith in the doctrine of election; and our faith must be made manifest by our works and every honorable exertion made to elect General Smith.
>
> Agricultural pursuits will take care of themselves, regulating their own operations and the rich also; but the poor we must gather and take care of, for they are to inherit the kingdom.

---

[85]"Synopsis of the History of Heber C. Kimball," *Millennial Star* 26 (1864): 728–729. The reference to Wight has respect to his habitual intemperance.

> Nauvoo will be a "corner Stake of Zion" forever, we most assuredly expect. Here are the house and the ordinances, extend where else we may.
>
> Press the bills through houses if possible. If Congress will not pass them, let them do as they have a mind with them. If they will not pass our bill, but will give us something, they will give us what they please, and it will be at our option to accept or reject.
>
> Men who are afraid on "hazarding their influence" in the council or political arena are good for nothing. 'Tis the fearless, undaunted, and persevering who will gain the conquest of the forum. . . .[86]

Orson Hyde arrived back at Washington on June 8, meeting Kimball and Wight, who presented him with the council's letter of May 16. From the immediate reply written by Hyde on June 9, its contents can be quite fully conjectured. The letter was very severe in tone. It inquired whether Hyde had so little regard for Joseph Smith's honor that he should let it perish through fear or cowardice. It instructed Hyde that the council stood on the summit of all earthly power, and that Joseph Smith, presiding over the council, was God's messenger to execute justice and judgment in the earth, so that any neglect or delinquency in failing to maintain Smith's dignity and honor demanded the censure and reproof of the council. It informed him that the people were sovereign, and that senators and representatives were sent to Washington to do the will of the people who sent them, not their own will, so that he should have stood upon sterner ground, and not easily accepted any man's verdict as to the constitutionality or unconstitutionality of the council's projects. In a word, Hyde stood convicted in the council's eyes of grave dereliction in his duty.

In his reply Hyde apologized for everything in which he might have been delinquent, begging the council to remember that if he had committed errors of judgment, this had been done "with a heart unreservedly devoted" to the best interests of the council. He asked the council to review the motives which had underlain his actions. Concerning the contention that the people were sovereign, he said that he had previously had some conversation on this point with Senator Robert Semple, who had reasoned forcefully that a representative could not execute the wishes of his people when the people had not acquainted him with their wishes by forwarding to him their names in black and white, or at least, a respectable majority of their names. The Illinois delegation was not "the representative of the Mormons alone, but

[86]"History of Joseph Smith," *Millennial Star* 23 (1861): 643, 657.

of all the classes." Hyde defended his action in having withdrawn the clause in the Oregon bill by which Smith was to be appointed a member of the Army of the United States; he himself had not presumed to judge whether the clause was or was not constitutional, but only what action might be had upon it from Congress. A proposal, however entitled to the deepest and warmest sympathies, might arbitrarily be rejected by men who consulted only popular opinion. Hyde cited the visit of Smith and Rigdon to Washington in 1841. "If, then, bros. Smith and Rigdon with their superior skill and wisdom could not make 'one hair white or black', how can it be expected that I, with less skill and power, could make an impression upon the same flinty material?" Semple's opinion concerning the unconstitutionality of that one clause, Hyde said, had influenced him to do that which he should "probably never do again, that is, to alter the document." In striking out the clause, Hyde contended, he had acted for what he considered the best. If the appointment of some specific person was the province of the executive alone, nothing was to be lost by striking out the passage and letting the bill try its luck in Congress, for if it should pass, he would take the President that memorial which had originally been addressed to him, and which remained unchanged; it approving and signing this memorial, the President at once would dispose of the question of the appointment. If the bill should not pass Congress, he would still be free to present to the President the memorial addressed to him.

> The truth of the matter was, {Hyde said,} I wanted to save the knowledge of our prophet from being impeached by congress, by his asking a thing not constitutional, and as it was the universal opinion of all with whom I conversed that the bill would not, or could not pass, anyhow, I thought there could be nothing lost by erasing that part, and there might be something saved. The bill has been rejected in both houses,[87] and now I am prepared to go to the president, which will be tomorrow, and when that is done, I know not what more I can do. I cannot recall the memorials that have been laid before congress, and been acted upon and rejected. But I do repeat it again, that no measure can pass congress unless it is a popular one, for the

[87]The bill was introduced into the House of Representatives on May 25 by John Wentworth, representative from Illinois. He requested that it be read by the clerk of the house, but before the reading had been completed, objection was interposed by J.R. Ingersall, who had also objected previously. Wentworth moved a suspension of the rules, that the memorial might be read, but the motion was defeated, 86–79. There was no further action than the bill. *Congressional Globe*, vol. 13, p. 624. [On the question of the Mormons and Oregon cf. Orson Hyde to General Council, 25 April 1844, *Millennial Star* 23, no. 32 (10 August 1861): 502–504. —Ed.]

people are the rulers, and if a measure is not popular with them, they will not pass it right or not right. If our former experience has not proven this declaration to be true to our satisfaction, we shall find it to be so hereafter, if the present government shall be permitted to stand.

That my exertions to save brother Joseph from the charge of ignorance in the estimation of congress should be interpreted into a disposition to let his honor perish through fear or cowardice grieves me much. The west is not farther from the east than my heart if from acting upon a principle of that kind, and that my course should meet the decided disapprobation and indignation of the council grieves me more. Then I received the memorials and left home, it was in good faith that congress would do something for us, and I asked brother Joseph something about responsibility, etc. His own words to me were "go and do the best you can, act like a king and get the very best things done for us that you can." Also my letter of commendation over his signature as Mayor authorized me to transact such business as I may deem expedient and beneficial for the party I represent. These are not direct authority to do as I have done, yet I considered them a shadow of authority, and where I could see no injury or loss to be sustained in the operation, but a little prospect of saving something, I ran the venture to make the alteration.

After being here eight days and talking with the members, and reasoning with them, it wanted no more of a prophetic spirit to tell what congress could do, or rather what they would not do, than it does to tell a man's back must be towards the south if his face is towards the north. Brother Wight says it is now said in council, that it was not expected that congress would do anything for us. The memorials were only to tease them, and that we might as well tease them with one thing as another. If I had left home with such instructions, I should never had altered a letter, but as I said before I say again, that it was in good faith that they would do something that I left home. Pursuant to that impression I went to work as industriously and prudently as possible, but instead of meeting your approbation, I have met your decided disapprobation and indignation. Your discernment is superior to mine. I therefore say that I am sorry that I have committed the error, and if the council will forgive this offense, I will assure them that I shall never again, under any circumstances, be inclined to take a like responsibility. If I knew of anything more that I could say or do to give you satisfaction, I would most certainly do it. . . .[88]

On June 11 Hyde wrote once more to describe a brief interview with President Tyler.

I presented him with the memorial. He read it attentively through, and then remarked that the object was most unquestionably a good one. "The possession and settlement of Oregon appears to be the leading feature in the

[88]Journal History, 8 June 1844.

memorial," said he, "and you will recollect," continues he, "that in my annual message I commended to congress the establishing of a line of forts through to that Territory. Now, does not this embrace all you want?" I answered, "No, sir, we shall go in bodies sufficiently large to protect ourselves through the Indian territories. Mr. Smith wishes the executive to throw a shield over him while his operations are confined to the United States in raising and fitting out said volunteers." He said, "Mr. Smith may go on and do as he wishes, and this government will extend the same protection to him that it will to any other citizen." I observed to him that this memorial originated upon the ground, that the same protection had not heretofore been extended to him, that had been to others. He replied that that was oweing [*sic*] to peculiar circumstances, wherein the state government was in the fault, not the general government. He says further, the laws of the respective states will afford you protection in raising the emigrants or volunteers, and the general government cannot interfere with the laws and regulations of the states. "But," says he, "the moment you get beyond the states into the United States territories, then you come under the immediate protection of the general government, also on the high seas, but when you are within the territory of a state, you must look to the state government for all the protection you can have. I wish you to distinctly understand this difference. This memorial asks me to do that which the constitution does not authorize me to do. It is very complex, and would require a joint action of the executive and congress. The general government have it already in contemplation to adopt measures for the protection of all its subjects emigrating to that country, but to limit its protection to only one part, and to confer any particular privilege upon one, more than on another, is not the business of the general government, neither can they do it. I will extend all constitutional protection to Mr. Smith with the greatest pleasure, and will pledge myself that he shall have equal protection with any and every other American citizen. This is all the executive can do in this case. Equal rights, is our nation's motto. But now, distinctly and pointedly, I cannot comply with the wishes of the memorialist, because he asks me by the memorial to exceed my constitutional limit."

He was very frank, open, and condescending, but seemed to feel that I should be satisfied with a few words because of the press of business. He spent a good deal more time with me than with any others who were there at the same hour. So I came away and took my pen immediately to acquaint you with the results.

☆ ☆ ☆ ☆ ☆

We are now thrown back upon our own resources. We have tried every department of government to obtain our rights, but we cannot find them. If we will look for them any longer, we must look to our swords. Diplomatic

> intercourse has ceased, and the ministers of heaven have called for their passports. Two left his morning with anger and disgust, Elders Wight and Kimball, and if God permit, I shall leave tomorrow morning for Long Island and Connecticut. Brother Kimball said he got the word of the Lord before he left that government had it in their hearts to do nothing for us, and that the sooner they left the better. . . . Now farewell for the present. May God open some door of deliverance through you, and save his people from dissenting power.[89]

It is possible that the missionaries in the East, electioneering for Joseph Smith, gave the congregations they addressed some idea of what was in the wind. Wight and Kimball, writing on June 24, described a local conference at Wilmington, Delaware, on June 22. "The brethren came in from the adjacent country, and after much instruction from bros. Kimball and Wight, we took a vote to know whether they would go withersoever the Presidency, and Patriarch, and Twelve went, should it be to Oregon, Texas, or California, or any other place directed by the wisdom of Almighty God. The saints numbering about 100 rose to their feet and exclaimed, withersoever they go, we go, without a dissenting voice. This was truly an interesting meeting: we have not the least idea that any one will back out, they are nearly all men of wealth, and have commenced this morning to offer all surplus property for sale, that whenever you say, go, they are ready. We ordained ten as promising young elders as we ever laid hands upon, they pledged themselves to start this week and go through the State of Delaware from house to house, and proclaim that the Kingdom of Heaven is at hand.["][90]

This whole involved structure of plan and action was now, however, to wreck upon the murder of Joseph and Hyrum Smith in the jail at Carthage in Illinois.

Although the Council of Fifty had voted, on May 6, to send Lucien Woodworth to Texas to confirm arrangements he had made with officials of the Republic of Texas, it does not appear that Woodworth went. In his journal Smith noted on May 27 that Woodworth accompanied him to Carthage, and other references indicate that Woodworth remained in Nauvoo throughout the period of violence which culminated in the murders at Carthage. In all probability his retention at Nauvoo was purposeful; the Mormon leaders perhaps wanted to see how the presidential winds would blow before committing themselves too directly in the matter of the Texas venture.

---

[89]Journal History, 11 June 1844.

[90]*Millennial Star* ___ [i.e., *History of the Church* 7: 157–158].

It would seem, however, that something of what the Mormons proposed doing may have leaked out in Texas; a letter written [to] Joseph Smith on June 3 from Galveston is perhaps, in its message, not merely coincidental. Smith almost certainly never saw the letter before his death, although the exact date of its arrival in Nauvoo is not clear.

In this letter a Mr. John H. Walton, giving his address as "Galveston City, Galveston Co. Republic of Texas, in care of John D. Groesbeck," offered for sale "a tract of land lying in latitude 33 degree extending from the Red River almost to the trinity containing sixty leagues." The letter attempted to play flatteringly upon a thirst for power. It began by observing that if Smith were to remove to Texas with all his adherents, he would at once acquire a controlling vote in Texas, and might aspire to and obtain any office in the Republic. In view of the fact that Mexico was "doomed . . . {to} fall a victim either to the open warfare or the stealthy encroachments of the Anglo-Saxon," Walton suggested that a man of Smith's energy, commanding his resources, might crush Mexico at a blow and make it tributary to Texas which "would stand alone unsupported and unsurpassed in wealth power and resources by any nation on the globe." He concluded: "In Texas you will find no dense population to contend with, no bigot to oppress, no overwhelming power to crush you in your infancy, but a new field open to the enterprising pioneer, as yet free from the civilized needs of superstition oppression and pride where every hand would be extended to you in friendship, and when you and your adherents in stead of forming a small third party in an inferior State, would at once assume and retain a commanding influence in a Republic doubtless richer in resources than any country in the world, and needing only a cool head and ambitious mind and unshrinking arm at the head of her affairs to assist and maintain that rank among nations which is justly her due."[91]

But by the time this letter was written, events in Nauvoo were taking their fatal turn with respect to the *Nauvoo Expositor*. On the 10th the *Expositor* was smashed; by the 22nd the situation had become so serious that Smith decided on flight—it is significant that this flight was directed toward the unoccupied Rocky Mountains rather than toward semi-occupied Texas. On the 23rd however, he returned to Nauvoo, and on the 24th surrendered to Governor [Thomas] Ford. Jailed at Carthage, on the 27th he was slain.

If his death was a paralyzing blow for the church, for the grandiose

[91]Journal History, 3 June 1844.

plans of salvation by migration it was almost a mortal blow. But all that underlay the struggle for succession to the power that had been Smith's, and the eventual migration from Nauvoo, relates intimately to these affairs that have been brought to light. Men and events profoundly were motivated in the next two years by the concept of the temporal "Kingdom of God."

Seventeen days after Smith's death on July 14, 1844, Lucien Woodworth wrote from Nauvoo to Samuel Houston, president of the Republic of Texas, concerning the misfiring of plan:

> Sir: With this, I forward you the Book of Mormon, Doctrine and Covenants, Mr. Pratt's "Voice of Warning"; which set forth the views of the Church of Jesus Christ of Latter-day Saints, or "Mormons", as they are called. Also "The Times and Seasons" of July 1st, in which you will find a correct statement concerning the horrid murder of Generals Joseph and Hyrum Smith, in Carthage jail, on the 27th ult., by a mob of 150 or 200, painted and disguised men, whose names are well known, but Gov. Ford, as yet, has taken no action to bring them to justice, and some, I am informed, have already started for Texas. This does not seem to discourage the members in the least, but they feel more disposed than ever to carry out Gen. Smith's views in all things. The great excitement around us, have been sufficient apology for all seeming neglect, and I hope Your Excellency will favor me with a letter; stating anything new which may have occurred, and you shall hear from me again, more particularly when I get a little more leisure. Recent occurrences have prevented my making the propositions desired. If you still consider the plan practicable, communicate, and a reply shall be forthcoming.
>
> Of the particular views of the Mormons, I have not time now to write. This you may expect hereafter.[92]

The absence from Nauvoo of almost all the ranking authorities of the church, sent out for electioneering purposes, left the church, for almost six weeks after Smith's death, in a position almost of supinity. One by one the authorities made their way back to Nauvoo, the most important arrivals being those of August 6 of Brigham Young, Lyman Wight, Orson Pratt, Wilford Woodruff, and Heber C. Kimball. George Miller, however, had arrived on or shortly before July 24, and Miller, who had a restless thirst for action, seems almost immediately after his arrival to have started a chain of action which had far-reaching effects.

On July 29 he called on Willard Richards and George A. Smith to request "the privilege or passing some resolutions against the murderers of Joseph

[92]Journal History, 14 July 1844.

and Hyrum. The brethren told him to be quiet and wait and see what the governor and the state authorities would do, that Dr. Richards had pledged himself that the brethren would be quiet, and the Lord had said, 'Vengeance is mine, I will repay.' Miller left the council, saying, 'Fat men for patience.' "[93] Next day Miller met again with Richards and George A. Smith, together with John Taylor. Supported by Alexander Badlam he requested the three apostles "to call together the Council of Fifty and organize the church. They were told that the Council of Fifty was not a church organization, but was composed of members irrespective of their religious faith, and organized for the purpose of consulting on the best manner of obtaining redress of grievances from our enemies, and to devise means to find and locate in some places where we could live in peace; and that the organization of the church belonged to the priesthood alone."[94]

In itself this minor occurrence of July 30 would perhaps have no significance, but considered in the light of the problems faced by Brigham Young upon his return it almost certainly had its influence in crystallizing many of Young's attitudes.

Arriving on August 6, Young found himself three days later than Sidney Rigdon, only surviving member of the First Presidency. Rigdon had arrived on August 3, and on the 4th he had preached to the congregation to assert that the Lord had vouchsafed him a vision concerning the situation of the church, that there must be appointed a guardian to build up the church as Joseph Smith had begun it, and that he was the appointed man. No action was taken, but it was agreed that a general meeting should be held on Thursday, August 8, when some decision could be made. Unfortunately, for Rigdon, Young returned to Nauvoo on the 6th. On the 7th the Twelve Apostles, the high council, and the high priests met in council, and Young called on Rigdon to make a statement concerning his position. Rigdon related a vision he had received at Pittsburgh on June 27, and asserted that he had been ordained "a spokesman to Joseph"; it had been required of him that he should come to Nauvoo and see that the church was properly governed. "Joseph," he said, "sustains the same relationship to this church as he has always done. No man can be the successor of Joseph. The Kingdom is to be built up to Jesus Christ through Joseph: there must be revelation still . . . I have been consecrated a spokesman to Joseph, and I was commanded

[93] *Millennial Star* [25 (1863): 136.]
[94] *Millennial Star* [25 (1863): 136.]

to speak for him . . . I propose to be a guardian to the people; in this I have discharged my duty, and done what God has commanded me, and the people can please themselves whether they accept me or not."[95]

Young's reply was non-committal except in one thing: he asserted flatly that he had "the keys {of the Kingdom of God} and the means of obtaining the mind of God on the subject"; furthermore, "no man or set of men can get between Joseph and the Twelve in this world or in the world to come." He proposed that the people should assemble next morning, and his proposal was carried by unanimous vote.[96*]

The following morning Rigdon addressed the people for an hour and a half. His remarks are lost, but those of Young, to a second meeting which convened in the afternoon, sufficiently survive to indicate his shrewd grasp of the occasion and the opportunity; before his speech was done he had so powerfully established himself in the heart of church authority that never in his lifetime was there to be a serious challenge of his position. Quickly and shrewdly he disposed of Rigdon. His remarks of Joseph Smith emphasized the irreplaceable loss; almost at once he then inquired of the congregation whether they wished to establish someone in his place. ". . . Do you . . . want to choose a Prophet or a guardian? Inasmuch as our Prophet and Patriarch are taken from our midst, do you want some one to guard, to guide and lead you through this world to be into the kingdom of God, or not? All that want some person to be a guardian or a Prophet, a spokesman or something else, signify it by raising the right hand."

There were, of course, no votes. Now, as shrewdly, Young implied that Rigdon—or any other individual aspiring to lead the church—had it as his purpose to lead off a faction rather than to preside over the church as an organic whole. "All that want to draw away a party from the church after them, let them do it if they can, but they will not prosper." If any man were ambitious to attempt this, he was welcome to try, but he would find that the Apostles, despite him, would "build up and defend the church and kingdom of God." The keys of the Kingdom, he said, rested with the Twelve. Joseph had

---

[95][*Millennial Star* 25, no. 14 (4 April 1863): 215; cf. *Times and Seasons* 5, no. 16 (2 September 1844): 637–638 and *Deseret News* 7 (20 January 1858): 361–363. Morgan inserted a note number but left this and the following references blank. —Ed.]

[96][*Millennial Star* 25, no. 14 (4 April 1863): 215.]

*[Past this point the author leaves only unfilled blanks in place for note numbers and makes no citations. As this is a draft, abandoned early in the writing process and never completed in this form, the omissions did not represent a problem for him. Where possible, these omissions are filled. —Ed.]

placed them there. "You cannot fill the office of a prophet, seer and revelator: God must do this." Like the sound of a trumpet was his affirmation: "I will tell you who your leader or guardians will be—the Twelve—I am their head."

In this crucial speech to the Saints, Young established himself in vital points. Shrewdly, he urged no personal ambitions; he himself stood within the impersonality of the Twelve. He cast doubt on the motives of individual leaders, whom he measured against the dead prophet. He entrenched himself solidly in righteousness. Altogether, he established a command over the main body of the Saints in Nauvoo; and those who should follow other leaders from Nauvoo would necessarily stigmatize themselves and their leaders as apostate groups. Young's masterly insight into the people he led was never better exemplified than on this crucial day of his life.

Young came victorious out of this initial skirmish. But none, perhaps, realized better than he his precarious situation. If consciously Young did not grasp the state of affairs—and this would bel[ie] all that he showed himself to be—subconsciously he did, without question.

There had been on foot, before Joseph Smith's death, plans for the removal of the Saints from Illinois. Presumably Young had joined in these plans as wholeheartedly as anyone. Now, however, it was tremendously important that he consolidate himself in his position at Nauvoo. Nauvoo stood as the visible symbol of all Mormon accomplishment. Here the Temple was being built; here were all the sanctified associations of Joseph Smith; to here came the constant stream of emigrants from England, to whom had been so constantly preached "the spirit of gathering." To abandon Nauvoo to any of the ambitious men whom he had eclipsed on August 8 would have been the act of a fool.

It is no more coincidence that meetings of the Council of Fifty are not mention[ed] for a period of almost nine months after Young's accession to power. The philosophy on which the Council of Fifty had been organized—flight for the church—ran counter to his own necessities in the struggle to consolidate his position. Additionally, Miller's proposal of July 30, that the Council of Fifty be convened to organize the church, must have appeared as another danger, another threat to organizational unity and his authority over the church.

Almost at once, in Lyman Wight and James Emmet, Young was presented with the concrete problem of having to handle the migrational impulses which had been loosed during the spring.

On Sunday, August 11, as Young recorded, "Elder Lyman Wight preached about leading a company away into the wilderness."[97] Wight had in mind the plan previously decided upon, to send the Black River Lumber Company to Texas to prepare the way for removal thence of the entire church. Wight was hot-tempered and obstinate, not an easy man to deal with. He must have given Young some uneasy moments. George Miller writes, concerning this period:

> Lyman Wight became disaffected with his brethren of the Twelve. The man left in charge of the mills in the pinery sold out possession of the whole concern (the mills being on Indian land possession was the best title) for a few hundred thousand feet of pine lumber. Those mills and appurtenances, worth at least $20,000, thus passed out of our hands for a mere trifle, by the act of an indiscreet man.
>
> He brought part of the lumber to Nauvoo, and all the company that had been engaged in the pineries. Lyman, ever fond of authority, placed himself at the head of this company. And as it had been announced by the Twelve from the stand that Joseph had laid out a work that would take twenty years to accomplish, Lyman averred that he would commence his work then, and solicited me to take my place and go with him to locate the Black River Company.
>
> I told Lyman there was a way to do all things right, and we would get Woodworth and [A. W.] Brown, and get the authorities together and clothe ourselves with the necessary papers, and proceed to meet the Texan Congress, as before Joseph's death agreed upon. Woodworth and myself waited on Brigham, requesting him to convene the authorities that the proper papers might be made out, so that we could be able to complete the unfinished negotiations of the treaty for the territory mentioned in my former letters. And to my utter astonishment, Brigham refused having anything to do in the matter; that he had no faith in it, and would do nothing to raise means for our outfit or expenses. Thus all hopes cut off to establish dominion of the kingdom, at a time that there seemed to be a crisis, and I verily believed all that we had concocted in council might so easily be accomplished, I was really cast down and dejected.[98]

[97 *History of the Church*, 7: 248. "The History of Brigham Young" concludes in the *Millennial Star* 26, no. 23 (4 June 1864): 359 with a summary account of Rigdon's excommunication. Further quotations are taken from the "Manuscript History of Brigham Young." This record was first extracted and published in the *Deseret News* beginning in 1858 before being collected by B. H. Roberts in the early 1900s for the seventh volume of the *History of the Church*, which Morgan would have used. He made copious transcripts of the Journal History (which also collected the accounts in scrapbook form). Elden J. Watson collected and edited a monograph under the same title, *Manuscript History of Brigham Young* (Salt Lake City: Elden J. Watson, 1968). For convenience, citations will be made to the more widely available *History of the Church*. —Ed.]

[98 Miller, *Correspondence*, 24.]

On August 12, the day after Wight's address, the Quorum of the Twelve did agree "That Lyman Wight go to Texas as he chooses, with his company, also George Miller and Lucine {Lucien} Woodworth, if they desire to go,"[[99]] but evidently the church itself was being dissociated from the Texas venture. On the 18th, indeed, Young said, in the course of a sermon to the Saints,

> I discover a disposition in the sheep to scatter, now the shepherd is taken away. I do not say that it will never be right for this people to go from here or scatter abroad; but I do say wait until the time comes, or until you are counseled to do so. The report has gone forth through the city that the Twelve have a secret understanding with those men who are going away and taking companies with them, that they shall take away all they can; and although the Twelve will blow it up in public, yet privately they wish it to go on, but if they were the last words I had to say before going into the eternal worlds I would swear by the Holy Trinity that such a report is utterly false, and there is not a word of truth in it. There is no man who has any right to lead away one soul out of this city by the consent of the Twelve, except Lyman Wight and George Miller, they have had the privilege of taking the 'Pine Company' where they please but not another soul has the consent of the Twelve to go with them. There is no man who has any liberty to lead away people into the wilderness from this church, or to lead them anywhere else, by the consent of the Twelve or the church, except in the case above named—and I tell you in the name of Jesus Christ that if Lyman Wight and George Miller take a course contrary to our counsel and will not act in concert with us, they will be damned and go to destruction—and if men will not stop striving to be great and exalted, and lead away parties from us, thereby weakening our hands, they will fall and not rise again—and I will destroy their influence in this church with the help of God and my brethren. I wish you to distinctly understand that the counsel of the Twelve is for every family that does not belong to the Pine Company to *stay here in Nauvoo,* and build up the Temple and get your endowments; do not scatter; 'united we stand, divided we fall.' It has been whispered about that all who go into the wilderness with Wight and Miller will get their endowments, but they cannot give an endowment in the wilderness. . . . Let no man go from this place but the pine country brethren, but stay here and sow, plant, build and put your plowshares into the prairies: one plowshare will do more to drive off the mob than two guns. Let us stay here where the bones of Joseph, Hyrum, Samuel, Don Carlos, and Father Smith are. . . . Concerning those who are wishing to lead away parties contrary to counsel, I would not wish them damned worse, than to have a company after their own liking go with them, for they will soon quarrel among themselves. . . . To those who want

[[99]*History of the Church,* 7: 249.]

> to go away from this place, I would say wait until the time comes. I will give you the key. North and South America is Zion and as soon as the Temple is done and you get your endowments you can go and build up stakes, but do not be in haste, wait until the Lord says go.[100]

On the 21st the Twelve met with Wight, and again on the 24th, when "Elder Lyman Wight was counseled to go north instead of going south."[101] Young's prejudice against the Texas venture, aside from the possible motives mentioned, may have been his mistrust of semi-occupied country, or possibly a mistrust of the consequences of moving the church into slave-soil. It is also quite probable that he wished the authority for Wight's adventure to spring from the Quorum of Twelve, instead of from the mandate of the Council of Fifty. In any event, Wight at first proved somewhat tractable. Miller says that Wight had a conference with Young and Kimball, who advised him to go up the river to Prairie La Crosse, and this he did. Wight, however, did not long remain at Prairie La Crosse. Texas had too strong a hold upon his imagination. His company he finally took to Texas where he founded the settlement of Zodiac, near present Fredericksburg. The story of Wight's colony in Texas, which removed to a number of new locations, is one of great interest, but only of such incidental interest as will hereafter be noticed with respect to this particular study.

In addition to Wight, Young had also to reckon with James Emmett, who likewise was obsessed with the idea of leading a company from Nauvoo. Emmett like Wight, had no apparent ambitions to lead the church itself, but he was headstrong and self-willed. He had been named as one of the Oregon exploring company in February, and either from this or some subsequent development (Miller says "he had received a mission to go among the Indians by appointment of Joseph and sanction of the council") he derived the idea that he was privileged to lead west from Nauvoo another company of Saints. On September 9 Kimball and George A. Smith "labored diligently with James Emmett that he might be persuaded to desist from his intended course of taking away a party of misguided saints into the wilderness"[102] but evidently with little effect* [*draft manuscript ends*]

[100 *History of the Church*, 7: 254–260.]

[101 *History of the Church*, 7: 261.]

[102 *History of the Church*, 7: 269.]

*[Morgan later edited a key account of the Emmett company, a reminiscent narrative by James Holt. See vol. 2, this edition. —Ed.]

Chapter 4

Mormon Story Tellers (1942)

Editor's Introduction

This little digression was a personal project, a confection or a compensation, perhaps, for the fact that he never could squeeze a novel out of the *Salt Lake Tribune* for review. During college Dale planned for a career in commercial art (graphic design) and hoped for a side career in modern literature. He generated angst-ridden short stories that saw publication mostly in the campus student magazine, but he found it very difficult to break into fiction. As a book reviewer for the *Salt Lake Tribune,* Dale Morgan had to content himself with reviewing non-fiction. He began writing a fictionalized treatment of his experience as a deaf teen and college student, but gave it up after producing an incomplete draft and partial revision, and upon going to work for the Historical Records Survey.

This article mirrors the critical approach and sentiment about writing that was exhibited in an earlier piece of criticism titled "On Realism in Literature," published while he was a student at the University of Utah.[1] Never interested in experimental writing or poetry, Morgan was attracted to character study and realism. He maintained a link to Utah's small literary scene by reading avidly across literature and by contact with Ray B. West, Jr., and his *Rocky Mountain Review,* a small and short-lived journal of criticism and original writing. In the 1940s Mormons did not have an established tradition of fictional literature, though as he notes, there were isolated examples. Morgan considers none of them to be "serious" literature in his review. This literary survey illustrates Morgan in the role he had once hoped to fill—at least occasionally—as a literary critic within Mormondom.

[1] "On Realism in Literature," *University Pen* (Winter 1937): 8–9, 22–25.

Mormon Story Tellers*

Even three years ago it would have seemed that the columns of the *Rocky Mountain Review* could be occupied to better advantage than by an article on this subject. The whole Mormon story, one of the richest, most variously faceted, and altogether extraordinary American history affords, awaited discovery like another Comstock Lode. Placer miners down the gulch had panned day wages from these riches, but the lode itself was inviolate, shrouded in sage and sand and piñon. The Mormon lode differed from the Comstock, however, in that everybody could see the proportions of the wealth, and it was not ignorance of its existence but the lack of a technology to mine it which prevented its exploitation. A prospector's eye and the drunken aberrations of an Old Virginny might suffice to open the Comstock, but the writing of an adequate Mormon novel required a glowing vision, an integrity of purpose, and above all a technical equipment which, in 1939, was nowhere in evidence. Three years ago, the Mormon riches was untouched and therefore inexhaustible.

In the autumn of 1942, however, we can number nine novels that have proceeded from the presses since *Children of God,* in 1939, ushered in the new dispensation. These nine novels represent the individual response of an astonishing variety of authors to an anomalous literary vacuum, and will have their weight in all further writing on the Mormon theme—if not as a direct impact upon the literary consciousness of individual novelists, then as a limiting factor in the willingness of publishers to accept books written out of the Mormon experience.

Some attention must be directed to Mormon fiction published before the fall of 1939. To the turn of the century, one hunts almost in vain for fiction concerned with Mormons. This is not altogether surprising. The violence of Mormon group relations was not conducive to the encouragement of fiction. For their part, quite aside from the fact that their society was notably a frontier culture for which fiction, under any circumstances, constituted a luxury expensive and suspect, the Mormons had more pressing uses for the literary talent of the Church. Polemical writing, aside from its social utility, had also an affirmative value in advancing a man's stature in the priesthood. Polemical writing and the expounding of the Gospel, as compared to the

---

**Rocky Mountain Review* 7, no. 1 (Fall 1942): 1, 3–4, 7. Republished in *The Rocky Mountain Reader,* ed. Ray B. West Jr. (New York: Dutton, 1946), 404–413. Cf. DLM to Ray B. West, 10 November 1946.

writing of fiction, brought greater social rewards and answered to a greater social need. Under these circumstances, it would be extraordinary if any Mormon writer to 1900 had produced a novel of distinction. Edward W. Tullidge, who may possibly have been capable of portraying Mormon society, chose to occupy himself with heavy historical plays at such times as he concerned himself with other than journalism and expository history. There were a few other native writers who now and then tried their hands at playwriting, the drama enjoying a certain social acceptance in Utah, hut Mormon literature remained barren.

Mormon materials fared hardly better in non-Mormon hands. Except, perhaps for Lily Dougall's *The Mormon Prophet* (1899), a novel centering upon Joseph Smith's life which is chiefly important (to history, not to literature) for its psychological explanation of Smith's puzzling character, there is not a single work of fiction, dealing with the Mormons, worth anyone's attention. Joaquin Miller's *The Danites in the Sierras,* published in its final form in 1881, vaguely incorporates Mormon materials, but is worthless from any point of view. Most non-Mormons who felt impelled to write about the Mormons did so out of an urge to attack the hydra-headed monster, and fiction was just another instrumentality; the anonymous and typical *Apples of Sodom* (1883) frankly closes with the pious hope that the book "may serve as drop to overflow the bucket of popular prejudice against polygamy."

The quarter century after 1900 did hardly better by the Mormons, although the assimilation of the Mormons by American society, following upon the Woodruff Manifesto and the granting of statehood to Utah, permitted a more stimulating contact of artists with Mormon experience on the American frontier. That there was no important Mormon novel written is, in part, of course an accident of time and place. Another Mark Twain could have been born in Utah. But he wasn't. Books about the Mormons, during this quarter century, were pedestrian endeavors.

Alfred H. Henry's *By Order of the Prophet* (1902) somewhat anticipates Susan Ertz' *The Proselyte,* written 31 years later; but this is not a novel of distinction, or even of much interest. Harry Leon Wilson published in 1903 *The Lions of the Lord,* but this was what today we would call "slick fiction," stock characters expertly manipulated in a never-never land. In 1909 Susa Young Gates published *John Stevens' Courtship,* a romance of the "Echo Canyon War" serving much the same purpose as the autobiographical narratives of the

"Faith-Promoting Series" written nearly a generation earlier. Pierre Benoit's *Le Lac Sal,* published in France in 1921 and printed next year by Knopf in English translation as *Salt Lake, A Romance,* is by long odds the most astonishing production of the period. This novel of intrigue after the Utah or Echo Canyon War reads like greased lightning (in pleasant contrast to most other novels here mentioned) but Benoit's conception of Utah as a more singular Graustark is almost absurd.* *Salt Lake,* like *The Lions of the Lord,* has nothing to do with the realities of Mormon life; it is a projection of the writer's interior fantasy into the Mormon environment.

There are, however, two books out of this second period that may be read with interest and pleasure, a pair of juvenile adventure novels by Walter Nichols, *Trust a Boy!* and *The Measure of a Boy.* While these books, published in 1923 and 1925, respectively, have no pretensions as literature, as a picture of boy life near and upon Great Salt Lake in the [eighteen] eighties they are unique, and possessed of considerable charm.

Bernard DeVoto's *The Chariot of Fire* (1926) announced the imminent assault of responsible artists upon the Mormon story. This novel, which followed by two years and was followed in two years by Mr. DeVoto's novels of a West in which the Mormons were conspicuous by their absence, used the Mormon story by complete conversion; essentially, *The Chariot of Fire* is a study of a phenomenon: frontier religion. It drew upon Mormon materials sufficiently that members of the Church heartily disliked it as a caricature of Mormon beginnings, but it did not come directly to grips with what writers were now beginning to see as "the Mormon epic."

In 1928 Vardis Fisher, with *Toilers of the Hills,* published his first novel, an account of farm life in the Snake country which only incidentally was concerned with Mormon society, but which was important as marking the first realistic use of native materials by a native artist. In later books that preceded *Children of God,* primarily his autobiographical tetralog, Mr. Fisher occupied himself to some extent with contemporary Mormon society, but he was engaged in exorcism, and Mormonism and the Mormon environment were only incidental in that.

Norton S. Parker's *Hell and Hallelujah!* (1931), laid principally in Nauvoo during the strenuous years, 1844–46, inaugurated in modern Mormon fiction

*[Graustark was a mythical European country that provided settings for the novels of George Barr McCutcheon. The novels revolve around royal intrigue, romance, and characters in disguise. —Ed.]

a kind of novel that has since been seen with increasing frequency. The exterior violence of Mormon history has much to attract tale-tellers; history itself is already an involute plot, and it is only necessary to lash the chief characters to the mast and let them run before the wind. *The Rocky Road to Jericho* (1935), by Frank Chester Field (Frank C. Robertson), has many points of similarity to Parker's novel, as has also Jeremiah Stokes' *The Soul's Fire,* 1936 (one of the few novels of orthodox Mormon viewpoint), and several of the new crop, though Mr. Robertson's book exhibits a greater earnestness in trying to resolve the contradictions of Mormon history than is expected of this type of work.

In popular consciousness, Susan Ertz, with The *Proselyte* (1933) was first to discover the Mormons. More weight has attached to *The Proselyte* than it deserves on its merits as a novel, primarily because Miss Ertz was already known as a writer of distinction. Although Miss Ertz brought sympathy and discernment to her theme, and was first to exemplify the dignity and integrity of Mormon social life, her novel peers out upon Mormonism from the shuttered window of an English parlor. It misconceives the vigorous Mormon story at vital points, its detail sometimes falls strange on the ear, and altogether it gives somewhat the effect of having been written at the tea table.

Rather more significant than *The Proselyte* were George Snell's *The Great Adam* (1934) and *Root, Hog, and Die* (1936). The former, concerned with the rise and fall of a banker in a small town of southern Idaho, is, despite the impression it gives of the arbitrary imposition of a classical pattern, a novel rather more richly conceived and well-rounded than the book which followed it. *Root, Hog, and Die,* a realistic picture of Mormon life over three generations, is an exciting exploration into the possibilities of the Mormon theme, but it seems more the outline of the story Snell wanted to write than the story itself. More important than the actual achievement, in the case of either novel, was Snell's evident consciousness of the literary potentialities of a life to which he is native.

Although I have not attempted a complete catalogue of writing by and about the Mormons to 1939, the authors and books mentioned represent most of what could be called significant in this writing, and this catalogue roughly indicates the status of Mormon fiction in 1939. A very few novels, distinguished for one reason or another, stood out in a wasteland, and none of these novels was possessed of such force and individuality as to inhibit any writer from making any use he chose of Mormon materials. It is important now to consider the change in this state of affairs produced by the nine novels already mentioned.

I should begin by listing these specifically: They are Vardis Fisher's *Children of God* (1939), Jean Woodman's *Glory Spent* (1940), Paul Bailey's *For This My Glory* (1940), Rhoda Nelson's *This Is Freedom* (1940), Maurine Whipple's *The Giant Joshua* (1940), Lorene Pearson's *The Harvest Waits* (1941), Hoffman Birney's *Ann Carmeny* (1941), Elinor Pryor's *And Never Yield* (1942), and Virginia Sorenson's *A Little Lower Than The Angels* (1942). Of these novels the first, fifth, sixth, and ninth may be regarded, for various reasons, as important. *This Is Freedom* is a treatment of the Mormon theme for adolescent readers, and not strictly of a kind with the others here mentioned, while *Ann Carmeny,* a tale of glittering derring-do in the Salt Lake basin in 1860, is more particularly of the genus of historical novels of adventure currently in vogue.

Fisher's novel, because most ambitious, is most important among these nine books. Subtitled "An American Epic," *Children of God* endeavored to swallow the Mormon story whole. Although the degree of success that attended the effort is illustrated by the fact that the book was the Harper prize novel in its year, that it sold well, and that it attracted a considerable measure of critical acclaim, *Children of God* is by no means a front-rank novel. Mr. Fisher has reached directly into Mormon history for the majority of his characters, and, his Joseph Smith, Emma Smith, Lyman Wight, and Brigham Young, for example, are warm with life—within the limitations of his intention. The panoplied movement of Mormon history itself was sufficient to give this novel a magnificent color and direction, granted an initial success in the recreation of the book's basic historical characters. *Children of God* was not, however, the successful epic it aimed to be.

Although he adopted orthodox Mormon views for the greater part of his novel, Mr. Fisher's sympathy and understanding were something less than whole hearted, and this emerges in the impact of the book as a whole. Perhaps a kind of lifelessness about the novel is a consequence of the fact that Mr. Fisher clothed the bones of history with Mormon flesh of the kind he knew in the Snake River Valley. Dock Hunter and his tribe are the legitimate offspring of the Mormons who saw glories in the sky and praised God for a latter-day prophet, but Dock Hunter is the product of the interaction of Mormon society with the desert environment; in peopling his pageant with a congregation of Dock Hunters, Mr. Fisher achieved a flavor of the frontier but lost qualities of personal fulfillment and deep spirituality that were profoundly important in the inception and growth of Mormonism.

With all its merits, and it should be understood that they are many, *Children of God* does not emerge as a finally important treatment of the Mormon story as an epic in itself, history immediately invaded by fiction. There is still room for such a novel. But *Children of God* will remain as a formidable barrier in its field to anything except a really front-rank novel. To that extent limitations have been imposed upon exploitation of the Mormon literary wealth.

Maurine Whipple's *The Giant Joshua* derives its strength from its warm humanity and from Miss Whipple's delighted absorption in the sensual splendor of Clory MacIntyre's world. Nowhere in Mr. Fisher's book, despite his greater technical competence, is there a comparable abundance of life; perhaps this reflects the greater nearness of Miss Whipple to the people of whom she writes, and the exactitude of her frame of reference. In the magnitude of its intention and the extent of its accomplishment *The Giant Joshua* has claims to be considered the best of the Mormon novels so far published, though its character as a first novel is clearly evidenced in a technical incapacity; the book structurally seems to run-in circles; it is repetitious and its feeling for romance sometimes flounders in sentimentality,

A novel of the type of *The Giant Joshua* tends to be a law unto itself. Any writer on the Mormon theme whose book overflows with life may be assured a hearing, for such a novel is richly rewarding to the reader who would find, in fiction, a renewed and deepened apprehension of his own life and all human living. Mormonism and Mormon materials theoretically need not intervene upon this function of literature. Practically speaking, however, writing is hardly to be divorced from its social context, and anyone, writing out of the Mormon theme, who can feel so deeply and write so eloquently will probably have something to say that will be of interest and importance first of all to the people in the Mormon country. Apart from such considerations, Miss Whipple's novel must be said to have laid these restrictions upon use of Mormon materials: On the romantic plane it got very nearly all that is to be gotten out of the problems of matured polygamy (especially, from the woman's viewpoint), and of warfare with the desert by the Mormon community. Additionally, the abundance of Miss Whipple's local color, which gives her novel at times a lushness almost overwhelming, will require of new

Mormon writing that it stand upon its feet without the props and crutches of quaintness and mere novelty of background.

Lorene Pearson's *The Harvest Waits* is radically dissimilar in point of view and choice of materials to any other among the Mormon novels. Although "realism" has been employed to a greater or lesser extent in half a dozen of the novels about the Mormons, Mrs. Pearson's book most nearly approaches the classical ideal. Her realism is a cumulative effect of her detached and broken viewpoint, of her deliberate de-emphasis, and of her choice of subject-matter and detail. It cannot be said that Mrs. Pearson's novel of the struggles of Mormons to live together during and after the period of the United Order, is altogether successful, but it is perhaps most thought-provoking of any of the Mormon novels. *The Harvest Waits* attempts to come to grips with its people without the marching and counter-marching of mobs and armies, the passage of glittering personalities, and all the lovely violences. This novel does not suggest itself for best-sellerdom, and it is probable that neither author nor publisher had any illusions upon this score, but its solidity, its quality of detail, its dignity, and its unexcited earnestness are rare qualities in a Mormon novel. Writers projecting Mormon novels would do well to review Mrs. Pearson's book for the wide bases of its approach to a Mormon community, and its ease of manner in the utilization of distinctive Mormon detail, though also, negatively, they may find instruction in observing its defects in its confusing progression of viewpoint, its insistent ellipses, and its determined repression of emotion at times when sustained emotion is not only valid but essential to the book. *The Harvest Waits* is a constructive performance that need not be inhibitory in further writing on the Mormon theme.

The fourth of the new novels that I have called significant is Virginia Sorenson's *A Little Lower Than the Angels.* Mrs. Sorenson's excellent novel of life in Nauvoo exhibits several fundamental differences form its fellows. The growth of a society, and the relationships of people, one with another, in this developing society, occupy her less than the age-old questions that are always new, on what terms a man and a woman may live together, what they can possess of life, and what life can do to their possession of each other. Although it would be misleading to say that the Mormon background and the events of Mormon history woven in to the fabric of this novel are inessential to its development, it seems clear that Mrs. Sorenson could have adapted her characters to, and worked out their problems in, another environment. Miss Whipple's characters, by contrast, are clearly the direct product of their time and environment; Abijah and Sheba and Clorinda MacIntyre, in the very stuff of their life, are inseparable from the Mormon frontier. We shall probably see more books of the general type of *A Little Lower Than the Angels.* I would guess however, that such novels are likely to be important to Mormon fiction primarily for their contributions to technique.

Attention must be directed, finally, to the other novels that have appeared since 1939. Jean Woodman's *Glory Spent* must be praised for the honesty of its intention, and Mrs. Woodman remains the only writer who has had the courage or the insight to attempt a depiction of Mormon society as it is today. Unfortunately, *Glory Spent* is primarily an essay in ideas, and the novel, as a work of fiction, is something less than adequate. *Glory Spent* has, for this discussion, the importance that it has brought into the open Mormonism's problems in a modern world; it relieves other authors of the responsibility of stating those problems for the record, and imposes upon them the responsibility of creating from this material a deep humanity, a richly felt life. There is no question of the need for a good novel of contemporary Mormonism, and Mrs. Woodman must be commended for her discernment of the need, whatever is said of her book itself.

Comment was made earlier on a type of adventure novel that has appeared in the Mormon fiction. Paul Bailey's *For This My Glory* is one of the more unfortunate efforts in this field; the novel is harnessed to various Mormon experiences of violent interests—the Missouri and Illinois persecutions, the march of the Mormon Battalion, the discovery of gold, the Utah War, the "polyg hunts"—and this flow of events, rather than the characters concerned, gives the book such an interest as it commands. Elinor Pryor's *And Never Yield* has certain points of similarity, but it is written in the tradition of *Anthony Adverse,* a now familiar kind of pageantry. Miss Pryor's book, once more to adopt the viewpoint of this discussion, is chiefly important because it makes further inroads upon Mormon history conceived as an epic. Mrs. Nelson's book, and Mr. Birney's, may here be regarded as primarily important because their bulk weighs in the possible exhaustion of the Mormon theme.

The broad outlines of what has been accomplished with Mormon materials should be fairly clear. A long period in which novelists more or less neglected the Mormon story has ended with a series of novels which, with varying success, has attempted to translate this story into a fiction of integrity and depth. It will be observed that the ambition to write on the epic plane has forcefully influenced the majority of these books. It is inevitable that the Mormon story should commend itself first of all as an epic, for it possesses historical continuity, spectacular violence, cross-grained social texture, and tragic content. Epics, however, feed voraciously upon their own being, and the measure of preoccupation with the Mormon theme that we have seen in the last three years establishes a probability that Mormon fiction will not be given over to writers less opportunistic and more serious in their purpose.

Chapter 5

The Deseret Alphabet (1941–1942)

Editor's Introduction

Heady with the critical response to *The State of Deseret,* Morgan's first step toward a larger work was to retreat a pace from the Deseret study to look into the sectarian origins of the idea of a theocratic state, among other possibilities. He began and then set aside a study of the Kingdom of God (chapter 3 in this volume) as too involved, only to have his attention immediately attracted to the followers of Joseph Morris, an idealistic and vocal but semiliterate prophet who nonetheless collected a group of followers out of the Latter-day Saints to a fort built in the Weber River bottoms. By June 1941 Morgan wrote to Reorganized Church (Community of Christ) librarian S. A. Burgess with a query on the subject, noting that "during the last six months or more, in such spare hours as I could manage" he had been gathering material on Morrisites, planning to write a monograph "as complete and authoritative in its way as that I wrote last year on the State of Deseret."[1] Despite that collecting effort, the writing of the piece went nowhere.

Morgan quickly perceived, however, that Utah and Mormon history was full of unexplored corners and curiosities. Having been turned on to history, Morgan exploited the opportunity the HRS enjoyed to collect source material. Beyond the extra carbon of transcripts gathered by the HRS workers, he conscientiously compiled notes and transcripts on topics of personal interest, including the Joseph Morris schism; Brigham Young's curious orthographic experiment, the "Deseret alphabet"; and the Danites. "The controversial aspects to Mormon history especially arouse my attention, and I intend to write special monographs on these in advance of the larger Mormon work

[1]DLM to S. A. Burgess, 8 June 1941, P79-2 f3, Community of Christ archives, Independence, Mo.

I have in progress," he informed Burgess. However, he confessed to a friend from his Writers' Project service that the Mormon-related projects were "being written purely for my own satisfaction; other stuff I am working on [*The Humboldt: Highroad to the West,* specifically] is being written for vulgar money."[2] He extended his grasp of each topic with additional research in the Library of Congress and National Archives after moving to Washington, D.C., in 1942.

The Deseret alphabet was not exactly a controversial topic, but it was an arcane one. A uniquely Mormon curiosity, the new alphabetic representation of spoken English was partly an attempt to set the saints apart from the world, partly a practical experiment in acculturating Scandinavian and Continental converts. Morgan became interested in the attempt at literacy engineering as he studied the attempts to establish Deseret as a state.

A few days before the Japanese navy dragged the U.S. into the Second World War with the Pearl Harbor attack, Dale typed a letter to novelist and former faculty advisor Wallace Stegner, who was teaching at Harvard University. Stegner had inquired about Utah and LDS themes, which would be woven into his 1942 book *Mormon Country.* Morgan responded with an update of his interest on one particular subject, the Deseret alphabet, but admitted that there "doesn't seem to be any likelihood that I'll be able to get that Deseret Alphabet piece done within the next day or week." He had not yet deciphered the articles printed in *Deseret News* issues to see what they were, yet he was able to generally summarize the history of the experiment and phonography in Utah.[3] Before the end of following January, the piece had been drafted once and Morgan was at work on revisions.[4] Unlike *The State of Deseret,* this study had been written, he later explained, mostly for his own information and to help Stegner with historical context. The sheaf went off to Boston with the Kingdom of God draft in May 1942. Once Stegner had seen it, Morgan felt the piece had served its chief purpose and filed the manuscript.

A couple of months after moving to Washington, D.C., and a year after picking up the topic with Stegner, while he busily cut his *Humboldt* manuscript to fit the publisher's page allotment, Morgan mentioned the Deseret alphabet draft to Utah Historical Society secretary Marguerite Sinclair. In April 1943 he retyped a corrected manuscript, which had expanded to present nearly every scrap of information on the topic the author could locate.

---

[2]DLM to S. A. Burgess, 30 November 1943; DLM to Grace [Winkleman] and Marguerite [Sinclaire], both 25 November 1943, Dale Lowell Morgan papers, Utah State Historical Society.

[3]DLM to Wallace Stegner, 3 December 1941.

[4]DLM to Wallace Stegner, 28 January 1942.

Miss Sinclair wrote Morgan in early December 1944 that the UHQ wished to publish his study, but that it was too long for the journal's limited capacity. He declined, and a week later proposed a shorter study on "Brigham Young as Indian Agent." The UHQ staff decided that neither the piece on Young's Indian affairs career nor the one on his odd alphabet would fit within the limits Morgan required and the magazine had available.[5]

This work is important to Morgan's development for at least two other reasons. First, by the time of its writing in 1943, Morgan's concept of "good" history had crystallized into a narrative approach that erred on the side of hard documentation while it unintentionally minimized broader contexts and dismissed interpretation almost entirely. At virtually the same time that the Deseret alphabet manuscript was posted to the *Utah Historical Quarterly*, Morgan wrote Roderick Korns a telling letter that explained his approach to writing and research. "I pretend to speak with maximum authority on two subjects only, and on these because I know more about them than anyone else now alive. The first is the Mormon State of Deseret, and the second is the Deseret Alphabet. I have published a monograph on the first of these, and written one presently to be published on the latter of these; in each case, I have gathered every scrap of fact available to me." While he busily strung "scraps of facts" on the thread of narrative, extrapolations did not belong in history; nor did interpretation, except of documented facts. While this approach made him into a thorough and tenacious researcher, it made the feelings and faith that motivated many Latter Day Saint converts and their leaders impossible for him to comprehend.

Secondly, the letter laid out for Korns a set of tentative directions in early Western American history, growing out of the undeveloped fur-trade study he had hoped to produce with Maurice Howe. This tangent eventually formed a parallel path to his interest in Utah and the Mormons. But, he observed,

> Until the facts begin to assume a reasonably complete pattern in my mind, I shall try to keep from forming absolute judgments. This is particularly

---

[5]A revised version of the Indian affairs article was eventually published as "The Administration of Indian Affairs in Utah, 1851–1858," *Pacific Historical Review* 17, no. 4 (November 1948): 383–409. The full history of that study and its place in Morgan's larger career can be found in Richard Saunders, "Dale L. Morgan and the Study of Indian Affairs," *Shoshonean Peoples and the Overland Trails: Frontiers of the Utah Superintendency of Indian Affairs, 1849–1869*, ed. Richard L. Saunders (Logan: Utah State Univ. Press, 2007), 7–31. Part of the reason the study remained a manuscript, despite the work he had poured into the subject, is because of close friend Stan S. Ivins's subsequent article "The Deseret Alphabet," *Western Humanities Review* 1, no. 3 (July 1947): 223–239. It is unlikely that Morgan knew of Samuel C. Monson's "The Deseret Alphabet," MA thesis, Columbia Univ., 1947.

> the case about western explorations and the fur trade. I paid only incidental attention to this subject until I contracted to do my book on The Humboldt. As an essential part of that job, I probably quadrupled my knowledge about the West, and I can now talk with a fair degree of intelligence about the Ashley-Smith expeditions, Peter Skene Ogden, the Walker venture to California, and the California migrations of 1841–46. . . . As far as [Harrison] Dale goes, I have one specific project in mind: Sooner or later I want to publish in one of the historical reviews a documentary collection of all the source material bearing on the Ashley-Smith expeditions. . . . The facts have been out of the reach of most investigators, and I consider that I will be doing everybody a favor if I can make these facts available.[6]

After his plan for *The Mormons* fell apart in the opening days of 1952, the road into Western Americana he had laid out for Roderick Korns represented the only immediately available path out of fiscal peril. Those familiar with Morgan's later writing can see here the first glimmers of *The West of William H. Ashley* (1964), *Overland in 1846* (1963), and *Jedediah Smith and the Opening of the West* (1953).

After being rejected by the state historical magazine in 1944, the Deseret alphabet manuscript was consigned to a folder among his files and was thereafter hardly mentioned throughout the rest of his writing career. In early 1945, a few months later, Dale began compiling a research fellowship application to the John Simon Guggenheim Memorial Foundation for research toward a three-volume history of the Mormons.

The Deseret Alphabet

Anyone who interests himself in Mormon history sooner or later encounters the Deseret Alphabet. The sense of rediscovery is like that of an archaeologist who comes suddenly in a desert on a weatherworn stone inscribed in some language of the dust. The hieroglyphs challenge the imagination.

Even patient investigation of the Deseret Alphabet does not dispel the sense of mystery that attaches to it, for the Alphabet is inseparable in the puzzling larger facts of Mormon history, in the ambiguities, the paradoxes, and the singularities that clothe this history in an uncertainty where facts always seem to mean something more or less than they should. As part of the Mormon folk experience no less than as an experiment in education, the Deseret Alphabet will always remain a fascinating chapter in Mormon history.[1]

---

[6]DLM to Rod [Korns], 20 April 1943, Charles Kelly papers, Utah State Historical Society.

[1]I have been led to make this study of the origin and development of the Deseret Alphabet as much for my own satisfaction, in establishing the facts about an obscure and misunderstood, if not overwhelmingly

On July 30, 1857 the initial nine English converts to the Church of Jesus Christ of Latter-day saints presented themselves for baptism in the Ribble River, at Preston, England. First to yield himself to the elders for baptism was a young man of twenty-two, George D. Watt.[2] The baptism and the year were alike propitious. In this year, 1837, Isaac Pitman published in England his *Stenographic Soundhand*, the first great contribution to "phonography."[3] Five years later, Pitman commenced publication of his *Phonographic Journal*, and by further coincidence, it was in this year, 1842, that George D. Watt emigrated to America. During those five years he seems to have acquired a knowledge of Pitman's shorthand, and he came to Nauvoo the first "phonographic reporter" among the Mormons.[4]

Watt's talents for phonography seem at first to have been less useful to his people than his strong body and his convert's zeal. He is listed among

important phase of Mormon history, as for the benefit of other historians. However, I have quoted extensively from my sources, not only to document my conclusions but to spare others from any necessity for originating into the dust piles from which I brought these facts. Alvin Smith, librarian in the L.D.S. Church Historian's Office, generously made available to me not only the resources of the Journal History of the Church, but also other documents and newspaper files; and I am also indebted to the WPA Writers' Project, for use of the manuscript collection [i.e., research files], and to the Salt Lake Public Library, for access to its admirable collection of early Utah newspapers.

[2]Andrew Jenson, *Church Chronology*, 13.

[3]Shorthand itself is very old. It was employed as early as 63 B.C., when Marcus Tullius Tiro, a friend of Cicero, invented a system of *notae* which in some respects was superior to any shorthand system since developed. The rise of the Christian church and a desire for the recording of exact utterances led to a re-emphasis on shorthand. Development in England began in 1588, but the first "orthographic system"—based on the alphabet—was John Willes' *Arte of Stenographic*, which dates from 1602. The first published system using a phonetic base was that of William Tiffin (1750). Pitman's system, however, inaugurated modern shorthand. Stephen Pearl Andres, at Boston, 1844, first introduced Pitman to America. Benn Pitman, brother of Isaac, came to the United States in 1852 and was influential in the spread of Pitmanic shorthand in this country. Pitman's system maintained itself superior to all rivals until after John Robert Gregg published in 1888 his *Light-Line Phonography*. Gregg's system, more in harmony with the movement of handwriting, rapidly gained adherents and in the United States is now predominantly used. For a brief discussion of shorthand history, see the *Encyclopedia Britannica*.

[4]Robert L. Campbell, in his annual "Report of the Territorial Superintendent of Common Schools," February 15, 1869, noted that "Pittman's system of phonetics" had been introduced by Watt in Illinois in 1845, whereupon it was generally adopted by Mormon reporters. Watt was born in Manchester, Lancashire, England, January 16, 1815. Some part of his life history is developed in the monograph. In 1835 he conceived the idea of publishing the discourses of the Church authorities in pamphlet form; these regularly published pamphlets were bound into yearly volumes, and constitute the famous series, the *Journal of Discourses*. Most of the early sermons so published were reported by Watt, though occasionally he was aided by others. In his capacity as church reporter, he accompanied Brigham Young on many of the memorable journeys the great Mormon leader made to the far-flung settlements of the Saints. In the Seventies, however, he had difficulties with the authorities, and on May 3, 1874, was excommunicated from the Church. He died October 24, 1881, at Kaysville, Utah. An obituary was published in the *Salt Lake Herald*, October 25, 1881, and reprinted in Kate B. Carter, ed., *Four Outstanding Activities of the Pioneers*, 5–6 [cf. Ida Watt Stringham and Dora Dutson Flack, *England's First Mormon Convert: The Biography of George Darling Watt* (n.p., [1958]); Ronald G. Watt, *The Mormon Passage of George D. Watt: First British Convert, Scribe for Zion* (Logan: Utah State Univ. Press, 2009), ch. 7–8. —Ed.].

those whom, in February, 1844, Joseph Smith and the Quorum of the Twelve Apostles proposed to send to the Rocky Mountains in search of a haven for the Saints. Events in Nauvoo matured too swiftly; Watt was sent to electioneer in Virginia for the presidential candidacy of Joseph Smith. He was, perhaps, still in the mission field when the mob burst into Carthage jail to assassinate Joseph and Hyrum Smith.

Returning to Nauvoo, Watt for the first time emerges to view as a "phonographer." On April 26, 1845, "Pres. Brigham Young, in company with Brother Heber C. Kimball, Geo. A. Smith, Amasa M. Lyman and others, attended Brother Geo. D. Watt's phonographic class from 9 o'clock a.m. till noon."[5] This class did not long continue, for almost at once Watt was sent to Warsaw to report proceedings in the trial of some of those men who had participated in the murder of the Smiths. The value of his "phonographic" talent was immediately evident, and the Church authorities voted, on June 1, 1845, to provide him with a quarter-lot and to build him a home thereon, repayment to be made through his "reporting labors."[6]

For the present Watt's knowledge of Pitman was subdued to a stenographic function. Yet the seed was sown in the mind of Brigham Young, who united with a stubborn streak of practicality an inveterate interest in experiment and novelty. The Church archives do not picture any growth of interest in Pitman among the people of Nauvoo during the year and a half after Joseph Smith's death that preceded the exodus from Nauvoo. But schools in the new orthography apparently functioned to some purpose; Allen J. Stout, whose education had not been extensive, so far mastered the idea that he kept unskillful "scrap journals" in the new orthography,[7] and his brother, Hosea, found time amid his duties as captain of police to write several pages of a "phonographical chart book" into his journal.

In February, 1846, phonography among the Mormons came to a temporary standstill. On the 4th of the month the advance companies of the Mormon emigration crossed the Mississippi into Iowa, and on the same day Watt was given his letter of recommendation to the English Saints, to whom he was now to return and preach the gospel.

Watt labored in England during the four eventful years while Zion was being established in the tops of the mountains. In the "Third General

[5]Journal History, 25 April 1845.

[6]Journal History, 19, 30, 31 May, 1 June 1845.

[7]Allen J. Stout wrote in his Journal for the period June–July 1845, "About those days I wrote my Scrap Journal in phonography, but was not well skilled in that science, so it is hard to read it."

Epistle of the Presidency," however, on April 12, 1850, it was observed that "Elders Orson Pratt and George D. Watt are wanted at this place {Great Salt Lake City}, with their families; and we shall expect them as early in 1851, as circumstances will permit."[8] On April 21, 1851, "our able phonographic reporter and lecturer" as the *Frontier Guardian* characterized him,[9] arrived at Kanesville on the Iowa frontiers; he soon set out on the trans-plains journey and arrived in "the valley" early in the autumn.

Soon after his arrival, on December 17, 1851, Watt "gave a lecture on Phonography in the Council House"; and ten days later, following another lecture, "the Board of Regents of the {Deseret} University met in the same room to investigate whether Stenography could be introduced into the schools to advantage, which was discussed with spirit." The position finally taken by the regents is not clear, but on January 1, 1852, Brigham Young, Thomas Bullock, Thomas W. Ellerbeck, William C. Staines, Nathaniel H. Felt, Albert Carrington, and Daniel H. Wells presented themselves as scholars in a "school of phonography" taught by the young English Saint.[10] The pressure of other duties seems to have prevented any extensive development of the school thus commenced, but Brigham Young had become definitely sold on the desirability of reconstructing English orthography, and it required only time and circumstance to bring forth a new written language for the Mormons.

The greatly expanded field of missionary activity may have precipitated for Young the pressing need of a revision of the language. From Norway, Sweden, Denmark, Germany, and France, as well as from that greatest mission field of all, the British Isles, thousands of zealous converts were now commencing to make their way toward Zion. The converts presented difficult problems of assimilation. The Mormon gospel had brought them to Utah's desert valleys, but if they were to be knit into the Kingdom of God, they should have to learn to speak and write a common language.

There was no question as to what the language should be. Mormon thinking has always taken its particular force and vitality from its grounding in American feeling. The international gospel of the Mormons returned again and again for its vitality to the driving forces of American life. America was in Mormon thought the chosen country, and the Mormons the chosen among

[8] *Millennial Star* 12 (1850): 245.

[9] *Frontier Guardian*, 30 May 1851.

[10] Journal History, 17, 27 December 1851; 1 January 1852.

the Americans. There might be defects in the English tongue; it might not be suited to the uses of the Kingdom of God; but between that tongue and any other there was no choice.[11]

Newly returned from his mission to China, and attending "at early candle light" a meeting of the University regents at the Council House, Hosea Stout on December 17, 1853, found his former associates in the Regency struggling with this problem of a new orthography for the English language. "They are endeavoring," he recorded in his journal, "to get up a new and simpler alphabet on the Phonetic principal so far as sound is concerned. Their object is so to shape the letters that they will answer for both writing and printing and take up as little room as possible. To do this and maintain the necessary dissimilarity of letters is no easy task but I think they will succeed."[12]

The effort was already two months old. In October, Parley P. Pratt, Heber C. Kimball, and George D. Watt had been appointed by the regents a committee "to prepare a small school-book in characters founded on some new system or orthography, whereby the spelling and pronunciation of the English Language might be made uniform and easily acquired. . . . After

[11]John V. Long, in a lecture at Seventies Hall on 12 February 1864, excellently typifies Mormon thinking as it would touch upon the subject of language. He "tried to prove that the English was destined to be the 'pure language' spoken of by the Prophet Zephaniah (Zeph. 3:9). He reasoned that the English language had borrowed a great number of words from almost all other languages—that it was the chosen medium through which the Mormon Gospel was revealed in this last dispensation, and that too, occurring about the same time, or at least only seven years previous to Pitman's spelling reformation—all went to prove, as he would have it, that the English is, or will be, the pure or universal language spoken in the Last days." (Letter by "A Hearer," in *The Daily Vedette*, 17 February 1864.) The *Vedette* correspondent discusses the tendency of all people to think their own language the pure language. Are we to believe, he asks, that after the confusion of the tongues at the Tower of Babel, and the continued confusion through the centuries, confusion has become purification, and the language which borrowed most has become most pure. English is the best language we have at present, he concludes, but it is hardly pure.

Those interested in Mormon thinking on the subject of communication in the world hereafter may consult Orson Pratt's discourses of 22 October 1854, published in the *Deseret News*, 28 December 1854, and reprinted in the *Journal of Discourses*, 3: 97–105, in which is advanced a concept of what might be called multi-dimensional communication independent of the tongue.

[12]Hosea Stout, Journal, vol. ___, p. ___ [This incomplete citation was intended to be made to a carefully typed transcription made in May 1941 under Morgan's direction. The quote appears in the published version of the diary in *On the Mormon Frontier: The Diary of Hosea Stout*, ed. Juanita Brooks, 2 vol. (Salt Lake City: Utah State Historical Society, 1963), 2: 499. Stout's remarkable diary remained accessible only in the family-held original manuscript form and Morgan's careful transcription for nearly two more decades. —Ed.]. The University of the State of Deseret was incorporated by the General Assembly of the State of Deseret on 28 February 1850. The act of incorporation appropriated $5,000 to the institution, but this money was not in the treasury, and until 1867 the University had its principal identity in the periodical meetings of its Board of Regents. Although it [the Board of Regents] is sometimes found [to be] concerned with the problems attending the functioning of the common schools, a preoccupation with the Deseret Alphabet primarily marks its existence during its first eighteen years.

some previous discussion, it was agreed that each regent should prepare an alphabet of his own contrivance and present I to the board."[13]

On November 22, 1853, the Board of Regents, sitting with Brigham Young and Heber C. Kimball, "adopted six new letters for the alphabet of the English language,"[14] but the archives fail to identify the contributions of the individual regents to the alphabet finally adopted. Except for the certain fact of Watt's phonographic knowledge, and the known inventiveness of mind of Parley P. Pratt and Heber C. Kimball, who were his fellow committee members, the Alphabet is almost the anonymous production of Mormonism itself.[15]

To the world the advent of the new alphabet was announced in the *Deseret News* on November 24, 1853.

> "We have observed the frequent sittings of the Board of late that has the fatherly supervision of education in the Territory of Utah, and are happy to learn that their discussions are calculated to call forth a searching investigation into the elementary sounds of language, and also into the nature and structure of such characters, and also into the nature and structure of such characters as are employed to express the radical and multiplied sounds of language. The Governor and other members of the First Presidency find times, in the midst of all their onerous duties to mingle in these meetings. The traditions that have come through the misty labyrinths of past ages are most powerfully assailed by the Governor, whose keen eye looks with suspicion upon the corruptions and perversions of language which was originally pure.[16] Thus far

[13]Hubert H. Bancroft, *History of Utah*, 712. Bancroft comments, "Parley Pratt was in favor of adopting one in which each letter should represent a single sound, but as some of the letters represent no sound except when in combination with other letters, and others are of uncertain sound, depending on such combination, the task would seem a difficult one." Bancroft's information on the inception of the Alphabet was apparently derived from a manuscript, "Deseret University." I am informed that this manuscript is not now to be found in the archives of the Bancroft Library at Berkeley.

[14]Journal History, 22 November 1853.

[15]Jules Remy, in *A Journey to Great Salt Lake City*, 2: 185, asserts positively that "the idea originated with the apostles[.] W. W. Phelps, one of the regents of the University, and that it was he who worked out the letters." There is no other authority for Phelps's participation in the origin of the Alphabet, and since Remy was making a point about the intellectual attainments of Phelps, he may not have been careful in his statement of fact. Only once does Phelps appear in the record of the Alphabet; he was one of a committee of three named in 1855 to make an investigation of the innovation for the Deseret Typographical Society. When any individual was credited with originating the Alphabet, it was usually Watt, as citations presently will show. Historians sometimes have credit Orson Pratt with creating the new orthography, but this is a confusion of mind arising out of his association with the Alphabet in its last years. Actually, he was in the East when the regents first occupied themselves with the idea, and in all probability the first intimation he had of the Deseret Alphabet was Brigham Young's letter of November 30, 1853: "The Regency of our University are quite busy at present, in trying to form a new, and better Alphabet, but have not time to agree definitely upon the different characters, hence will diligently continue their labors until a final result is arrived at." (Letter quoted in A. L. Neff, *History of Utah, 1847–1859*, 851).

[16]This conception of "pure" language, harks back, of course, to the Tower of Babel and its fruits.

it appears that the present orthography of the English Language is too full of absurdities to be tolerated by an enlightened people without a gradual and complete reformation. It is considered an easy matter to make many obvious improvements in this department of literature, but a query has arisen and occasioned some warm debate whether the present old Roman alphabet is sufficiently perfect to carry forward this reformation. It is objected by some that the characters of the old alphabet are like the white man (as the Indian says) too uncertain. That is, their sounds are too variable; too many letters enter into the composition of single words, and some of these letters are often silent and unmeaning. Now in the present stage of the discussion it is proposed by some to change a small portion of the English alphabetical characters and attach invariable certainty to the sounds of others, in order that words may be palpably shortened, and the spelling becomes natural and simple and easily acquired. Others are for carrying the reformation still further, thinking that a people of progressive intellect will not be contented with only a partial reformation, and that it requires an entirely new set of alphabetical characters to effect a clean handsome reformation that will be abiding. All seem to be agreed that both the written and printed language should be one and the same.

"Some of the Board have even offered the phonographic handwriting as a better hand for printed language than the phonetic hand, the latter being rather clumsy. . . . One thing seems quite certain in regard to language—especially the language of this people; it ought to be adapted to the urgency of these peculiar times. The focal point where the diverse languages of the people of all nations must be brought to harmonize into one common standard of speech renders the selection of a language for this purpose worthy of devout consideration. Can it be expected that the Apostles at Great Salt Lake City will speak by the immediate power of God so that people of every nation and language will forth with understand them? Or should we rather look for the power and wisdom of God to be displayed in forming a simple, easily acquired language, in which barbarians and Christians, bondmen and freemen, of every grade of intelligence, out of every tribe, caste, language, and country, can in a short time, interchange their sentiments and praise God unitedly in spirit and understanding.[17]

"If such a language is ever demanded at all, it seems to be required without delay, even now. It is not for a future generation, but for the present. Now the people are gathering, and the varied and most general influx of the diverse

[17]This occurrence of an important Mormon philosophy in the development of the Deseret Alphabet merits emphasis. Critics of the Mormons, attracted by the millennial features of the religion, have not observed how characteristic is this conception of the evolutionary, rather than the revolutionary, intervention of God in Mormon affairs. In my view, few things were more important to the growth of stable institutions amongst the Mormons than the emergence of this philosophy. I have pointed out a more striking instance of it in the monograph I prepared for the Historical Records Survey, "The State of Deseret," *Utah Historical Quarterly* 8, no. 1–4 (1940).

> tribes, nations, kindreds, and tongues, is even at our doors. Provision must be speedily made for this forthcoming crisis and event. Can we suppose that a few interpreters will answer the demands of a constant intercommunication between several thousand languages? May we not, and must we not, look for a *standard* to be lifted up? Should not that language be such as can be acquired by the most ordinary minds within a few days or months at the outside? Now it is possible to simplify and reduce the English language or in any way remould it so as to answer the emergency that awaits the saints of this generation? Tell us ye wise men! Will the old bottles answer for the deposit of the new wine? Or shall we construct new bottles for the new wine? The English language may be as good as any other known language, but is there any other known language whatever fitted to meet the great emergency of the great gathering and great work of teaching the law of the Lord to all people? Let wisdom speak, and her voice shall be heard."[18]

In a further announcement, to the Territorial Legislature in his gubernatorial message delivered December 13, 1853, Brigham Young laid less stress on the religious function of the developing Alphabet, and more on its scientific utility. "While the world is progressing with steam engine power, and lightning speed, in the accumulation of wealth, extension of science, communication and dissemination of letters and principle, why may not the way be paved for the easier acquisition of the English language, combining as it does great extension and varied expression, with beauty, simplicity, and power, and being unquestionably the most useful and beautiful in the world? But while we freely admit this, we also have to acknowledge that it is perhaps as much abused in its use, and as complex in its attainment as any other. The correction of its orthography, upon some principle of having characters to represent the sounds which we use, has occupied the attention of many scientific gentlemen from time to time,[19] but through lack of influence, energy, or some other cause, they have failed to accomplish so desirable an object. If something of this nature could be introduced which could be brought into general use, I consider it would be of great utility in the acquirement of our language. I am happy to learn that the Regency are deeply engaged in investigating this interesting subject; and hope that ere long, they may be able to produce something that will prove highly beneficial."[20]

18"Regency," *Deseret News*, 24 November 1853.

19That philosopher of inexhaustible interests, Benjamin Franklin, may be numbered among these. Noah Webster was also interested in the reform of the language, though, paradoxically, his Spelling Book and Dictionary did much to formalize the orthodoxies he personally disapproved.

20"Message of Governor Brigham Young," *Journals of the Legislative* (1854), 115–116; also printed in *Deseret News*, 15 December 1853, and in *Millennial Star* 16 (1854): 213.

A more concrete idea of what had been done by the Board of Regents was offered by the *Deseret News* in January:

"The Board of Regents, in company with the Governor and heads of departments, have adopted a new Alphabet, consisting of 38 characters.—The Board have held frequent sittings this winter, with the sanguine hope of simplifying the English language, and especially its orthography. After many fruitless attempts to render the common alphabet of the day subservient to their purpose, they found it expedient to invent an entirely new and original set of characters."

"These characters are much more simple in their structure than the usual alphabetical characters; every superfluous mark supposable, is wholly excluded from them. The written and printed hand are substantially merged in one."

"We may derive a hint of the advantage to orthography, from spelling the word *eight,* which in the new alphabet only requires two letters instead of five to spell it, viz: at. [*sic*] There will be a great saving of time and paper by the use of the new characters; and but a very small part of the time and expense will be requisite in obtaining a knowledge of the Language."

"The orthography will be so abridged that an ordinary writer can probably write one hundred words a minute with ease, and consequently report the speech of a common speaker without difficulty."

"As soon as this alphabet can be set in type, it will probably be furnished to the schools of the Territory for their use and benefit; not however with a view to immediately supercede the use to the common alphabet—which though it does not make the comers thereunto perfect, still it is a vehicle that has become venerable for age and much hard service."

"In the new alphabet every letter has a fixed and unalterable sound; and every word is spelt with reference to given sounds. By this means, strangers can not only acquire a knowledge of our language such more readily, but a practice reporter can also report a strange tongue so that the strange Language when spoken can be legible by one conversant with the tongue."[21]

The Alphabet had now crystallized in a form that could be presented to the public. The Alphabet originally approved by the Regency was by no

[21]"The New Alphabet," *Deseret News,* 19 January 1854, reprinted in *Millennial Star* 16 (1854): 293–294. The editorial goes on to mention a recent lecture on the Alphabet by Parley P. Pratt, which developed the apparently unrelated idea that it was "radical to all hopeful education" for the Spirit of God to predominate in families, as otherwise a "perverse, hateful jealous, envious, and contentious spirit" would produce a pernicious impression upon the mind of the infant that would be increased "by the force and meaning of words" after the child could talk and understand language.

Pratt's *Autobiography* could have supplied very illuminating information as to the origin of the Alphabet, but he contents himself with saying (p. 457), "The remainder of the winter {of 1853–54} was spent in the ministry; in the active duties of a Regent of the University of Deseret (being one of a Committee on the Deseret Alphabet and a New System of Orthography; in teaching a class in the Spanish language; in ministering in the ordinances of the endowments in the house of the Lord; and in studying, writing, etc."

means identical with that which characterized its final history, but most of the characters adopted in 1854 are to be found in the three other distinct forms of the Alphabet seen in Remy, Burton, and the four publications in Deseret Alphabet type.

The earliest representation I have found is that which Hosea Stout copied into his journal on March 24, 1854. Complete reliance cannot be placed on Stout's version as representing the appearance of the new orthography at this time, for Stout observes that "this is quite awkwardly executed as it {is} the first time I ever attempted to write any of the characters, & only inserted them to have some kind of a Specimen in my journal."[22] In the main, however, Stout's representation may be taken for what it purports to be.

The thirty-eight symbols in Stout's journal represent the long and short sounds of *e, a, ah, aw,* and *oo,* and the sounds of *I, ow, woo, ye, h* or *he, p, b, t, d, che, g, k, ga, f, v, eth, the, s, z, esh, zhee, r, l, m, n,* and *ng*.* In *A Journey to Great Salt Lake City* (1861), Jules Remy reproduced a facsimile of the alphabet executed at San Francisco in January, 1856, "after some genuine specimens we brought from the Salt Lake" the previous September. Remy's characters differ slightly from Stout's, but these differences may arise from the fact that they were obtained eighteen months later. Remy prints forty characters, rather than thirty-eight, the two additional symbols representing U and OI.[23] Variations between the Stout and Remy symbols are found in *ow,* which Stout represents as a kind of reversed *B,* with an internal loop, while Remy pictures it as identical with the *w*-like symbol for *aw* except for a looped extension of the right-hand stroke; and in the symbol for *e,* which Stout writes as a kind of script capital *F* while Remy uses the symbol which became standard, a cross with oblique cross-line.

The alphabet in use in August, 1860, when Richard F. Burton arrived in Great Salt Lake City, differs much more markedly from Remy's characters of 1855 than Remy's from Stout's of 1854. The Burton version has thirty-eight

[22]Stout, [*On the Mormon Frontier,* 2: 509]. This is hardly an enthusiastic comment on the Alphabet, especially in view of the fact that he was now again a member of the Board of Regents.

*[American Heritage Dictionary phonetic equivalents for the sounds Morgan had not heard for a decade and could only reproduce with the letters on his manual typewriter are ē, ā, ă, ä, and oo [barred double o], and the sounds of ī, ou, hw, y, h (aspirant), p, b, t, d, ch, j, k, g, f, v, th, *th*, s, z, sh, zh, r, l, m, n, and ŋ. —Ed.

[23]The Alphabet originally, and finally, comprised thirty-eight characters, but it would seem that several additional characters were added in 1855 and later. Remy found it to consist of forty symbols, and in 1857 an editorial comment on the Alphabet (see p.____) gave a total of forty-one [See note 52. —Ed.]. The version reproduced by Burton totaled only thirty-eight, but at the time the *Deseret News* announced the intention of adding two more in future (this was never done). The tendency to variation in the Alphabet is indicative of dissatisfaction with its adequacy.

characters only. The long vowel sounds in Remy and Burton are identical, but there is some variation in the short vowel symbols. The check-mark which in Remy denotes *a*, in Burton denotes *ah*; the somewhat similar check-mark which in Remy denotes *o*, in Burton denotes *a*; while the symbol for *ah* in Remy is entirely transplanted in Burton to represent *n*, *o* in Burton being represented by a symbol resembling a printed *r*. A perpendicular line which in Remy and Stout depicted *n* is eliminated entirely in Burton, while diagonal lines which entered into the structure of the angular symbols representing *p* and *eth* in Burton are made perpendicular, so that these symbols become right-angular. There is also an unimportant difference in the structure of the symbol for *r*.

The three initial versions of the Alphabet had dispensed with [the letter] *i*, evidently on the theory that *e* sufficiently captured the effect of this sound, but the final version of the Deseret Alphabet, used in 1868–69, incorporated a symbol for this sound, in addition to making other alterations of the symbols for short vowels. The symbol for *e* became *i*; that for *a* became *e*; that for *ah* became *o*; that for *o* became *u*; while the symbol for *oo* (as in *book*) remained the same. A further change is that the symbol for *a*, which resembled the number 3 in earlier versions, in the final version was reversed so as to resemble the script letter *E*.

Less easily traced than this physical evolution of the Alphabet is the derivation of the original symbols. Burton thought the Alphabet "a stereographic modification of Pitman's and other systems,"[24] but there is no marked physical resemblance between the Pitman and Deseret characters; Burton was reading into the structure of the Alphabet its unquestionable identity with Pitman in basic idea. Thomas W. Ellerbeck wrote Franklin D. Richards in 1885 that "the alphabet was designed principally by George D. Watt. . . . The forms of some of the letters were designed or originated by Mr. Watt—those of others were selected by Mr. Watt from some of the ancient alphabets found in the front of Webster's unabridged dictionary, but with a view to making the type wear well, neither tops nor tails to the letters were allowed."[25] H. H. Bancroft thought he perceived resemblances

[24]Richard F. Burton, *The City of the Saints and Across the Rocky Mountains to California* (New York: Harper & Bros., 1862), 419.

[25]Thomas W. Ellerbeck to Franklin D. Richards, letter dated 24 February 1886, printed in Carter, [*Four Outstanding Activities of the Pioneers*], 3. Richards at the time was preparing for H. H. Bancroft manuscripts relating to various phases of Mormon history, and Ellerbeck's letter contributed importantly to Richards' discussion of the Deseret Alphabet in the manuscript called by Bancroft, "Utah Miscellany" (now at the Bancroft Library) and so in turn to the Bancroft *History of Utah*.

92 Tuesday 21 March 1854
Sent my children to their grand mother's to day, by Joseph Taylor, where they will stay this summer
Wednesday 22 March 1854.
overhauling to day preparitory to going to Green River this summer
Thursday 23 March 1854
overhauling as yesterday.
Friday 24 March 1854
overhauling as yesterday
attended the meeting of the Regents at dark The subject was the new Alphabet which was printed and presented to the Board to night. It is anticipated to send by F. D. Richards to England for type &c also to introduce it there & use it hereafter in our correspondence also to immediately introduce it into our schools here. It is termed the Deseret alphabet and is as follows.

e. a. ah. aw. o. oo Long Sound.
e. a. ah. aw. o. oo Short sound
i. ow. woo. ye. h or he.

P. B. T. D. che. g.
K. ga. F. V. eth. the.
S. Z. esh (S Thae) R. L. M. N. Ng

The earliest representation of the Deseret Alphabet,
written into the Hosea Stout diary for 24 March 1854.
Courtesy of Utah State Historical Society.

to Greek, which, he said, "is also the case in the plates from which the book of Mormon is said to have been translated, where the letter[s] *pi, rho, tau, phi, chi,* some of them as in manuscript and others as in printed Greek, can be distinctly traced." Endeavoring to trace further the resemblance of the Alphabet to Greek, he adds, "Thus the long sound of the letter *e* in meter was represented by a character resembling the Greek *sigma* reversed, the double sound of *woo* in wood by one resembling *omega,* the aspirate by *phi,* and the articulate sound of *f* by *rho.*"[26] There are certain resemblances to the Ethiopic alphabet, also phonetic, which the originators doubtless saw in Webster's dictionary; this similarity was observed by an eastern paper in 1857: "The new characters are forty-one in number, and bear a striking resemblance to those of the Ethiopic Alphabet; in fact, some of the letters are identical in shape. . . ."[27] In all probability, the physical structure of the alphabet owed to all these sources without borrowing absolutely from one of them.[28]

Creation of an adequate alphabet for the phonetic rendition of English represented merely a beginning in the problem shouldered by Brigham Young and the Board of Regents. They now had to bring the Alphabet into effective everyday use. The history of the Alphabet through the next three years devolves about this problem of acquainting the public with it and converting them to its superiority.

Hosea Stout, who again had been elected a regent by the legislature in December, records in his journal through 1854 a variety of facts about the Alphabet. There were meetings of the regents on December 29, January 5, and January 12, at which the Alphabet presumably was the order of business; at a further meeting, on March 9, the regents were shown new type for the Alphabet, but there are no details about this. Meetings on March 16 and 17

[26]Bancroft, *History of Utah,* 712, 714.

[27]*New York Daily Times,* 26 August 1857, reprinted in *The Mormon,* 29 August 1857.

[28]No one who has written about the Deseret Alphabet has commented on the far more remarkable Cherokee Alphabet invented by the Cherokee Sequoyah. A casual glance at printed material in either alphabet gives one a striking impression of their similarity which, however, disappears on closer inspection. Sequoyah, whose English name was George Guess, never learned to read or speak English, but was impressed with the means of written communication. Unaided, he worked out an alphabet of 68 characters which for the first time enabled men to reduce the Cherokee language to writing (the English alphabet was inadequate to the task). So simple was this alphabet, moreover, the Cherokees were able to master it in a few days. Sequoyah required twelve years to evolve this alphabet, a labor he began about 1809, and has been called "the only man in history to conceive and perfect in its entirety an alphabet or syllabary." See Grant Foreman, *Sequoyah* (Norman: Univ. of Oklahoma Press, 1938). It is of interest that the Mormons maintained a mission among the Cherokees for some year after 1855.

were also concerned with the Alphabet, but not until March 24, the date he copied the new alphabet into his journal, is Stout very informative. On this night, however, he says that the new alphabet "was printed and presented to the Board."[29] It was decided "to send by F. D. Richards to England for type &c also to introduce it there and use it here after in our correspondence also to immediately introduce it into our schools here." On April 4 the regents met at the Social Hall theater "and exhibited the Deseret alphabet to the Public which was well received." A week later, the regents again met at the theater to make public demonstration of the Alphabet, and it may be presumed that efforts were made throughout the year to popularize the innovation.[30]

It is recorded that on November 29 the regency "met at Pres. Young's office where Pres. Young gave some instructions in regard to the new alphabet."[31] On December 7 the *Deseret News* advised that among the duties to be assumed by the regents and their assistants was the responsibility to "Enjoin upon the Trustees and Board of Examination to make it an indispensable requisite in teachers to forth with qualify themselves to teach the Deseret Alphabet in their respective schools"; and on December 16 Hosea Stout, returning to Great Salt Lake City from the Green River Mission, found the regents preoccupied with "the new Alphabet which is now becoming a subject of interest in the primary schools in the Territory." The Church Authorities seem to have found it desirable to practice what they preached—at least, to the extent that George A. Smith wrote John Taylor on February 7, 1855, "Elder B. B. Messenger is now engaged teaching the Clerks of the Historian's Office, the Deseret Alphabet."[32] And when "Educational Classes," conducted in connection with the Polysophical Institution, were announced on February 8, the Deseret Alphabet was listed among the subjects to be taught. Traveling in Utah County in March, George A. Smith found that John B. Milner was teaching the Alphabet to 160 scholars at Provo, 60 at Lehi, 28 at American Fork, 25 at Mountainville {Alpine}, 28 at Pleasant Grove, and 22 in the Provo First Ward.[33]

George D. Watt on June 6, 1855, lectured to the Deseret Theological Institute in Great Salt Lake City, but the greatest attention given the Alphabet

---

[29]By "printed" in all likelihood is meant carved wooden type which would serve for experimental purposes.

[30]Stout, [*On the Mormon Frontier,* 2: 511].

[31]Journal History, 29 November 1854.

[32]George A. Smith to John Taylor, letter dated 7 February 1855, *The Mormon,* 31 March 1855.

[33]Journal History, 11 March 1855.

by any single group in this year appears to have been by the Deseret Typographical Association—logical development in view of the fact that the territorial printers sooner or later would have to master it if it were to come into effective use.

On July 5 Watt "introduced for consideration the subject of the Deseret Alphabet," and after some discussion a committee of three, consisting of Watt, W. W. Phelps, and James McKnight, was appointed "to draft resolutions expressive of the views of this association relative to the Deseret Alphabet."[34] The report of the committee, on August 2, was all that might have been expected:

> "Whereas, the Regency of the University of Deseret, assisted by the First Presidency of the Church of Jesus Christ of Latter Day Saints, have invented a new Alphabet:—and,
>
> "Whereas, the present system of English orthography is very imperfect, and inadequate to the end it is designed to serve:—and,
>
> "Whereas the Deseret Alphabet supplies a simple character to most of the simple sounds of the human voice, substantially correcting the absurdities of English spelling,—rendering more definite the pronunciation of words, and more easy the acquisition of other languages, and lessening to a very great extent, for the rising generation, the labor of learning to read:—therefore,
>
> "Resolved, that justice to ourselves, and to our posterity, demands our serious attention and endeavors be directed towards rendering universal in our midst the practical adoption of this New Alphabet:—And that we may be more capable of fulfilling this resolution,
>
> "Resolved, that Elder Geo. D. Watt be solicited to instruct this Association in the principles of the Deseret Alphabet."
>
> Watt gave notice that he would give his first lesson in the New Alphabet on August 9, at 6 p.m.[35]

The Alphabet was a major item of business at each of the three succeeding monthly meetings of the Association. On September 6 "Prest. Young expressed his hearty concurrence in the resolutions; and action of the Association relative to the Deseret Alphabet; urged its claims upon our attention and that of this community; recommended measures for the speedy formation of a library."[36] On October 4 Samuel W. Richards "thought the Deseret Alphabet was indeed worthy [of] our attention," and heartily recommended it to the consideration of the Association. Robert Campbell discussed the Alphabet

[34] *Deseret News*, 11 July 1855.

[35] *Deseret News*, 15 August 1855.

[36] *Deseret News*, 12 September 1855.

as a means of communication, exhibiting "a letter from an elder on a mission, written in the new Alphabet, the writer being unable to write in the common style, and having received but six lessons in the new. It was indeed a pleasing illustration of the practical utility of the new Alphabet." James McKnight, further, "observed that it was the wish of President B. Young that the new Alphabet should be introduced among this entire people. It had not been prepared without much labor and patience."[37] On November 1 the Association listened to an address by Watt "upon the general principles of language," and resolved that they should meet again next evening "to receive instructions from G. D. Watt, in the Deseret Alphabet."[38] All this earnest effort came to nothing. In the Annual Address to the Deseret Typographical Association, on February 8, 1856, John B. Davies remarked, "The Typographical Association, since the last festival, have been busily engaged in their literary pursuits, in instruction one another, and learning the Deseret Alphabet."[39] But the Alphabet apparently never figured again in the activities of the Association.

Apart from this activity in connection with organized groups, the Alphabet seems to have made some popular headway during 1855. When Jules Remy reached Great Salt Lake City in September, he observed, "We have known {these singular characters} used in private correspondence, and seen them on some shop signs."[40] And by someone in Cedar City, at least, the future of the Alphabet seemed so certain that the stone erected upon the grave of "G ON M O UR I S," who died February 20, 1855, was carved wholly in Deseret Characters, barring only the place of his Welsh birth, *Lanfair Talhairn*, which may have seemed too tough a nut for even the Deseret Alphabet to crack. This tombstone, perhaps unique, is hereby called to the attention of those who specialize in the curiosa of graveyards.[41]

Lack of type in which the new Alphabet could be published was a serious obstacle. The *Deseret News* reported on August 15, 1855, "Punches, matrices, and moulds are being prepared by br. Sabins, for casting type of the New Alphabet; and we are in hopes of seeing ere long, a font of handsome letter case, and primary books in the new style, printed for the use of our schools."

---

[37] *Deseret News*, 17 October 1855

[38] *Deseret News*, 7 November 1855.

[39] *Deseret News*, 13 February 1856.

[40] Remy and Brenchley, *Journey to Great Salt Lake City*, 2: 184.

[41] A photograph of John Morris' gravestone in the Cedar City cemetery is printed in this issue of the *Quarterly*. I am indebted to Charles Kelly for calling it to my attention and to Horace Roundy of Kanarraville for photographing it. [This photo now joins the study for which it was taken. —Ed.]

[John Morris's gravestone in the Cedar City, Utah, cemetery, photographed by a WPA worker in 1944. The original stone has since been replaced by a modern one, which reproduces the text. —Ed.] *Courtesy of Utah State Historical Society.*

It was further noted that "Large letters of this Alphabet have been cut by two enterprising young lads in this office, which, together with an illustrative card, can be obtained at the Post Office."[42] But no local foundry ever produced an acceptable type,[43] and even as the *News* wrote, the Church may have been endeavoring to get what they wanted in St. Louis, for Remy says that the new characters, "intended for the printing-presses of the Salt Lake, were cast at St. Louis."[44]

When the Territorial Legislature met in December, it was proposed that $2,500 should be appropriated for procuring fonts of Deseret Alphabet type and for publishing books with this type. An act to this effect was passed December 23, 1855.[45] It appears that some further legislative measures of support were rejected; on January 2, 1856, Hosea Stout records that "An act adopting the Deseret Alphabet and Legalizing the laws of Utah" was adversely reported out of the Joint Committee on Education, and consequently was "laid on the table indefinitely."[46]

On February 4, 1856, the Chancellor and Board of Regents of the University met with Brigham Young, Heber C. Kimball, Jedediah M. Grant, Lorenzo D. Young, Frederick Kessler, and Robert Campbell to discuss the preparation of copy for the publication of elementary school books in the Alphabet. A committee consisting of Wilford Woodruff and S. W. Richards, regents, and George D. Watt, Secretary of the Board, was named to prepare the literature for publication, and report progress at each succeeding meeting, "that they may have the advantage of the information, judgment and experience of those who feel interested in the subject of education."[47] Woodruff,

---

[42]*Deseret News*, 15 August 1855.

[43]Cf., however, note 51.

[44]Remy and Brenchley, *Journey to Great Salt Lake City*, [2:] 184. Remy's book, however, was not published until 1861, and he may have incorporated later information than he derived first-hand in 1855.

[45]The Act in full reads as follows: ["]An Act appropriating money for educational purposes and defining certain duties of the Chancellor and Board of Regents of the University of the State of Deseret: Sec. 1. Be it enacted by the Governor and Legislative Assembly of the Territory of Utah; That the sum of two thousand five hundred dollars is appropriated, to be drawn by the Chancellor, and expended under the direction and control of the Chancellor and Board of Regent in procuring fonts of Deseret Alphabet type, in paying for printing books with said type, and for other purposes. Sec. 2. The Chancellor and Board of Regent are authorized and required to furnish, or cause to be furnished, copy for all publications they may order, to control the sale thereof, and to apply the profits arising there from to the most advantageous promotion of education, including such payments to the Superintendent of common schools for services rendered under their direction, as they may from time to time deem proper." *Laws of Utah* (1856), 5.

[46]Stout, [*On the Mormon Frontier*, 2: 590–591].

[47]*Deseret News*, 6 February 1856. Stout says [in an entry for 4 February that] the First Reader was to be printed in Liverpool "next spring."

Richards, and Watt accordingly spent most of their time, during the next week, on this work. "They commenced," the chronicle says, "to write upon such subjects as the pioneers, Mormon Battalion, Salt Lake Valley and Utah Territory, Grisly bears and buffalo bullfights, etc."[48]

On February 11, at a meeting of the regents, "The work of the committee was read and accepted. The greater part of the evening was occupied by exercises upon the blackboard, and then the Committee of Revision or examination was appointed, to assist those appointed as the first committee.

> "Pres. Young has had his mind deeply exercised upon the getting up of the 'Deseret Alphabet' and carrying it into practical use; he has labored diligently from the beginning upon this subject and the committee are now making books under his direction to be published in the Alphabet."
>
> "They have to get new type made as the letters are entirely different from any others now in use."
>
> "The Committee on the whole are satisfied that great good will grow out of the Deseret Alphabet. . . . The Committee who were last appointed were Albert Carrington, Daniel H. Wells and Wm. Willis."[49]

Two weeks later, at another meeting of the Board of Regents, Wilford Woodruff, chairman of his committee, "reported quite an amount in readiness for revision preparatory to being copied. The committee on revision had been so much occupied with other public duties that they had not been able to pass upon but a small portion of the manuscript resented. On this account, Messrs. E. Smith, O. Pratt and P. P. Pratt were added to the committee on revision, and it is presumable that the work will progress with greater rapidity."

"The pronunciation and of course the spelling of several classes of words, where custom invariably differs from that found in Webster's dictionary, was unanimously decided upon, and a record thereof made by the secretary."[50]

The record is unfortunately obscure as to the casting of type in St. Louis, which is the only important development involving the Alphabet for the next three years. Orson Pratt is said to have been sent to St. Louis to insure accuracy in the casting of the new fonts of type,[51] but except that a specimen

[48]Journal History, 6 February 1856.

[49]Journal History, 11 February 1856.

[50]*Deseret News*, 27 February 1856.

[51]Neff, *History of Utah*, 852. Matthias Cowley writes, in *Wilford Woodruff, Fourth President of the Church of Jesus Christ of Latter-day Saints: History of His Life and Labors as Recorded in His Daily Journals*, ed. Matthias F. Cowley (Salt Lake City: Deseret News, 1909), 367, "On the 3rd of March Elder Woodruff was called on a mission to the East to secure type for the *Deseret Alphabet*," but Woodruff remained in Utah throughout

fell into the hands of an eastern newspaper and was published in August, 1857, with the observation that the *Deseret News* would "probably hereafter be a profound mystery, at least in part, to all but the initiated,"[52] and that after conclusion of hostilities with the United States over the period of the "Utah War," the new type was freighted to Great Salt Lake City, and the way this opened for the further adventures of the Alphabet, little is recoverable about the Alphabet during these three years.[53]

On November 20, 1858, Woodruff came around to tell Brigham Young that all the works in the Alphabet formerly compiled had been lost. Young asked Woodruff "to take hold with Geo. D. Watt and get up some more." Five days later, at a meeting of the regents, "The board made arrangements

1857–58. F. D. Richards (Bancroft, *History of Utah*, [712–714]) told Bancroft that the type used in 1859–60 "was made in this city by John W. Rumell["]; although Richards must be given respectful attention, it appears that this first type was not manufactured in Utah. George D. Watt informed the Territorial Legislature in January 1857, that "A facsimile of the letters of said alphabet, was sent early in the spring of '56 to the United States, for the purpose of getting punches and matrices made for casting the letters, but they could not be made in time to be forwarded by this fall's emigration." No expenditures had been made by the University, he said, since 1852. *Journals of the Legislature* (1857), 32. [The Bancroft citation does not include the Richards statement cited here, a point that, because this is an unpublished manuscript, might have been corrected had Morgan completed the piece for publication. —Ed.]

[52]*New York Daily Times*, 26 August 1857, quoted in *The Mormon*, 29 August 1857. Note a comment of similar character, in the *San Francisco Globe*, 15 December 1857: "The Mormons, remarks an exchange, are a progressive people. They not only want more wives than is wholesome, but more letters to their Alphabet. Letters written with this Alphabet are as incomprehensible as the movements of woman or the hieroglyphics of the Chinese and the Egyptians. The Mormon alphabet consists of about forty letters, which have been so arranged and named as to cause the greatest possible annoyance to outsiders. The Saints not only wish to convert Utah into an oyster, but to close the shell against all knives except those found in the vicinity of the Great Salt Lake. The Mormons wish to isolate the 'generation of vipers' which are to succeed them. For this reason they wish to get up a new alphabet, a new spelling book, and a new language. The idea is ingenious, but it will not succeed. To get a new language in this country is as difficult as to bore a hole through the Rocky Mountains with a leather auger."

[53]Contemporary comment on the Alphabet by the rank and file of Mormondom is hard to find. Oliver B. Huntington, who was teaching a school at Centerville, remarks in his journal under date of 4 February 1856, that he had "commenced an evening school in the new or Deseret Alphabet," though whether as teacher or student is not clear. George Washington Bean, then with the Indian Mission located at Las Vegas, makes occasional reference in his journal to the Alphabet. Under date of 13 March 1856 James H. Martineau wrote George A. Smith from Parowan, "I see by the 'News' that arrangements are being made to print school books in the Deseret Alphabet. If it would not be asking too much, I should like to get a copy as soon as possible, as I feel quite interested in it." (Letter in Journal History.) I am informed by Mrs. Juanita Brooks of St. George that one of the ward records for Cedar City in 1856, kept by Martineau, is written in the Alphabet, so that he evidently was supplied with a copy of the Alphabet, and proceeded to learn it. During the Alphabet's period of activity in 1859, the conscientious Charles L. Walker, who evidently felt learning the Alphabet to be one of his responsibilities in the "living of his religion," wrote in his journal on 30 November, "At night studying the Deseret Alphabet"; and again on 2 December, "At night learning the Deseret Alphabet." In all this not much enthusiasm for the Alphabet itself, is to be discerned.

for the printing of the Deseret alphabet primers." On the 27th, the record notes, the Historian "was presented with a card for his {Young's} office, being the first printing done with the Deseret type." From November 29 to December 3 members of the regency and others, often including Brigham Young, labored on the Deseret primer; there were occasional lectures by Watt, and once "a spirited debate on the pronunciation of the word 'rule.' "[54]

This reawakened interest in the Alphabet soon brought misgivings. Something of the enormous dimensions of the task facing the Mormons was expressed in a meeting of the Quorum of the Twelve on January 23, 1859. It was estimated that it would cost about a million dollars to furnish books and stationery to educate only those people then in the Territory. Even though the English language was inferior to the Deseret, the English books would have to be continued, as but few Deseret books could be printed by the Mormons.[55]

Brigham Young was irritated by these objections. "I think we are the Head and not the tail," he told the Board of Regents on January 31, "and now if I had my way, I will tell you what I would do, I would put books into the hands of children in this Territory printed in the Deseret alphabet, I don't want man's books to teach children. . . . I would classify all the children. I would put the little children all together, and I would take a girl, or some one capable of teaching them, and I would have a good blackboard and I would teach the alphabet upon that. One book would be enough in the room. I do not believe in putting books in the hands of little children to pore over and make them sit on a hard bench until they ache all over. If I were a teacher, I would make them rise up and march around the house and I would try to interest their minds so they would delight to learn, but many persons who have learning enough to teach a school yet they are not fit to teach children. As soon as a child does something that does not please the teacher, he begins to pound the child with a rattan over the head and back or slap him on the side of the head with his hand. This is not the way to teach children. You put a work into the hands of a German, Frenchman, Dane or Swede, or any other nation printed in the Deseret Alphabet, and in a little time they will all read and spell alike, much sooner than they could learn a new language." The chronicle adds, "The rest of the brethren spoke,

[54]Journal History for the cited dates. I don't know whether it has any significance that this resurgence of the Alphabet came during the period when Young was in seclusion, following the establishment of [Albert Sidney] Johnston's army in Utah.

[55]Journal History, 23 January 1859.

Daniel H. Wells said that he was satisfied that the Lord has inspired the mind of Prest. Young in this matter."[56]

Over the next three days Brigham Young and others labored to prepare in the Alphabet Christ's Sermon on the Mount, for publication in the *Deseret News*; the regents also began to give some attention to a dictionary of the Deseret Alphabet.[57] February 16 was made notable by the appearance in the *Deseret News* of the first fifteen verses of the Sermon on the Mount, from the fifth chapter of Matthew; this was the first formal publication of anything in the Alphabet. The column of Deseret type was prefaced by an English introduction which almost invariably prefaced all the selections printed in the *News*:

> "We present to the people the Deseret Alphabet, but have not adopted any rules to bind the taste, judgment or preference of any. Such as it is you have it, and we are sanguine that the more it is practiced and the more intimately the people become acquainted with it, the more useful and beneficial it will appear.
>
> "The characters are designed to represent the sounds for which they stand, and are so used. Where one stands alone, the name of the character or letter is the word, it being the only sound heard. We make no classification into vowels, consonants, &c., considering that to be of little or no consequence; the student is therefore at liberty to deem all the characters vowels, or consonants, or starters, or stoppers, or whatever else he pleases."[58]

Webster's dictionary, it was noted, would be generally followed, though Webster would be varied from when general usage demanded. Words having the same pronunciation would be spelled alike, and the reader would have to determine the meaning from the context. When they could be procured, new characters would be added to represent the sound of *ew*, in *new*, and *ai*, in *hair.*

If in its news columns the *Deseret News* was unpersuaded about the Alphabet, no such backwardness is evident in the editorial published in the same issue: There was probably no language, living or dead, at once so perfect and exhibiting so many imperfections and inconsistencies as English. Composed of "the very pith and marrow of the tongues which have found their graves in the advancement of civilization," English had made its conquering way among the languages, and in due course probably would crowd out all other

[56]Journal History, 31 January 1859.
[57]Journal History, 9 February 1859.
[58]*Deseret News*, 16 February 1859.

languages, appropriating to itself whatever might be good in them. But the orthography of this language was filled with imperfections and absurdities; to talk English and to write it were two different things. Deseret proposed not to correct the language, nor to make any innovations upon the language itself, but Deseret did propose to effect an entire revolution in the orthography of English.

> "Our Regency have struck out for themselves a new path. They present us with new characters. Each character had its own independent sound. The sound is arbitrarily retained in the words where the character is found. The characters will appear crude and impracticable at first sight. We deemed them so when we were first shown them. But it was not long before we saw our error. We do not say that they are perfect. In fact we believe we can ourself see where improvements might be made. But we have so far scrutinized them as they are now presented, that we can say unhesitatingly they are not only a great improvement but easy of adoption. We look for improvements, and earnestly commend the subject to the further careful study and unremitting attention of the Chancellor and Regents. . . . We are fully confident that they will do honor to their important trust. At the same time we urge upon our fellow-citizens to encourage and support them in their labors. A few men can do but little in such a business. It requires, nay, to be effectual, must have the popular support. It must have it heart and soul, without squirming, and hesitation. It is the floodtide of improvement, and we strip off our traditions and make the plunge. Surely it does not require long arguments to prove the superiority of a system which gives in a common tuition perfection of orthography to a child, over one around whose labyrinths the maturity of college-bred manhood can scarcely wind itself.
>
> "We shall from time to time present our readers with short articles or selections in the new characters. . . . At present we give preference to selections from the Old or New Testament, as being more accessible for comparison to all parties."[59]

Brigham Young was probably more sold on the Alphabet than anyone in Utah. Yet he by no means shared the enthusiasm of the *News*. To John W. Rumell, who called this day to see him, proposing "to get up the pinnacles and mattrasses [i.e., punches and matrices] to make a set of new type for the Deseret Alphabet," and proffering to do the job himself satisfactorily or lose the labor, provided Young would furnish the materials, Brigham Young

[59]*Deseret News*, 16 February 1859. A naïve faith in the Alphabet is evidenced in the choice of editorial matter. For purposes of *comparison* the Bible was a matchless choice. But human nature is such that original editorial matter, with news or other interest, might have constituted a greater incentive to readers to learn something of the Alphabet and wade through the column of material set up in Deseret type.

said he did not like the present type, and intended to have a new set cast, but would wait until it had been thoroughly revised and improved, when he would send the job to England and have the casting done there, where the facilities were better. "He also said that he intended to get up a Speller containing all the words in Webster's Dictionary, and have it printed in England as they got up work, in good style in that country."[60]

The series of articles in the *News* continued intermittently until May 2, 1860. Except for an omission on March 30, 1859, the series was uninterrupted until October 5, but the weekly article after that date was occasionally omitted, and on four occasions in 1860 the article of the previous issue was reprinted. Until July 20, 1859, all selections were from the New or Old Testament, but thereafter they were as frequently taken from the *Book of Mormon,* or *Doctrine and Covenants.*[61] To aid readers, the *News* began advertising, on February 23, "A POCKET EDITION of the Deseret Alphabet, printed on card or flat-cap," for sale, wholesale or retail. There is no indication of how this card sold, except that advertising of it quickly ceased.[62]

Meanwhile Orson Pratt, Chancellor of the University of the State of Deseret, was engaged with George D. Watt in copying all the words in Webster's unabridged dictionary into the Alphabet, "for a speller and pronouncer in the Deseret Characters."[63] He quickly got enough of this. To the regents on March 21 he reported that "in consequence of the situation of his family and their present necessities, he had discontinued writing the Mss. Of the Deseret Alphabet Dictionary, that although he had not named it, his family had actually been in a suffering position, having had all his bread to purchase since his return from Europe. He also remarked that although it had fallen to his lot to write much when he was abroad, he naturally disliked it, and all the Gold in California could not hire him to engage in copying and arranging Websters Unabridged into the Deseret Alphabet as a Speller and Pronouncer or for a Dictionary; his eyes were affected and close application would be such that Gold would not be a temptation enough to hire him to do it."

---

[60]Journal History, 16 February 1859. It may have been this entry in the records that led F. D. Richards to think Rumell had made type for the Alphabet. cf. note 51.

[61]A complete bibliography of articles and books published in the Alphabet is printed at the end of this monograph.

[62]It is probably one of these cards that is reproduced in Burton, *City of the Saints,* 420, as a specimen of the Alphabet.

[63]Journal History, 14 March 1859.

Robert L. Campbell thought the getting up of such a dictionary "a Herculean task for which we were unprepared, and unable without involving ourselves and that should it be got up, we would find it uncalled for and unsaleable. He argued the propriety of getting up Juvenile readers, and a concise speller, which he thought would be needed, and as the Deseret Alphabet gained ground, and the inhabitants of the Territory increased, larger works could be profitably introduced."

Brigham Young, who subsequently came in, suggested to Pratt the propriety of getting up a Juvenile Reader, or Book of Mormon speller and dictionary, and since he did not feel able to write the MSS., to employ clerks who would labor under the superintendence of Pratt and Watt. It was voted that this be done, and Daniel H. Wells, Levi W. Richards, and Robert L. Campbell were named a committee to find clerks.[64] These clerks were hired during the first part of April, but by the 14th of that month Brigham Young found a logical reason to change his mind; he "dismissed the young men employed on the Deseret Alphabet Dictionary . . . stating that it was business for women and that the Regency had no funds to pay for the labor."[65]

The story of the Alphabet through 1859 is one of the lively interest. The *Valley Tan* had been by no means impressed. "This idea to get up a peculiar vocabulary," the editor thought, "is about as ridiculous as Mormonism itself." Education was much needed here, but a sound education in the rudiments of the English language. Children of the Territory should be educated, "not in Dutch or Deseret dialect, but in one that will enable them to read and understand other matters besides the precepts and dictates of the Church."[66]

The *News* disdained its local contemporary, but on May 14 took up the cudgels against the *New York Journal of Commerce,* which had inspected the new alphabet and come to the conclusion that it was "part of a scheme originally devised by the Saints to render their community quite exclusive, and to debar all Gentiles and outside barbarians from a too critical surveillance of the workings of the internal machinery of the State." This was, the *News* contended, an asinine observation in view of the fact that e key to the alphabet was published with it. Since the editor had rendered into English the *News*'s Matthew excerpt as *"Maetheoo sekseth cheahptaur,"* he might profitably

[64]Journal History, 21 March 1859

[65]Journal History, 14 April 1859. Campbell seems to have construed this action to mean that Young proposed to find women to do the work, but if so, this was not arranged.

[66]*The Valley Tan,* 22 February 1859.

adopt his own gratis advice: he might "better devote his time to mastering the English language than to criticizing, in such a blundering manner, a system of which he knows little or nothing."[67]

On June 4 Brigham Young had a visit from Marion J. Shelton, who for some ten years had been adventuring in the Indian country, from the Dakotas to Mexico. Shelton expressed the opinion "that the Spanish and most of the Indian languages could be written in the Deseret Character as far as he understood it."[68] Three months later on September 7, Shelton, who seems to have been thinking about the Alphabet in the meantime, had another conversation with Young and Wells. He appears to have raised some objections, to which Brigham Young replied that "these technicalities are the result of education and if the alphabet was taught to children who had not learned any other they would never realize the difference."[69] Shelton went on south, and in November he rode with Jacob Hamblin to "Oribe [Oraibi] Village" of the Hopi Indians, south across the Colorado River. Left to labor there, he added quite an amazing chapter to the story of the Alphabet. "I employ my time," he wrote George A. Smith, "in studying the Language, and in instructing them {the Hopis} in the Deseret Alphabet. I find that I acquire the language very readily, and those to whom I have given lessons have taken right hold to the alphabet and several of them know the first six characters, and we can hear them hollowing the sounds throughout the village. They have some peculiarities in their tongue that I never have heard in any other. You will please tell the President that I have had to introduce another character which I sincerely hope will meet with his approval. It is simply, I, a straight mark."[70]

Meantime Brigham Young in his own office and in the Historian's Office had instituted the keeping of a number of ledgers and office journals in the Deseret Alphabet. Thomas W. Ellerbeck in 1885 recalled that for one whole year "the ledger accounts of President Young were kept by me in those characters, exclusively, except that the figures of the old style were used, not

[67]*Deseret News*, 14 May 1859. As a matter of fact, the *Journal of Commerce*'s translation of the Alphabet was irreproachable, and the *News* was ungrateful to object that this rendition would require "more 'tongue'" than they were gifted with. An argument for the Deseret Alphabet was the English was absurd in attaching variable meanings to letters—for example, that "child" was not pronounced "chee-ild." The *Journal of Commerce* properly rendered the sounds assigned to the characters; the *News* implies that the names of the letters were rendered. This distinction does not ever seem to have been clearly thought out by the promulgators of the Alphabet.

[68]Journal History, 4 June 1859.

[69]Journal History, 7 September 1859.

[70]Marion J. Shelton to George A. Smith, letter dated 30 November 1859, in Journal History.

having been changed.[71] At Young's request, Watt had begun instructing the clerks of the Historian's Office on June 6, 1859. Inspecting "the history record in the Deseret Alphabet" on May 3, 1860, Young declared himself "very well pleased with it; said if he had influence enough he would have the old system dropped"; and when Richard Bentley, a clerk in the Historian's Office, departed on a mission on September 28, 1860, it was noted not least among his accomplishments that he had copied into the Deseret characters 92 pages of the "Autobiography of Brigham Young" and 88 pages of the "History of Brigham Young" into record "H."[72]

Discontinuance of the weekly articles in the *News* did not occur before the appearance of two defenses by "A. B.," published in the issues for March 14 and April 16, 1860.

The first of these articles implies that the Alphabet had received no very grateful reception: The circumstances attending the introduction of the Alphabet "are similar in their character to the reception which usually attends innovations upon an established system, whether scientific, theological or philological. The originators of every new system have always encountered the prejudices which flow as a consequence out of the existing ignorance of the newly discovered system or invention." After commending the form of the characters, with their lack of looped and long-tailed letters, the writer expresses the opinion that the Alphabet will be a boon to all who use it, and that adoption of the system "must greatly facilitate the student in his pursuit of literature and science."[73]

The second article dwells on some of the absurdities of English orthography, as for example the varying vowel sound in *bough, dough, cough,* and *enough.* We might as well, he contends, use hieroglyphics to represent our meaning as conventional English expressions—the eye, rather than the ear, has been employed. The merits of the Deseret System are dissolving the prejudices against it; already many among the people of Utah can read rapidly in the new alphabet. "The cobwebs of tradition are being removed from those who have fairly investigated it, and its reception clearly argues that in a few years its adoption will be general. . . ."[74]

[71]Ellerbeck, in Carter, *Four Outstanding Activities of the Pioneers,* 3.

[72]Alvin Smith, Librarian, in January 1942, could not venture an opinion as to how many journals and ledgers in the Historian's Office had been kept in the Deseret Alphabet.

[73]*Deseret News,* 14 March 1860.

[74]*Deseret News,* 18 April 1860.

On contrary, the reception had been such that within two weeks the *News* ceased to publish further matter in the Alphabet.

A sidelight to this period of Alphabet activity, of considerable numismatic interest, is the five dollar gold coin minted by the Mormons which bears in Alphabet characters the inscription "Holiness to the Lord." The Mormons had begun a coinage of their own in 1849; the coins so minted were of virgin gold. In 1858 Brigham Young had a new die prepared for the five dollar gold pieces. A pattern piece was struck for him, and this pattern piece he is said to have worn to the time of his death, as a charm attached to his watch chain. After his death, the executors of his will realized $300 from the sale of this watch, chain, and charm.[75] Coins from this die issued from the Mormon mint in 1860 and 1862, but apparently no Mormon coins were minted after this date, as Governor Alfred Cumming is said to have prohibited further minting in Utah.

If the Alphabet for eight years after 1860 made no further headway, it did remain an influence in the mind of Brigham Young. When on May 22, 1862, Robert L. Campbell presented for inspection a manuscript First Reader for the schools, Young "emphatically said he would not consent to have his type, ink, or paper used to print such trash (which he considers such works to be, seeing they are in the English characters). He wishes the Deseret Characters to be patronized."[76] Young may have been influenced somewhat by the belief prevailing among the Mormons at this time that great events were at hand in the world, that the establishment of the Kingdom of God was imminent.[77] Yet, beginning in 1864, he evinced an interest in phonography apart from the Deseret Alphabet. Sometimes these two interests clashed, but on occasion they did not.

On March 18, 1864, he expressed a desire to have the Regency called together and the system of phonography introduced in the place of the Deseret Alphabet;[78] and ten days later he met with Heber C. Kimball, Wilford Woodruff, George A. Smith, and the Regency, "trying the merits of the phonotypic systems, and comparing it with the Deseret system."[79] His

---

[75]John S. Dye, *Dye's Coin Encyclopedia* (Philadelphia: Bradley & Co., 1883), 1103–1105. The information apparently was supplied to the publisher about 1883 by Brigham Young, Jr., and Joseph L. Barfoot. A photograph of the coin bearing the Deseret characters is reproduced in Nels Anderson, *Desert Saints*, 86.

[76]Journal History, 22 May 1862.

[77]Cf. Historical Records Survey, [*State of Deseret*], 132–149.

[78]Journal History, 18 March 1864.

[79]Journal History, 28 March 1864.

conclusions are not evident unless the reappearance in the *Deseret News* of articles printed in the Alphabet is indicative. On May 11 the *News* presented P UR AU V O UR B Z CHE AH P. 24 [Proverbs Chap. 24]; and weekly selections from the *Bible, Book of Mormon,* and *Doctrine and Covenants* continued until August 24, with only one omission. One letter, (s), was left off the key July 13 and thereafter, and on July 20 four letters were left off the key—apparently as a move to "wean" readers of reliance on English equivalents. But publication of these articles ceased on August 24.

The Deseret Alphabet subsided into quietude. At a meeting of the Regency on December 3, 1866, Watt and George Q. Cannon informed their brethren that Young "had talked about adopting Pitman's orthography or letters";[80] and, S. W. Richards wrote his brother, "the Board gave attention to the propriety of adopting, and immediately introducing to general use in this community, Pitman's system of spelling, reading, and writing. This is considered a very great improvement upon the old style, and might materially aid in the future development of what was originally designed in introducing the 'Deseret alphabet'. Only one definite action was taken, but the subject was discussed in view of action at another meeting soon to be held. President Young, who has ever manifested a very lively interest in this subject, was not able to be present on account of illness, but his views will no doubt come before the Board."[81] Richards' is a conservative statement; one can be quite sure that Brigham Young's views would "come before the Board" before any action was taken on such a matter.

A last period of indecision precedes the final renaissance of the Alphabet. The year 1867 saw a general awakening of interest in phonography in the Territory of Utah, with perhaps an equivalent interest throughout the country.

Robert L. Campbell, in his annual report as Territorial Superintendent of Schools, wrote on January 18, 1867, "The superintendent takes great pleasure in noting the recent movements of the Board of Regents of the University of the State of Deseret in relation to the adoption of the reform in orthography known by many as the Phonetic system, and the adoption of those printed characters used by Phonetic publishers. This is certainly a step in the right direction, and one which the age of progress in which we live demands we should immediately take. This system has stood the test of years, and where it has been investigated by Legislative Committees, by

[80]Journal History, 3 December 1866.

[81]S. W. Richards to F. D. Richards, letter dated 2 & 3 February 1866, in *Millennial Star,* 29 (1867): 75.

eminent friends of education has been pronounced superior in every respect to the Romanic system."[82]

In June Edward L. Sloan advised the phonographers of the Territory that the idea projected in April, for the organization of a "Phonetic Society," had now matured, with a Parent Society organized in Great Salt Lake City; members would be divided into three classes—practical phonographers offering to correct gratuitously the exercises of beginners; students and practical phonographers not disposed to correct beginners' exercises; and, finally, persons not themselves phonographers but interested in furthering its development. Sloan was president, Alexander McRae, David W. Evans, and George A. Burgon vice presidents, John C. Graham secretary, Charles B. McGregor corresponding secretary, and Thomas Latimer treasurer.[83]

The *Deseret Evening News* on January 27, 1868, was pleased to learn of the ["]progress made in the dissemination of this valuable art in the cities and settlements throughout the Territory." John B. Milner was teaching classes in Provo, and George Burgon classes in Farmington, Kaysville, Ogden, North Ogden, Plain City, and Willard. Several phonographers were teaching in Great Salt Lake City, including Watt in the Mercantile Department of the Deseret University, and a number of classes were being taught in Cache Valley. The Phonographic Society may have contributed to this spread of interest.

It was to a session of this Society, in April, 1868, that the erstwhile Alphabet instructor of the Hopis, Marion J. Shelton, now of Fillmore, presented a new system of phonography claimed to be superior to Pitman's. "Unlike many glaring plagiarisms on Pitman's phonography which would-be inventors have called their own," the *News* told its readers, "this is entirely different to anything ever before presented as phonography since Pitman invented the art. Its characters are new, and their arrangement and combination are the author's own, and not borrowed. It has . . . one very great advantage over the phonography now in use,—a word can be written in full, with all its sounds represented, without lifting the pen to vocalize. And any number of words can be written together—forming a line of indefinite extent, without lifting the pen, if the writer so desired, every sound being faithfully represented by its appropriate character, ..."[84] Following the scheduled exhibition, the *News* reporters expressed themselves as most favorably impressed, and

[82] *Journals of the Legislature*, (1867), 156–157.
[83] *Deseret News*, 17 June 1867.
[84] *Deseret Evening News*, 11 April 1868.

hazarded the opinion that if this new shorthand fulfilled the expectations entertained concerning it, they should adopt it in preference to Pitman's, which they now used.[85]

While phonography was thus flowering, the Deseret Alphabet was preparing once more to take over its vested rights in Utah letters and linguistics.

As late as December 20, 1867, the *Deseret Evening News* was warmly commending the "phonographic system." A plan, it was noted, had been presented to the last session of Congress proposing that a commission of eminent American and English scholars be named to simplify English orthography on a phonetic base. It could not be hoped that anything would come of this plan, for "hoary-headed tradition would cry out in thunder tones against it, and Parliament and Congress could not resist the pressure that would be brought to bear against them." But what could not be done by other peoples could be done by the people of Utah Territory.

"Our population," pronounced the *News*, "is diverse in its origin and free from binding traditions. They would eagerly adopt any alphabet that had authoritative sanction, and that would come recommended to them by its simplicity and the ease with which it could be learned. For years this subject has been under consideration. It has rested with great weight upon the mind of President Young, and his interest in it has never flagged. Under his direction, years ago, characters were adopted, matrices for them were imported and a quantity of type was cast. But, whether from ignorance or design, the matrices were very rudely made and did the characters great injustice. The difficulty in obtaining a beautifully formed type of these characters kept the proposed reform in abeyance. Until, finally, it has been decided by the Chancellor and the Board of Regents of the University of the State of Deseret—President Young meeting with them, and taking great interest in the discussion—to adopt the Pitman Phonetic Alphabet and recommend it to the people for their adoption. This alphabet contains forty-three letters. It has several more shade vowels in it than were deemed necessary in what is known as the Deseret alphabet. These shade vowels are deemed superfluous by some, and it was suggested that they should be rejected; but, finally, it was thought advisable to adopt the alphabet in its entirety.

"Pitman's characters are available. This is the reason of their selection, and not because they were thought to be the best characters for an alphabet.

[85] *Deseret Evening News*, 16 April 1868. Notwithstanding all these merits, no more is heard of Shelton's invention.

The introduction of the system of phonetics is the great point to be now gained. The form of the characters is a somewhat secondary consideration. By the introduction of the system of spelling by sound our children and foreigners will be relieved from a heavy tax upon their time and brains. The portals of the temple of knowledge will be thrown open to all; and the ease with which an education can be received will be surprising. Among other great benefits which will follow the introduction of this system will be uniformity of pronunciation.

"This great reform lies in the pathway of our progress. We have effected an entire revolution in religion and morals since the organization of our Church; there is nothing to prevent our accomplishing this much-needed reform in our mother-tongue. This business should be taken in hand by our school-trustees and school-teachers throughout the Territory, and be carried through with energy."[86]

The paradoxical effect of this persuasive editorial seems to have been the resurrection of the Deseret Alphabet. Reading it, Brigham Young may well have been set to thinking. What, after all, were the advantages of Pitman over the Deseret Alphabet? Merely, that it was available and that no pleasing type had ever been cast for the Deseret characters. If suitable fonts of type were obtained, and books printed, these advantages would disappear. He had, moreover, been long convinced of the superiority of the Deseret Alphabet. . . .

The Board of Regents convened on February 3, 1868, with Brigham Young and Daniel H. Wells present, and voted to strike out of the minutes the vote of the former meeting by which the "former characters of phonotypy" was adopted, and to petition the Legislature for $10,000 to print school books in the Alphabet.[87] S. W. Richards outlined to his brother an ambitious project: "The Board of Regents met this evening and agreed to petition the Legislature for ten thousand dollars, and then send a practical printer to the East, and have the type made for the Deseret Alphabet, and publish and import this season, spelling books, primers, readers, &c., to be introduced immediately among our children, and so continue from year to year, until we have published in that alphabet the cream of all knowledge relating to theology, science, history, geography, and all necessary educational works. Brother O. Pratt will probably be employed in compiling matter for these books."[88]

---

[86]*Deseret Evening News*, 20 December 1867.

[87]Journal History, 3 February 1868.

[88]S[amuel] W. Richards to F. D. Richards, letter dated 2 & 3 February 1868, *Millennial Star* 30 (1868): 157.

A few days later George Goddard wrote F. D. Richards, "President Young strongly advocated the general introduction of the Deseret Alphabet, and that the same be taught throughout the Territory in all our Sabbath schools; said the Regency would be instructed to send for new type of the same, and have thousands and tens of thousands of small interesting books published, to be disseminated through our Sunday schools, which, by-the-by, are established in nearly every settlement throughout the Territory; and all who were willing to aid him in this important undertaking were asked to uplift their right hand, when every Bishop, Councillor, Teacher, and Elder present raised their hands: he then said, 'God bless you brethren.' This was about two hours ago, at the Bishop's meeting."[89]

On February 19, in his annual report as Territorial superintendent of common schools, Robert L. Campbell took pleasure, he said, in seconding the efforts "of President Brigham Young and the Board of Regents of the University of Deseret" in the introduction of the Deseret Alphabet. There was no question as to the need of reform in English orthography. "To follow in the footsteps of our venerated fathers in a system of orthography so inconsistent and ridiculous and which has never helped to make the comers thereunto perfect, is unworthy of a people whose constant and highest aspirations are to be associated with truth and intelligence, and who discard error in whatever form it is presented." In its childhood English had been spelled without system. The pronoun "it" alone was spelled eight different ways in Tyndale's translation of the New Testament.[90] The result of throwing together Anglo-Saxon and Mormon French orthography was a confusion to be found nowhere else except, perhaps, in the spelling of the native Irish. Learned bigots had frustrated the efforts of reformers. "It may be looked upon as Herculean effort to attempt the reform of English orthography; but it is a reform so much in keeping with the progress of the age, in which we are privileged to live, and which portends so much advantage and blessing

---

[89]George Goddard to F. D. Richards, letter dated 12 February 1868, *Millennial Star* 30 (1868): 190. Comment will be made later on some of the religious implications of this communication. [This essay did not so comment. —Ed.]

[90]It may be remarked that cheerful informalities were normal to English spelling until after Samuel Johnson published his famous dictionary in 1755. Noah Webster's dictionary, published in 1828 and setting up American standards, tended like his earlier and even more influential speller to enforce uniformity in American spelling. Unorthodoxies in spelling frequently crop up in pioneer journals. Descendants of those pioneers often display an absurd sensitivity about the "illiteracy" of their ancestors, failing to appreciate the charming independence and naiveté of those who, like William Clark of the Lewis and Clark Expedition, in their journals show themselves "determined enemies of the dictionary."

to our children, that we should be recreant to ourselves and to the cause of truth did we not unitedly take hold of the subject."[91]

Obediently, the Territorial Appropriation Bill of February 21, 1868, allocated "To the University of the State of Deseret, to be drawn by the Chancellor and expended under the direction and control of the Chancellor and Board of Regents in procuring books for Common Schools in Territory, ten thousand dollars."[92]

On April 18, in the Historian's Office, Orson Pratt commenced his labors on the school books to be printed in the Deseret Alphabet. On May 15 the Regency named Robert L. Campbell to act with Albert Carrington "as an executive committee to carry out the wishes of the regency in getting out books, etc." On May 21 Campbell furnished Pratt "letters" to transcribe into the alphabet for the primer, and on the 23rd Pratt was "engaged in transcribing a catechism into the Deseret Alphabet," a job on which he was still occupied May 27. On June 5 he was busy "revising his second book on the Deseret alphabet," and next day "was transcribing the catechism into the Deseret alphabet." On June 25 he and Campbell sent off the second book of the Deseret Alphabet by Wells, Fargo Express.[93]

David O. Calder, meanwhile, was sent East to arrange for the casting of fonts of type and the actual printing of the manuscripts being prepared by Pratt. He finally came to terms with Russell Brothers, a New York firm which published for the Mormons all of their books in the Alphabet. The primer, and possibly the second reader as well, issued from the presses by August. These were slender books, octavo, the Primer running to 36 pages and the Second Reader to 72. Illustrations used were derived from *Willson's Readers* ("so justly popular, and so universally used in the Territory") by permission of the publishers.[94] Twenty thousand copies of each work were published.[95]

[91]Robert L. Campbell, "Annual Report of the Superintendent of Common Schools, 1867," 170–171.

[92]*Laws of Utah* (1868), 31.

[93]Journal History for these dates.

[94]*Willson's Readers* in 1864 were made standard in the Territory, though they had not wholly displaced *McGuffey's Readers* in 1868. (Cf. Campbell's cited Report, 19 February 1868, p. 172).

[95]Report by Daniel H. Wells, chancellor of the University, 17 February 1870, in *Journals of the Legislature* (1870): 107. The Day Book of the University of the State of Deseret affords interesting data on costs. D[avid] O. Calder was allowed $841.04 for his bill, which included coach and rail fares, lodgings, and incidentals; Russell Brothers was allowed $2,897.47, the bill for printing the two school books including punches, matrices, electroplates, type, leads, rules, etc. Various freight bills amounted to $949.23. Orson Pratt was paid $414 for translating the two readers and the (apparently not printed) catechism. Robert Campbell was paid $189 "for composing lessons for readers & arranging same as per bill." With another $26 for clerical expenses, the total cost of these school books was $5,316.74. ("Day Book of the University of the State of Deseret," 20–21.)

With school books now available, the *Deseret Evening News* on August 13, 1868, argued to the public "The Deseret Alphabet—Its Advantages." Any system that would simplify the methods of educating the young "ought to be hailed by mankind as an invaluable boon." It now required years of close and persistent study by children to acquire even a moderate education; this was attributable primarily to a defective spelling system. After years of work acquiring a vocabulary, a writer might have to resort to the dictionary to satisfy himself as to the spelling of a word. "To acquire a sufficient knowledge of our language to be able to speak[,] read and write it correctly is an immense task for the memory, and strains it more than we can well realize." There were serious objections to sending young children constantly to school; health often had been undermined by unremitting application to study, but in many cases if children were not sent steadily to school when young, they would grow up illiterate, for by the time they were physically able to undergo the strain of schooling, their labor was frequently required by their parents.

> The introduction of the Deseret Alphabet, [affirmed the *News,*] will remedy the evils of our system of orthography, and facilitate, to a wonderful extent, the acquirement of education by the children. By its aid, in a very brief period, any person will be able to learn to read. It will also bring about a uniformity of pronunciation, for every word will be spelled as it is pronounced, and *vice versa*. If a person understands the sound of a language, by the aid of the Deseret Alphabet he can write it correctly; for the characters of that alphabet represents the sounds.
>
> A few moments' reflection will convince one what a great advantage such a system presents, and what time it will save the learner. Instead of spending years in learning to spell and read, it will only require, at the farthest, a few weeks. We are pleased to have it in our power to announce that there is every prospect that this system will soon be generally introduced into our schools. {Primary school books had been printed in the East; a specimen was now at hand.} The characters, to a person unaccustomed to them, may look strange; but to the eye to which they are familiar they are beautiful. Their chief beauty is their simplicity. A person of ordinary intellect, by applying himself to their study for a few hours, would be able to read a letter or book written or printed in them.
>
> The introduction of these books into our schools will be a highly important step in the right direction. The thinking, liberal portion of educated men in America and England have long felt the necessity of a change in our system of orthography. They have in some instances advocated such a reform, and steps have been taken to make it effective by publishing papers

> and books in phonetic characters. Many, however, while freely admitting that such a reform would be very desirable, have despaired about it ever being accomplished. To them the obstacles in the way of its universal adoption have seemed insurmountable.
>
> If our community were situated as others are, it might be quixotic to attempt the introduction of this reform among us with the hope of carrying it into practical operation. But our position is unique. We are united. This system can be made universal among us with but little trouble. We have effected important reforms in other directions, and done so successfully, and we can also make the correction of the orthography now in vogue a success. It is a labor worthy of us and our destiny. Some have an idea that if a child be educated in the system of spelling and writing by sound, it will be a detriment to it in learning the present system. But those most familiar with phonotypy assert that it is an aid to a child, if familiar with that system, in learning our present orthography; of course the Deseret Alphabet holds the same relation to our present system that phonotypy does; the principle of the two is the same; the characters only are different.
>
> It will probably be advantageous to children to have some knowledge imparted to them of the present system, even after the Deseret alphabet is generally adopted; but with us this should be a matter of secondary consideration. If they could find no better reading than much of the miserable trash that now obtains extensive circulation, it would be better, in our opinion, if they never learned to read the present orthography. In such a case ignorance would be blissful. Our own literature would be open to them, and though it might be limited, the minds of those who perused it would be more healthy and strong, than if they had a wider range of reading of an inferior character. The greatest evils which now flourish, and under which Christendom groans, are directly traceable to the licentiousness of the press. It sends forth a prurient and dangerous literature, which corrupts and distorts the minds and judgments of men. It is our aim to check its demoralizing tendencies, and in no way can we better do this, than by making the knowledge of the Deseret alphabet general and by training the children in its use.[96]

In this long editorial the *News* touched indirectly on a genuine difficulty. The alphabet could be learned, but except in communication it was functionless. It provided no access to the literature of the world, and provided no substitute for that literature. Consequently, although Orson Pratt on November 2, 1868 "commenced his labors again getting up lists of errata for the Deseret 1st and 2nd books,"[97] he also began a work of wider scope.

---

[96] *Deseret Evening News*, 13 August 1868; also printed in the *Deseret News* (weekly), 19 August 1868.

[97] Journal History, 2 November 1868.

George A. Smith advised Albert Carrington, "The Regent of the Deseret University are at work again and have employed Elder Orson Pratt to transcribe the Book of Mormon into the Deseret characters. The first and second readers, already published, are to be distributed throughout the schools in the Territory."[98] Pratt met with the Regents on November 9. They approved his bill for work already done, and accepted his proposition "to translate or rather transcribe" the Book of Mormon into the Alphabet for $1000.[99]

Parenthetic remark may here be made on the complete identity of religious with temporal purpose, apparent throughout the history of the Alphabet. The choice of the *Book of Mormon* as a "reader" for the schools can occasion no surprise. The Regency of the University of the State of Deseret from the beginning functioned as an adjunct to the First Presidency of the Church; when Brigham Young talked to the regents, and told them what he wanted done, he talked to them as President of the Church, although at first he was governor as well. A historian's dismay[100] at the fusion of church and state, here evidenced, is more than a little absurd, for if this fusion is to be criticized, it must be criticized on more fundamental issues and inter-relationships, of which the Deseret Alphabet may only be interpreted as vaguely symptomatic. It must also be remembered that the canons of historical objectivity do not always, or easily, apply to early Utah society. It is to be doubted, for example, whether in 1869 there were in Utah twenty Gentile children. Non-Mormons who had come to Utah had not, as a rule, brought with them wives, least of all children; moreover, in the Mormon view, non-Mormons were in Utah only on sufferance, for it was the Mormons who by the hard labor of body and soul had created this civilization in the desert after expulsion from other areas. The Mormons were not, in their employment of the Alphabet, perverting the school system of the Territory "from service to the commonality of its citizenry to the furtherance of the sectarian ambitions of a denominational group"; the "commonality of its citizenry" was the Mormon people, and schools were as much subject to their interested control as religion. The Saints might have argued, had the necessity of such an argument ever occurred to them, that in their Sabbath schools wherein was taught the Deseret Alphabet without cost to the Territory, they made a contribution to Territorial welfare far outmatching the cost of texts provided by the Territory.

[98]George A. Smith to Albert Carrington, letter dated 4 November 1868, in Journal History.

[99]Journal History, 9 November 1868.

[100]Neff, *History of Utah*, 852–853.

In his annual school report to the legislature, on February 16, 1869, Robert Campbell gave much space to the Alphabet. He reiterated the criticisms of English orthography, and mentioned that many new alphabets had been invented and published to the world, Pitman's having enlisted the most disciples, though the converts were few and the influence of Pitman relatively limited, compared with the extent to which the English tongue was spoken. Pitman, following upon its introduction into Illinois by Watt in 1845, had come into immediate use among the Mormons, and had subsequently been taught throughout Utah. The anomalous and contradictory character of the English alphabet, as related to spoken English, does "greater violence to the moral perceptions of the child than is commonly imagined. The Persians said, the first thing to teach a child is to speak the truth; the first thing we teach children seems to be not unlike a mass of literal falsehoods." The difficulty of acquiring English was such as nearly to preclude a foreigner from obtaining a perfect knowledge of it, while even for the native scholar, the task was immensely difficult. The influence of English literature upon the world was thus restricted. The Deseret system reduced to simplicity the spelling and reading of English; the acquirement of reading was divested of "the uncertainty, contradiction, and difficulty which attend the acquisition of the present system."

> As the subject of orthography meets us at every step in the school-room, [Campbell concluded,] "and as laudable efforts are being put forth to introduce this important and indispensable reform, the Superintendent could not do less than endorse a movement which augurs so much good to the cause of education. Could sufficient reasons be assigned for following in the footsteps of the fathers in this false system of orthography, we might forbear an innovation which completely upsets the present system, but to hold on to the same, and weave the web of inconsistency and falsehood around the feet of the present and future generations, which tradition and learned bigotry have woven around the past, would be to allow our children to turn round and have it truthfully to say of us as we can of our ancestors.
>
> 'Surely our fathers have inherited lies, vanity, and things—wherein there was no prophet.'[101]

Apparently it took Orson Pratt about four months to transcribe the *Book of Mormon* into the Alphabet. At a meeting of the Regents on March 1, 1869, he reported his labors finished and was appointed agent to go east and see the book through the press.[102]

---

[101]"Report of Territorial Superintendent of Schools," dated 16 February 1869, 176–181.

[102]Journal History, 1 March 1869, quoting them Historian's Office Journal.

Through March, however, he and Campbell were occupied in proofreading his transcription of the Book of Mormon,[103] and it was not until after a second session with the Board of Regents, on April 12, that he left for New York.[104]

It seems originally to have been planned to publish the *Book of Mormon* in three parts, "to take the place of the readers generally used in our schools," as Brigham Young wrote Albert Carrington.[105] After reaching New York, Pratt seems to have come to the conclusion that it would be better to publish a small edition of the entire Book of Mormon, and a considerably larger edition of the first part (the "Book of Nephi"). Writing for instructions on this and other matters, he was answered by Daniel H. Wells and Robert L. Campbell:

> "As to getting large capitals,[106] you will be the best judge. Get what is needful so far as practicable, having an eye to future use.
>
> "We are pleased to learn that you have negotiated with Russell Bros. for the execution of the present job."
>
> "You must have applied yourself very closely to have revised the seven hundred and sixty-eight pages of Mss. a second time We hope you will not overwork yourself at any time, for by so doing you might render yourself unable to hold on till the completion of the Book."
>
> "The binding estimates are reasonable and your intention of getting the first part in boards meets the President's approval."
>
> "The brethren are much pleased to find that your mind is exercised in relation to maturing plans for the future success of the printing in the Deseret characters. We will have a long talk with you on these matters when you get home. . . ."[107]

By June 19 the *News* was able to tell its readers that proof sheets of the new edition of the *Book of Mormon* were at hand, the clear type presenting a very neat appearance. A letter from Pratt is quoted, mentioning the he gives the proof sheets four careful readings to insure accuracy. The large capitals were not yet finished but in due course would be inserted in the proper place. "The compositors," Pratt added, "make a great abundance of mistakes in setting the type, which greatly increases my labor in the corrections."[108]

---

[103]Journal History, 15 March 1869.

[104]*Deseret Evening News*, 14 April 1869.

[105]Brigham Young to Albert Carrington, letter dated 9 December 1868, *Millennial Star* 31 (1869): 29. In his address to a Conference assemblage on 8 April 1869, George A. Smith said, "It is designed to publish an edition of ten thousand copies, suitable for the use of the schools." *Millennial Star* 31 (1869): 348.

[106]The question of capitals had been considered as early as 14 March 1859, when specimens were presented to the Regents for approval, but nothing was done at the time.

[107]Daniel H. Wells and Robert L. Campbell to Orson Pratt, letter dated 29 May 1869, quoted in Journal History for this date from Historian's Office Letterbook No. 6, p. 832.

[108]*Deseret Evening News*, 19 June 1869.

After twenty-three weeks' absence, Pratt returned on September 26. Eight thousand copies had been printed of the *Book of Nephi*, and five hundred of the *Book of Mormon* itself, at a total cost of $7,137.12.[109]

Two days after Pratt's return, the *Deseret Evening News* hailed completion of his task. "This is the greatest stride yet made in the world towards phonetic reform. For over thirty years the Phoneticians in England and this country have been laboring constantly for the introduction of phonetics and the advancement of phonetic reform. In England the *Phonetic Journal*, edited by Mr. Pitman, of Bath, has been published for many years, and latterly, we believe, this gentleman has printed the New Testament in the same characters. The Deseret Alphabet, though differing in form from the phonetic characters invented by Mr. Pitman, is precisely the same in principle; and the people of Utah have set an example worthy of imitation by all the English-speaking nations of the earth, in having printed sometime since, first and second readers, and now the Book of Mormon on this principle. It will do more towards spreading a correct style of speaking English among the polyglottian people of this Territory than anything else ever attempted."[110]

Three months later the *News* returned to the subject. The labors of fifteen years were briefly recapitulated, and the necessity for alphabetic reform reiterated. Although effort from time to time had been made to teach the alphabet, this effort had not been continuous, from lack of books, and those who had learned to read and use the alphabet had allowed this knowledge to fall into disuse. Now, however, four books had been printed, "and the

---

[109]The itemized bill includes twenty-three weeks' labor by Pratt, from 19 April to 26 September 1869, which at $36 per week totaled $828; Pratt's miscellaneous expenses while in New York, totaling $665; Russell Brothers' bill "for type and materials for stereotyping & printing and binding," $4,494.12; and costs earlier incurred, which included the thousand dollars paid Pratt for the transcription, an additional $75 paid him for comparing the *Book of Mormon*, and a further $75 paid him "on a/c of services." It will be noted that no freight cost is shown; although the completion of the railroad may have simplified that matter, it is improbable that Pratt brought some 8,500 books in his personal luggage. The cost of the *Book of Mormon* added to that of the First and Second Readers make the total cost of this publishing enterprise $12,453.86. The legislature had appropriated only $10,000, but an additional $2,000 was donated to the treasury of the University from tithing funds of the Church. A deficit of $453.86 would remain to be made up; it was expected that this would be taken care of by book sales. In this connection Chancellor D[aniel] H. Wells reported to the legislature on 17 February 1870, "There are yet some balances due for services rendered in prosecuting these labors, which will be liquidated as soon as possible out of the sales of the above books and it is designed, as means accumulate from these sales, to use them in procuring further works of the kind." *Journal of the Legislature* (1870), 169.

The cost figures above are derived from "Daybook of the University of the State of Deseret," 20–22. If sales did not cover the deficit, Church funds probably were used for that purpose, as there is no record of a legislative appropriation.

[110]*Deseret Evening News*, 28 September 1869.

Book of Doctrine and Covenants, a dictionary and probably other works, will doubtless soon follow. . . . The books that have already been printed should be used in the Sunday schools, in households, and in every schoolroom in the Territory. If the books at present offered for sale by the Regency were disposed of, they would then have funds at their disposal with which to publish other works, and we should soon have a literature published in our own characters.

"What a great advantage it will be to us," the *News* concludes, "to have a means of writing and printing which even children can learn with such ease and despatch! The advantages of such a system are apparent. Philologists have long perceived them, and many have denounced our present system of orthography as barbarous and utterly unsuited to the progress of the age, and have advocated the adoption of the Phonetic system of spelling; a number of books have been printed and at least one paper is published in Phonotype. But there is really no good prospect of the system becoming general in its use. It has the prejudices of the age to contend with, and it meets with strong opposition. If the system of spelling the English {language} by sound shall ever become general, it will have to be through the efforts of the people of this Territory. We have affected a great reform in religion, in politics, in social matters, and in many other directions; it remains for us to correct the faults which exist in the present method of writing our language.—We are better prepared than any other people to accomplish this, for we are united; and let it be known by the people of this Territory that a new and better system should be adopted, and they will not hesitate to carry it out.

"Every child in the Territory should be taught the Deseret Alphabet; the first and second readers and the Book of Mormon, printed in the character, should be in every house. By giving them a wide circulation the Board of Regents can pursue their labors, and but a few years will pass away until we shall have all our Church works and many standard works on history and science printed in our own characters."[111]

Reporting to the legislature on January 19, 1870, Robert L. Campbell also displayed optimism. "The Superintendent {Campbell}, in his recent school visits, has advocated the introduction and adoption of the Deseret characters and system of orthography in our common schools, and takes pleasure in stating that many teachers feel alive to the importance of the

[111] *Deseret Evening News*, 17 December 1869.

subject, and that the school authorities, in every district visited, have given it their hearty endorsement. The work of the reformation of English orthography and the introduction of a new character, in which to write and print our language, is a stupendous task, requiring time, means, patience, and unyielding perseverance; but the ease with which it is attained and the facility imparted by the system to the acquisition of English orthography, enables us to hope that when sufficient means are available to carry on the printing in that method, that but a few years will pass until the *News*, the *Instructor*, the *Ogden Junction*, and a host of other intellectual lights, will spring up, clothed in the unique, novel, and simple dress of the Deseret character. If the Legislative Assembly, in their economical and judicious distribution of the public money, would appropriate two thousand dollars to be expended in getting up a spelling book or elementary dictionary, another step could be taken which is very necessary and important in the further prosecution of this important reform."[112]

The bright dream persisted for a while—sufficiently long that the Board of Regents instructed Orson Pratt to translate, among other works, the Bible and *Doctrine and Covenants*. On January 16, 1872, Pratt petitioned the legislature for payment of his bill, rendered two years since and still unpaid, for lack of funds in the university treasury. He had written 3,996 foolscap pages "in Manuscript for educational purposes," and for this and other services he asked an appropriation of $6,537.87.[113]

The House Committee on Claims on February 13 reported "that they had no doubt of the justice of said claim, and recommended that a liberal appropriation be made to enable said Institution to enable them to fill all contracts and successfully carry on the same"; the Committee on Claims was thereupon instructed to incorporate into the Territorial Appropriation Bill the sum of $10,000, for the use and benefit of, and to liquidate all claims against, the University of Deseret.[114] Three days later the Council Committee of Education recommended that the figure of $10,000 be stricken from the appropriation bill, and "six thousand and thirty-eight dollars and five cents" be inserted instead, thus scaling down the Pratt claim.[115] The legislature did not strictly follow this recommendation, but Pratt was the loser thereby, for

[112]"Annual Report of the Superintendent of Common Schools," 191–192.

[113]Journal History, 16 January 1872.

[114]*Journals of the Legislature* (1872), 129.

[115]*Journals of the Legislature* (1872), 161.

the final Territorial Appropriation Bill, setting aside $9,000 to the Board of Regents of the University, provided that the Timpanogos Branch should receive $3,000 of the total sum.[116] If Pratt was given all the remainder, he received $6,000 on his claim. The total direct cost to the Territorial treasury of the Mormon venture in phonography thus approximated $18,500.

All the time and thought and effort that had gone into the creation and the development of the Alphabet was quickly shown to have been wasted. For the schools the Alphabet was impracticable, and for the general public it had none but a curiosity interest. Thomas W. Ellerbeck disposes of it as well as any. "Busier times coming on," he says, "the characters of the Deseret Alphabet gradually disappeared."[117] Franklin D. Richards told Hubert H. Bancroft, "It was found that the tailless characters, however economical in the wear and tear of type, were inimical to the eye, the monotonous evenness of the lines making it more difficult for the eye to follow and distinguish the words than when set in the ordinary type. It was also difficult to insure uniform pronunciation and consequently uniform orthography with the Deseret characters. As is the case in other communities, the people generally did not take kindly to the new characters, so that in a short time the Deseret alphabet fell into desuetude, from which it has never been resurrected, and no desire for its use appears now {188[6]} to exist."[118]

For awhile, however, there continued like a leaven in Mormon society some part of the force which had produced the Alphabet and its four books. In 1876 William Willes, one-time regent of the University, forwarded to the *New York Sun* a new alphabet to be submitted to the consideration of the American Philological Association. "We presume," said the *Sun*, "that Mr. Willes is aware that scores, if not hundreds, of new alphabets, some of them very ingenious, have been invented and published within the past half century, and he may know that the question of changing our alphabet in the interest of spelling reform has been under deliberation for a year past by the American philological association, which lately held its convention in this city. But that body took ground against all the proposed schemes of alphabetical change, and declared that the Roman alphabet is so widely and firmly established among the leading civilized nations that it cannot be

[116] *Laws of Utah* (1872), 41.

[117] Ellerbeck, in Carter, *Four Outstanding Activities of the Pioneers*, 4.

[118] F. D. Richards, ["Utah Miscellany," 15, Bancroft Library; quoted in part in Bancroft, *History of Utah*, 714].

displaced; therefore, in adapting it to improved use for English, the efforts of American scholars should be directed toward its use with uniformity and in conformity with other nations. Under these circumstances it would be useless to publish in the *Sun*, for the sake of the association, the curious alphabet sent to us from Salt Lake by Mr. Willes."[119]

To the end Brigham Young clung to his vision of a reformed English orthography. It is curiously fitting that his death closed the final endeavor. In July, 1877, it was decided that Orson Pratt should go to England to investigate the possibility of publishing some of the Mormon scriptures in Pitman. He left Salt Lake City on July 18, and next month arrived safely in England. To a conference at Leeds, on September 2, 1877, he said, "I am not on a mission specially to preach, but am preparing the 'Book of Mormon' and 'Doctrine and Covenants' for publication in the phonotype characters adopted by Mr. Pitman and others." He thought "there was sufficient union among the Saints to establish this reform,—a reform which the lack of union in England and the United States prevents. It was not the intention to discard the old system at present, but to retain most of the characters of the old alphabet."[120]

But Brigham Young died in the Lion House at Salt Lake City on August 29. On September 3 Pratt and Joseph F. Smith were called home. They sailed on the 12th, and arrived in Salt Lake City on the 27th. Mormon experimentation in alphabetic and orthographic reform never again lifted its head.

Viewed with seventy years' perspective, the Deseret Alphabet never had a chance of success. It complicated, rather than simplified, the problem of education. Mastery of the alphabet did not relieve the student of the necessity for mastering the intricacies of unreformed English orthography. The Deseret Alphabet could be dispensed with; ultimately, the Roman alphabetic representation of English language could not. Nothing could relieve the Mormon people of their dependence on that great cultural heritage of the world, English literature . . . unless these were indeed "the last days" when things-as-they-are no longer had an indefinite permanence.

Apart from its theoretical impracticability, the Deseret Alphabet was physically impracticable. Whatever superiority through its phonetic structure it may have enjoyed over the Roman Alphabet as an instrument for the rendition of English, was more than counterbalanced by the physical clumsiness of the

[119] *Salt Lake Daily Herald*, 6 September 1876.

[120] *Millennial Star* 39 (1877): 605.

characters. It had been an announced purpose of the originators to produce an alphabet lending itself equally to print and to script; if the published examples of the Alphabet are faithful to this ideal, a more difficult script would be hard to find. Even for the printed page the tailless characters and monotonous evenness of the lines made the characters unsatisfactory, as the words were difficult to distinguish. The structural complexity of many of the letters, moreover, rendered the Alphabet greatly inferior to Pitman as a shorthand for conventional English, and there is no record that anyone, including Watt himself, ever used the Alphabet for any "phonographic" purpose.

Nor could the Alphabet meet the expectations entertained concerning it as an instrument for the establishment of uniform pronunciation. Reflecting upon the incidence of dialect among people who nominally speak the same tongue, one would conceive that a system of writing founded upon the ear would be a system in constant grave danger of disintegration into unintelligibility. It was doubtless in appreciation of this danger that the regents of the University displayed such anxiety to complete an Alphabet version of Webster's Unabridged Dictionary. But even an accessible dictionary would be inadequate [to] combat the doctrine that a word is properly written when written in accordance with its apparent sound. Further, the arbitrary simplification of English pronunciation proposed by the Alphabet entailed a host of complications. The signs adopted for sounds were inadequate to meet all the demands made upon them, so that problems of orthography were occasionally solved in a most astonishingly arbitrary manner, as when the stonecutter rendered, on John Morris' tombstone, the wordy "Denbyshire" as D E N B ESH UR. The Alphabet was Procrustean in its demands upon the language, and sound was mongrelized, thickened and distorted to meet conditions of its Alphabet orthography, as in the rendition of "sixth" as S Ě K S ETH, "edition" as Ě D ESH Ǒ N, or "suspension" as S Ǒ S P Ǎ N ESH N. So little aural sensitivity was displayed in the creation of the Alphabet that it was not until the final version was brought forth in the books published in 1868–69 that *ǐ* was rendered other than as an indistinguishable variation of *ě*.[121]

[121] Accenting was also a problem, first taken up, according to Hosea Stout, on February 25, 1856 [*On the Mormon Frontier*, 2: 593]. The article in the Alphabet printed in the *Deseret News* on 7 September 1859, was accompanied by a brief explanatory note, also in the Alphabet, which is translated, "The ' {apostrophe} when used denotes a suspension of the voice [i.e., a vocal stop]." Examples were taken from [Noah] Webster's *Elementary Spelling Book* [Hartford, Conn.: Brown & Parsons, 1843], 63. Since the Alphabet dealt rather arbitrarily with syllabification, difficulties teachers would have encountered, using the Alphabet in the elementary grades, may be readily imagined.

Jules Remy was among the first to evaluate the Alphabet except with the eye of faith. The characters he thought "as simple as they are inelegant," and although some persons had supposed the object of the Alphabet that of preventing access to Mormon books and writings, "it is more probable that the only thing intended was to simplify the reading of the English language by establishing a determinate and uniform relation between the sign and its sound." Although it might be regrettable that there should be in any language a discrepancy between a sound and the sign that represents it, and although efforts to simplify the language by adopting signs which would make the sounds invariable might be both desirable and praiseworthy, nevertheless he thought that "the orthographic innovation proposed by the Mormon philologists will have no success, and will be abandoned by its own authors, on account of the difficulty that must be experienced in its application, not to speak of the inconveniences to which it would give rise, such as the effacement of etymologies, and the disconnection of roots from their derivatives."[122]

Sir Richard F. Burton, in 1860, remarked that as man prefers two alphabets to one, the Deseret Alphabet would "probably share the fate of the 'Fonetik Nuz.'"[123] The opinion of a New York editor in 1857, that institution of the alphabet was a step in the furtherance of Mormon exclusiveness, was picked up by others, notably by Bancroft, who commented in 1889 that a Mormon object in the experimentation with the Alphabet was exclusiveness, "a separate people wishing to have a separate language, and perhaps in time an independent literature."[124] Notwithstanding the fact that this idea was vigorously disputed by Brigham H. Roberts in 1914,[125] when it was pointed out that the Mormons throughout their history worked "for closer union of the Latter-day Saints with their fellow citizens of the United States, not exclusiveness, either in community life or literature,"[126] a reputable

[122]Remy and Brenchley, *Journey to Great Salt Lake City*, 2: 184–185. In his cited report of 19 February 1868, Robert L. Campbell indirectly replied to Remy when he quoted an authority who referred to "the original and proper office of orthography, to indicate pronunciation"; and to "the improper office of orthography, which some would assert for it, of a guide to etymology." But no teacher of English could with any happiness regard the loss to the language of the two functions mentioned by Remy.

[123]Burton, *City of the Saints*, 419.

[124]Bancroft, *History of Utah*, 712.

[125]In *Americana Magazine*, later reprinted in his *Comprehensive History of the Church*, 5: 79–80.

[126]In view of the social relations of Mormons with non-Mormons, and the attitude, for example, toward marriage outside the Church, Roberts' statement cannot be accepted as properly representing Mormon society in local terms. In the large, however, his contention seems borne out by the acts, and the question of the Deseret Alphabet has primary reference to the total relationship of the Mormons to society.

historian[127] suggested in 1917 that the Alphabet could bear investigation as an effort toward establishing a private language serving a separatist function.

The late A. L. Neff examined the Alphabet more carefully than anyone before him, and made the valuable point that for a Territory so relatively impoverished as Utah in pioneer times, it was a signal misfortune that so much money should have been sunk in financing so bootless an undertaking, thus retarding the evolution of the educational system generally.[128*] However, Neff interpreted this experiment as merely a freakish divagation on the part of the Mormon leaders. Such a view reads the Alphabet out of context. One must remember that the Deseret Alphabet was, after its fashion, no more startling, incongruous, or unreasonable an innovation than was brought forth by the Mormons in other fields of human endeavor. The Mormons considered that they broke all bounds in their introduction of their religion itself. No social or cultural experiment could be other than incidental to the tremendous fact of Mormonism. Mormon history is full of sudden unorthodoxies. The Deseret Alphabet can hardly be evaluated outside its place in the large picture. To dwell largely on its utter futility, in the light of history, is to say merely that, conspicuously, it did not work, that it is without defenders, that—in a word—it is a dead horse to be flogged.

The Deseret Alphabet originated in the restless receptivity of the Mormon people to their time-spirit. Orthographic reform was abroad in the age, and this reflected in Mormon society as did countless other forces of custom and idea. The relationship of Mormon thinking to the religious ferment of the eastern frontier has been often enough remarked. In an age of group experimentation with the sexual relationship, ranging all the way from free love to celibacy, the institution of polygamy by the Mormons

---

[127]Franklin D. Daines, "Separatism in Utah," *Annual Report of the American Historical Association for the Year 1917* (Washington, D.C.: GPO, 1917): 348. However, the late Professor Daines was sketching a method of thinking for the critical evaluation of Mormon history, not offering a serious historical judgment.

[128]Neff, *History of Utah*, 854–855. Neff assumes that money spent on the Alphabet otherwise would have been spent on other educational purposes. This cannot be substantiated, and the probabilities are against it. The Alphabet was educational in purpose and character, but the force behind it was religious at base, and the expenditures must be considered as of semi-religious nature. The case actually was one of appropriations made for the direct benefit of the Alphabet, rather than of educational appropriations made, from which a proportion was diverted to furthering the cause of the Alphabet—the University of the State of Deseret thus was merely a channel through which the money flowed.

*[Morgan drafted a slightly longer and more forceful but less focused closing argument which was replaced by the text reproduced here. The superseded pages (71–74) are filed with the manuscript at the conclusion of the article, and the versions diverge after note 128. —Ed.]

does not surprise the sociologist. Experimentation with socialistic societies and with small communes, and characteristic feature of the social development of America after 1800, is reflected in Mormon history by the United Order and by a variety of "joint stock" enterprises. Even so small a matter as experimentation in dress for women, instanced in the revolutionary costume popularized by Mrs. Bloomer, has its Mormon echo in the "Deseret costume" unsuccessfully prescribed for Mormon women in 1855. Adoption of a Deseret Alphabet was wholly logical for a people who seized upon the ideas of their time in the firm conviction that they had or could arrive at a better way of doing almost anything.

The Alphabet began as a movement of linguistic reform, and this was always its character. Derivatory ideas might have become important had the Alphabet possessed genuine vitality. Thus, one must note that the *Deseret Evening News* thought that the Alphabet could operate toward selectivity in the reading of the Saints. A repression of the reading range of the people had its undeniable advantages for a leadership that always preached unity and decried an initiative outside the sanctions of authority. A Deseret Alphabet, accepted by the people, can be conceived as an instrument of social control, a means to shape the patterns of thinking and seeing—an instrument, in short, for the social regimentation of the Mormon people. Such a regimentation, the achievement of such a docility, might not have been desirable, but the early Mormon leaders thought it was, and they labored indefatigably to accomplish it as "unity in all things." The might-have-beens of the Deseret Alphabet, apart from considerations of national and international acceptance, are endless and need not be explored.

There is no reason, however, to believe that the Alphabet ever captured the imagination of the Saints. Not even of the other leaders besides Brigham Young. Preaching of the Alphabet was motivated by religious zealotry rather than by educational conviction; there was a right way to think about the Alphabet as there was a right way to think about all the problems and projects of the Saints.[129] But the Alphabet had no vitality of its own; it merely reflected the vitality of a religion.

Innovations by the Mormons in the sphere of religion and social relationships were, essentially, innovations in the realm of ideas. Polygamy and the

---

[129]Cf. the loyal submissiveness of Daniel H. Wells in his comment on 31 January 1859. (see p.____ [i.e., comment cited in note 56]).

United Order had only stubborn social environments and the paradoxes of human nature to contend with. The Deseret Alphabet had a sterner antagonist. It was crushed by the majestic weight of English literature.

Works Printed in the Deseret Alphabet

Books.

The Deseret First Book. New York: Russell Brothers, 1868. 36 pp.
The Deseret Second Book. New York: Russell Brothers, 1868. 72 pp.
The Book of Nephi. New York: Russell Brothers, 1869. 116 pp. {This is the cover title. It is printed from the same plates as *The Book of Mormon,* and its title page is identical with that of the latter except that it is denoted "Part I."}
The Book of Mormon. New York: Russell Brothers, 1869. 443 pp.

Articles printed in the Deseret News.

There is much variance in the style of the titles used for these excerpts, with numbers sometimes spelled out and sometimes not, the chapter number sometimes preceding the title of the chapter, and sometimes not. As no useful purpose is to be served by a literal "translation," an arbitrary style has been adopted for this newspaper bibliography. [Morgan's use of Roman numerals in chapter references is also converted to standard form here. —Ed.]

February 16, 1859: Matthew 5: 1–15.
February 23, 1859: Matthew 5: 16–48.
March 2, 1859: Matthew 6: 1–12.
March 9, 1859: Matthew 6: 14–26.
March 16, 1859: Matthew 6: 27–34.
March 23, 1859: Matthew 7: 1–10.
April 6, 1859: Matthew 7: 11–20.
April 13, 1859: Matthew 7: 21–20.
April 20, 1859: Proverbs 16: 1–10.
April 27, 1859: Proverbs 16: 11–20.
May 4, 1859: Proverbs 16: 21–29.
May 11, 1859: Proverbs 17: 1–10.
May 18, 1859: Proverbs 17: 11–20.
May 25, 1859: Proverbs 17: 21–28.
June 1, 1859: Psalm 52: 1–9.
June 8, 1859: Isaiah 34: 1–6.
June 15, 1859: Isaiah 34: 7–13.

June 22, 1859: Isaiah 34: 14–17.
June 29, 1859: Psalm 26: 1–12.
July 6, 1859: Psalm 66: 1–10.
July 13, 1859: Psalm 66: 11–20.
July 20, 1859: Book of Mormon, Second European Edition [Liverpool, 1849], p. 301[–302] [Alma LDS 33: 1–11; Alma CC 16: 174–184]
July 27, 1859: Book of Mormon, Second European Edition, p. 44. [1 Nephi LDS 19: 1–2; 1 Nephi CC 5: 218–22]
August 3, 1859: Book of Mormon, Second European Edition, p. 248. [Alma LDS 13: 27–31; Alma CC 10: 27–31]
August 10, 1859: Psalm 87: 1–7.
August 17, 1859: Proverbs 22: 1–7.
August 24, 1859: Isaiah 27: 1–6.
August 31, 1859: Doctrine and Covenants, Fourth American Edition [Nauvoo, 1846], p. 91, sec. 2, par. 1. [*D&C* LDS 20: 1–4; *D&C* CC 17: 1a–c]
September 7, 1859: Doctrine and Covenants, Fourth American Edition, p. 91, sec. 2, par. 2. [*D&C* LDS 20: 5–12; *D&C* CC 17: 2a–g]*
September 14, 1859: Revelation on Prayer, Given October, 1831. [*D&C* LDS 65: 1–6; *D&C* CC 65: 1a–f]
September 21, 1859: The Testimony of Eight Witnesses of the Book of Mormon.
September 28, 1859: Matthew 18: 1–9.
October 12, 1859: Isaiah 43: 1–7.
October 19, 1859: Ecclesiastes 4: 1–6.
November 2, 1859: First Epistle General of John 1: 1–6.
November 9, 1859: Ecclesiastes 5: 1–7.
November 16, 1859: Deuteronomy 8: 1–6.
November 23, 1859: Deuteronomy 7: 7–12.

*[Morgan failed to note that following the extract is a short uncaptioned section which reads: "this ' when used denotes a suspension of the voice. Webster's elementary spelling book, page 63. Number 79," followed by a triple column of words spelled with the mark in place, each showing a slight vocal stop between syllables, as transliterated here: a'ria'l (aerial), no'tib'l (notable), interio'r (interior) in the first line; an'ooi'ti (annuity), ma'teri'al (material), imperi'l (imperial) in the second line; mi'mori'l (memorial), imperi'l (imperial, a second time), aksteri'r (exterior) in the third. The stops are not phonological and were probably no more than vagaries of common dialect or pronunciation. My thanks to Larry Draper for confirming the *D&C* citations against volumes in the BYU collections. —Ed.]

November 30, 1859:	Deuteronomy 8: 13–17.
December 14, 1859:	Deuteronomy 8: 18–20.
December 21, 1859:	A Revelation, Given May, 1833, sec. 1. [D&C LDS 93: 1–11; D&C CC 90: 1a–g]
December 28, 1859:	A Revelation, Given May, 1833, sec. 2. [D&C LDS 93: 12–17; D&C CC 90: 2a–d]
January 4, 1860:	A Revelation, Given May 1833, secs. 3–4. [D&C LDS 93:18–28; D&C CC 90: 3a–4e]
January 11, 1860:	A Revelation, Given May 1833, sec. 5. [D&C LDS 93: 29–35; D&C CC 90: 5a–f]
January 25, 1860:	A Revelation, Given May 1833, sec. 6. [D&C LDS 93: 36–43; D&C CC 90: 6a–f]
February 1, 1860:	A Revelation, Given May 1833, secs. 7–8. [D&C LDS 93: 44–49; D&C CC 90: 7–8d]
February 8, 1860:	{Article of previous week reprinted.}
February 15, 1860:	Doctrine and Covenants, Second European Edition [Liverpool, 1849], sec. 12, par. 1. [D&C LDS 38: 1–6; D&C CC 38: 1a–e]
February 22, 1860:	{Article of previous week reprinted.}
February 29, 1860:	Proverbs 7: 1–10.
March 7, 1860:	{Article of previous week reprinted.}
March 14, 1860:	{Article of previous week reprinted.}
March 21, 1860:	Proverbs 26: 1–8
April 11, 1860:	Psalm 144: 1–6.
April 18, 1860:	Doctrine and Covenants, Fourth European Edition [Liverpool, 1849], p. 269, sec. [part] 6. [D&C LDS 76: 71–78; D&C CC 76: 6a–f]
April 25, 1860:	{Alphabet itself was printed, but no text, perhaps crowded out by other matter.}
May 2, 1860:	Luke 5: 20–23.
May 11, 1864:	Proverbs 24[: 1–12]
May 18, 1864:	Doctrine and Covenants [Nauvoo, 1846], sec. 103, par. 13. [D&C LDS 124: 40–46; not in D&C CC]
May 25, 1864:	Doctrine and Covenants [Liverpool, 1852], p. 283, par. 12. [D&C LDS 101: 85–95; D&C CC 98: 11d–12e, both with slight variation]

June 1, 1864:	Doctrine and Covenants [Liverpool, 1849], p. 303, par. 15. [D&C LDS 124:49–51; not in D&C CC]
June 8, 1864:	Revelation Given February, 1834; Doctrine and Covenants [Liverpool, 1849, section 101], p. 291 [D&C LDS 103:1–4; D&C CC 100:1a–b]
June 15, 1864:	Revelation Given February, 1834, par. 2 [Cincinnati, 1864] [D&C LDS 103:5–10; D&C CC 100:2a–d]
June 22, 1864:	Doctrine and Covenants [edition unknown], p. 206, par. 54 [D&C LDS 31:1–5; D&C CC 31:1a–e]
June 29, 1864:	Doctrine and Covenants [Nauvoo, 1846], sec. 38, pars. 1–2 [D&C LDS 6, 11, 12, 14:1–5; D&C CC 6, 10–12:1a–2c]
July 6, 1864:	Ecclesiastes 8[: 1–3]
July 13, 1864:	Proverbs 18[: 1–7]
July 20, 1864:	Zephaniah 3[: 1–7]
July 27, 1864:	Micah 4[: 1–4]
August 10, 1864:	Joel 2: 18[–22]
August 17, 1864:	Isaiah 10[: 1–4]
August 24, 1864:	Nahum 1[: 1–5]

Chapter 6

The Danites in Mormon History

Missouri Phase (1944)

Editor's Introduction

In 1944, at about the same time that he began claiming to be at work on a "rough draft of the Mormon history on which I have worked so exhaustively at the research [through] the past five years,"[1] Dale Morgan also began thinking of related narrow topics which would be short enough to produce quickly, but substantive enough to garner attention and important enough to be a profitable expenditure of time and energy. He considered and ultimately discarded writing about the followers of Joseph Morris, who led a millenarian schism in the midst of 1860s Utah, and a number of fur-trade topics. One of the topics which actually did filter through his typewriter into written form included a serious study into the origins of the mythical "avenging angels" of nineteenth-century anti-Mormon folklore, the Danites. "I have paid particular attention to all the questions in Mormon history most argued over, most confused in the literature, and most distorted as to presentation of the actual facts," he wrote to *Pacific Historical Review* editor Louis Koontz. "On some of these questions I have organized monograph studies."[2] "Organized" was a loosely used word; it would be more accurate to say that he had formed an interest in the topic and began gathering source material. The major difference between Morgan's early idea for studies of the Morris schism and the Danites was that he actually committed the latter to paper.

[1]DLM to Rod Korns, 19 May 1944. This statement was a misrepresentation, unless one consider the Kingdom of God study set aside in 1940 as part of the process. He did not begin conceptual drafts for his history until July 1948 at the earliest.

[2]DLM to Louis Koontz, 22 July 1944.

This particular topic had its origin in a discussion by letter with Fawn Brodie in September 1943, but actual composition on the Danites piece dates nearly a year later to the following August.[3] Dale felt that a study of the Danites illustrated Joseph Smith's reliance on expedience and called into question the idea of revelation in the second Missouri period (1833–1839). Hints also show up among Morgan's letters that he might have felt that understanding the origins of the group could hold a clue to the thinking or emotions behind the Mountain Meadows massacre of 1857. By the mid 1940s he had established a reciprocal arrangement with Juanita Brooks of St. George, Utah. Each shared with the other what documentary material they uncovered. Brooks would rely heavily on Morgan's research to complete her study of the massacre in 1949 and see it to publication the next year.

That was not the only reason for the study. With "The Danites in Mormon History" Morgan also clearly intends to wag a historiologic finger at contemporary Mormon writers: if Latter Day Saint historians did not expect history to reinforce their religious belief and looked without patriotic bias at the documents that were directly in front of them, they could not reach any other conclusion than what he reaches. "It is my experience that if you gather enough facts, and organize them properly," Morgan had written RLDS archivist S. A. Burgess in 1943, "they provide their own conclusions."[4] This attitude sets the tone for his later work, but it is also here that he first strays into the thorny area of imputing facts with motivation, a problem which would plague his later attempt at broader cultural synthesis in *The Mormons*. His invocation of "persecution complex, frustration complex, religious dementia" relative to Rigdon's 1838 Fourth of July oration is lifted straight from Freud, a clue about how thoroughly that he had absorbed both the language and categories—with the implicit assumptions rooted in positivism—straight from post-collegiate readings in the literature of 1920s psychology, a time when the major writers in the field claimed almost unequivocally that human motivation had been circumscribed with scientific certainty.

As good as it is, the Danite study also stands as a clear example of Morgan's failure to look for larger contexts in favor of looking at immediate details. Convinced that a naturalistic explanation could be found primarily

[3]DLM to Fawn Brodie, 10 September 1943, *Dale Morgan on Early Mormonism: Correspondence and a New History* (Salt Lake City: Signature Books, 1986), 46–49; DLM to FMB, 8, 14 February 1944 (duplicated in Madeline McQuown papers, Marriott Library Special Collections, Univ. of Utah); DLM to Brodie, 3 August 1944, McQuown papers.

[4]DLM to S. A. Burgess, 26 April 1943.

in Joseph Smith's mind and personality, Morgan failed to look beyond the saints themselves to see what tensions and forces were at play between the Mormons and established Missourians, and Missouri in the context of national politics. While internal factors within the LDS church certainly drove the unfolding tragedy, the work of scholars a generation later has shown how intertwined both internal and external factors were across the conflict, a much more accurate view of human existence.[5]

Whatever his immediate motivation, Morgan's study of the Danites was probably the first credible attempt to understand the group and its origins. Despite never being published, the work was path breaking within Latter Day Saint history. Morgan sees the second phase of the Saints' trouble in Missouri as a direct extension of the social tensions present in the messy social meltdown in Kirtland, Ohio, in 1836–37. There the leadership had allowed dissent to grow effectively unchallenged until the community of believers was riven. Having fled Ohio and seeing that toleration of differences did not work, in Missouri, Morgan paints leaders as overreaching their response again but in the opposite direction. To Morgan's eyes, the Latter Day Saints' leadership, making defensive but heavy-handed attempts to prevent a repeat of the Kirtland apostasy of the previous year by refusing dissenters a place within the community—forcibly if necessary—took a tack precisely opposite to the one taken in Ohio. This move was circumstantially coupled to the Sidney Rigdon's intemperate oratory, all shackled by the opportunistic machinations of individuals, particularly Sampson Avard. It was a subtle interpretation. In this piece he neatly dismisses the old anti-Mormon folklore while playing true to source material and offering a new set of interpretations.

The Danites in Mormon History: Missouri Phase

The Danites are one of the most cherished themes of frontier taletellers.[1] The idea of bearded zealots banded together in a fellowship of murder,

[5]Cf. Ronald K. Esplin, "The Emergence of Brigham Young and the Twelve to Mormon Leadership, 1830–41," (Ph.D. dissertation, Brigham Young Univ., 1981); John E. Thompson, "A Chronology of Danite Meetings in Adam-ondi-Ahman, Missouri, July to September 1838," *Restoration* 4 (January 1985): 11–14; Steven C. LeSueur, "Missouri's Failed Compromise: The Creation of Caldwell County for the Mormons," *Journal of Mormon History* 32, no. 3 (Fall 2005): 113–144.

[1]Later phases of the controversial Danite history will be examined in a study to follow. With respect to the present monography [*sic*], I wish to make special acknowledgement to Fawn M. Brodie, who for her forthcoming biography of Joseph Smith, the first work of proper scholarship done on the founder of Mormonism, has paralleled my own research. Mrs. Brodie has been generous in (*continued, next page*)

pursuing hapless apostates and quaking wayfarers along the Western trails in the name of the Lord God Jehovah, has a purple magnificence which a hundred years has not faded. Historians, however, have found the Danites a thorny topic, an irritating and baffling problem in any assessment of the history of either Mormonism or the West.

It has not been possible to accept the contention of the Mormons that the Danites have been principally an invention of anti-Mormon malice and of sensation-mongers, but neither has it been possible to accept the spectacle of wholesale slaughter painted by the enemies of the Mormons. Historians have walked away gingerly in this no-man's-land, not sure what to believe and unwilling to evaluate the Danites as a reality, although the importance of the facts is not confined to Mormon history, being significant also in evaluation of the journals of overland travelers after the discovery of gold in California.

Evidence that there was a repressive or terroristic organization among the Mormons prior to the appearance of the Danite society in Missouri is so unsatisfactory as to add up to little more than malicious gossip. The anonymous biographer of Porter Rockwell asserts that such a group was organized among the Mormons at Kirtland, Ohio, about 1835. Rockwell, Joseph Smith, Sidney Rigdon, Oliver Cowdery, and Simon (i.e., David W.) Patten are named as the original five Danites, and accused of the assassination of one Jamison, "said to be the leader of the party that tarred and feathered Joe Smith in 1838 or 1839."[2] But no credence can be given this statement,

---

contributing materials, and I am especially indebted for permission to quote from the valuable manuscript narrative of Reed Peck. [See note 8. The treatment of the "later phases" that Morgan promises was never written, nor pursued so far as I have been able to find. The second Missouri period has since been addressed by Steven C. LeSueur in three works, *The 1838 Mormon War in Missouri* (Columbia: Univ. of Missouri Press, 1986), *"A Scarter Man Than One of Them Was I Never Saw": Attitudes and Perceptions of Missourians during the 1838 Mormon War* (Sandy, Utah: Mormon Miscellaneous, 1986), and "Missouri's Failed Compromise: The Creation of Caldwell County for the Mormons," *Journal of Mormon History* 31, no. 3 (Fall 2005): 113–144; and by Leland H. Gentry, *A History of the Latter-day Saints in Northern Missouri from 1836 to 1839* (Provo, Utah: Joseph Fielding Smith Institute for Latter-day Saint History and BYU Studies, ca. 2000), and "The Danite Band of 1838," *BYU Studies* 14, no. 4 (1974): 421–450; and Alexander L. Baugh, "A Call to Arms: The 1838 Mormon Defense of Northern Missouri," Thesis (Ph.D., Brigham Young University, 1996). —Ed.]

[2]Achilles [pseud.], *The Destroying Angels of Mormondom* (San Francisco: Alta California Printing House, 1878), 8. The Bancroft Library possesses a copy of this pamphlet, so rare as to be possibly unique. [Seventy years later the Bancroft copy remains unique. At this writing Morgan had not yet encountered the note in the *Salt Lake Daily Herald*, 6 August 1878, identifying "Achilles" as Samuel D. Sirrine. The author was later a notary in Yountville, Calif. —Ed.]

and effort made to bolster the idea of a band of "Kirtland avengers" has adduced no useful proofs.[3] Concerning the Danite society actually organized in Missouri, however, the principal facts may be readily established. The Danites may be regarded as an immediate consequence of the break-up of the Mormon church in Ohio.

The disruption in Ohio followed directly from the failure of the Kirtland Bank and the collapse, under the impact of the Panic of 1837, of inflated land values in the Kirtland area. Dangerous dissensions appeared in the church, extending not only to the membership generally but to the Quorum of the Twelve Apostles and the First Presidency. By December the Kirtland dissension had progressed so far that, as Joseph Smith writes, the dissenters "openly and publicly renounced the Church of Christ of Latter-day Saints and claimed themselves to be the old standard . . . and set me at naught, and the whole Church, denouncing us as heretics, not considering that the Saints shall possess the Kingdom according to the Prophet Daniel."[4] Within a month the debacle was complete, and on January 12, 1838, Smith and Rigdon fled Kirtland. Smith arrived at Far West, Missouri, March 14 and Rigdon three weeks later.

The Kirtland disintegration had been an experience of a kind to arouse in the Mormon leaders a corroding bitterness, an angry apprehension, and a thorough determination to root out dissenters and obstructionists. The entire position of the church was dangerously insecure. Kirtland was in violent apostasy, and the state of things even in Missouri was not good. Just prior to the arrival of Smith and Rigdon, a cleavage had developed in Far West and David and John Whitmer and W. W. Phelps were summoned to be tried on various charges. These three men, the local presidency, denied the right of the local council to try them, the consequence of which was that John Whitmer and Phelps were summarily disfellowshipped, an action taken also, soon after the arrival of Smith and Rigdon, in the cases of Oliver Cowdery, David Whitmer, and Lyman E. Johnson.[5]

---

[3]cf. Charles Kelly and Hoffman Birney, *Holy Murder: The Story of Porter Rockwell* (New York: Minton, Balch & Co., 1934), 15–18. This sensationalized biography of Porter Rockwell contains much misinterpretation and misstatement of fact, and too many of its conclusions are inacceptable, but it has served a useful purpose in floodlighting facts in Mormon history which should have critical attention.

[4]*History of the Church of Jesus Christ of Latter-day Saints,* ed. B. H. Roberts, 7v. (Salt Lake City: The Church, 1902–1912), 2: 509–511.

[5]*History of the Church,* 3: 3–7, 16–20.

All these men had been powers in the church from the time of its foundation. Cowdery had written most of the manuscript of the Book of Mormon to Smith's dictation, and he was the church's second elder. The Whitmers were among the witnesses to the Book of Mormon. Phelps had established in 1832 the first newspaper published by the church, and Johnson was one of the original Quorum of the Twelve. Their influence among the membership was potentially great; there was reason to feel that a considerable sympathy existed between them and the Kirtland rebels; and what had just happened in Kirtland was a staggering example of what could be accomplished by an organized opposition. Excommunication of these men by no means eradicated the danger, as they had no disposition to leave Far West, and they might readily become the spearhead of a new apostasy. The strongest logic called for their physical expulsion from the community.

In law there was no means by which this might be accomplished. But western Missouri in 1838 was the farther frontier. The frontier had its own laws; and, moreover, Missouri itself less than five years before had provided a precedent when the "old settlers" in Jackson County drove the Mormons from their Promised Land.

Apart from these considerations, powerful and compelling emotions were abroad among the Mormons. In the Last Days the Lord had enjoined upon them the duty of gathering to His revealed Zion, and yet they had been forcibly expelled from Zion into the northern counties of Missouri. With their outrage, their smouldering anger and their bitterness, was mingled a high sense of self-consecration and an unreasoning zeal—an incipient fanaticism of dangerous potentialities.

Sidney Rigdon touched fire to this tinder. A man of violent emotions, vindictive, and with a command of invective unrivaled in Mormon annals except by James J. Strang, Rigdon gave evidence of an inflammatory state of mind almost immediately after his arrival in Far West. At a meeting in April Joseph Smith announced bluntly that he intended having no more processes served on him, that "the officer who attempted it should die; that any person who spoke or acted against the Presidency of the Church should leave the county or die; and that he should suffer no such to remain there; that they should lose their heads." George W. Harris interposed, "The head of their influence, I suppose," and Smith, perhaps brought back to reality, agreed to that interpretation. But Rigdon intervened harshly. By "the head of their influence," he said, he meant "the ball of their shoulders, called the head, and that they should be followed to the ends of the earth."[6] Such language may have been designed to overawe factious spirits, but the intransigent feeling displayed was exactly calculated to arouse the membership of the church.

There were, moreover, unsettling ideas and emotions abroad among the Mormons during the spring of 1838. For eight years they had lived under a sense of crisis; the imminence of the establishment of the Kingdom of God was a deep conviction in all their thinking, religious and social. The prophet vision of Daniel was soon to achieve fulfillment, a kingdom established which should break in pieces all other kingdoms and stand forever. In the fall preceding, Joseph Smith had intimated to the Saints in Missouri that the principles of consecrations were again to be practiced among the Saints; one of the issues with Cowdery and the Whitmers had been their coolness toward this idea. Elaborate preparations were being made for the gathering here of the Saints from the far places of the earth, and a temple was to be builded to the Lord in Far West. Anything less than perfect unison imperiled the rolling forth of the Kingdom, and the very presence of the dissenters was a profound irritant. By mid-June that refractory element in the community had become intolerable.

To drive from Caldwell County all those who dissented from the Mormon church was, Sampson Avard says, the original object for which the Danite Band was formed,[7] and this is the implication also of Ebenezer Robinson and John Corrill.[8] The origin of the Danite movement can apparently be traced directly to a meeting at Far West the second week of June, called by Jared Carter and Dimick B. Huntington. At this meeting, Reed Peck says, a proposition was made to rid the community of the dissenters by killing them, but owing to the opposition of John Corrill and Thomas B. Marsh,

---

[6]Missouri General Assembly, *Documents Containing the Correspondence, Orders &c in Relation to the Disturbance with the Mormons. . .* (Fayette, Mo.: Printed at the Office of the Boon's Lick Democrat, 1841), hereafter cited as *Missouri Documents* [The documents were reprinted not quite in full for Congress under the title *Document Showing the Testimony Given Before the Judge of the Fifth Judicial Circuit of the State of Missouri . . .*, 26th Congress, 2nd session, Senate Doc. 189 (Serial 378). Although he worked from the printing cited, Morgan's manuscript does not include a single complete reference for any citation to the *Documents Containing*, which Morgan cites here by the abbreviation *Missouri Documents*. Since the congressional reprint is the more widely available version, page numbers from that edition are given here, in editorial brackets, rather than from the original Missouri state publication. —Ed.]. Quotation is from the testimony of John Whitmer at the hearings in Richmond, Missouri, in November 1838 (p. [33]). W. W. Phelps corroborated his account of this meeting (p. [43–44]).

[7]Avard's testimony, *Missouri Documents*, [1].

[8]Ebenezer Robinson, ["Items of Personal History," n.6] *The Return* 1, no. 10 (October 1889): 146–147; Corrill's testimony, *Missouri Documents*, [13].

the latter of whom was president of the Quorum of the Twelve, the meeting broke up without accomplishing anything.[9]

When, however, Rigdon encountered Corrill on the street, he told him brusquely that he ought to have nothing to do with the matter, that they should do as they pleased,[10] and on the Sunday following, June 17, 1838, he delivered in the presence of a large congregation at Far West what has since been famous as the Salt Sermon.

> S. Rigdon took his text {Peck says} from the fifth chapter of Mathew "Ye are the salt of the Earth but if the salt have lost its savor wherewith shall it be salted, it is henceforth good for nothing but to be cast out and be trodden underfoot of men" From this Scripture he undertook to prove that when men embrace the gospel and afterwards lose their faith, it is the duty of the Saints to trample them under their feet He informed the people that they have a set of men among them that have dissented from the church and were doing all in their power to destroy the presidency, laying plans to take their lives &c., accused them of counterfeiting lying cheating and numeour other crimes and called on the people to rise en mass and rid the county of such an nuisance He said it is the duty of this people to trample them into the earth and if the county cannot be freed from them any other way I will assist to trample them down or to erect a gallows on the square of Far West and hang them up as they did the gamblers at Vicksburgh and it would be an act at which the angels would smile with approbation.
>
> Joseph Smith in a short speech sanctioned what had been said by Rigdon though said he I don't want the brethren to act unlawfully but will tell them one thing Judas was a traitor and instead of hanging himself was hung by Peter, and with this hint the subject was dropped for the day having created a great excitement and prepared the people to execute any thing that should be proposed.[11]

[9]Reed Peck, "Mormons So Called," [Cake, *Peepstone Joe,* 88]. The original of this important narrative, written at Quincy, Illinois, in 1838, is now in the possession of Fawn M. Brodie, Washington, D.C. It was printed by Lu B. Cake in his *Peepstone Joe and the Peck Manuscript: Mormonism Exposed* (New York: Author, 1899), copies of which are owned by the Library of Congress and the New York Public Library. [Brodie gave Peck's manuscript to the Huntington Library in August 1946, but Dale made a complete transcription in 1942 or 1943, which may be found in carton 20 among his papers at the Bancroft Library. Instead of citing the unpaginated original document or Morgan's transcription, the references given here are to the one reasonably widespread publication of the document in Cake's negative polemic. —Ed.]

Peck had his information from Corrill and Marsh. Corrill himself adverted [*sic*] to this meeting in testifying at Richmond: "About last June, I was invited to a private meeting, in which an effort was made to adopt some plan to get rid of the dissenters. There was something I did not like, and opposed it, with others, and it failed. . . . None of the First Presidency was present at the meeting." *Missouri Documents,* [12].

[10]Corrill's testimony, *Missouri Documents,* [12].

[11]Peck [Cake, *Peepstone Joe,* 88–89]. This is the most extended account of the Salt Sermon, and the only one to date it precisely. Many writers have confused the Salt Sermon with Rigdon's even more famous

The Salt Sermon was implemented by Rigdon with a blunt letter which was sent to the five principal dissenters. Accusing them of theft, slander, disturbance of the peace, fraud, counterfeiting, institution of vexatious lawsuits, incitement to riot, and other crimes past and present, the letter warned the five men that they had three days to get out of the county, failing which "a more fatal calamity" should befall them. Eighty-three prominent Mormons signed their names to this document.[12]

Alarmed at these developments, John Whitmer asked several influential Mormons whether the supremacy of the law was not to be maintained. He got little satisfaction. Alanson Ripley told him that "as to the technical niceties of the law of the land, he did not intend to regard them; that the kingdom spoken of by the Prophet Daniel had been set up, and that it was necessary every kingdom should be governed by its own laws." George W. Robinson, Rigdon's son-in-law, had to say only that "when God spake he must be obeyed, whether his word came in contact with the law of the land or not; and that as the kingdom spoken of by Daniel had been set up, its laws must be obeyed." As to its being contrary to the law of the land to drive men from their homes, such things had been done of old, and the gathering of the Saints must continue, and dissenters could not live among the Mormons in peace. Whitmer went to talk to Smith himself, asking how he could allay the excitement. He was told that if he would place his property in the hands of the Bishop and High Council to be disposed of according to the laws of the church, that might improve the state of public feeling, as after a while the church might have confidence in him. "I wish to be governed by the laws of the land," Whitmer insisted stubbornly, to which Smith replied only, "Now you wish to pin me down to the law."[13]

Advised to flee by John Corrill,[14] and informed that preparations were

---

Fourth of July oration. Peck's account of the Sermon is corroborated by the Richmond testimony of Avard, Corrill, John Whitmer, and himself. *Missouri Documents,* [9, 12, 33, 20–21. The citation to the "Vicksburgh gamblers" refers to an 1835 lynching of five alleged gaming men in Vicksburg, Mississippi. cf. John E. Thompson, "The Far West Dissenters and the Gamblers at Vicksburg: An Examination of the Documentary Evidence and Historical Context of Sidney Rigdon's 'Salt Sermon,'" *Restoration* 5 (January 1986): 21–27; Joshua D. Rothman, "The Hazards of the Flush Times: Gambling, Mob Violence, and the Anxieties of America's Market Revolution," *Journal of American History* 95, no. 3 (December 2008): 651–677; Thomas Rhys Smith, "Independence Day, 1835: The John A. Murrell Conspiracy and the Lynching of the Vicksburg Gamblers in Literature," *Mississippi Quarterly* 59, no. 1/2 (Winter 2005/Spring 2006): 129–160. —Ed.]

[12]The entire letter, dated merely "June 1838" is printed with Avard's testimony. *Missouri Documents,* [6–9]. Hyrum Smith, brother of the prophet, was among those who signed it.

[13]Whitmer's testimony, *Missouri Documents,* [33].

[14]Corrill's testimony, *Missouri Documents,* [12].

being made to hang them, the Whitmers, Cowdery, and Johnson fled on the Tuesday night following the Salt Sermon, leaving their families and property in the hands of the Mormons.[15] Phelps having a good deal of property, and feeling he would lose it if he fled, stayed behind to make his peace as best he could.[16]

In retrospect it seemed to Reed Peck that the wrath of the presidency and the threats of hanging had been simply a farce acted out to frighten the men from the county. This object had been achieved, but many in the community did not approve, and next Sunday in a public discourse Rigdon felt impelled to explain "the principles of republicanism." "Some characters in the place," he said, "have been crying, 'You have broken the law; you have acted contrary to the principles of republicanism.' When a country, or body of people have individuals among them with whom they do not wish to associate and public expression is taken against them remaining among them and such individuals do not remove, it is the principle of republicanism itself that gives that community a right to expel them forcibly, and no law will prevent it." He added, "It was not against the principles of republicanism for the people to hang the gamblers at Vicksburgh, as it was a matter in which they unanimously acted."[17]

The bold preaching of such doctrine, and the spectacular success of the measures taken against the dissenters, brought the Danite organization out into the light of day. With it came a forceful new personality.

Of Dr. Sampson Avard not much is known. He seems to have left no mark except upon Mormon history, and the distaste Mormon historians have felt for him has not been conducive to research about him in the church archives. Avard joined the church perhaps in 1836 or 1837, for Joseph Smith said of him a little later that he had been a member "but a short time." The first record of him seems to be an entry of April 3, 1837, wherein he is mentioned as an elder in the First Quorum of Elders in Kirtland.[18] By October 18 he had evidently been taken into the High Priests' quorum, for a disciplinary action by that body in on record.[19] But it is as the central genius of the

[15]Peck [Cake, *Peepstone Joe*, 89–90].

[16]Phelps' testimony, *Missouri Documents*, [44]. Phelps apostatized in the autumn, but rejoined the church in 1841, and remained in good standing till his death in 1872.

[17]Peck [Cake, *Peepstone Joe*, 91].

[18]"Record of the First Quorum of Elders belonging to the Church of Christ at Kirtland, Geauga County, Ohio," original document in the library of the [Community of Christ], Independence, Missouri.

[19]*History of the Church*, 2: 519.

Danites, in June, 1838, that he makes his definite entry into Mormon history. Perhaps it is significant that his name stands first among the signatories to the threatening letter to the dissenters.

John Corrill could not say who originated the Danites, but he named Avard as "the most prominent leader and instructor." Inclined to think that the first presidency stood "as the wireworkers behind the curtain," although seeming not to have* much to do with it at first, he found Avard "very forward and indefatigable in accomplishing their purposes, for he devoted his whole talents to it, and spared no pains."[22] Although denying any personal responsibility for Avard, Smith later concurred in this estimate, admitting that "by his smiles and flattery" Avard persuaded his followers to believe "that he had the sanction of the heads of the Church for what he was about to do."[23]

There is some reason to accredit Jared Carter with initiating the Danite society. He had been associated with Dimick Huntington in that abortive first meeting; he was named "captain-general" when the Danites organized on a military basis; and it was as a play upon his name that the Danites first became known. But if Avard was not the person initially responsible for the Danites, he quickly became the society's dominant personality.

The organization at first was called, cryptically, "The Brother of Gideon." This was not a scriptural allusion but a literal reference to the Danite chief himself, as Jared Carter in fact had a brother named Gideon.[24] Effective public allusions were made for some weeks to the "terrible brother of Gideon," the scourge of evil-doers, but within the society itself another and more satisfactory name was sought.

"The Big Fan" was used, presumably figurative of an intention to cleanse the chaff from the wheat, but "The Daughter of Zion" was the name first formally adopted. Micah [4: 13] was the warrant for this name: "Arise, and thresh, O! daughter of Zion; for I will make thy horn iron, and thy hoofs brass; and though shalt beat in pieces many people; and I will consecrate

*[The manuscript pages numbered 7 and 8, though numbered sequentially, seem to both be typed from an earlier and no longer extant draft. They are nearly identical, except that note 19 is repeated, though the notes continue through the remaining pages in sequence. Morgan probably left off and later resumed typing without checking where he had left off. Only the last line of text on 8 is necessary to bridge pages 7 and 9, which inserts an unavoidable gap into the note numbering. —Ed.]

[22]John Corrill, *A Brief History of the Church of Christ of Latter Day Saints, (Commonly Called Mormons)* (St. Louis, Mo.: Author, 1839), 31.

[23]*History of the Church*, 3: 179.

[24]Peck [Cake, *Peepstone Joe*, 92, 97]. Gideon Carter was killed at Crooked River in October.

their gain unto the Lord, and their substance unto the Lord of the whole earth." Scripturally fitting as this name may have been, the gender was faulty. Genesis [49: 17] yielded a better name: "Dan shall be a serpent by the way, an adder in the path, that biteth the horses heels, so that his rider shall fall backward."[25] It was as the Sons of Dan or Danites that the organization finally came to be known.[26] At a later date, in the popular mind, "Destroying Angels" came to be synonymous with Danites, but this name properly had a quite different application which will presently be seen.

The original object of the Danite Band, in John Corrill's view, was to operate upon the dissenters, "but afterwards it grew into a system to carry out the designs of the Presidency; and if necessary to use physical force to uphold the Kingdom of God, as it was to be done by them."[27] Commenced as a rowdyism granted dignity by religious and social sanctions, the Danites were now given a rationale and a discipline which progressively enlarged the society's function into something of critical importance for the evolution of the church itself.

Corrill asserts that the basic tenet of the Danites was that they "should be agreed in all things."

> they secretly entered into solemn covenants, before God, and bound themselves under oath, to keep the secrets of the society, and covenanted to stand by one another in difficulty, whether right or wrong, but said they would correct each others wrongs themselves. As the presidency stood next to God, or between God and the church, and was the oracle through which the word and will of God was communicated to the church, they esteemed it very essential to have their word, or the word of God through them, strictly adhered to. They therefore entered into a covenant, that the word of the presidency should be obeyed, and none should be suffered to raise his hand or voice against it; for, as they stood at the head of the church, it was considered no more than reasonable that they knew more of the will of God than any others did; consequently, all things must be in submission to them, and, moreover, all tattling, lying, and backbiting must be put down, and he

---

[25]Corrill, *Brief History*, 32, is the original source on these names. John C. Bennett, John Hyde, and others have expanded [upon] his references [to scripture].

[26]In his official explanation of the Danites, Joseph Smith was at pains to say that Avard had come forward as "a spokesman, and a leader of this band, which *he* named *Danites*." *History of the Church*, 3: 180. But at a session of the Nauvoo City Council on 3 January 1844, he made a curious admission in the course of an investigation the council was pursuing: "The Danite system alluded to . . . never had any existence. It was a term made use of by some of the brethren in Far West, and grew out of an expression I made use of when the brethren were preparing to defend themselves from the Missouri mob. . . 'If the enemy comes, the Danites will be after them, meaning the brethren in self-defense.'" *History of the Church*, 6: 165.

[27]Corrill's testimony, *Missouri Documents*, [14].

that would not submit willingly must be forced to it, or leave the country. . . . They said they meant to cleanse their own members first, and then the church. In order to carry on their operations, they organized themselves into companies of fifties and tens, with a captain to each company, that they might be ready to act in concert on any occasion.[28]

Reed Peck's account closely corroborates Corrill's. He says that the secret meetings being held in Far West excited much curiosity among those not permitted to attend, as obviously something out of the ordinary was going on. On the invitation of George W. Robinson and Philo Dibble,[29] he attended a Danite meeting toward the end of June and heard "a full disclosure of its object."

> Jared Carter Geo W. Robinson and Sampson Avard, under the instruction of the presidency, had formed a secret military society, called the "daughter of Zion" and were holding meetings to initiate members The principles taught by Sampson A{v}ard as Spokesman, were that "as the Lord had raised up a prophet in these last days like unto Moses it shall be the duty of this band to obey him in all things, and whatever he requires you shall perform being ready to give up life and property for the advancement of the Cause When any thing is to be performed no member shall have the privilege of judging whether it would be right or wrong but shall engage in its accomplishment and trust God for the result
>
> It is not our business or place to know what is required by God, but he will inform us by means of the prophet and we must perform
>
> If any one of you see a member of the band in difficulty in the surrounding country contending for instance with an enemy, you shall extricate him even if in the wrong if you have to do with his adversary as Moses did with the Egyptian put him under the sand and both pack off to Far West and we will take care of the matter ourselves. No person shall be suffered to speak evil or disrespectfully of the presidency The secret signs and purposes of the Society are not to be revealed on pain of death" &c &c[30]

Avard was at no time the titular leader of the Danites. This may or may not have been a matter of personal choice. But he was so obviously the energizing spirit in the society that Smith ultimately placed all the blame on his shoulders, accusing him of having plotted "to form a secret combination by which he might rise a mighty conqueror, at the *expense and overthrow of the*

[28]Corrill, *Brief History*, 29, 30. Though Corrill came to be classed as an apostate by his brethren, they never challenged the factual accuracy of his book. Indeed, in 1844 it was advertised for sale along with official church publications in *The Prophet*, the church organ in New York City.

[29]*Missouri Documents*, [17].

[30]Peck [Cake, *Peepstone Joe*, 93–94].

Church," of professing to the membership that he had official sanction for all his teachings, and, by effectually binding them to secrecy, providing against discovery of his machinations and of his "rascality."[31]

It may well be that Avard had more on his mind than he ever acknowledged to anyone; it is possible also that in example and precept he went to extremes of which his superiors were not informed, that he exercised a license that had not been granted. But Smith is disingenuous in his entire explanation of the Danites; it is clear that he knew more of the Danites, over a longer period of time, than he cared subsequently to acknowledge, and he has a final responsibility for Avard regardless of whether Avard expressed his actual desires and ideas.

Avard's testimony is no more disinterested than Smith's on the point of ultimate responsibility. However, it was his contention that he was "continually in the society or company of the presidency, receiving instructions from them as to the teachings of the Danite band; and I continually informed them of my teachings; and they were well appraised of my course and teachings in the Danite society."[32] Whether or not he was honest in this statement, there is no question but that he succeeded in convincing the Danites he directly represented the presidency. Corrill testified at Richmond that this was his understanding, and he reiterated this conviction in his book.

Reed Peck at Richmond was scrupulous to describe what he himself actually knew, as distinguished from what he might have inferred. Depicting a meeting which the presidency attended, he said Avard "stated that he had procured the Presidency to come there, to show the society what he was doing was according to their direction or will; and while there, the Presidency approved of Avard's course in the society. Dr. Avard, however, did not explain to the Presidency what his teaching had been to the society."[33]

The larger responsibility of Smith and Rigdon becomes better apparent as one studies the use of the Danites as an instrument in their hands, but their immediate responsibility is clear also, in that they gave Avard and the Danites their public approbation and the weight of their authority. That responsibility is not mitigated if it is argued that they did not realize what they were doing.

In one respect, at least, Avard's testimony is well supported. He says the officers of the band, according to their grades, were brought before Joseph and

---

[31]*History of the Church*, 3: [179].

[32]Avard's testimony, *Missouri Documents*, [21].

[33]Peck [testimony, *Missouri Documents*, 18].

Hyrum Smith and Sidney Rigdon at a school house. Joseph "blessed them and prophesied over them, declaring that they should be the means, in the hands of God, of bringing forth the Millennial Kingdom"; he stated "that it was necessary that this band should be bound together by a covenant, that those who revealed the secrets of the society should be put to death," and he instructed the Danites that "if any of them should get into a difficulty, the rest should help him out, and that they should stand by each other, right or wrong."[34]

John Corrill attests that there was such a meeting, at which took place "a ceremony of introducing the officers of the society to the presidency, who pronounced a blessing on each of them, as introduced, exhorting to faithfulness in their calling, and they should have blessings. After this, President Smith got up, and made general marks . . . relating to the impressions the society had suffered and they wanted to be prepared for future events, but said, he wished to do nothing unlawful, and if the people would let him alone, they would preach the Gospel and live in peace. Towards the close he observed to the people, that they must obey the Presidency, and if the Presidency led them astray, they might destroy them."[35] John Cleminson adds that "to satisfy the people, Dr. Avard called on Joseph Smith, junior, who gave them a pledge that if they led them into a difficulty, he would give them his head for a foot-ball; and that it was the will of God these things should be so."[36]

With respect to the Danite Band itself, there are curious details of organization, the paraphernalia of secret societies from time immemorial. Avard claimed later that a constitution was drawn up soon after the letter to the dissenters was drafted. "This paper was taken into President Rigdon's house, and read to the First Presidency, Hyrum Smith being absent, and was unanimously adopted by them as their rule and guide in future. After it was thus adopted, I was instructed by the council to destroy it, as, if it should be discovered, it would be considered treasonable. This constitution after it was approved by the First Presidency, was read, article by article, to the Danite Band, and unanimously adopted by them."[37]

There is some doubt about the authenticity of this constitution. Joseph Smith and four other prominent Mormons flatly denied Avard's story;[38]

[34]Avard's testimony, *Missouri Documents,* [2].

[35]Corrill's testimony, *Missouri Documents,* [12].

[36]Cleminson's testimony, *Missouri Documents,* [15].

[37]Avard's testimony, *Missouri Documents,* [4–5].

[38]*History of the Church,* 3: 281.

perhaps more to the point, Corrill stated at Richmond that he "never heard it read in the society, no did ever hear it until lately,"[39] and John Cleminson testified similarly that he never heard of the document until Avard himself disclosed it on being captured.[40] This constitution may well have been a product of Avard's own intricate mind, absorbed with the Danites as a plaything. It seems clear, however, that whether with their foreknowledge and consent or quite blindly, the Danites were organized on such a basis as the constitution provided. Not particularly sensational, it merely stipulated that executive and legislative powers should be vested in the presidency of the church, and outlined a general military organization.[41]

The binding oaths and secret signs of the Danites are a matter of general record.[42] Avard says that all who entered the Danite Band covenanted that anyone revealing the secrets of the society should be put to death. "The covenant taken by all the Danite Band was as follows, to-wit: They declared in the name of Jesus Christ, the Son of God, 'I do solemnly obligate myself ever to conceal and never to reveal the secret purposes of this society, called the Daughters of Zion; Should I ever do the same, I hold my life as the forfeiture.' "[43]

Writing many years later, John D. Lee said that the Danites were placed "under the most sacred obligations that language could invent. They were sworn to stand by and sustain each other. *Sustain, protect, defend,* and *obey* the leaders of the Church, under any and *all circumstances unto death;* and to disobey the orders of the leaders of the Church, or divulge the name of a Danite, was to be punished with death."[44] William Swartzell describes the sign of

---

[39]*Missouri Documents,* [14].

[40]*Missouri Documents,* [17]. Ebenezer Robinson, who had been a Danite, refers to this document as merely a "purported" constitution. *The Return* (October, 1889): [145].

[41]It is printed in *Missouri Documents,* [5–6], and in B.H. Roberts, *Comprehensive History of the Church* [*of Jesus Christ of Latter-day Saints,* 6 vol. (Salt Lake City: Desert News Press, 1930), 1: 501–503].

[42]Smith himself says (*History of the Church,* 3: 179–189) that Avard administered to "the few under his control" an oath binding them to everlasting secrecy as to everything that should be communicated to them by himself. "Thus Avard initiated members into his band, firmly binding them, [by] all that was sacred, in the protecting of each other in all things that were lawful. . . . He held his meetings daily, and carried on his crafty work in great haste, to prevent mature reflection upon the matter by his followers, until he had them bound under the penalties of death to keep the secrets and certain signs of the organization by which they were to know each other by day or night." Cf. also Rigdon's statement of 1 July 1843 (*History of the Church,* 3: 453).

[43]Avard's testimony, *Missouri Documents,* [2]. Several versions of the Danite oath have been printed. Cf. William Swartzell (see note 45), John C. Bennett, *History of the Saints* (Boston: Leland & Whiting, 1842), 267, 271, and Achilles, *Destroying Angels,* 8–9.

[44]John D. Lee, *Mormonism Unveiled* (St. Louis, Mo.: Bryan, Brand & Co., 1877), 57–58.

recognition and distress. The Danite was to clap his right hand to his right thigh, and then raise it to the right temple, the thumb extending behind the ear. The password, which was to be spoken at the moment of giving the hand of fellowship, was "Who be you?" The answer was "Anama," which was interpreted as meaning "a friend."[45]

To all this there is a comic character. But the comic shades into the sinister. In this frontier microcosm there is an uncomfortable anticipation of the Klansmen, of Blackshirts and storm troopers. In retrospect it is easy to condemn the Danite movement as something at once ridiculous and dangerous. Certainly, the Mormons were playing with fire in their absorption with a secret and highly integrated organization answering to no law except internal loyalties and the word of an unstable religious authority. The mere existence of the Danites represented a danger—even more to the Mormon people themselves than to their enemies, because consciousness that such an instrument was ready to their hand was calculated to give the Mormon authorities a heady sense of their own power. Their intoxication could persuade them to extravagances likely to spur the Danite Band to serious excesses. Granted further the explosive potentialities of the Mormon relationship with the Gentile settlers in Missouri, what the Danites portended for the Mormons is clear.

In the society itself there was no doubt a leavening of rascals, firebrands, and bigots. Yet the Danite Band to the majority of its members may very probably have seemed an expression of the high religious purpose, the consecration beyond self, the loyalty, devotion, and belief, which they had brought to their conversion; and many of them, as former Free Masons, could have found nothing peculiar in this general character as a secret fellowship, even though a religio-military fellowship. In the emotional climate of 1838 the social dangers implicit in the Danite organization were not readily apparent. Even John Corrill, who from the outset was not in sympathy with the Danite society, testified a few months later that he "took exceptions only to the teachings as to the duties of that society, wherein it was said that if one brother got into any kind of difficulty, it was the duty of the rest to help him out, right or wrong."[46]

---

[45]William Swartzell, *Mormonism Exposed: Being a Journal of a Residence in Missouri from 28th of May to the 20th of August, 1838* (Pekin, Ohio: Author, 1840), 22–23. Copies of this rare narrative are owned by the Missouri Historical Society and the New York Public Library. Lee also describes the "sign" made by raising the right hand to the right ear (Lee, *Mormonism Unveiled,* [57–58]).

[46]Corrill's testimony, *Missouri Documents,* [12].

The conception of the Danites as a military arm of the church evolved swiftly. Reed Peck says that Jared Carter was named "Captain General of the Lord's Hosts," and that his subalterns were Major General Sampson Avard, Brigadier General Cornelius P. Lott, Colonel George W. Robinson, Lieutenant Colonel Philo Dibble, and Major Seymour Brunson, together with an adjutant, "secretary of war," and captains of fifties and tens, all "under the administration of the presidency of the church an wholly subject to their control." Peck was himself named adjutant, a position he found it impolitic to refuse.[47]

Below the general officers, this military organization incorporated the structure of the 59th Regiment of the Missouri militia, organized under authority of the governor in Caldwell County in the early spring. Robinson, Dibble, Brunson, and Peck carried their rank from the military regiment into the "Lord's Hosts."[48] As was to be expected in an Army of Israel below the officer level, however, organization followed the Biblical pattern. The unit was a captain with ten men, and the units combined into companies of fifty and one hundred. Once the groundwork was laid, men were initiated into the society wholesale, forty and fifty at a time,[49] and the organization

[47]Peck [Cake, *Peepstone Joe*, 94]; *Missouri Documents*, [17]. At Richmond, as near as he "could recollect it," Peck recalled Lott to be the major general and Avard the brigadier general.

[48]"Philo Dibble's Narrative," *Early Scenes in Church History*, [Faith Promoting Series, vol. 8] (Salt Lake City: Geo. Q. Cannon & Sons, 1882).

[49][Cake, *Peepstone Joe*, 94] Joseph Smith admitted existence of the Host of Israel but denied that there was any relationship or similitude to the Danites (cf. *History of the Church*, 3: [182]). Lee distinguishes between the two also (Lee, *Mormonism Unveiled*, [57, 112]) but clearly the organizing meeting for the Host of Israel to which Lee refers at Adam-ondi-Ahman is the "Daranite" meeting of 28 July 1838 which William Swartzell attended (Swartzell, *Mormonism Exposed*, [25–26]). The point is difficult to determine with finality, and it is possible that a distinction existed akin to that in the German army between regular and S.S. troops [during the Second World War]. However, the term Danite came into such regular use among the Mormons themselves, and in military context, that the conclusion represented in the text seems best to fit the facts. Three entries in the unpublished journal of Hosea Stout, when the Mormons were migrating from Illinois, are illuminating in this connection. On 21 March 1846 [*On the Mormon Frontier: The Diary of Hosea Stout*, 2 vol. (Salt Lake City: Utah State Historical Society, 1963), 1: 140–141], when in company with some horsemen of the guard, he wrote, "we then went on again performing as we rode some Danite evolutions of horsemanship as practiced in the War in Davi{es}s County Missouri in the fall of 1838." Again on 22 September 1846 [1: 197], taking command of the drill muster at Winter Quarters, he "took them through the old Missouri Danite drill. This was new to most and very entertaining, also to them and more so because it was such a short & simple method of maneuvering small companies." And on 5 June 1847 [1: 259], also at Winter Quarters, on going out to receive some Omaha Indians, he says his company was "formed on horse back according to the Danite system of horsemanship and consequently I was in the center of the line." Thus also Luman Shurtliff journals. During the summer of 1838 he "was invited to unite with a society called the Danite society. It was got up for our personal defense, also for the protection of our families, property and religion. Signs and pass words were given by which members could know the other wherever they met, night or day. All members must {settle} difficulties if he had any with a member of the society, before he could be received.["] Both Stout and Shurtliff lived and died faithful saints.

was extended to the Mormons in Daviess County, where Lyman Wight held the colonelcy. This army came finally and publicly to be known among the Mormons as "The Hosts of Israel."[50] Concurrently, for all practical purposes, the 59th Missouri Regiment ceased to exist.

A cloudy vainglory now began to characterize the speech of the church authorities. The most fiery language was Rigdon's, but Smith had reckless things to say also. In Corrill's store one day, shortly after the dissenters were driven from Far West, he had some rather wild remarks to make about Mahomet, "that he believed Mahomet was an inspired man, and had done a great deal of good, and that he intended to take the same course Mahomet did. That if the people would let him alone, he would, after awhile die a natural death; but if they did not, he would make it one gore of blood from the Rocky Mountains to the State of Maine." He added that he had "as regular an inquisition as ever was established, and as good a set of inquisitors as ever was."[51]

There was increasingly extravagant talk about setting up the "kingdom" which had been foretold by Daniel. Inevitably, as a millennial church, the Mormons had identified their church with Daniel's prophetic vision. In Corrill's words, "the church always believed that judgments, pestilence, disease, famine, great troubles and vexation, were sooner or later to be poured out upon all the wicked, and cut them off in the course of time . . . the object of gathering together was that they might purify themselves, and stand in holy places appointed of God for that purpose, and thus escape these judgments. But, now, it began to be taught that the Church, instead of God, or rather, the church in the hands of God, was to bring about these things."[52] George Hinkle agrees that there had come a reversal of the earlier idea that the Kingdom of God should be set up peaceably; the doctrine, he says, was now boldly advanced that "the time had come when this Kingdom was to

---

[50]Peck [But such a comment does not appear in the Cake printing of the Peck document. —Ed.]; Swartzell, *Mormonism Exposed,* [25–26 notes the existence of officer corps among the group, but nowhere in the rest of the Swartzell's work does the term "Hosts of Israel" appear].

[51]George Walter's testimony, *Missouri Documents,* ____. Marsh affid. [Morgan's tentative citation is in error. George Walter, W. W. Phelps, John Cleminson, George M. Hinkle, and John Corrill signed a "Certificate of Mormons as to the conduct of Gen. Clark and his troops," dated "Richmond, November 23, 1838," which appears in the Missouri state document but not the federal reprint. Walter is only named as a deposed witness on p. 43; no testimony is recorded. The citation to Marsh is a manuscript emendation and probably refers to the Thomas B. Marsh affidavit of 24 October 1838 in *History of the Church* 3: 167–168n. —Ed.]

[52]Corrill, *Brief History,* [31].

be set up by forcible means, if necessary . . . the time had come when the riches of the Gentiles were to be consecrated to the true Israel."[53]

July 4, 1838 was a day of double significance, the 62nd anniversary of the Declaration of Independence, and the day set for laying the cornerstones of the temple the Lord had commanded to be builded in Far West. Sidney Rigdon had been designated orator of the day, and W. W. Phelps was told by David W. Patten that Rigdon's speech would declare the church independent. When he objected that such a thing would be treasonable, Patten replied that it would not be if they could maintain it—or die fighing.[54] Phelps and many another, doubtless, listened with great attention for what Rigdon would say.

Much of the oration was unexceptionable. But midway in his course Rigdon passed from sonorous acclaim of the principles of the Republic to a bitter résumé of the persecutions of the Saints, and he swept on to a peroration savagely eloquent:

> We take God and all the holy angels to witness this day that we warn all men, in the name of Jesus Christ, to come on us no more forever; for, from this hour, we will bear it no more; our rights shall no more be trampled on with impunity; the man, or the set of men, who attempts it, does it at the expense of their lives. And that mob that comes on us to disturb us, it shall be between us and them a war of extermination; for we will follow them till the last drop of their blood is spilled, or else they will have to exterminate us; for we will carry the seat of war to their own houses and to their own families, and one party or the other shall be utterly destroyed. Remember it, then, all men! We will never be the aggressors; we will infringe on the rights of no people, but shall stand for our own until death.
>
> We claim our own rights, and are willing that all others shall enjoy theirs. No man shall be at liberty to come into our streets to threaten us with mobs, for if he does, he shall atone for it before he leaves the place; neither shall he be at liberty to vilify and slander any of us, for suffer it we will not in this place. We therefore take all me to record this day, that we proclaim our liberty this day, as did our fathers; and we pledge this day to one another, our fortunes, our lives, and our sacred honors, to be delivered from the persecutions which we have had to endure for the last nine years, or nearly that time. Neither will we indulge any man or set of men in instituting vexatious lawsuits against us, to cheat us out of our rights; if they attempt it, we say woe be unto them! We this day, then, proclaim ourselves

[53]Hinkle's testimony, *Missouri Documents,* [23]. In his introduction to vol. 3 of Smith's *History of the Church,* Brigham H. Roberts discusses the Missouri problems in detail, including "the unwisdom of the Saints" in interpreting the revelations as to Zion too immediately, with a consequent outburst of injudicious and open talk by individual Saints. cf. p. xlvii.

[54]Phelps' testimony, *Missouri Documents,* [44].

free, with a purpose and a determination that never can be broken, "no, never! no never!! no, never!!!"[55]

With these words the Mormons were carried over a fateful borderline. To the church Rigdon had given a fighting doctrine; these were sentiments the membership, many of them now enrolled in the Danite Band, could interpret for themselves. But, fully as important, the Missourians were put on their notice that after two years of peace, a new factor had entered into their relations with the Mormons. There was no one to interpret Rigdon's oration in terms of persecution complex, frustration complex, religious dementia. But its significance as announcement of the breakdown of law was unmistakable. News of the oration, spreading through the upper country, created a sensation.[56]

The first of the explosions came a month later. Meantime the Mormon authorities began overturning life in Far West.

In a public discourse at the end of June Rigdon had advised the church members that they would soon be called upon to consecrate their property.[57] Those who would not comply with the law of consecration, he said, should be delivered over to the brother of Gideon. The building of the "Lord's House" in Far West would enhance the value of property ten-fold in its vicinity and proprietors who would not consecrate the whole of that increase for the building of the temple and other church uses should be "delivered over to the brother of Gideon and be send bounding over the Prairies as the dissenters were a few days ago."[58]

Rigdon's forecast was fulfilled on July 8, four days after the corner-stones were laid for the temple at Far West, when Smith brought forth the revelation on tithing. Church members were to give to their bishop "all their surplus property" for the building of the temple and the laying of the foundation of Zion "and for the debts of the Presidency of my Church"; thereafter, all

---

[55]A copy of Rigdon's oration, as originally printed in pamphlet form at Far West in 1838 [Flake/Draper, *A Mormon Bibliography*, n.7284], is owned by the Chicago Historical Society. It has been reprinted in James H. Hunt, *Mormonism: Embracing the Origin, Rise and Progress of the Sect, With an Examination of . . . Their Troubles in Missouri* (St. Louis, Mo.: Ustick & Davies, 1844), 167–180, and thence in Joseph & Heman C. Smith, *Church History*, 6 vol. (Lamoni, Iowa: Board of Publication of the Reorganized Church of Jesus Christ of Latter Day Saints, 1897), 2: 157–165. [Flake/Draper, n.4142, notes that the Hunt book cited here was made up from a new title page and the unbound sheets of an earlier title, *A History of the Mormon War*, published the same year. —Ed.]

[56][No note contents. Darn. —Ed.]

[57][Manuscript note:] The law of consecration had been instituted among the Mormons in 1831, but except as an [*illegible*] by [*illegible*] in force by the fall of 1837, at that time it began to be preached, and it had been a factor in the Cowdery-Whitmer dissension. It was now revived in the heat of religious passion.

[58]Peck [Cake, *Peepstone Joe*, 92].

who had been thus tithed should pay one-tenth of all their interest annually, "a standing law unto them forever." All who gathered unto the Land of Zion were to observe this law "or not be found worthy to abide among you." Unless by this law the land of Zion were sanctified unto the Lord, "verily I say unto you, it shall not be a land of Zion unto you."[58]

History has obscured the immediacy of purpose of this revelation, because it had a continuing importance as a revenue-producing measure after its original object became meaningless and was forgotten. It was designed originally for reconstituting Zion.

The temple to be built in Far West through the instrumentality of this revelation was to be made in effect the center of the world. All the Saints were to turn over to the church their lands and property. By sale of the outlying lands, and with the funds realized from the consecrations generally, all non-Mormons would be bought out within a twelve-mile radius. Within the tract thus secured to the church two square miles would be laid out in one-acre lots, centering about the temple lot.* The lots nearest the temple would be distributed to the High Priests and the dignitaries of the church. A group of lots father removed, ranging in size from five to ten acres each, would be allotted to individuals as homesteads, the size of each man's lot depending upon the size of his family. At the extremities of the twelve square miles would be laid out four lots of a thousand acres each, east, west, north, and south, and these thousand-acre lots would be the general farming lands of the church. These who tilled these lands would be given their foodstuffs and seed-grain, and in return they would give to the church for its support each year's surplus. Overseers would direct who was to work, and where and when.[59]

Giving force to this program was the warning that unless God's requirement were met, "the Saints would be driven from State to State, from city to city, from one abiding place to another, until the members would die and waste away, leaving but a remnant of the Saints to return and receive their inheritance in Zion . . . in the *Last Days.*" Harangued by Rigdon and promised that the Lord

[58]*Doctrine and Covenants* [LDS 119; D&C CC 106]. There is a possibility, verging upon a probability, that the revelation on tithing is one pole of a dual revelation of which the other half has been lost or suppressed. John D. Lee (*Mormonism Unveiled*, 60–61) describes a revelation which exactly instructed the Saints as to the procedure to be followed in carrying forward the work of consecration. Such a revelation may well have been one of the three which Joseph Smith says he received on 12 January 1838, the day he left Kirtland, and which he read to the public congregation in Far West on the day the Revelation on Tithing was received (*History of the Church*, 3: 44).

*10 acre = Winchester letter [Marginal note. —Ed.]

[59]This account is based principally upon Swartzell, p. [9–15]. cf. also Lee, *Mormonism Unveiled*, 61.

had revealed to Smith that if they obeyed they should nevermore be driven from their homes because He "would then fight the battles of His children," the Saints by upraised hands gave unanimous sanction to the consecration.[60]

But in retrospect Lee concluded that the people had voted to please the priesthood and then acted to suit themselves; and as a practical matter, many in the community may not have felt themselves bound by the action of the congregation. Many, Reed Peck says, consecrated lands in Jackson, Clay, and Caldwell counties, and others brought forward furniture, horses, and other properties, "but it all added little to the church fund & I conclude fell far short of satisfying the presidency for the business of consecration was immediately followed by the formation of four large firms and it was required by the 'Word of the Lord' that every member of the church should become a partner in some one of them[.] All the land and personal property of each individual were to become property of some one of these firms and subject to an individual head. . . . All branches of business were to be carried on by these companies, mercantile mechanical and agricultural and all laborers were bound to work according to the special directions of their superintendent[.] Very many were violently opposed to this new church order but after much *argument, preaching teaching* and *explaining* by S Avard the excitement was allayed and all but a few consented to give up their property and we may say subject themselves to a *driver.*"[61]

The kind of pressure exerted against individuals not inclined to look with favor upon the consecration program is described by W. W. Phelps, who was present at a meeting, attended by the presidency, which had as its object "to make persons confess and repent of their sins to God and the Presidency," and to arraign them for giving false accounts of their money and effects, they said, whenever they found one guilty of these things, he was to be handed over to the 'Brother of Gideon.'" One man rose to defend himself and though ordered to leave the house, nevertheless commenced speaking. Avard at once demanded, "Where are my ten men?" Thirty or more men stood up, whereupon the man

[60]Lee, *Mormonism Unveiled,* [61].

[61]Peck [Cake, *Peepstone Joe,* 99. A loose fragment filed behind the page in the typescript bears Morgan's handwritten note that looks like "add 61"; it reads (with the citation corrected): "John Corrill (*Brief History,* 46) says that shortly after their organization the Danites undertook to enforce the law of consecration, 'but this did not amount to much. Then they undertook another plan in which Doctor Avard was very officious and forward, viz., to constitute large firms, so that every male member of the Church could become a member of the firm.' He describes the operation of these firms much as Peck does, and adds, 'Many joined these firms, while many others were much dissatisfied with them, which caused considerable excitement and feeling in the Church. Smith said every man must act his own feelings, whether to join or not, yet great exertions were used, and especially by Doctor Avard, to persuade all to join.'" —Ed.]

agreed to leave the house.[62] To Corrill and Peck[,] Avard said sharply that "all persons who attempted to deceive and retain property that should be give up would meet with the fate of Ananias and Saphira who were *killed by Peter.*"[63]

A little later Corrill observed to one of the Saints that he did not think it his duty to unite with the firm and had no confidence in the revelation that required it; thereupon he was publicly rebuked by Smith and Rigdon. "If you tell about the streets again that you do not believe this or that revelation," Smith told him, "I will walk on your neck, Sir," smiting his fists the while in evidence of his rage. "If you do not act differently and show yourself approved, you shall never be admitted into the Kingdom of Heaven—I will stand at the entrance and oppose you myself and will keep you out if I have to take a fisty cuff in doing it."[64]

The iron hand of authority, in fact, was now being clamped down upon the Mormon community in earnest. Ironically, one of the earliest victims was Jared Carter. On complaining to Joseph Smith about some observations made by Rigdon in a sermon, the Danites' Captain-General was tried for finding fault with one of the presidency, and deprived of his station. Elias Higbee was appointed in his stead.[65] In another instance, a young man from Ohio reported to have said something about Smith and Rigdon was taken in hand by the constable, Dimick Huntington, and several others, compelled to sign a libel, and to kneel before Rigdon and ask pardon as the only alternative to a caning.[66]

Acting so ruthlessly to suppress any criticism, the authorities were not in the least disposed to let the courts be employed against them. When Lyman E. Johnson filed suit for trespass against Smith and others, the latter told John Cleminson, clerk of the Caldwell County Circuit Court, not to issue the writ, "that he did not intend to submit to it; that it was a vexatious thing, and I had a right to judge of it; and that he would see me out on it."[67] Phelps, one of the justices of the County Court, discussed the matter with

[62]Phelps' testimony, *Missouri Documents,* [44].

[63]Peck [Cake, *Peepstone Joe,* 99].

[64]Peck [Cake, *Peepstone Joe,* 100]. For Smith's version of this encounter, see his entry for 30 August 1838 (*History of the Church,* 3: 65–66).

[65]Peck [Cake, *Peepstone Joe,* 97–98]. Carter was tried by a council which included the presidency [Joseph Smith, Hyrum Smith, Sidney Rigdon], Avard, Higbee, Dimick Huntington, and David W. Patten. From what Peck was told by Huntington immediately after the trial, some rough language was used. Smith is characterized as having said that "he should have cut out Carters throat on the spot if he had been alone when he made the complaint," and Huntington averred that "on his trial Carter came within a fingers point of losing his head." If all this is discounted as oratory, its effect upon the listeners must still be reckoned with.

[66]Peck [Cake, *Peepstone Joe,* 93].

[67]Cleminson's testimony, *Missouri Documents,* [16].

Smith, observing that as the clerk's fee had not been paid, a refusal to issue the writ could be based on legal grounds. Smith replied that "he did not care for that; he did not intend to have any writ issued against him in the county."[68] In the face of the Danite Band, Cleminson had no disposition to go ahead and issue the writ. If he needed an object lesson, the case of George Walter would have sufficed him. When Johnson was arrested on some charge, Walter provided bail for him. Thereupon, he testified, "I was taken to task and warned that I would suffer for it, and on leaving town that evening, in company with Johnson, there were a number of guns fired at us, as I heard the balls whistle near us. In a day or two I returned to town, and saw Rigdon, who took me to task for going Johnson's bail."[69]

Election day in Missouri was the first Monday in August. On the Saturday preceding, Peck says, a meeting was called in the afternoon and Avard informed those present that they had been guilty of neglect of duty in not inquiring of the Lord through the prophet what persons should be supported as candidates. "You may," he said, "elect the identical persons that God would choose, but even if you do, they will prove a curse to the county because you did not inquire as you ought."

Forthwith a committee was appointed to wait on the presidency, a result of which it was ordered that printed tickets should be sent about the county to each precinct, that all might know for whom to vote. The tickets were struck off, and next day Avard distributed them among a large gathering of Danites from all parts of Caldwell County, with word that they were according to the will of God, "which," Peck remarks, "was sufficient to make nearly every person vote that ticket and no other." Peck thought it beyond doubt that some candidates who would ordinarily have got the votes of three-fourths of the people by this intervention polled no more than 15 or 20 votes, and he attributed this interference in the election to the desire of the presidency to obtain more malleable office holders.[70]

68Phelps' testimony, *Missouri Documents,* [44].

69Walter's testimony, *Missouri Documents,* [*Documents Containing the Correspondence,* 87]. cf. also Corrill's testimony and that of Abner Scovel, *ibid.,* ____. [Morgan's incomplete citation does not leave enough clues to complete the note with authority. —Ed.]

70Peck [Cake, *Peepstone Joe,* 102]. The official history of the church makes no mention of this episode, but there is no reason to doubt it, as elections in Utah for a quarter of a century after the Mormon[s] settled there were conducted on such a basis. Elias Higbee told a Senate Committee in February, 1840 "that it was all false about a Revelation on voting: and the reason of our voting that ticket" was in consequence of popular adherence to the Democratic party, whose principles had "been taught us from our infancy. . . ." But he added, "It was true we advised our brethren to vote this ticket, telling them we thought that party would protect our rights, and not suffer us to be driven from our lands, as (*continued, next page*)

John Corrill corroborates Peck's story, adding that the people supposed the ticket was from headquarters, and "that it was the will of God that all should go for it. But many saw that it was taking an undue advantage of the election, and were extremely dissatisfied; not so much with the ticket itself, as with the principle in which it had been got up. . . . There was some murmuring and finding fault after the election, by those opposed to the proceedings, but this was soon put down by the Danite influence."[71]

In Caldwell County the election went off to the general satisfaction of the Mormon authorities. But at Gallatin, across the line in Daviess County, the fuse Rigdon had lighted on the Fourth of July reached powder. An election fight involving a group of Danites blew off the roof and set in motion an avalanche which swept the Mormons out of Missouri.

For some time resentment had been rising in Daviess County against the increasing Mormon settlement there, held by many of the settlers to be in violation of the agreement by which Caldwell County had been created specifically for the Mormons' benefit. Moreover, the political situation in the county was delicately balanced between the Democrats and Whigs, and the voting weight of the Mormons gave them a disturbing balance of power.

On August 6 the polls opened at the county seat, Gallatin, with some forty or fifty Missourians present, and eight or ten Mormons. The Missourians rushed to vote, after which the Whig candidate, and old enemy of the Mormons, mounted a whisky barrel and began to harangue the crowd to inflame their passions against the Mormons and so prevent them from voting. Swearing that the Mormons had no more right to vote than the niggers, the mob bully began browbeating one of the Mormons, and when another Mormon caught the bully by the arm, half a dozen of the Missourians began beating the second Mormon with clubs and boards. A general brawl broke out.

John L. Butler had gone a little aside and was at first not involved in the melee, but on seeing one of his brethren attacked, "from four to a dozen on

---

we had hitherto been. . . ." *History of the Church,* 4: 85–86. [Morgan moved the note number from the end of the paragraph and circled the remaining 6½ lines but did not mark them for deletion. Because he thus leaves open a question about his intent for that text, I include it here: "In his mind, however, the 'prettiest part of the affair' was that nearly half a day before the committee went to inquire as to the candidates, he saw the self-same ticket in the hands of the compositor at the printing office. It had already been made out by the Smith, Rigdon, and Robinson—'the transactions in the afternoon were no doubt to take off a little of the glare by making it appear that the people consulted them respecting the ticket to be voted and not have it understood that they interfered voluntarily.'" —Ed.]

[71] Corrill, *Brief History,* [33].

a man and all damning 'em and God damning the 'Mormon,'" he remembered the covenants entered into by the Danites as to protecting each other, and he shouted out at the top of his voice, "Oyez, you Danites, here is a job for us!" A giant of a man, he seized an oaken club and waded into the middle of the battle. He said later that he felt himself seven or eight feet tall and "when I called out for the Danites there was a power rested upon me such as . . . I never felt before." With his club he did terrible execution; and others, like John D. Lee who saw the Danite sign and plunged furiously into the battle, helped utterly rout the Missourians. The entire action was over in two minutes. At an election in Kentucky Butler had seen 200 men fighting six or eight minutes with clubs, knives, brickbats, and the like, and not a tenth part of the execution done; there were perhaps as many as 30 men with bloodied heads, and some of them badly hurt. It was surprising, John D. Lee reflected, what a few resolute men could do.

The little band of Mormons was now in possession of the field of battle, and the officials cleared a road to the polls for them. But it seemed to Butler that in the poll box he should be defenseless with his enemies so close around him; not many of the Mormons voted, and within a few moments they withdrew from town. Having reason to believe that the Missourians were gathering for retaliatory raids, they returned to their homes, gathered their families, and hid them in a thicket of hazel, the men standing guard in the rain throughout the night.

In itself this election brawl need have amounted to nothing; its like had occurred time and again. But there were two unfortunate preconditions of this short and savage fight. Rigdon's challenging Fourth of July oration, no doubt made even more sensational as it passed from mouth to mouth, had disquieted the whole upper country, and for many Missourians, the rumor of the Gallatin affray had the substance of an overt act of war by the Mormons. And for their part, the Mormons were wrought to such a pitch, confident in their strength to the point of arrogance, and reckless of consequences, that they were psychologically prepared to react violently and immediately to an aggression.

An express carried the first wild story of the Gallatin affair to the Saints at Adam-ondi-Ahman. The reports had it that the Missourians had raised a mob and killed two of the brethren, whom they would not permit to be buried. Immediately an express was sent to Far West with the news, where

Sampson Avard called for twenty men to accompany him to Adam-ondi-Ahman.* Something like 150 volunteers reported for duty, and by noon of the 7th "were marching for Daviess County breathing vengeance against 'the mob' for the attack made the previous day on their brethren." Smith and Rigdon accompanied the party.[72] Adam-ondi-Ahman was reached by nightfall, and during the night 180 Mormons, William Swartzell estimates, stood guard against the attack which was hourly expected.

The Pukes, however, did not put in their appearance.[73] Reed Peck says, indeed, that the inhabitants of Daviess County had been so alarmed at the size of the Mormon force that they "fled from their houses to make the woods their covert until the storm should pass or assistance be procured to expel what they termed a band of invaders."

It would have been the part of wisdom on the part of the Mormons to return to Far West, as it was now clear that the reports which had aroused them to arms were largely without foundation. The state of their feelings, however, demanded expression. Early on the morning of the 7th the Mormons were paraded in a hollow square on the prairie, the horsemen on one side and the foot soldiers on the other, with the uniformed officers in the center. Rigdon drew his sword and harangued the troops in the vein of his Fourth of July oration:

> We have been imposed upon and persecuted, ever since the rising of this Church—have been driven from Kirtland, Ohio, to Jackson county, now we are in Daviess county. We are the people of God, and the only people that believe in His word. We fear God, our Almighty Protector: and we will be no more driven from this blessed land. Now, we, as the people of God, do declare and decree, by the great Jehovah, the eternal and omnipotent God, that sits upon his vast and everlasting throne, beyond the ethereal blue, we WILL bathe our swords in the VITAL BLOOD of the Missourians, or DIE in the attempt!

The company shouted their approbation and gave three cheers. Then in silence they marched behind smith to the home of Adam Black, judge-elect of the county, and justice of the peace. Black previously had sold his

*Avard [testimony, *Missouri Documents*, 2. This note is an incomplete in-text occurrence. —Ed.]

[72]Peck [Cake, *Peepstone Joe*, 104]; *History of the Church*, 3: 58 says 15 or 20 started from Far West and were joined by an unspecified number en route. Avard says "about 120" were in the company. George W. Robinson is asserted by Smith to have been the commander, while Peck, speaking more generally, says Smith and Rigdon were "at their head." Corrill, *Brief History*, 34 says about 150 went.

[73]It may be observed in passing that some contemporary historians have thought this term as applied to Missourians a misreading of "Pikes," a nickname familiar in the literature of the gold rush. "Pikes," however, was in common usage a decade before the discovery of gold in California. cf. Swartzell, *Mormonism Exposed*, 31.

pre-emption right to one of the leading Mormons, Vinson Knight, for $1000, half of which had been paid in hand. Some disagreement had arisen, however, and in Smith's words, Black had "united himself with a band of mobbers to drive the Saints from, and prevent their settling in, Daviess county." Demand was now made upon Black that he should agree to administer the law in justice. He refused to sign the document presented to him by the Mormons, but agreed to write one of his own, which certified that as he was bound to support the Constitution of Missouri and of the United States, and as he was not attached nor would attach himself to any mob, so long as the Mormons would not molest him, he would not molest them.[74] The Mormons then took their leave of him, though not without some hard words as to what his fate should be if he violated his agreement.[75] The following afternoon, the Caldwell County Mormons returned to their homes.

Smith's conversation with Black may have been expressed in polite terms, as he says, but with upwards of a hundred armed men around his house at the time, Black took another view of the matter. He made his way to Richmond, in Ray County, and swore to an affidavit asserting that he had been threatened with instant death in the event he did not sign an instrument binding himself as a justice of the peace not to "molest the Mormons, and averring further that the Mormons said they intended to have satisfaction for abuse they had received on the Monday previous [at Gallatin], and that they could not submit to the laws."

Writs were sworn out against Smith and Wight, and after a period of negotiation Smith and Wight agreed to be tried before Judge Austin A. King, in Daviess County just over the Caldwell County line. The hearing took place on September 7, after which Wight and Smith were bound over to the court in a $500 bond. "There was no proof against us to criminate us," Smith remarks, "but it is supposed he did it to pacify, as much as possible, the feelings of the mobbers."[76]

The excitement, it was generally believed, would now die down. But the forces unloosed in the upper Missouri country were such that a violent final resolution of the Mormon problem had become inevitable. The Missourians living closest among the Mormons who had more especial reason to fear or hate them, had wild and alarming tales to tell, tales they were first to believe,

[74] *History of the Church,* 3: 59–60.

[75] Swartzell, *Mormonism Exposed,* 30.

[76] *History of the Church,* 3: 72.

and which grew in the telling. They had disliked the Mormons from the beginning, and the avowed Mormon determination no longer to respect a law which was administered only against them destroyed all belief in the efficacy of the law as a secure foundation for society; in this condition of legal anarchy, the Missourians were impelled to organize their own protection of what the Mormons were swift to brand as mobs.

The Mormons, in turn, had had an unfortunate experience with the law in Missouri; it had seen them driven into the northern counties of the state not merely with complacence but with its active complicity. Though the root of their present difficulties was the supremely unfortunate oration Rigdon had delivered on the Fourth of July, that oration was now seen not as a cause but as a precondition of their present situation—a line drawn upon which they should now stand. The Mormons had no great faith in the law except as they administered it themselves; and more importantly, growing in their midst was the reality of "the Kingdom," a core of righteousness in any decision taken for resistance. The Mormons had come to the point where they would not yield another inch. It was to be the misfortune of the Mormons, however, that the orientation of their religious philosophy through this year with its [*illegible*] political, social, and economic [*illegible*] led them to look to their own strength and to God for a solution. More practically, the Missourians invoked the forms and the mechanism of state law. Armed resistance the Mormons were prepared to offer was thus translated into resistance against the state itself. It was inevitable that the Mormons should be crushed. But in the history of their downfall the Danites have a final arresting chapter.

There were two particular sore spots as September wore on, the turmoil in Davies County and conflict over a settlement the Mormons had made at DeWitt, in Carroll County some 50 miles southeast of Far West. Two Mormon families had located at DeWitt in June, on the invitation of some of the townsfolk, but as early as the second week of August they were asked to leave. The DeWitt Mormons held their ground, however, and except for passing resolutions in mass meeting, nothing was done by the inhabitants of DeWitt until late September, when a company of Saints emigrating from Canada settled down at the Carroll County town. Gunfire then broke out around DeWitt.[77] [*end of draft manuscript*]

---

[77]Peck observes ironically that in determining to eject the Mormons from Carroll County, the citizens of DeWitt were "acting on the principles of republicanism as defined by S. Rigdon." (Peck [Cake, *Peepstone Joe*, 107]).

Chapter 7

Early Book Reviews (1945–1951)

Editor's Introduction

Well before being introduced to history as a discipline in the Historical Records Survey, Morgan was already a practiced critic of current American literature. One of the experiences that attracted the interest of HRS administration was nearly a score of contemporary reviews that Morgan generated as an occasional book reviewer for the *Salt Lake Tribune*. Between 1937 and 1939, Morgan reviewed a variety of non-fiction volumes for the newspaper. He had once proposed that the paper publish a daily book-review column; he had to settle for an informal stint as an occasional reviewer for the Sunday-issue books page.[1] Though Dale expected to follow a career as a copywriter for an advertising firm, he also harbored literary aspirations and hoped that he could at least moonlight as a book reviewer. Reviews were integral to his self-directed effort at establishing a literary career. Since he sat outside the world of journalism looking to break in, he was unaware that for a decade the proportion of time the public once spent in recreational reading was rapidly being reallocated to new diversions, notably to radio listening and attending motion pictures. The Depression pushed the trend deeper, and the consequences of declining sales rippled through the publishing world. By the mid-1930s, American newspapers had cut back their story and review pages drastically. Papers that had published a full page of reviews and notices reduced their reviews to a couple of columns. Many newspapers that published book reviews only occasionally abandoned them altogether.[2]

[1] DLM to Jerry Bleak, 16 July 1937, Bleak letters.

[2] James D. Hart, *The Popular Book: A History of America's Literary Taste* (New York: Oxford Univ. Press, 1950), 246–282; David Welky, *Everything Was Better: Print Culture in the Great Depression* (Urbana: Univ. of Illinois Press, 2008).

In the three years during which Dale Morgan reviewed books for the *Tribune,* none of his opportunities involved books on the Mormons, the state of Utah, or even the West. He typically reviewed non-fiction and only occasionally the serious literature which he coveted. His contributions netted him little for the effort besides keeping the book he reviewed and the byline opportunity, but as a budding writer, reviewing books was one means of keeping himself in touch with the writing of the time. As he became progressively more focused on HRS activities, he reviewed progressively fewer books for the *Tribune.* The end of his book reviewing for the paper coincided with beginning the research effort that eventually became *The State of Deseret.*[3] Following his move to the national capital, in 1943 Morgan began plaguing the editor of *The Saturday Review of Literature* and other mainstream magazines with non-fiction article ideas, hoping for a break. None were accepted, but his zeal did secure his first book-review commission, for Richard Scowcroft's novel *Children of the Covenant,* perhaps because he had personally known and worked with the author when both were students at the University of Utah. Published weekly, this national publication inverted Morgan's earlier relationship with reviewing, since he reviewed nothing *but* non-academic Western or Mormon-related works for the *Review* between 1945 and 1965. As you can see, each was for a Mormon-related book from a nationally significant press or author.

What is not represented in this section are the manuscript reviews and critiques done privately by letter for friends and correspondents. Just as editor Maxwell Perkins shaped his generation of writers on the 1920s, particularly Ernest Hemingway, Morgan exerted a current of critical influence in the small amount of serious writing being done about the Mormon West. Writers whose work he shaped before publication included Nels Anderson's *Desert Saints* (1942), Wallace Stegner's *Mormon Country* (1942), Bernard DeVoto's *Year of Decision: 1846* (1943), two turns through the manuscript of Fawn Brodie's *No Man Knows My History* (1945), and Juanita Brooks's *Mountain Meadows Massacre* (1950), among others. These were mass-market rather than academic writers; very little scholarly writing involved the Latter Day Saints at all until the publication of Leonard Arrington's *Great Basin Kingdom* (1959). To this list can be added the private criticisms in the vein of the second edition of Francis W. Kirkham's *New Witness for Christ in America* (1947).

[3]A complete list from across his career is available in Saunders, *Eloquence from a Silent World: A Descriptive Bibliography of the Published Writings of Dale L. Morgan* (Salt Lake City: Caramon Press, 1990), 53–64.

Also not represented is the advice and resources he heaped on correspondents, some of whom were writers but many who never published their work. This list would include Community of Christ historian Inez Smith Davis, LDS apostle John A. Widtsoe, William H. Cadman, Stanley Ivins, and Fawn Brodie's uncle, Dean Brimhall. Writers in the church's mainstream, like Joseph Fielding Smith and popular scholar E. Cecil McGavin, studiously ignored Morgan, holding him and his work at arm's length, though they were concerned about his grasp of facts and documentation.

Book reviews are broad statements, and Morgan's reviews for *The Saturday Review of Literature* were written for general readership. In a review, an author is handed an opportunity to sit in formal judgment, so reviews reflect the author's view of a field that is not well covered by other forms of written work. Book reviewers do not tend to make a career out of criticism, and Dale Morgan was no exception, but in a collection such as this, reviews provide not only a judgment of the work under review but also a particular type of window into the writer. In this case, the reviews illuminate the shades and fissures in Morgan's perspective as a cultural participant and critic. His voracious reading habits as a youth and college student helped ground him in good (and bad) literature and provided a foundation in language and reading that he drew on for his reviews. Thus, he could deftly pillory Maurine Whipple with understatement as effectively as he could reach into the purple to praise Fawn Brodie. Morgan regarded review criticism—both positive and negative—as a charge of public duty. He was not immune, however, from the temptation to use a well-placed review to promote an interpretation of Mormonism that he shared (an in the case of Brodie's *No Man Knows My History*). Morgan's career as a book reviewer was relatively short, but the reviews produced for the *Saturday Review of Literature* kept him emotionally anchored in the field of Latter Day Saint culture and its history as the currents of life flowed on around him.

"They Happened to be Mormons"[4]

Children of the Covenant. By Richard Scowcroft.
Boston: Houghton Mifflin Company. 1945. 292 pp. $2.50.

With Mr. Scowcroft's novel something different and long overdue has come into Mormon fiction. There has been a great deal of writing about

[4] "They Happened to be Mormons," *Saturday Review of Literature* 28, no. 33 (18 August 1945): 16.

the Mormons of late, but the majority of the novelists have yielded to the almost irresistible impulse to write an epic of the pioneer years.

"Children of the Covenant" breaks so completely with this developing "romantic" tradition as to be somewhat misrepresented in being called a "Mormon novel" at all. It is, more properly, a mature and absorbing novel about some people who happen to be Mormons. Although the Mormon culture and pioneer energies are central forces in their lives, it is as individuals that we are concerned with them. The milieu could as well be Methodist and the locale Kansas, for this novel is an interpretation of the Mormons in terms of what is universal, rather than merely peculiar, in their lives.

Square-jawed daughter of one of Brigham Young's square-jawed empire builders, Esther Burton had married Harry Curtis in 1895 because he was available, because there might be no one else, and because she knew that "if one's husband couldn't build cities and railroads, one could bring up one's children so that they could." But the eldest boy, Hank, had taken up with cigarettes and girls and gone off to the Coast and unforgivably become successful. The lovely Irene had willfully married a Gentile, Julian, and died after the birth of the plain little Caroline.

Only [younger son] Burton, coming home from his mission to England, remains a justification for Esther's life. Burton feels, as he is expected to feel, that the two years given to the Church were the happiest of his life, that he values the mission more than a college education. But the mission has not given him any basis for adjustment to adult life, and as he flounders around, finally drowning in marriage, he makes progressive wreckage of Esther's contracting life, a ruin set in its ultimate clear perspective by the patient and even kindly Julian, in whom the little girl, Caroline, at last discovers her father.

To summarize Mr. Scowcroft's story in anything less than its own length is unsatisfying, for it is a searching novel of character, often sensitively imagined, exact and thoughtful in its observation, opening unhurriedly into the deep recesses of the family's life. In tone it ranges from an almost ascetic detachment to a tenderness that is close to tears. The writing is lucid and relaxed, with a vein of irony that underlies the narrative to crop out occasionally as a broader humor. Sometimes the portraiture is uneven in that the irony is not altogether consistent in its application. Burton, especially, often seems the butt of this irony beyond the immediate incongruity of situation, and one sometimes feels that Burton is too ruthlessly whittled down from his proper dimensions. But these things in no way burden the total effect of the novel. One will be able to ponder Mr. Scowcroft's people and come back to them for a more intimate understanding of them. That is achievement of a high order.

Mr. Scowcroft has avoided any such error as attempting to portray "a typical Mormon family." His people have something in common with every

Mormon family, and one has constant recognitions, but Mr. Scowcroft is concerned not with types but with human beings, and it is a tribute to his insight and depth that he could now write a novel about a family next door without in any degree exhausting our interest.

Yet, though it is no thesis novel, the book is significant as reportage. No one has stated so clearly or so forcibly the dilemma of Mormonism as the pioneer energies run down. The will to achieve is still passionately alive, but history has caught up with the Mormons and there is no place to go, no place for the Church to turn except in upon itself. As Julian says at last, one does not object to Mormonism, necessarily; one may even acquire an admiration for it. But one can object to "some of the zealous old brethren who have nothing to be zealous about. You can't be an evangelist if you've lost your message. The Mormons need a new message, a new cause."

The novel has a further importance as social history. Mr. Scowcroft depicts his native Ogden graphically, and that Ogden of twenty years ago provides a useful vantage point for surveying the social erosion one perceives to have operated since that time upon people and ideas. The free-spirited Liz Templeton, Mike Bradley, and, yes, even the sardonic Albert whose church membership is not incompatible with a corrosive vulgarity encompassing the Authorities themselves, are recognizable prototypes of people one meets on the street today; one would have to look much farther for a Burton with such elementary ideas about girls, or for a girl, in turn, with a mind calibrated to nothing more profound than chocolate pie and Ronald Colman. Intermarriage with Gentiles and use of tea, coffee, and tobacco still occasion a certain social discomfort and some blindfolding of the conscience, but they have ceased, at least in the urban areas, to constitute the raw stuff of sin and social ostracism.

"Scenic Backdrop With People"[5]

This Is the Place: Utah! By Maurine Whipple.
New York: Alfred A. Knopf. 1945. 222 pp. $5.

It is almost twenty years now since Bernard DeVoto, in the *American Mercury*, assaulted the pained citizenry of his native state with something more than a hint that there was more to be said about their culture than they took in on Sundays at church or on Fridays at the Rotary Club luncheon. Mr. DeVoto and the State both have mellowed since he blew off that accumulated steam, but a full-length portrait of Utah set in a frame of scholarship and painted with an urbane, sufficiently astringent, yet sympathetic touch has waited for other hands and the present decade.

[5]"Scenic Backdrop, with People," *Saturday Review of Literature* 28, no. 45 (10 November 1945): 17.

Maurine Whipple's is the third such book about Utah in five years. The Writers' Program's "Utah: A Guide to the State" (1941) is the basic account of the state, and Wallace Stegner's "Mormon Country" (1942) is an immensely readable report on the region, its history, and its people, by a vigorous critical intelligence with a novelist's eye for the flare and color of a people and a land. Owing a great deal to both these books, "This Is the Place: Utah" has also an individuality that is a reflection of Miss Whipple's lusty, gusty, sometimes bumptious personality, and it is set off with some of the most breathless photographs of Utah (and therefore of the West) ever brought between two covers.

"This Is the Place: Utah" is half picture book, with four magnificent photographs in full color, and ninety-eight black and white photographs hardly less striking. The sun is in them, and the wind, and the desert fragrances, and the blood and bones of an immortal naked land, "17,000 square miles standing on end," with a people tucked in at the crevices. The other half of this book, Miss Whipple's prose contribution, is more difficult to characterize—a crazy-quilt Chamber of Commerce daydream in no way belying the reality, a record of good times with good fellows, an elliptical history, a hardheaded thinkpiece, a cookbook, an easychair course in the contemporary a gossip of Mormondom. . . . It's these and a large variety of other things.

Miss Whipple's first novel published in 1941, "The Giant Joshua," is still the best of the romantic novels about the Mormons. Her new book partakes both of the flaws and the virtues of her first. It often proceeds by exclamation, it is at times crushingly romantic, and it is a spasmodic engulfing of Mormon history, in places disorganized and overmuch cluttered with Miss Whipple herself. But also it has a matchless eye for the sensuous splendor of the red rock country, an impetuous, not to say explosive, interest in people, a shrewd and sometimes summary skepticism.

The introduction and the first section of the book, "Do They Really Have Horns?," are least well done, with many of the facts not quite straight, the personal effect distinctly contrived, and the narrative only at intervals catching fire. But in the second section, wherein Miss Whipple takes as her text dour Ebenezer Bryce's imperishable summation of the glories of Bryce Canyon—"Hell of a Place to Lose a Cow"—the land smokes and glows in its farthest corners as she roams it, "the whole landscape—the white, the green, the gray, the yellow, and the red—bucking like a wild steer," and through it all "wonderful sunny silences, freedom and smell of space," with a full complement of "hardgutted" people having a capacity for living.

The Mormons, "A Peculiar People," in the third section are dissected with professional aplomb; at the same time Miss Whipple is full of stories new and old about the Mormon way of life. Some of these are likely to be remembered. But out in Zion, what is going to bring the natives to this chapter like bees to a honeypot is the frank reporting of the state of things in Mormondom, the adversities of the Church in prosperity. Some of the internal cleavages of which Miss Whipple writes are more apparent than real, but they certainly exist and must be reckoned with. The final chapter, "The Arsenal of Democracy," is an arresting picture of the impact of the war upon Utah; it is vigorous journalism but in the sequel, I suspect, will prove indifferent history.

Miss Whipple closes her book with acknowledgements for services rendered. The list runs to incredible proportions, but something would seem to have been left undone. A number of the Utah Guide's best lines she has wedded without benefit of quotation marks, and she has an unexpressed major indebtedness to Nels Anderson's discerning book on Utah's frontier era, "Desert Saints." A certain justice follows in the omission to credit literary sources, however, for she has taken to herself from these works not only facts, ideas, and language, but for good measure a number of their errors.

"A Prophet and His Legend"[6]

No Man Knows My History: The Life of Joseph Smith, the Mormon Prophet.
By Fawn M. Brodie.
New York: Alfred A. Knopf. 1945. 476 pp. and index. $4.

As with his contemporary, Abraham Lincoln, and to even more marked degree, there is about the life of Joseph Smith extraordinary difficulty in getting at the man himself inside the encrustation of legend. Apotheosis has been the lot of each man, but in the case of the Mormon prophet something exactly akin to deification has been at work. Vilification of him has largely disappeared with his generation, while among his followers faith and the will to believe have worked upon his memory, expurgating his history of the grotesque, the absurd, or the merely inconvenient, softening his faults, and investing his character with a sweet serenity and an infinite love—a being who withstood the devil and all his archangels and died a martyr.

Nor is the task of searching out the man inside this temple of belief the only difficulty confronting a biographer. The life of Joseph Smith was an outrageous melodrama any playwright would tremble at placing on a stage, yet at the heart of this melodrama was a character infinitely complex and steadily enigmatic. Joseph Smith was a man who wrote largely about himself, yet revealed himself almost in nothing, and a man, moreover, of abundantly contradictory interests, motivations, and ambitions. He, became the most celebrated of modern prophets, and revised his history accordingly; his followers have gone on revising it to suit their needs and tastes, and his enemies

6"A Prophet and His Legend," *Saturday Review of Literature* 28, no. 47 (24 November 1945): 7–8.

have contributed their full quota of obfuscation. Between the suppression and the manufacture of fact, it is not strange that it has required a hundred years for the writing of a definitive biography.

In "No Man Knows My History," Fawn M. Brodie has taken up the challenge Joseph Smith himself laid down in a sermon to his people two months before his death: *"You don't know me; you never knew my heart. No man knows my history. I cannot tell it; I shall never undertake it. I don't blame anyone for not believing my history. If I had not experienced what I have, I could not have believed it myself."* Mrs. Brodie has pursued that history through quiet country towns in Vermont, New York, and Pennsylvania, through religious revivals, land booms, and panics, through civil wars and "mobbings and drivings" across the breadth of the Mississippi Valley, and through temples, courtrooms, bedrooms, and jails to its violent end in a little town in Illinois.

Joseph Smith's story is all he says of it—so fundamentally incredible that notwithstanding the million present day Mormons and the stupendous literature about him, one is sometimes persuaded that no such person ever existed. But in Mrs. Brodie's book an eminently human and entirely understandable being stares into peepstones, communes with God, kicks the tax collector the length of his walk, rebukes the powers of his time, drinks with the boys, marries some fifty wives, parades with the Nauvoo Legion, and has his people distinctly to understand that a prophet is a prophet only while he is working at the job. The result is the finest job of scholarship yet done in Mormon history and perhaps the outstanding biography in several years—a book distinguished in the range and originality of its research, the informed and searching objectivity of its viewpoint, the richness and suppleness of its prose, and its narrative power.

It is with wit and vigor and learning that Mrs. Brodie has reexamined some of the most cherished and most fundamental conceptions of Mormon history, the first sober application of modern techniques and criteria of research to a history fiercely irreconcilable in its details and overlaid with both passion and duplicity. The story of Joseph's intercourse with God in the coming-forth of the Book of Mormon she pictures as essentially an afterthought on the part of the Prophet, and hers is a fresh point of view which will give pause to scholars in and out of the several Mormon churches. The Book of Mormon itself she subjects to a remarkably original analysis of its character, its content, and the sources of its ideas; in her hands it emerges as a work of imaginative creation by a variously gifted young man, a work which began as a simple speculation and ended as the touchstone of a new religion to which its author had become committed. Though this theory is not new, its implementation is.

If the Spaulding theory relative to the origin of the Book of Mormon has retained any adherents in the face of forceful criticisms by B. H. Roberts on the one side and Bernard DeVoto on the other,* the appendix Mrs. Brodie devotes to this subject should lay that theory to rest once and for all. But Mrs. Brodie's demolitions have been carried still further: those who have accepted Mr. DeVoto's persuasive theory that Joseph Smith was a paranoid will find no comfort at all in this book. That theory rests initially upon an acceptance of the historicity of Joseph Smith's own account of his visions, and it will be quite an undertaking for scholars to reestablish the authenticity of those visions in the light of Mrs. Brodie's exploration of the facts; moreover, Mrs. Brodie's skilful integration of Joseph Smith with the turbulent times in which he lived, together with the surgical job she has performed in laying open the quality and character of his personality, does not encourage the thesis that Joseph's was a personality for which death barely intervened upon complete disintegration.

Having faced up to the hard fact that Joseph Smith must have been initially a conscious fraud and imposter, Mrs. Brodie is not so undiscerning as to leave the question there. Joseph's capacity for fantasy was entirely adequate to persuade him ultimately of the actuality of his own pretensions; though Mrs. Brodie thinks it doubtful if he ever escaped "the memory of the conscious artifice that went into the Book of Mormon," no one can explore his history without reaching the conviction that he came to believe utterly in the role to which destiny led him.

Mrs. Brodie's point of view is essentially sympathetic throughout, yet, as her publishers say, "inexorably searching as to the facts and the probabilities." A constant flood of light is thrown on Joseph and his church, an illumination that penetrates to the obscurest corners of their joint history and lights up details at which other historians have fumbled ineffectually. Of particular importance is her investigation of the origins of polygamy, culminating in an amazing appendix documenting the Prophet's relations with almost fifty wives—a total which will doubtless shock even the better informed among the Mormons themselves. Nor has she been nonplused by the stand of the Reorganized Church, which has hitherto stood uncontradicted in its claim that Joseph had no children by plural wives (and therefore could have had no plural wives), although from the nature of the facts no absolute determination can be made. And with all these solid merits, the biography has the pace and sweep, the bizarre incidents, and impelling suspense of the most extravagant

*[The "Spaulding theory" was an early attempt to explain the *Book of Mormon* by crediting Campbellite minister Sidney Rigdon with the book's origin. Proponents argued that Rigdon absconded with a literary romance by one Solomon Spaulding, rewrote the story, and then passed it off to Joseph Smith, Jr., for publication as *The Book of Mormon*. Spaulding's original manuscript was rediscovered in the late nineteenth century. Since it exhibits only the barest thread of similarity to the foundation text of Mormonism, adherents subsequently proposed the existence of an earlier, unrecorded Spaulding manuscript. The works to which Morgan alludes are B. H. Roberts, *A New Witness for God* (Salt Lake City: George Q. Cannon & Sons, 1895), which went through subsequent editions as *New Witnesses for God*; and Bernard DeVoto, *Forays and Rebuttals* (Boston: Little, Brown, 1936), 92–95. —Ed.]

historical novel, and its violent climax under the walls of Carthage jail has all the power and emotional impact of a personal experience.

Some criticisms suggest themselves. Perhaps the spotlight is too insistently kept on Joseph, and it is questionable whether quite so searchingly sympathetic a viewpoint has operated in the analysis of the lesser persons who figure in the drama. Mrs. Brodie is less inclined to recognize the chiaroscuro of character with these others than with Joseph and Emma Smith. Inadequate attention also may have been given to the developments of those in the church who upon Joseph's death took hold upon power with a firm, grasp and "carried off the kingdom" with a strength and decision that could hardly have been foreseen. In the interests of narrative sweep, again, Mrs. Brodie selects her thread of fact without always indicating the complexity of the possibilities; there are more difficult problems about both the selection and the assessment of fact than is always clear from the text. And, finally, it may be said that in summing up the Prophet's life, what he was, what he stood for, what he accomplished, and what his legacy was and is, Mrs. Brodie's judgment may be subject to both a kinder and a far more rangingly objective reinterpretation.

When all reservations have been made, however, "No Man Knows My History" stacks up as almost certainly the definitive treatment of its subject. At the very least it is the book that had to be written before a finally authoritative biography could be written. It is not to be expected that members of the Mormon churches will accept the biography as either final or authoritative, striking as it does at the very sources of their faith. But if their feelings are to have any weight outside their own sentiments, they will have to unearth from their archives facts to modify or to contravene Mrs. Brodie's conclusions. Thus her book is going to serve a valuable function as a benchmark and a corrective in Mormon scholarship. "No Man Knows My History," altogether, is an extremely difficult and important job, well done.

"Fruits of Rebellion"[7]

The Evening and the Morning. By Virginia Sorensen.
New York: Harcourt, Brace & Co. 1949. 341 pp. $3.

"The Evening and the Morning" is a fine and in every way distinguished work, as satisfying a novel as I have read in several years, and one which abundantly realizes every promise of Virginia Sorensen's first three novels. In these pages two years ago I complained of a dissociation in her work, that she seemed to be writing stories about people, not writing about people directly. I have no such objection now. The experience of reading her new book is that of

[7]"Fruits of Rebellion," *Saturday Review of Literature* 32, no. 17 (23 April 1949): 13–14.

having lived with people—and people who disturbingly, inexorably, through all their diversity and complexity, are yourself. That is the power and the beauty of this novel, that somehow or other it is everybody's autobiography.

To tell her story, Mrs. Sorensen has returned to the scene of her second novel and of her own childhood, the town of Manti in Utah's Sanpete Valley, a place for which she has a profound feeling and about which she writes with a penetrating understanding. The settlers of this high mountain valley were predominantly Danish, as is Mrs. Sorensen herself, and she writes about them as the generations have worked upon and "Americanized" them. Because these people whom she knows were Mormon converts, Mormon themes here as elsewhere occupy Mrs. Sorensen's pages, but let us make this clear, she is no writer of "Mormon novels." It is only by accident of her birth or theirs that the people she writes about are Mormons rather than Amish or Pennsylvania Dutch, and their problems are the problems of people everywhere who somehow must make good lives for themselves, each bringing order out of his individual chaos.

In this new novel it is Kate Alexander's life that we are mainly concerned with, but Kate's life is inseparable from the whole life of her family, her children, even her grandchildren. Kate's desires and needs have shaped the desires and needs of her daughter, antithetical as these are, and Dessie's imperatives in turn have molded her husband's life, and her children's. All of them alike seek something to hold to, emotional security, but for some this security is attainable only by the route of rebellion. That becomes perhaps the major theme of the book, the necessity, the difficulty, and the fruits of rebellion.

Eighteen-year-old Kate Black had married the slender widower Karl Alexander because he was good, because he was kind, and because he was the first man who asked her. But Kate came to learn that there are deeps within a woman which simple goodness can never be adequate to plumb. Eventually she had to seek from the young fiddle-maker Peter Hansen, as he from her, the ecstasy and misery that existed for neither of them within the blank walls of their marriages. Yet Kate and Peter were responsible persons who had to recognize their marriages and families as realities from which they could not run away. Only Marya, sister of Karl's dead first wife and of Peter's own wife, came to suspect what existed between them and that Dessie was the child of Peter. What came of this relationship finally, the emptiness and the irony, is brilliantly and compassionately chronicled.

Kate's story is told on the occasion of her visit to her daughter's home during six hot July days of 1922, and the story proceeds in two dimensions, the six days of the present and whole lifetimes of the past, which is not the past at all but the urgent present. The opening pages are a little difficult, as difficult as Kate's absorption into the bloodstream of her daughter's family life, but as we begin to know Kate we are caught up in the spell of her story, not to be released until she sits at last in a railway coach by night, her granddaughter's sleeping head pillowed on her lap, remembering how evening follows morning, and morning evening—nothing ever ended that is not also a new beginning.

In the space available to me it is impossible to convey the whole richness of this novel, the sharply etched portraits of so many different people, the many avenues of entrance into universal experience. This is a major novel that with all its technical brilliance is honest, simple, and direct, and distinguished for its understanding, its justness, its intelligence, and its feeling.

"Deseret News That Is Fit to Print"[8]

Voice in the West. By Wendell Ashton.
New York: Duell, Sloan Pearce. 424 pp. $5.

This book is a "centennial biography" of the Salt Lake City *Deseret News,* which as one of the twenty newspapers established north of Texas and west of the Missouri River got out its first issue June 15, 1850. Save for the Santa Fe *New Mexican,* which celebrated its hundredth anniversary two years ago, it has outlived all its contemporaries. In a country of notably high press mortality the feat of achieving a centennial issue is enough, surely, to justify a history.

The *News* has come safe and sound through its century principally because it has been the organ of the Mormon Church. In its first precarious years the Church was alert to see that unhealthy competition did not choke its growth and the Church has steadily beaten the bushes for subscribers to maintain it. Even this powerful aid would have been insufficient had the Church not been able also to lick the paper problem, and perhaps the most appealing chapters of Mr. Ashton's book are those which describe the struggles of a pioneer paper industry.

Rarely over its long history has the *Deseret News* been an exciting paper, but it has contrived to represent the interests of the Mormon people and of Utah in a sober fashion which on the whole has done it honor.

It remains Utah's most influential paper, in the sense that public personalities and institutions fear it more than its contemporaries—not as a newspaper so much as an expression of Church attitudes which may influence local elections and legislative appropriations. On the other hand, it is so ultra-conservative, dominated by the prejudices which have their finest flowering in J. Reuben Clark, that it is regarded with a certain suspicion and dislike even by many members of the Church, to say nothing of other elements of the community. In part as a result of historical circumstance, in part because it represents so narrow a pressure interest, the *News* long

[8]"Deseret News That Is Fit to Print," *Saturday Review of Literature* 33, no. 23 (15 July 1950): 27.

has lagged behind its morning contemporary both in news coverage and in circulation, and as the *Tribune* can be more things to more people, there is no early prospect that the *News* will gain the preeminence it so much covets.

Neither by first nor last intention is this a critical history. Mr. Ashton was hired to serve up the pièce-de-résistance for a birthday party and there is no use pining after gamier fare than is produced for the occasion. If the inner history of the *News* is ever written, its struggle to be a newspaper in the great tradition with the managing authority in the hands of men whose real interest is religion rather than newspapering, obviously it will have to be done outside the *News* organization. Such a history will be much more entertaining than anything that is to be found in the present book and a wonderfully amusing chapter will deal with the crotchets of the paper, how its busybody concern with the morals of the community sits upon editorial policy and practice, even the most innocuous of comic strips not secure from the censorious chisel of the stereotyper. But we may have to wait a long while for another cook than Mr. Ashton, and if it is mutton rather than venison that he serves up, after all, a good joint of mutton has its uses.

The early chapters are much the best, a useful contribution to the history of American printing and publishing, since Mr. Ashton was given access to the archives of the Church and to important diaries still in private hands which have been withheld from students. This part of the book also exhibits a greater objectivity than is characteristic of the chronicle of the last half-century and Mr. Ashton points out some of the more obvious failings as well as the special virtues of the *News* as a true newspaper during its pioneer period. Unwilling to trample on any tender corns, Mr. Ashton is not so successful in dealing with the paper and its personalities since the turn of the century, its vicissitudes as a metropolitan daily, and its renaissance since throwing overboard an old Church prejudice to begin publication of a Sunday edition.

The style in which the whole is told demonstrates once more what a mingled curse and blessing *Time* has been to the prose of our generation. Well illustrated and documented, the book is marred by an index more lengthy than adequate.

"Gallant Lady"[9]

Family Kingdom. By Samuel Woolley Taylor.
New York: McGraw-Hill Book Co. 302 pp. $3.30.

Several years ago in *Holiday* magazine Samuel W. Taylor published an account of his remarkable father and the life he led his six families as one of the last great Mormon polygamists, a reminiscence so full of zest, of high

[9]"Gallant Lady," *Saturday Review of Literature* 34, no. 19 (12 May 1951): 17.

good humor, and refreshing social insights as to have retained a warm place in the recollection of all who read it. Now he has written an entire book about John W. Taylor and his variegated families, a book which has every good quality of the original article and particular virtues besides.

I am sure it will delight many as a tale; at the same time it has a certain value as a contribution to our understanding of the mechanics and the infinite complexity and variety of the society in which we live. By intention "Family Kingdom" is the story of Mr. Taylor's mother, Nettie May, the third of John W.'s six wives. But, of course, her story is inseparable from that of her husband, and to all intents and purposes it comes to its end with John W. Taylor's death in 1916. Not exactly a formal biography even of his mother and not even remotely one of his father, Mr. Taylor's "Family Kingdom" actually is an impressionistic portrait of both his parents, gay and altogether engaging yet with an underlying sadness. For Nettie M. Taylor, still living today, has seen herself become a quaint and uncomfortable anachronism even among her own people. The sacrifices she made were in pursuit of an ideal which in the perspective of time is seen to have been vain and impossible and which the Mormons themselves would prefer to have forgotten.

A son by a plural wife of the third president of the Mormon church, John W. Taylor was a young man of distinguished presence, gay and gregarious, headstrong to the point of wilfulness, brimming over with energy, a born promoter and plunger, yet a man whose essential spirituality was his most striking quality. He brought snap and sparkle into the lives of everyone who knew him, warmth and a sense of the richness of life, so that each of his friends regarded himself as his best friend and each of his six wives felt assured in her heart that she was his favorite wife, while he was adored by, as he adored, not only the three dozen children his own wives bore him but all the children of any neighborhood he lived in.

But he was a man born too early or too late. In a time when the survival of his church depended upon its capacity for compromise and change he was hostile to compromise and incapable of change. He had taken his first two plural wives just before his church formally renounced the practice of plural marriage; like a great many others of his generation, John W. Taylor could not bring himself to give up a principle he regarded as divinely enjoined, and thereafter he took three more wives. Inevitably it became necessary that the church hurl him from his high position as one of the Quorum of the Twelve Apostles. For, although at various periods in its history the church had found it necessary to talk from two sides of its mouth, during those times it also had to maintain a façade of impeccable integrity, depending upon the passing years to harden this into the real thing. Any one member could be regarded as expendable.

As history "Family Kingdom" would be a good deal more valuable if—granting that he had the desire—Samuel W. Taylor had the necessary information to develop the details of his father's estrangement from the church. The whole question of plural marriage and its abandonment by the church is still a Pandora's box the church authorities would just as soon keep closed for a long time.

But I do not wish to make too much of defects. Mr. Taylor's account of his mother's growing up depicts the patriarchal society of the Utah frontier in the time of its finest flowering and shows us also why and how that way of life came to an end. His mother's gallant years on "the underground" as a child-bearing "widow," the dizzy alternation of her life, emotionally, socially, and financially, between the heights and the depths, the rigid principle she had to live by, the disproportionate sacrifices that polygamy required from the women, and the complacence of the men in pursuit of heavenly blessings with earthly prerogatives, the complex relations which obtained between wives, and families—all this and much more is woven into a continuously fascinating story told with wit, warmth, and much wisdom. Only nine years old when his father died, Samuel W. Taylor writes about him with some detachment, but no one will doubt the affection with which he holds in remembrance his extraordinary father or the love and admiration he has for his mother.

Dale L. Morgan is the author of "The Great Salt Lake" and other books about the Mormon Country.

Chapter 8

The Mormon Ferry on the North Platte
The Journal of William A. Empey, May 7–August 4, 1847

Editor's Introduction

Dale Morgan travelled across the continent on a Guggenheim Foundation research fellowship in 1947 and 1948, gathering material and gaining a personal sense of the geography of Mormondom. After costly repairs to address engine trouble in California, he crossed the Sierras and the Nevada desert, limping into his mother's driveway in Salt Lake City on 28 March 1948. By then the car was working, but his finances were a wreck. He had hoped his research fellowship would be renewed another year but, flooded with applicants recently demobilized from military and industrial service during the Second World War, the Guggenheim Foundation opted to encourage scholarship as broadly as it could and chose not to renew fellowships. Morgan moved to an apartment and began working as a freelance writer as he tried to start writing on his Mormon projects. He remained in the city between April 1948 and October 1949. Over that year and a half, Morgan's attention to historical research fragmented, drawn in many directions at once by both opportunity and necessity. This book addresses only scattered segments of that process, projects that as a rule did not make him any money. The few Mormon-related projects that did net him some income are collected in chapter 10; the ones he actually worked on through this period occupy chapters 8 and 9.

Between 1948 and 1953, Dale Morgan engaged in a frenetic and fractured attempt at keeping as many options open as possible. In the first week of June

1949, while he waited for the University of Utah to decide about publication of his Mormon historical bibliography (Chapter 9 here) and in a short lull between several other projects, Morgan pitched the value of the William A. Empey diary to Wyoming state librarian Mary McGrath. As he noted in the published introduction, he had been alerted to the diary's existence at the Huntington Library by Juanita Brooks. When he arrived there himself in January 1948, Morgan invested some of his research time making a careful transcript. The document was a remarkable record. As the Mormons' initial Pioneer Company moved west in 1847, Empey and eight others had been assigned to remain at the last North Platte crossing to operate a ferry. The diary was not long, but it was detailed and short enough to make a good documentary article.

Like many state historical journals, *The Annals of Wyoming* conducted a ceaseless search for suitable material, and Morgan's proposal on Empey's journal was a godsend. Replicating the intense writing of *The State of Deseret* and some of his later manuscripts, Morgan required a month to pull notes together from his transcripts, all the time prodding various correspondents for additional information. Six weeks from the initial proposal date, he wrote Chicago book collector Everett D. Graff, mentioning that the notes were complete and he was at work on an introduction. The finished manuscript went to McGrath's successor, Ellen Crowley, on Pioneer Day, 24 July 1949. His submission went into production immediately and appeared in a double July–October issue late the same year.[1]

Such a tight schedule for the detailed editing of the Empey journal—measured in weeks rather than months—shows how closely entwined Morgan's research on the Mormons and the larger West really was. They were conjoined topics, even while he preferred to pin his hopes on his Mormon studies through the opening of his career. The Mormon settlement of Utah was a subset of the West's larger history, and Empey's stay on the central

[1]DLM to Mary A. McGrath, 7 June 1949; DLM to Everett D. Graff, 14 July 1949; DLM to Ellen Crowley, 24 July 1949. The Appleton M. Harmon diary, which figures prominently in Morgan's edited rendition, had been a transcription project of the Utah Historical Records Survey as early as 1936, so Morgan had been aware of the historical significance of the ferry ever since he began stirring around in Western history. The Empey diary, however, he transcribed himself from the original document at the Huntington Library, San Marino, Calif. His editing was enriched by the published *William Clayton's Journal* (Salt Lake City: Clayton Family Association, 1921), but as unpublished material in the Church Historian's Office was generally inaccessible, Morgan was unaware of the official diary of the Pioneer Company kept by Thomas Bullock. It is now available as *The Pioneer Camp of the Saints: The 1846 and 1847 Mormon Trail Journals of Thomas Bullock*, ed. Will Bagley (Spokane, Wash.: Arthur H. Clark Co., 1997).

Wyoming overland trail was a smaller subset of Mormon settlement. Mormon Utah and the broader West shared common archival resources at the federal level. Morgan had drawn notes, references, and transcripts on both subjects from the same research. As he had embarked upon a research regimen in the Library of Congress holdings in 1943, he had culled American newspapers for items related to the Latter Day Saints, trans-Mississippi exploration, the fur trade, and overland trail history. Continuing work in the National Archives records series in the late 1940s, he combed departmental records from Interior, State, War, and Justice, along with the General Land Office and select executive and legislative branch series, as well as manuscript collections. He also compiled an extensive and always growing collection of books and documentary publications in journals. By the time he proposed publication of the Empey diary in the middle of 1949, Morgan had amassed a peerless collection of primary-source material in print and transcript, one large enough that he could write authoritatively on a relatively obscure Western topic without leaving his apartment. As an exercise in documentary editing, of marshalling available facts, the Empey diary is the first project of the type that would secure Morgan his lasting reputation as a scholar of the American West—but it did not pay well.

Existing for a year and a half on occasional writing commissions and short-term employment, without a dependable income, nothing for Dale Morgan was ever simple or straightforward. At about the same time the Empey manuscript was mailed to Cheyenne, he finally decided Salt Lake City was unwilling to provide meaningful employment for him and began preparing to move back to Washington, D.C., for the city's better job prospects. Between July and November, as he read and corrected the Empey galleys and page proofs, he was also packing his apartment, sorting and prioritizing the research material he would take with him, and trying to produce at least a rough draft for the first volume of his Mormon book. As if that was not enough, during the same months he was also indexing the massive double-volume publication of the Colorado River exploration documents for the *Utah Historical Quarterly*; compiling, circulating, and submitting the Bickerton bibliography; taking over Roderick Korns's research on trails across Utah; advising the Utah Historical Society on collection development and its publication processes; conducting research and setting down occasional conceptual drafts for later chapters his Mormon book; abstracting the Oliver Olney papers for Edward Eberstadt & Sons; all the while writing between four and ten letters daily in a ceaseless round of queries, updates, requests, and answers to correspondents across the country. Juggling such a variety of demands represented not only a broad and inclusive interest in the West, but also an attempt to keep open as many options as possible, hoping one would eventually pan out into a salary. The number of projects he shuffled often also had the unintended effect of distracting his attention from larger goals and firmer opportunities.

Morgan's editing of the Empey diary is a marvelous document, full of collocated details and relevant historical context. The calculated risk he took producing the manuscript robbed time from the effort he could expend on his Mormon book, the one project to which he was contractually committed, but the short time he had to devote to the project makes the documentary result all the more remarkable.

"The Mormon Ferry on the North Platte: The Journal of William A. Empey, May 7–August 4, 1847" ed. Dale L. Morgan*

The nine men Brigham Young detailed in 1847 from his Pioneer party to remain at the Upper Crossing of the North Platte and operate a ferry for the benefit of the Saints and the convenience of the Oregon and California immigration established a famous institution in the history of the Overland Trail. There had been ferries to serve overland travelers before this time, across the Missouri and the Kaw, but the Mormon ferry at the Upper Crossing of the Platte marked the beginning of commercial ferry operations in the Rocky Mountains, foreshadowed similar ferries across the Green and Bear rivers, and for six years played a prominent role in the westward movement.

During 1847 and 1848 the Mormons had a monopoly in the operation of ferries at the North Platte, though immigrants sometimes stayed on at the river for a time to pick up an extra dollar or two by ferry work. The gold rush to California broke up the Mormon monopoly, such as it was, rival companies finding it to their advantage to come out from the States to compete for the business. The ever growing stream of overland travel finally rendered the ferries obsolete, by underwriting the investment required to bridge the river.

*[*Annals of Wyoming* 21, no. 2–3 (July–October 1949): 111–176. —Ed.]

The journal of William A. Empey, as here published with supplemental extracts from the journal of Appleton M. Harmon, presents an almost complete picture of the operations of the Mormon ferry during its first year. No such records exist for the following years, but a general picture of the ferry can be gained in 1849 and 1850, and at least one reference is to be found to the Mormon ferry as late as 1852, the last year before John Richard's bridge permanently swept the ferries from the river.

The nine men selected to run the Mormon ferry as first established were Thomas Grover, John S. Higbee, William A. Empey, Appleton M. Harmon, Edmund Ellsworth, Luke Johnson, Francis M. Pomeroy, James Davenport, and Benjamin F. Stewart.[1] After the greater part of the Oregon and California immigration had passed, Grover, Ellsworth, Pomeroy, and Stewart turned east to meet their families, who were coming along with the great migration following in the track of the Mormon Pioneers. Of those who waited at the ferry, three were to be disappointed in any expectations they may have had that their own families would be along, and these three, Empey, Harmon, and Johnson, after the Mormon immigration passed by, rode on down the Platte to wait at Fort Laramie for the Pioneers returning from the Great Salt Lake. Harmon found employment at the fort as a blacksmith, and stayed there until March, but Johnson and Empey journeyed on back to the States. All three men appear to have migrated to Utah with the immigration of 1848, and of the three only Harmon had any further connection with the Platte ferry.

Although little is known about their experiences or identity, a company of Saints journeyed to the Platte in the spring of 1848 for the dual purpose of operating the ferry and of taking East teams for the year's Mormon immigration. It is probably these of whom Eliza R. Snow writes in her diary on May 18, "Hancock, Ellsworth & others start with teams to meet the immigrants." And again on May 23, "Another com{pany} start with 35 wagons to meet the immigrants." In August, she and others having gone on an excursion up into the mountains above Salt Lake Valley, she noted that they returned in company with, "Ellsworth & Hancock who came up with us on Mon{day} from the Platte, & arriv'd in the valley on Fri{day} the

---

[1]Brief biographies of all these men are printed by Andrew Jenson in his *Latter-day Saints' Biographical Encyclopedia*, vols. 2 and 4, though it will be seen in the light of the information in Empey's journal that most of these biographies are faulty insofar as they relate to the ferry.

18th."[2] From these notations, it would seem that Edmund Ellsworth and Levi Hancock were among those who served the ferry in 1848. The identity of the others is not easily established.

It was a forceful precedent that the ferrymen this year came from the West rather than from the East. After 1848, each year till the Platte Bridge was built, a company set out from Great Salt Lake City to reach the river in advance of the year's immigration. The overland journals of 1848 are few in number, and only one daily diary of an Oregon or California immigrant is known. Riley Root, headed for Oregon, arrived at the ferry on June 15 to find a group of Saints already there. "The Mormons from Salt Lake," he commented, "had arrived a few days previous, and prepared a raft for crossing." He crossed the river next day, though whether ferried by the Saints he neglects to say.[3]

Six weeks later, when the Mormon immigration reached the Upper Crossing, their brethren were awaiting them. Hosea Stout wrote in his journal on August 4, "several from the Valley . . . had come to meet us & had been also ferrying the Oregon Emegrants over the Platte."[4] Their presence was welcome, not so much in crossing the river, which by August could usually be forded, as in the fresh teams they had ready to take up the burden from the failing oxen of the immigration.

Rather more is known about ferry operations in 1849. Appleton Harmon was one of a company of nine who traveled to the ferry, and in his autobiography he gives a condensed account of their experiences. They arrived, he says, on the 27th of May, "and commenced ferrying the 28 a very heavey emegration ware passing to California and in July 2 battalions of U.S. troops crossed at our ferry on their way to Oreigon[5] and one Company of our own emigrants going to the Valley. a bout the last of July and after the river became fordable we having earned and divided $646.50 cts to each of us. we bought each of us a waggon and oxen to draw it and Started to the alley."[6]

[2]"Pioneer Diary of Eliza R. Snow," *Improvement Era* 47 (April 1944): 239.

[3]Riley Root, *Journal of Travels from St. Josephs to Oregon* (Galesburg, Ill.: Gazetteer and Intelligencer Prints, 1850), 20.

[4]Hosea Stout, Journal No. 4, typed transcription in the WPA Collection of the Utah State Historical Society [*On the Mormon Frontier: The Diary of Hosea Stout*, ed. Juanita Brooks, 2 vol. (Salt Lake City: Utah State Historical Society, 1963), 1: 321].

[5]See the narrative by Osborne Cross, as edited by Raymond W. Settle, *The March of the Mounted Riflemen* (Glendale, Calif.: Arthur H. Clark Co., 1940), 110–112. The army officers found it more expedient to have their wagons ferried across by the Mormons at $4 each than to build rafts and hazard their wagons to them. The river was crossed 2–3 July 1849.

[6]Appleton M. Harmon, Autobiography, typed transcription in the WPA Collection of the Utah State Historical Society; printed in *Appleton Milo Harmon Goes West* (Berkeley: Gillick Press, 1946), 53–4.

Besides Harmon, the ferrymen this year were Charles Shumway, Madison [D. Hambleton], James Allred, John Greene, Andrew Lytle, one Potter, and two others whose names do not appear. Shumway was evidently in charge, for a letter from him in the archives of the Church, written apparently at the end of May from the "Upper Platte Ferry," advises that his company "arrived there on the 27th, raised their boats, and found them in good order. . . . On the 29th the first company of emigrants for the California gold mines reached the ferry, who stated that the road thence to the Missouri river was lined with emigrant wagons for the same destination."[7]

Numerous overland journals of 1849 make mention of the Mormon ferry. Among the earliest was William G. Johnston, who noted in his journal on June 3, "Contrary to expectation, based upon the common reputation of these Latter-Day Saints, we found those in charge of the ferry men of respectable appearance, well informed, polite, and in every way agreeable. They showed us specimens of California gold, the first we had seen, and their accounts as to the Eldorado were as extravagant as any we have had."[8] William Kelly, who came along a day later, adds that the ferrymen were "strongly entrenched in a heavy timber palisading, for their own protection and the security of their animals," the Crows just then being troublesome in the extreme. As Kelly describes the ferryboat, it was similar in all respects to that of 1847; it was perhaps the same craft, even, consisting of a large platform constructed on two dug-out canoes. "This structure they worked with three large oars, one at each side, and one as a rudder, getting over smoothly enough, but at a terrible slant, which gave them hard labour in again working up against the stream, even with the assistance of two yoke of oxen pulling on the bank as on a canal."[9]

William Johnston's cordial opinion of the Saints at the ferry was echoed by a Dr. Caldwell, who came along on June 27. "Entered our names to cross," his diary says, "when our turn comes. This is 5 miles below the old crossing, of Fremont & others. They have but one boat here, which is a good one, & very careful hands. The Mormons appear honest so far as dealing with them{.}

[7]Documentary History of the Church, 1849, p. 85, MS. in LDS Church Historian's Office, Salt Lake City, Utah.

[8]See Johnston's *Experiences of a 49er* (Pittsburgh: [n.p.], 1892), or the edition printed at Oakland, Calif.: Biobooks, 1948, under the title, *Overland to California*.

[9]William Kelly, *Across the Rocky Mountains, from New York to California*, 2nd. ed. (London: Sims and M'Intyre, 1852), 126–127. The first edition, *An Excursion to California over the Prairie, Rocky Mountains, and Great Sierra Nevada* (London: Chapman and Hall, 1851), has different pagination.

They conduct matters very well here, & have a smithery with 2 forges, but charge high. They are numerous at this place. Swim the cattle, & charge $3.00 per wagon for ferrying."[10]

But the Mormon ferrymen did not fare so well in every passerby's opinion. Israel F. Hale remarked on June 24 that the Saints apparently had "removed the ferry a few miles lower down that the emigrants may cross and leave the grass unmolested for their Mormon friends"[11] to arrive later in the summer. More violently stirred was J. Goldsborough Bruff, on July 16, who found the Saints so importunate in drumming up trade for their ferry that he threatened to blow a hole through one of the brethren.[12]

This struggle for business is more understandable when it is realized that rival ferries were operating all the way from the Mormon ferry site to Deer Creek. Amos Batchelder, who crossed on July 17 by the ferry just above Deer Creek, noted that it was maintained by a small company made up of men, women, and children, with three wagons and several cows, butter from which was an unexpected luxury.[13] Captain Howard Stansbury on July 25 crossed by this same ferry, paying $2 per wagon, which he thought by no means extortionate, considering that "the ferryman had been for months encamped here in a little tent, exposed to the assaults of hordes of wandering savages, for the sole purpose of affording this accommodation to travelers." He was informed that 28 men had been drowned trying to ford the river this year, though he received the information with all due skepticism.[14] Stansbury was near the tail end of the immigration, and the river was about to become fordable, hence it is quite possible that the Mormon ferry was abandoned by the time he passed its site.

In 1850 Appleton Harmon was destined for England as a missionary, rather than for the North Platte as a ferryman, but his journal is nevertheless once more a useful source on the ferry. The company of missionaries of which he was a member left Salt Lake Valley on April 20, and soon over-took

10 Diary of {T.G.?} Caldwell, printed as an appendix to the diaries of J. Goldsborough Bruff in Georgia Willis Read and Ruth Gaines, *Gold Rush: The Journals, Drawings, and Other Papers of J. Goldsborough Bruff*, 2v. (New York: Columbia University Press, 1944), 2: 1255.

11 "Diary of Trip to California in 1849: Written by Israel F. Hale," *Quarterly of the Society of California Pioneers* 11, no. 2 (30 June 1925): 85.

12 Read and Gaines, *Gold Rush*, 1:46.

13 Amos Batchelder, "Journal of a Tour Across the Continent of North America from Boston, via Independence, Missouri, the Rocky Mountains, to San Francisco in 1849," MS., typed transcription in my possession [carton 4, Morgan papers].

14 Howard Stansbury, *Exploration and Survey of the Valley of the Great Salt Lake of Utah, Including a Reconnaissance of a New Route Through the Rocky Mountains* (Washington: R. Armstrong, Public Printer, 1853), 60, 61.

"Captain Andrew Lytles Company who ware goin to establish a ferry on the platte river." This year the California immigration had got the jump on the ferrymen, being met by the eastbound Saints as early as May 15, and as far west as the Dry Sandy.

Under date of May 25 Harmon writes: "we camped on the Platte bottom the river being verry high and our oxen being some what fatienged, we thought to Stop a fiew days and recruit. Capt. Lytles Co. ware here one day before us and had commenced a flat boat. we took hold and helped them and suceded in launching one on the 28 Tuesday and with that commenced operations in ferring this boat was maned with a crew. while the remainder of us went to work and Built a larger one. they went to the mountain for the gunwhales, and brought them down to the river and sawed plank out of the Cotton wood and put it together with wooden pins. Calked and pitched it."

Finally, on June 3, "we launched this big boat and commenced ferrying with it. it worked nice and the emigrants were anchously waiting to give us $4 a waggon to take them over the Platte was about 10 feet deep and one hundred and fifty yards wide. during this delay we had exchanged our oxen and waggons for four horses harness and wagon. . . . Capt Lytle gave us $125 for what we had done on the Boats. this we divided equally between us and we Crossed the River with our new team on the new Boat, took leave of Capt Lytle and Company and Started."[15]

Jesse W. Crosby, who also was enroute to the English mission, and who also had helped in the boat building, says there were 16 in the party left at the ferry, and adds that the boats "were managed by means of large ropes stretched across the stream, then with pully blocks working on the before named rope, then Guy ropes attached to each end of the boat, and to the two blocks with pulleys, then drop one end of the boat so that the force of the current pressing against it will push the boat across, then reverse the process and the boat will recross and make in about five minutes."[16]

Evidence of continued stiff competition for business is preserved in the year's overland diaries. Lorenzo Sawyer, arriving June 3, found "four boats running, one of which belonged to the Mormons."[17] Madison Berryman Moorman, on June 29, clarifies this somewhat by explaining that there were "four boats belonging to two parties:—one called the 'Missouri Ferry' &

[15]Appleton M. Harmon, Autobiography, MS. cited in Note 6.

[16]"History and Journal of the Life and Travels of Jesse W. Crosby," *Annals of Wyoming* 11, no. 3 (July 1939): 187, 188.

[17]Lorenzo Sawyer, *Wayside Sketches* (New York: Edward Eberstadt, 1926), 39.

the other the 'Mormon Ferry.' The latter had but one boat & and the former three—all Buoyboats. They are decidedly the best boats I ever saw—much better than steam on as rapid a stream as this foaming Platte. . . , The Mo. Ferry, as I was told by the ferryman—averages about three hundred wagons a day at five dollars each, besides multiplied hundreds of oxen—horses & mules at from fifty cents to one dollar a piece."[18] Sawyer had found the fees slightly more moderate than Moorman, $4 per wagon and 25 cents per head for animals. These prices marked a stiff advance over those which prevailed in the first year of the ferry, and are evidence of the pressure upon the ferry facilities. This year, as in 1849, it seems to have been necessary for immigrants to register and wait their turn at the ferry.[19]

For the last two years the Mormon ferry presumably was maintained, little information seems to have survived. Although I have not searched the overland journals exhaustively, I have not seen a Mormon ferry mentioned in 1851, and only by the Clark-Brown party in 1852. John Hawkins Clark wrote on June 22, 1852, that his company paid $32 for the passage of the river, adding plaintively, "these plainsmen do not forget to charge. All have to ferry their wagons, but most of the immigrants swim their stock. Many cattle have been lost at this point and the ferryman has a record of fifteen men drowned within the last month. The boatman had, I think, located this ferry on a difficult place in the river in order to force custom over it." Clark does not say specifically that the ferry was run by Mormons, but Godfrey C. Ingrim, a member of the party whose reminiscences are quoted by Louise Barry in editing the Clark journal, says that "there was some Mormons that had a ferry here they charged five dollars a wagon and men had to swim their teams or stock."[20]

The end of the Platte ferries was foreshadowed in 1851, when the first mention of a bridge appears in the overland journals.[21] John S. Zeiber, on July 12, 1851, noted the presence of a bridge one mile above Deer Creek, or some 27

[18]*The Journal of Madison Berryman Moorman 1850–1851* (San Francisco: California Historical Society, 1948), 33.

[19]C. S. Abbott, *Recollections of a California Pioneer* (New York: Neale Publ. Co., 1917), 40, 41.

[20]"Overland to the Gold Fields of California in 1852: The Journal of John Hawkins Clark, Expanded and Revised from Notes Made During the Journey," ed. Louise Barry, *Kansas Historical Quarterly* 11, no. 3 (August 1942): 257.

[21]Irene D. Paden, in *The Wake of the Prairie Schooner* (New York: Macmillan Co., 1943), 198, remarks that in 1849 "a few travelers noted a precarious bridge three miles below the site of the later bridge near the ferry," built by a fur company, and "apparently of no importance or use to the emigrants." She does not cite a source and I have seen no reference to a bridge across the Platte before 1851.

miles below the site of the original Mormon ferry, but as he himself was here traveling up the north bank of the river, a route first used by wagons in 1850, he had no occasion to resort to either bridge or ferry.[22] Albert Carrington, who had gone east in the fall of 1850 with Captain Stansbury, and who was enroute back to Utah, commented on this bridge on August 2, 1851, but he too was traveling up the north bank and did not use the bridge.[23] Robert Robe, who was one of those to travel up the south bank this year, wrote in his journal on June 22, "Travelled from Deer creek, which is a good camping place and arrived in the evening at the upper Ferry. There is a bridge over Platte at Deer creek but this does not seem to be much used. There is also an intermediate ferry but this {*i.e.*, the upper ferry} is generally used."[24]

A year later another traveler coming up the north bank of the Platte wrote in his journal on June 29, "Our camp tonight is a few miles above the crossing of the North Platte, where the emigrants who traveled on the south side of the river crossed over to the road of those who traveled on the north side of the Platte. We understand that there is a bridge at this crossing of the Platte."[25] This diarist did not himself see the bridge, and his hearsay information does not permit an authoritative answer to the question whether the bridge actually was at the Upper Crossing or near Deer Creek.

The idea has been prevalent that the first substantial bridge across the North Platte was built in the winter of 1858–59, but the universal testimony of the overland journals is that such a bridge existed from 1853 on.[26] The later bridge is supposed to have been built by John Richard, but he was probably concerned in the bridge from the beginning. The 1853 diaries I have examined do not specifically mention Richard, but his name appears early enough in the overland journals to make it a reasonable certainty that the

[22]"Diary of John S. Zeiber, 1851," *Transactions of the Forty-Eighth Annual Reunion of the Oregon Pioneer Association, 1920* (Portland, Ore.: Association, 1921), 317.

[23]"Diary of Albert Carrington," in *Heart Throbs of the West* (Salt Lake City: Daughters of Utah Pioneers, 1947), 8:121.

[24]"Robert Robe's Diary While Crossing the Plains in 1851," *Washington Historical Quarterly* 19 (January 1928): 53.

[25]"Diary of E. W. Conyers; a Pioneer of 1852," *Transactions of the Thirty-Third Annual Reunion of the Oregon Pioneer Association, 1905* (1906), 453.

[26]See, *e.g.*, the diaries of 1853 kept by Orange Gaylord, *Transactions of the Forty-Fifth Annual Reunion of the Oregon Pioneer Association, 1917* (1920); Celinda E. Hines, *Transactions of the Forty-Sixth Annual Reunion of the Oregon Pioneer Association, 1918* (1921); Velina A. Williams, *Transactions of the Forty-Seventh Annual Reunion of the Oregon Pioneer Association, 1919* (1922); John (or David) Dinwiddie, *The Frontier* (*Missoula, Mont.*) 8, no. 3 (March 1928); and Thomas Flint, *Annual Publications of the Historical Society of Southern California* (Los Angeles: Reprinted for Dawson's Book Shop, 1923). Flint wrote on 29 July 1853, "Passed a bridge across the Platt—a very strong one built of hewn timbers. Reported to have cost $14,000."

Platte Bridge was his enterprise from its inception. J. Robert Brown wrote in 1856, "The brothers Richards (pro. Rashaw) {*sic*} own the post and bridge here, and are coining money from it; they have made over $200,000 apiece, but that demon, gambling, keeps them down. They appear to be very clever men. They are from Florisant, {Missouri}."[27]

A correspondent of the *Missouri Republican*, writing in that paper as early as November 2, 1853, called the Platte Bridge a "substantial" affair, but it is not inconceivable that it was replaced by another structure early in 1858, for a later correspondent of the *Republican*, writing from Rulo, Nebraska, under date of August 22, 1858, comments, "Our fellow-citizens, Charles Martin and Wm. Renceleur, have just arrived from the Platte Bridge. They made the trip to this place in seventeen days. Their partner in the bridge, John Richards Esq., came with them."[28] They brought news of the high excitement over the Pikes Peak gold discoveries, which doubtless gave a healthy fillip to their business.

But it is not my purpose to pursue the history of the Platte Bridge, noted as it became in the history of Wyoming. A more useful object will be served by providing some biography of William A. Empey as an introduction to his diary of 1847.

William Adam Empey was born July 4, 1808, at Ossnabrook, Storment County, Canada, the son of Adam and Margaret Steenbergh Empey. His parents and grandparents were born in upper New York, but at some indeterminate date before William's birth moved to Canada. It is not known just when William became a member of the Church of Jesus Christ of Latter-day Saints, the Mormon Church, but it was at some time anterior to the death of Joseph Smith, the Mormon prophet.

In accordance with Mormon doctrine of the time, before the evacuation from Nauvoo Empey was "sealed" to Brigham Young as an "adopted son," and subsequently he often signed his name "William Y. Empey." When Brigham Young set out from Winter Quarters in 1847 to find an abiding place for the Saints, Empey was enlisted as a member of the fifth company of ten. After the formation of a night guard became prudent, he was one of 50 men selected, a distinction he found onerous, as the entries in his diary make plain. He had a reputation as a sober, conscientious, entirely dependable person, and his journal exhibits all these qualities.

[27] J. Robert Brown, *A Journal of a Trip Across the Plains of the U.S., from Missouri to California, in the year 1856* (Columbus, Ohio: Author, 1860), 51, 52.

[28] *Missouri Republican (St. Louis, Mo.)*, 1 September 1858.

The first pages of his journal are missing, the record beginning on May 7, three weeks after the journey commenced, and a week after the Mormon Pioneers came down to the north bank of the Platte near Grand Island. The laconic, somewhat monotonous entries made in the early pages of the diary do not compare in interest with other records of the Mormon Pioneer party. But fortunately, just where Empey's diary has most to offer, with the inception of the Mormon ferry, it becomes richest in detail. Though some pages are gone, depriving us of his record of the events of June 27–July 10, information about which must be had from the journal of Appleton M. Harmon, his journal is our sole record of the ferry from July 17 to August 4, Harmon's journal not extending beyond July 16.*

With four others, Empey stayed on at the ferry until the arrival of the Mormon family immigration in mid-August of 1847. His journal would lead one to think that he had expected his family with the Second Company. If so, he was disappointed, and accordingly journeyed back to Winter Quarters during the fall.

It is not known absolutely when Empey settled in Salt Lake Valley, but he is included by the Daughters of Utah Pioneers with their lists for 1848,[29] and this seems reasonable because a Great Salt Lake City ordinance of November 10, 1849, appointed him from the Fifteenth Ward as one of a number of assistant supervisors of streets, which probably would not have happened had he just arrived in the Valley.[30] In February, 1850, he was given by the legislature of the State of Deseret a franchise for a ferry across the Bear River, and he was active at this business during the spring and summer of 1850.[31] The following winter he volunteered or was "called" for the Iron County Mission which settled Parowan, in southern Utah,[32] but evidently he retained an active interest in the operation of ferries, for the first legislature of the Territory of Utah, meeting during the winter of 1851–52, granted to

*[This edition corrects two dates in this sentence as given in DLM to Ellen Crowley, 17 October 1950, Morgan papers. —Ed.]

[29] *Heart Throbs of the West* (Salt Lake City: Daughters of Utah Pioneers, 1948), 9: 484. [The LDS Church's index to "Mormon Pioneer Overland Travel, 1847–1868" lists Empey and family arriving with the Brigham Young company that arrived in the valley 20–24 September 1848. As Morgan later notes in his introduction, Empey also led a company westward in 1854 from Westport, Missouri, and was a member of the ill-fated 1856 James G. Willie handcart company. —Ed.]

[30] *Utah Historical Quarterly* 8 (1940): 237, 238.

[31] *Utah Historical Quarterly* 8 (1940): 99; Journal of Lt. John W. Gunnison, MS., typed transcription in my possession [carton 25, Morgan papers. —Ed.].

[32] George A. Smith, Journal of the Iron County Mission, MS., typed transcription in the Utah State Historical Society's WPA Collection.

him, Joseph Young, John Young, and David Fullmer the ferry rights for Bear River—meaning of course the lower river above its mouth in Great Salt Lake, rather than the upper river in present Wyoming.[33]

In the summer of 1852 he was one among the Saints called to serve a mission in England—a mission principally interesting because it was the first sent out after the public avowal of the principle and practice of plural marriage, and had the duty of defending that doctrine to the world. The only other diary by Empey known to exist, apart from the one here printed, describes this mission, beginning with his departure from Great Salt Lake City on September 15, 1852, and ending April 20, 1854, when he was again on the frontier preparing to set out for Utah.*

Following his return to Utah, he again became associated in the operation of a ferry across the Bear River, but in 1862 was one of those called to strengthen the "Cotton Mission," and the remainder of his life was spent in Utah's "Dixie" country. He established a farm at Tonaquint, at the junction of the Virgin and Santa Clara rivers, and subsequently a ranch between Central and Pine Valley. His last years were devoted to viticulture. He died at St. George, Utah, August 19, 1890, at the age of 82. A Saint who practiced as well as preached the doctrine of plural marriage, he had three wives, Mary Ann Morgan (b. 18—?, d. February 24, 1891), whom he married in 1840 and by whom he had 10 children; Mary Harriet Porter (b. January 4, 1832, d. March 24, 1869), whom he married October 27, 1855, and by whom he had 6 children; and Martha Fielding (b. April 20, 1833, d. February 12, 1912), whom he married March 17, 1857, and by whom he had 9 children.[34]

The journal here reproduced has been deposited by his daughter-in-law, Mrs. Ida Terry Empey of St. George, Utah, in the Henry E. Huntington Library, San Marino, California, and is printed with her permission and that of the library. The manuscript is a loosely sewed notebook 24.8 × 19.5 cm., apparently consisting originally of 16 leaves of 32 numbered pages. Pages 1–8 and 19–22 have been lost, while p. 32 is blank. The first part of the extant manuscript, to p. 18, is written in blue ink, with the last part in brown.

In writing his diary, Empey ran all the first section of it together, with no paragraph breaks whatever until the entry for June 26. To make this part of

[33]*Laws of Utah, 1852*, 167–169.

*[This diary is now in the holdings of the Church History Library, Salt Lake City. —Ed.]

[34]Biographical details when not otherwise documented are from a manuscript biographical sketch of Empey's life in the possession of Mrs. Ida Terry Empey. A copy is in the Utah State Historical Society.

the diary more easily read, arbitrary paragraphing has been enforced upon it, though without eliminating his characteristic use of the conjunction "and," which is left at the end of many a paragraph. After June 26, perhaps influenced by the example of Appleton Harmon, from whose journal Empey seems at times to have copied, Empey characteristically wrote the date centered on the page, with the entry under it, an arrangement which has also been altered slightly in this printing.

The important hiatus in the Empey diary for the period June 27–July 10 has been filled, in the interests of a complete record of the Mormon ferry during 1847, from a transcription of the Harmon journal in the possession of the Utah State Historical Society, obtained through the courtesy of Harmon's daughter, Mrs. Julia Kessler, of Bountiful, Utah. Harmon's journal, itself incomplete, has recently been printed by Maybelle Harmon Anderson as *Appleton Milo Harmon Goes West* (Berkeley[, Calif.: Gillick Press], 1946), though unfortunately with some excisions and some not always well-considered corrections of his spelling. [It was also published the same year as *The Journals of Appleton Milo Harmon* (Glendale: Arthur H. Clark Co., 1946).] The original of Harmon's diary is in the custody of the L.D.S. Church Historian's Office [presently the Church History Library].

Other records of the Mormon Pioneer party which have been used in editing the Empey diary include *William Clayton's Journal* (Salt Lake City: Deseret News, 1921); Howard Egan's *Pioneering the West, 1846 to 1878* (Richmond, Utah: Howard R. Egan Estate, 1917), used in conjunction with Egan's original manuscript diary, now in the Coe Collection at Yale; the *Autobiography of Pioneer John Brown* (Salt Lake City: Stevens & Wallis Inc., 1941); Matthew Cowley's *Wilford Woodruff, His Life and Labors* (Salt Lake City: Deseret News, 1909); Orson Pratt's "Interesting Items Concerning the Journeying of the Latter-Day Saints from the City of Nauvoo, Until Their Location in the Valley of the Great Salt Lake," printed originally in the Liverpool *Millennial Star* 11–12 (1849–1850), and lately reprinted separately at Salt Lake City by N.B. Lundwall as *Exodus from Modern Israel*; the diary of Erastus Snow, first published in *Improvement Era* 14–15 (1911–1912), and subsequently reprinted in part and evidently with greater fidelity to the original manuscript in the *Utah Humanities Review* 11 (1948); the diary of Lorenzo Dow Young and his wife Harriet, in *Utah Historical Quarterly* 14 (1946); the diary of Heber C. Kimball, published incomplete (because of the suspension of that magazine in 1940) in *Utah Genealogical and Historical Magazine*, 30–31 (1939–1940); and the extracts from the diary of Horace K. Whitney published in *Improvement Era* 49 (1947). Some diaries in manuscript which have also been used, from typed transcriptions in the collection of the Utah State Historical Society, include the important record by Norton Jacob, the no less important diary kept by Albert Carrington for Amasa Lyman (Carrington kept another, almost identical, for George A. Smith,[35] which like the original of the Lyman diary, is in the custody of the L. D. S. Church Historian's Office), and the journal of Levi Jackman. Other diaries of the Pioneer party, not normally accessible to students, are in the possession of the Historian's Office.

Information helpful in the editing of William Empey's diary has been provided by Mrs. Juanita Brooks of St. George, who first brought the record to my attention, Mrs. Ida Terry Empey of St. George, Utah, Mrs. Effie Miller, Payson, Utah, and Mrs. Ruth Gubler, Panguitch, Utah, grand-daughters of Empey; Mr. Everett D. Graff of Chicago and Mr. Thomas W. Streeter of Morristown, N.J., well-known Chicago book collectors who examined certain rare titles in their collections for my benefit; Mrs. Brenda R. Gieseker, Librarian of the Missouri Historical Society, St. Louis, Missouri; Miss Priscilla Knuth, Research Associate in the Oregon Historical Society, who searched the manuscript collections of the Society for information and clues to information about the 1847 Oregon immigrants, and who also sent me numerous helpful references from Sarah Hunt Steeves' *Book of Remembrance of Marion County, Oregon, Pioneers* (Portland, Ore.: Berncliff Press, 1927); and the Utah State Historical Society, which has been helpful in more ways than I could hope to list. Numerous references to contemporary newspapers in the notes are from transcripts in my possession, gathered in connection with my researches for a larger history of Mormonism, for which I must express an obligation to a fellowship granted me by the John Simon Guggenheim Memorial Foundation.

The Journal of William A. Empey
May 7–August 4, 1847

noon it is a valley of dry bones for it looks as thousands of buffalows killed in the big platt it is a Delight ful country it appears as though there were milions

[35]Extracts from the diary of George A. Smith are being printed in *The Instructor*, organ of the Deseret Sunday School Union of the L. D. S. Church, and as this issue of *Annals of Wyoming* goes to press (July 1949), *The Instructor* has reached the beginning of Smith's account of the Pioneer journey of 1847. [Cf. The complete series, "My Journal," abridged by Alice Merrill Horne, which included an autobiography and diary entries between Zion's Camp in 1833 and July 24, 1847. It appeared in *The Instructor* 81, no. 1 (January 1946)–84, no. 7 (July 1949). —Ed.]

of buffelows killed on this place The platt is about one mile in weadth and is about 2 feet and a half on a everage some of Brother Brigham teams give out on account of the of the pararie being burnt and the buffalow being so numerous that they have eaten the pararie bare we have averaged a bout 10 miles per Day, up to this preasant time being being the 7th of the month;

we Started as usesial on the 8 and all was peace and quietness but our teams bing gun to fail the weather is cold for the time of the year we saw some hundreds of buffalow this morning where we camped at night near the Big platt[1] and we was a blige to sent out men to keep the buffalow from our cattl wee had a good nights rest and

persued on our jurney on the 9 {8} of the {?} we saw severl thousands of buffalow they would follow us for miles and we would set out Dogs on them to see them run. some times they would fight the dogs we this Day saw a bout 50 thousand but if I would com to the in particalar I think I could say with in bounds that there were 1.00 thousand we travled 14 {11-1/4} miles and they were so thick in places that that no person could see through them, for they were like a cloud strung along both sides of the river and in {?} every ille lan {*i.e.*, island} a long the platt[2] the woolfs are so numers that as son as you shoot a calf or buffalow that before you can get to the camp and back to fetch the meat the wolves has got persession of them; no grass for our teams on account of buffalows there is many Lies Dead I think on account of faood {?}, we have made an estament of the distance up to this presant Date up to the bluffs being the 9 of May, thea numbrs of miles is 3,39 miles[3] we rested this night in peace and

we arose as usesial by the sound of the bugal being the sabbath day and made preperations for a march on account of no food for our teams it being the 9 {10} of the month traveled 5 {3-1/2} miles and camped, the brethren

[1]The night encampment was 6 miles northwest of the site of Gothenburg, Nebraska. On this day William Clayton made the first effort at mechanical measurement of the distance traveled, an idea which had its fruition a few days later in the roadometer built by Appleton M. Harmon to Orson Pratt's specifications. From May 8 the distances traveled were measured.

[2]The Saints were enormously impressed with the buffalo, which they first encountered on May 1. "No pen nor tongue," William Clayton wrote, "can give an idea of the multitude now in sight continually, and it appears difficult to keep them away from the wagons." Their numbers presented a serious problem in obtaining feed for the Mormon livestock, as Empey notes in his entry for 10 May. The whole face of the earth, Norton Jacob commented, was "eat up here by the thousands upon thousands of buffalo."

[3]By William Clayton's reckoning, posted up for the Mormon companies that were to follow, the distance from Winter Quarters (north of present Omaha) was 300 miles at the end of this day's travel. The encampment was 9-1/2 miles northwest of present Gothenburg.

took a rope and run up to a buffalow caught him around the horns and Drove him for a little Distance and let him go we enjoided our selves well through the Day we had a meeting Br Amasy Lyman opined the meeting by prayer and Brother Orson pratt give us a fine Lecture on the good feelings that existe amoungst the Brethren he said he traveled to far west but he never traveled amongst so many men that observed so good ordar and he new that the spirit of god weighs {?} in the camp Brother Amasy Lyman followed by making some good remarks that was applicable to our case and so Did Brotherly woodruff and Br Benson[4]

On May 10 we jurney on and and traveled 10 {9-3/4} miles and campeped[5] Shot one buffalow and one Deer and rested in peace and

on the 11 we started on wards to wards the mountains the weather is fine and we had but one shower of rain[,] the season [a]peares to be verry Dry we are now a bout the south faulk {fork} and north faulk on the big platt near the bluffs we are enjoining good health through the camp and all peace except Zebedee Coulter {Coltrin} he and Brother {Sylvester H.} Earl separated this morning; Coulten has Done all the Rangling in the camp; with in a few exceptions he is counted by the majority of the camp a quarles some man Brother Earl appears to be a fine man and is well thought of by the camp of Pioneers the north Faulk a bout 1 mile in weadth the water is like the Masuira {Missouri} water we camped for the night and rested in peace we traveld 8 {8-1/3} miles[6] and

on the 12th we started by the sound of the bugal and saw severl flocks of buffalow and also saw were the indians killed severl and took the hides and skin and tongs And leff the meat Lie on the psrarie the food is Giting better on account of the buffalow is not so numers it apears that the indians has hunted them a great deal the Land where we traveled to Day we traveled 12 miles campped for the night;[7] the hunters Shot 1 buffalow and we had to use

---

[4]The most interesting account of the day's discourses is that of Norton Jacob. Orson Pratt, Jacob writes, "said that some had supposed that we should be able to get over into Bear River valley in time to put in spring crops, but he had not thought so, but we must prepare for difficulties that we should be in condition to cope with whatever circumstances we should be thrown into and make the best of it. If we do not get there in time enough, to return next fall we must winter there and make the best of it." In the journal Albert Carrington was keeping for Amasa Lyman, he writes that Lyman "spoke upon the principle of learning all the time to be patient in the school we are in, which would be better to us than gold or silver." This theme of the necessity for obedience occupied the Mormon leaders throughout the journey.

[5]The night's camp was made approximately 8 miles southeast of present Pawnee, Nebraska.

[6]The encampment was on the site of Pawnee, Nebraska.

[7]On Whitehorse Creek, 4 miles north and slightly west of the present city of North Platte, Nebraska.

buffalow chips for fewel to cook with the weather is verry Disagreeable it is cold for the season of the year; we have traveled riseing of 300 and 50 miles and have not traveled 25 rods through the timber so you may perceive that there is verry little timber; we rested in peace for the night, and

made ready for to persue on our jurney it being the 13 of the month we traveled a bout 5 miles and bated our teams one our and then made cur way on our jurney and came to the bluff, conjunction fork river[8] we traveled 12 miles and camped for the night and rested in peace

we arose as usesial by the sound of the signal and paid our Devotions to to our Father in heaven; and had to clime the bluffs a bout 3 miles this Day we Shot 2 antilopes and 2 buffalow this was on the 14 of the month we traveled 11 {8} miles and 3 quarters and camped[9] about 11 o clock at night one of the gard {Rodney Badger} shot at what he supposed to be an indian he said he was a bout to take hold of one of the mules we all gathered our teams and rested in peace for the night, and

on the 15 of the month we started and traveled a bout 3 {2-1/4} miles and camped on account of rain it cleared off and then we started on and traveled about 8 {6} miles and 3 quarters and camped for the night[10] we Shot 1 buffalow and 2 antilopes the weather is getting a little mileder this was Done on the 15 of may we rested in peace for the night and

on the 16 of thee month we rested on the sabath Day in peace the hunters shot 1 buffalow and 1 antilope Brother {Willard} Richard{s} and B heber {C. Kimball} and some others preached to the camp telling them the importance of our mishion, and the responsibility that rested on us as peoineers in keeping the commandments of god, he said he traveled to far west with a bout 2 hundred but he said he never traveled with a company that keept so good order and he feelt theat god was with us and he knew that the angels was continualey a round and a bout us to open our way to the place where god Desire for the saint to have a resting place where kings and quenn and all the rich would come to hear the word of the Lord and we as peioneers

[8]Empey's language is somewhat confused. The night's encampment, at the end of a 10-3/4 mile journey, was on Birdwood Creek, 5 miles north and a little east of present Sutherland, Nebraska. Variant names are applied to Birdwood Creek in the Mormon journals: Conjunction Fork River, Junction Bluff Creek, or, as Brigham Young preferred, North Bluff Fork.

[9]This night's encampment was made on the bank of the Platte 6 miles northwest of Sutherland, Nebraska.

[10]On the Platte about 14 miles east of present Keystone, Nebraska. The whole day's travel was 6-3/4 miles, not 11-3/4, as Empey's language would suggest.

would be look on as angels of god and many more blessings to numerous to mention[11] this Day and night pased in peace and

on the 17 we prepareed to start on our jurney we passed severl butifull springs which came out of the bluffs and we traveled a bout 2 miles over the bluffs and came to a butifull flatte[12] and the hunters shot 3 buffalow and 1 antilope and we camped for the night and we traveled 12 miles and 3 quarters and we rested from our Day travel and paid our Devotions to almighty god for his kind care over us; and

we arose as usesial by the sound of the bugal and prepared to take our march brother Brigham called the capttians to gether and addressed them teling them the evil of killing so much game and wounded so many buffalow and wasting so mutch aminution and teling the camp to be care full of the meat that they had on hand they should not shoot any birds of any kind without orders from him; the bugle sounded and we started as usesial a long the platt we crossed a butifull stream of water wich proceded out of the bluffs[13] we also passed a little island wich was full of read sedar {red cedar} and on the opposite side of the river the bluffs {Cedar Point} came to the waters edge wich was butifull ly a dorrend with butifull read sedar and the cliffs of rocks we traveled 7 miles and a half and bated our teams the game is plenty buffalow antilopes Deers and fowls & hares we traveled 15 miles and 3 quarters and camped for thee night and rested in peace and

a rose at the sound of the bugal at 5 o clock and started and traveled 3 miles to git better food for our teams we bated on our and refreshed our selves with a good breakfast and started on our jurney as usesial and came to the bluffs[14] were we crossed the bluffs was a mile and a quarter and came to the platt on the leaver the wather bein rather wet and rainy we halted for about 3 ours and started on and when started it began to rain we halted for the night and camped in a half a circle we traveled 8 miles it being the 19 of the month, and

on the 20 we arose and made ready for our jurney and started at the sound of the bugal and traveled 7 miles 3 quarters and bated our teams 1 our we have

---

[11]Kimball's allusion is to the march of Zion's Camp from Kirtland, Ohio, to western Missouri in 1834, for which see his "Journal," *Times and Seasons* 6, no. 1 (15 January 1845): 770ff. Nine members of Zion's Camp were in the Pioneer party.

[12]The "butifull flatte" is the site of Keystone, Nebraska.

[13]The stream was Whitetail Creek, named by Brigham Young "Rattlesnake Creek." Immediately west of the stream rise bluffs which, the Mormon journals note, were called by Frémont in 1842 Cedar Bluffs. The encampment this night was on Sand Creek, 13 miles farther west.

[14]These bluffs, lying immediately west of Otter Creek, a stream Brigham Young named "Wolf Creek," extend to the bank of the Platte. Camp was made near the river, three-quarters of a mile east of present Clear Creek.

traveled a bout 90 miles without seeing on the north side of the platt a tree large anught for a hand spike till to Day we passed a read sedar a bout 3 feet a cross the stump the bluffs on both sides of the north bank is bluffs with legges of rocks and on the opposite side is groves of read sedar and mulbry trees and a fee scrubs of brush I have benn chosen as a Capt of ten for the purpose of night gard and have to stand every 3 night witch makes it purtey Sevear but it is nessay for it to be so[15] we camped to Day at noon the boys took skiff and crossed the platt and found where the road came Down from the south platt as {?} across to the north right opposite of us the place is knon by the nane of it is the ash hollow there an indian killed a white man for his horse and Brother Brown helped to berry him,[16] so we prepared to start and crossed cassel Creek a butifull Stream and sand bottom[17] we traveled 15 miles and 3 quarters and camped for the night and rested for the night; an

made ready for a start on the 21 of may and crosse an nother Creek {Lost Creek} and travele 7 miles and 3 quarters and halted and bated our teams one our and Started on our jurney as usesial the weather being in our favour it was arfine Day and the bluffs and legges of rock on the opposite sid of fork. We camped for thee night in a circle[18] there came 3 indians to us Dressed in mens clothing they started back on their horses over the bluffs their horses appeared to be team horses[19] we rested in peace for the night,

---

[15]This appointment to the guard was not made on this night, as Empey's language might indicate, but on April 17. He was captain of the second ten in the guard.

[16]The reconnaissance across the Platte, made at William Clayton's suggestion to aid the Saints in orienting themselves in relation to Frémont's map, was by Orson Pratt, Amasa Lyman, Luke Johnson, and John Brown. The year before, Brown had led west along the Oregon Trail a small company of Saints from Mississippi, who had hoped to meet somewhere in the Platte Valley the large Mormon immigration out of Nauvoo. When the Mississippi Saints, here at Ash Hollow, on July 2, 1846, met James Clyman's eastbound company from California and learned that no Mormons were ahead of them on the trail, the 43 persons who comprised Brown's party went on in some perplexity to Fort Bernard, a few miles below Fort Laramie, and then south to Pueblo, on the Arkansas River, where they wintered in company with the Sick Detachment of the Mormon Battalion. Brown himself, once his company was settled at Pueblo, journeyed down the Plains to the States, returning to the mountains with the Pioneer party of 1847.

The reference to Brown's having helped bury a man is not understood. Neither Brown nor the records of 1846 refer to such an incident, though at Ash Hollow Brown's party lost a few horses to Pawnees. Perhaps the man killed was Edward Trimble, but this happened farther east. See Joel Palmer's account in his *Journal of Travels over the Rocky Mountains* (Thwaites edition, [*Early Western Travels,* vol. 30 (Cleveland, Ohio: Arthur H. Clark Co.], 1906), 251–255.

[17]Castle Creek, now Blue Creek, was so called by the Saints because the bluffs along its west bank, which they named Castle Bluffs, seemed so much to resemble "the rock on which Lancaster Castle is built." The night encampment was 5 miles northwest of present Lewellen, Nebraska.

[18]On the bank of the Platte near the mouth of Mutton Creek, the day's travel being 15-3/4 miles.

[19]There were two, not three, Indians, a brave and a squaw. They were Sioux, and Appleton Harmon identifies them as *Sants* [i.e., Sans Arc, a Lakota sub-band]. The editor of Harmon's journal (*Appleton Milo Harmon Goes West* [Berkeley: Gillick Press, 1946]) has metamorphosed this to "Saints" and called them "Mormon Indians."

on the 22 we started as usesial by the sound of the bugal to persue our jurney the weather being fine and pleasant; the sous indians has caves in the legges rocks of the bluffs so that you come up on them un a wares it is not safe for one man to leave the Camp we traveled a bout 15 and a half a bout 6 miles was over a Dessert place a bout 2 miles over the bluffs we passed severl Dry creeks there were a butifull groves on the opposite side of the river we camped for the night and rested in peace[20] and

arose on the 23 of thee month on the sabbath Day and rested and had Brother Brigham preach to us and said that he was sasfied with the Brothren for their be haveiour was good fore he said that he never asked them or required any request but what it was done the weather Darkened and it began to thunder and lighting and the wind began to blow and Rain and hail it was a Disagreeable night it being the 23 of the month and

on the 24 we arose and made ready for a start it being colder then I ever saw at this time a year it snowed a Little the bluffs was 2.35 feet, a bove the Level of the water we started at the sound of the bugal on our jurney and traveled 10 miles and bated our teams and while we were taken our Dinner there came 2 indians up to the camp and we gave them some Dinner they went off and a bout 2 ours after there came 35 indians and squaws {*Here interlineated is:* We traveled 15 miles 1/2} Dressed in the most genteal manner[21] we gave them their suppers and they camped with us all night we risted in peace and in quieeness[22]

we arose in the morning and made ready for our jurney being the 25 of the month thoes were the sous indians we travele 12 miles and camped and rested in peace a little below Chimley {Chimney} rock this rock is 2.60 feet in height and 10 by 12 in seadth on the top[23]

we arose as usesial being the 26 of the month the hunters shot 5 antiopes and camped and took our Dinners and started on the bluffs is a great height no wood growing on this side of the platt in situ the weather is pleasant but cold nights we reached Chimley rock wich is 2.60 feet in height it is a

---

[20]The encampment was at the Remsburg Ranch near present Lisco, Nebraska.

[21]Clayton says of them, "They are all well dressed and very noble looking, some of them having good clean blankets, others nice robes artfully ornamented with beads and paintings. All had many ornaments on their clothing and ears, some had nice painted shells suspended from the ear. All appeared to be well armed with muskets. Their moccasins were indeed clean and beautiful. One had a pair of moccasins of clear white, ornamented with beads, etc. They fit very tight to the foot. For cleanness and neatness, they will vie with the most tasteful whites. They are thirty-five in number, about half squaws and children. They are Sioux and have two recommends certifying as to their friendship, etc."

[22]This night's camp was on the Platte 2 miles southeast of present Northport, Nebraska.

[23]They encamped about 3 miles southeast of Bayard, Nebraska, which is just east of the meridian of Chimney Rock.

Delightfull country the atmus phere is pleasant and clear, we traveled 12 {12-1/4} miles and camped for the night[24] and rested in peace, and

started on the 27 and traveled 6 miles and bated our teams one our the mountains is a great height there is one lone thwer {i.e., tower} on the opposite side of the river the hunters killed 4 antilopes; we travele 13 miles and 3 quarters and camped in a circle for the night[25] and rested in peace; and

a rose by the sound of thee bugal as usesial and made ready for our jurney it being 28 of the month it rained a little through the night and at Day Light there was a fine mist of rain the country is in Different places Dersert and barren except what they call Devils toungs which grows on a Dersert[26] the mountains is a great height a Long the platt the country is a Live with woolves & it rained till 10 oclock be fore we started on our jurney and had a fine Day for traveling we Drove 11 miles and a half and camped for the night[27] I planted my men on gard as usesial and at 12 oclock it began to rain a litle and

at Day light we a rose as usesial and paid our Devotions to our Father in heaven it being 29 of of {*sic*} the month it keept on raining a so it hindered us from starting at our regular our we was called together and Brother Brigham addressed us with the Word of the Lord to repent of uur sins and and folleys wich we was giltey of before the Lord sutch as Dansing and Dice playing and card playing wich {?} jumping Loud Lafter and all such habbits wich was a bomation in the sight of god and was a stink in his norstels he went on to tell us our Duty towards our god that we might better Spend our Luiser moments in prayer or in reading some good Books or in strutting each other in rightousness for he knew that if we did not reform and turn to the Lord and repent that we would be cut of and would not have a preavilege to go on the mishion that we was appointed to be called for the {?} the cats {i.e., captains} of tens to call out their men for he said he was

---

[24]The night's encampment was approximately a mile southeast of Minitare, Nebraska. The lone tower Empey refers to in the next day's entry was evidently Castle Rock, which the Saints passed on the afternoon of the 26th.

[25]The campsite was 3 miles northwest of the site of the modern town of Scottsbluff, Nebraska, on the north bank opposite the famous Scottsbluff, now a National Monument.

[26]Empey's "Devil's Tongue" was described by Orson Pratt in his journal for 8 May. "On the top of some of these sand hills, in the driest places, grew a vegetable, the top of which very much resembled a pineapple; one being dug, the root was about one and a half inch in diameter, and two feet in length. It was called by some of the company, a Spanish soap weed. The roots being pounded up, they make a very good suds, and are used in Mexico for washing raiment, etc." The plant is a variety of yucca, familiar throughout the Southwest as Spanish bayonet or "oose."

[27]This night's encampment was on the bank of the Platte immediately south of Morrill, Nebraska.

not in a hurry nor would not go with men that had such a trifeling spirit he then called for a vote and a covnant of all thoes that would sererve the true and Living god he called on the twelve first wich was unanimous then on the high priest and then on the seventies and then on the elders and all and all thoes that that was not willing to reform would have the privileg to go back and he request all sutch would go we all as a man, covenanted before god and man that we would reform and serve the true and Living god he then requested us as to morrow was the sabbath that we would fast and pray that god would have mercy uppon us and wood give us more of his holey spirit he then pronounced the blessing of god uppon us as his people and many others blessings that is to numers to mention and said that we was Discharged and every man to his waggon to start it being 9 oclock when we started[28] we traveld over a Dersert 4 miles and came to where there were grass and we passed horse Creek on the opposite side of the platt wich is 40 miles from fort Larama we traveled 8 miles and a half the weather being rainy we camped for the night in peace and in Love one with another we retired as usesial by the sound of the bugal and paid our Devotions to god and rested in peace[29]

we a rose as usesial called on the Lord and had a meeting at 8 oclock and the good Lord was preasan and blessed us our meeting brok up at 10 and commenced at 11 and we per took of the Lords supper there, when good instructions to all and our prayers was offered up in the behalf of all saints under all surcumstances that they might recieve more of the spirit of god to gide them in all truth; it commenced raining a littl a bout 3 o clock this Day being 30 of the month we rested in peace and called on the Lord as usesial

we arose in the morning at 4 oclock and returned thanks to almighty god for his Loveing kindness to wards us as his servants we then started at 9 oclock and traveled 10 miles and bated our teams and took our Dinners it being the 31 of may we started and traveled over a Dersert all after noon we traveled 16 miles and 3 quarters and camted for the night a loung side of a creek called Raw Hide[30] we rested in in peace and

---

[28]This memorable dressing down Brigham Young gave the Saints electrifies every Mormon journal of 1847.

[29]The encampment was nearly on, perhaps a little west of, the present Wyoming-Nebraska state line.

[30]The Rawhide, still so called, had been named by the fur traders, how early is not known, but very likely after the establishment of Fort Laramie in 1834. The encampment was about 8 miles northwest of present Torrington, Wyoming.

started at 9 oclock it being the first Day of june the weather pleasant and fair we traveled 12 miles and 1/2 half {12} an came to the fort—Larramie[31] and camped for the night in peace and found some of our Brethren from the missippie 3 famleys 9 men 5 women and 3 children wich came out in the year 1836 {1846} they went to fort perbolo [Pueblo —Ed.] and wintered and came to meet the rest of the saints in the spring[32] we hired a boat and ferried our teams and waggons[33] part of them on the 3 of june and visited the fort they treated us with kindness, and on the fort 4 of june we finished ferring through the night it rained Rappedly; the jentle men of the fort said they had no rain for 2 years before this spring it is a Deloate country by all appearances thoes jentle men has got squass for their companions we gathered quite a quantity of beads on the pis aunts houses; the fourt is made of large green {unburnt} brick and is 100 and 68 {?} by a 1.00.16 in weadth and also an old fort a bout the same sise[34] we started about 11 oclock and traveled a bout 8 miles a halted and rested in peace for the night[35] and

started on our jurney on the 5the of june and we saw and traveled a long thee black hills {Laramie mountains} it is al Seder and pine and ash and some other kinds of timber we traveled on till a bout 12 oclock and halted by the warm spring wich proceeded out of the Mountain[36] while we bated our teams there came a 11 waggons in company for oragon and passed

---

[31]The camp remained on the north bank of the Platte about three-quarters of a mile above its confluence with the Laramie River. They stayed there over the next day while Brigham Young and others crossed the river to visit the fur company's establishment at Fort Laramie, situated on the Laramie River, two miles farther south.

[32]The little detachment of the Mississippi Saints here mentioned had come on in advance of their brethren from Pueblo. They consisted of Robert Crow, his wife and 8 children, a gentile son-in-law, two grandchildren, and three unattached men. One of these latter, Lewis B. Myers, was a mountain man who had joined the Crows at Pueblo; he acted as their hunter, and he was to play a part in the establishment of the Mormon ferry at the upper crossing of the Platte.

[33]The traders at the fort had a flatboat which the Saints rented for $15. The average time to get a wagon across, according to William Clayton, was 11 minutes.

[34]The "old fort" was a rival post called Fort Platte, established in 1840 or 1841 and abandoned in 1845. It was located on the south bank of the North Platte, three-quarters of a mile above the confluence with the Laramie, or nearly opposite the point where the Mormons crossed the river. Ground plans of both forts, as drawn by Thomas Bullock, clerk to the Mormon camp, are reproduced in L.R. Hafen and F.M. Young, *Fort Laramie* (Glendale, Calif.: Arthur H. Clark Co., 1938), 127.

[35]The night's encampment was on the south hank of the North Platte, some 8 miles northwest of Fort Laramie.

[36]The Warm Spring was a famous watering place on the Overland Trail. The Saints reached it by following the bank of the Platte to the mouth of Warm Springs Canyon, then ascending that canyon to where the spring broke out.

us[37] we then started as usesial and over took the same company and camped for the night we traveled 17 miles. and rested in peace[38] and got up by the sound of the bugal and paid our Devotions to our Father in Heaven it being the Sabbath Day; we fasted and prayed one with another and Spoke of the goodness of god to wards us as a people wich was rejected from the jentiles nation I can sureley say that god poured out his spirrit up on us and we enjoided our selves well while at meeting there was reported that there was an nother company our meeting was brought to a close and there passed 19 waggons 72 yokes of cattle besides the Loose stock and horses[39] this {?} we then made preperations to start to it being the 6 of the month to travel 6 miles to a good camping place we starte and over took one of the camps

[37]This is Empey's first mention of the year's Oregon immigration, but a pack party had brought news of the immigration to Fort Laramie 2 June, before the Saints resumed their journey west. Orson Pratt wrote in his journal on 3 June, "Yesterday afternoon we saw with our glasses three or four white men coming in on horseback; they were on the opposite side of the Platte, and soon arrived at the fort. This morning brought us the news that they were from the States, having made the journey in seventeen days, passing about 2,000 wagons in detached companies on their way to Oregon. One small company is expected in to-morrow, another larger the next day, and one still larger the day following. We understand that these emigrants are principally from Missouri, Illinois, and Iowa." Howard Egan says that these men, four in all, had come from St. Joseph. Erastus Snow says they estimated 5,000 immigrants to be with the 2,000 wagons, but William Clayton exhibited some skepticism at these numbers, a skepticism well justified, as the year's Oregon and California immigration did not total more than 1,000 wagons.

None of the Mormon journals name the captain of this company which had overtaken the Saints at the Warm Spring, but Clayton noted that they had left Independence 22 April and intended to stay ahead of all companies on the road. They brought news that two more companies had arrived at Fort Laramie as they were leaving, and that three other companies were within 20 miles of the fort. Albert Carrington, in the journal he was keeping for Amasa Lyman, noted that these Oregon immigrants were mostly from Illinois, not far from Chicago, and that the 11 "wagons" Empey refers to consisted in reality of 9 wagons, 1 cart, and 1 handsome 2-horse carriage. With them, Carrington observed, was "one Gabriel Priedeaum . . . who belongs at the missionary station on St. Mary's, a tributary of the Columbia, 4-1/2 days ride on horseback from Ft. Hall. This man, he was interested to learn, had been over the trail before. As a matter of fact, in Gabriel Prudhomme, Carrington was talking to a person of some distinction in the history of the West. He was the half-breed interpreter, "Gabriel," who had served Father [Pierre-Jean] De Smet so well in 1841–42, and taken him down the Missouri to St. Louis. He had then returned to the mountains, for De Smet had found him at the Catholic mission station on the St. Mary's (Bitterroot) River in Montana on returning there in 1844. Probably he had again taken De Smet to St. Louis in the fall of 1846 and was on his way back to the mountains. Prudhomme's death at Fort Owen, 15 January 1856, is recorded in *The Journals and Letters of Major John Owen*, 2v. (New York: Edward Eberstadt, 1927), 115.

[38]On Cottonwood, or as it was sometimes called, Bitter Cottonwood Creek, a little south of present Wendover, Wyoming.

[39]The Mormon journals are not in entire agreement, but evidently this second Oregon company consisted of 19 wagons and 2 carriages. Carrington says they were from Illinois and Missouri; Levi Jackman adds that they had all ox teams, from 3 to 5 yoke to the wagon; and Norton Jacob comments that they had a large drove of cattle and horses. Anybody from Missouri was regarded with grave suspicion by the Saints, and the members of this company were no exception. See Clayton's journal [*William Clayton's Journal* (1921), 219].

that went by us the same Day and we camped we trave 5 miles and rested in peace[40] and

arose at the sound of the bugal being the 7, of the month there is four companys behind in about 20 miles the country a pears to be helthy and pleasant the Land in the flats is good the mountains is a great height my gard is a blight toe Stand every 3 night half of the of the night we are united in Love and in harmany the spirit of the Lord is with us continuley we started as usesial by the sound of the bugal on our jurney and traveled 7 miles and a half and bated our teams oposite of fourt john {Laramie} peak it is a chain of the rockemountains wich is south west course there is quitee a quantity of snow on the mountains; while we were a bating our teams there passed a 13 waggons and teams going to oragon from Illinois[41] this is the 3 company that has passed us in going 40 miles they said that the waar is still going on in Illinois one side a gainst annother[42] we traveled 13 miles and camped for the night a Long horse shoe creek[43] the hunters shot 2 Deer the Deer has black tails and one antilope with suplied our wants for the preasant we took our suppers and paid our Devotions to our god and rested in peace for the night the mountains is covered with pine and all over the bluffs a Long thee creeks is thee broade Leaf willow and cotton wood

we started on our Jurney on the 8 Day of june the weather being verry cold we traveled 25 miles and a half and camped for the night a Long side of big timber Creek[44] the hunters shot 2 antilopes and one Deer & there came 6 traders from the mountains with 5 teams Loded with furs[45] we rested in peace for the night and

---

[40]The night's camp was on a run called Bear Creek, some 5 miles south of Cassa, Wyoming. It was not the practice of the Saints to travel on Sundays, but an exception was made in this case because it was more than a day's journey from Cottonwood Creek to the next water west of Bear Creek.

[41]The other Mormon journals agree that this company was not from Illinois but from Andrew County, Missouri.

[42]Agitation by the anti-Mormons did not die down in Illinois immediately, even after the formal expulsion of the Saints, from Nauvoo in September, 1846; and in Massac County a species of civil war was being carried on by and against some "Regulators."

[43]The stream is still so named. The camp site was some 4 miles to the southwest of present Cassa, Wyoming.

[44]Empey's "Big Timber Creek" is more readily recognizable as LaBonte Creek or River.

[45]The Saints had been looking for this party from the mountains ever since their departure from Fort Laramie. Brigham Young's journal records, "Met James H. Grieve, William Tucker, James Woodrie, James Bonoir and six other Frenchmen from whom we learn that Mr. Bridger was located about 300 miles west, that the mountaineers could ride to Salt Lake from Bridger's Fort in two days and that the Utah country was beautiful." The Mormon journals disagree considerably as to how many actually composed this company, the discrepancy presumably arising because the traders' encampment was west of that of the Mormons, and not all of the mountain men visited the Saints. Albert Carrington (*continued, next page*)

arose on the 9 of the month and started at sun rise to go to better feed and camped and took our break fast and started on as usesial the Day is pleasant but cold wind from the mountain we trave 10 miles and bated our teams and started on our way and Traveled in all 19 miles and a quarter and camped a Lonng side of Alapier Creek[46] were we enjoided our selves in peace and in Love and

started on in the morning it being the 10 of the month we sent of on the 9. 18 waggons and some horse men to secure the bull hide boat that the traders gave us the priviledg of crossing with there were so many companys a head that we knew that if we Did not send some a head we would be Deaiad {delayed}[47] we traveled over the black and read hills on the 9 & we traveled 8 miles and a quarter and bated our teams a Long side of Fourche Boisce Creek; we then started on and traviled this 17 miles and 3 quarters and camped a Long side of Deer creek it is a Delightful place situated a Long side of the Platt we left the platt 18 miles a bove Ft. john on the 5 of june and we traveled over the Black and read hills and came to the platt on the 10 of the month; we rested in peace and in quiteness and

started on the 11 of june at the sound of the bugal the country is more beautiful then we saw it since we Left winters quarters; Brother B Young say he will have a few famley farm it on Deer Creek for it is a Delightful place[48]

notes that a squaw was included among their number and that they had 3 carts and 1 wagon loaded with furs. Appleton Harmon says the men "ware a goin to fort John from thare to fort Lookout on the missouri river with 3 waggon loads of peltry from thare I under stood that one of them would go to Councilbluffs by water thare ware Some letters sent by them."

The meeting with these traders led directly to the establishment of the Mormon ferry at the upper crossing of the North Platte. William Clayton writes that they "had left a kind of ferry made of three buffalo skins {*i.e.,* a bullboat} hung in a tree on the Platte and wanted Brother Crow's company to have it." This generous inclination undoubtedly was born of their prior acquaintance with Lewis B. Myers, the mountain man who had rallied to the fortunes of the Crow family.

[46]Present-day La Prele Creek, probably given originally the French name "a la prele," most recurrently appears in the Mormon journals as Alapier or a la Pierre.

[47]See Note 45 above. William Clayton writes concerning this party, "It was decided to send a company ahead to overreach the Missouri companies and get the ferry before they could arrive, and also build a raft for us to cross on, kill game, etc. . . . Nineteen wagons were sent ahead and about forty men to attend to this business. All of Brother Crow's company went, Aaron Farr, J. Redding, the cutter {the Saints' leather boat, the *Revenue Cutter*}, etc., being five wagons from the 1st division and fourteen from the 2nd." They were commanded by John S. Higbee. John Brown was one of those sent ahead to the ferry, but of their experiences he says only, "A company of us were detached and sent on to get the boat before the emigrants got it. We reached the ferry first but could find nothing of the boat. We turned out and killed a fine lot of meat by the time the camp came up." Ferrying of the Oregon immigrants, nevertheless, began immediately on the arrival of the advance party at the river, the *Revenue Cutter* being employed.

[48]Such a settlement was actually made by the Saints, but not until 10 years later, as a station for the short-lived express company established by Brigham Young. The settlement, like the express company, was broken up in the summer of 1857 by the affair of the Utah Expedition.

we found a coal mind a half a mile Long and 10 feet thick of first quality of coal[49] we traveled 9 miles and a quarter in the fouer noon a long side of the platt in cotton wood grove and we traveled in the after noon 7 miles and 3 quarters which makes 17 miles and camped a Long side of the platt in a butifull valley[50] we rested in peace for the night I for got to say that I shot one antilope on the 11 and there were 7 or 8 shot the same Day shot

we started on our jurney as usesial by the sound of the bugal it being the 12 of june we traveled and Traveled 11 miles and a quarter and came to were our company was ferreying the Emmagrants a cross the platt[51] we had a Dollar and a half a waggon for 22 waggons we got flour at 2 Dollars and a half per hundred and bacon at 6 Dollars per hundred.[52] we rested in peace for the night and

---

[49]The coal outcropping was discovered by Albert Carrington who says that it was "the first ever found to our knowledge on the Platte or any of its tributaries, it rests upon a fine grit sandstone, commonly called grindstone, grit of excellent quality of a whitish or light grey color, except where stained by sulphuret of iron, then yellowish, as far as it shows, from the creek to coal bed is from 40 to 50 ft. thick, then the coal bed, probably from 6 to 10 ft. thick traced nearly 1 mile, then overlaid by a brown micaceous slate, could not determine its thickness without mineing. . . ." The coal was subsequently used by the Mormon blacksmiths at the ferry but found to be of less than first quality. Coal had been noted here at least as early as 1846.

[50]The night's encampment was about 8 miles east of the site of Casper, Wyoming. Here, William Clayton writes, "we came to a halt on account of seeing a number of wagons about a half mile ahead which proved to be two of the Missouri companies camped on the banks of the river and preparing to cross here. It was also ascertained that there is no camping place beyond them unless we go some distance. . . . These Missourian companies inform us that the regular crossing place is twelve miles farther and that our brethren are gone on there and also the balance of the Missourian companies. These men have got a light flat boat with them and have already got one load over." Orson Pratt says of these same immigrants, "A short distance above us, two small companies which had passed us a few days before, were encamped; they were building a raft to cross at that place. The day before their teams took a fright by the running of a horse, upsetting two of their wagons; one woman and two children considerably injured, but no bones broken: some crockery, &c destroyed."

[51]On the morning of 12 June the Saints traveled 7-1/4 miles to the vicinity of Casper, where, Norton Jacob makes note, "there is an excellent fording place which has been much used by emigrants. James Case and Stephen Markham forded the river experimentally here, finding the water about 4-1/2 feet deep in the channel, and the current very swift. "Of course it could not be forded with loads in the wagons," William Clayton records, "but the loading would have to be ferried in the boat. They made a report of this kind on their return to camp and about the same time Brother {Alexander} Chesley came down from the brethren ahead and reported their progress and the nature of the crossing place, etc. A number of the brethren in company with Elder Kimball and Chesley went to the river opposite the camp to decide whether to cross here or go on. Brother Markham and Case again went over, but it was finally concluded to go up to the other ferry." The Saints moved on up the river 4 miles and made their night encampment half a mile below where the provisional Mormon ferry was being operated, which was some 3-3/4 miles above present Casper.

[52]William Clayton writes, concerning the inception of the ferry, that the brethren sent ahead had arrived at the river about noon of the 11th. "Two of the Missourian companies arrived about the same time. The brethren concluded that a raft would be of no use on account of the swiftness of the current. The Missourian company offered to pay them well if they would carry their company (*continued, next page*)

on the 13 of the month was the Sabbath we held a prayer meeting and had Br Kimble Speak to us and also Br Young we truley was blessed with the spirit of the Lord was in our midst after metting Br young counciled us to take one team to each ten and a few men with guns and axes and go to the mountains {Casper Range} and cut pine poles for ferrying a cross the Platt so we Started and went accordingley and Got to the mountains and there we found plentey snow on the 13 of june we washed our faces with snow we came back with our poles at 9 oclock at night it being 7 miles to the mountains opposite of of the ferry on the platt and

on the 14 of june we commenced ferriing a cross the platt takeing 2 waggons side of each other and put holes {poles} under the the waggons and Lashed them fast and took a Long rope a cross the stream and some {worked} on raffs and as we come menced our opperations we soon found that this would not Do[[53]] we then made 4 or five raffs and we on the 15 of the month we got a bout 2 thirds a cross the platt the weather being rather to our Disadvantage it being stormmey[54] on the 16 of the month in the

---

over in the boat and a contract was made to do so for $1.50 per load, the brethren to receive their pay in flour at $2.50 per hundred. They commenced soon after and this evening {12 June} finished their work, and received the pay mostly in flour, a little meal and some bacon. They have made $34.00 with the cutter all in provisions which is a great blessing to the camp inasmuch as a number of the brethren have had no bread stuff for some days. . . . The Missourian company seem to feel well toward us and express their joy at having got across the river so soon." [The commencement of the ferry is likewise addressed by company's official diarist, Thomas Bullock, *The Pioneer Camp of the Saints: The 1846 and 1847 Mormon Trail Journals of Thomas Bullock*, ed. Will Bagley (Spokane, Wash.: Arthur H. Clark Co., 1997), 193ff. —Ed.]

[53][The *Annals'* typesetter neglected to place a note number in text, and Morgan neglected to catch the omission in reviews. Placement here is an exercise of editorial license on my part. —Ed.] Experiment proved that attempting to take across more than one wagon at a time, so far from saving time and energy, multiplied the problems and resulted in serious damage to the wagons. When the Saints quit work on the 14th, Clayton makes note, 23 of their wagons had been ferried over the river. "There was no difficulty in getting the freight over for one man can carry it in the cutter faster than all the rest of the camp can get the wagons over." On the 18th the Saints put into service a ferry boat to replace their makeshift rafts, and it was this craft that served the immigration through the rest of the season. Appleton Harmon describes it as "built of 2 dugouts 23 feet long & ties a crost they being placed 6 feet apart and run plank lengthwise."

[54]William Clayton remarks that on this day it was concluded "to leave several brethren here to make a boat and keep a ferry till the next {Mormon} company comes up. By that means they will probably make enough to supply a large company of emigrants coming up on the north side of the Platt above Grand Island. There are doubtless some of our brethren and if so they will probably reach us before we get through." The rumor Clayton alludes to was without foundation—the Mormon Second Company of 1847 on this date was just setting out from Winter Quarters, on the Missouri River, but the rumor played its part in the establishing of the ferry.

The company of Missourians referred to is noted by Appleton Harmon as being "an Oregon company of 18 wagons commanded by Capt Smith . . . Judge Kimsey with him." It would seem likely that the Captain Smith referred to was Doctor Smith, the father of Moses Ira Smith. Sarah Hunt Steeves writes concerning the son, in her *Book of Remembrance of Marion County, Oregon, Pioneers* (Portland, Ore.: Berncliff Press, 1927), 118, 120: "Doctor Smith and his wife, Nancy Scott-Wisdom Smith, were his parents.

four noon we passed over severl waggons and the the wind began to blow and the water began to rise some did not not do much in the after noon but prepair our craffs on {?} for the night there come too companyes of emagrants one was from Masura and the others from ohiwa and came to us to make a bargan for to have us to Cross them we a greed to Do so for pay[55] Br Young then thought it would be wisdom for some of our Brethern to go to work and make toe canoes and make a ferry and pint some good faith full men to stay at the platt and cross all the companeys that would come so we might get means to sustains thee saints and he would not have any men to stay that would not come on when our Brethren came that we might go on with them The wind a bated a bout 4 oclock in the after noon and we ferried over severl teams and rested in peace for the night and

on the 17 of the mont we commenced ferriing and ferryed over severl waggons and then the wind commenced blowing so we was a blige to stop we got too canoe màde to ferry with and too raffs the canoes worked first rate so we Laid by the rafts and worked with the canoes we finished ferring our teams and waggons on the 17 of the month;[56] and on the 19 of june the

---

Doctor was just a given name. . . . Moses' father had been elected captain of the train, that started out with about thirty wagons, and others joined them, until in time there were two hundred white-covered wagons. . . . At the second crossing of the Platte (North Platte) they overtook Brigham Young, the great Mormon apostle, who was camped here with his many followers and five hundred wagons {actually, 77 wagons and 1 cart}, preparing to cross the river, on their way to the Great Salt Lake. He had sent men to the timber in the hills about fifteen miles away, where they dug up whole trees and from them made dug-out canoes. By fastening two of these together as a basis for rafts, they would carry a loaded wagon across in safety, returning again for another. Brigham Young was very kind to the immigrants in many ways. He proposed to take their train across on his rafts, before he did his own and only charged at the rate of fifty pounds of flour per wagon for this service. Moses' father had known Brigham in Missouri, and no doubt these two men were glad to renew their old acquaintance and enjoyed talking over things in old Missouri. . . ." Doctor Smith, captain of this train, died at Green River.

[55]It is difficult to disentangle the companies of the Oregon immigration during this and the next couple of days—perhaps because, as Norton Jacob declares, "there was one hundred eight emigrant waggons within four miles all wanting to cross the river." Some, he adds, "hired us to cross them at $1.50 paid in flour and at $2.50 per hundred, and others crossed themselves." Although the 16th was principally occupied in getting across the Saints' own wagons, Appleton Harmon says that "a company of ten {Oregon} wagons, came up and we engaged to ferry them for $1.50 per waggon."

Historians of the overland trail having commented on Brigham Young's great shrewdness, if not tight-fistedness, in fixing the ferry fees at low States' prices for the provisions accepted in payment, it is worth noting that the standard fee was established, by bargaining between the Oregon immigrants and the Saints sent to the ferry, before Young arrived on the scene.

[56]William Clayton adds a footnote which illustrates the ingenuity of the Saints in turning an extra dollar. After the last Mormon wagon was got over, there remained two Missouri companies which had made application to be set over at $1.50 per load. "When the contract was made with the first company to be sent across as soon as our wagons were over, the other company of ten wagons offered to pay the brethren 50¢ per man extra if they would set them over first, making $5.00 over the stated price for ferriage being ten of the brethren to work at it. Colonel {Albert} Rockwood {commanding (*continued, next page*)

camp started on their jurney; we ferried a cross the platt besides our teams of the Emagrants 64 waggons wich a mounted to 94 dollars wich we took provishions for flower at 2 Dollars and 50 cents per hundred, and pork at 6 per hundred; on the 18 we ferried all Day for the emagrants and on the 19 we ferried 16 waggons wich finished ferring for them the twelve set in council and appointed 9 men to stay and ferry till our Brethren the 2 camp came up so that we might assis them in crossing and we might have all we made in ferring we then was called together thoes that where chosen to stay and Brother Brigham young gave us in struct how to proceed with the jentiles

North Fork of Platt River Upper Ferry: Juene 18; 1847
125 miles west of Fort
Laraie or St john[57]

Instructions to Thomas Grover John J {S} Higbee Wm Empey; appleton m Harman. Edmund Elsworth. Luke johnson[,] Francies m. Pomera, James Devenport & Benjamine F Stewart: Brethren as you are a bout to stop at this place for a little season for the purpose of passing Emagrants over the river, and assisting the saints. We have thought fit appoint Thomas Grover Superintendent of the ferry, and of your Company; which if you approve; we want you to agree that you will follow his council implicitly and, without gainsaying; and we desire that you will be agreed in all your operations, actions in Concert keeping together continually, and not scatter to hunt, &c, and at your leisure moments put up a comfortable room that will afford yourselves and horses protection against the Indians should a war partey pass this way; but, first of all, see that you boat is propperley coupled; by fastining Raw Hides over the tops of the Canoes, or some better

the second division} had made a contract to the above effect with the first company and did not like to break it. However, he received a hint that this was Colonel {Stephen} Markham's day for the use of the boat and consequently Colonel Markham {commanding the first division} had a right to take the last offer if he chose. He took the hint and they went to work forthwith at a dollar and a half a wagon in provisions at Missouri prices and 50¢ extra per man in what they preferred for themselves. . . . The ferrying was continued all night and till daylight at which time many of the Missourians' wagons in the two companies were over."

[57]The nine men named to stay at the ferry were Thomas Grover, John S. Higbee, William Empey, Appleton Harmon, Edmund Ellsworth, Luke Johnson, Francis M. Pomeroy, James Davenport, and Benjamin F. Stewart. A tenth man, Eric Glines, stayed on without Brigham Young's sanction. Of him William Clayton wrote on 18 June, "The President . . . referred to Brother Glines who was wishful to stay but the president said he had no council for him to tarry, but he might do as he had a mind to. Some explanations followed by Glines, but the unanimous feeling of the brethren was to have him go on." Glines remained at the ferry until the 23rd, but then had a change of heart and set out after the Pioneer party, which he overtook on the 26th, three days' journey west.

process. Complete the Landings and be carefull of the Lives and property of all you labour for, remembering that you are responsible for all accidents though your carelessness or negligence and see that ye Retain not that which belongeth to the Traveller

For one wagon . . . Familey &. you will charge $1.50 fo payment in Flower and Provisions at state prices; or three Dollars in cash, but you had better take young stock at a fair valation in stead of cash. and. a team if you shall want the same to remove

Should generl Emagration cease before our brethren arrive—Cachet your effects and return to Laramie and wait thier arrival and come on with them to the place of location and we promis you that, the superintendent of the Ferry shall never lack wisdom or knowledge to devise and council you in righteousness and for your best good; if you will always be a greed; and in all humility watch and pray without ceasing

When our Emigration companies arrives: if the river is not fordable, ferry them, and let them who are able pay a reasonable sum, the the council of their camp will decide who are able to pay.

Let a strict account be kept of every mans labour also of all Wagons and teams &c ferried and of all receipts and expenditures allowing each according to his labor and justice; and if any one feels aggrieved let him not murmur; but be patient till you come up, and let the council decide and the way not to be aggrieved is for every man to Love his brother as him self

By order, and in behalf of the council
We remain your Brethren in Christ
Brigham Young President

we the Subscribers whose names inserted in the foregoing instructions fully concur therein and cheerfulley agree that we will implicitly follow the Council theirein contained; and that of our Superintendent according to best of our ability relying on our Heavenly Father continually for his assistance in testimony whereof we have here unto set set our hands at the time and place above specified

Thomas Grover	Edmund Ellsworth
Appleton M. Harmon	James Devenport
John S Higbee	Benjamin F Stewart
Frances m Pomeray	Luke Johnson

and

on the 20 we finished Ferying the company[58] and on the 21 Capt grover chosed too men to go to Deer creek for a load of coals at Deer creek the Distance of 30 miles Wm Y Empey and steward was appointed to go wich was Disagreeable on account of indians but we went[59] we traveled within 2 miles of Deer creek and there we on 22 we got our Load of coal and returned on our jurney on the 22. and on the 23 we arrived to our Ferry;[60]

on the 23 there came 4 Canadian Traders and one squaw with 6 horses and they stopped all night with us[61] and

[58]For this date Appleton Harmon's journal has an amusing entry showing that the benefits of competition in free enterprise were no more appreciated in 1847 than they have been in many a year since: "br Empy & Sturart Started with 4 horses & a waggon after coal back to Deer crick 28 *ms* a companied by F.M. Pumeroy & glines who went to rekanorter the ferry below & see if it could be chartered for laramie post they returned Jest at evening & reported that the boat was on the opposite Side the river & 3 men thare with a waggon apearent ly waiting for a nother company Luke Johnson, Edmund Elsworth, went down on the north Side to make a more close examination but returned about day light having found it well guarded & a faith ful watch dog[.]"

[59]Harmon's journal, as quoted in Note 58, would indicate that Empey and Stewart set out on the 20th, rather than the 21st. While they were gone, Harmon records (21 June) an important change in the affairs of the Mormon ferry: "I arose early & in company with John Higbee by the request of Capt grover went down to the lower ferry hunting horses & to see how long those men ware to Stay there, they sed that they expected to Stay until a company of 27 waggons should bee crossed that they expected they would git thare to night, we got our things together finished blacsmithing got a cow in pay ment put our things most of them on to the boat Capt Grover my Self J. Higbee, F.M. Pumeroy & J Debenport, shoved of with the ferry boat & leather skift leaving. Luke Johnson & Edmund Elsworth with the 2 waggons & things that remain thair while we floted down the river in quest of a ferrying ground below those a bove mentioned we Stuck on 2 Sand bears but got of with but verry little difficulty we halted a short time at their ferry Capt grover asked them if they ware willing for us to fery at the Same place with them, and working in concert with them but they seemed to choose to run the risk a lone of gitting what they could So we moved on down the river a bout 2 ms & landed on the South Side the river in a grove of Scatering cotton woods close by the road whare the feed is good & a good Cite for a ferry after a few moments consultation we unamously agreed that this should be the Spot We acordingly unloaded our things br debenport put up his black Smith tools &c Herick glines Started with the cattle to drive them down to whare we ware a going, but when we landed we found that he was a head of us, we Set up some punchaon & bords that we had on the boat to break the wind offrom us & made our beds on the ground, we ware called to gether by capt Grover & returned thanks to the God of Jacob as usial & retierd to our lodging."

It would appear that the rival ferry was something over a mile below Casper, and the reestablished Mormon ferry from 2 to 2-1/2 miles farther down.

[60]Harmon's journal says that Empey and Stewart were gone from the 20th to noon of the 22nd, whereas Empey makes it from the 21st to the 23rd. Being more full, Harmon's journal is presumably more reliable. Harmon adds that the two men put up an advertisement at Deer Creek as follows:

NOTICE

To the ferry 28 ms the ferry good & safe maned by experienced men black Smithing horse & ox Shoing done all so a wheel right

Thomas, Grover,

The 28 miles given as the distance from Deer Creek was correct for the original location, but now of course the Mormon ferry was about 7 miles closer.

[61]The 4 French traders, so Harmon writes, "enformed us that the Soldiers {Sick Detachment of the Mormon Battalion} from Peublo w are at fort John {Fort Laramie} when they lift & would be here in a few days."

on the 24 there came 2 men in a carriage and got some work done in the Line of black smithing they told us that there were severl Companies between St john and were we was at the ferry the Companies of our Brethren from Purbelow was on there way to California on our rout

Friday the 25th in the morning we ferried John Battice[62] & 3 of his companions french men & one squaw they had 10 horses with them Capt Wm Vaugn[63] & his company arived a bout noon & imploy us to Ferry him & company not with standing a man from the upper ferry met them some 8 miles below here & proffered them the use of the Ferry boat gratis we ferryed 5 of their waggons & way obliged to stop on a count of winds blowing. Capt Hodge arived with with 11 waggons[64] we a greed to ferry them for 5 {50} cents a waggon thinking if we gave the uper ferry no chance of employment they would not remain Long. a bout 5 oclock P. M. John Higby discovered the baby {i.e., body} of Wesley T Dustin[65] floting down the river that was drowned june the 19. 2/2 {2-1/2} ms a bove here at Hill Ferry[66] Capt bounyn {Vounyn?} went with the boat picked up the corpes, he was interd by Capt Vanghns Company near our ferry their was found in his possessian a pocket knife & a dollar and 60 cents cents in money wich a jentle man Said he would forward to his parents that ware a head

Saturday the 26th we ferried this day 40 waggons which ampleted the 2

[62]John Battice, or Jean Baptiste, figures often in the annals of Fort Bridger, trading in association with Jim Bridger.

[63]Vaughn's company is not clearly distinguished in the Oregon annals, but is mentioned in a report of the 1847 immigration in the St. Joseph *Gazette*, 28 May 1847. The *Gazette*'s informant met "Vaughn's company," then consisting of 48 wagons, on May 17, apparently on the Little Blue. Empey's journal entry for the 25th is almost word for word the same as Harmon's indicating that one diarist copied from the other.

[64]Captain Hodge was possibly Jesse Monroe Hodges, or his son, D.R. Hodges. Bancroft notes in his *History of Oregon*, 2v. (San Francisco: History Company, 1886), 1: 628, 629, "Jesse Monroe Hodges was born in Melbourne Co., S.C., Dec. 18, 1788. In 1811 he married Catherine Stanley of N.C. He served in the war of 1812, and fought under General Jackson at Horse Shoe Bend. In 1817 he moved to Tenn., thence to Ind., and thence in 1839 to Mo., making his last remove to Oregon in 1847, and settling in Benton County. He died at the residence of his son, D.R. Hodges, March 27, 1877. His mental condition was sound up to his latest moments, though over 88 years of age."

[65]Harmon had written on June 20, before the change in location of the ferry, "A Young man got Drowned 5 ms below here by the name of Wesley Tustin aged 18 years while Swiming a horse he was not found." Albert Carrington, who heard of the incident on the trail two days later, was informed that the young man was from Morgan Co., Illinois. Harmon and Carrington spelled the name Tustin, which was evidently right; the [George H. Himes's "Death List of Oregon Pioneers,"] *Oregon Historical Quarterly* 20, no. 1 (March 1919): 139, records the death of Caleb S. Tustin, born in Illinois in 1830, came to Oregon in 1847, died at McMinnville, 11 February 1919. Caleb was apparently Wesley's younger brother.

[66]The name, "Hill Ferry," is explained by an entry in Harmon's journal of 23 June, to the effect that James Davenport had "Done some black Smithing for Mr. {Henry?} Hill that has remained 2 miles a bove us with the ferry above mentioned."

companies a bout $15.00 dollars worthe of black smithing in the after noon the ferry boat that was a bove us came floating down past us Cut to peices the companies that had went up they all got across & they seeing no chance of specalation dis troyed their boats & went a head our arrangement for Labour for this Day is as follows for this Day is as John Higbee[67]

{EXTRACT FROM THE JOURNAL OF APPLETON M. HARMON, JUNE 26–JULY 10, 1847}

Amasa Lyman Roswell Stephens Thomas Wolsey & 2 of the soldiers arrived a bout 6 P. M. having left Capt {James} Brown & his battalion a few miles back[68]

Sunday the 27th a Company of 11 wagons drove up Mr Cox foreman[69] ferryed them for $16.00 in cash & done $3.75 worth of blacksmithing for them Capt Brown arived with his Battalion a bout 8 A. M. Capt Saunders[70] company arived a bout 2 P. M. and refused to pay us 75 cts a wagon for ferrying

[67]At this point two leaves are gone from the manuscript, comprising pp. 19–22 and the entries from 26 June to 10 July. Fortunately the gap can be filled with an extract from Appleton Harmon's journal. In Harmon's own journal, however, the first part of the entry for June 26 is evidently missing.

[68]Amasa Lyman, Roswell Stevens, and Thomas Woolsey, together with John H. Tippetts, had been detached from the Pioneer party at Fort Laramie on 3 June, to go south and meet the Mississippi Saints and the Sick Detachment of the Mormon Battalion. They met on 11 June, according to a letter now in the Church archives, written by Lyman on 28 June from "Grover Ferry, on Fork of Platte." John Steele was a member of the detachment commanded by Brown, and he writes, "On the 27th of June came to the crossing of the Platte, found there Brother Groves & Co. ferrying missionaries across the river on their way to Oregon and charging $1.50 for crossing. . . . There are hundreds of emigrants here and find the Mormons a God-send to help them across the river. We crossed over July 1st, 1847." See Steele's journal, ["Extracts from the Journal of John Steele,"] *Utah Historical Quarterly* 6, no. 1 (January 1933): 16.

[69]The company was evidently that of Thomas Cox, alluded to as the Chicago company, and consisting originally of some 14 wagons. Bancroft (*History of Oregon*, 629, 630) writes of him that he "was by birth a Virginian. When but a small child he removed with his parents to Ross Co., Ohio. In 1811 he married Martha Cox, who though of the same name was not a relative. He removed with his family of three children and their mother to Bartholomew Co., where he built the first grist and carding mills in that place. He afterward removed to the Wabash River country, and there also erected flour and carding mills at the mouth of the Shawnee River. He also manufactured guns and gunpowder, and carried on a general blacksmithing business. In 1834 he made another remove, this time to Illinois, where he settled in Will County, and laid out the town of Winchester, the name of which was afterward changed to Wilmington, and where he again erected mills for flouring and carding, and opened a general merchandise business. During the period of land speculation and 'wild-cat' banks, Cox resisted the gambling spirit, and managed to save his property, while others were ruined. In 1846 he made preparations for emigrating to Oregon, in company with his married son, Joseph, and two sons-in-law, Elias Brown and Peter Polley." Cox settled in Salem and set up a store with goods brought across the Plains. Later he turned to fruit-raising, and died at Salem 3 October 1862. See also Ralph C. Geer's account in *Transactions of the Seventh Annual Re-Union of the Oregon Pioneer Association for 1879* (1880), 40, which says the Cox store at Salem was the first such establishment south of Champoeg.

[70]If "Captain Saunders" was L. W. Saunders, he was from Oskaloosa, Iowa, subsequently taught school at Waiilatpu, and was killed in the Whitman Massacre, leaving a widow and 5 children. It is more likely that L. W. Saunders was a member of the Chapman company. See Note 115.

them & got a raft that was left thare by Some of the former Companies & commenced operations Some Jobs of Smithing Commenced for Capt Browns Company 7 of Capt Saunders Co got Sick of raft ing & returned to us & we ferryed them for 75 cts a wagon the morning of the 28th

Tuesday June 29th we then ferryed Br {Elam} Luddington for $1.00 2 waggons for Thomas Willeams $2.00 1 waggon for {William or Benjamin} Matthews $1.00 & one waggon for Mis {Mrs. Nicholas} Kelly gratis making 75 waggons during the day

Wednesday the 30eth Capt Brown & his Detachment Started as all So Amasa Lyman[71] we ferryed Capt Saunders Co or the remainder of it who had refused to give us 75 cts a waggon they havein worked 2 days & got 2 waggons a crost only, & then returned to us & wated until we ferryed 90 waggons that ware a head of them & they paid us $1.00 a waggon for the 12 waggons remaining we then ferryed Capt Higgins Co of 23 waggons for $23.00 in cash[72] allso

---

[71]Brown and Lyman carried west a letter, now in the Church archives, from Thomas Grover to Brigham Young:

Platte river, June 29, 1847.

President Young.

Dear Sir. Having an opportunity of communication a few lines to you by Brother Amasa Lyman, we embrace the same. We are all well at present, but are rather lonesome since you left us. We have just finished ferrying Capt. Brown and company consisting of 19 wagons, four extra loads, three dollars per trip, and also 150 men and women, who are in the United States service at twelve and a half cents and also for Blacksmithing.

$66.00
18.75
22.50
$106.25

Capt. Brown has left with us six oxen that could not be driven any further for us to bring on if they should be able to travel when our brethren come on with a promise to settle the bill as you say is right when we come on.

We remain as ever, your brethren,
Thos. Grover.

Grover's arithmetic would seem to have been somewhat faulty, but not his adherence to a long-established American practice, of soaking the government twice as much as a private individual for services rendered. At rates charged the Oregon immigration, the fee for ferrying the 19 wagons and four extra loads would have been $34.50.

[72]At first glance Captain Higgins most plausibly would seem to be Captain Nelson Higgins of the Mormon Battalion, since no Higgins appears in the lists of the year's Oregon and California immigration. The 23 wagons, however, is so unaccountably large a number for him to be captaining, even if some of them belonged to the Mississippi Saints, as to suggest that the name may have been Wiggins rather than Higgins. William Wiggins seems to have started out from Independence as guide to the contingent with which the Blanchets traveled. His party was belated on the trail, and he attempted to get through to California by a route substantially that of the Lassen Cutoff of 1849, but he had to turn north into Oregon and finally reached California by sea. The safety of his company was a constant theme of anxiety for the California newspapers during the fall and early winter of 1847–48, especially so because of the tragic experiences of the Donner party in the mountains the year before.

Capt McCloys {?} Co of 23 waggons[73] & Capt Taylors Co of 12 waggons[74] & Capt Patter Sons Co of 16 waggons[75] & done $6.50 worth of black Smithing this day we have ferryed 73 waggons & made 2 extra trips, 2 of the trips Namely, {Jonathan} Pugmyer & {Marcus} East man Stade here on a furlow[76]

Thursday July the 1st we ferryed Capt F A Collards Co of 18 waggons,[77] Capt Turpens Co mulkey Pilot[78] of 23 waggons Capt Elisha Bidwells Co of 15 waggons[79] & done $12.85 worth of blacksmithing making 56 waggons this

---

[73]Captain McClay or McCay is not identifiable. A John McCoy is listed by Bancroft as an Oregon immigrant of this year.

[74]I cannot distinguish which Taylor this may be. Christopher, John F., and L. Taylor were Oregon immigrants of 1847. There may have been others.

[75]In *To Oregon by Ox-Team in '47* (Portland: Fred Lockley, n. d. [1924?]), Fred Lockley develops the history of the Hunt family, whose train Elijah Patterson captained, as told by a grandson, Jeptha Hunt. The Hunts were from Indiana, and Jeptha says, "At Independence grandfather {J. S. Hunt} met a young man, Elijah Patterson, who was anxious to go to Oregon but did not have sufficient money to outfit himself for the trip. An arrangement was made whereby Elijah Patterson would furnish a yoke of oxen and a yoke of young cows in exchange for his board while crossing the plains. At Indian Grove a wagon train consisting of 21 wagons was organized and Elijah Patterson was elected captain of the train. . . . On the North Platte they overtook a large company of Mormons enroute for the Great Salt Lake. . . . Jeptha adds that in 1851 his grandfather married Mrs. Nancy Smith, the widow of Doctor Smith (see Note 54).

Sarah Hunt Steeves' *Book of Remembrance*, 97, quotes George Washington Hunt, Jeptha's father, as saying, "After we arrived at Independence, Mo., my father's money running short, he took in an excellent young man from Texas by the name of Elijah Patterson. . . . From Independence we made our way to Indian Grove, our next camp on the line of the Indian Territory (now Kansas). Here Patterson was elected captain of 21 wagons and we rolled out for Oregon. . . . The Mormons crossed us over North Platte in a rather loose affair called a ferry."

[76]Jonathan Pugmyer, Jr., and Marcus N. Eastman were members of the Mormon Battalion evidently furloughed to meet their families coming along in the Second Company, or to return to the States. See Harmon's journal entry for 4 July.

[77]Felix A. Collard is listed in the pioneer index of the Oregon Historical Society. He was born in Kentucky in 1810, settled in Illinois, and then journeyed to Oregon in 1847; he was a farmer, merchant, blacksmith, and member of the Oregon legislature.

[78]Captain Turpen presumably was William Turpin, included in Bancroft's list of the 1847 immigrants. The Oregon Historical Society has a typescript of reminiscences by Cyrenius Mulkey, "Eighty-One Years of Frontier Life," which relates that he and his family crossed the plains in 1847, when he was only 15. His father, a preacher whose given name does not appear, or his father's brother, Johnson Mulkey, might have been the Mulkey referred to as pilot for "Captain Turpen." They started from Missouri and of course traveled the North Platte. The *Transactions of the Twenty-Ninth Annual Reunion of the Orgeon Pioneer Association for 1901* (1902), contains an address of welcome by "Frederick W. Mulkey, son of Marion F. Mulkey and grandson of Mulkey, pioneers of 1847," but this contains no information on the family and does not supply the given name of the grandfather. The only Mulkey appearing in Bancroft's list is Johnson Mulkey, but "Westly Mulkey" has been listed with the immigration of 1844.

[79]Elisha Bidwell, the E. Bidwell of Bancroft's list, is presumably the Elisha Bedwell who appears in the pioneer index of the Oregon Historical Society, though without any evidence that he came as captain of a company. He was born in La Fayette County, Missouri, 9 September 1819, moved to Texas, returned to Missouri, and started across the plains 12 April 1847, arriving in Oregon the following October. He settled in Yamhill.

day & we ware all very tiard & wanted rest Capt Palmers Co of 35 waggons[80] went up a bove & we afterwards learned that they crossed on our raft

Friday July the 2ond we ferryed Capt Snooks Co of 17 waggons,[81] Capt Dodsons Co 11 waggons[82] Capt Daniel Putman Co of 11 waggons[83] & done $7.60 worth of blacksmithing Saturday the 3rd Weather rather clowdy & a Strong wind from the South Mr. James Bridger of Bridgers fort[84] arived bout 11 A. M. & brought a line from prest Young as follows

June 29, 1847 Little Sandy

Mr Thomas Grover and Company
we introduce to your notice Mr James Bridger who we expected to have seen at his fort he is now on his way to Fort Laramie we wish you to cross him & his 2 men on our a count B Y

he was agoing to Laramie & expected to return to his fort in in time to Pilot the Pioneers through to Salt Lake he said that he could take us to a place that would Suit us, thare ware 4 of our Soldiers form Browns detachment

---

[80]Joel Palmer was the most significant figure in the Oregon immigration of 1847. He went to Oregon in 1845, returned east in 1846 to publish his famous Journal, and then immediately returned to the Pacific at the head of an immigrant company. Palmer set out from St. Joseph, and the *Gazette* of that place on 28 May 1847 printed the report of an informant who had met Palmer's party of 99 wagons on May 18, then the ninth company in line along the trail. "Capt. Palmer had taken the census of his company, which was as follows:— 129 males and 72 females over 16 years of age; and under 16 years, 85 males and 83 females. His company had also 1012 head of cattle, 66 horses, 2 mules, and 45 sheep. After the usual fashion of immigrant companies, by the time Palmer reached the Mormon ferry, his company had split up into smaller segments. The *Oregon Spectator*, 19 August 1847, printing news of the oncoming immigration, was pleased to learn of Palmer among them. "Mr. Palmer, who, but a short time since, was a citizen of this country, and has numerous friends here, we are happy to learn, is on his return, and has been honored with the command of a large company of wagons, principally from Missouri. . . ."

[81]Captain Snooks remains unidentified. A person of this name was mentioned by James Clyman as among his fellow wayfarers to Oregon in 1844, and Charles L. Camp has suggested that he may be the P. Snooks who was wounded in the Cascade fight in the Yakima war of 1856. Bancroft, [*History of Oregon*], vol. 2, p. 457, alludes to a major of the 68th Ohio Regiment during the Civil War as "a former resident of Oregon named Snooks, of the immigration of 1844." Possibly all these are one and the same man.

[82]The only name resembling Dodson in the lists of the immigration is D. D. Dostins, but there were Dodsons in Oregon as early as 1845.

[83]The pioneer index of the Oregon Historical Society lists a Daniel B. Putman, born in Illinois 15 April 1810, who came overland to Oregon in 1847, arriving 3 October; he was a millwright who settled at Oregon City.

[84]Jim Bridger, eastbound to Fort Laramie, had met the Mormon Pioneer party at the Little Sandy on 28 June. He and the Saints interrupted their journey for a long conference through the afternoon and evening, the remarkable account of which is found, in particular, in the journals of William Clayton and Norton Jacob. It was then thought that Bridger would return to his fort in time to aid the Saints in finding a location. These plans, however, did not work out. [*William Clayton's Journal* (Salt Lake City: Deseret News Press, 1921), 273–278. Morgan would have used the Jacob journal in typescript, but it appears in print as *The Mormon Vanguard Brigade of 1847: Norton Jacob's Record*, ed. Ronald O. Barney (Logan: Utah State Univ. Press, 2005). —Ed.]

came back with Mr Bridger on a furlow & was agoing to the States,[85] we ferryed Capt Ingersols Co of 11 waggons & 1 extra load for $12,[86] the Oregon mail arived a bout Sun down thare ware 8 men of them & several pack horses & mules they had been ever since the 5th of May on the rout they came by way of California, we ferryed their packs for $1.00[87] I wrote a line by the

[85]Who the four furloughed Battalion members were does not appear.

[86]Chester Ingersoll wrote apparently the only contemporary account of the year's California immigration, in 10 letters published in the *Signal* (*Joliet, Ill.*), reprinted in 1937 at Chicago by Douglas C. McMurtrie as *Overland to California in 1847* [Chicago: Black Cat Press, 1937]. Ingersoll's letters, sent back as opportunity offered, are in effect an intermittent journal of the trip. He set out from Independence, embarking upon the plains on May 10. There were 78 wagons in the company originally, but this number was unwieldy, and split up into smaller detachments, Ingersoll's section consisting of "30 wagons, and 45 able bodied men, with a guide that has traveled the route eight times." He writes on July 2, "Travelled 18 miles to the place of crossing the river which was too high to be forded, but we found a company of Mormons at the ford with a boat. They ferried us over for one dollar per wagon." Next day, "Most of the day was occupied in crossing the river." From Harmon's notation as to the size of the company, it had undergone some further fission since mid-May. Ingersoll reached Johnson's Ranch, above Sutter's Fort, on October 2. Bancroft's index of the California pioneers records that Ingersoll died in San Francisco in 1849, leaving a family.

Additional notes on the California immigration of 1847 were published by Charles L. Camp in "William Alexander Trubody and the Overland Pioneers of 1847," *California Historical Society Quarterly* 16, no. 2 (June 1937). The Trubody family reached California under the guidance of Charles Hopper, but if Hopper commanded a company east of Fort Hall, the record does not appear in the Mormon journals kept at the Platte ferry. The total number of wagons that reached California this year seems to have been 70.

[87]There are some difficulties about identifying the eastbound parties from Oregon in 1847 because they all seem to have split up and recombined in a greater or lesser degree. These 8 men were evidently those who had been encountered by the Mormon Pioneer party at South Pass on the night of 26 June, their guide at that point being the famous mountain man, Moses "Black" Harris. Clayton observes that they had "over twenty horses and mules with them mostly laden with packs of robes, skins, etc.," while Orson Pratt remarks that they had left the Oregon settlements on 5 May.

They were evidently one division of the company of 19 men guided by Levi Scott who left the Rickreal Valley on 5 May and came east by the Applegate Cutoff, the so-called southern or "California" route to which Harmon's journal alludes. Their departure was noted in the *Oregon Spectator*, 15 April, 13 May, and 10 June 1847. Levi Scott went, evidently, only as far as Fort Hall, since he guided back to Oregon by the Applegate Cutoff some 60 wagons of the year's immigration, his return noted in the *Spectator* of 14 October 1847. Where the party split up is not certain, but it is reasonably clear that the second party from Oregon whose passage Harmon notes on 7 July was a subdivision of the larger party by the Applegate Cutoff. The Mormon leader in California, Sam Brannan, who crossed the Sierras in May, in a letter of 18 June written from Fort Hall, remarks that a company from Oregon had arrived at the fort the day before and that he had sent letters in their care (*Millennial Star* 9 (15 October 1847): 304, 305), but otherwise gives no information about them.

Niles' National Register 72 (14 August 1847): 370, records the arrival on the frontier of Messrs. Shaw, Bolden, and Thompson, "direct from Oregon, having left the frontier settlement on the 5th of May, and made the trip to St. Joseph's in 83 days." They had met Brannan at Fort Hall, which makes it likely that they were the party by the Applegate Cutoff. The *St. Louis Daily Union*, 5 August 1847, notes the arrival last night of Mr. Huber, who "left the principal settlements in Willamette Valley on the 7th of May, and arrived at St. Joseph, Mo., on the 28th of July. He was accompanied by fourteen men." Evidently 15 men were in the Oregon company (whose arrival at St. Joseph on 28 July was noted in the *Gazette* of 30 July.) If the 16th man was Black Harris, this would indicate that the two parties of 8 recombined in traveling through the Sioux and Pawnee territory, Harris remaining behind.

request of Capt grover to our next Co Notify fying them that we ware here keeping a ferry & intended to stay until they came up giving them all so the latest news we had from the Pioneers, & sent it by mr Bridger to Laramie Ingerslos Co ware agoing to Calafornia

Sunday July the 4th 1847 morning Clowdy & apearnce of rain I wrote a letter to my wife several of the breathering wrote to their wives or relatives & sent the letters by Makas {Marcus} Eastman who went back with the 4 a bove mentioned they Started a bout 10 A. M.[88] F. M. Pumeroy bought a horse of one of them for $25.00 we ferreyed Capt John McKinneys Co of 27 waggons for $27.00 & done $2.35 cts worth of blacksmithing[89]

Monday the 5 of July we ferryed 6 waggons for Retford & Bodall[90] for $4.00 each

Tuesday the 6th we ferryed Capt Wards Co of 18 waggons[91] for 50 cts a wagon & 3 of them went of with out paing their ferage we done $3.63 cents worth of blacksmithing for them Capt Whitcoms Co of 22 wagons[92] went above to ford which could be done by raising their wagon beds for the river

[88]It is difficult to trace the movements of these 5 men, except for what may be learned from a letter by Orson Hyde, dated St. Louis, 5 August 1847. "In coming from the {Council} Bluffs to St. Joseph's, about five days ago, I met five of our battalion of soldiers returning. They came to fort Laramie, from Purbelo, in company with about 150 others.... Upon their arrival at the fort, the soldiers, all except these five whom I met, went on with brother Amasa after the pioneers. A small party from Oregon overtook our five returning soldiers. They met our pioneers beyond the 'south pass' in the mountains. All well." The 5 Battalion men may thus have been with the company which reached St. Joseph 28 July. (*Millennial Star* 9 (15 September 1847): 272–273.)

[89]Sarah Hunt Steeves, *Book of Remembrance*, 137–138, writes: "Rev. John McKinney was born in Tennessee, April 3, 1798.... From Tennessee the family moved to Jackson county, Missouri.... Of the party to start across the plains from the McKinney farm in 1847, many came from St. Joseph and other places. Of this company were a Mr. Doty; John and Hugh Harrison, with their families; Hadley Hobson and family; Mr. Thompkins and family; Dr. Prettyman and family; the two McKinneys; Rev. John McKinney, William McKinney and wife Matilda; a Mr. Davis, who was hauling a set of mill burrs across the plains; Mr. Luellyn who had planted an embryo nursery in a wagon bed ... ; Dick Adams, and a Major Magoon, with many others. The company numbered about one hundred wagons, with Major Magoon in charge ... Very soon, however, dissension arose over who should be officers ... caused the train to divide into ten groups of ten wagons each, with Major Magoon as head over all companies. Each ten wagons elected a captain and thus they were enabled to travel with more harmony.... Rev. John McKinney was chosen captain of the ten wagons comprising the two of the McKinneys, Mr. Davis ... , Mr. Doty, the Harrisons, Hobsons, Dr. Prettyman, Thompkins, the Luellyn family with the nursery stock and Major Magoon." When his father was sick, William McKinney acted as captain.

[90]Retford and Bodall are unidentified.

[91]Ward also for the present defies identification.

[92]Whitcom is presumably Lot Whitcomb, whose name is found in Bancroft's list of the year's Oregon immigration. *The St. Joseph Gazette*, 28 May 1847, referred to Whitcomb's as having been on 20 May the twelfth company in line on the trail, consisting then of 109 wagons.

hass been for Some days falling verry fast. Capt Hocketts Co of 20 wagons[93] arived here & got Some work done

Wednesday the 7th 1847 we ferryed Capt Magones Co of 36 wagons for $1.00 a waggon 8 waggons of the same Co went above to ford making 44 waggons in Said Co[94] I furnished Capt Magone with the Names of the Captains of all the Companies & the Number of wagons, which he said would be published thare was a catholick bishop & 7 priests in Capt Magones Co 2 of their names ware Blachets the others I did not learn,[95]—8 men from Oregon arived with pack horses & mules[96] we ferryed them & their packs for $1.00 & done $7.75 cts worth of blacksmithing Capt Hocketts Co went above to ford

Thursday the 8th thare was done $6.40 cts worth of black Smithing & Some other jobs commenced Luke Johnson got $3.00 for cleaning teeth & Doctoring which was put into the jineral pile

Friday the 9th our men ware imployed this day in the following manner T Grover Wm Empey John Higbee—Johnathan Pugmyer worked at Black

---

[93]Captain Hockett is not readily identifiable. He may have been the J. C. Holgate on Bancroft's list, "identified with the early histories of Oregon, Washington, and Idaho," and killed in a mining difficulty at Owyhee in March 1868.

[94]The "Reminiscences of James Jory," *Oregon Historical Quarterly* 3 (September 1902): 271–283, describe the experiences of Joseph Magone's company, which started from Independence. "Magone was from New York, an unmarried man, young, handsome, and deservedly popular. He had hired his passage with the train, and was out for an adventure, but when it was represented that he was the best man for captain, being free-handed and well-informed, he set aside personal considerations and accepted. He proved to be one of the best emigrant captains ever on the Plains, alert, cheerful, watchful of the needs of every one, and promising all that he would see the last one through safely to the banks of the Willamette, and he most bravely redeemed his promise. . . . Magone was married after reaching Oregon to a Miss Tomlinson that he met on the Plains; and long afterwards, indeed after the railroad was built, illustrated his original love of adventure by walking back East for a visit." See also Note 89.

[95]The Catholics alluded to by Appleton Harmon were Francis Norbert Blanchet, newly consecrated archbishop of Oregon, his brother, A. M. A. Blanchet, who on reaching Oregon was to become the first bishop of Walla Walla, and six others whose names are not recorded. F. N. Blanchet had opened Catholic missionary activity in Oregon in 1838, returning to Quebec by sea in 1845 to receive his ordination as archbishop. He had then gone to Europe to raise funds and was now returning to his vicariate. Chester Ingersoll, *Overland to California in 1847*, 17 on setting out from Independence early in May, noted the presence of the 7 priests and the bishop among his fellow travelers. A. M. A. Blanchet's account of his journey (*Rapport sur les Missions du Diocese de Quebec*, Quebec, April 1849, p. 19), mentions his arrival at the Mormon ferry on 6 July, the Mormon blacksmithing operations, and the fact that many of his fellow immigrants preferred to go up the river 8 miles and ferry themselves across than to pay the Mormon fee: "Aprés avoir passé la Riviére aux Chevreuils, nous etions a la nouvelle traverse de la Platte. Des Mormons y avaient etabli une forge pour réparer les chariots, et un bac pour les transporter sur la rive gauche. Nous fumes contents de donner une piastre pour chacun des notres; mais plusiers de nos compagnons préférérent aller traverser, á 8 milles plus haut." ["After crossing Deer River, we arrived at the new Platte crossing, where Mormons had built a smithy to repair the chariots [wagons], and a ferry to take them over to the left bank. We happily gave one dollar for each, but several men in our party preferred to ride to a crossing eight miles upstream." (translation by Dr. Alice-Catherine Carls) —Ed.] The Catholic travelers reached Walla Walla on 5 September.

[96]See note 87 above.

Smithing Setting tyer &c I A M Harmon put in an exaltree for Elsworth, & a hown for 1 of the emegrants & assisted in putting on tyer &c L Johnson Doctor ing & cleaning teeth B. F. Stuart at herding Cattle F m Pumeroy hunting his horse Elsworth & Devenport sick—done this day a bout $30.00 worth of blacksmithing $2 1/2 worth of waggon work $3.00 Doctoring &c Capt Whiles {White's} Co of 50 waggons passed up a bove us to ford[97]

Saturday the 10th $7.20 cts worth of blacksmithing done, L Johnson Shot a buffalo a bout 3 ms from here 1 of the emegrants that ware camped here brought it in the Company all together bought about $100.00 worth of goods of Mr H. Quelling a Quaker[98]—he had a Rhoadometer on 1 of his waggons—Capt Bonsers Co of 12 waggons[99]

---

[97]White was, according to a member of his company, Loren B. Hastings, a Methodist preacher, but his first name does not appear. (Bancroft['s *History of Oregon*] lists a "Luther," a "Rev.," and a "Thomas" White.) Hastings' journal, published in *Transactions of the Fifty-first Annual Reunion of the Oregon Pioneer Association, 1923* (1926), is a document of considerable interest. White was elected captain on 20 May, shortly after the departure from St. Joseph. Hastings does not say how many wagons they had on setting out, but this information is supplied by the St. Joseph *Gazette*, 28 May 1847, which gives the number as 37, and their place 13th in the line of travel. Hastings writes:

"July 9. This day arrived at the Mormon ferry and blacksmith shop; the 20 wagon (Captain Bonsers Co. as it is called) had gone ahead, but we found them here; my company (called Captain Whites Co.) went ahead; myself and some others remained with Captain Bonsers Co. to set our wagon tires, etc.

"July 10. This day the Mormons set my wagon tire; the boys killed a buffalo.

"July 11. This day, Sunday, intended to move, but some of our cattle were minus. Mr. Taylor and myself went out on mules to hunt our cattle. . . . Six wagons went" up to the ford on the south side of the river, crossed over and camped. The Mormons ferried over the balance at the shop and we moved up on the north side of the river and camped three miles below the other wagons."

[98]Henderson Luelling, a Quaker from Salem, Iowa, is memorable in the immigration of 1847 for the "traveling nursery" he took along. Ralph Geer (*Transactions, 1879*, 40–41 [Ralph C. Geer, "Occasional Address for the Year 1847," *Transactions of the Ninth Annual Re-union of the Oregon Pioneer Association for 1879* (Salem, Ore.: E. M. Waite, Steam Printer and Bookbinder, 1880), 32–42]) recalled that Luelling made two boxes 12 inches deep, and just wide and long enough to fill the wagon bed, filling them with a compost composed principally of charcoal and earth, into which he planted about 700 trees and shrubs, from 20 inches to 4 feet high, protected from the stock by a light but strong frame fastened to the wagon box. He permitted no one to discourage him in the undertaking, and reached The Dalles with his nursery about 1 October. "That load of trees contained health, wealth and comfort, for the old Pioneers of Oregon. It was the mother of all our early nurseries and orchards. . . . That load of living trees and shrubs brought more wealth to Oregon than any ship that ever entered the Columbia river." [cf. Thomas C. McClintock, "Henderson Luelling, Seth Lewelling, and the Birth of the Pacific Coast Fruit Industry," *Oregon Historical Quarterly* 60, no. 2 (June 1967): 153–174.]

Harmon's mention of a roadometer [i.e., odometer] on one of Luelling's wagons is interesting, for Harmon was the mechanic who constructed the first Mormon roadometer. Credit for absolute invention and first use of the roadometer for Plains travel has long been given to the Mormons, but Luelling's device makes it obvious that roadometers were simultaneously evolved in several places to answer the exigencies of trans-Plains travel, and that the question of first use must be left open.

[99]Luelling traveled as a member of Stephen Bonser's company. As seen in note 97, Loren B. Hastings consistently referred to Bonser's as being a company of 20 wagons rather than 12, as here recorded. Bonser was one of those who set out from St. Joseph. Geer says that he "brought a herd of fine cattle and improved the herds of the Columbia bottoms vastly."

{The Journal of William A. Empey resumes on July 11.}

Sunday 11 the[100] Received for Blacksmithing $16. Dol and 45 cents worth for waggon work $1 Dol for Ferrying 12 waggons of Capt Bonser Co $10.55 cents in cash we ferryed a nusery of 700 Trees they ware apple peach plumb pare Curnd Grapes rasberry and cherryes all growing in a clover patch and were owned by Mr H Lieuelling a Quaker from Salim Iowa & Phineous Young Aaron Faf, Gorge Wodward Herrick Glines Wm Waker, John Cazar arrived from the Camp of Pioniers they Left. the camp at Green River july the 4the & got here a bout 10 A M they were a going back to pilot our Brethrening through that ware a coming[101] the rive is fordable the Emagrants is nigh done for this year Emagration & our Bretheren, that were at the ferry thought it adviseable to go back with thoese that had come from the campt, to meet their famleys Capt Grover stated that he thought that we would Devide our substance of what we had gained equally amoung us it was a greed so to do

Monday the 12the the Bretrening ware prepareing to go back to Larama When, we Discovered 2 buffalow on the north side of the platt river coming towards us. Luke Johnson & Phineous Young started off persuity [in pursuit] of them and soon killed one of them Luke johnson gave him the Death wound and we fetched the buffalow to the campt and Dryed the meat for our Brethren and our selves

Theusday the 13 the Capt Grover Called together our company and addressed us as our capt in the most feeling manner how the Lord had prospered us on the mishon thatt the presadent had appointed to us and said that he was a bout to Leave for a short time to go to meet his famley and he would nomiate Wm Y Empey for Capt in his Abscence till his return it was second and carried there were six of us to stay nameley John Higbee Who is quite sick Luke johnson james Devenport A M Harmon and Br Glines, and after they went off we went to work at cuting up our meat to Drye it for the compy Devenport refused to work and said that if we moved his tools he would not

[100]Here William Empey's journal again picks up the story from Appleton Harmon's. The entries in the two diaries from 11 July to [the] 14, however, are so strikingly alike as to make it obvious one journal is based upon the other. The style being more characteristic of Harmon, it is likely Empey was the copyist.

[101]Phineas Young, Aaron Farr, George Woodard, Eric Glines, and Rodney Badger were detached from the Pioneer party on the west bank of Green River, on 4 July, to go back and meet the Second Company of the Mormon immigration. Just as they were setting out, 13 men of the Sick Detachment of the Mormon Battalion overtook the Pioneer party, and one of their number, William Walker, turned back with the other five to meet his wife. Rodney Badger did not go as far as the Platte ferry, turning about instead to guide the Mississippi Saints and the Sick Detachment of the Battalion. Evidently John Cazier of the Battalion was furloughed to take his place.

set them up a gain to work he told Br Glines that if he went to work he would hire a man he told Br Luke johnson the same Br Appleton harmon the same Wensday the 14 the we moved our waggons to the upper Ferry were there was good feed for our teams and stock on the platt river according to Council of our capt[102] and shorteley after there came 24 waggons and teams of Emagrants and Capt McGee at their head[103] they camped a Long side of our camp and we went to work at setting tyre we sot 15 for 15 Dollars and some other work.

Thirsday the 15 the We finished moveing our effects and made preperations to take care of our meat and so passed the Day working at Diferent work at hawling coals &[104]

Friday the 16 the month[105] We arose as usesial in good helth and in good spirits although in a strange Land and in a willderness the Lord has benn verry mercifull towards us and blessed us with health to labour and gain a sustanance for our selves and famleys we went to work at chopping coal wood while Luke johnson cooked Devenport and Br A. M harmon at blacksmithing Br john Higbee herding cattle Br Glines and my self chopping

[102]Harmon says under this date, "we prepaired to move our effects up the river to whare thare is better feed acording to Capt Grovers request Br Empy went up with 1 waggon at a time, Makees Co of 24 Wagons arived a bout noon & wanted some work done & as the feed was poor they thought best to assist in moving the black Smith tools up whare we ware a going they acordingly done so Br devenport set up his tools a gain at our camping place 6 ms a bove & commenced work setting tyer &c I assisted him Br glines assisted a bout moveing Br Higbee is a gitting Somebetter Luke Johnson Stayed at the old camp to watch the things until to morow." From these remarks, the third location of the Mormon ferry was very near its original site, from 3-1/2 to 4 miles above present Casper.

[103]Variously named McGee, Makee, and McKee by Empey and Harmon, the captain of this Oregon company was possibly Joel McKee, listed by Bancroft.

[104]Harmon gives a fuller account of the day's activities: "my Self & James Devenport went to work at the Black Smith shop Br Glines went below after some Coal & the ballance of the things that ware left there Br Empy & Higbee took care of the Buffalo meat & Cattle &c I would here mention that Br luke last night while watching our buffalo meat &c below was mutch troubled by the wolves & had ocation to fire on them he wounded one reloaded & fired again the the gun bursted, it burnt his face & arm & hand Considerable & Slightly wounded his hand & arm, a piece of the loak or Something alse passed through his hat with great violinc which closely graced his head."

[105]This day's journal entry terminates Appleton Harmon's record of the Mormon ferry: "worked at black smithing &c Capt McKees Co Stil remained here gitting work done near evening a young man by the name of Jacob Cooper was married to Kittean Huckelbee by ex Squire Tullis of said Company from the State of Indiana a Company of 14 men arived from Oregon with 50 pack horses & mules a going to the States a part of which came by way of fort Bridger & met our Company of Pioneers with in 15 ms of that place

Doct L Johnson Cook

J. Devenport Black Smith

A. M. Harmon Blacksmiths assistant

Wm Empy & Erick glines Coliers

John Higbee Herdsman, is the order of this day Quite a Shower Came up some vapers of clowds hung of between us & the Mountains"

coal wood for to kee the work a going on so we might have all things in readeness when our Brethren comes & about sunset there came fourteen men in company from oragon with 40 horses and mules a going to ohio thef told us that could not get through this season they started from oragon the 6 of may and reached here on the 16 of the month of july[106]

Satterday the 17the month We a rose in good health and strenght and went about our work as usesial we went to Drawing wood for a coalpit and set it up and covered it, and sot it a fire while the rest of Brethren were a bout their work & Capt McGee started on their jurney a bout 4 oclock in the Evening which Left us a lone 6 men of us

Sunday the 18the july the 12 waggons a bove mentioned started & and we enjoid a short season of rest I would here mention that 2 or 3 of the last Co. have lost a great No of their Cattle which the say is occationed by the murrin but I think it is over driving & going with out water as the Last Emagrants have Lost some hundred head of cattle

Capt. Mc Kees Co Lost 7 head with in the Last 30 miles

Monday the 19 the Month of july Luke johnson & Erick Glings went a hunting—

A. P. M Harmon J Devenport Staed at home My Self and Brother Higbee went down to the old Ferry ground to secure thee boat a bout 2 P M. Luke johnson & Eric Glines returned to the Camp with the meat & hide of a large Griselly Bear & tells the following story they had been up near the foot of the mountain each of them on horse back Dr johnson had his 11 Shooter they as yet having Seen no game within shot had turned their Course home ward & ware following down a little Crick or Spring branch when all of a sudden their horses took fright at some thing to their riders un seen but thought it

[106]This company from Oregon seems to be that described in the St. Louis *Missouri Republican*, 24 August 1847: "On Saturday evening, Captain T. G. Drake, of the British ship Modeste . . . and Mr. John G. Campbell, arrived in this city from Oregon. They left Oregon on the 6th of May, and travelled to Fort Hall in company with a brigade of the Hudson Bay Company. They left Fort Hall with only four men, but overtook another party of seven, and arrived in the settlements with a party of fourteen. . . . Between Fort Hall and Soda Spring, they were overtaken by a party of four men from California. This party left California on the 4th of June.

Ralph Geer (*Transactions, 1879*, 35) gives the names of two others with Drake and Campbell, presumably the whole group which set out from Oregon together: "At the snow bank we met J. G. Campbell, of Oregon City, and Wm. and Samuel Campbell, who were going back east for their father and family." *The Oregon Spectator* of 10 June reported that Captain Drake and J. G. Campbell had reached Fort Wallawalla on 23 May and started forward early the next morning. Although Harmon's journal says this company had met the Mormon Pioneer party within 15 miles of Fort Bridger, singularly enough not one of the journals of the Pioneer party mentions such an encounter.

either was indians or a bear but keeing a good Loukout soon Discovered a young cub through a thicket of under woods they road a round to an opening which Lead in to the thicket where they Discovered the Damb Diging roots for the cubs within 50 feet of them Dr johnson sliped Carefully of of my mare & perpared for the Combat the moment he struck the ground the bear Discovered him & came to wards him at the top of her Speed with her mouth wide open & each Jump a companied with an awah awah oo the Dr let go my mare that he might not bee in cumbered & it not until the bear was within 20 feet of him with 3 of her cubs at her heels coming in the Same fright in ful position, with that he fired with un uring aim at his antagonist which Cause her to turn & run som 8 rods & fell Dead the ball having struck her in the breast passed through the heart Lights liver &c.

Tuesday the 20the James Devenport & A. P. M Harmon went down the river in search of our cattle they having strayed of the Evening previous they followed their tracks down the road some 10 or 11 miles until they met met a Company of Emagrants of 33 waggons formely belonging to Capt Davis Co.[107] they had picked up our cattle some 7 miles below where we met them a ware of Driving them a Long they took our cattle & drove them to the campt & Dr Johnson Erick Glines and my self went in search of the cubs that they had seen the Day before but did not find them Dr johnson wounded a buffalow but did not get him & all is peace but no word of our company

Wednesday the 21eth a Company of 18 men from oragon with 60 horses & mules a going to the states passed us 2 of them that Came by way of Fort Bridger said they saw the campt of peioniers at the fort there ware in their Company 1 famley a going back on horse back 3 of them Famley were woomin[108] & Devenport done 65 cts worth of black smithing for the com. a

[107]Bancroft's list includes an Albert G., C., Eli, Henry W., and a Leander L. Davis. I cannot determine which if any might be "Captain Davis." A more likely choice may be D. D. Davis, from Green Bay, Lee County, Iowa. The Oregon Historical Society has a letter from James N. to Daniel Harty, dated "Platt River, June 29th 1847," which alludes to the election of Davis as Captain of Harty's company. At the time, there were apparently 47 wagons and 75 men in the company. *The Oregon Spectator*, 25 November 1847, indicates that 11 wagons under a Captain Davis took the Applegate Cutoff. See also Note 89.

[108]This company from Oregon may, from the language used, have been constituted from two or more smaller groups. From the reference to the Mormon Pioneers at Fort Bridger, one of their number was Colonel William Finley, who had gone out to Oregon in 1845, for in a letter Brigham Young wrote Amasa Lyman from the fort on July 8, a letter now in the Church archives, he commented, "Col. Findley left here this morning for the states, direct from Oregon, doubtless you will see him." There is frequent mention of Finley's intended departure east in the *Oregon Spectator*, and in the diary of George Gary at Oregon City (see *Oregon Historical Quarterly* 24, no. 4 (December 1923): 398–401). The *Spectator* of 10 June reported that Finley's party had reached The Dalles on 30 May and left next day. (*continued, next page*)

bove mentioned Com of 33 waggons passed us about 10 A. M. the remainder part of the Day passed a way verry Lonesom we being in a strange Land and far from our homes and famleys being near to us we would often talk what we would give if we oneley knew the situation of them it gave a many a Lonesome our medtetation &

Thirsday the 22the we a rose in good spirits and in good helth the Day being pleasant and fair we took breckfast and we happended to cast our eyes towards the mountains we saw 2 buffalow Dr johnson said if I would get my mares he would go and try and Shoot one of them so him and Br Glines went they went of together they Did not return till Dark and they shot 2 buffalow and fetched part of them home & there came a company of 10 men from oragon with a bout 40 ponies and mules there were also a famley with them going to the states[109] Devenport bought a poney and started with them back to winters quarters on Friday[110] they started on their jurney there came

---

How it happened that only one or two of this group went by way of Fort Bridger is not clear. Perhaps some of Finley's original group were among those who arrived at St. Joseph with Drake and Campbell.

Loren Hastings, who had met this party 5 days earlier on the Sweetwater, commented, "In the company was a man and his wife and family. They were going back to Adams County, Illinois. The woman rode with one foot on the one side of her pony and the other foot on the other side. This is the greatest curiosity I have seen yet, it knocks everything else into the shade." Perhaps this is the same family Ralph Geer tells of (*Transactions, 1879*, 35–36), though Geer recalled the man as being from Missouri: "At the last crossing of Sweetwater, we met a man by the name of Grant, with his whole family on his way back to Missuri. When asked what his objections to Oregon were, he said: In the first place they have no bees there; and in the second place, they can't raise corn, and whar they can't raise corn they can't raise hogs, and whar they can't raise hogs they can't have bacon, and I'm going back to old Missouri whar I can have corn bread, bacon and honey.' "

[109]When Nathaniel V. Jones, with [Steven Watts] Kearny's escort, overtook this company at Wolf River on 19 August, almost a month later, he observed that among them "was a missionary by the name of Little-John." ("The Journal of Nathaniel V. Jones," *Utah Historical Quarterly* 4, no. 1 (January 1931): 23). P.B. Littlejohn had gone to Oregon with his wife in 1840 as an independent Presbyterian missionary, and during the seven years he was there, appears frequently in the correspondence of Narcissa Whitman. In one of her last letters, under date of 23 August 1847, she commented, "Mr. Littlejohn and family have gone home to the States; they started this spring. . . . {Mrs. Littlejohn} was Adeline Saddler. . . . She was very unwilling to leave the country, but her husband has become such an hypochondiac that there was no living with him in peace. He wanted to kill himself last winter. It is well for him that he has gone to the States, where he can be taken care of." (*Transactions of the Twenty-First Annual Reunion of the Oregon Pioneer Association for 1893* (1894), 213). George H. Gary's diary (ed. Charles Henry Carey, OHQ 23, no. 1–2 (Mar–Jun 1923): 399), on 6 May noted that the Littlejohns with their 2 children were leaving. Loren Hastings wrote concerning him on 18 July, "Met another returning company from Oregon. In the company was a missionary who had been in Oregon seven years and his family with him. His ladies rode like the ladies we met yesterday (that is, astride). A little child not old enough to talk was lashed on to a pony and they drove the pony before them."

[110]Although Davenport left with this party evidently on the understanding he would serve them as a guide to Winter Quarters, the company kept to the route south of the Platte, and when overtaken by Kearny, as seen in the previous note, had nearly reach St. Joseph. Jones noted the presence of Davenport with this group. Notwithstanding his falling out with his brethren, Davenport maintained his fellowship with the Saints, migrating to Utah in 1848 and living there until his death at Richmond about 1885.

a company of 19 waggons & Capt Fredrick Company 17 in com[111] & Capt Smith 24 waggons in com[112] Br johnson and Br Glines went out a hunting and came back but Did not succeed in geting a game to Day Devenport Done some Blacksmithing a mounted to $400 as near as I could find out he said to them that he would go to council bluffs with them & pilot them the road if they would sell a horse & waitt until the next morning till he could get ready they concluded to do so and in the Evening I said james Devenport as you are a bout to leave us it be comes my duty to have a Settlement with you to have our our substance Eaquley Devided a moungts the company according to council of our supeiriors I them Called upon Br A. P. M Harmon he being the clerk for the company and stated to him to read the a mount over that we have earned since Cap Grover Left us it was Done accordingly the a mount $29.85. Cts with the exception of what he had Done that Day a bout $4.00 I said that I was willing that he should keep that providing the rist of the Bretheren was willing rather then to have any hard feelings a bout it, it was a greed that he should have the 4 Dollars extra but I wanted an Eaquel Division of the $29.86 Cets {?} for we all helped to earn it but Br Devenport was not willing to Do so saying that was robing him of his Earnings & he would not stay with such a people & as we Done the coking and burned the coal and helped him at the shop we herded his cows and it being according to greement &c thought ourselves, justifiable in Shareing equal with him there were a part of it earned other wise be sides Blacksmithing we pressed {?} to make an equal Division all tho he was not satisfied Br John Higbee bought his cow & gave him $10.00 for her it being $2.00 more than he gave & all he asked for her & A P M Harmon bought some salt he could not carry Brother Johnson bought his trunk Some other things

Friday the 23d 1847 James Devenport started having bought a horse for $25.00 a saddle & Larett for $4.00 and the Com was to pack his things for him through to council Bluffs he went of dissatisfied and refused to tak 50. cts that was tendered to him to make an equeal Division of our Last Earnings & he went and told Co that he was going with that we robed him; Erick Glines heard it & told them the circumstances &c Capt Fredderick

[111]Captain Frederick remains unidentified.

[112]Captain Smith was Cornelius Smith, as identified by the disappointingly laconic journal of a member of his party, Mrs. Elizabeth Dixon Smith, later Mrs. Geer, published in *Transactions of the 35th Annual Reunion of the Oregon Pioneer Association, 1907* (1908). Although her company crossed the Platte on either July 22 or 23, in her diary she merely notes that they traveled 15 miles on the one day, and 16 on the second. She herself was from LaPorte, Ind. It is not clear whether Cornelius Smith was her husband.

Co bought a stear of Luke johnson belonging to E. Elsworth; Co {? lo?} he had Lost his whole 5 yoke of oxen & 2 horses they ware run of by the buffalow he said as I under stood some 20 head of horses {were lost} at the same time in the same way & there was a widdow moving in the same company belonging to our church a going to oragon with her Brother[113] She said she would go to the church the first oppertunity She had she was acquainted with Br Higbee

Satterday the 24th there passed here 4 men from California with 12 mules & 1 horse a going to the States they saw the camp of peioniers with in 4 Days travel of the salt Lake on the 10 Day of july[114] they met the soldiers at green river & Capt Chapman Co of 16 waggons passed here on their way to oragon[115] they said that they ware the Last Co this Season that is they Knowed of no others on the road they had lost all their horses since they Left the States there started 17 head ran of at 1 time a mongst the buffalow &c

[113]One of the unsolved, and perhaps insoluble mysteries of Western history is how many Mormons went West before the organized Church immigration to Utah began. C. G. Coutant, *History of Wyoming from the Earliest Known Discoveries*, 3v. (Laramie: Chaplin, Stafford & Methison, printers, 1899), 1: 341, relates a purported reconnaissance of the Great Salt Lake country by Mormons in 1846, but his source has been printed in *Annals of Wyoming* 6 (July–October 1929): 240, and this is just the maundering of an old mountain man. Nevertheless, it seems certain that Mormons passed through Salt Lake Valley in 1846 as members of the Harlan-Young and Donner-Reed parties. There are fugitive glimpses of some others in California in 1846–47. Several dozen of the Saints, in all, may have anticipated Brigham Young in coming west. [The Murphy family of the Donner-Reed party were Mormon converts from Weakley County, Tennessee, who moved to and then returned from Nauvoo to west Tennessee before making the fateful move to California. —Ed.]

[114]These 4 men had come east from California with Miles Goodyear, the red-headed mountain man who built the first home on the site of Ogden. They met the Mormons at Bear River, some 6 miles southeast of present Evanston, on July 10. Learning that the Oregon immigration was earlier than usual, Goodyear and his two Indian helpers separated from the others, going on down Bear River to intersect the immigration where it came down Bridgers Creek to the Bear Valley. The four who continued on east were a Mr. Craig of Ray County, Missouri, a Mr. Truete of Shelby County, Illinois, and two others, names not given. Craig was the John Craig who with Larkin Stanley got the first immigrant wagons to California in 1846 (see Edwin Bryant, *What I Saw in California* (New York: D. Appleton, 1848), 210, 373; and Maude A. Rucker, *The Oregon Trail and Some of Its Blazers* (New York: W. Neale, 1930), 240). Craig and Stanley joined Frémont's California Battalion, but Stanley died of typhoid on the march south. Next spring, in the *California Star*, 3 April 1847, Craig announced his intention of going east, and the *New Helvetia Diary* on 22 May notes his departure. The records do not disclose who his companions were, except that the "Mr. Truete" remarked on by Albert Carrington may have been Samuel Truitt.

[115]Sarah Hunt Steeves, *Book of Remembrance*, 143, writes concerning Wiley Chapman, "Born in Tennessee, he married a young girl of the same place. . . . They then moved to Pike county, Illinois. . . . Illinois was only the frontier at that time, and they had not much to leave behind, so these young folk decided to cast their lot with an immigrant train of about 40 wagons, made up of Isaac Baker, the Canfields, Robinsons, Wrights, Matlocks, Truesdales, Saunders and others. . . . The train was known as the Oscaloosa, Iowa, train. . . ." Chapman was chosen captain. See also Fred Lockley, "Reminiscences of James E. R. Harrell," *Oregon Historical Quarterly* 24 (June 1923): 186–192.

for the Last week the Companies that have past says that the buffalow ware tremendious thick a Long on thee south platt they crossed from the north platt over the river to the south the rest of the companies saw none at tall

Capt Chapmans Co said that 40 head of their stock ran off with with the buffalow & they hunted 2 Days but Did not git them a tall

Sunday the 25th july 1847 John s Higbee bought a cow for which he paid $4.00 She was a little Lame he bought her of mr Canfield[116] from Oskaluey of Capt Chapmans Co & this Day passed of verry Lonesome as we can get no news of or from the Long expectted co of our Breathering & the matter for journalism is rather Scarce of this Day unless I sould record the expreshsions of anxiety now & then droped from the breathering of the Long looked for appearance of our Comp from Winters Quarters Monday the 26 1847 A heavey Shower last night attended with thunder & light ning, which raised cannon Creek[117] full to the edge of the banks the Days pleasand butt the nights cool Nothing more worth recording to Day

Thursday the 27th my Self Br A.PM harmon and Br Johnson went a hunting & tokk with us waggon & went a bout 10 ms up cannon Creek on the north side of the platt we saw a large herd of buffalow we wounded 2 but did not git them Br Johnson Killed 2 antelopes & we returned back to our camp

Wednesday the 28th We a rose in good helth and attended to our antilopes that we killed we put it out to day and Dressing the Skins, this evening Cold & Clowdy & and Severl panthers has been seen with in a few Days past & our ears has been Saluted with their terific yells by night

Thursday the 29 the 1847 we a rose in good helth and strenght and we a greed that Eric Glines and A.P.M. Harmon went a bout 15 ms down the river with the horses and waggon after the Iron of an old waggon that was left there by the Emegrants they got it. Br Luke johnson took my Grey mare and went up the river a bout 3 or 4 ms to hunt his Knife and gun strap that he Lost the Day before on his return he saw an antilope wich caused him to follow to the river he spied a trail where Indians traveled a bout 2 or 3 ours before he turned a bout and came to wards the camp at Lenght he heard a report of a gun towards our camp he then thought within him self that the indians had got to us he then gave speed to the mare and came in haste and it being off of the road made suspect it was a war party of Indians at this juncture he heard a gun fire in the direction of our camp by Jorge

[116]Possibly Robert or W. D. Canfield.

[117]Casper Creek. See Note 123.

says he to him self I dont know but hostilities has commenced & if so they will want my help he took a straight short cut for home & he said that my mare tail Stuck out be hind Like a skillet handle & he soon joined us and told us the kness we had not as yet Discovered the party & soon Discovered his apprehentions to us we loaded all our guns & pistols Cashed our best goods and more esspecially our purses Br johnson made a kind of breast work of some Chests & boxes with 19 shots al ready & amuition at his hand my self with 6 shots posted in a tree as a spy to watch the 1st appearance of the enemy I soon Discovered 2 men on the opposite Side of the river riding up & Down it at Length 1 of them crossed the river at the ford & came to wards our camp which at that Distance had the appearance over the hills of an Indian at at this Junc ture Gen Carny made his appearance over the hills some 2 ms Distant with 40 men & about 140 head of Anamials which at that Distance we could not tell but what they were indians I then mounted my mare by the council of Br Luke johnson and B Higbee to goo and Look to the cattle before I reached the cattle I had got of a bout a 1/2 a mile when I looked back and saw the a bove mentioned personage approaching on horse back at full speed riding after me Spanish custom I turned back as quick as my horse could go and met him at the waggons Brother Higbee with 3 Shots ready he went and met him without arms a few rods from the waggons and behold it was Br Binley[118] & it was not until he was with in a few steps of him that he did distinguish whather it was a White man or an In dian and behold their a mag anry antagonists ware proved to be Gen. Carney & severl of our breathrn and many other officers from the Battalion[119] Col Fremont Soon hove in sight be tween us & the mountains having Crossed the river a

[118]John Binley, one of the 15 members of the Mormon Battalion included in Kearny's escort. The discharge given him next day was granted, Nathaniel Jones remarks, because he was unwell.

[119]General Stephen W. Kearny had left [John] Sutter's 16 June. There were 64 in the party, increased to 66 on 17 June when Edwin Bryant and his servant joined the company. Their guide, according to the official report of the march written by Kearny's aide, Captain Henry A. Turner, was a Mr. Murphy. They picked up Black Harris in the Bear River Valley apparently on 19 July. They reached Fort Leavenworth 22 August. Under date of 28 July, leaving the Sweetwater, Turner writes in the report, "Met the rear-most party of emigrants; who seemed to despair of getting farther than Fort Hall this Season—Cool. With very few exceptions the entire emigration this year is to Oregon: a few families were destined to California; a good deal of pains having been taken to obtain correct information, the following statistical list is the result & may be relied on: 1336 Men—789 women—1384 both sexes under 16 years of age—929 Horses & Mules—7946 Cattle—469 Sheep—941 Wagons." (Journal of Gen. Kearny's Return from California in 1847, Records of Adjutant General, War Department, National Archives, filemark 249 Kearny Sept: 30/47.) Notwithstanding Turner's pains with his statistical table, it was defective to the extent that it could not have included those who were late on the road and took the branch of the trail via Fort Bridger, Kearny having taken the Greenwood or Sublette Cutoff.

bove the old ford with a bout 200 head of animals. Spanish horses & mules passed down by us a bout 1 mile from the road[120] our boys came home at Dark and all was well Br Binley stated that he saw ware some 50 souls of the Emmagrants had perished Last winter a crossing thee {?} mountains he helped to berry severl one women in paticular she was sawed to peaces her head was sawe 4 peaces her legs was sawed of by her body one of the men was a Long that was in that awful situation and told how they was a blige to eat each other to keep a Live some of them made their escape to the settlement and got releif from them the snow was so Deep that may souls perished[121]

Friday the 30th Br Binly got his Discharge from Gen Carney and Stoped here with us to wait until his famley Should Come up for he expected them with the camp we sold major Sword {Thomas W. Swords} $200 worth of Dryed buffalow meat Br Binley stoped here with us he also bought him self a horse {*lower quarter of p. 30 left blank*}

Saturday the 31st 1847 I and Brother A.P.M. Harmon worked a little at Blacksmithing &c mad some pickets pins &c towards morning had quite a gale of wind from the west 13 head of our cattle went off our hole stock is 24 head of horned cattle 2 calves and 4 head of horses we have for our night guard 5 dogs &c I set a trap and caught a wolf in the Evening for we wanted the oil to Dress our Antilopes Skins with &c

August the 1st 1847 Sunday, the 1.st of August a storm of wind from the S.W. Brother Glines went off on horse back after our cattle that went off in the storm &c we begin to think that Some aciident has happened our Brethren that they Do not Come for when we stopped here we Suposed 3 or 4 weeks at the out side would bring them here[122] as Br Glines returned a bout Noo[n] with the cattle he found them a bout 8 ms below Where

[120]Under technical arrest, Frémont was proceeding east for the famous court martial that grew out of his conflict with Kearny. He had asked permission to be relieved from all connection with his topographical party of 19 men, and allowed to return to the States with a small party made up by his private means, but in a letter of 14 June 1847, dated "Camp near New Helvetia, Calif.," Kearny brusquely refused. (Kearny letterbook, 1846–1847, pp. 164, 165, Missouri Historical Society, St. Louis.) Seemingly, Frémont crossed the Platte above the old ford which was near the Red Buttes.

[121]Nathaniel V. Jones's journal gives a graphic picture of conditions at the Donner camp in the Sierras when Kearny's force marched past. Empey declares that a member of the Donner party was actually in Kearny's escort. It is difficult to say who this might have been. Though the guide was a Mr. Murphy, and though Murphy is a famous name in the annals of the Donner party, the sons of the widowed Lavinia Murphy were only in their early teens in 1847.

[122]The brethren at the ferry still had a long and lonesome wait ahead of them. It was not until August 18 that the Second Company reached the Platte ferry. See the journal of Jesse W. Crosby in *Annals of Wyoming* 11 (July 1939): 178.

we camped &c it seems some Like the fall of the cold nights and cold high winds we feel verry Lonesome to Day in a barren wilderness severls hundred miles from any in habitance but the wild men of the forest and all kinds of wild Animals roaring at Knight time

Monday the 2.ond quite a pleasant morning Br Luke johnson & Br Binley went up to wards the mountains a hunting Br Luke killed a Large fine fat antilope, he shot him Through the heart at the Distance 1.95 yards the returned in the after part of the Day with 5 feasants & the above mentioned antilope &c I and Br harmon went to work at Blacksmithing set 3 tyre & Done some other Little jobs Tuesday the 3d Done some little jobs of Blacksmithing Br Luke johnson. Eric Glines & Br Binley went down the river a hunting &c—

Wednesday the 4th we a rose in good helth the Day being pleasant Brother Luke johnson & Br Binley went a hunting up Canno Crick, for that is the name of the Crick that comes in on the north side of the river as we ware in formed by Gen Carneys Guide it having arrived its name from the fact that a cannon was cashed on east as I understand on said Creek a bout 4 years a go by a Co of dragoons under col Carney &c[123]

[123]This explanation of the derivation of the name "Cannon Creek," as applied to present Casper Creek, is the last entry in the diary. The allusion is evidently to Kearny's dragoon expedition to South Pass in 1845. Two howitzers were taken along, but none of the journals or reports mention caching one of them.

Chapter 9

The Mormon Bibliographies, Part 1 (1949–1950)

Editor's Introduction

Few scholars and fewer general readers will pick up a bibliography. Librarians and book collectors, on the other hand, look at bibliographies as invaluable tools. Bibliographic volumes are usually relegated to the reference stacks of a library, where they sit dully as monuments to scholarly minutia. In 1906 New York Public librarian and early bibliographer Victor Paltsits claimed that "Anyone can compile a list, many can make a catalog, but very few can agonize to bring forth a bibliography."[1] He was referring to the qualities of awareness, patience, and attention to detail that was nourishing an emerging branch of scholarship. The potential behind one branch of bibliography eventually drew the attention of a young Dale Morgan—and as his experience as a bibliographer unfolded, *agonize* sadly became an entirely appropriate word, though not for the reason Paltsits implied.

The commitment Dale Morgan lavished on the Latter Day Saints' little-known print culture is difficult to understand if one looks only at his reputation as a historian of the American fur trade and overland trails. Nevertheless, Morgan was deeply interested in the early books, pamphlets, and broadsides the Latter Day Saints produced. His interest led to several pathbreaking works of LDS historical bibliography. Morgan's legacy as a bibliographer is perhaps his sole lasting contribution to the field of Latter Day Saint studies. His three published historical bibliographies were almost the only substantive studies of the respective subjects for a generation. He also generated a bibliographic list that was converted to a heavily used card

[1] "A Plea for an Anatomical Method in Bibliography," Proceedings and Papers of the Bibliographical Society of America, v.1 pt.2 (New York: Society, 1907), 124.

file by the Utah State Historical Society, and still later became the major catalogue for the subject when supplemented and expanded by Chad Flake, a librarian at Brigham Young University. Because Morgan's bibliographic works grew out of essentially the same research and writing processes and were so closely related by time and effort, this introduction addresses four of his five major bibliographic projects: the title checklist of Mormonism (of which only the introduction is included in these volumes), the sample pages of the incomplete and unpublished "master" historical bibliography of Mormonism 1830–1849, and the first two of the three completed installments to the "Bibliographies of the Lesser Mormon Churches" published in 1949 and 1950. A separate introduction for the third published bibliography and an afterword to conclude his bibliographic career follow in the second volume. Morgan's own recollection of how his work came into being was included as an introduction to the published "Flake" catalogue and again in the revised and expanded second edition of the work. It is found in the second volume of this book as well.

Though called by different names in different disciplines, the practice of bibliography occupies a respected position in reporting research results. Often writers will discuss the arguments, conclusions, or shortcomings of earlier works to introduce their own work. Academic writers routinely summarize prior scholarly or scientific publications as part of a writing project either as part of the text or in the notes. A "review of literature" illustrates where a work fits within the larger discipline, extending knowledge or contributing to the field. Most readers are familiar with bibliography as the name for a long list of works in the back of nonfiction books. This sort of "Bibliography" is not quite the same as a section listing "Works Cited." The latter is self explanatory, but bibliographies provide readers with more than a list of what an author used. They present a list of *relevant* works that might not have been used or cited by the author: a guide to the publications in the field (and sometimes its printed sources) built around the topic. This type of bibliography was practiced in the 1930s as well, but in the documentary historical projects like the American Imprints Inventory, Historical Records Survey, and Writers' Project, compiling bibliographic lists served a slightly different practical purpose.

Research access to original documents was comparatively limited. The earliest form of facsimile reproduction—microfilm—was just becoming

BX8611 MORMON CHURCH
.G8 Gunnison, John Williams, 1812-1853.
The Mormons, or, Latter-day saints, in the valley of the Great Salt Lake: a history of their rise and progress, peculiar doctrines, present condition, and prospects, derived from personal observation: during a residence among them. Philadelphia, J.B. Lippincott & Co., 1856.
1v, 13-168 p. front.,illus. 19 cm.

1. Mormons and Mormonism.

The Mormon menace
F826
.L475 Lee, John Doyle, 1812-1877.
The Mormon menace; being the confession of John Doyle Lee, Danite and official assassin of the Mormon church under the late Brigham Young; introduction by Alfred Henry Lewis ... New York, Home Protection Pub. Co. [c1905]
1 p.ℓ., xxii [23]-368 p. front.,3 plates, port. 20 cm.

An abridged reprint of an earlier edition (St. Louis, 1881) published under title: Mormonism unveiled; including the remarkable life and confessions of John D. Lee ...

Manually typed subject and title cards of the sort used in library catalogues before electronic automation. A book was represented with a group of cards filed alphabetically by the top line on the card, each representing a research "entry" in the catalogue. The note on the "Lee" card shows why searching individual library catalogues was bibliographically important. The numbered heading on the "Gunnison" card represents cards for the same book filed elsewhere in the same subject catalogue. A large library would likely have separate title, author, and subject catalogues; small ones might have an "integrated" catalogue where all cards were filed together. *Courtesy of Tennessee State Library and Archives.*

common technology; much more was available in print. Publication of key manuscripts in the form of documentary editions became a common nineteenth-century practice for making source material widely available. Publication of congressional deliberation in the *American State Papers* set the stage for public reporting and documentation in the United States. The Congressional "Executive Documents" in the U.S. Serials Set laid the pattern, publishing reports and letters by the hundreds annually. Feeding on a self-conscious antiquarianism, perhaps a manifestation of civic boosterism or fascination with the passing of the West's founding generation, documentary monograph series such as the Champlain Society (1905–present), Hudson's Bay Record Society (1938–1983), and the Arthur H. Clark Company's *Early Western Travels* (1904–1906) became common. By the mid-1930s, state historical journals also became rich sources for disseminating edited documents. For HRS researchers, bibliography existed as a form of documentary research. One of Dale's major functions as an HRS historian was to figure out just what sort of historical source material was available to inform county-history "sketches." To do that, compiling bibliographies—finding out what books described the history of a given place, pinning down what copies existed and where—was a critical preliminary step in historical writing. Hunting down books was supplemented by a systematic quest for unpublished primary materials still in descendants' keeping, approaching families across the state to see what original documents existed in private hands. Once relevant items were identified, HRS workers typically made extensive notes or complete transcriptions.

Keep in mind that large academic research libraries did not exist beyond a few institutions like the University of Chicago, Ivy League schools, and the University of California at Berkeley. The present luxury of remote electronic access to library catalogues and digital collections was inconceivable. Library research required on-site effort, thumbing through ranked and filed drawers of typed cards, each listing a single item. Identifying titles and copying details about books was one means workers used to group source material for use in the office. Out-of-print books were difficult to buy reliably, not every book could be checked out of a library, and the contents of library collections varied dramatically, especially in Morgan's day, when private giving was often the only way a library acquired important out-of-print works and virtually all rarities it housed. Utah's HRS workers were dispatched to public libraries in Ogden, then in Salt Lake City. The largest publicly accessible collection with a Mormon component in Utah existed in the few hundred volumes at the Salt Lake Public Library.[2]

The immediate practical result of HRS research was notes and transcripts organized into workable research files, the chief source of historical data for the writing projects. With photocopiers not yet invented and microfilm still uncommon, the research files contained tens of thousands of pages of notes, data, and direct transcriptions. In at least the Utah HRS office, staff maintained a three-part central file of transcripts and notes that all writers drew upon: a subject file, an author file, and a geographical location file. The files represented hundreds of hours of work locating the sources, but also transcribing relevant extracts or reproducing a document in its entirety, character by character on manual typewriters. Today typewriters are curiosities, but they were the fastest and most effective recording device and duplication machine of the period. Typewriter keys activated a series of levers, which struck the paper through an inked ribbon to produce the sharply defined top or "ribbon copy." Duplicates could be produced with no extra effort by backing a page with a sheet of carbon paper and blank "onionskin" sheet for each copy desired, up to about four. The extra paper dampened the blow from the key, requiring a much harder strike to generate a clear mark, so that the typed image on each carbon copy was progressively muddier than the one above it. Notes and transcripts could be duplicated for files only by rolling a sandwich of carbon paper and "onionskins" through the typewriter—or by laboriously retyping the entire document, which was a common activity.[3]

Dale Morgan was not just an end-user of research files, he put himself into the thick of this process. In November 1938 a reassignment made him effectively the research director for the state HRS office, which gave him direct control of the bibliographic study and production of notes and transcripts for the research files. It was hardly his only assignment, which included the technical editing and publicity he had initially been hired to do, as well as

[2]M. Wilford Poulson, "Library Resources for the Scientific Study of Mormonism," *Utah Academy of Sciences Proceedings*, 7 (15 July 1930): 37–38; *Mormon Americana: A Guide to Sources and Collections in the United States*, ed. David J. Whittaker (Provo, Utah: BYU Studies, 1995).

[3]The HRS typists actually produced a ribbon copy and three carbons of notes and transcripts, but the bottom copy was typically not used. Morgan got permission to keep these himself when they were marked for discard, and they formed the core of his massive personal collection, now at the Bancroft Library (DLM to Bernard DeVoto, 1 May 1944). Because of the small number of duplicates needed, stencil duplicator or mimeograph machines were not particularly useful to the HRS staff, except for producing the short-run publications the office generated. Chester Carlson invented the light-sensitive process behind photocopiers in 1937 but was unable to mechanize or scale-up the process until the late 1960s.

historical writing and indexing for the project. By the following February, Morgan was interested enough in historical source material that he was reviewing library catalogues and bound periodicals himself when not at work. Morgan's introduction to bibliography in the late 1930s, and its utility to him as a mature writer, was as a means of exploring the boundaries of a subject, filling in gaps of the available source material, and sight-lining possible approaches. "I have become interested in bibliography myself only by the back door, as a means of finding out things I need to know in the field of history," Morgan wrote Denver book dealer Fred Rosenstock in 1944.[4] But even in the 1930s bibliography was a loose word, and practical differences existed between *citations, cataloguing,* and *bibliography.* It is perhaps helpful to digress a bit to explain the different types of bibliography and bibliographies of Morgan's day.

Perhaps the most common form of bibliography is a collection of *citations.* Citation often included merely the relevant information needed to identify a work for an interested reader, and as long as its format was consistent within a citation list, adherence to some larger, abstract standard was less important. The present all-powerful citation forms of the American Psychological Association (APA), Modern Language Association (MLA), and University of Chicago Press were barely internal conventions in the 1930s and 1940s. We can assume that few HRS or Writers' Project workers came to the job having been so exposed. Even a college graduate like Morgan probably would have had little or no experience. Since modern bibliography and citation forms did not exist in the 1930s, and since no uniform descriptive standards existed outside of libraries, the HRS produced its own citation standards as a style guide for its writers, an eighteen-page document loosely based on library cataloguing "designed to bring about uniformity in the publications."[5] The federal programs required standardization among the research files generated by its scores of individual projects to streamline manuscript reviews and approvals. Survey administrators and workers knew the project was temporary, but the research files, identified by uniform citation standards

[4]DLM to O'Neil, Hugh F. O'Neil collection, BANC MSS P-F 311 5:28, Univ. of Calif., Berkeley; DLM to Fred Rosenstock, 27 May 1944, Morgan papers.

[5]American Imprints Inventory, *Manual of Procedure,* 3d ed. (Chicago: The Historical Records Survey, 1938) (this might be the manual Morgan was handed by supervisor Hugh F. O'Neil [O'Neil to DLM, undated (ca. October 1938)]); *The Form and Use of Footnotes and Bibliography in the Publications of Historical Records Survey Projects* (Washington, D.C.: Federal Works Agency, Work Projects Administration, Division of Professional and Service Projects, 1940).

across the country, would be left to the respective states. Standard citation forms would simplify the work of later scholars and make the research material useful beyond the offices which generated it. The citation guide was intended to accomplish both goals, but it was updated so frequently by the national office that coping with the ceaseless swirl of style updates and mandatory requirements was a common frustration shared just as uniformly by its employees. At the time Dale Morgan was employed by the Utah HRS, the American Imprints Inventory, an arm of the Historical Records Survey, released a new edition of its *Manual of Procedure* in October 1938. This basic introduction to the way published items were to be listed and cited was uniformly applicable. As the HRS historian, it is inconceivable that Morgan was unfamiliar with the publication, as he also must have been with *The Form and Use of Footnotes and Bibliography* issued in 1940.[6]

The polar opposite of straightforward citation forms in notes is the discipline of *analytical* or *descriptive bibliography*. Based on the work of British scholar W. W. Greg, Fredson Bowers of the University of Virginia was busily codifying American analytical bibliography at about the same time Dale Morgan was beginning his career. This branch of bibliography provides highly detailed catalogues of typographic and physical minutia of individual printed works. Descriptive bibliography was created in the days before facsimile reproduction was common and microfilm was reserved mostly for newspapers. It is designed to identify and describe a printed item as a technological object. Ideally it provides detail to a degree that small differences in physical forms (typography, page layout, spelling, paper choices, and broken or reset type) from which printed and reprinted items can be identified and accurately described—the "thousand words" that a picture is said to be worth. Attention to physical detail helped determine precedence between different printings of a work over time and space, identifying items produced at different times or places. Descriptive bibliography was particularly important in the study of literary culture prior to the Industrial Revolution. Descriptive bibliographers identified traces and inferred the history behind printed works to tease out precedence and publishing history, especially of often-reprinted plays and popular works. Study of books at this level of descriptive detail was a

[6]American Imprints Inventory, *Manual of Procedure,* 3d ed. (Chicago: The Historical Records Survey, 1938); *The Form and Use of Footnotes and Bibliography in the Publications of Historical Records Survey Projects . . .* (Washington, D.C.: Federal Works Agency, Work Projects Administration, Division of Professional and Service Projects, 1940).

bridge to understanding the place a work occupied within the intellectual and market history of society, which ultimately informed a work's textual, literary, or historical criticism. This type of description requires not only a discerning eye for detail, but also a specialized understanding of printing and typography. It has always been the venue of experts, making descriptive bibliography serious overkill much beyond specializations within the field of literature and some rare-book markets.[7] Morgan had no experience with Bowers's discipline if he knew about it, and likely had no interest in it. For his needs—understanding the authors and the forces that generated specific items—descriptive bibliography was excessive.

The practice of *annotated bibliography* might be considered a midpoint between the two descriptive extremes. More than merely a list of citations in the back of a scholarly study, annotated bibliographies are typically narrowly focused on a discrete subject and are created to encompass a field of published knowledge—they *are* the study. As the term implies, annotated bibliographies list a variety of publications based on the compiler's criteria, but with the citation include notes or annotations about each entry's scope, its significance, or some other aspect of importance to a reader. They are more common in scientific circles and less so in the humanities. One annotated bibliography Morgan is known to have used before setting forth on his bibliographies of Mormonism is "The Great Salt Lake: A Selected Bibliography with Annotations."[8] Rather than listing all relevant works, this focused sort of list presented the key publications with a succinct summary and explanation why they were relevant or historically significant.

Cataloguing, also a form of recording bibliographic detail, refer to two different forms. First, the process of compiling descriptions for a sale catalogue is essentially a form of historical bibliography that focuses on illustrating why a given work is important but also desirable. Descriptions are compiled with an eye of attracting the informed buyer. Issuing printed sale catalogues distinguishes a fine book dealer from a used book dealer. They were (and still are, though much less frequently) often compiled to present groups of books organized around specific theme or topic.

---

[7]Fredson Bowers, *Principles of Bibliographic Description* (Princeton: Princeton Univ. Press, 1949). A very good explanation of descriptive bibliography for non-experts is Terry Belanger, "Descriptive Bibliography," *Book Collecting: A Modern Guide*, ed. Jean Peters (New York: R.R. Bowker, 1977), 97–101, which can be found on the Bibliographical Society of American website.

[8]Ralf R. Woolley and Ray E. Marsell, "The Great Salt Lake: A Selected Bibliography with Annotations," *Transactions of the American Geophysical Union* 27, no. 1 (February 1946): 103–107.

A second use of the word refers to library cataloguing, a specialized and very rigid form of description. Driven by rules and standards, this form of cataloguing was created to objectify description. Reducing description to specific forms and rules was grounded on the premise that any two trained individuals looking at different copies of the same item and following the rules could generate essentially identical catalogue records. About the only truly standard descriptive format in the 1930s for books existed in library card catalogues, the massive ranks of cabinets with long, narrow drawers and alphabetically arranged cards. Scholarship in the humanities and emerging social sciences hung on library catalogues before the digital age. We often think of books as the measure of a library's value, but it was the rational, predictable order of its catalogue that made a library collection useful and was a library's chief asset. The earliest library catalogues were simply printed lists of books. In the early nineteenth century, libraries became large enough that lists gave way to card files, which grew exponentially as the world's published knowledge exploded on steam-powered printing presses. These library tools, typically divided into separate author, title, and subject catalogues, were governed by filing rules for the way headings were arranged and conventions that accounted for multiple-word alphabetization to simplify filing, reduce the likelihood of error, and make topical research possible. Title or author cards had the book's data arranged in a rigid pattern of indented paragraphs and punctuation. Cards in subject catalogues added a typed heading line at the very top of the card to facilitate filing and browsing. Catalogue cards typically included much more information than was relevant for the needs of any one researcher. For Dale Morgan and other researchers of his day, it was the process of selectively extracting data from catalogue cards that characterizes the work *they* called bibliography.

We usually think of bibliography in terms of a list of relevant works in the back of a scholarly volume. Morgan's practice of bibliography is at heart a variation on that type of research product, but it involved more than merely listing works, or "checklisting." In the documentary projects of the 1930s, bibliography involved compiling an organized list of titles (usually including author, title, subtitle, and stated publication data), supplemented by a census of copies located in libraries. This was the sort of bibliography adopted for the formal bibliographic enumeration of the country, the American Imprints Inventory. The AII aimed at identifying individual American imprints and creating a list of copies in institutional keeping. AII workers devoted their time to transcribing library catalogue cards, and the project's checklisting procedure was understandably built on the library catalogue model. The result produced little detail beyond enough data to distinguish separate titles or editions. The ultimate goal of the AII was to organize a record of the nation's printed legacy by creating annualized or regional checklists of individual imprints—all the material printed in 1767, or the printed work of early Kentucky, for instance—with a census of copies, so that scholars could see what books existed and where they were.[9] The AII did not operate in Utah, and the state had no AII office staff or specific employees dedicated to the project, though the national office accepted any bibliographic cards generated by the Utah HRS office. Other than the census of located copies, the straightforward AII checklists did not provide much context for later researchers. Generating carefully collated lists of published items—imprints—by itself was an important contribution to national history and kicked off a movement of similar undertakings. Until the 1970s it was common practice for library science students to produce a topical checklist as a final project. Under the post-war leadership of Luther H. Evans, former head of the national HRS project, the Reference Section in the Library of Congress adopted bibliography as a means of improving service and as sources of prestige among reference staff.[10]

By the time Morgan began his work as a bibliographer of the Latter Day Saints, these various ingredients were being cooked into a form of annotated bibliography that has since been called "historical bibliography." This approach grew out of the local-history antiquarianism of the late nineteenth century. It was adopted widely by the talented amateur scholars and the librarians who produced some of the great volumes of the genre.

There are few rules to historical bibliography, but common traits. Historical bibliographies typically include a transcription of the title (sometimes marking line divisions as well), include pagination and occasionally a collational formula describing page makeup, and supplement the descriptive data by adding notes about the history of the printed item itself or its place in history. Such works may be alphabetically arranged, catalogue-like affairs,

[9]Cf. Douglas C. McMurtrie, "Locating the Printed Source Materials for United States History," *Mississippi Valley Historical Review* 31, no. 3 (December 1944): 369–406.

[10]Mortimer Taube and Helen F. Conover, *Manual for Bibliographers in the Library of Congress* (Washington, D.C.: The Library, 1944); Verner Clapp, "Three Ages of Reference Work," *Special Libraries* 57 (July/August 1966): 379–384; Josephus Nelson and Judith Farley, *Full Circle: Ninety Years of Service in the Main Reading Room* (Washington, D.C.: Library of Congress, 1991).

with bare summary notes, as was Cadwell A. Raines' early *Bibliography of Texas* (Austin, Tex.: Gammel Book Co., 1896), or exhaustively researched masterpieces, like Thomas W. Streeter's five-volume *Bibliography of Texas* (Cambridge, Mass.: Harvard Univ. Press, 1955–1960). The pinnacle of historical bibliography as far as the American West is concerned is undoubtedly *The Plains and the Rockies,* which appeared in three editions during Morgan's lifetime—works that Dale Morgan knew well.[11] Historical bibliography was particularly well suited to saying something meaningful about rare publications with curious histories or backgrounds. The approach attempted to stake out the boundaries of available resource material and provide researchers with a window into a work and its significance. This is the style of bibliography that Morgan adopted in most of his work on the Mormons.

Morgan's appreciation of imprints and of bibliography did not grow merely from varied technical approaches to listing published works. Early in his career as a researcher and practicing historical writer, he crossed paths with a contemporary pioneer of Mormon institutional collecting. Twenty years Morgan's senior, M. Wilford Poulson was a professor of psychology at Brigham Young University, an avid collector of Mormon books, and the point man for BYU's budding institutional collection of early LDS manuscript material. More significant, Poulson employed an antiquarian's cultivated sense about the significance of imprint collections to both print and social history, as well as a discriminating awareness of the significance of variation in printed matter. In August 1941, as Morgan was laying the administrative groundwork for a Writers' Project history of Provo city, he stopped at BYU specifically to meet Poulson. He found a thoughtful professional with a developed sense of historicism about Mormonism and its founders. Poulson had compiled lists of specific library holdings and particular books well before meeting Morgan. Importantly, his interests (and collection) included the publications of dozens of barely known Latter Day Saint schismatic organizations and their own offshoots, and he had bought and sold scores of rare works in pursuing his avocation. Though the pair

[11]Henry R. Wagner, *The Plains and the Rockies: A Bibliography of Original Narratives of Travel and Adventure, 1800–1865* (San Francisco: J. Howell, 1921); 2nd ed. Charles Camp (San Francisco: Grabhorn Press, 1937); 3rd ed. (Columbus, Ohio: Long's College Book Shop, 1953). In 1948 Morgan wrote book collector Everett Graff that "When and if I find time to get all my papers in order, I shall send Camp a long letter of further additions and corrections for P&R besides those I sent him some years ago" (DLM to Graff, 20 July 1948). He never did, so far as I can determine. A fourth edition was expanded to a form closer to descriptive bibliography; ed. Robert H. Becker (San Francisco: John Howell Books, 1982).

met only occasionally and did not correspond frequently, it seems each met a kindred spirit with regard to books. Morgan encouraged Poulson in his never-completed study of James J. Strang and his church; Poulson supplied Morgan with bibliographic details from his own extensive book collection, occasional expertise, and reviews of checklists.[12] In 1951 Morgan inscribed a copy of the Strang bibliography offprint "To Professor Poulson, who got into Mormon bibliography while I was still wet behind the ears and also commands a knowledge of the field as do few others."[13] The early acquaintance with Wilford Poulson seems to have deepened and broadened Morgan's interest in Mormonism beyond Utah's valleys. It also shaped the younger man's awareness of bibliography's general importance to historical research in a way that familiarity with institutional collections did not.

Dale Morgan's determined passion for Latter Day Saint bibliography stemmed not only from plans to write about Mormonism but also partly resulted from the degree of relative unsophistication at which Mormon history existed in the 1930s. He and other historical writers and book collectors knew about scriptures, hymnals, and periodicals like the *Saints Herald, Millennial Star, Deseret News, Times and Seasons,* and various *Messenger and Advocate* incarnations, but no one had an inkling either how much or precisely *what* else had been published by or about the Mormons in pamphlets, books, and broadsides. No one had a grip on the literature of Mormonism because no one had yet bothered. Wilford Poulson perhaps came the closest. Knowing abstractly *that* material existed was less useful than knowing *what* existed. By October 1942, as he rode the Union Pacific's *Challenger* eastward for wartime Washington, D.C., Dale Morgan had privately committed himself to putting together a "really worth while" history of the Mormons. What he needed was sources from which to do it, and for those, he had to identify what existed. That is why he became interested in Mormon bibliography.

After being hired by the Office of Price Administration in late 1942, Dale found himself with a desk in its central administrative office, located a few blocks north of both the new National Archives and the Library of Congress. He paid comparatively little attention to printed material as a rule, other than buying heavily in published primary sources that flourished in state

[12] Cf. DLM to Maurice Howe, 20 August 1941; DLM to Poulson, 25 June 1944; Poulson to DLM, 1 October 1941, 7 May 1948, 14 February 1954; Miscellaneous notes in MSS 823, M. Wilford Poulson Collection, 20th-century Mormon and Western Americana section, L. Tom Perry Special Collections, Harold B. Lee Library, Brigham Young University. My grateful thanks to Andy Mickelson for research help with this point.

[13] Inscription in the Poulson copy, L. Tom Perry Special Collections, Brigham Young Univ.

historical society journals, and what was fed him by book dealers across the West. Between his workaday services for the OPA, he began taking time to read through the Library of Congress catalogue to identify anything Mormon related. His appreciation of systematic bibliographic research changed somewhat after beginning his lunch-time and after-hours research. That massive collection had a fully developed catalogue to its contents and far more material than Morgan could hope to buy for himself; the catalogue's institutional subjectivity also complicated research somewhat, either lumping together everything relating to the Latter Day Saints without regard to which schismatic branch produced it, or segregating it entirely. In late 1943 Dale observed to Community of Christ archivist S. A. Burgess that the Library of Congress card file of holdings on the Mormons was badly arranged and simply excluded all RLDS material.[14] As frustrating as that was, the dozens of new items and later printings reflected in the Library of Congress catalogue underscored how incomplete his knowledge of Mormon history was, even of merely its printed material. Works and comments on the Mormons were produced across the country and abroad; some of the material was very rare and much existed only in unique copies. For Dale Morgan, the first part of landing that firsthand information was to identify Mormonism's printed material itself, *then* to understand the social and institutional contexts of its production. If he were to write a valid history of Mormonism, he needed to know what works documented and commented upon the faith. That would require at having at least a list in hand for reference, but it was already abundantly clear that the works of the Latter Day Saints were both rare and widely scattered. To compile such a list he could not rely on a single library collection. He would have to broaden his inquiry.

In August 1943 a five-day trip to visit his sister and her husband in New York doubled as an opportunity to look over one of the largest discrete collections of Mormon materials on the East Coast: the William Berrian collection at the New York Public Library.[15] The visit was revelatory. For

[14]DLM to S. A. Burgess, 25 September 1943.

[15]DLM to Alvin Smith, 12 August 1943. The Berrian collection has been rumoured to contain many items from Charles L. Woodward's nearly legendary "Bibliothica Scallawagiana" gathering, which had been sold at auction in 1880. That catalogue was the first bibliographic listing of Mormon material. *Bibliothica Scallawagiana: A Facsimile Reprint of the 1880 Catalog Concerning Mormons and Mormonism* (Spokane: Arthur H. Clark Co., 1997). The library's complete holdings were checklisted quite imperfectly in "List of Works in the New York Public Library Relating to the Mormons," *Bulletin of the New York Public Library* 13, no. 3 (March 1909): 179–239.

the first time Dale was able to see a collection of Mormon material that had been collected systematically rather than haphazardly. By the time he returned to his apartment in Alexandria, Virginia, the need to resolve descriptive inconsistencies for items between the collections he had seen in Utah, Washington, and New York induced him to begin his own list of works by and about the Latter Day Saints. By February 1944 his bibliography note sheets had expanded to the point that Dale felt mired in tracking down detail about the works of schismatic groups and had arrived at a decision. "I have been occupying myself to some extent, in recent months, with a practical bibliography of works on Mormonism," he wrote to Church Historian's Office librarian Alvin Smith in Salt Lake City. "By 'practical bibliography,' I mean that only books actually found in libraries have been included, though ultimately I will doubtless extend the bibliography to include titles to which I have found references, even though the works themselves cannot be located."[16] This plan to list *all* works on Mormon culture was new ground, something that not even the two major Restoration church libraries had attempted. Fired by the uniqueness of his project to identify and describe the culture comprehensively, including material not even seen, Dale's lunch-hour, after-work, and weekend research trips soon involved searching page by page through Latter Day Saint periodicals available in Washington's libraries. By June 1944 he was forwarding queries about early serial publications to Restoration churches across the country. Out of the process grew an entirely new project, to create a descriptive list of the works from and about Mormonism prior to 1870. "If I ever get around to it, in fact, I might do a comprehensive Mormon bibliography myself," he wrote Denver book dealer Fred Rosenstock. "A proper annotation of Mormon literature is something badly needed."[17]

What did Dale Morgan have in mind as a "proper annotation"? First, he used the term loosely, but it is clear that he is thinking terms of historical bibliography. To accomplish a work of that scale, however, he would have had to identify first what existed, and that meant creating a simple list of what items he could identify. As he began studying Mormonism as an entity, Dale Morgan was chiefly interested in identifying and listing items—checklisting—rather than describing their physical forms. He understood checklists: author, title,

[16]DLM to Alvin Smith, 17 February 1944.

[17]DLM to Fred Rosenstock, 27 May 1944.

publication details, and pagination data.[18] At the time he conceived it, the compilation was an attempt to draw an inclusive and defining line around Latter Day Saint culture. It was an ambitious and pathbreaking work.

Early in 1945 Morgan applied for and was awarded a "post-service" research fellowship by the John Simon Guggenheim Memorial Foundation to pursue a sociohistorical study of the rise of Mormonism. The fellowship stipend, paid in installments over the term of the grant, would be available to the recipients at the conclusion of their war-related service. His growing bibliography was not an explicit part of the work, but three years it later became a major project on his cross-continental research trip funded by the fellowship. After the end of the war, as the Office of Price Administration and its price-control policies were dismantled for free-market consumer production, Morgan used up his accumulated leave to subsidize research in Washington through the spring of 1947. By that fall he had already given enough thought that he could name a goal for his interest. As he began the long drive that would take him first through New England, then to Chicago, St. Louis, California, and home to Salt Lake City, he wrote to Huntington Library's Leslie Bliss that he had "been constructing a bibliography of everything published about the Mormons up to 1849, the first contribution to a genuine critical bibliography."[19]

After shipping crated books and notes to his mother, the drive from Washington to New York City was the first leg of the trip. He arrived in December 1947. There he spent an afternoon at the Parke-Bernet auction galleries to check his bibliographic notes against auction lots from the Herbert S. Auerbach collection and made additional corrections to his list against the Berrian collection holdings. He stopped in New Haven, Connecticut, to see part of the Coe collection that was arriving at Yale, crossed Massachusetts to Vermont and the birthplaces of Joseph Smith and Brigham Young, then turned westward following the Smith family's steps to Palmyra and Rochester, New York. From upstate New York he drove south into Ohio. By the time he reached Cleveland for an extended stop at the Western Reserve library, he explained to a cousin that he had begun his list "with the light-hearted idea that it would be a useful job to have all the titles for that

[18]On the broader subject of checklisting, I'd like to think that Morgan had at least noticed a pair of Luther Evans's comments on the discipline, "History and the Problem of Bibliography," *College and Research Libraries* 7 (July 1946): 195–205, and "Bibliography by Cooperation," *Bulletin of the Medical Library Association* 37, no. 3 (July 1949): 197–212, since he put into practice elements discussed in both pieces.

[19]DLM to Leslie Bliss, 4 November 1947.

period listed, and that they wouldn't total more than about a hundred."[20] The number proved to be a dramatic miscalculation. Within a short time, the list had swelled to five times that size. Faced with such an obvious lack of hard data about the church, Morgan changed his basic research plan. "It is my expectation to publish in advance of my history a critical bibliography of every title and edition of works by or about the Mormons printed down to 1849," he informed Community of Christ president Israel A. Smith. By December 1947 he had arrived at Fort Leavenworth and would write to Americana book dealer Edward Eberstadt that in addition to the basic Mormon research, he had been pulling together his bibliography and was able to generate a list of not-yet-located items, just from the cursory searches he had made in periodicals.[21]

At the turn of 1948, reporting to the Guggenheim Foundation about the progress of work being made on his fellowship, Dale revealed how deeply he had immersed himself in the history of Mormon printed works. Dale justified his attention to bibliography and explained the circumstance in terms its officers were certain to understand: "One of the most interesting things about this work that I have performed is the feeling I have had that I am being instrumental in the creation of a whole body of history."[22] For someone exhibiting talent and ability with no formal training, the idea of contributing substantially to a field of study was an intoxicating thought. The idea that he was doing fundamental work in any field drove him relentlessly for the rest of his career. Identifying works by checking catalogue cards and compiling a title checklist was an important first step, but it was, at best, preliminary. Seeing such a specialized study into print represented a potentially massive undertaking of time and effort. Privately he was less confident and confided to former national HRS director Luther H. Evans, now the Librarian of Congress, that he had not the "remotest idea yet who will want to publish a critical bibliography of the first phase of Mormon history." He was willing to speculate on spending time devoted to the project, however, because "the need for such a bibliography is so bad that I can probably scare up a publisher in some neck of the woods or other."[23]

[20]DLM to Doug Hardy, 19 April 1948.

[21]DLM to Israel A. Smith, 20 December 1947; DLM to Edward Eberstadt, 31 December 1947.

[22]DLM to Henry Moe, 3 January 1948, "Morgan, Dale L.," John Simon Guggenheim Memorial Foundation archives, New York.

[23]DLM to Luther H. Evans, 15 January 1948.

From Fort Leavenworth Morgan drove straight through to California, where he visited the Huntington and Bancroft libraries, and concluded his Guggenheim-sponsored research trip by returning to Salt Lake City on 28 March 1948. From his mother's home the next day, he composed a confident, almost brash request to church president George Albert Smith for access to the Church Historian's Office manuscript collections and included a request for bibliographic help. "As a byproduct of my major researches," he wrote, "I have taken an interest in constructing a bibliography of everything relating to the Mormons published between 1830 and 1849. This has assumed astonishing proportions; it must run close to 500 titles."[24] By this time the preliminary checklist of Mormon material had burgeoned to an almost unmanageable size, and his request dangled the opportunity to see the checklist for the church's own information in exchange for comparing the entries against the Church Historian's Office largely uncatalogued book holdings. Two weeks later the secretary to the First Presidency, Joseph Anderson, wrote denying the request. Still smarting from Fawn Brodie's biography of Joseph Smith, and doubtless noting Morgan's name listed prominently in the acknowledgments, church officers declined to allow access to its manuscript holdings. The church was, however, cautiously willing to cooperate on the bibliographic project, particularly after Dale sat down with the church's assistant historian, A. William Lund, and showed him the sheaf of entries. Lund was stunned. Morgan's single-spaced draft notes actually listed over seven hundred items, with more titles, more editions, and broader coverage of Latter Day Saint and Latter-day Saint material than existed in even the Church Historian's Office holdings.[25] Lund was willing to admit to the limits of his knowledge and agreed to cross-check the checklist against the church's holdings once Morgan had it finalized.

But first he had to produce one.

Immediately upon arriving in Salt Lake City in March 1948, Morgan had also dispatched a flood of queries to resolve bibliographic details on the checklist. "I've been working constantly to get my bibliography [that is, his the initial checklist] in shape so that I can try to get it published," he wrote close friend Darel McConkey back in Washington. "I don't know what [publication] arrangements can be made, but I am going to press that point in likely places as soon as I can put the manuscript in shape."[26] "Practically

[24]DLM to George Albert Smith, 29 March 1948.

[25]DLM to Lucie Howe, 27 April 1948.

[26]DLM to Darel McConkey, 22 April 1948.

all the preliminary work is now done on this," he noted with a tone of curiously inaccurate optimism to Maurice Howe's widow, Lucie, in April, 1948.[27] He was waiting on a dozen outstanding inquiries, then planned to retype the checklist in a form that libraries could check readily. Once the duplicate carbons returned (a round-robin process), he could compile the final list and census from the various carbons, type a final manuscript with historical notes and comments, and hunt up a publisher. He fully expected to complete and publish the bibliography by the end of the 1948 summer, but once the leaves began turning to blaze and crimson in the Wasatch canyons above the city, he had to confess to Americana book collector Everett Graff in Chicago that "I have not even been able to take the time to complete my checklist for the Mormon bibliography, which must go out to the libraries before I type up the manuscript . . . it is stalled in the 'J's, where it has been since mid-summer."[28]

The reason the bibliography was stalled was because Morgan had signed a book contract. After his arrival in early 1948, Dale was forced to scratch together a living from what he could find in Salt Lake City. Four months after arriving home, Dale was no closer to meaningful employment when Utah State Historical Society editor J. Cecil Alter abruptly resigned his post and moved to California. Morgan assumed the managing editorship of the *Utah Historical Quarterly* on a small stipend to keep both him and the journal alive, but otherwise life as a freelance historical and technical writer was thin living. Finally, more in desperation than preparation, in July he reluctantly submitted a book proposal for a general history of the Mormons. "[I] am only getting involved in such a proposition now because it seems the best of the several expedients open to me," he explained to John Selby of Rinehart & Company.[29] The firm had published his *Great Salt Lake* the previous year and were very pleased with the work and its sales. They were willing to accept another Morgan manuscript. What Dale did not tell the firm was that he was not prepared to write just yet. The first part of that process, he felt, was to complete the bibliography. Thus, even as Dale was preparing his proposal for *The Mormons* to the Rinehart firm in July 1948, he

[27]DLM to Lucie Howe, 27 April 1948.

[28]DLM to Everett D. Graff, 31 October 1948. He had instead been working on the Powell journals on contract for the UHQ and the *Utah Historical Trails Map* on another contract, done a Utah Indian affairs article for *Pacific Historical Quarterly*, and tried to complete an article on the American fur-trade firm of Smith, Jackson & Sublette.

[29]DLM to John Selby, 26 July 1948, *Dale Morgan on Early Mormonism: Correspondence and a New History* (Salt Lake City: Signature Books, 1986), 158–160; DLM to Fredrick R. Rinehart, 31 August 1948.

was already pressing forward on a separate bibliographic study of Mormonism. Bibliography looked like it would provide the rock-solid foundation for later work, so Morgan's personal attention leaned most heavily toward pursuing that line of research. The problem was, his January letter to Evans implied, that committing a publisher to the project would be problematic and probably not very lucrative. For someone who wanted to make living by writing, that obviously presented a problem. In the short run, however, the contract for the history of Mormonism presented an immediate and desperately needed $250 advance against royalties. Dale quickly paid his outstanding bills and set to work—not on the book nor even on the title checklist, but instead at least nominally on the opening pages of a historical bibliography of Mormonism beginning with the New York impression of *The Book of Mormon* in 1830 and expected to conclude in 1849.

Why he embarked on the historical bibliography—one more project that ate up time he did not have and could not afford—is inexplicable until one other piece of data is supplied: the Utah Humanities Research Foundation at the University of Utah occupied an office on the alluvial bench a few hundred yards directly above his apartment. The foundation had been established with a Rockefeller Foundation grant in 1944. Its mission was to collect and preserve cultural expressions from Utah's unique cultures and those of the surrounding areas. A small-scale fellowship program dispatched graduate students and others into the state and surrounding regions to conduct oral interviews, document folkways and folklore, record music, and establish the beginnings of a regional study collection.[30] Funded as a folk-culture project, the foundation staff also published the *Utah Humanities Review* (later the *Western Humanities Review*) and had just proposed the founding of an academic press partly to disseminate the work being generated. The new academic press sounded like an ideal publisher for Morgan's bibliographic work and just might net him another research fellowship in the process.

With so much to do on a large-scale volume of history for which he already had signed a contract, what was Morgan hoping to accomplish with a Latter Day Saint bibliography? One clue is in his 1942 letter to S. A. Burgess, where he explained that he expected his study to involve the Restoration as inclusively as possible. Certainly by 1948 he had come to view "Mormonism" as

[30]Utah Humanities Research Foundation records, Marriott Library Manuscripts Div., Univ. of Utah. A file of promotional material discussing the journal and its stated aims in official detail may be found in box 12, folder 1.

no longer merely the church in which he grew up, nor even its main competing claimant, the Reorganized Church of Jesus Christ of Latter Day Saints (today the Community of Christ). His view of Mormonism was catholic rather than specific. By the time he wrote George Albert Smith about access to the Church Historian's Office collections, Dale Morgan viewed Mormonism inclusively—drawing in the full scope of commonly shared cultural background of faith and belief. The schismatic groups that sprang up and flew apart after 1844 were as important to his forthcoming history as was the body led by the apostles that moved west to found Great Salt Lake City. Morgan's view of Mormonism had become solidly ecumenical, and it was critical that he study these small movements on their own terms rather than on what was said about them by members of the two mainline denominations. "It is . . . a matter of moment to me what [Charles B.] Thompson was doing in Iowa, [Alpheus] Cutler in Minnesota, or [Lyman] Wight in Texas, not less than what the Reorganization and Utah churches were doing," he had written RLDS president Israel A. Smith while still travelling in the first week of 1948, "and it is important to me to be able to develop their history from their own point of view. Hence I am in need not merely of a few hasty notes but the whole corpus of their writings, [to] which I may give thoughtful study."[31] Dale Morgan's work in Latter Day Saint bibliography accomplished two purposes for him. Foremost, a checklist and historical bibliography would circumscribe public Mormonism, defining its nether limits and helping him form a view of not merely the core of the tradition but its fringes as well, just as research in contemporary newspapers helped him judge its reach and influence. Second and just as importantly, he recognized that Mormonism was documented by extraordinarily scarce publications; he expected that publication of a bibliography would bring to light unrecorded works that could inform his larger Mormon histories. He wanted everything, but by the summer of 1948 his attention to Latter Day Saint bibliography had expanded to the point that it could consume almost fully the sliver of the clock he could devote to his own work, and he still had to make a living, which ultimately pushed aside both the bibliography and the Mormon history.

In fact, by the fall of 1948 Dale Morgan had created a delicate tier of research priorities that was beginning to look uncomfortably like a house of cards. Each project was interrelated to the others and partly depended on the

[31] DLM to Israel A. Smith, 5 January 1948.

ability of everything to be moved forward simultaneously. Initially he would compile the title checklist of Mormon works for 1830–1849. While carbon copies were circulating for cross-checking by libraries and some selected book collectors, he would begin writing the master historical bibliography on the church; meanwhile he would generate draft material for the Mormon history as thoughts struck him and opportunities were presented. By the time the bibliography was done and ready for publication, the first volume of the history should be done as well, ready for Rinehart & Company. The flaw in this plan, of course, was that the whole process hinged entirely on finding a steady job. Employment might eat into his week, but a salary would free his after-work time to attend to the varied steps in his research and publication scheme.

On his frequent trips to the state capitol basement as UHQ editor, Historical Society secretary Marguerite Sinclair lobbied him repeatedly to allow the Utah State Historical Society to publish the 1830–1849 historical bibliography as a three- or four-number monographic volume of the *Quarterly*, just as *The State of Deseret* and a number of other documentary collections had been. In the first week of 1949, with only a few draft entries for "The Mormons" committed to paper and going nowhere with the checklist, Dale needed to get the logjam moving and responded. He was reluctantly willing to let the UHQ have the historical bibliography, on certain conditions: that three hundred pages of the journal would be committed for the work, that he would have the assistance of a Historical Society typist, that the Historical Society would take care of copyright registration, and that at least fifty separate offprints or extra-issue copies were printed. Sinclair readily agreed, but ultimately Dale backed out of publishing the historical bibliography in the *Quarterly*, concerned that if his historical bibliography appeared in a periodical, it would be buried in libraries' shelves of bound serials and not catalogued as a distinct volume. Monographs, he observed, were much better controlled and accessible through libraries and had a better chance of being useful to succeeding generations.[32] Though he held out hope that such foundational work would find a publisher, time would prove that Sinclair's offer was as close to publication as "The Mormons, 1830–1849" would ever come.

Thinking that he would soon be prepared to begin the historical bibliography in earnest, at the beginning of March 1949 Dale approached

[32]DLM to MSR, 2 February 1949.

Harold D. Bentley of the *Western Humanities Review.* Bentley was the motivating factor behind the creation of scholarly press at the University of Utah. Administrators' cautiously positive response to the idea of a university press had induced Bentley to begin looking for manuscripts. Dale asked, would the new press like first chance at a historical study of publications in and around Mormonism? Bentley nodded that yes, a bibliography on this scale was something of the sort he would consider, and asked Morgan how large he expected the finished manuscript to be.[33] Morgan demurred giving either an immediate or precise response. Through the winter and spring of 1948–1949 he or the Historical Society typist had transformed his reams of notes and queries into a preliminary title checklist that would form the backbone for the historical bibliography, but he was busily engaged with the last difficult task in checklisting: identification and translation of Welsh-language publications, which was accomplished with the help of Salt Lake City podiatrist and Welsh speaker Dr. John E. Thomas.[34] He needed to get at least the master title checklist circulating before Bentley could have a set of sample pages for review.

The ribbon copy of a master checklist was backed by a sandwich of three carbons. When the painstaking retyping was complete, the first step was to compare the list to the holdings of several book collections and libraries he had not visited.[35] The introduction to that checklist manuscript is included in this volume, although the pages of entries themselves are not. While his checklist carbons were pirouetting around the country, Dale began

[33]Hal Bentley to DLM, 9 March 1949.

[34]DLM to John E. Thomas, 18 March 1949. Though missionaries were preaching in other European countries and several South Sea islands, Welsh was the only foreign language in which Mormon imprints appeared in 1849.

[35]Through the spring of 1949, the duplicates circulated to institutions willing to check their catalogue against his extensive list (librarians actually did that for researchers once upon a time). Two copies bounced between research institutions and academic libraries including Harvard (which held the first Eli J. Pierce book collection), the Wisconsin and Iowa historical societies, the University of Iowa, and several others. Another set shuttled between an increasingly incredulous Will Lund at the Church Historian's Office and the California Historical Society. Neither of these carbons survive. The single surviving set, part of Dale's papers at the Bancroft Library (carton 8), was the carbon set forwarded to four major book collectors whose collections includes substantial Mormon holdings: Everett D. Graff in Chicago, then Thomas W. Streeter in New Jersey, followed by Americana dealers Edward Eberstadt & Sons in New York City, and finally Yale University Library, which had been recently given the fabulous William R. Coe collection. In time the sets returned to Salt Lake City, Morgan collated notes, new entries, and other data, and forwarded the sheaf to the Library of Congress for checking against the Union Catalogue. Until that set returned with the Library of Congress's annotations, emendations, and corrections, he suspended all effort toward adding further items to the list.

two projects. The first he confided to Chicago book collector Everett D. Graff a week later when sending carbon copies of the "Checklist of Works on Mormonism, 1830–1849": he was embarking "immediately" on a rough draft of what would become an historical bibliography of the Mormons' first twenty years.[36] When he could steal time, he worked hard to collate his notes and generate a clear working copy of the basic form for his historical bibliography—individual entries in a chronological arrangement with historical annotations on their authors, influences, and histories, beginning with the *Book of Mormon.*

Between 18 March and 7 April 1949 Morgan drafted twenty-one pages of historical bibliography for "The Mormons, 1830–1849," describing the first forty-five items identified through 1836, all of the attention he could spare for the moment. This was merely a sample of what such a work would look like in manuscript, not a complete draft. He carried the sheets to Hal Bentley at the University of Utah. Morgan's draft pages were intended to nudge the administration further toward chartering the press, as well as tip the balance his directions in negotiations for a possible book contract.[37] The entries he managed to compile are here reproduced from the manuscript of "The Mormons, 1830–1849" among his papers. The sample draft provides just enough detail to make modern scholars wish he had finished the list. As noted in the introduction, this bibliography was to include not merely works produced by Mormons, but also works produced about them. The resulting work would have provided an interesting view of the unfolding religious tradition in terms of "mass media" of the day. The list was informed by a decade of research through Latter Day Saint publications and American newspapers. If he included newspaper stories, as he planned, then it would have been possible to virtually track the unfolding of Mormonism as a newsworthy topic across America's social landscape.

Opening draft pages of "The Mormons, 1830–1849" were barely out of his typewriter and into Bentley's hand when the sample draft of the historical bibliography became a casualty of mission creep. Dale entertained a nagging fear about the tenor of his work and its possible effects for at least a year. He had long since personally concluded that Mormon origins lay strictly

[36]DLM to Everett D. Graff, 25 March 1949.

[37]DLM to Fawn M. Brodie, 7 April 1949, *Dale Morgan on Early Mormonism,* 168; DLM to Thomas W. Streeter, 1 April 1949, Morgan papers.

within historical circumstances of 1820s New York and Joseph Smith's psyche. He felt he had the documents to prove the point, but a treatment of the religion that laid out the documentary basis of his conclusion risked offending believers across the Latter Day Saint spectrum. Though he had no more than a few conceptual drafts on hand for the earliest chapters of his Mormon book, he expected that his history of the Mormons would challenge the very foundation of the claims advanced by the religious tradition. That was not so much of a problem for the Latter-day Saints and the Reorganization or Community of Christ since he had on hand a decade's worth of research notes and transcripts involving the two major Restoration churches and their history, but what if the smaller churches, about which much less was known, "clammed up" once the first volume appeared? If they did, it would be impossible to gather necessary source material for the second volume, which would address the Mormon Diaspora between 1844 and about 1880. So little was known about the small groups or their history that Morgan was forced to rely exclusively on their good graces for access to the unpublished material in their hands. If they became as unwelcoming as the Salt Lake church, then it might be impossible to move forward with his historical volumes. That was a potential problem. "It would be smart of me to do what can be done about the church archives before the situation becomes further complicated," he had told close friend Madeline McQuown early the previous spring. He was in good company. "One of the first things I learned in my studies of the history of printing, both in Europe and in the United States," wrote contemporary printing historian Douglas C. McMurtrie, "is that you can never trust any statement [about printed works] that is not based on first-hand information." Dale determined to first pry necessary historical data from the various organizations before his book on the early years of Mormonism potentially insulted everyone into ceasing cooperation.[38]

On 7 April 1949 Morgan abruptly quit typing the draft for the 1830–1849 historical bibliography. He immediately reordered research priorities once again and dragged to the foreground still another bibliographical project

[38]DLM to Brodie, 7 April 1949, *Dale Morgan on Early Mormonism,* 168; DLM to MRM, 12 March 1948, Madeline McQuown papers, Marriott Library Special Collections, Univ. of Utah; DLM to Beatrice Johnson, 24 January 1948, to New York Public Library, 16 May 1949, Morgan papers; Douglas C. McMurtrie, *A Historical Background of Printing* (Washington, D.C.: Apprentice School of the Government Printing Office, 1937), 2.

or projects: a series of bibliographies of "the lesser Mormon churches." It was a calculated but rather desperate risk. Making a few hopefully quick digressions into something as non-threatening as a historical bibliography would provide the research leverage with the churches, he explained to Fawn Brodie the same day in early April. These publications would extend his bibliographic understanding across the extended Latter Day Saint heritage, cementing him a place within the research field. Individually they looked small enough that they would probably not require large commitments of time or energy. He had patiently coaxed historical data and publications from schismatic organizations over the previous decade and discovered that approaching a church with something as non-threatening as a bibliography allowed him to establish credentials as a respectfully interested outsider, providing an opportunity to pull relevant historical sources from the various groups to inform his descriptive work (and, incidentally, his larger cultural history), and helping him get at least a bibliographic grasp of the frustratingly large and complicated legacy of Mormon denominations. To correspondents across the country he wrote variations of "When I can afford the time, I mean to publish a series of bibliographical contributions on the publishing history of each of these."[39]

Morgan hardly had time to watch the rest of April 1949 as it blossomed into a Great Basin spring. Rather than focusing on one group, Dale immediately launched into his various digressions and began writing inquiries to many small Latter Day Saint offshoots. By May, and as he waited impatiently for query responses to return through the mail, he began to suspect that the University of Utah administration either could not resolve or would not act upon the administrative and fiscal issues incident to beginning a scholarly press. If they did not, he was stuck. Writing on *The Mormons,* his history, could not yet effectively begin, despite the contract; writing on "The Mormons, 1830–1849" was set aside for the moment as the checklists circulated and while he attended to bibliographies of the small Restoration churches. On 9 April, employing a bit of overstatement, he wrote to Clarence L. Wheaton of the Church of Christ (Temple Lot) in Independence, Missouri, that "I have in the last stages of completion a huge bibliography of all works published between 1830 and 1849 which in any way relate to 'Mormonism,' but at the same time

[39]DLM to Brodie, 7 April 1949, *Dale Morgan on Early Mormonism,* 168; DLM to New York Public Library, 16 May 1949; DLM to Fred Rosenstock, 19 April 1951.

I am working at a bibliography of the publications of each of the several churches."[40] At this point the draft of the historical bibliography was hardly begun, certainly not in what other scholars would consider "the last stage of completion." The other bibliographies were merely ideas. Similar letters were dispatched to libraries with specific items he wanted to include and to county courthouses, which could supply background data from public records.

As he set to work on this project, June 1949 brought a rash of bad news. First, Hal Bentley informed him that University of Utah administrators supported the creation of a university press, but it would be months or longer before the school was prepared to actually begin a publication program. Bentley returned Morgan's 1830–1836 draft bibliography pages with compliments but no publication nor fellowship offer.

The U did not initiate its press until a few years later, by which time Morgan had no time to work further on the historical bibliography that had driven him for a half a decade.[41] The second blow to his plans, also landing in the first week of June and just after proposing publication of the edited Empey journal to the *Annals of Wyoming*, was the hospitalization of close friend Roderick Korns following a major heart attack. The *Utah Historical Quarterly* had just offered to publish a multi-issue volume of Korns's research on emigrant trails across Utah, but its author was now in no condition to generate a manuscript. Having worked with Korns nearly every step of the way through his research, Morgan gamely volunteered to put the notes into shape so that his friend could revise and amend it during his convalescence.[42] After Korns's sudden passing on 2 July, Dale generously but rashly promised the widow that he would see her husband's lifework to publication. The effort needed to gather and edit (and correct and expand) this work added yet another thick layer of commitments to his already overcommitted budget of energy and time.

By summer the dead weight of the grounded historical bibliography suddenly lightened to buoy up his sinking financial hopes. After Korns's funeral Morgan wrote his good friend Darel McConkey in Washington, D.C., and asked him to make some discrete inquiries at the Library of Congress. Morgan had realized the "Mormon bibliography" could be a competitive funding proposal toward a Library of Congress fellowship in bibliography, history, or

[40] DLM to Clarence L. Wheaton, 9 April 1949.

[41] Hal Bentley to DLM, 1 June 1949; DLM to Stan Ivins, 7 June 1949.

[42] DLM to Virginia Sorenson, 7 May 1949. The University of Utah Press did, however, eventually publish the catalogue that Morgan began.

American culture. In his letter Dale tipped his hand about his research and writing method. He noted that "the work," by which he always meant *research*, "has mostly been done, except for the laborious chore of typing out the whole manuscript and annotating it"—in other words, almost nothing had been committed to written form; the thousands of details simply occupied stray corners of his remarkable mind, to be set down and rechecked as necessary when he did get around to actual writing. McConkey's reply in October came too late to rescue Morgan's plan to quit Salt Lake City for Washington: McConkey had put off responding for over a month, and Luther Evans, the Librarian of Congress and one of Morgan's earlier supporters, was by then out of the country.[43] Without Evans's direct support, securing a fellowship for a bibliographic project was not a practical possibility.

Morgan's hope to publish the grand historical bibliography of the first twenty years of Mormonism evaporated by the time he left the West a second time for the East. He never added another page to the manuscript nor expended more effort on its completion, though he busily circulated the three carbon copies of the master title checklist which would have informed it. Morgan abandoned Salt Lake City and moved to Washington, D.C., in October 1949, even without a commission for the historical bibliography as a financial life-preserver, to fruitlessly chase positions in the civil service.

Had he been able to complete it, the finished bibliography of Mormonism would have been huge, consisting of over nine hundred entries and historical notes. Unlike the work of later scholars, it would include not only works by church members but also the work of detractors and antagonists as well. He anticipated presenting a picture of Mormonism from its earliest days to the high point of the Mormon Diaspora. The final form would have resembled the pages reproduced here. The detailed transcriptions and notes familiar to descriptive bibliographers would have been omitted in favor of straightforward titles, reproducing only the word order and not line breaks or the typefaces used. The page description would have followed much more closely the standard library description of the time rather than the detailed collational formulae of descriptive bibliography specified by Fredson Bowers. Just this data, drawn straight from his checklist, would have been useful to researchers, but the analytical historical notes appended to the entries would have been the prize for later scholars. The sample pages reproduced here

[43]DLM to Darel McConkey, 1949 Jul 30; McConkey to DLM, 1949 Sep 17, Morgan papers.

provide merely sparse hints of what would come; in final form *The Mormons: A Historical Bibliography, 1830–1849,* would have looked much more like his *Churches of the Dispersion,* which follows in the second volume of this edition. The completed bibliography would have provided the skeleton of relationships and influences on which he would hang the muscle of his historical work. Instead, it never really got off the ground. To historical novelist Virginia Sorenson he lamented that "The Mormons, 1830–1849" bibliography had eaten up a year of time and yet would net him nothing financially.[44]

Completion and publication of the historical bibliography was not the only measure for the value for his bibliographic research. Morgan had managed to cast a broad net around Mormon publications and he would draw upon that research for the three bibliographies he would complete. His discoveries would also at least inform and enrich the text of *The Mormons*—if he could ever get sufficient support to get that writing project started.

Despite these pressures, Dale plowed ahead with his work on the lesser Mormon churches. In the spring of 1949 he took the time to draft a sample project, a bibliography of the Church of Christ, a group organized around Sidney Rigdon's post-martyrdom claim to leadership by William Bickerton in the 1860s and carried into the twentieth century by William Cadman. Tucking into his briefcase the manuscript for the Bickerton/Cadman bibliography, Morgan walked or caught a streetcar up the hill from his apartment to the university and paid a visit to Bill Mulder at the *Western Humanities Review* office. With the jerky combination of his nasal and too-loud voice, hand gestures, and notes scribbled between them to clarify the details of spoken conversation that Morgan could not hear, Dale advanced a new idea. If the prenatal University of Utah Press was unable to act on the large historical bibliography of Mormonism, perhaps the *Western Humanities Review* would publish the series of discrete and much smaller bibliographies that discussed distinct facets of Restoration culture. Unlike his larger and more historically detailed 1830–1849 bibliography (which was still circulating as a preliminary title checklist), this smaller study included all works of a denomination (and any of its offshoots) up to the moment. Mulder liked the promising idea of looking at cultural Mormonism by following its tracks left in print and took the idea to director Hal Cannon. Cannon concurred and approved publication. Morgan was delighted—his first piece had slid

[44]DLM to Carroll D. Hall, 21 June 1949.

(almost) effortlessly into place. As a venue for cultural studies, the *WHR* was certainly the easiest venue to approach about publishing his bibliographic work. Given the nature of cultural studies at the time, since the *UHQ* could not deliver, it may have been the only other venue in the country that would have seriously considered the piece for publication. A few weeks later Bentley also agreed to abide by the arrangements Mulder had made, and Dale promised to have the first manuscript to the journal on short order.

The Bickerton/Cadman list appeared in the last *Western Humanities Review* issue of 1949, and two succeeding bibliographies appeared in 1950 and 1953. They broke entirely new ground for Restoration studies and demonstrated that the author was deadly serious about approaching "Mormonism" as constituting not merely the Utah mainstream, but as a diverse cultural whole. These studies represented virtually the first time that any of the smaller schismatic denominations had been studied seriously by someone outside the sect, the Strang group (though not its own offshoots) being the exception. In a historiographic sense, including the smaller churches, groups, and claims as legitimate historical entities in their own right elevated the past and the ideas of each small church to the same level as either the LDS or RLDS churches—Mormonism's mainline denominations. If that point had been parsed from his publications by the Church Historian's Office staff, its church leadership would not have approved; the LDS church regarded its own tradition as the sole authoritative heir to Joseph Smith's spiritual and organizational legacy. Conversely, having grown out of the period known later as the Mormon Diaspora (1840–1870), and with much of its early membership drawn from the movements discussed by Morgan, the Reorganization was more ecumenical on the subject and sympathetic to the project.

As new, insightful, and well-documented as they might be, the bibliographies of lesser Latter Day Saint sects contributed absolutely nothing to the author's pocketbook—they were expensive luxuries rooted in free time he did not have. In the tension between interest and necessity, the demands of real life eventually won out. Deciding Salt Lake City could not provide him a writing career, while the master-checklist carbons were circulating between libraries and shortly after the Bickerton/Cadman manuscript was accepted for publication, the author abandoned Salt Lake City for Washington, D.C., again, hoping that the larger town held attendantly greater chances to find work. Desperate for an income and despite contractual commitments to

Rinehart & Company for the Mormon book, once he arrived he set aside *The Mormons* manuscript and even the lesser-Mormon-churches lists. Between 1949 and 1951 Morgan supported himself by compiling catalogue descriptions on commission for New York Americana book dealer Edward Eberstadt & Sons. His role as sales cataloguer paid the bills while putting into his hands some very rare Latter Day Saint, fur-trade, and Western Americana material.

As he could snatch time from what paying work he managed to scavenge, Morgan completed and routed a checklist for a second historical bibliography on the James J. Strang sect and its defenders in May 1950. Toward the end of the same month the Eberstadts commissioned a detailed review of Milo M. Quaife's book and manuscript collection on Strang and his church. The Quaife commission set the subject for his second Dispersion bibliography and entirely displaced work on the Mormon book.[45] Morgan had seen the collection briefly during his Guggenheim excursion three years earlier; now on the sale block, it was destined for the Coe collection at Yale. Needing the money from the commission as a cataloguer and craving the opportunity to see the Strang material in detail at his convenience, Dale laid everything else aside and snatched up the chance willingly. Through the first three weeks of June 1950, Morgan spent virtually every waking moment with the Quaife-Strang papers strewn across the tiny workspace in his sister's apartment in Alexandria, Virginia, typewriter clattering out abstracts and notes. Since the largest gathering of Strang-related historical material was immediately at hand, the manuscript for the Strang imprint bibliography, which was finally dispatched westward in November, was far more historically substantive (not to mention twice the length) than the preceding Bickerton/Cadman listing.

A year later, in the summer of 1951, Dale was still stuck in Washington, D.C., still without a job, and desperate for any dependable income. Unable to work on *The Mormons* because he utterly lacked fiscal support that would allow him to do so, Morgan made a desperate proposal to the Utah State Historical Society that would provide at least a brief financial reprieve. He offered to crosscheck his lengthening checklist of Latter Day Saint publications against the National Union Catalogue and Library of Congress holdings and to give the result to the Utah State Historical Society. Since he feared he would never be able to complete the "The Mormons, 1830–1849" as historical bibliography, the investment would at least allow the Society to generate a card file of Mormon-related works from Morgan's notes. In

[45]DLM to Stan Ivins, 5 June 1950.

September, 1951 the board of directors agreed.[46] This commission netted him enough for Morgan to devote six weeks to painstakingly checking each entry for accuracy and broadening his search through the catalogue to unearth others. The resulting card file of the Mormon bibliography, carefully retyped and accessible at the Historical Society's new office in the Kearns Mansion on North Temple Street, became one of the Society's most heavily used resources and eventually took on a life of its own.[47]

Dale Morgan's historical bibliographies plowed entirely new ground in Mormon historiography, and his large title checklist—which in his hands never progressed further than a typed list with three carbons—was the first substantive attempt to circumscribe Latter Day Saint intellectual and social culture. Bibliographic progress came with a high cost reckoned in time and effort, however. With his checklist dispatched to Utah, Morgan set about again working on *The Mormons,* revising the first chapter and pushing out a few additional conceptual drafts. It was not enough. Having seen no substantive progress on the history of Mormonism, under contract since 1948, Stanley Rinehart cancelled the publication agreement for *The Mormons* in January 1952. Losing the contract for his Mormon book was more than simply a financial setback. The cancellation forced Morgan to redirect his entire effort toward the historical subjects for which he is still remembered as a giant: the American fur trade, North American continental exploration, and the transcontinental overland trails. Work on a third bibliography (contained in volume two) was delayed for two years while Morgan worked quickly to draft *Jedediah Smith and the Opening of the West* (Indianpolis: Bobbs-Merrill, 1953).

Dale Morgan focused attention on Mormon bibliography because he recognized that it provided not only a window into ideas, but because he understood that print was the nineteenth-century equivalent of mass media. Printed work legitimates and perpetuates Western societies. Printing allowed groups to organize, represent themselves, and disseminate their message. If he were to understand Mormonism as a society, part of his attention would

[46] DLM to MRM, 15 September 1951, McQuown papers.

[47] The original file of typed cards has disappeared, probably discarded when the file was converted back into a manuscript for use in compiling the published catalogue. This was published by a consortium of Utah libraries and compiled by the instrumentality of BYU librarian Chad Flake. Morgan was a consultant for the project. Chad J. Flake, *A Mormon Bibliography, 1830–1930* (Salt Lake City: Univ. of Utah Press, 1978); Chad J. Flake and Larry W. Draper, *A Mormon Bibliography, 1830–1930,* 2nd ed. (Provo, Utah: BYU Religious Studies Center, 2004).

profitably be focused on the form, the content, and the history surrounding its printed works.[48] Work on the bibliographies expanded Morgan's understanding of the Latter Day Saint movement. Over time, the series also reflected stylistic development. The Bickerton/Cadman list provided readers little beyond a standard library checklist of publications, a document of the type that would be found in any large library of the time. The Strang list added brief notes about each work and was a much more interesting and historically useful production. *Churches of the Dispersion,* published in 1953 and found in volume 2 of this collection, is a remarkable resource of context and historical detail in a style that Peter Crawley would adopt a generation later, first for two library exhibition catalogues, *A Mormon Fifty* (Provo: Friends of the BYU Library, 1984) and then *Mormon Imprints in Great Britain and the Empire, 1836–1857* (Provo: Friends of the BYU Library, 1987), and would expand upon as a stylistic foundation for his multi-volume *Descriptive Bibliography of the Mormon Church* (Provo: BYU Religious Studies Center, 1996–). Had it been completed, "The Mormons, 1830–1849" would likely have resembled the narrative scope displayed in *Churches of the Dispersion.*

A few dated manuscript notes on "The Mormons, 1830–1849" suggest that Dale picked up the manuscript again as Chad Flake began working on an expanded card file around 1965. Morgan checked entries for the serial items against the newest edition of the *Union List of Serials,* but in a career that only grew more frantically busy—if that were possible—Morgan was never able to find time to return to his notes and complete the larger historical bibliography. The four works presented here are then both introductory and seminal, incomplete and anticipatory, a view into one of Dale Morgan's greatest, most frustrating, and influential research priorities.

A Checklist of Works on Mormonism, 1830–1849

Introduction

The checklist has been prepared primarily for census purposes. No effort has been made to achieve any consistency in style, or even in description of the books in such technical matters as statement of pagination. Enough information has been provided in all cases, however, so that titles may be fully differentiated from one another.

---

[48] Cf. Richard Saunders, *Printing in Deseret: Mormons, Economy, Politics, and Utah's Incunabula, 1849–1851* (Salt Lake City: Univ. of Utah Press, 2000), ix, 5–16.

The titles have been sent up in five categories: (1) By author, where the author is known with reasonable certainty. (2) By title of entry, where author is unknown. (3) Broadsides. (4) Hymn books. (5) Titles in Welsh.

Occasionally, by an inadvertence in the typing up of the checklist, an author or title will be found a few entries before or after his place in the strict alphabetical order. In the case of broadsides, a few will be found in category (1), placed there in the first instance, and overlooked when all such entries were moved to a special broadside category.

The finished bibliography will adhere to a strictly chronological presentation, beginning with the Book of Mormon in March, 1830, and ending with the last title published in December, 1849, so far as this can be done. In final form, the bibliography will also contain complete bibliographical information, including the vertical and horizontal dimensions of the title pages in centimeters, and notes on content, historical value, place and date of authorship and publication, and other information of interest, including census lists of all copies of these works known to me.

Apart from works usually thought of as belonging to the general category, "Mormons and Mormonism," this checklist includes peripheral works which refer incidentally to Mormonism or the Mormons; no doubt it is less complete which respect to such titles, however, as I have not attempted an exhaustive examination of almanacs, encyclopedias, gazetteers, and such works in the various states, or dealing with the various states, published during the limiting dates, 1830–1849. Anyone examining this checklist who may be aware of additional titles referring to the Mormons, including travel books that may have escaped me, is solicited to send me information of these. In one respect the checklist is incomplete; it does not include all the books published in 1849 which incorporated Colonel [Richard Barnes] Mason's report to [James] Polk concerning the California gold discoveries, in which the Mormons were mentioned in passing. An effort may be made hereafter to add a complete list of such books as printed the Mason report.

The bibliography is limited to books, pamphlets, and broadsides, and does not include material in newspapers and periodicals, though some allusions will be made to such material in the notes. An appendix, not now present, will be added to the printed bibliography, listing all newspapers and periodicals published by the various Mormon churches during the period 1830–1849.

Dale L. Morgan*

*[The five-part checklist in the Morgan papers that follow this opening statement runs to forty-seven pages, including addenda, and is omitted from this publication. —Ed.]

The Mormons
1830–1849
A Bibliography of the First Twenty Years of Mormonism

Preface

This bibliography is essentially a history of the Mormons in terms of the immense literature that burst into being between 1830 and 1849 around this dynamic arrival on the American religious scene. To the extent that resources of inquiry have permitted, the works listed are presented in the actual order of their publication. Thus they exhibit the whole social evolution of Mormonism—its beginnings with the publication of the *Book of Mormon,* the early rebuttals to that book and the attacks upon the character of its adherents, the geographic spread of Mormon proselyting, the developing doctrinal system, the appearance, character, and resolution of local controversies, the social and theological pressures brought to bear against the new religion, the arguments in defense, counter-attack, and offense brought forth by the Saints, the emergence of the Mormons as a group of genuine national concern and significance, the tragic death of the prophet, Joseph Smith, in 1844, the fission which then took place in the church, and the final scattering of the fragments of the church to the far corners of America.

By reason of the nature of this immense literature, each title an organic part of the whole, the creation of this bibliography has been a fascinating employment, though involving so great an expenditure of time, energy, and money that like many another bibliographer I should never had undertaken the labor had I understood in the beginning what I was getting into.

I had been doing exploratory researches through more than a decade for a comprehensive history of the Mormons, and I labored with this bibliography originally out of a curiosity to see what the proportions would be of a list of works concerned with the opening era of Mormon history, subsequently because I conceived that publication of such a book in advance of my history would serve to bring to light unknown titles that might have a significant bearing on that history, still later because the need for such a work became dramatically apparent as research unearthed dozens of unimagined titles, and finally because the bibliography had assumed so imperious an existence that I was no longer free to lay it aside.

Works regarded as germane to the bibliography are all books, pamphlets, and broadsides published between 1830 and 1849 which in any way refer to the Saints, even if only in passing allusion. Newspapers and periodicals published by the various Mormon churches are included, as are two newspapers published at Nauvoo in 1846–47. With this exception, articles and comments in the contemporaneous press are excluded; they would swell the bibliography to unmanageable proportions. Moreover, research in this field is not far enough advanced to justify a bibliography of it. I commend further labor in this direction as a worthy and difficult subject for a doctoral study, or indeed several doctoral studies; not only should the literature be catalogued but also a work in Mormon history is called for that would explore the impact of Mormonism upon the American churches as shown in their periodicals. The difficulties presented by such studies are serious, the materials being scattered through hundreds of obscure periodicals which must be sought out in depositories all over the United States. The notes that have accumulated from my months of preliminary spade-work in this field are at the disposal of any scholar with the time and ambition to go on from where I have left off.

Naturally, the works commonly thought of as belonging to a Mormons-and-Mormonism category are more completely represented in this bibliography than peripheral works. I have no doubt that many incidental mentions of the Saints in travel narratives, gazetteers, almanacs, and kindred works have escaped me, and I would appreciate having brought to my attention any that may hereafter come to light, as also copies of works herein listed which none of my ingenuities have sufficed to locate.

In general I have chosen to assign a number to each edition of each book, and have placed it in accordance with its individual date of publication. An exception to this rule is the treatment of certain travel narratives; I have elected to print consecutively after their first appearance in the bibliography the various editions of Samuel Parker, Josiah Gregg, John Charles Frémont, Edwin Bryant, and some gold-rush literature of 1848–49, all of which are only incidentally concerned with the Saints. Any method adopted for a bibliography always presents its problems but having decided upon a chronological method as being most fruitful for my purposes, I have supplied at the end an author index and a short-title index which should make it possible to refer easily to any title. As the authors of a number of these works have been positively or tentatively identified for the first time, this three-fold approach seems all the more desirable and necessary.

The terminal date to be adopted for the bibliography presented many difficulties. The immense literature germinated by Mormonism forbad any idea of a comprehensive bibliography for the entire period since 1830, both from limitations in the time that I could afford to give to such a work and from considerations of space. My purpose originally was to end the bibliography with the year of Joseph Smith's death, 1844, but as the work developed, this date became obviously unsatisfactory, and I considered fixing as a terminal date the year of the Mormon expulsion from Nauvoo, 1846. Eventually the year 1849 was adopted because it rounded out the first two decades of Mormon history, covered the beginnings of Mormon settlement in the Great Basin and the commencement of printing there, with the virtual cessation of Mormon publishing activity elsewhere except in England; and also covered comprehensively the publishing history of most of the schismatic groups which sprang up immediately after the death of Joseph Smith (if it did not completely cover the bibliographical history of James J. Strang's church, it did with one exception include all the publications of his church at Voree, before its removal to Beaver Island in Lake Michigan).

Virtually every title herein listed I have personally examined. The point of view has been that of the practical historian seeking information, rather than that of the printer and collector, and I have been more concerned with content than with bibliographical niceties of description. In the case of purely polemical or doctrinal works with a limited present-day interest, I have curtailed my notes; and conversely, have written more extended notes on works of key significance or works still unlocated about which clues may prove helpful. The dimensions of the entries, stated first vertically and then horizontally in centimeters, are those of title-pages, which has seemed to me a more logical procedure than to state the dimensions of bindings, the more so because a high proportion of the entries had only paper wrappers or none. The dimensions given are usually those of the tallest copies that came to my attention.

References to *Doctrine and Covenants* in the notes are to the Utah edition, which varies from that of the Reorganized Church; the former having been more widely distributed, use of it seems better to suit general convenience. In this connection it might be remarked that "Mormons" and "Saints" are used as interchangeable terms, though some of the churches that have sprung from the 1830 church vehemently decline the words "Mormon" or "Mormonism" as proper terminology; the Utah church, the Church of Jesus Christ of Jesus Christ of Latter-day Saints, is however if not reconciled at least resigned to this appellation. Also as a matter of convenience in reference, the annals of the Saints are usually referred to by the instrumentality of the *History of the Church of Jesus Christ of Latter-day Saints*, published at Salt Lake City in 7 volumes, 1902–1932.

It has seemed to me that provision of a census must be a primary consideration of such a work as this, though no census can hope to be complete. My attempt at a census began with the Union Catalog in the Library of Congress, including all holdings reported to September, 1947, by cooperating libraries. It continued as I personally examined the collections of Princeton University, the New York Public Library, the New-York Historical Society, the New York State Library, the Rochester Public Library, Yale University and the notable W. R. Coe collection now domiciled there, the Connecticut State Library, Harvard College, the Boston Public Library, the American Antiquarian Society, the Vermont State Library, the Western Reserve Historical Society, Western Reserve University, the Cleveland Public Library, the Detroit Public Library, the Strang collection of Dr. Milo M. Quaife of Detroit, the Newberry Library, the Chicago Historical Society, the Missouri Historical Society, the St. Louis Mercantile Library, the St. Louis Public Library, the State Historical Society of Missouri, the Reorganized Church of Jesus Christ of Latter Day Saints, the Henry E. Huntington Library, Stanford University, the Bancroft Library at the University of California, the Salt Lake City Free Public Library, the Utah State Historical Society, University of Utah, Utah State Agricultural College, Brigham Young University, and the Historian's Office of the Church of Jesus Christ of Latter-day Saints. By correspondence and the courtesy of librarians and collectors, the census also reflects the holdings of the State Historical Society of Wisconsin, the Illinois State Historical Library, the California State Library, the California Historical Society, and two distinguished private collectors of Americana, the late Everett D. Graff of Chicago, and the late Thomas W. Streeter of Morristown, N.J. Individual titles in other libraries that have been reported to me are also listed. Location symbols employed are those adopted by the Union Catalog in the Library of Congress.

Since the bibliography grew throughout the period of research, it is not to be supposed that the census perfectly reflects the holdings of all these libraries, particularly in the realm of peripheral works, but a special effort has been made to have a final check performed in the key libraries: the Historian's Office of the Church of Jesus Christ of Latter-day Saints, the Reorganized Church of Jesus Christ of Latter Day Saints, the Salt Lake City Free Public Library, the University of Utah, Brigham Young University, the Bancroft Library, the Henry E. Huntington Library, the State Historical Society of Wisconsin, the Chicago Historical Society, the Illinois State Historical Library, the Newberry Library, the Western Reserve Historical Society, the New York Public Library, Harvard College, the Coe Collection at Yale University, and the Library of Congress. By the courtesy of Mr. Hugo Hespen, acting head of the Union Catalog Division of the Library of Congress, a final check has also been made in the Union Catalog.

To the John Simon Guggenheim Memorial Foundation, as to myself, this bibliography comes as a surprising by-product of my professional interests in history. The Foundation granted me in 1945 a fellowship in connection with my projected history of the Mormons, and this fellowship, activated in March, 1947, materially expedited if it did not alone make possible the transcontinental researches without which this bibliography would not now exist. Throughout the period of research and preparation I have been immensely indebted also to the staffs of all the libraries mentioned, the names of many members of which I do not even know and cannot hope to thank. First noting a special obligation to Dr. John Thomas, a director of the Cambrian Society in Salt Lake City, who translated for me the numerous Welsh titles that came to light and thus made it possible for me to deal with them authoritatively, I would like to extend warm thanks and appreciation to: [*text ends*]

1830

JOSEPH SMITH, JUNIOR

The Book of Mormon: An account written by the hand of Mormon, upon plates taken from the plates of Nephi. Wherefore it is an abridgment of the record of the People of Nephi; and also of the Lamanites; written to the Lamanites, which are a remnant of the House of Israel; and also to Jew and Gentile; written by way of commandment, and also by the spirit of prophesy and of revelation. Written, and sealed up, and hid up unto the Lord, that they might not be destroyed, to come forth by the gift and power of God unto the interpretation thereof; sealed by the hand of Moroni, and hid up unto the Lord, to come forth in due time by the way of Gentile; the interpretation thereof by the gift of God; an abridgment taken from the Book of Ether.

Also, which is a record of the people of Jared, which were scattered at the time the Lord confounded the language of the people when they were building a tower to get to heaven: which is to shew unto the remnant of the House of Israel how great things the Lord hath done for their fathers; and that they may know the covenants of the Lord, that they are not cast off forever; and also to the convincing of the Jew and Gentile that Jesus is the Christ, the Eternal God, manifesting himself unto all nations. And now if there be fault, it be the mistake of men; wherefore condemn not the things of God, that ye may be found spotless at the judgment seat of Christ. By Joseph Smith, Junior, Author and Proprietor.

Palmyra {N.Y.}: Printed by E.B. Grandin, for the Author. 1830. iv, {5}–588, (2) pp. 18.8 × 11.7 cm.

The Book of Mormon was presented as the record of the peopling of the New World by two different waves of migration from ancient Israel, preserved upon engraved metal plates, the existence of which were revealed to Joseph Smith by an angel in 1823, and translated by him, through the power of God, between 1827 and 1829. The first edition contains a two-page preface explaining that 116 pages of the manuscript as first written had been stolen and kept from the author for probable ulterior purposes, and that their place had been supplied by translation from other plates, all these plates having been "found in the township of Manchester, Ontario county, New-York." This preface was not republished in later editions. The "Testimony of Three Witnesses," and the "Testimony of Eight Witnesses," printed on the last leaf of this edition, were moved to the front of the book in later editions. Some copies of the first edition contain a printed index of iv pages, inserted after the last fly-leaves, and headed "References | to the | Book of Mormon." The provenance of this index has not been absolutely determined, but it was probably printed {at} Palmyra before distribution of the first edition was completed. The book was copyrighted by deposit of the title-page at Lansing, N.Y., on June 11, 1829. Five thousand copies were printed, first advertised for sale in the Palmyra *Wayne Sentinel,* March 26, 1830. Prior to publication, some extracts were printed in *The Reflector,* January 2, 13, and 22, 1830, published at Palmyra by "O. Dogberry" {A[bner] Cole}, who according to the Prophet's mother, Lucy Mack Smith, only desisted under threat of suit for infringement of copyright.

Scattered references to the book while it was in press are found in the *Wayne Sentinel*, June 26, 1828, and March 19, 1830; in the Palmyra *Freeman*, as reprinted in the Rochester *Advertiser and Telegraph*, August 31, 1829, and the Rochester *Gem*, September 5, 1829, and in *The Reflector*, September 2, 16, 23, 30, October 2, December 9, 1829, and January 2, 13, 1830. When the book was reprinted at Kirtland in 1837 (no.____), various changes, principally grammatical, were made in the text; for these, see Lamoni Call, *2000 Changes in the Book of Mormon* (Bountiful, Utah: 1898). The 1830 edition has been reprinted intact only by the Hedrickite faction, as: *The Nephite Records*{.} *An Account written by the hand of Mormon upon plates taken from the plates of Nephi. . . . Translated by Joseph Smith, Jun. Published by the Church of Christ. Printed from the Palmyra edition, which edition was printed from the original manuscript.* (Independence, Mo., 1899). {v}–xiii, 721 pp.

At least two copies of the Book of Mormon manuscript existed. Fragments of one are now preserved by the Historian's Office of the Church of Jesus Christ of Latter-day Saints at Salt Lake City, while the other copy was preserved in its entirety by Oliver Cowdery, David Whitmer, and the Whitmer heirs, and since 1903 has been in the possession of the [Community of Christ] at Independence. While the manuscript was still in the possession of Whitmer, it was examined by a committee from the [Community of Christ], which thereafter, in 1908, published its own authorized version, based on a proofreading of the 1837 edition against the original text. Editions of the Book of Mormon down to 1849 are listed chronologically in this bibliography. For an account of the innumerable editions in all languages since that times, see Joseph Sabin and Wilberforce Eames, *A Dictionary of Books Relation to America*, Vol. 20, pp. 304–329.

Woodward 230*

1831

ALEXANDER CAMPBELL

2. Mormonism. The Book of Mormon reviewed, and its divine pretensions Exposed. Delusions. By A. Campbell.

{Bethany, Va., 1831} 12 pp.

Not located. Title derived from the Painesville, O., *Telegraph*, March 1, 1831, the pamphlet being reprinted in the issues of the *Telegraph* following March 8 and 15, 1831. The pamphlet had evidently been reprinted as a separate from Campbell's periodical, *The Millennial Harbinger* 2 (February 7, 1831): 85–96. Campbell's critique is usually known from the 1832 edition, our No. 8. It was not only the first widely read but also the ablest of the earliest rebuttals to the Book of Mormon.

---

*[The citations to "Woodward" refer to an 1880 book sale catalogue reproduced as *Bibliothica Scallawagiana* (Spokane: Arthur H. Clark Co., 1997). This edition of the manuscript incorporates Morgan's scribbled 1967 amendations as numbered footnotes but does not include Morgan's sixty-year-out-of-date imprint census. —Ed.]

DAVID MARKS

The Life of David Marks, to the 26th year of his age. Including the particulars of his conversion, call to the ministry, and labours in itinerant preaching for nearly eleven years. Written by himself. . . .

Limerick, Me.: Printed at the Office of the Morning Star. 1831. {3}–396 pp. 17.9 × 10.5 cm. Portrait.

The preface is dated Limerick, Me., September 26, 1831. Marks, a Free-Will Baptist preacher, was traveling in western New York at the time the Book of Mormon was published. On March 29, 1830 he stayed at the Whitmer home in Fayette, and talked to some of the Whitmer sons, who were among the witnesses to the Book of Mormon. Marks thought the new scripture a money-making device, "full of absurdity, and too dull to charm the soul." The verso of the title-page has a paragraph of "Errata in a part of the copies."[1]

1832

W. W. PHELPS

{Prospectus of} The Evening and [the] Morning Star. {Signed:} W. W. Phelps, February 1832.

Not located. The prospectus is reprinted in *Millennial Star* 14 (1852): 146–148, and is of larger significance than a simple prospectus because it was the first statement in a Mormon imprint of the latter-day importance of the *Book of Mormon* and the doctrinal position of the new church. Most of the prospectus is devoted to these larger questions, and what is said about the prospective publication is mostly limited to the information that it would be issued monthly on a royal sheet quarto, at one dollar a year. The *Star* would borrow its light from sacred sources, and be devoted to "the revelations of God as made known to His servants by the Holy Ghost, at sundry times since the creation of man, but more especially in these last days, for the restoration of the house of Israel." From this press also might be expected "as soon as wisdom directs, many sacred records, which have slept for ages." Phelps had been editor of an anti-Masonic weekly, the *Ontario Phoenix*, at Canandaigua, N.Y., but in the spring of 1831 had joined his fortunes with those of the Mormons in Ohio. He was welcomed with a revelation which declared that he should be ordained to assist Oliver Cowdery "to do the work of printing, and of selecting and writing books for schools in this Church." A second revelation in July, 1831, declared that Phelps should be established at Independence, Missouri, as "a printer unto the church." A conference at Kirtland in the fall of 1831 instructed Phelps to stop at Cincinnati on his way to Missouri, to purchase a press and type for establishing *The Evening and Morning Star.* In his history, apparently under date of March, 1832, Joseph Smith recorded that he "received a letter from the brethren who went up to the land of Zion, stating that they

[1]"Reprinted in 1846 and 1847 q.v." and "His debate in 1841 (T & S)." [The latter reference cannot be located. —Ed.]

had arrived at Independence, Missouri . . . with a printing press and a store of goods." The prospectus came with this letter. From this it would appear that the prospectus was printed at Independence, on the indicated date.

LILBURN W. BOGGS

{5} Star Extra. To the People of Missouri. Fellow-Citizens:— {Signed:} Lilburn W. Boggs. Jackson county, Mo. May 21, 1832. Broadside.

Not located. Title derived from the Columbia *Missouri Intelligencer and Boon's Lick Advertiser,* June 2, 1832, which reprinted what it called Boggs' "circular" in full. The Democratic convention at Jefferson City the previous November having placed Boggs before the electorate as "a suitable person to be voted for as Lieutenant-Governor," he here sets forth his political views: in favor of the reelection of Jackson, against the tariff, and against rechartering the Bank of the United States. This broadside appears to have been the second issue from the Mormon press at Independence.

THE EVENING AND THE MORNING STAR

{6} The Evening and the Morning Star. Independence, Mo., June, 1832. Vol. 1, No. 1. Published every month at Independence, Jackson County, Mo., by W. W. Phelps & Co. ____ cm.

Publication continued monthly until the Mormon press at Independence was broken up in July, 1833. The paper was then reestablished under the same name at Kirtland, Ohio, beginning with Vol. II, No. 15, December, 1833, and was continued monthly to the end of the volume, September, 1834. The 14 issues published at Independence numbered 112 pp., and the 10 issues published at Kirtland continued the pagination, pp. 113–192.

The first number of the *Star* evidently issued from the press in mid-June, 1832, for receipt of it was announced by the *Missouri Intelligencer and Boon's Lick Advertiser,* June 23, 1832, termed "not only neatly but even handsomely executed." The content of the *Star* ran so heavily to doctrinal matters that it aroused some dissatisfaction at church headquarters in Kirtland, and Joseph Smith wrote Phelps on January 14, 1833, "We wish you to render the *Star* as interesting as possible, by setting for the rise, progress, and faith of the Church, as well as the doctrine; for if you do not render it more interesting than at present, it will fall, and the Church suffer a great loss thereby." Thereafter more secular news appeared, less so at Independence than at Kirtland, after the violent events in Jackson County. The issues of the *Star* printed at Independence (June, 1832–July, 1833) were reprinted in the Church of Christ's *Evening and Morning Star* at Independence, June, 1911–June, 1913. See also No. 24.[2]

[2]Add further re the Kirtland issues and beginning of printing there. [The newspaper was republished, not really reprinted, at Kirtland, Ohio, following the saints' expulsion from the Independence area. —Ed.]

THE UPPER MISSOURI ADVERTISER

The Upper Missouri Advertiser. Independence, Mo. {June 27?, 1832}. No. 1. By W. W. Phelps & Co.

54 × 35 cm.

The date of the first number is assumed from the only copy located, July 11, 1832, No. 3, in the American Antiquarian Society. The *Advertiser* was to be "published weekly at Independence, at the rate of seventy five cents a year till the sheet is printed on both sides—then one dollar a year: in advance." The third issue was a 3-column broadside with no local news and two-thirds of its space given over to advertisements. It is presumed that publication continued weekly until the destruction of the Mormon press in July, 1833, but the only reference picked up from the contemporary press is in the *Missouri Intelligencer and Boon's Lick Advertiser,* November 10, 1832, reporting the arrival of Captain Bent & Company from Santa Fe.[3]

ALEXANDER CAMPBELL

Delusions. An analysis of the Book of Mormon, with an examination of its internal and external evidences, and a refutation of its pretences to divine authority. By Alexander Campbell. With prefatory remarks by Joshua V. Himes.

Boston: Benjamin H. Greene. 1832 {3}–16 pp. 22.2 × 13.6 cm.

The preface by Himes is dated Boston, August 14, 1832. As a Baptist minister anxious to combat Mormon proselyting, he had sent 600 miles for a copy of Campbell's review, to reprint and circulate it in New England, a course he thought Campbell would approve. Himes inveighs against the Mormons as a set of swindlers. He reprinted this text in 1842 {No. ____}, at a time when he had become a convert of William Miller, prominently identified with Adventist activities. Campbell's text was twice reprinted in London in 1850 as: *Mormonism weighed in the balances and found wanting: being an analysis of the internal and external evidences of the Book of Mormon.* The 1832 pamphlet itself was reprinted by the Morgan-Bruce Book Company, Salt Lake City, 1925.

Woodward 32

NANCY TOWLE

Vicissitudes illustrated, in the experience of Nancy Towle, in Europe and America. Written by herself. With an appendix of letters, &c. An engraving—and preface by Lorenzo Dow. (The profits, will be devoted to charitable purposes.) . . .

---

[3]It may be inferred that publication continued into 1833 since George A. Smith, *Journal of Discourses,* XI: 178 says "the Latter-day Saints established the first printing press in western Mo the *EMS,* pub at Indep in 1832–3 and the *Upper Mo Adv* in 1833 by W. W. Phelps." [Only a single issue of the *Upper Missouri Advertiser,* from July 1832, is recorded. —Ed.]

Charleston {S.C.}: Printed for the Authoress, by James L. Burges. 1832. (6), {5}–11, (1), {5}–294 pp. 14.5 × 8.5 cm. Front.[4]

The preface is dated Charleston, November 4, 1832; Dow's preface is dated Baltimore, May 21, 1832. Nancy was born in 1796 and began itinerant preaching in 1821. In mid-October, 1831, she made a voyage on Lake Erie and visited Kirtland, Ohio, where she met Joseph Smith, Sidney Rigdon, Martin Harris, and W. W. Phelps. She gives an unfavorable account of these men, of the inception of Mormonism, and of the distinctive doctrines of the Book of Mormon.

1833

NANCY TOWLE

{10} Vicissitudes illustrated, in the experience of Nancy Towle, in Europe and America. Written by herself. With an appendix of letters, &c. An engraving—and preface by Lorenzo Dow. (The profits, will be devoted to charitable purposes.) . . . Second edition.

Portsmouth {N.H.}: Printed for the Authoress, by John Caldwell. 1833. (6), {9}–310 pp. 15 × 9 cm. Front.

This edition is materially the same as that of 1832, but with some small verbal changes; and names rendered by initials in the first edition are spelled out.

Woodward 278

{10A JOSIAH PRIEST, AMERICAN ANTIQUITIES} [Inserted by hand. —Ed.]

{W. W. PHELPS}

{11} "The Evening and Morning Star" Extra. July 16, 1833.

{Independence: 1833} Broadside?

Not located. Title from *History of the Church*, 1: 378–387, which reprints the content of the extra in full. This was the last number of *The Evening and the Morning Star* to be published in Independence. The July issue of the *Star* had contained an editorial by W. W. Phelps, "Free People of Color," which though innocuous aroused the violent anger of the anti-Mormons in Jackson County. Phelps rushed this *Extra* into print in an effort to undo the damage, but it added fuel to the flames, and on July 20 the anti-Mormons, assembled as a mob, demanded the discontinuance of the Mormon printing establishment. When compliance was refused, they tore it down and pied the type.

---

[4] "Flake = 3 p.l. {5}–11 {1} 5–294 p. plates. 15 cm." [The manuscript notes citing "Flake" would have been added after at least the first meeting with Chad Flake of BYU, who began work compiling a comprehensive list of Mormon works from the Utah State Historical Society card file in 1967. —Ed.]

JOSEPH SMITH, JUNIOR

A Book of Commandments, for the government of the Church of Christ, Organized according to law, on the 6th of April, 1830.

Zion {Independence}: Published by W. W. Phelps & Co., 1833. {3}–160 pp. 11.9 × 7.5 cm.

The title-page is known in two states, with and without an ornamental border, the latter being more common. This work is the most celebrated rarity in Mormon bibliography. At the time of publication it was the westernmost American imprint, and it was also the first appearance in book form of Joseph Smith's revelations, though some had appeared surreptitiously in Ohio newspapers and by authority in *The Evening and the Morning Star.* The Book of Commandments was more important than the Book of Mormon, because the latter purported to be simply the record of God's dealings with a lost American civilization, whereas the Commandments were the voice of God heard in the Saints' own day specifically for their welfare. The social structure of Mormonism today is founded upon these and revelations subsequently given. At a special conference in Kirtland, November, 1831, it was decided to print the revelations in an edition of 10,000 copies but on May 1 following, a church council in Independence reduced the number to 3,000, W. W. Phelps, Oliver Cowdery, and John Whitmer being appointed a committee to review and prepare "such revelations for the press as shall be deemed proper for publication," to be printed at Independence under the style of "W. W. Phelps & Co." The printing had progressed to p. 160, near the end of Chapter LXV [*D&C* LDS 64, *D&C* CC 65], when the *Star* office was destroyed, in July, 1833. Perhaps a hundred copies of the incomplete work were bound from sheets preserved.

Among the Mormon churches the question of the completeness of the Book of Commandments has been extensively argued, but this argument is definitely settled by a fragment of the printer's manuscript surviving in the possession of the Reorganized Church, preserved by David Whiter, along with the Book of Mormon manuscript. A portion of this manuscript extending beyond the last part set in type, and exhibiting the printer's marks, has been photographically reproduced in Journal of History, April, 1921. This part of the manuscript comprises in all p. 117–122. A separate leaf which has also been preserved, two pages numbered 139 and 140, contains as chapter 83 the revelation now appearing as Section lxxxi of Doctrine and Covenants [*D&C* LDS 81, *D&C* CC 80].

The great historical interest of the *Book of Commandments* is that a number of the revelations were materially revised before they again issued from the Mormon press, e.g., those revelations now appearing in the Utah edition of Doctrine and Covenants as Sections v, vii, viii, x, xix, xx, xxvii, and xliii [*D&C* CC 5, 7, 8, 3, 18, 17, 26, 43]. Merely verbal changes were made in some others.

The Book of Commandments has been four times reprinted, by the Salt Lake *Tribune*, 1884, 1903 by C. Wickes, Lamoni, Iowa, 1903; and by Charles F. Putnam and Daniel Macgregor for the Church of Christ, Independence, 1926. + ?[5]

Woodward 17

---

[5]Haskins | Josiah Priest [Morgan's placement of these items in the margin suggests he planned to add both to the list. The Haskins reference is unqualified but seems to relate to the manuscript "+ ?" marks inserted at the end of the entry; note that only three subsequent editions of the *Book of Commandments* are cited. The reference to Priest is probably an item accepted as a contemporary parallel (*continued, next page*)

{James?} HIGBY

{13} {Pamphlet on the Mormons.}

{1833?}

Not located. Known only from a passage relative to speaking in tongues quoted in E.D. Howe's *Mormonism Unvailed* {No. 23}, and from this source reprinted in other works. It seems probable that it was printed in New York or Ohio. The first name of the author is not given by Howe, but very likely he was the James Higby who in a Mormon conference at Westfield, N.Y., June 23, 1833, was cut off from the church "for circulating false and slanderous reports, and not observing the order of the Gospel." The council, upon evidence submitted, "and from Brother Higby's own mouth, and the spirit he manifested," declared him guilty and "demanded his license and the Church record, which he utterly refused to give up." See *History of the Church*, 1: 355–356.

JOSEPH SMITH, JUNIOR

{14} {Revelation of December 16, 1833}

{Kirtland: 1833?}

Not located. Known from the Painesville *Telegraph*, January 24, 1834, which says that soon after news of the Mormon expulsion from Jackson County, "the following document (which they call a revelation) was printed and privately circulated among the deluded followers of the imposter, Smith." As a printed revelation, this is also referred to by Parley P. Pratt, *Millennial Star* 1 (1840): 65; the revelation, he says, "was printed at the time, and a copy of it sent to the Governor of Missouri, and another to Prisident {*sic*} Jackson. . . ." The revelation now appears in Doctrine and Covenants as Section ci [*D&C* LDS 101, *D&C* CC 98].[6]

1834

PARLEY PARKER PRATT, NEWEL KNIGHT, AND JOHN CORRILL

{15} {Expulsion of the Mormons from Jackson County, Missouri.}

{Liberty, Mo.?: Kelly & Davis?, 1834?} Broadside.

Not located. Described as a "voluminous" handbill, this broadside was published to voice the Mormon outrage over the expulsion from Jackson County. It was dated December 12, 1833, but had a postscript dated sometime after December 23, and was printed presumably on the only press immediately available to the Saints, that of Robert Kelly and William Davis, who had purchased W. W. Phelps' press to begin publication at Liberty on January

to the *Book of Mormon*, Josiah Priest, *American Antiquities, and Discoveries in the West* (Albany, N.Y.: Packard, Hoffman and White, 1833). —Ed.]

[6] Also add notes from Cowdery letterbook and *History of the Church*. [Probably a reference to the Oliver Cowdery letterbooks at the Huntington Library. —Ed.]

11, 1834, of the *Upper Missouri Enquirer*. Extracts from the handbill were printed in the *Missouri Intelligencer and Boon's Lick Advertiser*, February 1, 1834, and a summary in the St. Louis *Missouri Republican*, January 20, 1834. From these extracts it can be determined that the official Mormon history of the expulsion from Jackson County, as published in *History of the Church*, 1: 426–469, *passim*, is directly adapted from the handbill. Two copies were sent to President Jackson with a letter of April 10, 1834 (see *History of the Church*, 1: 483), but these have not been found among Jackson's imperfectly preserved papers, now in the Library of Congress. If Jackson referred the letter to one of the government departments, a specimen of the handbill may yet come to light in the National Archives.

} Reprint of the handbill by the Kirtland press. Cf Cowdery's letter to F. H. Denton, Feb 20, 1834

{A. T. CROW?}

} {Pamphlet on Mormonism.}

{Galena, Ill.: Office of The Galenian, 1834.}

Not located. Known only from references in *The Galenian* of March 14, and 21, 1834. in the former issue was printed an advertisement under the heading, "Book of Mormon, Extra—Chap. 1," which, parodying the style of that book, announced that the writer had published a work now available at a Galena store. The advertisement was signed, "Mahomet, J—s C—t, Jo Smith, & Co." In the next issue of *The Galenian* appeared an editorial apologizing for the advertisement. This said that a "young gentleman of the town, who was in the frequent habit of corresponding with the Galenian, made an arrangement at the office to have a pamphlet printed. . . . When the job was completed, the author was anxious to let the public know the fact, as many gentlemen of the town and country had subscribed for it . . . we conceived . . . that no well founded objection existed to the insertion of an *advertisement* for a patron of the office. He wrote it—it was put in type, the proof read by himself. Nor did we read it, until the paper had been circulated, and the advertisement pointed out to us by a *friend*. . . ." With this apology was printed a letter exculpating *The Galenian* by the author of the advertisement, signed "Editor Auxiliary No. Western Examiner. The *Western Examiner*, a free-thinkers' journal was published weekly at St. Louis during 1834–35 by J. Bobb. The paper's list of agents included Dr. A. T. Crow of Galena, who presumably was the author of the pamphlet.

See Byrd 214

W. W. PHELPS, D. WHITMER, JOHN WHITMER, {*ET. AL.*}

7} An Appeal.

{Kirtland, Ohio: Star Office. 1834} Broadside.

Not located. An extract, "merely a small portion," is reprinted in the *Missouri Intelligencer and Boon's Lick Advertiser*, October 11, 1834, where it is referred to as "a publication entitled 'An

Appeal,' issued from the Mormon Press, at Kirtland, Ohio . . . signed by W. W. Phelps, D. Whitmer, John Whitmer, E. Partridge, J. Corrill, Isaac Morley, P. P. Pratt, L. Wight, R. Knight, T. B. Marsh, S. Carter, Calvin Beebee. The object of this 'appeal' is to enlist the sympathies of the public in their behalf. . . ." Evidently it was published as a separate from its occurrence in the *Evening and Morning Star,* August, 1834. It seems to have been written early in July in Clay County, Missouri, and carried back to Kirtland by the returning members of Zion's Camp, the Mormon "army" which had journeyed to Missouri that spring in the hope of reinstating the outcast Mormons on their land in Jackson County. The text is reprinted in *History of the Church,* 2: 126–134.

LATTER DAY SAINTS' MESSENGER AND ADVOCATE

{18} Latter Day Saints' Messenger and Advocate. Kirtland, Ohio, October 1834. Vol. 1, No. 1. Whole No. 1 {Published by F. G. Williams & Co.} 25.5 × 15.5 cm.

The *Messenger and Advocate* was the successor to the *Evening and Morning Star,* and continued through three volumes of 12 numbers each, October, 1834–September, 1837, before giving way to the *Elders' Journal.* Pagination was continuous throughout, and had reached p. 576 (574?) when the publication was discontinued in 1837. F. G. Williams was publisher from October, 1834, to April, 1836. No publisher is stated for the issue of May, 1836, but in June, 1836, Oliver Cowdery became "editor and proprietor," so continuing through November, 1836. No publisher is stated for December, 1836, but the January, 1837, issue was published by "O. Cowdery & Co." Beginning with February, 1837, "J. Smith, Jr. & S. Rigdon" became publishers. Owing to the economic and legal situation arising from the failure of the Kirtland Bank, ownership passed to William S. Marks, as proprietor, beginning with April, 1837, and presumably so continuing to the end of the volume, September, 1837, though no publisher is stated in the last two issues. Oliver Cowdery was the first editor, serving in this capacity from October, 1834, to May, 1835. John Whitmer was editor from June, 1835, to March, 1836, when Cowdery again became editor. With the number for February, 1837, Oliver was succeeded by his brother, Warren A. Cowdery, who remained editor to the close of the volume. In the break-up of the Mormon society at Kirtland during 1837 Warren Cowdery became disaffected. By legal process the *Messenger and Advocate* establishment passed into his hands, and it appears that he intended continuing the periodical as a dissenting organ. The establishment was destroyed by fire on the night of January 15, 1838, however, and nothing came of these plans.

During its period of publication, the *Messenger and Advocate* was the official organ of the church; with letters, minutes of meetings, and doctrinal articles, it is an indispensable source for this period of Mormon history.

Sabin 50743, Woodward 122

NORTHERN TIMES

{19} {Northern Times, Extra.}

{Kirtland: 1834.} Broadside. ____ cm.?

Not located. What is known of this broadside is derived from the contemporary Ohio press. The *Northern Times,* though apparently projected in the fall of 1834, did not make its appearance until February following (see No. 28 [i.e., 27]). This and another broadside (No. 20) were occasioned by a political struggle in Geauga County over the removal of the county seat from Chardon to Painesville. The Painesville *Telegraph,* October 10, 1834, relates that on the previous Saturday night Samuel Butler and I. C. Paine had sent an emissary to the Mormons at Kirtland "for the purpose of obtaining a handbill that would call a public meeting" in opposition to the position taken by the *Telegraph.* Such a handbill was printed, for the *Telegraph* says, "We have been unable as yet to find any one to avow himself the author of the handbill, and therefore conclude it must have been procured from the Mormon prophet 'by way of revelation.' Upon the strength of the notice two meetings were held and attended by from 20 to 30 persons." The broadside thus appeared sometime between October 4–10. It was again referred to by the *Chardon Spectator and Geauga Gazette,* February 21, 1835, on noting the appearance of the first regular number of the *Northern Times,* the contents of which, it said, appeared to have been written six months earlier, "probably bout the time the two little black half sheets, under the same title, were sent out just before our late election."

{NORTHERN TIMES}

[illegible]} {Northern times, Extra.}

{Kirtland: 1834.} Broadside.

Not located. It was published during the week of October 4–10, 1834. See note to No. 19 above.

JOHN MASON PECK

[illegible]} A *Gazetteer of Illinois,* in three parts: containing a general view of the State; a general view of each county; and a particular description of each town, settlement, stream, prairie bottom, bluff, etc.—Alphabetically arranged. By J. M. Peck, Author of a Guide for Emigrants, etc.

Jacksonville {Ill.}: Published by R. Goudy. 1834. {iii}–viii, 376 pp. 14.8 × 10.3 cm.

The preface is dated Rock Spring {Illinois}, October, 1834. According to the 1837 edition {No. ___}, 4,200 copies were printed. In his remarks on "ancient Indian fortifications" in the Mississippi Valley, Peck makes a derisive allusion to the *Book of Mormon* and "that distinguished antiquarian Joe Smith," as being possible sources of information concerning these curiosities. In this section on religion, Peck speaks of the existence of "a small society of *Mormons* in Green county."

Byrd 191

DANIEL DUNKLIN

{22} Governor's Message. {To the senate and House of Representatives of the State of Missouri. Signed at end:} Daniel Dunklin. City of Jefferson, November 18, 1834.

Ordered by the legislature to be printed, but no copy located. Dunklin calls attention to the wrongful expulsion of the Mormons from Jackson County the previous November, and suggests the propriety of so amending the State laws as to make it possible to obtain convictions for violence committed against Mormons in Jackson County. The message was reprinted in the Senate and House journals {No. 25 and No. 26}, and in Floyd C. Shoemaker, *Messages and Proclamations of the Governors of the State of Missouri* (Columbia: [State Historical Society of Missouri], 1925), 1: [229–59]. The paragraph alluding to the Mormons is reprinted in *History of the Church*, 2: 171–172.

EBER D. HOWE

{23} Mormonism Unvailed or, A faithful account of that singular imposition and delusion, from its rise to the present time. With sketches of the characters of its propagators, and a full detail of the manner in which the famous Golden Bible was brought before the world. To which are added, inquiries into the probability that the historical part of the said Bible was written by one Solomon Spaulding, more than twenty years ago, and by him intended to have been published as a romance. By E. D. Howe.

Painesville: Printed and published by the Author. 1834. {v}–ix, {11}–290 {i.e., 292} pp. {The pagination is faulty, pp. 175 and 176 appearing twice in the numbering.} 17.9 × 10.6 cm.

This was the earliest formal history and is still one of the most important and fiercely controversial of the books about the Mormons, its influence felt in all that has been written about the Saints since 1834. Publication of the work was announced in Howe's paper, the Painesville *Telegraph*, on November 28, 1834. In his *Autobiography and Recollections of a Pioneer Printer*, Painesville: 1878, Howe says that he himself "wrote and compiled" this book, but a significant contribution to it he remarks more justly in a statement dated April 8, 1885 [*sic*], now in the Chicago Historical Society.* In 1833–1834, as he relates, several leading citizens of Geauga County employed doctor Philastus Hurlbut, who had been a Mormon elder but who had been excommunicated for alleged immorality, to go to New York and Pennsylvania to obtain affidavits concerning the bad repute of the Smith family during its residence there. Hurlbut did this, but also by accident stumbled over the story of a clergyman of Conneaut, Ohio, who in 1810–1811 had written a romance dealing with the pre-Columbian history of the American aborigines. Hurlbut concluded that with the connivance of Sidney Ridgon Joseph Smith had plagiarized the unpublished Spaulding "Manuscript Found," and on his return to Ohio commenced lecturing against the Mormons. {In the Painesville *Telegraph* for January 31, 1834, a committee of Kirtland citizens published a card on the subject, saying they were making arrangements for the

*[Morgan flagged this badly constructed sentence for further work, but since the manuscript was never revised, he did not correct the phrase. —Ed.]

publication and extensive circulation of a book to prove the *Book of Mormon* "a work of *fiction* and *imagination*."} Hurlbut's threats against Joseph Smith and the Mormons brought him afoul [of] the law, however, and he was put under bonds to keep the peace. He "finally came to me," Howe says, "to have the evidence he had obtained published. I bargained to pay him in books which I sent to him at Conneaut, O. Before publishing my Book I went to Conneaut and saw most of the witnesses who had seen Spaulding Manuscript Found and had testified to its identity with the Book of Mormon as published in my book and was satisfied they were men of intelligence and respectability and were not mistaken in their statements. I published only a small part of the statements Hurlbut let me have.... I was not acquainted with Hurlbut until he came to me to have his evidence published. He was good sized fine looking full of gab but illiterate and had lectured on many subjects." Hurlbut, it appears, was not a medical doctor, but as a seventh son had been named "Doctor Philastus Hurlbut" by his mother. Mormon rebuttals to Howe's book have always attributed the whole work to Hurlbut, meanwhile attacking his character, but apart from the affidavits and possibly the long introductory description of the contents of the Book of Mormon it seems to have been written and compiled by Howe himself from his own experience, his own inquiries, and the back files of his paper. The historically interesting feature of its information concerning the probable antecedents of the Book of Mormon is that the affidavits set up two antithetical propositions; the Spaulding affidavits, which powerfully conditioned all theorizing about the origin of the Book of Mormon from this time on, were not readily reconcilable with the affidavits from the former neighbors of the Smith family, which had portrayed them generally as ne'er do wells, and Joseph Smith specifically as a peeper in seer stones and a digger after buried treasures. According to the weight historians of Mormonism have given to one set of affidavits or the other, their books have been colored ever since. Within the Church, writers have rejected all the affidavits. An important feature of the book was the section given over to reprinting nine letters Ezra Booth had published in the Ravenna *Ohio Star* between October 13 and December 15, 1831, the first significant apostate publication against the church, Booth having traveled to Missouri in the summer of 1831 only to return to Ohio and break with the Saints.

The book was reissued in 1840 with a new title-page {No. ___}. Ezra Booth's letters were reprinted by R[obert] B. Neal as: *Anti-Mormon tracts, No. 6: Booth's Bombs*, Grayson Ky. 190–.[7]

1835

EVENING AND MORNING STAR

] Evening and Morning Star. Independence, Missouri, June, 1832. Vol. 1, No. 1.

{Kirtland: Reprinted and published by F.G. Williams & Co. 1835.} ___cm.

Nominally a reprinted version of the octavo size of the periodical that had been printed in Missouri and subsequently in Ohio in quarto size, actually this version of the *Star*

[7]Woodward 99 remarks the "Curious Frontispiece." Incorrectly gives title as *Mormonism Unveiled*. [The Neal item is described in Flake/Draper n.574. —Ed.]

embodied so many changes that it must be regarded as a separate work. The "reprinting," which had been promised in September, 1834, commenced in January, 1835, and continued serially to October, 1836. Revisions were made not only in letters and news items but in the revelations which had been printed in the original *Star*, the revelations as amended taking on the form in which they were printed later in 1835 in the first edition of *Doctrine and Covenants* {No. 37}.[8]

GENERAL ASSEMBLY OF THE STATE OF MISSOURI

{25} Journal of the Senate of the Eighth General Assembly of the State of Missouri, begun and held at the City of Jefferson, on Monday the seventeenth day of November, in the year of our Lord, one thousand eight hundred and thirty-four.

Fayette: Printed by W. S. Napton 1835. {3}-412 pp. 22.8 × 14 cm.

Governor Dunklin's message of November 18, 1834, is reprinted on pp. 12–24. No action was taken on that part of it relation to the Mormon difficulties.

GENERAL ASSEMBLY OF THE STATE OF MISSOURI

{26} {Journal of the House of the Eighth General Assembly of the State of Missouri, begun and held at the City of Jefferson, on Monday the seventeenth day of November, in the year of our Lord, one thousand eight hundred and thirty-four.}

{Fayette: Printed by W.S. Napton. 1835. {3}–544 pp. 22.8 × 14 cm.

The copy seen, at the Missouri historical Society, lacked a title-page. Dunklin's message was printed on pp. 24–36. No action was taken on the part of it relation to the Mormon difficulties.

NORTHERN TIMES

{27} {Northern Times. Kirtland, Ohio, February 20? 1835, Vol. 1, No. 1. Published by F.G. Williams & Co. Edited by O. Cowdery.}

From the fact that only two issues of this paper survive, October 2 and 9, 1835, Nos. 27 and 28, exact description of the *Northern Times* presents many difficulties. A weekly newspaper at Kirtland in the interest of Jacksonian Democracy was projected as early as November, 1833. In a letter of Nov. 24, 1833 to Horace Kingsbury Oliver Cowdery wrote, "Please inform our Jackson friends we shall print the Democrat in this place {Kirtland} as circumstance render it impossible to print it elsewhere." The prospectus appeared in December. The Painesville *Telegraph* of January 3, 1834, quotes the Warren *News-Letter* as saying that "proposals have been issued for publishing a Jackson paper in Kirtland, in this county. From other sources we learn that said paper is to be under the guidance of the Mormon leaders." By the autumn of 1834 plans had sufficiently matured that two extras were published {No. 19 and No. 20

[8]Note dates of reprinted issues

above}, but it was February before the first regularly numbered issue appeared. February 20 is conjectured to be the date from the fact that Fridays and Saturdays were most favored as days of publication and from the fact that the Painesville *Telegraph* of February 20, which sometimes contrived to get in late news, noted that "A paper entitled the *Northern Times* has made its appearance at Kirtland, in this county, and purports to be published by F. G. Williams & Co. and edited by O. Cowdery, one of the Mormon prophets," but had not seen the paper until the following week, commenting on it at length in the issue of February 28. The second issue was some time in coming, only an Extra {No. 31} appearing before mid-April. Judging from the numbering, this second issue appeared April 10, or perhaps April 11. If Friday was the day of publication for the earlier issues, it would have been April 10; but the Painesville *Telegraph* of July 10 quotes an animadversion of the *Cleveland Whig* upon "the 'Northern Times' of the 4th," indicating that this number, at least, was published on a Saturday. Publication continued as late as Vol. 1, No. 42, Wednesday January 13, 1836, for a fragment bearing that date is described in the *Deseret News*, January 9, 1870. The two issues that survive contain no locals of specific Mormon interest.

Olive Cowdery was first editor of the *Northern Times*, but about the middle May 1835, gave way to Frederick G. Williams (*History of the Church*, 2: 227), a change recorded via the Warren *News-Letter* by the Painesville *Telegraph* of June 12, 1835. The paper was strongly pro-Jackson the first issue being given up to a seven-column attack by Cowdery on the U.S. Bank. No other weekly paper was published in Kirtland during the Mormon tenure, though James M. Carrel in February, 1837, circulated the prospectus of another Democratic organ, *The News*, this prospectus being published in the Painesville *Republican*, March 30, 1837. Carrel had designed commencing publication about the first week of May, but in a card published in the *Republican* of April 20 he announced relinquishment of this project.[9]

{JOHN MASON PECK?}

} Mormonism, one of the delusions of Satan, exposed. By a Friend of Truth.

{Galena, Ill.? 1835?} 4 pp. 19.7 × 14 cm.

A tract which drew largely on Howe's book for its onslaught against Mormonism, perhaps the first work so to be influenced. The copy described once belonged to John Mason Peck. The likelihood of his being the author, apart from this circumstance, is suggested by the fact that some incidental matter in the tract is signed "P," and even more so by a fortuitous entry in the transcript of the journal of Levi Jackman, in the Utah State Historical Society. On May 18, 1835, at Carrolton, Green County, Ill., Jackman heard a Baptist missionary, Mr. Lemmon, contend against Mormonism—he "cryed out delusion, false propets etc. etc. having to assist him a little sheet filled with falsehood written by the Revr. Mr Peck." The probable plane and date of publication appear from a weather note on p. 4 of the tract: "We had now another cold snap. At Galena on the 3rd February, the Thermometer stood at 32 degrees below zero." Mention is made of the eastern mail having gotten into the Embarras river on the night of the 7th inst. No Cincinnati mail had been received for

[9]USIC [i.e., Church History Library] fragment of January 13, 1836, Dec. 2, 1855 {!!} says Flake

three weeks. A paragraph also is printed concerning a young actor who, while pretending on the stage of a theater at Nashville to be stabbing himself, actually did so and died.

Byrd 242

E. S. ABDY

{29} Journal of a residence and tour in the United States of North America, from April, 1833, to October, 1834. By E. S. Abdy, Fellow of Jesus College, Cambridge. . . .

London: John Murray, Albemarie Street. MDCCCXXXV {1835}. {Vol. I:} {v}–xii, 395 pp.; {Vol. II:} {v}–viii, 415 pp.; {Vol. III:} {v}–viii, 408 pp. 20.2 × 12.3 cm.

While in New York State in the summer of 1833, Abdy visited the scene of the anti-Masonic excitement of 1837–31, the area in which Joseph Smith grew up. Abdy talked with a resident who had known Smith, and commented on the anti-Masonic character of the Book of Mormon text. Abdy journeyed through the slave states before turning back to England. On voyaging up the Ohio River, at Ripley, Ohio, he noted down a hearsay account of the Mormons and their recent troubles. Abdy embarked for England October 16, 1834, and arrived at Portsmouth three weeks later. His book probably appeared early in the new year.

D. GRIFFITHS, JUNIOR

{30} Two years' residence in the new settlements of Ohio, North America: with directions to emigrants. By D. Griffiths, Jun.

London: Westly and Davis; Jackson and Walford; Kettering: Toller; Northampton: Abel and Wheeler; Daventry: Tomalin and Potts. 1835. {v}–vii, {9}–197 pp. 18.5 × 10.7 cm.

The preface is dated Long Buckley, February 1835. Griffith[s] sailed from Liverpool March 28, 1832, arriving in New York May 4. He lived in the Western Reserve, especially Huron County. His Chapter VI is largely devoted to the Mormons, based on information obtained from a Mormon elder, but of only slight interest.

NORTHERN TIMES

{31} {Northern Times, Extra.}

{Kirtland: 1835.} Broadside. ____ cm.?

After appearance of the first regular issue of the *Northern Times* in February, publication lapsed, only to resume with this extra at the last of March or first of April. What is known of this *Extra* is derived from the *Chardon Spectator and Geauga Gazette,* April 4, 1835: "The Northern Times appears to observe neither times or seasons. After the lapse of four or five weeks, from the first and only regular number, an *extra* has made its appearance, making three *extras* to one regular, much like the *extra* allowances made to some of the mail contractors—being greater than the regular . . . in this *extra*-ordinary times he is out upon Church and State, but as he seems to bear most heavily against the editor of the

Cleveland Whig—we will leave the work of defending against such sharp shooting to him. One office which this 'latter-day saint' assigns to democracy is new to us, he says, it 'will be a barrier in their way,' (alluding to such editors as of the Whig and ourself,) 'and may it remain and grow firmer until the United States of America shall again become a *wilderness,*'—a consummation (he might have added) devoutly to be wished. The editor may have spoken more truly of the effect of the kind of democracy he supports, than he intended."

PARLEY PARKER PRATT

} A short account of a shameful outrage, committed by a part of the inhabitants of the Town of Mentor, upon the person of Elder Parley P. Pratt, while delivering a public discourse upon the subject of the gospel; April 7th, 1835.

{Kirtland? 1835?} {3}–11 pp. 18.9 × 10.9 cm.

In an effort to keep Pratt from preaching atop the steps of a church in the town of Mentor on April 7, 1835, Grandison Newell and Elias Randall paraded the militia and a brass band around him. When this did not silence him, he was pelted with eggs. This pamphlet was probably printed soon after the occurrence, for Pratt does not mention the sequel. He haled Newell into court, and in October Newell was fined $47 damages by the Court of Common Pleas at Chardon.

WILLIAM LEETE STONE

} Matthias and his impostures: or, the progress of fanaticism. Illustrated in the extraordinary case of Robert Matthews, and some of his forerunners and disciples. . . . By William L. Stone.

New-York: Published by Harper & Brothers, No. 82 Cliff-Street, and sold by the principal booksellers throughout the United States. 1835. {3}–347 pp. 15.4 × 9.7 cm.[10]

The preface, which occupies the first 8 pp., is dated New-York, June 12, 1835. Matthias was the subject of a newspaper sensation of 1834–35, an evangelist who claimed to have dealings with God, and who gathered a following in New York City. In April, 1835, he was tried on the charge of having poisoned one of his converts but was found not guilty; however, he was given a jail sentence for assaulting his daughter with a whip. The evidence brought out showed him at best to have been of highly unbalanced mind. Stone's biography of Robert Matthews, or Matthias, as he called himself, is only relevant to this bibliography from that fact that he alludes to Mormonism as one of the distressing fanaticisms of the day.[11] After Matthias was released from prison, he made a journey west, and had a series of interviews with Joseph Smith at Kirtland on November 9–11, 1835, recorded by the latter in *History of the Church;* 2: 305–307. A notation in *Niles' National Register,* September 4, 1841, indicates that Matthias died at Asheville, N.C., July 21, 1841, aged 60.

[10]Flake says 8, 13–247 p. plan 16 cm.

[11]p. 316?

WILLIAM LEETE STONE

{34} {The same.} Third edition.

This edition has the same imprint and collation as the first. No second edition has come to light, which indicates either that the second edition was printed without edition number from the type of the first, or that this "third edition" was erroneously so called. The latter may be the case, for there is another third edition" with a slight variation in imprint.

WILLIAM LEETE STONE

{35} {The same.} Third edition.

New-York: Published by Harper & Brothers, No. 82 Cliff-Street. 1835.

{Same collation as first edition.}[12]

PARLEY PARKER PRATT

{36} The Millennium, a Poem. To which is added hymns and songs on various subjects, new and interesting, adapted to the dispensation of the fullness of times. . . .

Boston: Printed for Elder Parley P. Pratt, Author and Proprietor. 1835. {3}–52 pp. 14.2 × 9.4 cm. The collation is: title-page, copyright on verso; contents, pp. {3}–4; preface by "Author's Friend," with added paragraph by author, pp. {5}–7; blank page; poem in VI chapters on The Millennium, pp. {9}–30; IX songs, pp. 31–48; "Mission of the Twelve," pp. 49–50: Farewell Song, pp. 50–52.

This, Pratt's first exploitation of a vein often characteristic of his writing subsequently, was probably published in September. On May 4 he had left Kirtland on a mission to the Eastern States with the Twelve Apostles, and as he writes in his *Autobiography*, "The month of August found us in the State of Maine, and the mission completed. We now returned to Boston, and from thence home to Kirtland, where we arrived sometime in October. . . ." Presumably he published this little volume enroute home. The poem, "The Millennium," he reprinted in 1840 {No. ___}.

JOSEPH SMITH, JUNIOR

{37} Doctrine and covenants of the Church of the Latter Day Saints: carefully selected from the revelations of God, and compiled by Joseph Smith, Junior, Oliver Cowdery, Sidney Rigdon, Frederick G. Williams, (Presiding Elders of said Church.) Proprietors.

Kirtland, Ohio: Printed by F. G. Williams & Co. for the Proprietors. 1835. {iii}–iv, {5}–257, xxv pp. 15 × 10.2 cm.

---

[12] 1836 ed at ODW? [i.e., Ohio Weslyan University] Flake

This book is of high importance in the doctrinal evolution and social organization of Mormonism because the early revelations here crystallized in a final form. The order of the revelations adopted, however, has not been employed for all editions subsequently published. In the Book of Commandments the revelations had been printed in chronological order, but in this first edition of Doctrine and Covenants they were organized according to subject matter, insofar as the nature of the revelations permitted.

Publication of this work had been authorized on September 24, 1834, when the High Council at Kirtland appointed Smith, Cowdery, Rigdon, and Williams a committee "to arrange the items of the doctrine of Jesus Christ, the government of the Church of Latter-day Saints." In return for their work, these men were to "have the avails of the same" on publication. The labor was evidently completed by February 17, 1835, this being the date of the Preface, but it was August 17, 1835, before a church conference in Kirtland gave final sanction to the book as expressing the faith and belief of the church. Possibly the book was not distributed until sometime in 1836, for lack of book binding facilities made it necessary for Oliver Cowdery to go to New York in November, and as late as April 2, 1836, an arrangement is spoken of by which W. W. Phelps, John Whitmer, and David Whitmer were to "have five hundred book of Doctrine and Covenants, when bound, and five hundred Hymn Books."

In addition to the revelations, the book contained a section on Marriage and one on Governments and Laws in General, setting forth the entirely conventional view of the church at this time upon these matters,; the minutes of the General Assembly which had approved the book, and nine lectures on faith delivered in the theological school in Kirtland. These lectures seem to have been delivered by Sidney Rigdon, since he conducted the school and in later years reprinted them in a *Messenger and Advocate* of his own {No. ___}.[13] The lectures were retained in Doctrine and Covenants until 1920, when they were dropped as being not properly a part of the canon. They have been reprinted by N.B. Lundwall, Salt Lake City: 194–, with attribution to Joseph Smith.

Woodward 240

EMMA (HALE) SMITH

8} A Collection of sacred hymns, for the Church of the Latter Day Saints. Selected by Emma Smith.

Kirtland, Ohio: Printed by F. G. Williams & Co. 1835. {iii}–iv, {5}–121, (1), v pp. 10.8 × 7.2 cm.[14]

Emma Smith had been designated to compile a hymn book in a revelation of July, 1830. She obeyed the commandment, for on May 1, 1832, at Independence, W. W. Phelps was instructed to "correct and print the hymns which had been selected by Emma Smith in fulfillment of the revelation." From this action it has sometimes been supposed that a hymn book was printed in 1832, but this was not done, for at Kirtland on September 14,

---

[13][The Rigdon periodical noted is the *Latter Day Saints' Messenger and Advocate,* which was published at Philadelphia and Greencastle, Pennsylvania, between 1844 and 1846. Morgan later described it as no. 6 of *Churches of the Dispersion,* in the following volume. —Ed.]

[14]Flake = iv, {5}–121 {2} ii–v p. 11-1/2 cm.

1835, a church council decreed "that Sister Emma Smith proceed to make a selection of Sacred Hymns, according to the revelation; and that President W. W. Phelps be appointed to revise and arrange them for printing." In the library of the Reorganized Church is a tattered hymn book said by Catherine Salisbury, sister of Joseph Smith, to have been used by Emma in compiling her own work described as a Methodist hymnal, it is without title-page, and leaves before and after pp. 38–654 are lost. The surviving part contains hymns from No. 50 "Infinite grace," to an incomplete No. 1089, "Triumphant death of a brother."

This compilation by the wife of the Prophet was the first hymn book published for the new church, and contains 90 hymns in all. Among the hymns of Mormon origin is one still a favorite, "The Spirit of God like a fire is burning," by W. W. Phelps. "The Role of Hymnody in the Development of the Latter-day Saint Movement" has been treated in a doctoral dissertation by David Sterling Wheelwright, submitted to the University of Maryland, 1944.

1836

J. NEWTON BROWN

{39} Fassenden & Co.'s Encyclopedia of Religious Knowledge: or, Dictionary of the Bible, theology, religious biography, all religions, ecclesiastical history, and missions; containing definitions of all religious terms; an impartial account of the principal Christian denominations that have existed in the world from the birth of Christ to the present day, as well as those of the Jews, Mohammedans, and heathen nations together with the manners and customs of the East, illustrative of the Holy Scriptures, and a description of the quadrupeds, birds, fishes, reptiles, insects, trees, plants, and minerals, mentioned in the Bible; a statement of the most remarkable transactions and events in ecclesiastical history; biographical notices of the early martyrs and distinguished religious writers and characters of all ages. To which is added a missionary gazetteer, containing descriptions of the various missionary stations throughout the globe, by Rev. B. B. Edwards, editor of Quarterly Observer. The whole brought down to the present time, and embracing, under one alphabet, the most valuable part of Calmet's and Brown's dictionaries of the Bible; Buck's Theol. Dictionary; Abbott's Scripture Natural History; Wells' Geography of the Bible; Jones' Biographical Dictionary; and numerous other similar works. Designed as a complete book of reference on all religious subjects; and companion to the Bible: forming a cheap and compact library of religious knowledge. Edited by Rev. J. Newton Brown. Illustrated by wood cuts, maps and engravings on copper and steel.

Brattleboro' {Vt.}: Published by Fessenden and Co. 1836. {iii}–vi, (1), {9}–1275 (iii) pp. 26.4 × 17.8 cm.

The three pages at the end are not numbered, and the last page and a half are devoted to the publisher's advertisement. The preface, signed "J. N. B.," is dated Boston, January 1, 1835. The book was copyrighted in Vermont, 1835, and stereotyped by Shepard, Oliver, & Co., Boston. A preliminary title-page, not included in the numbering, reads: The Encyclopedia of Religious Knowledge. Illustrated with maps & engravings. Brattleboro', Vt. Published by Fessenden & Co.

The entry on "Mormonites" is based largely on the affidavit of March 29, 1834, by Isaac Hale, father-in-law of Joseph Smith, first printed in Howe's *Mormonism Unvailed.* The editor expresses sympathy for the Mormons in the recent outrages in Missouri, but declares that the facts should be known which show the real foundation of "the imposture," and refers his readers to the *Cross & Baptist Journal,* 1834.

JOSHUA SEIXAS

Supplement to J. Seixas' Manual Hebrew Grammar, for the Kirtland, Ohio, Theological Institution.

New-York: Printed by West & Trow, for J. Smith, Jun., S. Rigdon, O. Cowdery. 1836. {7}–32 pp. 15.2 × 9.9 cm. Collation is: Cover, verso blank; title-page, verso blank; Hebrew Alphabet, verso blank; Preface by O. Cowdery, pp. {7}–8; text, pp. {9}–27, followed by a Hebrew text which runs from the back of the book, pp. {32}–28.

Seixas had published in 1833 and 1834 two editions of a small Hebrew grammar. A Hebrew class was established at Kirtland in the winter of 1835–36, the Saints being desirous of studying the sacred scriptures "in the original," and Oliver Cowdery brought back with him from New York in November a quantity of Hebrew books. It was then decided to import a Jew to teach the Mormon students, and in January, 1836, Joshua Seixas, then teaching at a seminary in Hudson, Ohio, was hired as instructor. He began his classes the last week of January, and continued until the last week of March. The only clue in the *History of the Church* as to the provenance of this "Supplement" to his grammars is an entry of February 22, 1836, "At four o'clock {Joseph Smith} met Professor Seixas and the school committee at the printing office, to make some arrangements for the advancement of the several classes." Oliver Cowdery's Preface to the "Supplement," however, sheds a little more light, if not on the exact date of publication:

"The following lessons, being a mere abridgement of Mr. Seixas' Hebrew Grammar, were copied and arranged by himself, for the benefit of a class under his instruction, at the 'Kirtland Theological Institution,' there being only a few copies of his grammar in the country. The progress of this class being so proficient, in acquiring a knowledge of this ancient sacred language, by the introduction of those simple lessons, without burthening the mind with a large volume, detailing the critical niceties of the same, the undersigned has been induced to arrange the whole in a book form, adding a small amount of matter from the 1st of Genesis, that young students may the better preserve their {Hebrew} Bibles, till they are able to read and translate from any part of the same. He is confident, that, under the tuition of a proper preceptor, a student may obtain sufficient from this little abridgment, to enable him to enter the more nice parts of the language with ease and success.

"As this book has been arranged for the express benefit of the institution, with which I am so immediately connected, and in the future prosperity of which I feel an uncommon interest, I cannot but hope, that it may serve to facilitate the acquisition of a perfect knowledge of one of the best of books—*the Scriptures*—the introduction of which has served to dispel darkness, and disperse light unto every clime, where it has been permitted to enter, and remain free for the inspection of all."

The copy described once belonged to John E. Page. The Reorganized Church and the Utah church both have Hebrew Bibles used by various students in this winter's study.

JOSEPH SMITH, JUNIOR

{41] Prayer, at the dedication of the Lord's House in Kirtland, Ohio, March 27, 1836,—By Joseph Smith, jr. President of the Church of the Latter Day Saints.

{Kirtland: 1836.} 1 leaf. 31.2 × 20 cm.

This prayer has been printed on the inside pages of a leaf folded to make four pages. The prayer has since been accepted as inspired, and is now printed in Doctrine and Covenants as Section cix.[15] In a discourse at [Salt Lake City] on November 15, 1864, George A. Smith remarked, "When the dedication prayer was read by Joseph, it was read from a printed copy. This was a great trial of faith to many 'How can it be that the prophet should read a prayer?' What an awful trial it was, for the prophet to read a prayer!" (*Journal of Discourses*, 11: 9)

ORSON HYDE

{42} A Proclamation to all the churches, of every sect and denomination, and to every Individual into whose hands it may fall. By O. Hyde, preacher of the gospel, and citizen of the United States.

Toronto: August, 1836. Broadside. 46.4 × 30.1 cm.

As the earliest publication by a Mormon elder in Canada that has yet come to light, this broadside started Hyde on a distinguished career of firsts. Under a variant title, this was also the first Mormon tract published in England {No. ___}, and Hyde was also first to publish the Mormon message in Dutch and German {No. ___ and No. ___}. This 3-column broadside warns the world that it is in apostasy, must repent, be baptized in water for the remission of sins in the name and by the authority of the Lord Jesus Christ, and receive the gift of the Holy Ghost by the laying on of hands. Before its separate appearance in print, it had been published in the *Messenger and Advocate*, July, 1836, under the title, "A Prophetic Warning: To all the churches, of every sect and denomination, and to every individual into whose hands it may fall. By O. Hyde, Preacher of the Gospel." It was there dated June 16, 1836. As the *Messenger and Advocate* said the article had been obtained "through the kindness of a friend," and in effect apologized for publishing it without the sanction of the author, it may be that Hyde was unaware of its previous appearance in print when he published it as a broadside in Toronto in August. Both versions had an "N.B." at the end,[16] advising that "it is the present intention of the Author to publish, as soon as circumstances will permit, his Exposition of the Ancient Prophecies, in book form, showing their application to the times in which we live, together with such other matter as he shall think most beneficial to mankind at this period, under the *same title which this*

[15][D&C LDS 109, not in D&C CC. —Ed.]

[16][Note left blank; "N.B." is an abbreviation for *nota bene*, or an explanatory note added for the benefit of readers. —Ed.]

bears." Apparently this was never done, perhaps because Parley P. Pratt, a year later, went forcefully over the same ground in his *Voice of Warning* {No. ___}.

JOHN HAYWARD

The religious creeds and statistics of every Christian denomination in the United States and British Provinces. With some account of the religious sentiments of the Jews, American Indians, deists, Mahometans, &c. Alphabetically arranged by John Hayward.

Boston: Published by John Hayward. . . . 1836. {3} 156 pp. 18.4 × 11.4 cm.

Perhaps the first effort at an impartial presentation of the Mormon story, as Hayward calls it, "the sum and substance of the Mormon scheme." He prints the adverse Isaac Hale affidavit, a summary of the *Book of Mormon*, a statement of Mormon belief furnished him in Boston by Joseph Young, and several of the revelations from the 1835 *Doctrine and Covenants*. The statement from Young is particularly important as one of the earliest efforts to express concisely the "Articles of Faith" definitively enunciated by Joseph Smith in 1842.

PARLEY PARKER PRATT

"Doth our law judge a man before it hear him?"

Kingston, Canada: 1836. Broadside.

Not located. Title from Pratt's *Autobiography*. This "printed handbill," he says, was an outgrowth of a controversy with one Caird, an English preacher "who pretended to be sent of God by revelation." It contained "a statement of his lying {about the Mormons, in a public discourse}, a copy of the line I had really sent to him, and a statement of our doctrine as Latter-day Saints. . . . We circulated the handbills in the streets by hundreds, and then sent plenty of them by mail to our friends in Toronto. The bill was headed: '*Doth our law judge a man before it hear him?*' These events took place, apparently, in the early fall of 1836.

PARLEY PARKER PRATT

{Second broadside against Caird.}

Toronto: 1836. Broadside.

Not located. Title from Pratt's *Autobiography*. He followed Caird from Kingston to Toronto where he "applied to Wm. Lyon McKenzie, a printer and editor, in King street, for some large public halls or rooms of his, which would hold hundreds of people. He gave us the use of them, and we put out a bill, advertising two meetings, and pledging to the public that we would prove to a demonstration that Mr. Caird, who was now preaching in this city, was a false teacher, whom God had never sent, and that no believer in the Bible, who listened with attention, should go away unconvinced of that fact, or the truth of the doctrine of the Church of Jesus Christ of Latter-day Saints. In the handbill Mr. Caird was again invited to attend."

[*end of manuscript*]

A Bibliography of the Church of Jesus Christ Organized at Green Oak, Pennsylvania, July, 1862*

Introduction

This bibliography of the Church of Jesus Christ is presented as the first of a series of bibliographical contributions to the history of what are commonly called the lesser churches of Mormonism. The size and the scope of activity of the two largest groups, the Church of Jesus Christ of Latter-day Saints, and the Reorganized Church of Jesus Christ of Latter Day Saints [i.e., Community of Christ], have tended to obscure from public awareness the smaller churches that trace their origin to the Book of Mormon, and little serious effort has been made to investigate the literature of these churches.

As a result of this historical neglect, the principles and point of view of the smaller churches have either been ignored by students of Mormonism or seen from a hostile viewpoint, it being characteristic of all the Mormon churches to regard their rivals as misguided even when well-meaning. Thus it has not been possible, down to the present day, for any interested inquirer to take an objective look at the whole cultural phenomenon, root and all the branches, that is Mormonism.

The several Mormon churches having made it a common practice to identify their rivals by the names of personalities dominant in their history—the Utah church being called the Brighamite, the Reorganized church the Josephite, and the Church of Christ the Hedrickite, among others—the Church of Jesus Christ which today has headquarters at Monongahela, Pennsylvania, has been known in turn as the Bickertonite and the Cadmanite church, in allusion to William Bickerton, William Cadman, and the latter's son, W. H. Cadman, who have presided through most of its history.

After the breakup of the original Mormon Church following upon the murder of Joseph Smith in 1844, one faction was established by Sidney Rigdon, at first in Pittsburgh and later in Greencastle, Pennsylvania. In 1845 William Bickerton was baptized into Rigdon's church, but as it soon disintegrated, Bickerton was left at loose ends. In May, 1851, he associated himself with a branch of the Utah church at West Elizabeth, Pennsylvania, but he broke with this church the following March, apparently in reaction to the teachings on plural marriage beginning to spread among the membership. Bickerton

*[*Western Humanities Review* 4, no. 1 (Winter 1949–1950): 45–70. —Ed.]

continued preaching the gospel, and gradually gathered about him at West Elizabeth a nuclear organization numbering, by 1857, as many as ninety-three adherents. In 1859 those who accepted his leadership acknowledged him as a prophet, and subsequently he brought forth a revelation foreshadowing the formal organization of a church. In October, 1861, he was sustained prophet and president, with two counselors, and at the July conference of 1862, twelve apostles and a number of evangelists were ordained. The organization of the church was considered to have been completed at this July conference, and the Church of Jesus Christ ever since has regarded 1862 as the year of its founding. It was legally incorporated at Pittsburgh in 1865.

The point of view of the Church of Jesus Christ is that it came into existence, not through fission from any faction of the original church, but, rather, "by way of revelation and heavenly experience" vouchsafed the members in the period 1859–62. Though claiming divine succession to the authority and priesthood restored through Joseph Smith in 1829, it accepts only the Book of Mormon from among the scriptures brought forth by Joseph Smith, and rejects as uncanonical the Doctrine and Covenants, the "Book of Abraham," and the Inspired Revision of the Bible. More philosophically than some of the churches, it rejects also the terms "Mormons" and "Mormonism," which from 1830 the outside world has found so convenient and insisted on applying to Joseph Smith's followers and doctrine. The Church of Jesus Christ has always been monogamic, and its teachings on marriage as a binding contract between man and woman remain so orthodox that even today divorce is countenanced almost solely on the grounds of adultery. An interesting feature of the church's doctrine is that it discriminates in no way against Negroes or members of other racial groups, who are fully admitted to all the privileges of priesthood. It has taken a strong stand for human rights, and was, for example, uncompromisingly against the Ku Klux Klan during that organization's period of ascendancy after the first World War.

The Church of Jesus Christ has always been strongest in numbers in Pennsylvania, Ohio, New York, New Jersey, and Michigan, but its conception of its responsibility to bring the gospel to the Indians has exerted a strong westward pull from the earliest days. In July, 1868, the church dispatched three elders to the Indian Nation on a "mission to the Lamanites," but a year later "practically laid aside and abandoned this mission." The project of an Indian mission nevertheless persisted, bound up with the concept of the "gathering" of the church to a "stake of Zion" in the West, and in July,

1874, a committee was appointed to devise ways and means. Next year the conference passed a resolution authorizing the removal of church headquarters to Zion Valley (now St. John) in southwestern Kansas. With William Bickerton president over the whole church, Eli Kendall became president of the church in the West, and William Cadman president of the church in the East. Bickerton himself settled with the western branch. Subsequently friction arose, and in 1880 Bickerton was disfellowshipped, Cadman being elected president over the whole church. Bickerton returned to the church in 1902, and died in the faith in January, 1905, the headquarters meantime (1887) having been returned to Pennsylvania.

By 1904 Cadman was the only apostle still living of those ordained in 1862, and accordingly the church was "reorganized," or the quorums filled up, eleven new apostles being ordained. Cadman died on November 6, 1905, and at the July conference following, Alexander Cherry was chosen to be third president of the church. New friction between the eastern and western branches arose, however, and became centered around a doctrinal dispute over the nature of life in the millennium. In 1907 half the Quorum of the Twelve broke away to establish a Re-Organized Church of Jesus Christ, with branches in Kansas and Pennsylvania. This church was incorporated on April 8, 1908, and is represented in this bibliography by a separate group of five titles.

Another schism developed in 1914, as a delayed reaction to an action taken by the church conference in 1908. At that time, in what was regarded as a return to the organizational pattern on which the church was established in 1862, a quorum of three had been elevated from the Twelve to direct the church. Under the leadership of James Caldwell, a few members in Monongahela organized a protestant group under the name "Primitive Church of Jesus Christ." With this church the surviving members of the Re-Organized Church eventually associated themselves. In 1949 the Primitive Church had a building and an organized congregation in Erie, Pennsylvania, with scattered members elsewhere, but details are lacking. The president of the church currently is Lawrence C. Dias, of Lawrence Park, Erie, Pennsylvania. Since 1914 the Church of Jesus Christ has carried on extensive missionary labors in the Eastern States, particularly among persons of Italian descent, a fact reflected in Italian-language editions of several works listed in this bibliography, including an Italian Book of Mormon. Renewed interest in the "Indian Mission" has also led to missionary work among the Indians on reservations in New York and in Canada.

Alexander Cherry died on August 31, 1921. William Henry Cadman, son of William Cadman, was chosen as president at the July conference, 1922, and has served in that office since. The church today has thirty-five organized congregations in eight states, including the province of Ontario in Canada, and has a total membership estimated at between 1,600 and 1,800. Headquarters are at the corner of Lincoln and Sixth Streets, Monongahela, Pennsylvania.

In the preparation of this bibliography I have had every assistance from the president of the church, Mr. W.H. Cadman. Mr. W. S. Crosby of Youngwood, Pennsylvania, has been most helpful in providing information about and copies of the publications of the Reorganized Church of Jesus Christ, and Mr. Lawrence C. Dias furnished me with a statement concerning the Primitive Church of Jesus Christ. Dr. George B. Arbaugh of Augustana College, Rock Island, Illinois, supplied me with a leaflet I had been unable to obtain elsewhere, while Professor M. Wilford Poulson of Brigham Young University, Mr. A. William Lund, Assistant Historian of the Church of Jesus Christ of Latter-day Saints at Salt Lake City, and Mr. S.A. Burgess, Assistant Historian of the Reorganized Church of Jesus Christ of Latter Day Saints at Independence, were helpful in furnishing information. The two latter also kindly checked the collections of their churches against the titles listed in my bibliography. The New York Public Library, the Library of Congress, and the Utah State Historical Society likewise have been of service.

Where place of publication and name of printer appear in brackets, the information has been derived from the work itself, other than from the title page; from Mr. Cadman's history of the church; or from correspondence with Mr. Cadman.

Location symbols employed are those of the Union Catalog in the Library of Congress. The census lists are not intended to be comprehensive, representing only the collections of a few key libraries.

DLC	Library of Congress, Washington, D.C.
MoInRC	Reorganized Church of Jesus Christ of Latter Day Saints, Independence, Mo. [i.e., Community of Christ]
NN	New York Public Library, New York, N.Y.
OClWHi	Western Reserve Historical Society, Cleveland, Ohio.
OO	Oberlin College, Oberlin, Ohio.
PMonC	Church of Jesus Christ, Monongahela, Pa.
UHi	Utah State Historical Society, Salt Lake City, Utah.
USlC	Historian's Office, Church of Jesus Christ of Latter-day Saints, Salt Lake City, Utah.
Morgan	Personal collection of Dale L. Morgan.*

*[Morgan's personal collection of publications from the lesser Mormon churches was given to the University of California and today is among the collections of the Bancroft Library. Much of his duplicated material (chiefly microfilm and photostat) was given to the Utah State Historical Society. —Ed.]

Bibliography

1855

{CHURCH OF JESUS CHRIST}

Hymns and Spiritual Songs, Original and Selected{.} For the use of the Church of Jesus Christ of Latter Day Saints. Revised and Compiled by W. Bickerton, T. Bickerton, and J. Stranger. Elders of the Church in West Elizabeth, Pa.

Pittsburgh: Printed by J. T. Shryock Book and Job Printer. 1855. 314 pp. 8.8 × 8 cm.

This first hymn book was also the first book of any kind published by the church, and in fact its publication anticipated by seven years the formal organization of the church. The need for hymn books of their own, even in advance of doctrinal works expounding their faith, has been felt by almost all of the Mormon churches. The compilers of this work were William and Thomas Bickerton and Jacob Stranger. Although the title page uses the words "revised and compiled," it is believed this means that a selection was made from hymn books outside the church at West Elizabeth, rather than that a still earlier hymnal had been published. The work has 339 hymns, and an index which is included in the pagination; the only copy known is bound in leather.

PMonC

CHURCH OF JESUS CHRIST

The Ensign: or a Light to Lighten the Gentiles, in which the Doctrine of The Church of Jesus Christ of Latter-Day Saints, is Set Forth, and Scripture Evidence Adduced to Establish it. Also, a Brief Treatise upon the Most Important Prophecies Recorded in the Old and New Testaments, which relate to the Great Work of God of the Latter Days. Published by the Authority of the Church of Jesus Christ of Latter-Day Saints. William Bickerton, Charles Brown, George Bonnes {Barnes}, William Cadman, Joseph Astin, Publishing Committee.

Pittsburgh: Printed by Ferguson & Co., 84 Fifth Street (Gazette Building). 1863. 26 pp. 21.5 × 14 cm.

The only known copy is in the possession of the church at Monongahela. Another copy, in the possession of the Reorganized Church of Jesus Christ of Latter Day Saints, at Independence, Mo., was apparently burned in the Herald Office fire in 1907. Extracts have been reprinted in the *Law and Order* book {No. 22}, in W. H. Cadman's *A History of the Church of Jesus Christ* {No. 50}, in the church periodicals, and in Joseph and Heman C. Smith, *History of the {Reorganized} Church of Jesus Christ of Latter Day Saints,* vol. 3, pp. 74–77. It contains a statement by William Bickerton concerning the founding of the church;

minutes of conferences and ordinations between 1861 and 1863; an undated revelation appointing Bickerton a seer, translator, prophet, apostle, and elder of the church; a declaration against polygamy; a subsequently well-known hymn by William Cadman, "The Lord did raise up Joseph Smith"; and an extract reprinted from Benjamin Winchester's *Gospel Reflector* (Philadelphia, 1841).

PMonC

1864

CHURCH OF JESUS CHRIST

{3} *The Ensign: or a Light to Lighten the Gentiles, in which the Doctrine of the Church of Jesus Christ of Latter-Day Saints, is Set Forth, and Scripture Evidence Adduced to Establish it. Also, A Brief Treatise upon the Most Important Prophecies Recorded in the Old and New Testaments, which Relate to the Great Work of God of the Latter Days.* Published by the authority of the Church of Jesus Christ of Latter-Day Saints. West Elizabeth, Allegheny Co., Pa.

Pittsburgh: Printed by Ferguson, 84 Fifth Street, (Gazette Building). 1864. {27}–52? pp. 21.5 × 14 cm.

The number of pages is assumed from the number in the 1863 *Ensign*, the pagination of which is carried on in this pamphlet or "church paper," as it was contemporaneously referred to by the membership. Both the known copies end in the middle of a sentence at the end of page 50, lacking what was presumably the last leaf. This issue of the *Ensign* is principally devoted to doctrinal articles, one of them signed by William Cadman, but also contains two hymns; a revelation given in 1859; extracts from the minutes of a conference held at "Greenock," Pa., on January 2, 3, and 5, 1864; an extract from the private journal of Cadman describing a missionary tour in Pennsylvania during July and August, 1863; some extracts from the Book of Mormon; and some doctrinal matter reprinted from Benjamin Winchester's *Gospel Reflector* (1841).

The caption title is: "The Ensign. All ye inhabitants of the world, and dwellers on the earth, see ye when He lifteth up an ensign on the mountains: and when He bloweth a trumpet, Hear ye.—Isaiah 18:3." At head of the cover title is a notice that copies of the *Ensign* are obtainable from Thomas Bickerton, West Elizabeth, Allegheny Co., Pa. From the church annals, it appears that this pamphlet was published sometime between January and March, 1864.

MoInRC, PMonC

CHURCH OF JESUS CHRIST

{4} *Hymns and Spiritual Songs Original and Selected{.} For the use of the Church of Jesus Christ of Latter Day Saints.* Revised and Compiled by the Elders of the Church in West Elizabeth, Pa., U.S.

Pittsburgh: Printed by Ferguson, 84 Fifth Street. 1864. 376 pp. 11.1 × 7.1 cm.

This second hymnal published by the church is, Mr. W. H. Cadman remembers, the one in use when he was a boy (he was born in 1876), and was not superseded until sometime in the nineties. It contains 390 hymns.

PMonC

1875

{D. L. SHINN}

The Adventure. Clarksburg, West Virginia. Edited by D. L. Shinn. Vol. I, Nos. I–V. 72 pp. June–October, 1875.

This periodical is known only from having been offered for sale in 1880 by the New York bookseller, Charles L. Woodward, in his catalog, *Bibliothica Scallawagiana.* His file, he said, was "Supposed to be complete. The 'Adventurer' was Eld. D. L. Shinn. . . . I sent him the amount of a year's subscription, but having myself witnessed the early death of many periodicals, requested him to send me two copies, and promised him that if I ever saw the sixth number, I would send him another dollar. He sent me but one copy, and I never saw the sixth number. Perhaps the Elder was translated." Although Mr. W. H. Cadman has never heard of this periodical, Shinn's name appears intermittently in the church annals as recorded by Mr. Cadman {No. 50}. At the January conference of 1870 at Wheeling, West Va., Shinn and John Stevenson were commissioned to go and preach the gospel; a vision by him is also recorded. At the Wheeling conference four years later, the church delegated a committee "to look into the matter of the Church buying a Printing Press." By 1876 the church had evidently acquired such a press, "which was to be shipped to Bro. Shinn, but instead it was wanted in Kansas by Bro. Bickerton." Except for a notation that a copy of the minutes of the July conference of 1880 were to be sent to Shinn at Clarksburg, there is no further mention of him.

189–?

CHURCH OF JESUS CHRIST

Hymns and Spiritual Songs, original and selected for use in the Church of Jesus Christ. Compiled by the Elders of the Church at West Elizabeth, Pa., U.S.A. Revised edition.

Greensburg, Pa.: Printed by "Press of Greensburg Press Co." n. d. 407, {11} pp. 11.4 × 10.2 cm.

This edition of the hymn book, according to Mr. Cadman, was published between 1890 and 1900. The eleven pages at the end are devoted to an index. The book was leather-bound, some copies having a flap cover.

PMonC

1894

WILLIAM CADMAN

{7} *Daniel's Little Horn*{.} By Wm. Cadman, West Elizabeth, Pa., U.S.A.

{Pittsburgh, Pa.?} {1894.} 16 pp. 25 × 15.5 cm.

Cover title. The caption title is: "The Little Horn by Daniel the Prophet. See Daniel—7th Chapter, 8th Verse." A doctrinal pamphlet applying the imagery of Daniel to modern history, the "little horn" being the United States. It was evidently published early in 1894, since the church resolved at the July conference of 1894 "that we endorse the contents of the Pamphlet, as a correct interpretation of the Prophecies of Daniel as recorded."

DLC, MoInRC, NN, PMonC, UHi, USlC, Morgan

1897

{WILLIAM CADMAN}

{8} *Faith and Doctrines of the Church of Jesus Christ,* Published by Order of the Church in 1897. Committee: Wm. Cadman, J. L. Armbrust, W. D. Wright. West Elizabeth, Pa.

{Pittsburgh, Pa.?} {1897.} 24 pp. 23.5 × 15.3 cm.

Cover title. The caption title is: "The Faith and Doctrine of the Church of Jesus Christ." At the April conference in 1897, "Bro. Wm. Cadman presented the manuscript of the 'Articles of Faith' for consideration. It was printed in Pamphlet form in this same year under the title, 'Faith and Doctrines of the Church of Jesus Christ'." The pamphlet contains twenty-seven articles of faith; declarations on marriage and on earthly governments and laws; rules governing conferences; and a definition of "Differences with People Called Latter Day Saints." A new edition was printed in 1948 {No. 53}.

MoInRC, PMonC, USlC, Morgan

1899

WILLIAM CADMAN

{9} *Religious Experiences and Expectations.* By Wm. Cadman, West Elizabeth, Pa. U.S.A.

Pittsburgh: Devine & Co., Printers, 444 Fifth Ave., 1899. 23 pp. 19.7 × 13 cm.

Cover title. The caption title is: "To Conference Assembled, October, 1899." The church annals record that at this conference Cadman "presented to the Saints an article he had written on the past experience of this Church and our future hopes," which was ordered to be published in pamphlet form. It is more especially concerned with the Indian Mission and the concept of gathering to a home in the West, but it also argues the relevance of certain Bible passages to the future of the church. Extracts are currently (1949) being reprinted in the *Gospel News* {No. 49}.

MoInRC, NN, PMonC, UHi, USlC, Morgan

WILLIAM CADMAN

Faith and Doctrines of the Church of Jesus Christ, Series No. 2. Published by Order of the Church in 1902. By Wm. Cadman, West Elizabeth, Pa., U.S.A.

Roscoe, Pa.: Roscoe Ledger Print. {1902} 20 pp. 23.2 × 15.5 cm.

Cover title. The caption title is: "Polygamy and Other Forms of Adultery Described, Etc." According to the church annals, William Cadman was authorized to prepare this pamphlet at the January conference, 1902. Five thousand copies were to be printed. Apart from its principal doctrinal purpose, described in the caption title, the pamphlet includes some reminiscences by Cadman concerning his early life and first association with the church.

MoInRC, PMonC, UHi, USlC, Morgan

1905

CHURCH OF JESUS CHRIST

Law and Order of the Church of Jesus Christ{.} Organized July 7, 1862.

{Roscoe, Pa.:} Roscoe Ledger Print. 1905. 12 pp. 17.7 × 10.3 cm.

Three variants of this pamphlet were published, one with a plain cover, one with a cover portrait of William Bickerton, and one with a cover portrait of William Cadman. Internally the three are identical, containing a list of apostles and evangelists of the church as it was incorporated June 10, 1865, and a list of apostles and evangelists named when it was reorganized July 6, 1904; rules governing conferences; order of business; laws governing the Church of Jesus Christ; and the scriptural law of offenses. The pamphlet seems to have been prepared by a committee consisting of Allen Wright, W. T. Maxwell, and W. S. Crosby.

MoInRC, PMonC, Morgan

CHURCH OF JESUS CHRIST

The Gospel Reflector. Roscoe, Pa. Edited by Alexander Cherry. Vol. I, No. 1, August, 1905. 4 pp. 33.1 × 25.5 cm.

The project of publishing a church periodical, brought up at the April conference in 1903, was finally sanctioned at the July conference, 1905. Alexander Cherry was named editor, to be assisted by Samuel Sanders. Publication continued monthly to August, 1910, Vol. III, No. 13, with 24 numbers to the volume. The only known file, at Monongahela, ends with the issue for August, 1910, and it is believed this was the last published. Many articles which appeared in the *Reflector* have been reprinted in the present-day Church organ, the *Gospel News* {No. 49}, and some others in Mr. Cadman's history {No. 50}. Cherry, then president of the Church, remained editor throughout.

PMonC

1906

CHURCH OF JESUS CHRIST

{13} *Constitution and By-Laws of the Missionary and Benevolent Association of the Church of Jesus Christ.*

Roscoe, Pa.: Roscoe Ledger Print. 1906. 8 pp. 12.3 × 8.9 cm.

The title explains the purpose of this little work. A revised edition was published in 1942. {No. 46}.

PMonC

1919

CHURCH OF JESUS CHRIST

{14} *The Saints' Hymnal.*

Monongahela, Pa.: Printed by Geo. Ashworth. {1919} 165 pp. 17.8 × 12.7 cm.

The need of a new hymn book, felt as early as July, 1913, was answered at the October conference of 1919, when 1,000 copies of a hymnal were ordered printed. The book contained 200 hymns. Published as a frontispiece was the portrait of Nephi Federer, who had been first counselor in the church and much interested in singing.

PMonC

1920

{W. H. CADMAN}

{15} *The Way of Salvation* {by} W.H. Cadman, Charles Ashton, Committee. Published by the Ladies' Uplift Circle of the Church of Jesus Christ.

Monongahela: Printed by Zimmer Printing. {1920} 7 pp. 20.4 × 10.2 cm.

A small tract setting forth the doctrinal argument of the church. It has twice been reprinted in English {No. 26 and No. 36}, and twice in Italian {No. 16 and No. 40}.

PMonC

1921

{W. H. CADMAN}

La Via della "Salvazione" Publicata del Circolo Sollevare delle Donne della Chiesa di Gesu Cristo.

{Monongahela: Printed by Zimmer Printing. 1921} 8 pp. 20 × 9.9 cm.

A history of the Ladies' Uplift Circle written by Mrs. Sadie B. Cadman, printed in Mr. Cadman's history of the church, notes that on March 24, 1921, the Circle "met and decided to print leaflets, 'The Way of Salvation' in Italian." The translation, Mrs. Cadman says further, was done by Sister Marietta Veneri of Monesson, Pa. Reprinted in 1938 {No. 40}.

PMonC

1923

{W. H. CADMAN}

Retrogression of the Primitive Church. Published by The Ladies' Uplift Circle of the Church of Jesus Christ. {Signed:} Wm. H. Cadman, Jr., President of the Church. Thurman S. Furnier, Recording Sec'y of the Church.

n.p. {1923} 7 pp. 20.5 × 9.7 cm.

Caption title. According to Mrs. Cadman, "In March, 1922 . . . a request was sent to the Church {by the Ladies' Uplift Circle} to write an article on the falling away and restoration of the Gospel," and the church annals note that at the April conference, 1923, Furnier and Cadman were delegated to write such an article. At the April conference, a year later, "The Article written by Bro. Cadman was read and accepted, then given to the Ladies' Uplift Circle to be put into print, under the title 'The Retrogression of the Primitive Church.'" Reprinted in 1936 {No. 35}.

PMonC, USlC

ZADOC BROOK

Introduction to the Book of Mormon. {At end:} Written by Z. Brook.

n.p. {1923} 7 pp. 20.5 × 9.7 cm.

Although several times printed by the Church of Jesus Christ, this commentary on the Book of Mormon was not written by a member of the church. Brook headed a small Mormon faction which in the 'Fifties and 'Sixties had headquarters at Kirtland, Ohio. His "Introduction" was first printed as the preface to a re-issue of an edition of the Book of Mormon printed in New York in 1858 as a commercial venture. It appears that the plates of the 1858 edition, which was printed by J. O. Wright & Company, were bought by Russell Huntley, a prosperous member of Brook's faction, and 4,000 copies reprinted sometime between 1859 and 1861, a new introduction by Brook replacing that of Wright. Although Brook's faction soon disappeared, this edition was used to supply the Reorganized Church until their own first edition was printed in 1874, Huntley himself eventually becoming a member of the Reorganized Church. Brook's "Introduction," was first reprinted in the text of an article by Walter W. Smith, "The Book of Mormon, Its Translation and Publication," in *Journal of History,* January, 1921, vol. XIV, pp. 19–26.

A copy of the Brook-Huntley edition of the Book of Mormon is in the possession of the Church of Jesus Christ, and was used in the publication of the Book of Mormon in its own title in 1934. The idea of printing the Brook "Introduction" in advocacy of the claims of the church was evidently conceived early in 1923, for at the April conference of that year, it was reported that this leaflet was in the hands of the printer, and that 1,000 copies were being printed. It was reprinted in 1934 in the church's own edition of the Book of Mormon {No. 31}, and again separately in 1936 {No. 33}.

PMonC

CHURCH OF JESUS CHRIST

{19} *Saints Hymnal of the Church of Jesus Christ.*

Monesson, Pa.: Printed by Goodlow Thomas. 1923. 120 pp. 19.8 × 13.7 cm.

At the July conference, 1923, it was reported by the Hymn Book Committee that 2,000 copies were being printed. A portrait of Alexander Cherry appears as the frontispiece.

PMonC

1924

{W. H. CADMAN}

{20} *What Is the Indian Mission?* {By W. H. Cadman.}

n.p. January 5th, 1924. 4 pp. 21.7 × 12.7 cm.

According to Mrs. Cadman, "The Italian Sisters from Glassport asked for a better understanding of the Indian Mission Work, so at our request Brother W. H. Cadman wrote the article 'What Is the Indian Mission?' which the Circle had printed." Reprinted in 1936 {No. 37}.

PMonC

ALEXANDER CHERRY AND CHARLES ASHTON

{21} *Article on "Book of Mormon and Latter Day Work."* Begun by Brother Alex. Cherry (Now Deceased) and Continued by Brother Charles Ashton.

n.p. {1924} 6 pp. 21.7 × 12.7 cm.

Alexander Cherry, then president, had been designated by the church at the conference of April, 1920, to write an article on the *Book of Mormon.* Left incomplete at his death in 1921, it was finished by Charles Ashton and at the April, 1923, conference turned over to the church for publication. A year later, 1,000 copies were printed. Reprinted in 1936 {No. 32}.

PMonC

1925

CHURCH OF JESUS CHRIST

Law and Order of the Church of Jesus Christ{.} Post Office Address Monongahela, Pa. . . . Organized July 7, 1862, and Incorporated June 10, 1865. Published 1925{.}

Uniontown, Pa.: Herald-Genius. 1925. {3}–29 pp. 19.7 × 12.9 cm.

The church annals note that at the July conference, 1925, the committee designated to arrange a code of law and order for the church made their final report, "and their work was accepted and ordered published." The pamphlet retained the substance of the 1905 *Law and Order* book {No. 111}, but defined the "Laws Governing the Church of Jesus Christ" at greater length, and also reprinted from the 1863 *Ensign* its account of the early history of the church. Two thousand copies were printed.

PMonC, Morgan

1927

SADIE B. CADMAN

} *Scriptural Lessons.* Composed by Sadie B. Cadman. Published by The Ladies' Uplift Circle. A. D. 1927.

Uniontown, Pa.: Herald-Genius. 1927. {5}–56 pp. 19.7 × 13.6 cm.

Mrs. Cadman having written a series of lessons suitable for Sabbath School work, and a committee having reported favorably, the church at its April, 1926, conference agreed to place the manuscript in the hands of the Circle for publication. Reprinted in 1941 {No. 44}.

PMonC

1929

CHURCH OF JESUS CHRIST

4} *The Last Witness Dead.*

n.p. {1929} 7 pp. 15.3 × 10 cm.

The church annals make note at the July conference, 1929, "The committee that had been appointed to take care of the printing of the dying testimony of David Whitmer (one of the three witnesses to the Book of Mormon) reported that it had been published by the Ladies Uplift Circle and was now ready for distribution. It was titled, 'The Last Witness Dead.'" The text of the leaflet consists of the remarks of the *Richmond* (Mo.) *Democrat* on the occasion of Whitmer's death, together with two short extracts from Whitmer's own writings affirming the truth of the Book of Mormon. Reprinted in 1936 {No. 34}.

PMonC

JOSEPH SMITH, JUN.

{25} *Il Libro di Mormon Sommario Scritto per Mano di Mormon Sulle Tavolette Preso dalle Tavolette di Nefi.* . . . Tradotto in Lingua Inglese da Giuseppe Smith, il Giovane. Publicato dalla Chiesa di Gesu Christo. W. H. Cadman, Presidente.

{Pittsburgh, Pa.: Stampato dalla Frediani Printing Co.} 1929. {8}, 638 pp. 19.2 × 13 cm.

This Italian-language edition of the Book of Mormon was projected at the January conference, 1927. Two years later, the Church authorized letting the contract for printing 1,000 copies at a price of $1,095. Including the translation, which I am informed by Mr. Cadman was arranged by the printer, the total cost was reported a year later as $1,395.

PMonC, USIC

1930

{W. H. CADMAN}

{26} *The Way of Salvation* {by} W. H. Cadman, Charles Ashton, Committee.

Monongahela: Printed by Harry Lorber. {1930.} Second Series. 7 pp. 15.6 × 11.4 cm.

Reprinted from No. 15.

PMonC

1931

CHURCH OF JESUS CHRIST

{27} *The Saints Hymnal{.} A Choice Selection of Hymns for Use in the Church of Jesus Christ. . . . Domicile of the Church Monongahela City, Penn. . . .*

{Pittsburgh, Pa.: Printed by Herbic & Held Printing Co.} 1931. 117 pp. 19.8 × 13.7 cm.

At the April conference, 1931, 3,000 copies were reported as in course of being printed.

PMonC

1932

{W. H. CADMAN}

A Brief History of the Origin of the Church of Jesus Christ with Headquarters at Monongahela, Pennsylvania. {By W. H. Cadman.}

n.p. {1932} 8 pp. w.p. 19.2 × 14 cm.

At the April conference, 1932, W. H. Cadman having previously been given authority to prepare a pamphlet setting forth the origin of the church, he "read an article he had written on the subject and a motion was passed, that the article be accepted with a few corrections." At the October conference, the same year, it was reported that the Ladies' Uplift Circle had had 2,000 copies printed. Reprinted in 1947 {No. 52}.

MoInRC, PMonC, USlC

1933

{W. H. CADMAN}

Una Breve Storia dell' Origine della Chiesa di Gesu' Christo con Sede a Monongahela, Pennsylvania. . . . La pubblicazione di Questo Lavoro e' finanziata dal Circolo Educativo Delle Signore{.} Pubblicato nell' Anno di Nostro Signore 1932.

n.p. {1933} {8} pp. 19.4 × 13.2 cm.

At the January conference, 1933, Frank Palermo was authorized to have 3,000 copies printed of this Italian translation of "The Origin of the Church." At the April conference he reported having done so. The Ladies' Uplift Circle paid the cost, amounting to $17.

PMonC, UHi, Morgan

OLIVER COWDERY

A Reproduction of A Series of Letters written by Oliver Cowdery by the Church of Jesus Christ with Headquarters at Monongahela, Pa. . . . The Publishing of this Work is Financed by the Ladies' Uplift Circle. Published in the Year of our Lord 1933.

{Washington, Pa. Ward Printing Co.} 1933. 44 pp. 22.9 × 15.3 cm.

These letters by Cowdery to W. W. Phelps concerning the early history of the church were originally printed in the *Latter Day Saints' Messenger and Advocate* at Kirtland, 1834–35, and first separately printed in Liverpool, 1844. They have been reprinted by nearly all the branches of the original church. Three thousand copies were reprinted in this edition.

MoInRC, NN, OClWHi, PMonC, UHi, USlC, Morgan

JOSEPH SMITH, JUN.

{31} *The Book of Mormon*{.} An Account Written by The Hand of Mormon Upon Plates Taken From the Plates of Nephi. . . . Translated by Joseph Smith, Jun. Published by the Church of Jesus Christ{,} Monongahela, Pennsylvania, U.S.A.

{Crafton, Pa.: Cramer Printing and Publishing Company.} 1934. {12}, 519 pp. 19.1 × 14 cm.

Though as early as 1872 the church displayed an anxiety to print its own edition of the Book of Mormon, the dream had to wait two generations for realization. In 1934 the church did not own a copy of the first edition (1830) of the Book of Mormon, though one has since been obtained, and accordingly, as the preface explains, this edition is based upon one of 1923, presumably that of the Reorganized Church, on the grounds that the publishers of that edition were guided by the wording of the original manuscript. The division into chapters and verses follows that of an edition of 1899 published by the Church of Christ at Kansas City, which was a reprint of the 1830 edition under the title, *The Nephite Record.* Other editions utilized in the work of revision included the Utah edition of 1920, and the New York edition, ca. 1859–1861, mentioned in the note to No. 18, the text of which was based upon the third American {Cincinnati, 1840} edition. Five thousand copies were printed. Subsequently the church purchased the type used to print this edition.

The twelve unnumbered pages at the beginning, collate as follows: Title page, verso blank; p. 1, picture of church building in Monongahela, with acknowledgement to the Missionary Benevolent Association; pp. 2–4, "The Following is a Brief Account of Joseph Smith's Experiences and the Rise of the Church of Jesus Christ," an unsigned article by W. H. Cadman, setting forth the claims of the Church; pp. 5–9, "Introduction," unsigned but by Z. Brook {see No. 18}; p. 10, Note concerning the publishing of this work, by Thurman S. Furnier, Charles Ashton, and W. H. Cadman, Committee; p. 11, "The Testimony of Three Witnesses And Also The Testimony of Eight Witnesses"; p. 12, Names and Order of Books in the Book of Mormon. The text of the Book of Mormon occupies pp. 1–465. P. 466 is blank, and pp. 467–519 are given over to the index.

DLC, NN, OO, PMonC, UHi, USlC, Morgan

ALEXANDER CHERRY AND CHARLES ASHTON

{32} *Article on "Book of Mormon and Latter Day Work"* Begun by Brother Alex. Cherry (Now Deceased) and Continued by Brother Charles Ashton{.}

{Monongahela: Gilkey & Underwood, Printers. Second Series, 1936.} 6 pp., with 7th page of advertisement. 19.2 × 12.8 cm.

Caption title, A new printing of No. 21.

PMonC, UHi, USIC, Morgan

Z. BROOK

Introduction to the Book of Mormon. {Written by Z. Brook. Reprinted by the Church of Jesus Christ . . . Monongahela, Pa.}

{Monongahela, Pa.: Gilkey & Underwood, Printers. Second Series.} {1936?} 4 pp. w.p. 19.2 × 12.8 cm.

Caption title. A new printing of No. 18, attributed to 1936 from its identity in format with the other tracts reprinted this year.

PMonC, UHi, USIC, Morgan

CHURCH OF JESUS CHRIST

The Last Witness Dead. {Published by the Ladies' Uplift Circle of the Church of Jesus Christ . . . Monongahela, Pa.}

{Monongahela.?} Second Series, 1936. 4 pp. w.p. 19.2 × 12.8 cm.

Caption title. A new printing of No. 24.

PMonC, UHi, USIC, Morgan

{W. H. CADMAN}

Retrogression of the Primitive Church{.} Published by the Ladies' Uplift Circle of the Church of Jesus Christ . . . Monongahela, Pa.

{Monongahela:?} Second Series, 1936. 4 pp. 19.2 × 12.8 cm.

Caption title. A new printing of No. 17.

PMonC, UHi, Morgan

{W. H. CADMAN}

The Way of Salvation{.} Published by the Ladies Uplift Circle of the Church of Jesus Christ . . . Monongahela, Pa.

{Monongahela: Gilkey & Underwood, Printers.} Third Series, 1936. 5 pp. and 6th page of advertisement. 19.2 × 12.8 cm.

The title page is not included in the pagination, which commences with p. 1 on the verso of the title. A third printing of No. 15.

PMonC, UHi, USIC, Morgan

{W. H. CADMAN}

{37} *What Is the Indian Mission?* Published by the Ladies' Uplift Circle of the Church of Jesus Christ{.}

{Monongahela: Gilkey & Underwood, Printers.} First published January 5th, 1924. Second Series 1936. 4 pp. 19.2 × 12.8 cm.

Caption title. A new printing of No. 20.

PMonC, UHi, Morgan

CHURCH OF JESUS CHRIST

{38} *Law and Order of the Ladies Uplift Circle of the Church of Jesus Christ.*

{Washington, Pa.: Ward Printing Co. 1936.} 8 pp. 11.5 × 7.7 cm.

Cover title. Caption title is: "Law and Order." A small handbook of rules and procedure, of which, Mrs. Cadman's history of the Ladies' Uplift Circle states, 300 copies were printed in 1936.

PMonC, Morgan

1937

CHURCH OF JESUS CHRIST

{39} *"The Saints Hymnal" A Choice Selection of Hymns For Use in the Church of Jesus Christ . . .* Domicile of the Church{,} Monongahela City, Penna. Reprinted in the Year of our Lord, 1937.

{Pittsburgh: Herbic & Held Printing Co.} 1937. {7}–119 pp. 19.8 × 13.7 cm.

The collation is as follows: Photograph of the church in Monongahela, verso blank, pp. {1–2}; title page, preface on verso, pp. {3–4}; hymns, pp. {5}–110; index of first lines, pp. 111–114; topical index, pp. 115–119. This hymnal is in all essential respects the same as that of 1931.

PMonC, UHi, Morgan

{W. H. CADMAN}

{40} *La Via della "Salvazione"*{.} Publicata del Circolo Sollevare delle Donne della Chiesa di Gesu Cristo. . . . Monongahela, Pa.

{Monongahela, Pa.: Printed by W. H. Cadman.} Secondo Serie 1938. 6 pp. 19.1 × 12.8 cm.

The collation is as follows: title page, with p. 1 of text on verso; text, pp. 1–5; photograph of the church at Monongahela, p. 6; imprint on verso of p. 6. A reprint of No. 16.

PMonC, UHi, Morgan

CHURCH OF JESUS CHRIST

The Gospel News, Monongahela, Pa. March, 1938. {Printed and published by Elder W.H. Cadman.} 4 pp. 25.4 $\times$ 19.1 cm.

Published as the first number, though without volume or issue numbering, of a contemplated monthly periodical. Cadman reported to the April conference, 1938, "I have purchased a Printing Press and some type, capable of printing a paper 10" by 15" which I intended to print monthly, providing I could obtain enough subscriptions to cover the expense of printing it. I calculated the cost would be approximately twenty dollars each for each issue of three or possibly four hundred papers composed of four pages. However our people did not seem much interested and thus far I have printed only one issue." A paper by the same name was finally established in 1945 {No. 49}.

PMonC, UHi, Morgan

ALMA B. CADMAN

} *The Seventh Day of Rest*{.} by A.B. Cadman, Monongahela, Pa.

Monongahela, Pa: Printed by W.H. Cadman. {1938.} 15 pp. 19.1 $\times$ 12.9 cm.

Cover title. The caption title is: "A Treatise on Scripture. By Bro. A.B. Cadman." The preface, on p. 1, points out that the contents of the pamphlet "are not necessarily the faith of the Church of Jesus Christ," and adds that "The dividing of sacrifices described herein, and the chronology of time which would usher in the seventh thousand years at, or about the year of 1970, is wholly the product of Bro. Alma B. Cadman who is one of the Apostles of the Church. His views on this matter has been heard [*sic*] by most all of us, and many have wanted them put into print. Hence the Church publishes this Pamphlet with the understanding that the writer bears the responsibility of the same."

In October, 1933, the church authorized Alma B. Cadman to prepare an article on "The Peaceful Reign of the Kingdom, While Living in the Flesh," and this was reported to the April conference, 1934. It was read and revised by several committees until its publication was authorized under the above title at the July conference, 1938.

PMonC, UHi, Morgan

1940

JOSEPH SMITH, JUN.

3} *A Prophecy by Joseph Smith.* Revelation and Prophecy given by Joseph Smith on December 25, 1832, was recorded in our record in October of 1874. . . . Printed by the Church of Jesus Christ, Monongahela, Pa.

{Monongahela: Printed by W.H. Cadman. 1940?} Broadside, 1 p. 19.1 $\times$ 12.8 cm.

This is the well-known prophecy on the breaking out of the Civil War which appears in the Doctrine and Covenants of the Utah church, though not in that of the Reorganized Church.

PMonC, UHi, Morgan

SADIE B. CADMAN

{44} *Scriptural Lessons Composed by Sadie B. Cadman*{.} Published by the Ladies Uplift Circle A. D. 1927 Second Issue—1941{.} Authorized by the Church of Jesus Christ . . . Monongahela, Pennsylvania.

{Washington, Pa.: Ward Printing Co.} 1941. 56 pp. 19.7 × 13.6 cm.

Collation is: Picture of the church, verso blank, pp. {1–2}; title page, p. {3}, with verso of title page bearing a preface, p. 4; text, pp. 5–54; table of contents, pp. 55–56. A new printing of No. 23.

PMonC, UHi, Morgan

UNITED STATES BUREAU OF THE CENSUS

{45} *Church of Jesus Christ (Bickertonites).* {In: *Religious Bodies:* 1936, Volume II Part 2 Denominations K to Z Statistics, History, Doctrine Organization, and Work{.} Prepared under the supervision of Dr. T. F. Murphy Chief Statistician for Religious Statistics{.}

Washington: United States Government Printing Office. 1941. xiv, 799–1695 pp. 23 × 14.7 cm.

The section, "Church of Jesus Christ (Bickertonites)," appears on pp. 828–833, as the fourth of six denominations treated under the general classification, "Latter Day Saints." This was the first time the Church of Jesus Christ had, been reported in the census of religious bodies. An article on "History, Doctrine, and Organization," prepared by W. H. Cadman, and occupying pp. 830–833, is printed with four statistical tables prepared by the Bureau of the Census.

DLC, MoInRC, NN, OClWHi, PMonC, USlC, Morgan

1942

CHURCH OF JESUS CHRIST

{46} *Constitution and By-Laws of the Missionary and Benevolent Association of the Church of Jesus Christ*{.} Headquarters The Church of Jesus Christ . . . Monongahela, Pa.

{Washington, Pa.: Ward Printing Co.} 1942. 12 pp. 14 × 8.8 cm.

A revised edition of No. 13.

PMonC, UHi, Morgan

ALMA B. CADMAN

Il Settimo Giorno di Riposo{.} {By} Alma B. Cadman Monongahela, Pa. Traduzione dall' Inglese dal Fratello Mario Milano From the Cleveland Branch.

{Cleveland: L'Araldo Publishing Co. 1942.} 16 pp. 18.1 × 13 cm.

Cover title. As noted in the title, this work was translated from the English version {No. 42} by Mario Milano. Fifteen hundred copies were printed.

PMonC, UHi, USlC, Morgan

1943

CHURCH OF JESUS CHRIST

} *Saints Hymnal of the Church of Jesus Christ.* Compiled by V{incent}. James Lovalvo, Clifford A. Burgess, Sadie B. Cadman. Headquarters of the Church . . . Monongahela City, Penna. Published 1943 by the Church of Jesus Christ. Printed in U.S.A.

{Pittsburgh: Rodeheaver-Hall-Mack Company.} 1943. {ii, 444} pp. w.p. 20.9 × 14.2 cm.

This was the first hymnal of the church printed with music, though such a book had been dreamed of at least since 1922. In 1929 Mrs. Cadman was authorized by the church conference to arrange such a hymn book, but it required many years to bring the project to fruition. Five thousand copies were printed, on a contract providing for the ultimate printing of 10,000. For a frontispiece the hymnal has a portrait of the church president, W. H. Cadman. Pages are not numbered, the numbering being by hymns, of which there are 449 with music, 47 more to be sung to music printed earlier in the book, and two final hymns, numbered 497 and 498, with music. At the end is a six-page index of first lines.

DLC, NN, PMonC, UHi, Morgan

1945

CHURCH OF JESUS CHRIST

9} *The Gospel News.* Monongahela, Pa. March, 1945. {Vol. I, No. 1.} {Edited by W. H. Cadman.}

Monongahela: {Printed and published for the Church of Jesus Christ by W. H. Cadman.} 8 pp. 25.4 × 19.1 cm.

The monthly periodical which had a tentative beginning in March, 1938 {No. 41}, recommenced with the issue of March, 1945. The first two issues, March and April, were printed without volume or issue numbering. After a lapse of one month, regular monthly publication began with June, 1945, Vol. 1, No. 3, the paper from this time being printed for the church by the Monongahela Publishing Company. The first volume closed with

December, 1945, Vol. 1, No. 9, and numbering since has corresponded with the calendar gear, at this writing having reached January, 1950, Vol. 6, No. 1. Each issue consists of 8 pages, without cumulative pagination. The circulation of the paper now approximates 550 to 575 copies monthly.

DLC Apr 1945
MoInRC Complete
PMonC Complete
UHi Apr–Jun, Aug 1945–Mar, Jun–Nov 1947; Mar, May 1949 to date
USIC Apr–Jun, Aug 1945–Mar, Jun–Nov 1947; Apr–Jun 1949
Morgan Apr–Jun, Aug 1945–Mar, Jun 1947 to date

W. H. CADMAN

{50} *A History of the Church of Jesus Christ Organized at Green Oak, Pennsylvania, U.S.A. in the year 1862.* Present headquarters at Monongahela, Pennsylvania. . . . By W. H. Cadman, Historian. Published by the Church in the Year of our Lord 1945{.}

{Lebanon, Pa.: Sowers Printing Co.} 1945. v–xvii, 413 pp. 23.1 × 15.2 cm.

Historically, this work is the most valuable publication of the Church of Jesus Christ. It is at once a history of the church in the form of annals, based upon minute books in the church archives dating back as far as 1852, and a personal history by Mr. Cadman, whose whole life has been bound up with the church. Relatively small space is given to general Mormon history prior to 1852, the emphasis fortunately resting on the later and less well-known history of this specific church. Though the introduction is dated April 12, 1934, the narrative continues to January, 1944. A last chapter, by Mrs. Sadie B. Cadman, is a history of the Ladies' Uplift Circle, 1920–1940. The book has in lieu of an index, a somewhat detailed table of contents and a list of the numerous illustrations. References in this bibliography to "the annals of the Church" are all drawn from Mr. Cadman's history.

DLC, PMonC, UHi, USIC, Morgan

ISHMAEL D'AMICO

{51} *My Testimony*{.} {By} Ishmael D'Amico{.}

{Rochester, N.Y.: 1945} 36 pp. 19.2 × 14.2 cm.

Cover title. An *apologia pro vita sua* by an Italian convert, the only thing of its kind so far to appear in the literature of the church.

PMonC, UHi, Morgan

1947

{W. H. CADMAN}

A Brief History of the Origin of the Church of Jesus Christ with Headquarters at Monongahela, Pennsylvania . . . The Publishing of this Work Is Financed by the Ladies Uplift Circle{.} Published in the Year of Our Lord 1932. Second series published in 1947{.}

{Monongahela: Printed by W.H. Cadman.} 1947. 7 pp. 19.1 × 12.8 cm.

Caption title is: "A Brief History of the Church of Jesus Christ." A new printing of No. 28.

MoInRC, PMonC, UHi, Morgan

1948

{WILLIAM CADMAN}

Faith and Doctrines of the Church of Jesus Christ, Monongahela, Pa. Published by Order of the Church in 1897{.} No. 1 Second Series—1948{.} Committee: Wm. Cadman, J.L. Armbrust, W. D. Wright. Headquarters: Monongahela, Pa. . . .

{Washington, Pa.: Ward Printing Co.} 1948. {5}–29 pp. 22.9 × 14.9 cm.

A new printing of No. 8.

MoInRC, PMonC, UHi, Morgan

1949

PAUL D'AMICO

.} *Un Riassunto Del Vangelo Ristorato.* {By} Paul D'Amico.

{Lockport, N.Y.: A. J. Laux & Co. 1949.} 3–28 pp. 20.3 × 12.8 cm.

A short compilation by an Italian brother of the history and doctrinal claims of the church, ending with a catechism of twenty-eight questions.

PMonC, UHi, Morgan

JOHN ROSS AND THOMAS ROSS

;} *Scriptural Lessons taken from the Book of Mormon*{.} Composed by John Ross and Thomas Ross{.} Authorized by The Church of Jesus Christ . . . Monongahela, Pa., U.S.A.

{Washington, Pa.: Ward Printing Company.} 1949. 95 pp. 19.6 × 13.4 cm.

Primarily designed for Sabbath School study, the sixty lessons in this pamphlet "were composed by Brothers John, and Thomas Ross of Aliquippa, Pa., and were examined by a committee of brethren delegated by the General Church." Three thousand copies were printed in October, 1949.

PMonC, UHi, Morgan

The Re-Organized Church of Jesus Christ[1]

ALLEN WRIGHT

{1} *A Conversation on the Thousand Years' Reign of Christ.* Written by Elder Allen Wright. St. John, Kansas. (No. 1.)

{St. John, Kansas: The County Capital.} 1907. 24 pp. 16.5 × 12.3 cm.

Cover title. Published by an apostle of the church, this pamphlet argues for the doctrine that blood life will exist during the time of Christ's return. It aroused the disapproval of the parent church organization in Pennsylvania, both for its content and for having been printed and distributed without sanction. As a result, the pamphlet was condemned as being contrary to the faith of the church. This action led directly to a schism within the church, five of the apostles joining Wright in his stand.

PMonC, Morgan

1908

{W. T. MAXWELL}

{2} *A Statement Issued by the Re-Organized Church of Jesus Christ July 4th, 1908*{.} J. L. Armbrust, Armbrust, Pa. {and} W. T. Maxwell, Greensburg, Pa. Publishing Committee{.}

{Youngwood, Pa.?} 1908. 6 pp. w.p. 15.1 × 9.8 cm.

Cover title. The caption title is: "Declaration and Statement by the Church of Jesus Christ." The statement is dated Youngwood, Pa., July 4th, 1908, and is signed by Elder W. T. Maxwell. This pamphlet was the first official statement of the position taken by those in association with Allen Wright, and reviews their position and the events which had led to the organization of their separate church.

MoInRC, PMonC, UHi, Morgan

SOLOMON VAN LIEU

{3} *A Trace of Prophecy, on the Second Coming of Christ. Or the Little Stone Kingdom, and the end of*

[1]This church has no connection with the Reorganized Church of Jesus Christ of Latter Day Saints, with headquarters at Independence, Missouri.

the Gentile Rule or Reign—the begin{n}ing of the Great Anti-typical Jubilee in 1914. Written by Elder Sol. Van Lieu{,} August 24, 1908. St. John, Kansas.

{St. John: The County Capital.} 1908. 36 pp. 15.1 × 11.7 cm.

Cover title. The caption title is: "What We Believe." The pamphlet sets forth the doctrinal position of the new organization, makes a numerical calculation from the prophecies of Daniel, and argues a conception of the millennium. Pasted to the inside rear cover is a printed slip, "This Pamphlet and Pamphlet Number One, Written by Elder Allen Wright On the Millennial, Can be Had by Addressing Allen Wright, St. John, Kansas Or W. S. Crosby, Greensburg, Penna."

PMonC, Morgan

19XX

RE-ORGANIZED CHURCH OF JESUS CHRIST

What Must We Do To Be Saved. Submitted by Re-Organized Church of Jesus Christ{.}

n.p., {19—} Placard. 8.9 × 12.7 cm.

This placard sets forth ten articles of faith, with an eleventh saying that these are an outline of the faith and doctrines taught and practiced according to the Scriptures. There is no evidence as to date or place of publication, but Mr. W. S. Crosby suggests that J. L. Armbrust had a small printing press and may have printed it at Armbrust, Pa., sometime between 1908 and 1929.

Morgan

1929

J. L. ARMBRUST

Reformation or Restoration, or Which Is the Church? Jesus Christ Established but One Visible Church. {Dated at end:} August 15, 1929.

{Armbrust, Pa.?} 1929. 4 pp. w.p. 21.6 × 12.9 cm.

Caption title. This tract argues the lack of authority in existing churches, and the necessity that arose for a restoration. Two copies were presented by J. L. Armbrust in 1930 to Dr. George B. Arbaugh, and one of these Dr. Arbaugh kindly presented to me. Armbrust died July 30, 1944.

Morgan

THE PRIMITIVE CHURCH OF JESUS CHRIST

No titles are known to have been published by this church.

II
Church of Jesus Christ of Latter Day Saints {Strangite}*

Save only the Utah church, none of the existing branches of the original Mormon church has an antiquity comparable to that founded by James J. Strang. This antiquity is reflected even in its name, which is identical with that of the church Brigham Young took to Utah, and may only be differentiated from it by the absence or presence of a hyphen in the spelling, the Utah church having adopted the usage, "Church of Jesus Christ of Latter-day Saints."

Once arch-rivals, the Utah and Strangite bodies have many things in common other than their name. As a result of historical pressures which forced them into social conflict with outside groups, both have accepted the nickname "Mormon" as a term of identification, though preferring to describe members as "Saints." Both accept unequivocally the life and works of Joseph Smith. Both were at one time polygamous, though neither church at present sanctions the practice of plural marriage. Many points of doctrine are held in common, though there are differences not only in emphasis but in some fundamentals, especially including the determined monotheism of the Strangite church and its insistence, with respect to the Succession, on the necessity for ordination under the hands of an angel. Both churches have a remarkable history, filled with high endeavor, spectacular conflict, and tragic event. The parallelism is noted by the Strangite church in this, that Brigham Young's church is the only rival accorded the dignity of being regarded as a "schismatic" rather than a "Pseudo Mormon" organization.

Bibliographically as historically, the Strangite church has a place of its own in American culture. Its early publications are sought after as are those of no other among the lesser Mormon churches; from their rarity and the singular circumstances of their publication, quite as much as for their content, they have excited historians and bibliographers. Yet, for all the interest they have aroused, these publications have consistently defied attempts at professional description. There is no bibliography of Strangite literature, on whatever scale, that is not full of misconceptions, [Joseph] Sabin's *Bibliotheca Americana* as overflowing with misinformation as the catalog of any harried

*[*Western Humanities Review* 5, no. 1 (Winter 1950–1951): 43–114. —Ed.]

bookseller. With its time-span of more than a century, many of the titles represented only in unique copies, still others as yet unlocated, and no great amount of information extant about the printing history of any, the Strangite bibliographical house is one exceptionally difficult to place in order. The present study is by no means to be thought of as definitive.

James Jesse Strang, the founder and continuing spiritual force of the Strangite church, was born in Scipio, New York, in 1813. Although he had the benefit of little formal schooling, he had a notable aptitude for learning and a quick and agile mind which was tempered in the lyceums and debating societies of the neighborhood. He taught school and read for the law, being admitted to the bar of Chautauqua County in 1836, and this experience contributed to the disciplined, orderly mind he subsequently displayed in the realm of religion. He served also as village postmaster, editor of a village paper, and temperance lecturer, this varied experience all standing him in good stead. In the autumn of 1843 he removed to southern Wisconsin. His brother-in-law, Moses Smith, and the latter's brother Aaron, were Mormon converts, and under their influence he visited Nauvoo in February, 1844, at which time he was baptized into the Church—it is said by the Mormon Prophet himself.

A few months later, immediately after the murder of Joseph and Hyrum Smith, Strang brought forth a letter said to have been received at Burlington in the regular course of mail, which purported to have been written by the Prophet June 18, 1844, nine days before his death. In effect, it named Strang as his successor. This remarkable letter, the original of which is now in the Coe Collection at Yale, Strang carried to a local church conference at Florence, Michigan, early in August, 1844. It got a somewhat mixed reception, and no sooner was a copy carried to Nauvoo than the Twelve Apostles denounced it as a forgery. Summarily excommunicated, Strang nevertheless persevered, gathering around him at Voree, near Burlington, Wisconsin, a little group of converts who aided him in getting out the first number of a paper, the *Voree Herald,* which blazoned his claims to the world. In January, 1846, Strang sallied south into Illinois to urge his claims upon the branches of the Church in person, and Reuben Miller, sent by the Twelve to combat him, was himself converted. Miller returned to Nauvoo to get out three thousand copies of a tract advocating Strang's cause, and thenceforth the Twelve had to reckon with a serious rival to the Succession.

By summer Strang was in a position to carry the fight for control of the Church to the eastern branches. His tour east approximated a triumphal procession, and he returned to Voree in October with prospects of rallying most of the Church to his standard. Had Brigham Young's Western migration come to grief, Strang might well have succeeded. Through revelation the Church was called to establish itself on the islands of the Great Lakes, Beaver Island in Lake Michigan finally being selected as the place of gathering. Headquarters was transferred there from Voree in June, 1850.

There were, however, many ruinous influences at work. Strang had come back from the East in the fall of 1846 to find the Church at Voree racked by schism. Headed by Aaron Smith, one of his First Presidency, the dissidents set up a rival church organization. Strang contemptuously dismissed the apostates as "Pseudo Mormons" or "Pseudoes," and in fact their church was short-lived, soon swallowed up by other factions, but the Church was shaken in all its far-flung branches, and Strang had to reckon with the "Pseudoes" as a corrupting force in everything he afterwards undertook. The removal to Beaver Island proved to be no solution to Strang's difficulties, either social or economic. Conflict arose between the Saints and the fishermen of Mackinac, and something very like a border warfare was carried on by the two parties for five years. Strang himself at last fell a victim in this embittered conflict, struck down in June, 1856, by the hand of an apostate.

After Strang's death, no leader of stature appeared to take his place. Most of the members evacuated the islands, settling on the mainland in Wisconsin or Michigan, and over the years they gave their adherence to one or another of the factions into which the Church of 1844 had split. After 1860 the Reorganized Church won the allegiance of many, a fact reflected in much of the polemical literature described in this bibliography. Nevertheless, a core of unyielding believers remained, and these in the end succeeded in preserving the integrity of the Strangite church. Shortly before his death in 1897, the apostle L. D. Hickey ordained Wingfield Watson to be presiding high priest, and in this office Watson served until his own death in 1923. The Church at this time had sunk to its lowest ebb, but in the generation since, it has exhibited renewed vitality and has again increased in numbers. Samuel H. Martin, ordained by Watson in October, 1922, to assist and succeed him, presided over the Church until his own death in 1935. Moroni ("Max") Flanders was ordained by Martin in 1928 to be his own assistant and successor, and he in turn presided between 1935 and 1946. Much of the burden of administrative responsibility in Moroni Flanders' last years was carried by Lloyd A. Flanders of Longlane, Missouri, and following the former's death in 1946, Lloyd Flanders was sustained presiding high priest at the 1947 general conference of the Church. At the present time the Strangite church has six organized congregations in five states, with a total estimated membership of 200. The archives are in the custody of the General Church Recorder, Stephen West, who lives on the site of old Voree, Rt. 2, Box 40, Burlington, Wisconsin.

The present-day Church makes little effort to invest money in lands or buildings, so many millions of dollars having been lost to persecution in the past. The Saints are not urged to "gather," except to branches where they may attend church regularly, or to Voree. All are urged to leave the cities and establish themselves upon land. No great emphasis is placed upon proselyting, the aim being to make strong converts out of those baptized, rather than to make a large number of converts. The expectation is that in the early future God will again send the Gospel to the world, and the membership, as Mr. Flanders has written, "aims to be ready and waiting, prepared in heart and in mind," with the eldership "awake, expectant, waiting, hoping, and praying for that day, and ready to go on in unity and peace under the leadership of that {as yet unknown} prophet to fulfill all the great prophecies of the Scripture regarding that dispensation of the Lord's Gospel." The standard works of the Church are the Bible (the King James version usually preferred), the *Book of Mormon,* and the *Book of the Law of the Lord. Doctrine and Covenants* is accepted insofar as its content was published before Joseph Smith's death. The Nauvoo edition is regarded as standard; when for convenience a modern printing is used, preference is given to editions published by the Utah church.

No history of the Strangite church, written from its own point of view, has yet been published. The colorful character of this history has led to studies of it by a number of outside observers, the most responsible treatment being that by Milo M. Quaife, *The Kingdom of St. James* (New Haven, 1930), but none of these works is regarded with conspicuous favor within the Church. The principal depository of Strangite documents is the Coe Collection at Yale, the Strang MSS formerly in the possession of Dr. Quaife having passed into this great archive. Other documents of importance are held by the Reorganized Church of Jesus Christ of Latter Day Saints, at Independence, Missouri, and by the Strangite church itself. Printed materials are located by this bibliography.

In addition to the 105 titles which comprise a bibliography of the Strangite church proper, seven titles appear in a category of their own as Dissenting Works. The first five of these emanated from schismatic activity at Voree, but only three properly represent the dissenting church there. Since this church was founded mainly upon opposition to Strang, it had no real vitality and was soon swallowed up by other factions, its president, Aaron Smith, being baptized into William McLellin's Kirtland church so early as February 13, 1847. Many of the Mormon factions which flourished near mid-century and after included members prominent at one time or another in the Strangite church, but these bodies must receive separate bibliographical treatment. Somewhere between the one category and the other is the case of Joseph Robinson. *The Gospel Herald* of May 30, 1850, said of Robinson that he had been "a regular member of a branch of the church in Franklin, Ill., who practiced talking in tongues on all his ordinary business, and even in driving his teams. Some two or three years since he came to Voree and commenced dictating the affairs of the church by the pretended interpretation of his pretended tongues, and being stoutly rebuked by the prophet commenced prophesying and building up a church. B. C. Ellsworth and J. W. Crane became the main pillars of his church, and ordained him to the prophetic office. They however soon fell off, and the spirit of his work died out." An approximate date for Robinson is provided by the *Herald* of February 10, 1848: "We are informed by letter from Franklinville, Ill., that John W. Crane has ordained one Joseph Robinson prophet &c., instead of Joseph Smith." Any publications by Robinson, or in his interest, have escaped my attention.

The data for this study of Strangite literature have been gathered over a period of several years, and particularly during 1947–1948 when I visited most of the major libraries of the country assisted by a grant from the John Simon Guggenheim Memorial Foundation. Facilities extended by the Library of Congress during the preparation of the manuscript have been very helpful, and I have been notably aided by Miss Carolyn Jakeman of the Houghton Library at Harvard, Miss Dorothy W. Bridgwater of the Yale University Library, Miss Gertrude Hassler of the Western Reserve Historical Society, Mrs. Elleine H. Stones of the Detroit Public Library, Mrs. Margaret Gleason of the State Historical Society of Wisconsin, Mr. Paul North Rice of the New York Public Library, Dr. George B. Arbaugh of Augustana College, Rock Island, Illinois, the late S. A. Burgess of the Reorganized Church of Jesus Christ of Latter Day Saints, Mr. A. William Lund of the Historian's Office, Church of Jesus Christ of Latter-day Saints, Mr. Stanley Ivins of Salt Lake City, and especially by Mr. Edward Eberstadt and his sons Charles and Lindley, who so well exemplify the fructifying role played in bibliographical research today by the creative bookseller. They have delighted in calling new finds to my attention, have furnished photostats and general information, and without stint have placed all their rich bookseller's lore at my disposal.

I am indebted as well to Dr. Milo M. Quaife, who gave me generous access to the Strang MSS while they were yet in his possession, and who has answered inquiries willingly and at length. When subsequently the Strang MSS were acquired by Mr. W. R. Coe for his great collection of source documents on Mormonism and the Far West, and before they were deposited at Yale, these papers and many of the printed works hereafter described were for some weeks given into my keeping, and the opportunity to study them at leisure was of great value to this work. I freely express my thanks, and desire to emphasize how essential are the MSS and rare printed works gathered into his collection by Mr. Coe for any scholar concerned with Mormon history. Even with such aid from so many sources, the bibliography must have been imperfect had I not enjoyed the full cooperation of Mr. Lloyd A. Flanders and Mr. Stephen West, who found time amid many pressing responsibilities to seek out copies of, and information about, many works here described. Except for their efforts, half a dozen or more titles must have escaped notice, being found in none of the institutional collections, and in many other respects this bibliography has been enriched by their interest.

Census

CSmH	Henry E. Huntington Library, San Marino, Calif.
CU-B	Bancroft Library, University of California, Berkeley, Calif.
CtY	Yale University Library, New Haven, Conn.
CtY-C	Coe Collection, Yale University Library, New Haven, Conn.*
DLC	Library Congress, Washington, D.C.
ICN	Newberry Library, Chicago, Ill.
IHi	Illinois State Historical Library, Springfield, Ill.
MH	Harvard University Library, Cambridge, Mass.
Mi	Michigan State Library, Lansing, Mich.
MiDdB	Burton Historical Collection, Detroit Public Library, Detroit, Mich.
MiU-C	Clements Library, University of Michigan, Ann Arbor, Mich.
MoInRC	Reorganized Church of Jesus Christ of Latter Day Saints, Independence, Mo.
NN	New York Public Library, New York, N.Y.
NNHi	New-York Historical Society, New York, N.Y.
NNUT	Union Theological Seminary, New York, N.Y.
OClWHi	Western Reserve Historical Society, Cleveland, O.
RPB	Brown University Library, Providence, R.I.
UHi	Utah State Historical Society, Salt Lake City, Utah.
USlC	Historian's Office, Church of Jesus Christ of Latter-day Saints, Salt Lake City, Utah.
ViU	University of Virginia Library, Charlottesville, Va.
WBuC	Church of Jesus Christ of Latter Day Saints {Strangite}, Burlington, Wis.
WHi	State Historical Society of Wisconsin, Madison, Wis.
Morgan	Personal collection of Dale L. Morgan.**

*[The Coe material was integrated into the Beinecke Library collection without attribution and remains that way today. —Ed.]

**[Morgan's collection of publications from the lesser Mormon churches was given to the University of California and today is among the collections of the Bancroft Library. Much of his duplicated material (chiefly microfilm and photostat) was given to the Utah State Historical Society. —Ed.]

Bibliography

1846

{CHURCH OF JESUS CHRIST OF LATTER DAY SAINTS}

Voree Herald. Voree, Wis. Vol. I, No. 1. January, 1846. 4 pp. 30.2 × 23.3 cm.

None of Strang's publications has a history more interesting and eventful than the *Herald.* With its appearance he assumed genuine stature among the rivals to the Succession, and it was the standard around which he rallied his church. The genesis of the paper may be traced in the manuscript Chronicles of Voree. On December 15, 1845, in a meeting of the Saints at Voree, it was resolved that Strang should "write an Epistle to all the Elders and get one thousand copies thereof printed to be put into immediate circulation." This epistle, the "First Pastoral Letter of James the Prophet," which bears date of December 25, 1845, was printed (with Strang's Letter of Appointment from Joseph Smith and much other matter vindicating him in his claims to lead the Church) as the first issue of the *Herald.* Strang said later that there were not a dozen subscribers at the time the *Herald* commenced publication, and in fact no copy of the first issue has yet been located, though its content is preserved {see No. 2}. It is possible that some of the copies comprising the first number bore date of December, 1845, or perhaps January, 1845; at any rate, the *Herald* of February, 1846, in calling attention to some misprints which had escaped notice until a part of the first issue had been worked off, declared that "The date of the paper should be Jan. 1846."

Under its original name, 10 issues of the *Voree Herald* were published, January–October, 1846. These were printed at various job offices; as explained in the *Northern Islander* of January 24, 1856, "Nos. 1, 2, & 3, at the office of the Southport (Kenosha) Telegraph; No. 4 at the office of the Ottawa Constitutionalist; Nos. 5, 6, 7, & 10 at the office of the Elkhorn Star (now Wisconsin Reporter); Nos. 8 & 9 at Calhoun's job office, Chatham Square, New York City." In other words, it was printed wherever Strang happened to be during this period. The need of a press of his own was manifest, and while in Philadelphia, in the late summer of 1846, Strang made arrangements for a press with the firm of L. Johnson & Co. As late as December 28, letters in the Strang MSS make clear, he had not succeeded in effecting delivery of the press, but once it passed into his hands he quickly got out the belated November and December issues, completing the first volume, and transformed his periodical into a weekly although his first intention had been to publish semi-monthly. The subscription price was $1 for the first volume, $2 thereafter. A three-column paper the first year, the *Herald* thereafter was printed in double columns.

Publication was carried on under a new name, *Zion's Reveille.* This name had been suggested to Strang by John C. Bennett as far back as April 16, 1846; in a letter preserved by the Reorganized Church, Bennett argued that "the 'VOREE REVEILLE' would *wake up* saints and sinners to a sense of their danger if they reject the new prophet of the living God." An explanation to this effect was published in the first (November, 1846) issue of the *Reveille.* Because Bennett had been prominently associated with the change of name, it became distasteful to Strang after he cut Bennett off the Church in the summer of 1847, and with the issue of September 23, 1847, Vol. 11, No. 27, he renamed the paper *Gospel Herald,* a name it bore until publication ceased. The first editor and printer, after Strang acquired his own press, was John Greenhow, late from the Philadelphia branch; the proprietors were listed as James J. Strang, James M. Adams, George W. Gregg, and Artemus Judd, these men having gone security for Strang in the contract to purchase the press. Greenhow published the paper weekly from January 14 to April 15, 1847, and then threw it into confusion by printing his resignation from both the Church and the paper. The issue which bears date of April 22 was not got out until mid-May, and only one other issue, June 1, until July. Regular publication was resumed on July 8, 1847, and though numbers were occasionally delayed and the issue of September 23–30, 1847, appeared as a combined or double number {No. 27–28}, weekly frequency was achieved until publication ceased on June 6, 1850, Vol. V, No. 12, Whole No. 180. Strang was nominally editor for the issues of April 22 and June 1, and formally so from and after July 8, 1847, but most of the editorial drudgery until the summer of 1849 was performed by John E. Page, and thereafter by Gilbert Watson and Frank Cooper. The *Herald* is by far the most important printed source for the history of the Strangite church, filled with letters, news, doctrinal articles, and disputations. Because it gave so much attention to the Mormon factions of the period, it is also one of the most important sources for the history of these, due allowance being made for the bias displayed.

No complete file of the *Herald* is known. As early as 1856 the *Northern Islander* could locate only one "entire set," that belonging to Strang. However, by utilizing the resources of all known files, a file may be constructed in microfilm, lacking only the issues of January and December, 1846, the first and twelfth numbers.

CtY-C May 1846; Jun 29, 1848; Jul 26, 1849.

MoInRC Mar, Jun*, Jul, Aug*, Sep*, Oct*, 1846; Feb 11*, 18, Mar 4–18, 25*, Apr 22–Jul 15, 22*, 29, Aug 5*, 12*, 19–Oct 7, 14*, 21–Dec 30, 1847; Jan 6–27, Feb 3*, 10–17, Mar 23–30, Apr 13–Dec 28, 1848; Jan 4–Dec 27, 1849; Jan 3–Jun 6, 1850. {Numbers which are imperfect are indicated with an asterisk. This file was microfilmed in 1948 by the Library of Congress.}

NN Apr, Sep 1846; Jan 14–21, Feb 11, Mar 11, Aug 26–Sep 2, 16–23, Oct 28, Nov 25–Dec 9, 1847; Jan 6, Feb 3, 17–24, Mar 9–30, Apr 13–27, May 25–Jun 8, Aug 17, Oct 5, 19, Dec 14, 1848; Jan 18–25, Feb 8–Mar 23, May 31–Jun 28, Aug 16, Sep 6, Oct 11, Nov 1, Dec 6–13, 1849; Jan 17–24, Feb 7–14, Apr 11, 25, May 16, 1850.

USIC Feb–Sep 1846; Dec 16, 1847.

WBuC Feb–May, Jul–Nov 1846; Jan 14, 28–Nov 25, Dec 23–30, 1847; Jan 6–Feb 3, 17–Mar 9, Apr 6–20, May 11–Dec 28, 1848; Jan 4–Mar 1, 15–Jul 26, Aug 16–23, Sep 27–Oct 11, 25–Nov 8, 22–Dec 27, 1849; Jan 3, 17, 31–Feb 21, Mar 7–Apr 11, 25–May 23, Jun 6, 1850. {This file was formerly Wingfield Watson's. Missing numbers have been supplied in photostat so as to complete it except for Vol. I, Nos. 1, 6, 12; Vol. II, Nos. 47, 52; Vol. III, No. 7, and Vol. V, No. 11.}

WHi Feb, Aug–Oct 1846; Jan 14, Jun 1, Sep 2, 23–Oct 7, Nov 18–25, Dec 16–23, 1847; Aug 24–Dec 28, 1848; Jan 4–Mar 15, 29–Dec 27, 1849; Jan 3–Feb 28, Mar 14, 28–May 9, 1850. {Missing numbers in this file have been supplied in photostat, principally from Wingfield Watson's file, so as to complete it except for those numbers listed as lacking in the WBuC file above.}

{REUBEN MILLER}

A Defence of the Claims of James J. Strang to the Authority now Usurped by The Twelve; And shewing him to be the True Successor of Joseph Smith, as First President of the High Priesthood. {By Reuben Miller.}

{Keokuk, Iowa: 1846.} 16 pp. 20.5 × 13.5 cm.

Caption title. The history of this first pamphlet published in advocacy of Strang's claims is developed through sources widely scattered but remarkably circumstantial. In a letter in the Strang MSS dated February 15, 1846, Reuben Miller wrote from Nauvoo, "We have had your paper {i.e., the first issue of the *Voree Herald*} published in pamphlet form with considerable additional matter (3,000 copies)." Its publication is referred to in a letter from Warsaw, Ill., printed in the St. Louis *Missouri Republican*, February 20, 1846, which gave information that the Strangites "have now a pamphlet in press at Keokuk the object of which is to turn the tide of emigration toward Wisconsin." Another letter in the Strang MSS from Hazen Aldrich, dated Willoughby, Ohio, April {15}, 1846, ties these two fragments of information together: "A friend of mine at Keokuk sent me a Pamphlet containing the truth but the Publisher has not given his name: neither the time of its being published." This is a sufficient description of the *Defence*.

The special importance of the pamphlet is that it fills the place of the still unlocated first issue of the *Herald*. It contains the Letter of Appointment of June 18, 1844, the "First Pastoral Letter of James the Prophet," dated December 25, 1845; quotations from *Doctrine and Covenants* supporting Strang's claims; his revelation of September 1, 1845, concerning the Voree Plates; the testimony of the witnesses who dug up these plates; Strang's translation of them; and the "Irresistible Conclusions" which follow from the whole. To this is added in double columns on pp. 15–16—perhaps the independent contribution made by Miller—a comparison of "The Doctrine of Primitive Mormonism" with "The Doctrine of Degenerate Mormonism." At the end is a song, "Primitive Mormonism Advocated." Apparently Reuben Miller placed a number of copies of this pamphlet at Strang's disposal, for the Strang MSS and the columns of the *Herald* during the next two years contain many references to what was called "the tract reprint of the *Herald*."

CtY-C

JOHN COOK BENNETT

{ 3 } *Practice of Medicine. Doctor Bennett, Professor of the Principles and Practice of Midwifery and the Diseases of Women and Children in the Willoughby University of Lake, Erie, (A. D. 1834 and '35); and Professor of Obstetric, Medicine, and Surgery, and the Diseases peculiar to Females and Infants, in the Literary and Botanico-Medical College of the State of Ohio, Cincinnati, (A. D. 1845 and '46,) Proffers his professional services to the citizens of Burlington and Voree, Wisconsin, and the circumjacent country.* {Dated:} Burlington, Racine County, Wisconsin, July 4th, A. D. 1846.

{Elkhorn, Wis.? 1846.} Broadside. 33.6 × 21 cm.

This broadside, really an advertising circular and therefore not strictly apposite to this bibliography, is included for its bearing on one of the most important (and unfortunate) conversions Strang ever made. Bennett had taken a prominent role in Nauvoo affairs in 1840–42 only to break spectacularly with Joseph Smith and publish a celebrated exposé. A man of great ability, something of a wayward genius, he early saw the potentialities of Strang's church, and in a letter of February 24, 1846, now in the Reorganized Church library, wrote Strang tacitly suggesting that they come to some arrangement. Although aware of the deep prejudice against Bennett that prevailed among the Saints, Strang permitted him to be rebaptized. Bennett promptly made himself conspicuously useful, showering his new leader with ideas, publicity notices, and promises of substantial aid, and Strang pledged that he should have back the position he had held under Joseph Smith. The present broadside was published within a few days of Bennett's arrival at Voree, and contains various testimonials as to his professional stature and skill.

Helpful as Bennett proved to be, he was found by Strang to be more of a liability than an asset. Most of the racking schisms which beset the Church, beginning in the fall of 1846, grew out of feeling about the doctor, but it was not until June, 1847, that Strang formally broke with him, the stated grounds being that he had suppressed letters addressed to Strang, taught unsound doctrine, and given instruction in the name of the First Presidency which was unauthorized and violative of known instructions and settled policy. Nearly two and a half years later, Bennett made new overtures to Strang, and letters in the Strang MSS reveal that the two men were on cordial terms as late as the spring of 1851. Bennett at that time was living in Plymouth, Mass., where he originated the celebrated Plymouth Rock breed of chickens and wrote a substantial book on poultry-raising. In 1854 he removed to Polk City, Iowa, where he died, a pauper it is said, in 1867.

CtY-C

{JAMES J. STRANG}

{4} *Warning to all People.* By James J. Strang, Successor Prophet to Joseph Smith. {Jefferson County, N.Y.? 1846.} Broadside. 74 × 11.4 cm.

Caption title. The only known copy, in the Harvard Library, has been mounted on 4 pages, but was originally a narrow broadside. Quite evidently, it was published by Ebenezer

Page in connection with his missionary labors in the Black River District of western New York. In addition to Page's letter of appointment as presiding high priest for that district, signed at Voree July 9, 1846, the broadside contains Strang's revelations of June 18 and 27, 1844, January 17, 1845, and July 1, 1846. Probably it was published in one of the towns of Jefferson County in August or September, 1846; had it been published between October and January, it would most likely have been mentioned in one of Page's letters preserved in the Strang MSS.

MH

GEORGE J. ADAMS

The Star in the East. Boston, Mass. Edited by G. J. Adams. Published by H. L. Southworth. Vol. I, No. 1. November, 1846. 24 pp. 23 × 13 cm.

The Star in the East was a monthly periodical established in Strang's interest by George J. Adams. Adams had been an apostle in Joseph Smith's church, not a member of the Quorum of the Twelve but a so-called "Apostle to the Gentiles." He fell out with his brethren in 1845, and early in 1846 was taken into Strang's church, an episode recorded in a number of remarkable letters preserved with the Strang MSS in the Coe Collection. After Strang abandoned hope of inducing Sidney Rigdon to enter his First Presidency, he gave the place to Adams, the letter of appointment, signed by Strang October 8, 1846, being given to the world in the *Star.*

The first issue of *The Star in the East* contained, besides the long prospectus and the usual documents backing up Strang's claims to the prophetic succession, 3 pages of "Intelligence and Miscellany" relating to the Boston branch. It has been supposed that this issue was the only one published, but the Strang MSS contain a letter inquiring about a comment in the *Star* to the effect that semimonthly publication of the *Herald* was contemplated, and in view of the fact that no remark of this character appears in the November issue, it must be supposed that a December issue, No. 2, was got out. A letter from H. L. Southworth to Strang, written on the prospectus of the *Independent Inquirer* {see No. 6}, indicates the probable content of this second number. Under date of November 18, 1846, Southworth wrote: "We have printed 1500 more of the first number making 2500 in all having faith that it would be noticed, and that it {would} be sold. We have received from Thomas Braidwood the Fac Simile of the plates—the copper plate engraving, which we shall publish in the second number. . . . We receive a good deal of encouragement with regard to this matter, but no returns of any consequence."

The lack of returns seems to have been only one of several causes contributing to the downfall of the *Star.* Adams was given to alternate appearances in the pulpit and on the stage, and in the first issue of the *Star* went so far as to incorporate a paragraph on the current drama in Boston. It would appear from a letter by James M. Greig in the Strang MSS that this gave offense to Saints as far distant as Pittsburgh, but the *Star* gave up the ghost when the Boston branch, on February 1, 1847, rose against Adams in uproarious rebellion. Belatedly *Zion's Reveille,* September 9, 1847, took note of the decease of its sister publication, informing the brethren that inasmuch as Adams, because of unexpected misfortunes, had failed to publish *The Star in the East,* subscribers would be furnished with the *Reveille* in its place. Probably two issues only were published, though it is conceivable that a third, for January, 1847, also appeared.

NN Nov 1846

{GEORGE J. ADAMS}

{6} *Prospectus of the Independent Inquirer, and Journal of the Times.* Charles P. Bosson, Editor, George J. Adams, Proprietor, H. L. Southworth, Publisher. Boston, Mass.: November 20th, 1846. Broadside. 25 × 20.8 cm.

According to the prospectus, of which the only known copy is in the Coe Collection, the *Independent Inquirer* was to have published a first number the first Tuesday in December, 1846, and then to have commenced weekly publication the first Thursday in January, 1847. In sending Strang the prospectus on November 18, 1846, two days before the date it bears on its face, Southworth wrote: "You will at once perceive the idea: which is to break down prejudice with regard to you & Mormonism; to reply to every thing that make{s} its appearance in derision and without advocating mormonism, to do much good. The editor, is a man, who's name is a tower of strength throughout the agricultural public; he wrote a pamphlet on the potato, a short time since, *15000* copies of which were printed and nearly all sold. He takes hold of it with all the energies of his mind, he is not in the church, but I have no doubt he believes *all things.* He has done a very extensive business in his day & he is still young. . . . The moment we get any copies from the printer which will not be before the 1st Dec. we shall send you 25 or 50 copies and we have no doubt you will do what is necessary to obtain subscribers &c."

The prospectus declares the intention "that the paper shall truly be what its title indicates. No subject, however sanctioned by custom and long toleration, shall be too sacred for examination, and none, however unpopular and despised, shall be prejudged. In short, the paper will be devoted to the truth, as it affects the interest of humanity. Every creed and belief,—all the diversified opinions of society may be given in this paper from the pens of those who hold the doctrine preached. Every class of community may speak for themselves, in their own language; for we believe that good men and good ideas are to be found among all classes. We believe also, 'that error may be tolerated if truth is left free to combat it.'" The *Inquirer* was to have sold at $2 per annum, single copies 4 cents.

It is uncertain whether any issues were actually printed; the *Independent Inquirer* went down in the same ruin that overtook *The Star in the East.* However, when the enterprising publisher, H. L. Southworth, two years later gave in his allegiance to the Brighamites and started West, he paid a call on the Saints at Voree; Gilbert Watson's letter of November 13, 1849, in the Strang MSS, mentions the visit and identifies him to Strang in this language: "He was connected with Bro. Adams in getting out the 'Star in the East' and the 'Independent Inquirer.'" So concrete an allusion may mean that one or more copies actually appeared, but as none have been located, the paper itself is not included in this bibliography. The prospectus consists of a leaf folded to make 4 pages. The dimensions stated are those of the third page, on which the printed text appears.

CtY-C

JOHN E. PAGE

{*A Treatise on Circumcision.* By John E. Page. Gospel Tract No. 1.}

{Voree: 1847. 20 pp.}

No copy known. Publication of this tract, the first separate publication of the Voree press, was announced in *Zion's Reveille,* August 19, 1847. The matter contained in it was first published in the *Reveille* for June 1, July 29, and August 5, described as having been written originally as a communication to the *Christian Watchman* in 1842, by that publication rejected, and printed in the Reveille unrevised as an essay "effectually overthrowing *pedo baptism.*" In reviewing the publications of Strang's press, the *Northern Islander,* January 24, 1856, remarks, "In 1847 we published an edition of nine hundred copies of a series of three tracts, by John E. Page, on the priesthood and covenants with Abraham," but copies of none of these have been located. Page had been a member of the Quorum of the Twelve in Joseph Smith's day, but separated from the Twelve at the time they left Nauvoo to become one of the principal figures of Strang's church, serving as president of the "College of Apostles" and de facto editor of the *Herald.* Cut off by Strang in August, 1849, he became associated with the Brewsterite faction, and still later with the Hedrickite organization.

JOHN E. PAGE

{*A Treatise on the Spiritual Covenant Made with Abraham.* By John E. Page. Gospel Tract No. 2.}

{Voree: 1847. 4 pp.}

No copy known. Publication of this tract, in 4 pages, was announced in *Zion's Reveille,* August 19, 1847. Such an article, declared to be concerned with the "spiritual covenant" with Abraham, in contradistinction to the "temporal covenant" which had been the subject of the *Treatise on Circumcision,* appeared in the *Reveille* for August 12 and was continued through the issues of August 19–26, September 9–23, and October 7. Either the article was extended beyond the original expectation, or the material furnished copy for two tracts, which was very likely the case.

JOHN E. PAGE

{*A Treatise on the Spiritual Covenant Made with Abraham.* By John E. Page. Gospel Tract No. 3?}

{Voree: 1847.}

The title is entirely conjectural, nothing being known of this tract other than the information developed in the notes to No. 7 and No. 8 above. Separate publication of the tract was not specifically announced in the *Herald,* and the determination of how it differed in its title from No. 8 must wait upon the finding of a copy.

INCREASE McGEE VAN DEUSEN AND MARIA VAN DEUSEN

{10} *Positively True. A Dialogue between Adam and Eve, the Lord and the Devil, called the Endowments as was acted by Twelve or Fifteen Thousand, in secret, in the Nauvoo Temple, said to be revealed from God, as a Reward for building that Splendid Edifice, and the Express Object for which it was built.* {By Increase McGee Van Deusen and Maria Van Deusen.}

Albany: Printed by C. Killmer. 1847. 24 pp. 21.5 × 14.2 cm.

The above title is that of the Yale copy, but an authoritative description of the first edition must wait upon the discovery of a copy intact with the wrapper; lacking the wrapper, the Yale copy quite possibly is a second rather than a first issue, as is here assumed. Van Deusen was one of Strang's converts of 1846, and participated in the conference at Voree in which Brigham Young and others of the Twelve were tried in absentia and cut off. Van Deusen went on East and some 20 months later got out this exposé. "Our apology for presenting this imperfect work to the public," he and his wife declare in the preface, "is, that we believe the farce which we are about to describe, as acted in the Nauvoo Temple, in our presence, tends to the ruin of thousands, and if we had followed out the principles contained in the farce, it would, in all probability, have resulted in literal death." The pamphlet describes seven degrees taken by Van Deusen and his wife in the Nauvoo Temple, more factual and less sensational than in later editions, comments on Brigham Young in highly critical vein, and goes on to say, "The following is designed to show the foundation and claims of the Second Mormon Prophet, now actively engaged in Wisconsin, by the Name of JAMES J. STRANG, a lawyer, formerly of the state of New-York." There follows an abridgment of Strang's Letter of Appointment from Joseph Smith and "a Sketch of Joseph Smith's Origin and First Vision," this latter derived from Orson Pratt's *An Interesting Account of Several Remarkable Visions.*

The *Gospel Herald,* September 21, 1848, prints a letter from Van Deusen to Strang dated in New York September 3, which says in part that after leaving Voree he had preached a few times, baptized 3, "then went to work for myself. I published the endowment as given by the impostor Brigham Young. When I commenced selling that I quit preaching entirely. ... The pamphlet does not meddle with doctrines. It reveals the endowment, Joseph's letter of appointment, your claims, &c. I have sold 10,000 copies." Strang received the pamphlet coldly, disapproving it "because by the account of the author it involves him in the crime of perjury." These remarks wounded Van Deusen's feelings, and he defended himself in the *Herald* of November 2; he also, in subsequent printings of his pamphlet, eliminated the Strangite material. However, in a penitent letter in the Strang MSS, dated New York, June 18, 1849, Van Deusen confessed "my folly in the course I have taken the last two years in leaving the work of God and turning to my own in publishing the Endowment as Given by the Impostor B. Young. I sined not that I believe it should be kept A secret but it was far beneath my calling to do so I stooped low in doing it. . . . I say therefore to all the world I hereby confess my sin which consists not so mutch in the doing that refered to Above As in departing from God and like Jonah going any where but to Nineva."

Van Deusen was violently unstable, and figured in an acrimonious conference of the Strangite church in New York the following October. At that time he made reluctant admission that he might have said "that Joe Smith & Jas J Strang & the Twelve were all of a piece that Mormonism & the Book of Mormon was a humbug that it was all a humbug from beginning to end," but declared that while "he might have said so for the purpose of selling his book . . . he never designed it in his heart." Eventually Van Deusen began publishing revelations of his own {see Dissenting Works, Nos. 6, 7}. The numerous later editions of Van Deusen's exposé are irrelevant to this bibliography, but he published thousands of copies, each edition more sensational than the last, and the bookseller Charles L. Woodward, in his *Bibliothica Scallawagiana,* preserves the memory of Van Deusen hawking these about the streets of New York.

CtY

INCREASE McGEE VAN DEUSEN AND MARIA VAN DEUSEN

Positively True. A Dialogue between Adam and Eve, the Lord and the Devil, called the Endowments as was acted by Twelve or Fifteen Thousand, in secret, in the Nauvoo Temple, said to be revealed from God, as a Reward for building that Splendid Edifice, and the Express Object for which it was built. {By Increase McGee Van Deusen and Maria Van Deusen.}

Albany: Printed by C. Killmer. 1847. 24 pp. 21.5 × 14.2 cm.

The wrapper has the title: *Second Edition. The Sublime and ridiculous blended; A Dialogue between Adam and Eve,* etc., as on the title page. The wrapper title became the title of the revised edition of 1848, and may or may not have been the wrapper title of the first edition. It would appear from the Note to No. 10 that of the first two editions, which alone are pertinent to the history of the Strangite church, 10,000 copies were printed.

MH, NN

1848

JAMES J. STRANG

} *The Diamond: Being the Law of Prophetic Succession, and a Defence of the Calling of James J. Strang as Successor to Joseph Smith.*

Voree, Wisconsin: Gospel Herald Print, MDCCCXLVIII {1848}. 20 pp. 19.4 × 12.6 cm.

Cover title. The caption title is somewhat different: *Gospel Tract. — No. IV. The Diamond: A Full Exposition of the Law of God Touching the Succession of Prophets Holding the Presidency of the True Church, and the Proof that this Succession Has Been Kept Up.* Later editions combine the wrapper and caption titles of the first.

The publication of a pamphlet of this character was forecast in *Zion's Reveille,* August 19, 1847, which announced as in preparation a tract on "The calling, appointment and ordination of Prophets, and the relative duties of Prophets and Apostles." The material contained in the pamphlet was published in the *Gospel Herald,* April 27–May 4, 1848, and when publication was announced in the latter issue, the *Herald* declared, "The Diamond cuts all things, and is destructive of the pretensions of all false prophets."

According to the *Northern Islander*, January 24, 1856, a total of 3,500 copies were printed, of which 200 copies remained on hand. Since there has been some speculation whether *The Diamond* was reprinted at Beaver Island, this comment by the *Islander* should dispose of the question. The pamphlet is organized in five chapters, the first dealing with "The Institution of the First Presidency and the Law of Succession, Extracted from the Book of Doctrine and Covenants," and succeeding chapters printing the Letter of Appointment, with a discussion of the evidences for its authenticity, Strang's vision of June 27, 1844, which constituted his ordination, and the "First Pastoral Letter of James the Prophet." All this material had appeared in substantially the same form in the first issue of the *Voree Herald;* to it, however, Strang added an epistle of "The True Shepherd to the Saints Emigrating from Great Britain and Ireland to America," dated at Voree, May 1, 1848.

The first edition contained on the back wrapper some remarks on Strang's rivals to the Succession; these were not included in later editions. It was claimed that about one-third of all the Mormons acknowledged Strang as their leader, "and the disproportion in the number of his followers and those of Brigham Young is gradually becoming less." Down through the years, *The Diamond* has been one of the most effective advocates of Strang's claims. It has been reprinted four times {Nos. 36, 53, 97, 105}, and the Church maintains that it has not been necessary to alter a single line in the century since it was first published.

CtY-C, MoInRC, USIC, WHi

JAMES J. STRANG

{13} *Catholic Discussion.*

{Voree, Wis.: Gospel Herald Print, 1848.} {5}–60 pp. 18.2 × 12.3 cm.

Caption title. The only copy known, in the Coe Collection, has somewhat peculiar pagination, which may indicate that it was intended to have a title page and preface, and it is barely possible that it was issued with one, since when advertised for sale some years later in the *Northern Islander* it was referred to as "A Discussion of the Roman Catholic Religion, between Charles Rafferty and James J. Strang." On the other hand, the Coe copy appears to be complete in signatures, and on first being announced for sale, in the *Herald* of May 4, 1848, was described as having 56 pages, which is in accord with the odd pagination. According to the *Islander*, 1,200 copies were printed.

The material was published originally as a letter from a Catholic layman, Charles Rafferty, dated Wellsville, Ohio, August 30, 1847, and six letters in reply by Strang, *Gospel Herald*, September 23–October 14, October 28–November 25, 1847. To this was added an appendix in which Strang discusses a question at issue between John Gaylord and himself, relative to the lineage of Christ. Two additional letters by Rafferty, and replies by Strang, written after publication of the *Catholic Discussion*, appeared in the *Herald* of November 16 and 30, 1848, and April 5, 1849. Strang's followers have always regarded this discussion as putting "a full end" to the Catholic claim to priesthood. See also No. 68.

CtY-C

GEORGE J. ADAMS

A True History of the Rise of the Church of Jesus Christ of Latter Day Saints—of the Restoration of the Holy Priesthood. And of the Late Discovery of Ancient American Records Collected from the Most Authentic Sources Ever Published to the World, Which Unfold the History of this Continent from the Earliest Ages after the Flood, to the Beginning of the Fifth Century of the Christian Era. With a Sketch of the Faith and Doctrine of the Church of Jesus Christ of Latter Day Saints. Also a Brief Outline of Their Persecution, and Martyrdom of Their Prophet, Joseph Smith, and the Appointment of His Successor James J. Strang. By G. J. Adams, Minister of the Gospel . . .

Baltimore: Hoffman, Printer, No. 218 Baltimore St. {1849?} 44 pp. 15.5 × 10 cm.

Wrapper title. A copy in the Utah Church Historian's Office, lacking the wrapper, has occasioned some bibliographical confusion, as it has been erroneously catalogued under the title, "Facts; Ancient American Records. By J. J. Strang. Michigan: 1844," and as such was included in the Historical Records Survey's *Preliminary Check List of Michigan Imprints 1796–1850* as No. 559. Even without this complication, the title is a problem, for with minor exceptions it is identical in text with a pamphlet of the same title by T. Horton {No. 15}, and it is difficult to establish which was published first.

Primarily the pamphlet is an adaptation of Orson Pratt's *An Interesting Account of Several Remarkable Visions, and of the Late Discovery of Ancient American Records,* of which half a dozen editions were printed between 1840 and 1849. After a 2-page introduction, pp. {3}–37 are given over to the "Facts In Relation to the Late Discovery of Ancient American Records," with the remainder of the pamphlet devoted to Strang's claims. The only internal evidence as to date of publication appears in the introduction, which refers to "the people that call themselves 'Mormons,' now located at the great salt Lake, with Brigham Young as their leader." Thus it was hardly published before the fall of 1848, yet was probably written before the gold rush placed the Mormon situation in the mountains in different perspective. The *Gospel Herald* mentions neither the Adams nor the Horton pamphlet, though such a title by Adams is listed for sale with other works by the *Northern Islander* of June 1, 1854, three and a half years after the final break between Strang and Adams. In his correspondence with the *Herald* and with Strang Adams does not mention the pamphlet, but his activities in Baltimore as recorded in the columns of the *Herald* serve to indicate the probable time and circumstances of publication. He organized the first Baltimore branch of the Strangite church in January, 1849, and the *Herald* of April 26, 1849, printed minutes of a conference at Baltimore on March 24 at which Adams "presented a brief view of the rise and progress of the church, together with the evidences from the Book of Doctrine and Covenants, and Bro. Joseph Smith's last letter, and the other evidences which establish the claims of Bro. Strang as the successor of Joseph Smith as the prophet and President of the church." This sounds very much as though Adams had read to the conference the manuscript of his pamphlet, with some added matter, which he may then have sent to the printer by way of raising funds to enable himself to attend the conference scheduled for Beaver Island the ensuing summer. Adams presided over another conference in Baltimore June 2, 3, and 6, and visited the city fleetingly in the fall, but did not stay there any length of time until February, 1850. In one of his letters in the Strang MSS, dated at Wilmington,

Delaware, November 1, 1849, he tells of his "friends and Brethren in Baltimore {who} last Sunday Nobly raised one Hundreed and fifty Dollors Towards paying my Debts—for Type, and various other things," but the "type" may as well as not refer to the handbills which customarily heralded his engagements in the pulpit and on the stage.

USIC, WHi

THOMAS HORTON

{15} *A True History of the Rise of the Church of Jesus Christ of Latter Day Saints—of the restoration of the Holy Priesthood. And of the Late Discovery of Ancient American Records, Collected from the most authentic sources ever published to the world, which unfold the history of this continent from the earliest ages after the flood, to the beginning of the fifth century of the Christian era. With a Sketch of the Faith and Doctrine of the Church of Jesus Christ of Latter Day Saints. Also a brief outline of their persecution, and martyrdom of their Prophet Joseph Smith, and the appointment of his successor James J. Strang.* By T. Horton, Minister of the Gospel. . . .

Geneva, N.Y.: Gazette Print. {1849?} 47 pp. 15 × 10.4 cm.

Cover title. With the exception of the name of the "Minister of the Gospel," it will be seen that this title is identical with that of No. 14, and their common source is further indicated by the fact that the back wrapper of each contains a certification by the Smith family, dated March 1, 1846, affirming their belief in Strang. This edition has been reset, however, and added at the end are some remarks and a poem on the subject of the materiality of God, together with a song, "Martyred Prophets." Very little information about Horton is to be had, but owing to his obscurity in Mormon history before and after 1849, it is more likely that he republished for his use a copy of the Adams pamphlet than vice versa. In the Strang MSS is a letter from Samuel Graham dated January 15, 1848 (but which perhaps was misdated for 1849), in which a Brother Horton is mentioned, apparently in the neighborhood of Bath Mills, Mich. Horton went to Beaver Island and there had a falling out with the brethren. A letter from M.M. Aldrich to Strang, dated September 14, 1849, comments, "There is a Bro. here by the name of Thomas Horton, who had become quite disaffected, and was on the point of pseudoing. And in a fit of wrath, and with indignant and shameful language, slandered the apostle L.D. Hickey, for which Bro. S. Graham preferred a complaint against said Horton for slander." He was excommunicated September 13, 1849, all this appearing in the *Herald* of October 4. Horton thereupon disappears from the annals of the Church, which makes it extremely unlikely that his pamphlet was published after July, 1849.

CtY-C, NN

CHURCH OF JESUS CHRIST OF LATTER DAY SAINTS

{16} *A Collection of Sacred Hymns; adapted to the faith and views of the Church of Jesus Christ of Latter Day Saints.*

Voree, Wis.: Gospel Press. 1849. 172 pp. 10.4 × 7 cm.

This first hymnal of the Strangite church was a long time a-borning. *Zion's Reveille,* August 19, 1847, announced that beginning early in September, a hymn book would be commenced, issued in semi-monthly numbers of 16 pages each—to consist of some 200 hymns and 160 pages of matter, and to sell at 25 cents or five for $1. On September 23 the members were advised that the hymn book had been delayed a few weeks to procure better paper, but there was evidently more to the story than that, for when the hymnal did appear it was noted that the attempt to raise money by subscription had been a failure, not realizing a quarter of the expense of the paper. The plan of publishing in parts was nevertheless carried out. In the *Herald* of May 25, 1848, Stephen Post wrote, "Of the hymn books I suppose I have received as fast as printed," and in the Strang MSS another letter from Post, dated April 20, 1849, inquires whether the hymn book is finished; he had received to that time up to p. 104. On August 16, 1849, the *Herald* announced, "We have just completed the printing of our long delayed hymn book," and bound copies became available shortly after, for a letter from Strang to Frank Cooper in the Strang MSS, dated Racine, September 1, 1849, advises that the hymn books are at M. Miller's, to be bound in marbled boards, 100 with cloth backs, 50 with skin backs, and to be ready September 15. These 150 copies evidently constitute the first issue and possibly even the entire number of copies with an 1849 title page. According to the *Northern Islander,* January 24, 1856, 1,000 copies were printed, but there is good reason to think this includes not only those sent out in parts but the sheets of which the second and third editions were made up {Nos. 17, 23}. The book itself has an "Advertisement" apologizing for the deficiencies of the work, the selection having been "attended by different individuals for each sheet as it went to press, without any systematic arrangement, and the mechanical work . . . done in distinct jobs, over a long period of time." It was hoped eventually to "revise and republish in better style and order a suitable collection for the use of the saints," but if this was done, it was not until 1856 {No. 30}. In all, 120 hymns were published. The collation is: Title page, verso blank, pp. {1–2}; "Advertisement," verso blank, pp. {3–4}; hymns, pp. 5–166; index of first lines, pp. 167–172.

DLC, NNHi

1850

CHURCH OF JESUS CHRIST OF LATTER DAY SAINTS

} *A Collection of Sacred Hymns; adapted to the faith and views of the Church of Jesus Christ of Latter Day Saints.* Second edition.

Voree: Gospel Press. 1850. 172 pp. 10.4 × 7 cm.

This second edition of the hymnal is a reissue of the 1849 edition with a new title page; this is shown by misprints common to both, e.g., p. 37, line 3, "dsscend"; p. 53, line 6, "aince." Following a mistaken catalog entry in the library of the Union Theological Seminary, the Historical Records Survey's *Check List of Wisconsin Imprints 1850–1854,* No. 20, attributed the compilation to John Hardy, no doubt because Hardy had published a Mormon hymnal in 1843. Hardy, however, broke with Strang at the time of the uprising of the Boston branch early in 1847 and had nothing to do with the Voree hymnal. In addition to the two copies listed below, a third was owned in 1945 by Prof. T. J. Fitzpatrick of the University of Nebraska.

NNUT, WHi

CHURCH OF JESUS CHRIST OF LATTER DAY SAINTS

{18} *Memorial. To the President and Congress of the United States, and to all the People of the Nation — We, James J. Strang, George J. Adams, and William Marks, Presidents of the Church of the Saints, Apostles of the Lord Jesus Christ, and Witnesses of His Name unto all Nations, and others, our Fellow Servants, send Greeting:—* {Dated:} Buffalo, April 6, 1850.

{Voree: Gospel Press. 1850.} 4 pp. 32.4 × 20 cm.

It has been erroneously supposed that this Memorial was printed in Buffalo, which however was only the place of its composition. The Memorial was printed in the final issue of the *Herald*, June 6, 1850, Vol. VI, pp. 92–95, as "A Testimony to the Nation. To the President and Congress of the United States, and to all the people of the nation—We, James J. Strang, George J. Adams, and William Marks, Presidents of the Church of the Saints, Apostles of the Lord Jesus Christ, and witnesses of his name unto all nations, send greeting:—" and was reprinted from the same type, with minor changes in the heading. The Memorial rehearses the historic wrongs of the Saints in Missouri and Illinois, and appeals for redress to "the highest authority known to the land," asking it "to pass a law giving the consent of the Nation that the saints may settle upon and forever occupy all the uninhabited lands of the islands of Lake Michigan, and to cease to sell the same to other persons." The President and Congress are also requested "by some public act, {to} condemn in behalf of the nation, the martyrdom of the saints and their exile from some of the States," for otherwise God cannot hold the Nation guiltless of the blood of saints and prophets. The Memorial was presented in the U.S. Senate June 15, 1850, and referred to the Committee on Public Lands over the objection of the chairman, who thought that the United States had no public lands on the islands. On September 21, 1850, the Committee asked to be discharged from further consideration of the Memorial, and this was agreed to. See *Congressional Globe*, Vol. 19, pp. 1221, 1907. The Memorial has been reprinted in Milo M. Quaife, *The Kingdom of St. James* [New Haven: Yale University Press, 1930], pp. 249–255, and in *Prophetic Controversy No. 14* {No. 98}.

CtY-C

{JAMES J. STRANG}

{19} *Traveling Theatre Royal, Late from Beaver Island. Adams' New Drama. The Famous Original Five Act Drama, "Improving the Household," by Mr. G. J. Adams, Author, Manager and Star Actor.*

{Saint James: Cooper & Chidester. 1850.} 5-column broadside. 55.2 × 36.9 cm.

This devastating broadside would seem to be the very first issue of the Beaver Island press. Its existence had gone entirely unsuspected before a copy was turned up in the summer of 1950 by Mr. Lindley Eberstadt. Evidently it was published by Strang as a rejoinder to the proceedings at Mackinac, October 26–28, 1850, where he had been tried on charges of threatening the life of Adams' wife, Louisa. The history of this quarrel between Adams and Strang was thus described, a few weeks later, in the first issue of the *Northern Islander*: "G. J. Adams, last winter, became acquainted with a woman of indifferent fame in Boston, by the name of Louisa Pray, *alias* Louisa Cogswell, whom he took to Baltimore and introduced to his family and friends as a wealthy widow just returning from a large estate in Charleston, South Carolina. In April he appeared at Beaver with Miss Pray as Mrs. Adams, alledging that his wife, who was known to be far gone with consumption, was dead, and he married to the rich widow. Soon the fact transpired that he had sent Mrs. Adams to New Jersey, and abandoned her. The regular acts of discipline were taken in the premises, and went on step by step until Mr. Adams lost his standing in the church. In the mean time his real wife, who was a most excellent and amiable lady, died. He left here for Mackinac, breathing vengeance on the Mormons in general, and the prophet in particular." Adams returned to Beaver Island October 20 with a writ against Strang charging him with having threatened the life of Mrs. Adams. Strang evaded service but went on his own account to Mackinac. In the court proceedings there, so the *Islander* declared, "Adams testified that he had no wife but this, and had not had for many years. But when Mr. Strang pressed him hard concerning his real wife, whom he had lived with some fifteen years down till last March, and who died in August, Mr. Justice [Charles] O'Malley abruptly closed the examination of the witness."

Although the broadside bears no date or place of publication, it must have been printed shortly after Strang's return to Beaver Island in November, 1850, and it may have been intended primarily for the Saints on the island, since the originals of the documents it contained were declared to be available "at the office of publication, for the inspection of literary connoiseurs." Attacking Adams at one of his most vulnerable points, his proclivity for the stage, the broadside is made up of five letters dealing with his tangled marital affairs, each constituting one act in this "famous original five act drama." Act First is "The great tragedian's anonymous letter accusing his wife of being a drunkard, and scolding her for not dying sooner." Act Second is "The rich widow's anonymous letter endorsing her own excellent and amiable character." Act Third is "The great tragedian in ill luck. Imposture exposed. Discovery on the testimony of the woman herself that his wife was not dead." Act Fourth is "The catastrophe. Letter of Mrs. Margaret Duff {apparently Adams' sister} to Mr. G. J. Adams. Death of Mrs. Adams." Act Fifth is "The after piece. Sorrow of the great tragedian, not for the dead, but the living. The strong minded man growing gray. Jealous of DR. AKENSIDE. Asking his friend to peep behind the scenes." This last letter is from Adams to Strang himself, dated Dark Co., Twin Township, Ohio, Aug. 14, 1850, written in his most extravagant vein: "James!! I love!! Louisa!!! My *Dear Wife!!!! Yes love her to* MADNESS." The letter asks Strang to watch over Louisa and keep her pure and inviolate: "She must Not be ruined, one in particular I Mean a *tall man under* the *Garb* of *friendship*, if he Suckceeds I am a lost ruined undone Man." With his polished irony Strang adds some closing remarks concerning "the great tragedian and his talented assistant," and aims a gibe at Charles O'Malley, the justice of the peace with whom he had lately contended at Mackinac.

CtY-C

{CHURCH OF JESUS CHRIST OF LATTER DAY SAINTS}

{20} *Northern Islander.* Saint James, Beaver Island {Michigan}. By Cooper & Chidester. Vol. I, No. 1. December 12, 1850, 53.3 × 35.6 cm.

Successor of a kind to the *Gospel Herald,* the *Northern Islander* was the first newspaper published in northern Michigan. In their salutatory Strang's printers, Frank Cooper and Edward Chidester, declared that the paper was to be "the gazette of the Islands; devoted to their interests; as well as a vehicle of general news, literature, science, and the arts. And issuing among a people exclusively saints (in derision called Mormons) it will of course strongly reflect their interests and feelings. Yet it is not intended as the official organ of the church, but a paper for general reading. The publishers will, nevertheless, as matters of news, keep their readers informed of every thing of interest, both relating to the Mormon colonies in this region, and all the various settlements commenced in the upper lake country." They also announced: "The *Islander* will be sent to the subscribers of the Gospel Herald, for the periods which they are severally entitled to that paper. We shall issue a periodical exclusively theological, as soon as we can obtain a supply of paper of the proper quality. We were disappointed in obtaining a supply before the close of navigation." It never did become possible to publish this "periodical exclusively theological," and the *Islander* served as the organ of the Church until the dispersion from Beaver Island. A 5-column paper costing $2 a year, the *Islander* was to have been published once a month while Lake Michigan was icebound, and once a week during the season of navigation, but so many and varied were the troubles which beset the Saints that publication throughout its history was highly irregular. As a nominal weekly, the *Islander* was published at St. James from December 12, 1850, to June 19, 1856. One known extra was published during that time {No. 24}, and a nominal daily was got out in connection with the weekly in 1856 {No. 29}. A legend has arisen that the *Islander* was printed on a press brought to Michigan by French Jesuits in the eighteenth century (see Douglas C. McMurtrie, *Early Printing in Michigan* {Chicago[: John Calhoun Club], 1931}, 323–324), but such legends have arisen in ignorance of the earlier printing history of the Strangite church in Wisconsin, and allusions in the Strang MSS make it quite clear, if logic did not, that this press, originally purchased in Philadelphia in 1846, was moved to Beaver Island in the summer of 1850.

Volume and issue numbering is confused, particularly for the year 1852, but Wingfield Watson's file of the *Islander,* preserved by the Church at Voree, and also to be seen in photostat at the State Historical Society of Wisconsin and the Burton Historical Collection of the Detroit Public Library, makes it possible to sketch the history of the *Islander* with reasonable accuracy. One issue, December 12, was printed in 1850. Volume numbering was generally in accordance with the calendar year, but the first volume was carried over into 1851, Nos. 2–13 being published on the following dates: January 9, February 6, March {__}, April 3, May 1–15, June 5, July 24–31, August 14, 28. If the numbering can be trusted, 29 issues were published in 1852, comprising the second volume, but the *Islander* of January 24, 1856, asserts that 26 issues were published that year, while the whole numbering, which commenced in 1854, would indicate that no less than 32 issues were printed in 1852.

Presumably the issue numbering is the best criterion, though the *Islander* was far from being uniformly reliable in this respect. Evidently the first number for 1852 was published in January or February, since the Watson file begins with No. 2, March 4 (dated inside March 18). The next number in the Watson file, April 22, is impossibly dated No. 9, more probably No. 6, since the lake as late as April 22 was not yet open for navigation. The third number in the Watson file for 1852, June 17, is also dated No. 9; an apology in this issue makes it clear that there had been a lapse in publication since mid-May, at least. Vol. II, No. 10, June 24, is lacking in the Watson file, but a copy, recently unearthed by Edward Eberstadt & Sons, is in the Coe Collection. From this date the Watson file constitutes a reasonably responsible index to the contents of the second volume, as it includes Nos. 11–18, 20–22, 24, 26–27, and 29—i.e., July 1–August 19, September 2–16, 30, October 14–21, and November 11. Obviously the *Islander* achieved weekly frequency from June 17 to November 11, except that it failed of publication on either October 28 or November 4. Assuming that no issues were published after November 11 and that the numbering of the first issues in this volume was not wholly confused, 29 numbers in all were published in 1852.

Owing to grave upsets in island affairs, only three regular numbers were published in 1853, April 28, May 5, and June 30. In 1854 Vol. IV was made up of 20 issues, January {__}, February 2, March 2, April 13, May {__}, June 1–22, July 13, 27, August {3 or 10}, 17–24, September 7, 21–28, October {__}, November 2, 30. Whole numbering began with this volume. How trustworthy this numbering may be is a matter of doubt; however, February 2 is Whole No. 49, and November 2 is Whole No. 66, the final issue for 1854 not being present in the Watson file. In 1855 Vol. V consisted of 16 numbers, May 31, June 14–21, July 5, 19, 26, August 9–23, September 6–20. October 11–18, November 1, December 6 (Whole Nos. 68–83). The last volume of the *Islander* comprised 8 numbers, January 24, February 14, March 13, April 3, May 1, 22, June 5, 19. By mistake the issue of May 1, "No. 4, Whole No. 87," repeated the numbering of the issue of April 3, and this error was not corrected up to the time publication ceased. By its own numbering, the last issue of the weekly *Islander* was No. 90. Adding the inaccurately numbered issue of May 1 would make a total of 91. But if the issues of the several volumes are added up, taking 29 as the correct number for 1852, it is seen that 89 regular numbers were published. The *Islander* of January 24, 1856, gave erroneous totals of the volumes not only for the year 1852 but for 1854, in which year, so it was said, 25 issues had been published.

CtY-C Jun 24, 1852; Mar 2, Sep 28 1854.

WBuC Dec 12, 1850; Jan 9, Feb 6, Apr 3, May 1–15, Jun 5, Jul 24–31, Aug 14, 28, 1851; Mar 4, Apr 22, Jun 17, Jul 1–Aug 19, Sep 2–16, 30, Oct 14–21, Nov 11, 1852; Apr 28, May 5, Jun 30, 1853; Feb 2, Mar 2, Apr 13, Jun 1–22, Jul 13, 27, Aug 17–24, Sep 7, 21–28, Nov 2, 1854; May 31, Jun 14–21, Jul 5, 19, 26, Aug 9–23, Sep 6–20, Oct 11–18, Nov 1, Dec 6, 1855; Jan 24, Feb 14, Mar 13, Apr 3, May 1, 22, Jun 5, 19, 1856.

WHi May 1, 1856.

1851

JAMES J. STRANG

{21} *The Book of the Law of the Lord, consisting of an inspired translation of some of the most important parts of the law given to Moses, and a very few additional commandments, with brief notes and references.*

Saint James: Printed by command of the King, at the Royal Press. A.R.I. {1851} viii, 9–80 pp. 17.8 × 11.4 cm.

None of Strang's publications has excited the interest of bibliographers more than this original edition of the *Book of the Law of the Lord.* One of the curiosities of American publishing because of the peculiarities of its title page and its bearing on the expanded book of the same title printed five years later, it has been extraordinarily rare. Of the 200 copies said (in the *Islander* of January 24, 1856) to have been printed, the only one known to have survived was Gilbert Watson's, presented in 1878 to Wingfield Watson, and after the latter's death in 1923, preserved by his daughter, Mrs. E.M. White. The present whereabouts of this copy among the late Mrs. White's effects is not known, but meantime a second copy has been brought to light by the Eberstadts, and this is the only one definitely located as this bibliography goes to press. It is doubtful that many more can be in existence; Watson told Dr. Quaife that most had gone the way of his own original copy, worn out in use. Mr. Lloyd A. Flanders writes me that he has been told by old-timers in the Church "that the original Small Edition was not authorized for general distribution but was printed in small numbers for use of the ministry and Saints only." The small number of copies printed, and the lack of a contemporary announcement of its publication, supports such a verbal tradition.

The *Book of the Law of the Lord* was the first book or pamphlet published after the establishment of the press on Beaver Island, and its odd dating, which evidently means Anno Regio I (In the First Year of the King) reflects the circumstance that Strang's followers had crowned him a "king in Zion" in an elaborate ceremony at St. James on July 8, 1850. The book contains revelations by Strang not given until February, 1851, so that it was published, presumably, sometime between February and July, 1851.

The name of the book may have been suggested by the fact that in Joseph Smith's day a manuscript record with such a title was maintained by the church scribes in Nauvoo; allusions to it are scattered through the "History of Joseph Smith" from 1841, by which it would seem to have been a catch-all record for revelations, tithe-payments, and other matters of church business. According to Strang's own preface, however, the Book of the Law of the Lord was the most important of all the lost books of the Bible, kept in the Ark of the Covenant and too sacred to go into the hands of strangers. "When the Septuagint translation was made, the Book of the Law was kept back, and the Book lost to the Jewish nation in the time that they were subject to foreign powers. The various books in the Pentateuch, containing abstracts of some of the laws, have been read instead of it, until even the existence of the book has come to be a matter of doubt. It is from an authorized copy of that book, written on metallick plates long previous to the Babylonish captivity, that this translation is made. And being made by the same spirit by which the words were originally dictated, it is beyond doubt as perfect as the language will admit of. The utmost pains have been taken to make the execution of it in all respects what it should be, and the editor flatters himself that no errour has crept into the body of the work, and none of importance into the notes." A note following the table of contents further explains that Strang's source was "the plates of Laban, taken from the house of Laban, in Jerusalem, in the days of Zedekiah, king of Judah," these being plates which figure prominently in the early chapters of the Book of Mormon. All of the 38 chapters comprising the book were translated from these plates except Chapter II, "written by the prophet James, by inspiration of God," Chapter V, "a revelation from Jesus Christ, given to James J. Strang, Aug. 9th, 1849," the first six sections of Chapter XII, "written by the prophet James, by inspiration of God," and the nine following sections, "the words of the angel of God when he conferred upon James J. Strang the prophetic authority, and made him the chief shepherd of the flock of God on earth"; the first three sections of Chapter XXVI, "a revelation from God, given to James J. Strang, July 8th, 1850"; Chapter XXX, "a revelation given Feb., 1851, except the first two sections"; and Chapter XXXVIII, "a revelation given Feb., 1851."

The preliminary matter includes the title, "testimony" of seven witnesses, preface, table of contents, and a statement (as noted above) of the origin of the several portions of the book. The main text begins with Chapter I, numbered p. 9, and ends on p. 80 with a summation of the entire contents, amounting to 38 chapters, 285 sections, 15,488 words, and 65,659 letters. This peculiarity of totaling the minutiae of printing is said to have been a precaution taken against future unauthorized changes in text. Strang himself, however, made some subsequent changes; for these see the Note to the expanded edition of 1856 {No. 31}. The title page is decorated with a vignette which in the context might be supposed to represent the Ark of the Covenant; however, this decorative device was reproduced in the *Gospel Herald* so early as June 1, 1848, and was used again in 1854 on the title page of *The Epistles of Oliver Cowdery* {No. 26}. No great amount of information has survived to document the actual writing of the *Book of the Law*. It seems to have been principally written in the winter of 1849–50 while Strang was living in Baltimore and Philadelphia, but the only definite allusion in the Strang MSS is a letter from George J. Adams, {February} 18, 1850, which expresses pleasure that Strang is "getting along So well with the translation of the plates." The idea of publishing such a work was much older, for on April 13, 1849, in a letter to Strang from North Bay, Oneida County, N.Y., Alden Hale wrote, "it might be well for you to give to br {Ebenezer} Page the name quality & amount of type you wish for the publishing the new translations also the cost of the same at Chicago & also the size quality & price per lb. of printing paper at your place it is ten cts here but a better quality than yours. & also the apparatus for binding & means." As an indication when typesetting began, the *Northern Islander* of February 6, 1851 printed the Decalogue, which constitutes the first chapter of the published book. Reprinted in 1927 {No. 91}.

CtY-C

{TOWNSHIP OF PEAINE}

{22} *Ordinances and By-Laws of the Township of Peaine, adopted in the years 1851–2. By Authority.*

Saint James: Cooper & Chidester Printers. 1852. 18, {4} pp. 17.8 × 13.1 cm.

This pamphlet was unknown until the Eberstadts, with their uncanny flair for such things, turned up a copy in the summer of 1950. It was not listed by the *Northern Islander* in its accounting of the publications of the Strang press, hence the number of copies published is not known, but there could not have been many. Except for the index, the content of the pamphlet was published in the *Islander* of April 22, 1852. The *Ordinances* has a wrapper title with the same text as the title page, but differently set up, and with "Township" misspelled "Towpship." Curiously, the wrapper is included in the pagination. The collation is: Wrapper title, verso blank, pp. {1–2}; title page, verso blank, pp. {3–4}; "Township Ordinances. 1851," pp. 5–8; "Township Ordinances. 1852," pp. 8–16; "Regulations of the Board of Health," pp. 17–18; "Peaine Organized," p. {19}; "Township Officers. 1852," p. {20}; index, pp. {21–22}. Peaine constituted "all that part of the county of Mackinaw designated as the Beaver Islands in Lake Michigan," and was organized under an act of the Michigan legislature approved March 16, 1847. The township officers notably included in 1852 James J. Strang as supervisor and George Miller as treasurer. The ordinances of 1851 are in two chapters, "Pound" and "Domestic Animals"; those of 1852 are in four chapters, "Quarantine," "Hospital," "Dogs," and "Gunpowder"; while the lone chapter constituting the regulations of the Board of Health is concerned with the exposure of stinking fish. The wrapper and the title page are decorated by a vignette of an Indian with bow and arrow. This cut appeared originally in the *Gospel Herald* of June 8, 1848, and in 1854 it was used again on the wrapper of *Ancient and Modern Michilimackinac* {No. 25}. This latter work has a considerable account of the political situation in which Peaine Township figured so large, and the maneuver by which Strang won himself a place in the Michigan legislature.

CtY-C

CHURCH OF JESUS CHRIST OF LATTER DAY SAINTS

{23} {A Collection of Sacred Hymns; adapted to the faith and views of the Church of Jesus Christ of Latter Day Saints. Third Edition.}

{Saint James: Cooper & Chidester. 1852.}

No copy located. This entry is conjectural, based upon an advertisement in the *Northern Islander,* September 16, 1852: "Hymn Books. Just received and for sale. St. James Sept. 15, 1852." It is highly unlikely that hymnals were imported to St. James, particularly with a press in operation there. It is much more probable that a third portion of the sheets printed in 1849 were bound at this time with a new title page. The hymn book is included here, even as a doubtful title, in the hope that the attention given it may serve in bringing a copy to light.

1853

{CHURCH OF JESUS CHRIST OF LATTER DAY SAINTS}

Northern Islander Extra. Murderous Assault—Attack on Sheriff Miller—Six Men Wounded.

Saint James: Thursday, July 14, 1853. Broadside. 52 × 23 cm.

The above description comes from a photostat made for M. M. Quaife of a copy of the original at one time in the possession of Wingfield Watson, this copy being at present unlocated. The text was reprinted in *A Few Historical Facts Concerning the Murderous Assault at Pine River* {Nos. 52, 88}, and again by Dr. Quaife in *The Kingdom of St. James,* 271–275. The attack upon the Mormons by the fishermen of Mackinac, chronicled in this *Extra,* was responsible for the fact that no further issues of the *Islander* were published in 1853, the printers being drawn away from their establishment in connection with the lengthy court action which followed.

1854

JAMES J. STRANG

Ancient and Modern Michilimackinac, including an account of the controversy between Mackinac and the Mormons.

{Saint James: Cooper & Chidester.} MDCCCLIV {1854}. 48 pp. 21.4 × 14 cm.

Cover title. In double columns, and with a paragraph of errata at the end. The principal content of this pamphlet appeared as a series of articles under the title, "Beaver Islands and Emmet County," in the first four numbers of Vol. IV of the *Islander.* In it Strang surveys the geography and history of Mackinac and the surrounding region, particularly the islands of Lake Michigan, and after giving an account of the Mormon settlement upon Big Beaver Island, addresses himself to the bitter controversies between the people of Mackinac and the Mormons. Although dealing with controverted matters and colored by Strang's indignation at the outrages he and his people had had to endure, the pamphlet is a responsible source on the events of which it treats, and is also interesting for the considerable measure of learning it reveals in Strang. The recto and the verso of the back wrapper are given over to "Notices of the Press" displaying an unwonted respect for Strang and the Mormons. The pamphlet was announced for sale in the *Islander* of June 1, 1854; 600 copies were printed. Strang published as a kind of supplement to this work "Some Remarks on the Natural History of Beaver Islands, Michigan," in the Smithsonian Institution's *Annual Report,* 1854, (Washington, 1855), pp. 282–288.

CtY-C, DLC, ICN, MiD-B, MiU[-C], OClWHi, WHi

OLIVER COWDERY

{26} *The Epistles of Oliver Cowdery, on the bringing in of a New dispensation.*

Saint James: Cooper & Chidester. 1854. iv, {5}–56 pp. 21 × 13.5 cm.

Cover title. In double columns. The preface, pp. {iii}–iv, and the Appendix, pp. {54}–56, are by Strang; the rest of the pamphlet, pp. {5}–53, is given over to the eight letters concerning the early history of Joseph Smith and the Church which Cowdery had published in 1834–35 in the *Latter Day Saints' Messenger and Advocate.* These letters, with the added material by Strang, appeared in the *Northern Islander,* June 1–September 7, 1854, and doubtless the pamphlet made its appearance by October. The title page, which is reproduced in M. M. Quaife's *The Kingdom of St. James,* p. 188, is decorated by the same cut which appeared on the title of *The Book of the Law of the Lord* {No. 21}. According to the *Northern Islander* of January 24, 1856, 1,100 copies were printed. Since the Cowdery letters have been reprinted many times by the various Mormon churches, the feature of chief interest in this edition is Strang's own contribution to it. The Preface declares that in the 20 years since the letters were first published, Mormonism "has ceased to be despised by any but fools and men of a past age." With its two or three hundred thousand believers, the present generation has to "look it in the face." Cowdery's little work "will live when the nations of the earth are broken. Though the language in which it is written shall be forgotten, it shall be fresh in the courts of heaven while truth remains and God lives." The Appendix defends the Book of Mormon against the many criticisms of its style and content voiced in the 24 years since it was first published. See also Nos. 38, 65.

CtY-C, MH

1856

JAMES J. STRANG

{27} {The Prophetic Controversy. A Letter from James J. Strang to Mrs. Corey. Saint James, Sept. 26, 1854.}

{Saint James: Cooper & Chidester. 1856?} 44 pp. 26.9 × 18 cm.

No copy of this work intact with the title page is known, the only specimen of the first edition which has turned up being that in the Coe Collection, which lacks the first 2 and last 4 pages. It is evident that if the pamphlet had a title page, it was not included in the pagination; possibly it had a caption title only, without date or place of publication. This view is the more probable in that three subsequent reprints had caption titles. The total number of pages stated, 41, comes from the *Islander* of January 24, 1856, which also notes that 1,000 copies were printed.

Strang's letter to "Mrs. Corey" (i.e., Mrs. Howard Coray) was first published in the *Islander* in the four issues beginning September 28, 1854, but was not republished in pamphlet form until at least a year after that date, for Strang added to it an extract from a letter George Miller published in the *Islander* of September 6, 1855. The fact that the pamphlet had not been announced for publication down to December 6, 1855, would indicate that it was published after that date; it is here assumed that it issued from the press early in January, 1856. The "Letter" itself is an eloquent restatement of the grounds on which Strang based his claims to authority, and recounts in considerable detail his efforts to establish his rights to the Succession, with attention to the shifting position taken by the Twelve between 1844 and 1847. The pamphlet has been thrice reprinted {Nos. 35, 44, 54}.

JAMES HUTCHINS

} *Guide to Eternal Life.* By James Hutchins.

{Saint James: Cooper & Chidester. 1856?} 12 pp.

Nothing is known of this pamphlet except that the *Islander* of January 24, 1856, in listing the publications of the St. James press, mentions that it had printed "1,000 copies 'Guide to Eternal Life,' by James Hutchins, 12 pages, double column." The tract would seem to have been published at the same time as Strang's *Prophetic Controversy.*

{CHURCH OF JESUS CHRIST OF LATTER DAY SAINTS}

} *Daily Northern Islander.* Saint James, Lake Michigan. {By} Cooper & Chidester. Vol. I, No. 1. Tuesday, April 1, 1856. 4 pp. 30.2 × 26 cm. {later issues 37 × 27.8 cm.}

The first issue of the *Daily Northern Islander* appeared April 1, 1856, in fulfillment of the announcement made in the weekly *Islander* of January 24, 1856: "We now announce that hereafter the Islander will be published as a daily and weekly paper. One weekly will be issued every week during the season of navigation, and every month during the suspension of navigation, at $2.00 a year, and the daily *Islander* every day, except Sabbath, during the season of navigation, and every week during the suspension of navigation, at $5.00 {later $6} a year." In their first number Cooper & Chidester observed dryly, "The *Daily* is out a little earlier than we anticipated, and we doubt not some years earlier than most men looked for it. Truly, we hardly consider it commenced yet, bur having the matter of this number in type, and wishing to preserve it, have made up number one without advertisements, or commercial matter; and shall get out number two in good season, and issue, in fact, daily, from the arrival of the first boat." The lead article deals with the imminent opening of the lake. The rest of the issue, 10 1/4 columns, is given over to an article, "Origin of the Book of Mormon," which apparently had been written—at any rate it was eventually published—as Note IV to the chapter on "Priesthood" in the enlarged edition of *The Book of the Law of the Lord.* The same matter appeared in the weekly *Islander* of April 3, and proofsheets of it may be extant, for Strang mentions that such sheets had been sent to Benjamin Ferris, author of *Utah and the Mormons,* for whatever rebuttal he might care to make of criticisms levied against his book. Only three issues of the *Daily* are known, the first and last, in the Coe Collection, and the eighth, May 5, in the library of the Reorganized Church. Because the matter published in the *Daily* was generally reprinted in the *Weekly,* 22 of the 33 issues can be dated. These include April 1, 29 (announcing the opening of navigation), April 30, May 1, 5, 7–9, 11–13, 19–20, 23, 25–26, 28–30, June 5, 8, 20. The last issue, June 20, 1856, Vol. I, No. 33, has a long account of the murderous assault on Strang which ended in his death, and with it a sad little paragraph stating: "In consequence of the laying up of Mr Strang with his wounds, and the disarrangement of affairs growing out of the occurrence, the *Daily Islander* will be suspended." As it turned out, this applied also to the *Weekly*.

The first number of the *Daily* was printed with a 3-column page, but when regular publication began, a 4-column page was adopted; the *Daily* for May 5 and June 20 have that character. A photostat of the issue for June 20 is in the Burton Historical Collection of the Detroit Public Library; a microfilm of that for May 5 is in the Library of Congress. A biographical sketch of Frank Cooper and Edward Chidester, co-publishers of the *Northern Islander*, together with a portrait of the latter, is published in *The Gospel Herald*, January, 1942 {see No. 101}.

CtY-C Apr 1, Jun 20, 1856
MoInRC May 5, 1856

CHURCH OF JESUS CHRIST OF LATTER DAY SAINTS

{30} {A *Collection of Sacred Hymns; adapted to the faith and views of the Church of Jesus Christ of Latter Day Saints.* Fourth edition.}

{Saint James: Cooper & Chidester. 1856. 172 pp.}

As with the supposed third edition of the hymnal, the above title is conjectural. It is included here on the authority of an advertisement published in the *Islander* from April 3, 1856: "We shall issue in May next 'Sacred Hymns,' a small volume, selected for the use of the Latter Day Saints. 172 pp. Price, in morocco binding, 50 cents. This is printed, folded, and ready for the binder." The sheets conceivably were destroyed at the time of the dispersion from Beaver Island, but as this book was in a more advanced state than *The Book of the Law of the Lord*, and as the sheets of the latter work were preserved, a copy may yet appear.

JAMES J. STRANG

{31} {*The Book of the Law of the Lord.*}

{Saint James: 1856.} {17}–336 pp.

Among the many publications of the Strangite church, none bulks so large in its doctrinal system or its complex bibliographical history as this expanded edition of the *Book of the Law of the Lord.* The unbound sheets comprising the book were carried along when Strang's followers left the islands after his death, and for safekeeping these sheets were deposited in small lots in the homes of various members. Over a period of years, portions of these sheets were bound for use, sometimes without title page or preliminary matter, sometimes with front matter printed for this purpose. Although bibliographers have been able to distinguish four principal variants, priority as to issue has been baffling. Some further light is here shed on the history of the book, including the probable number of copies, but it is by no means yet possible to deal definitely with the complexities of this history.

The first printed intimation that there was to be an enlarged edition of the *Book of the Law* appeared in the *Northern Islander* of January 24, 1856, when the office was declared to be "engaged on the 'Book of the Law of the Lord,' 2,100 copies, 320 pp." Extracts were printed in that issue of the *Islander,* and again on February 14, March 13, April 3, and May 1, 1856. An advertisement that ran from April 3 until the *Islander* ceased publication announced that the printing of the work was about three-fourths done. The book was to have been ready for the binder during that month, and for the market before the end of May, to comprise from 320 to 350 pp., and sell, bound in calf, for $2. Mr. Lloyd A. Flanders has suggested to me that the book, as it was carried in sheets from the island later that year, was probably incomplete, that Strang, had he lived, would have added a few more chapters. This, however, can apply only to the preliminary matter, for the completeness of the basic text is attested by the fact that on the last page, and only on the last page, appears a cumulative total of the number of chapters, sections, words, and letters, and this of course had been printed before Strang's death.

In a narrative written for the Coldwater, Mich., *Reporter* in September, 1896, seven months before his death, the apostle L. D. Hickey asserted that at the time of Strang's death there were 1,500 copies of the *Book of the Law* in the printing office ready for the binder. If this memory was exact, the plans for the book held in January, 1856, had been somewhat modified. Hickey was one of a committee of three who assumed the care of the church property on Beaver Island, including the sheets of the book, and according to a letter from Edward Chidester to Warren Post, dated August 3, 1856 (cited in Quaife, *The Kingdom of St. James*, p. 189), these sheets were boxed and shipped to Racine, Wisconsin, where Benjamin Wright, an apostle and father of one of Strang's plural wives, took them in charge. "As no one was able to get them bound," Hickey recalled, "we stored them with our people for safety. Some of them have been faithful and taken good care of them: others have been careless and let the mice and rain destroy them." Just when Strang's followers began having copies of the book bound for their own use is not known, but a letter in the Strang MSS from Wingfield Watson to Gilbert Watson, February 16, 1862, makes it evident that each had a bound copy of the book at that time. Probably the first copies thus bound lacked title page and preliminary matter; a number of such copies exist, bearing only the caption title at the head of p. 17: Book of the Law. | The Decalogue.

The earliest record of any disposition of the unbound sheets by formal action of the Church is found in the minutes of the conference at Hixton, Wisconsin, December 25, 1863, when authorization was given for binding 100 copies for the use of the Saints. These too probably had no front matter. As late as the spring of 1864, at least 915 copies of the book were still preserved in sheets; Mr. Flanders has among the Church records receipts for this many copies given between February 15 and April 24, 1864; the number of copies distributed among the Saints varied from 50 to 150, passed out "for safekeeping until called for by a Church Committee." The distributing committee consisted of C. S. Daniels and J. Raymond, and receipts were signed by J. C. Hill, Chester I. Linnell, C. S. Daniels, Nephi Nichols, M. R. Letson, J. Raymond, and George Wantz, all at Hixton.

It was probably 1878 or later before copies of the *Book of the Law* began appearing with a title page; this date is suggested because a resurgence of publishing activity began at about that time. The title page of the original or pamphlet edition of 1851 was followed (so literally as to repeat the dating, "A.R. I," rather than "A.R. VI," as it more properly would have been), and the rest of the front matter of the original edition was employed, with only such changes as the changes in the book itself required. Three variant issues have been distinguished having this front matter, for the first two of which L.D. Hickey seems to have been responsible, the other owing to Strang's son, Charles. The three issues with title pages may be described as follows:

{A} The | Book of the Law | of | the Lord | consisting of | An Inspired Translation of some of the | Most Important Parts of the law | given to Moses, and a very few | Additional Commandments, | with Brief Notes and | References. | Printed by command of the King | at the Royal Press | Saint James | A.R.I. In this issue the testimony on the verso of the title page is signed by three rather than by seven witnesses, and the rest of the introductory matter is completed in 7 pages. Some copies having this character contain a leaf preceding the title page, an "Explanatory" note signed in holograph by Charles J. Strang. One such copy in the Western Reserve Historical Society library bears a note by Wingfield Watson: "I see that in this edition L.D. Hickey has put the testimony of only three witnesses to the plates, from which this book has been translated, in this book, whereas there was seven witnesses to it in the first place, four of whose names I have attached."

{B} The | Book of the Law of the Lord; | consisting of an Inspired Translation of Some of the Most | Important Parts of the Law given to Moses, | and a very few Additional Commandments, with Brief Notes and References. | Printed by command of the King | at the Royal Press, St. James. | A.R.I. Aside from these slight variations in the makeup of the title page, this issue is like {A} above. Sabin has assumed that this particular issue appeared between 1890 and 1900, but there does not seem to be any concrete evidence which would either prove or disprove the assumption.

{C} The | Book of the Law | of | the Lord | consisting of | An Inspired Translation of some of the most important | Parts of the Law given to Moses, and a very | few Additional Commandments, with | Notes and References. | Printed by Command of the King. | At the Royal Press, | St. James, A.R.I. This issue differs from the two above in that the preliminary matter extends over 8 pages rather than 7, and that the testimony on the verso of the title is signed by seven rather than three witnesses. Sabin conjectured that this particular issue appeared about 1920, but the Church at Voree has Charles J. Strang's personal copy, noted as having been received from the binder on June 30, 1891, agreeing in all respects with the above description; I am informed that it was this copy which was employed in the 1949 reprint of the book {No. 104}.

A complication in determining when any particular copy may have been bound is that a supply of the various sheets of prefatory matter was for years preserved among the

Saints; thus when Dr. Quaife, in the 1920's, assembled a few complete copies from unbound sheets of the book which he had found in central Wisconsin, he was able to obtain front matter for them from Wingfield Watson, and the copies he placed in circulation differ only in the binding from the {C} variant described above. Similarly Mr. Flanders, who was baptized into the Church so late as 1922, informs me that sheets of the 1856 book were bound in Kansas City within his remembrance.

The principal difference between the expanded *Book of the Law* of 1856 and the original edition of 1851 is the great elaboration of the notes. The chapter which comprises the revelation on "Baptism for the Dead" is materially altered, and nine chapters, on "Oaths," "Benedictions," "Maledictions," "Prayer," "Thanksgiving," "Sacrifice," "Monuments," "High Priest," and "Priesthood" are added. Thus the enlarged edition has 47 chapters, 332 sections, 16,865 words, and 71,538 letters, exclusive of the notes.

CtY-C, DLC, IHi, MH, MiD-B, MiU-C, MoInRC, NN, OClWHi, RPB, USlC, WBuC, WHi

1871

JAMES HUTCHINS

} *An Outline Sketch of the Travels of James Hutchins.*

{n.p. 1871?} 123 pp. 19.8 × 13.2 cm.

Caption title. Although it does not appear from his narrative, Hutchins was a member of the Strangite Quorum of the Twelve at the time of Strang's death. His pamphlet is in part a sketchy autobiography and in part a collection of what might be called sermons. The autobiographical matter is written in the third person but (in the Coe copy, at all events) corrected by holograph to the first person. Hutchins was born in Tennessee and reared in southwestern Mississippi. Converted by a Mormon missionary late in 1843, he removed to Nauvoo next year, but was out in the mission field at the time of Joseph Smith's death. He followed Brigham Young as far as Council Bluffs, but after living in Iowa for some years made his way to Beaver Island, at which place, as he says, the kingdom foretold by Daniel had been set up. After the dispersion from the islands, Hutchins settled in Jackson County, Wisconsin, with many of his fellow Saints. Trouble arose, his home torn down in the course of it, and Hutchins removed to Black River Falls, where possibly this pamphlet was published. Incorporated into his narrative are addresses he wrote to Pres. [Andrew] Johnson, March 4, 1868, and Pres. [Ulysses S.] Grant, March 25, 1869, each of these dignitaries being exhorted to penitence and righteousness. Of greater interest is an account of a missionary tour made to Utah in August, 1870. Brigham Young denied him facilities to preach, and the pamphlet contains the epistles Hutchins wrote Young expressing his sorrow that the gates had been locked against him. Doubtless this was the first Strangite mission to Utah.

CtY-C, ViU

1876

JAMES HUTCHINS

{33} *An Earnest Appeal for Justice.* By James Hutchins.

Black River Falls, Wis.: Published by the Author. 1876. 62 pp. 20.1 × 13.5 cm.

Cover title. The text, beginning on p. {3}, is headed: "To the Honorable President and Cabinet Council of the Commonwealth of the United States of North America — Greeting:" Hutchins appeals "in the name of virtue and justice that we {the Mormons} may be restored to the state and national liberties and rights that constitutionally belong to us," by which he has reference to the Missouri outrages of 1833–39. He recites the circumstances under which the Saints were driven from Missouri, incorporating into his narrative Noah Packard's Memorial of 1844 to the Governor, Senate, and House of Representatives of Massachusetts, together with a long extract from Charles Mackay's *History of the Mormons.* All pleadings in behalf of the Saints, Hutchins declares, have been in vain; the United States has been deaf and blind to Mormon importunities for redress. As in the case of Hutchins' pamphlets of 1879 and 1881, this publication contains no history or doctrine specific to the Strangite church, but records in the possession of Mr. Flanders show that Hutchins was still officiating in its ordinances in the late seventies, and it may be assumed that he was a member at the time he published the "Appeal."

CtY-C, NN

1877

WINGFIELD WATSON

{34} *The Necessity of Baptism; and of Having Authority from God to Preach the Gospel.* {Signed:} Wingfield Watson, Boyne, Charlevoix Co., Mich.

Plano, Ill.: Printed at the Herald Steam Book and Job Office. {1877.} 8 pp. 32 × 23 cm.

Caption title. In triple columns. From the fact that this pamphlet bears the imprint of the press of the Reorganized Church, the New York Public Library *Bulletin,* March, 1909, p. 239, listed it among the publications of that church. Its content was, in fact, first printed in the *Saints' Herald,* "Baptism" in the issue for October 1, 1876, Vol. XXIII, pp. 579–585, and "Authority in the Name of God" in the issue for July 15, 1877, Vol. XXIV, pp. 209–212. This however was only in conformance with the policy of Joseph Smith III to admit variant points of view into the *Herald,* which between 1862 and 1883 printed a number of articles and communications by Watson. The argument of the pamphlet is broadly theological without proceeding necessarily out of the doctrinal system of the Strangite church.

NN

1878

JAMES J. STRANG

The Prophetic Controversy. A Letter from James J. Strang to Mrs. Corey.

{Boyne, Mich.? 1878?} 49 pp. {and page of errata}. 21.2 × 14.2 cm.

Caption title. The date of this first reprint of *The Prophetic Controversy* is not definitely established, but it is reasonable to conclude that it was printed in or close to 1878. About this time Wingfield Watson opened a new era in Strangite polemic, and in 1878 he acquired, from Gilbert Watson's widow, a considerable collection of the early publications of the Church. It is probable that this new edition of *The Prophetic Controversy* was published simultaneously with a new edition of *The Diamond* {No. 36}. All this is in the realm of conjecture, but in view of the fact that this 49-page edition was listed for sale in *The Revelations of James J. Strang* {No. 42} it is at least established that it was in print by February, 1885. Inasmuch as it was advertised for sale by Wingfield Watson, it may be reasonably supposed that it was printed in the vicinity of Boyne, Michigan, where he at the time was living.

CtY-C, MH, NN, WBuC, WHi

JAMES J. STRANG

The Diamond: Being the Law of Prophetic Succession and a Defense of the Calling of James J. Strang as Successor to Joseph Smith. {At head of title:} Gospel Tract No. IV. First published by the Church of Latter Day Saints at Voree, Wis., 1848.

{Boyne, Mich.? 1878?} 16 pp. 22.2 × 14.9 cm.

Caption title. In double columns. This 16-page edition was the first reprint of *The Diamond,* as is evidenced by its having been advertised for sale in *The Revelations of James J. Strang* {No. 42}, The date and place of publication, as conjectured on the basis of the considerations set forth in the Note to No. 35, find some shadow of substantiation in that on first acquiring the pamphlet, the New York Public Library gave it the tentative date 1878. The Library is now unable to say on what this judgment was based, but there is every reason to suppose that it was well-founded. This and other reprints having been attributed at times to Beaver Island, it should be emphasized that no evidence whatever exists that the press on Beaver Island between 1850 and 1856 reprinted any of Strang's polemical works, and there was no press on the Island after 1856. In the case of *The Diamond,* evidence against a St. James provenance is overwhelming {see No. 12, Note}.

CtY-C, NN, RPB, WHi, Morgan

1879

JAMES HUTCHINS

{37} *The Messenger, a Timely Warning, to a Thoughtless World.* {Signed:} James Hutchins.

{Independence, Mo.:} 1879. 23 pp. 20 × 11 cm.

A discourse on "the way of righteousness," about which the pamphlet is insistent because written in "these last days."

NN

1880

OLIVER COWDERY

{38} *Cowdery's Letters, on the Bringing In of the New Dispensation.*

Milwaukee, Wis.: Macrorie & Pitcher, 258 South Water Street. 1880. 33 pp. 19.5 × 14 cm.

A new printing of the letters by Cowdery on the early history of the Church. This is not precisely a reprint of the edition of 1854, for it lacks Strang's preface and appendix. Presumably it was published for Wingfield Watson, since it was one of the pamphlets he advertised for sale in 1885.

CtY-C, NN

1881

JAMES HUTCHINS

{39} *Truth Developed and Falsehood Shown.* {Signed:} James Hutchins, February 27, 1881.

{n.p., 1881.} 14 pp. 21.5 × 15.3 cm.

Another of Hutchins' "sermons in print," having no material specific to the history or doctrinal system of the Strangite church.

USIC

1884

WINGFIELD WATSON

{40} *The Book of Mormon. An Essay on its Claims and Prophecies,* by Wingfield Watson, An Elder in the Church of Jesus Christ of Latter Day Saints. {Dated at end:} Boyne, Charlevoix county, Mich., March 25, 1884.

{Boyne, Mich.? 1884.} 16 pp. 21.5 × 12.4 cm.

Caption title. In double columns. See also Nos. 63, 66.

CtY-C, WBuC

{WINGFIELD WATSON}

Modern Christianity. A Dialogue between a Baptist and an Infidel.

{Boyne, Mich.? 1884?} 10 pp. 20.2 × 13.5 cm.

Caption title. In double columns. No date or place of publication appears, but the tract was doubtless printed at Boyne about 1884, since it was offered for sale in *The Revelations of James J. Strang.* A prefatory note signed W. Watson explains that the dialogue "was written in 1849 during the prevalence of the cholera epidemic, and serves very well to illustrate the difference between the ancient primitive religion of apostles and prophets, and taught by the Latter Day Saints, and that of modern sectarianism. . . . The present publisher found this dialogue in an old file of Latter Day Saints papers, and thinking it too good to be lost, concluded to republish it, adding to it the Scripture references." Watson's source was the *Millennial Star,* Liverpool, January 1, 1850, Vol. XII, pp. 4–9, the author being John Hyde, who figured in a celebrated apostasy in the Utah church and wrote *Mormonism: Its Leaders and Designs* (New York, 1857). For another edition of this work under Strangite auspices, adapted to later proselyting, see No. 96.

CtY-C, WBuC, Morgan

1885

JAMES J. STRANG

} *The Revelations of James J. Strang.*

{Boyne, Mich.? 1885?} 22 pp. 23.4 × 15.6 cm.

Caption title. In double columns. Strang's revelations were not separately printed during his lifetime, and Wingfield Watson explains his reasons for gathering them "in some kind of book form." The revelations were "not in any shape for convenient reading and reference, being had complete only in the church record kept in Voree, Wisconsin," and he felt that making them available "might be followed with some good to others as well as myself and family." He adds: "It is not proposed to print the revelations contained in the letter of appointment, nor the words of the angel that ordained Mr. Strang; as these are already in print, in the Diamond and Prophetic Controversy; a copy of each of which should accompany these revelations, in order that the student of these revelations and claims of Mr. Strang may have them complete up to 1850. Neither is it proposed to print any revelations contained in the Book of the Law, as these would enlarge the work now aimed at beyond the limits intended. The intention is merely to print all Mr. Strang's revelations from 1844 to 1850, excepting the two before mentioned. Those following the latter date are had in the Book of the Law, copies of which may be had of several persons who have them in care." As published, the pamphlet is not the complete compilation aimed at, for it omits a revelation of December 21, 1846, pronouncing a curse upon Kirtland, which may be found in *Zion's Reveille*, January 21, 1847. This revelation, for some reason, was not copied into the Chronicles of Voree.

Watson's introduction runs to a little over 3 pages, followed by 10 revelations and inspired documents, a list of errata, some remarks discussing certain features of the revelations, and finally a list of six tracts offered for sale {Nos. 34, 36, 38, 40, 41 in this bibliography}. The copy of the *Revelations* in the New York Public Library has the holograph date February, 1885, written below this list of tracts, an obviously contemporary notation. The date of the pamphlet is therefore tentatively fixed for 1885, but it may have been late 1884. Aside from the evidence provided by the advertisement, which includes Watson's essay on the Book of Mormon (demonstrably published in 1884), Watson's introduction itself is of service in dating the *Revelations*. Referring to the Utah church membership, he says, "That they have been going into bondage since 1880, is very clear to anyone who is paying the least attention to affairs in Utah. Never has there been so much excitement in this nation against that people as in the last four years."

In addition to its integral features, the pamphlet has tipped in between pages 2 and 3 a separately printed leaf, 16.7 × 12.3 cm., headed, "A Vision, Which James J. Strang had on the day in which Joseph Smith wrote the Letter of Appointment"; and besides this, tipped in between pages 6 and 7, a leaf 22 × 11.5 cm., exhibiting in facsimile the three "Voree Plates" Strang claimed to have found in September, 1845, and to have translated by the Urim and Thummim. The former leaf is paper of poorer quality, the latter paper of better quality, than the pamphlet itself. Whether the plate of facsimiles was prepared especially for use with this pamphlet is not known. A great many copies of this leaf seem to have been printed, and occasionally it is found, tipped in, in some of the later pamphlets got out by Watson—especially the two subsequent editions of *The Prophetic Controversy* {Nos. 44, 54}. It is possible that the copper plate from which the reproductions were made dates back to 1846; see No. 5, Note. For later printings of the revelations, see Nos. 64, 99.

CSmH, CtY-C, MH, NN, WHi, Morgan

JAMES J. STRANG

{43} *Ancient and Modern Michilimackinac as published in 1854, with Supplement.*

St. Ignace, Mich.: The News and Free Press. 1885. 52 pp. 22 × 15 cm.

The provenance of this "outside" edition of *Ancient and Modern Michilimackinac* has been straightened out as the result of researches by Dr. George B. Arbaugh. Seeking to authenticate a document utilized in his *Revelation in Mormonism*, Dr. Arbaugh addressed some inquiries to Will A. Brown, son of Charles R. Brown, an early Michigan lawyer. Mr. Brown wrote in reply on November 18, 1930, "The old document you refer to . . . came into Father's hands sometime between the years of 1881 and 1885, while he was living at St. Ignace. . . . {At this time} father edited and had printed a pamphlet of some 50 odd pages (printed by the News and Free Press of St. Ignace) entitled 'Ancient and Modern

Michilimackinac, including an account of the controversy between Mackinac and the Mormons, as published in 1854, with Supplement. 1885.' I now have in my possession the printed pamphlet published by my father in 1885 (just one copy) but have never seen or possessed the pamphlet from which he made the copy." I am indebted to Dr. Arbaugh for this information. The "supplement," pp. 49–52, reprints the story of Strang's assassination from the *Daily Northern Islander* of June 20, 1856, and brings the history down to date with a description of Mackinac in 1885.

CtY-C, MiD-B, WHi

1886

JAMES J. STRANG

The Prophetic Controversy{.} *A Letter from James J. Strang to Mrs. Corey.*

{Boyne, Mich.? 1886?} 38 pp. 22.1 × 15.2 cm.

Caption title. In double columns. This third printing of *The Prophetic Controversy* may have been printed in 1885, but the 1886 date is regarded as a better approximation. That it was published prior to February, 1887, is evident from a citation in Wingfield Watson's *Prophetic Controversy No. 2*, p. 20, which can apply only to this edition. Equally, it was published after February, 1885, because the 49-page reprint rather than this 38-page reprint was offered for sale in *The Revelations of James J. Strang.*

CtY-C, MH, UHi, USlC, WHi, Morgan

REUBEN T. NICHOLS

The Ministerial Labors of Reuben T. Nichols, in the Church of Jesus Christ of Latter Day Saints. {Signed:} Reuben T. Nichols.

{n. p., 1886?} 11 pp. 23 × 15.5 cm.

Caption title. This little autobiography was probably published in 1886, since the concluding paragraph brings events down to "the present time (1886)." Nichols was born in 1807 and baptized into the Church in 1833. Over the years he did much missionary labor in the Black River District of western New York. He removed to Nauvoo in 1845, and next year was converted by Strang; some of his correspondence is in the Strang MSS. After further missionary work, he settled on Beaver Island in 1854. Nichols may have been one of the polygamous Saints, for he has an account of marrying the widow, Mary Demary, without making quite clear what became of his first wife. After Strang's death, Nichols lived in Wisconsin for a time, but from 1860 made his home in Antrim County, Mich. It would appear that most of the autobiography was written in 1864, and that the last paragraph was added immediately prior to publication. The autobiography of course does not mention the matter, but from the manuscript records of the Church it seems that Nichols committed an extremely grave personal transgression. Although forgiven by the

Church, he was permitted to retain his priesthood only on condition that he refrain from using it. Possibly this incident had something to do with his desire to place on record the constructive employment of his priesthood earlier in life.

CtY-C, UHi, WBuC, Morgan

1887

WINGFIELD WATSON

{46} *Prophetic Controversy, No. 2; Extracted from the Writings and Criticisms of John E. Page, James J. Strang, William Marks and Hyrum P. Brown, to which are added A Few Notes in Brackets, and a Short Commentary by the Transcriber, Wingfield Watson.*

{Boyne, Mich.? 1887.} 28 pp. 21.9 × 15.1 cm.

In double columns. The pamphlet is made up of a series of extracts from the *Gospel Herald* of 1848, in which the men named in one way or another uphold Strang's claims against his rivals of that period, followed by a long argument by Watson himself contending that "the prophetic office as held by Joseph Smith and James J. Strang has never yet been vacated one moment either by the death of Joseph Smith or James J. Strang." Watson believed that there was then on earth a prophet, seer, revelator, and translator who would yet appear with conclusive evidence of his calling. Although expressing sympathy for the people of Utah, Watson had "no faith in either Brigham Young or John Taylor's claims as legally appointed prophets of God." This discussion is dated at the end, "Boyne, Charlevoix Co., Mich., February, 1887," after which follows a postscript, dated March, 1887, critical of some statements in Franklin D. Richards' *A Compendium of the Doctrines of the Gospel.*

CtY-C, DLC, MH, MoInRC, NN, OClWHi, UHi, USlC, WBuC, WHi, Morgan

1889

WINGFIELD WATSON

{47} *Prophetic Controversy, No. 3; or the Even Balances by which Isaac Scott, Chancy Loomis, and the Founders of the Reorganization Are Weighed and Found Wanting. In Two Chapters.* By Wingfield Watson, an elder in the Church of Jesus Christ of Latter Day Saints, Bay Springs, Charlevoix County, Michigan. February, 1889.

{Boyne, Mich.? 1889.} 44 pp. 22 × 14.9 cm.

In double columns. There are two issues of this pamphlet, one with plain wrappers and one with some "Reflections" on the verso of the front wrapper and on the recto and the verso of the back wrapper. The pamphlet has as its principal purpose the defense of Strang against charges levied by various members of the Reorganized Church. Watson declared that the *Saints' Herald* had consistently attacked Strang since its founding in 1860, but that "lately for some reason or other the defamation and slander of Mr. Strang through that paper has greatly exceeded itself." In particular he replies to statements by Isaac F. Scott in the *Herald* of December 29, 1888; Scott had been one of the earliest members of Strang's church, and was prominent in the first apostasy which rent it (see Dissenting Works, No. 2), and his article in the *Herald* was a renewal of a controversy no less bitter than old. By way of rebuttal, Watson reprints attacks upon Scott which had been printed in 1847 in *Zion's Reveille.* Even though Strang could be proved an impostor, Watson adds, this would not substantiate the claims of the Brighamites and the Josephites to the prophetic authority; the leaders of neither church "have ever once showed any willingness to discuss in a fair, manly, public way, the claims made by them for young Joseph {Smith III} to the prophetic office, with any leading Strangite. They always dodge that some way, and no doubt they always will. I want no man as my prophet who dares not test his own claims." The "Reflections" on the wrapper deal with doctrinal questions in dispute, and inform the Josephites that criticisms they have made against the Brighamites apply quite as well to themselves.

CtY-C, MH, NN, UHi, USlC, WBuC, WHi, Morgan

EDWARD T. COUCH

Evidences of Inspiration. By Edward T. Couch. Bay Springs, Mich., Feb. 1890. . . .

{Boyne, Mich.?} 1890. 38 pp. 21.5 × 14.9 cm.

In double columns. Taking his text from Isaiah 8:20 and 1 Thes. 5:20, Couch argues that the two Latter Day prophets, Joseph Smith and James J. Strang, were men inspired from on high.

WBuC

EDWARD T. COUCH

The Sabbath and the Restitution. By Edward T. Couch, Bay Springs, Charlevoix County, Michigan. March 1891.

{Boyne, Mich.? 1891.} 51 pp. 21.4 × 14.7 cm.

Cover title. In double columns. The caption title is "The Sabbath," which is the first section of the pamphlet, pp. 1–21. The second section, "The Restitution," occupies pp. 22–51. The argument is of purely theological interest.

MH, OClWHi, UHi, USlC, WBuC, Morgan

L. D. HICKEY

Who was the Successor of Joseph Smith? {Signed:} L. D. Hickey, Coldwater, Mich., June 15, 1891.

{Coldwater, Mich.? 1891.} 5 pp. 23.5 × 16 cm.

This tract was written during a period when L. D. Hickey, the last surviving apostle of the Church, was not fellowshipped by it, and the tract advocates the views which had led to action against him. On the thesis that Joseph Smith III had been ordained by Strang a patriarch, viceroy, and vice king in 1846 (an ordination "Young Joseph" himself denied), Hickey sought strenuously to bring his fellow Strangites into the Reorganized Church. At Horton, Kansas, on October 24, 1888, he organized a conference at which it was resolved that Joseph Smith III should be received "as President of the Church of Jesus Christ of Latter Day Saints." This action, however, was repudiated by those of opposing views in a second conference at Horton on December 23 of the same year. A conference of a more general and representative character was held at Horton, April 7, 1889, at which it was resolved that Hickey and those who shared his views should not be held in fellowship as officers or members of the Church "during the continuance of their Schismatic Resolutions." He was not, in fact, readmitted until May 9, 1896, so that this and other tracts published by Hickey during that period do not, in a sense, belong with the other titles in this bibliography. It has, however, been found more suitable to list them here than with the Dissenting Works [i.e., works by dissenters from Strang's following, which followed this installment; here, pp. 468–72. —Ed.].

In the present tract Hickey insists upon the validity of Strang's claims to the Succession, but sets forth the terms upon which he is prepared to accept Joseph Smith III as President: "he don't hold the degrees of Priesthood that Joseph did; he don't hold the keys of Mysteries; he don't hold the Sceptre in his hand as did Strang, yet he will stand as President until God removes him and sends another. . . . I am not a Republican, yet I will hold Harrison as President whether he pleases me or not, until his term is out. Yet I will not endorse his veto or Bills he don't veto. I will stand back and say, Mr Harrison, go on, your time will run out! So I say of young Joseph, go ahead, I will not adopt nor endorse your teachings. . . ." Joseph Smith III declined to be accepted on these terms, nor was Hickey long able to feel at home in the Reorganization. He returned to fellowship with those who had held aloof from the Reorganized Church, and a week after he ordained Wingfield Watson to be presiding high priest over the Church, which was on April 18, 1897, he died at Coldwater, Mich. During the seven months before his death he wrote intermittently on the subject of his experiences in the Church, and to the extent that this narrative was completed, it was published in the Coldwater *Reporter.* The manuscript is now in the possession of the Church.

CtY-C, DLC, WBuC, Morgan

1892

WINGFIELD WATSON *AND* W. W. BLAIR

{51} *The Watson-Blair Debate which took place at East Jordan, Mich., commencing Oct. 22nd and ending Oct. 26th, 1891.* Published by W. J. Smith, Galien, Mich.

Clifford, Ont.: Printed at the Glad Tidings Office, Allan St. 1892. 244 pp. 15.9 × 11.5 cm.

The preface, signed Willard J. Smith, Galien, Mich., Dec., 1891, declares: "The debate was the result of repeated challenges by Mr. Watson to the leading officials of the Reorganized Church, and then to Mr. Blair in particular, to meet him in public discussion of the relative merits of the claims made that James J. Strang on the one hand, and Young Joseph Smith, on the other, was the rightful, lawfully ordained president of the Church of Jesus Christ of Latter Day Saints." The debate, as taken down by J. J. Cornish and Smith, is not verbatim, but the transcript was corrected by the disputants and certified by them. The preface occupies pp. {3}–6, and the main text pp. {9}–244, followed by two leaves of advertisement.

MH, MoInRC, WHi

{JAMES J. STRANG}

A Few Historical Facts Concerning the Murderous Assault at Pine River. Also the Life, Ministry, Ancestry and Childhood of James J. Strang.

Lansing, Mich.: Reprinted by Charles J. Strang. 1892. 7 pp. 20.7 × 14.5 cm.

This pamphlet consists of a reprint of the *Northern Islander Extra* of July 14, 1853, {see No. 24}, and a sketch of the "Ancestry and Childhood of James J. Strang Written by Himself 1855," the latter certified by Charles J. Strang, Lansing, April 3, 1892. The original of this autobiography is now among the Strang MSS in the Coe Collection. Charles J. Strang, son of the prophet, was never himself a believer, but like his brother Clement took an interest in correcting historical distortions concerning his famous father, and was instrumental in gathering the impressive group of documents now in the Coe Collection. For a later reprint, with additions, see No. 88.

WBuC

1893

JAMES J. STRANG

The Diamond: Being the Law of Prophetic Succession and a Defense of the Calling of James J. Strang as Successor to Joseph Smith, and a Full Exposition of the Law of God Touching the Succession of Prophets Holding the Presidency of the True Church, and the Proof that this Succession Has Been Kept Up. Voree, Wis., 1848. {At head of title:} Gospel Tract No. IV.—First published by the Church of Latter Day Saints at Voree, Wis. 1848.

{Burlington, Wis.? 1893?} 15 pp. 22.4 × 15.5 cm.

Caption title. In double columns. The exact dating is somewhat conjectural, but 1893 cannot be far off. This edition of *The Diamond* was not published earlier than 1887, for in that case a page reference in Watson's *Prophetic Controversy, No. 2* would have cited this reprint rather than the 16-page edition. Equally, it was not published after 1896 because a citation in Watson's *Open Letter to B. H. Roberts* {No. 61}can apply only to this printing. I am informed on the authority of Watson's grandchildren that he removed from Boyne, Mich., to Spring Prairie, Wis., in March, 1892. If this is correct, and if the date attributed to the pamphlet is also correct, it was doubtless printed at Burlington.

DLC, MoInRC, NN, OClWHi, USlC, Morgan

JAMES J. STRANG

{54} *The Prophetic Controversy. A Letter from James J. Strang to Mrs. Corey.*

{Burlington, Wis.? 1893?} 35 pp. 22 × 15.4 cm.

Caption title. In double columns. This third reprint of *The Prophetic Controversy* cannot be dated exactly, but the copy in the Library of Congress is provisionally dated 1893, which is in harmony with the general situation, including the evident appearance at the same time of a new edition of *The Diamond.* From references in Watson's *Prophetic Controversy No. 4,* pp. 10–12, it is at any rate established that this edition was in print prior to March, 1897.

CtY-C, DLC, MH, MoInRC, USlC, WHi, Morgan

JAMES J. STRANG

{55} *Ancient and Modern Michilimackinac, including an account of the controversy between Mackinac and the Mormons. MDCCCLIV.*

{Burlington, Wis.? 1894?} 48 pp. 21.6 × 13.4 cm.

Cover title. In double columns. Some copies have, tipped in, a 4-page preface, 19.2 × 12 cm., by Wingfield Watson, dated March 31, 1894. It is presumed that all copies with or without preface, were printed at Burlington in 1894. Evidently unaware of the St. Ignace reprint of 1885, Watson speaks of his reprint as "this second edition." Sabin alludes to a purported 40-page reprint of *Ancient and Modern Michilimackinac,* a copy of which was sold with the original edition of 1854 in the Paullin sale in 1929, with still other copies sold in the wake of that sale by Charles F. Heartman in 1930. This, however, is a mistake. The Paullin copy is now in the Coe Collection, and its accompanying reprint is found to be the present edition. Apparently, in disposing of some duplicates of the reprint, Heartman adopted the description in the Paullin catalog without verifying the collation.

CtY-C, DLC, MoInRC, UHi, WBuC, WHi, Morgan

L. D. HICKEY *and* D. B. ALVORD

{56} *A Card to the Public Defending Hon. James J. Strang.*

{Coldwater, Mich.? 1894.}

Not seen; described from the second edition {No. 59}. If the original tract was set up like the later one, p. 1 contained a testimony signed L.D. Hickey and D.B. Albert {i.e., D.B. Alvord}, while pp. 2–3, under the heading "Testimony of the Michigan Press," reprinted the early testimonials to Strang and the Mormons which Watson used on the back wrapper of the 1894 *Ancient and Modern Michilimackinac.* The second edition says that 500 copies of the "card" had been printed "some two years" before, most of them taken out to Utah, where they were so well received that a new edition was now called for. It appears that Hickey was in Utah from June to November, 1894, hence the "card" must have been printed in the spring of that year.

WINGFIELD WATSON

An Open Letter to B. H. Roberts, Salt Lake City, Utah. {Dated at end:} Spring Prairie, Wis., Nov. 13, 1894.

{Burlington, Wis.? 1894?} 18 pp. 22.3 × 15 cm.

Caption title. In double columns. Watson with this "open letter" intervenes upon a dispute which had been in progress between B. H. Roberts of the Utah church (*Succession in the Presidency of the Church*) and Heman C. Smith of the Reorganized Church (*True Succession in the Presidency of the Church*). Watson finds Roberts to be "a good reasoner and logician when you have sound premises to reason from," but as a Strangite tells him, "unfortunately you are not always in possession of such premises, and therefore, while your reasoning faculties are good, many of your conclusions are simply faulty and false." He regards Robert's arguments against the claims of Joseph Smith III as entirely just, and voices the opinion "that any man who reflects at all upon those claims, must come to similar conclusions." Thereupon, however, Watson attacks the claims made for Brigham Young, and tells Roberts that the whole people who went to Utah were rejected, with their dead, when they crossed the Mississippi to follow Brigham Young, "for God never called them to go there, or to follow any such man or men"; Young and his associates, Watson points out, were tried and found guilty at Voree on April 6, 1846, by a court "having lawful jurisdiction of the case," as usurpers, teachers of false doctrine, and men guilty of tyranny, oppression, robbery of the Saints, and other crimes, whereupon their priesthood and membership had been taken from them, and they "delivered over to the buffetings of Satan." For a later reprint, with other matter, see No. 61.

MoInRC, WBuC

1896

L. D. HICKEY

A Card to the Kind and Brave People of Utah. By Apostle L. D. Hickey.

{Monte Vista, Colo.? 1896?} 8 pp. 17.3 × 12.7 cm.

Caption title. A clipping from the Monte Vista, Colo., *Journal,* April 18, 1896, preserved among the Strang MSS, appears to establish the place and time of publication of this pamphlet. The *Journal* remarks that it has been "getting out some tracts this week for our Mormon friends which contain the letter of Joseph Smith" that launched Strang upon his career as prophet, and with this the letter itself is printed. No other tract of the period, apart from *The Diamond,* contains the letter, hence it is a reasonable presumption that the *Journal* had reference to this "Card." Moreover, Hickey's presence at Monte Vista at this time is recorded in the action of the branch there, which on May 9, 1896, received him back into full fellowship and resolved to sustain him in his office as apostle.

In his prefatory remarks, Hickey tells the Utah Saints: "After laboring with you from June until the 20th of October, 1894, and {when I} was about to bid you good bye, I was requested by some to send you the letters Joseph Smith sent to the Church and to James J. Strang, June 18th, 1844, just before he was taken. Also the Revelation God gave by Mr. Strang relative to the people who followed Brigham to Utah from Nauvoo in 1847. I now fulfill my promise and will give you the exact words of both." Then follows the letter, accompanied by "Strang's Rebut{t}al" of criticisms directed against it, and the text of Strang's revelation of July 8, 1846.

MH

L. D. HICKEY AND D. B. ALVORD

{59} *A Card To The Public.—Defending Hon. James J. Strang.*

{Monte Vista, Colo.? 1896?} 4 pp. w.p. 19 × 14.9 cm.

In double columns. A reprint of the tract of 1894 {No. 56}, with added material signed by L.D. Hickey and John Wake. This latter consists of "Testimony of the Old Pioneers of Burlington, Wisconsin," cordial to the memory of Strang. After remarks upon the success the first edition had enjoyed in Utah, the writers go on to say, "we have been requested to send out a second edition, adding the testimony of the old pioneers of Burlington, Wisconsin." These testimonies are declared to have been gathered by "the writer of this article" in the spring of 1894 in company with Wingfield Watson, the two having traveled extensively by horse and buggy to carry out their project. The copy of this tract in the Coe Collection so much resembles in paper and typography Hickey's *Card to the Kind and Brave People of Utah* that one may safely conclude it was printed at the same place and time. An oddity is that D.B. Alvord's name is misspelled "Albert." It would be interesting to know if this mistake was made in the first edition and carried over into this.

CtY-C, MoInRC

L. D. HICKEY

{60} *Who was the Successor of Joseph Smith?* {Signed:} L.D. Hickey.

{Monte Vista, Colo.? 1896?} 6 pp. 19 × 14.9 cm.

In double columns. Page 1 begins on the verso of the title. This reprint of Hickey's tract of 1891 is identical in format and typography with No. 59 above, and the only copy seen, in the Coe Collection, has been preserved in association with it, which makes it virtually certain that they issued from the same press. If so, the time element is interesting, for it would indicate that as late as April 18, 1896, Hickey was still advocating views which by May 9 he had formally renounced.

CtY-C

WINGFIELD WATSON

An Open Letter to B. H. Roberts, Salt Lake City, Utah.

{Burlington, Wis.? 1896?} 30 pp. 22.4 × 15 cm.

Caption title. In double columns. Watson here reprints his "open letter" of 1894 with two other items. These latter may have appeared separately, but if so, copies have not come to my attention. The letter to Roberts is printed on pp. 1–17. Pages 18–21 are given over to "A Word to George Q. Cannon," roundly rebuking him for some remarks critical of George Miller published in the *Deseret Weekly News* of March 14, 1896. The last item, pp. 22–30, is "A Full History of the letter of appointment written by the Prophet, Joseph Smith, to James J. Strang, and its reception at Burlington, Wis., as kept by the appointed church scribe." In this discussion Watson attacks positions taken by W. W. Blair in their debate of 1891 {No. 51}, and prints a considerable extract from the manuscript Chronicles of Voree.

WBuC, WHi, Morgan

1897

WINGFIELD WATSON

{[illegible]} *Prophetic Controversy No. 4. Mr. Strang Proved To Have Been Always an Honorable Man. The Theory that the Prophetic Office Goes by Lineal Right, and the Doctrine that Lesser Officers in the Priesthood Can Ordain to the Greater, Utterly Exploded.* {Signed:} Wingfield Watson, Spring Prairie, Walworth County, Wisconsin, March 15, 1897.

{Burlington, Wis.? 1897.} 38 pp. 21.3 × 14.5 cm.

Caption title. In double columns. After addressing himself to various slanders Strang had to combat during his lifetime, Watson undertakes—by disputing the validity of lineal right—to knock "the underpinning from under your so-called Reorganized church; a basis upon which it can never again be reared."

MH, MoInRC, UHi, WBuC, WHi, Morgan

WINGFIELD WATSON

{[illegible]3} *Latter Day Signs.* {Signed:} Wingfield Watson, Minister of the Gospel of Jesus Christ. Lyons, June, 1897.

{Burlington, Wis.? 1897.} 15 pp. 21 × 13.7 cm.

Caption title. In double columns. This pamphlet contains two tracts, "Latter Day Signs," pp. 1–10, and "The Book of Mormon," pp. 11–15. It is the latter that has Watson's terminal signature and date. In my notes is some indication that I have seen an 8-page *Latter Day Signs* in the library of the Reorganized Church, but if so a subsequent recheck has not brought the pamphlet forth. In the first of the present discussions Watson argues that these are indeed the last days, that we are living in the generation immediately preceding "the second coming of the Lord Jesus Christ, to judge the world," and cites the Scriptural evidences that support his thesis. The second article adopts the point of view that harmonious with the Bible as the Book of Mormon may be, it has a place of its own to fill, because it sets forth the gospel so much more plainly than does the New Testament. The discussion is independent of Watson's separately printed essays on the Book of Mormon {Nos. 40, 66}.

MH, MoInRC, OClWHi, UHi, WBuC, Morgan

JAMES J. STRANG

{64} *The Revelations of James J. Strang.*

{Burlington, Wis.? 189–?} 24 pp. 22.1 × 15.2 cm.

Caption title. In double columns. I have not been able to determine precisely when this new edition of the revelations was printed, the only clue being a note at the end which says, "This tract, and others on kindred subjects, may be had of the compiler. Address: Wingfield Watson, Spring Prairie, Wisconsin." It was therefore published sometime after Watson's removal to Spring Prairie in March, 1892—most probably between 1897 and 1899. This edition differs from that of 1885 principally in the introductory remarks by Watson. The original version had pointed reference to conditions in Utah, the "bondage" in which the people found themselves; but in this new printing Watson's remarks are more generalized, with emphasis upon the "One Mighty and Strong" who will appear to set the House of God in order. The revelations are printed as before, but in the absence of the plate of facsimiles a more extended description of the Voree Plates is provided. The "Vision" of June 18, 1844, which had been tipped into the earlier edition does not appear in this. At the end Watson adds 5 pages of "Testimonies" by "Unimpeachable Witnesses," including John E. Page, Jason W. Briggs, Johnathan Sumner, Lucy Smith, William Smith, George J. Adams, and George Miller, reprinted from the columns of the *Gospel Herald* and the *Northern Islander* and favorable to Strang's claims. Also published are two extracts from the writings of the Prophet Joseph Smith concerning revelation and prophets of God.

CSmH, CtY-C, MoInRC, UHi, USlC, WBuC, WHi, Morgan

1899

OLIVER COWDERY

{65} *Cowdery's Letters on the Bringing In of the New Dispensation.*

Burlington, Wis.: Free Press Print. 1899. iv, 31 pp. 19.4 × 13.4 cm.

In double columns. The wrapper title is not included in the pagination. The main text is given over to the eight letters by Cowdery. Watson's preface, signed at Spring Prairie

Jan. 13, 1899, quotes liberally from Strang's remarks in the 1854 edition, and adds some comment of his own contradicting the idea that revelation has ceased.

MH, OClWHi, UHi, WBuC, Morgan

WINGFIELD WATSON

The Book of Mormon. An Essay on Its Claims and Prophecies. By Wingfield Watson, An Elder in the Church of Jesus Christ of Latter Day Saints. {Dated at end:} Spring Prairie, Wis., March 24, 1899.

{Burlington, Wis.? 1899.} 18 pp. 19.5 × 13.7 cm.

Caption title. In double columns. An enlarged version of Watson's tract of 1884 {No. 40}.

CtY-C, MH, OClWHi, UHi, WBuC, WHi, Morgan

WINGFIELD WATSON

Baptism. What Is It Designed For?—How is It Administered?—Is It a Saving Ordinance?—And is It a Commandment of God? {Signed:} Wingfield Watson, An Elder in the Church of Jesus Christ of Latter Day Saints. Spring Prairie, Wis., Dec. 26, 1899.

{Burlington, Wis.? 1899?} 32 pp. 19.5 × 13.5 cm.

Caption title. In double columns. Dated so late in 1899, the tract may have been published in 1900. It differs materially from Watson's tract of 1877 {No. 34}, the subject matter being recast and revised; the subheads are "Baptism," "A Note on the Sacrifice of Christ," and "Authority to Act in the Name of God."

WBuC, WHi, Morgan

1902

JAMES J. STRANG

Catholic Discussion. {Signed:} Wingfield Watson, Lyons, Wisconsin, May 26, 1902.

{Burlington, Wis.? 1902.} 24 pp. 20.7 × 14 cm.

Caption title. In double columns. This edition differs so markedly from that of 1848 {No. 13} as to suggest that Watson reprinted the discussion from the columns of the *Gospel Herald* rather than from the original pamphlet itself. Strang's sixth letter to Rafferty, and his Appendix, are omitted entirely. The main text is republished on pp. 1–22, with the rest of the pamphlet given over to a note by Watson calling to the attention of the Brighamite and Josephite churches Strang's "able handling of the Catholic claim to priesthood," which in Watson's view demolishes that claim.

CtY-C, MH, MoInRC, UHi, USlC, WBuC, WHi, Morgan

1903

WINGFIELD WATSON

{69} *Prophetic Controversy No. 5.* {Signed:} Wingfield Watson, Lyons, Wis., April 18, 1903.

{Burlington, Wis.? 1903.} 27 pp. 21 × 13.7 cm.

Caption title. In double columns. The pamphlet publishes an open letter to Heman C. Smith of the Reorganized Church which was originally written, or perhaps commenced, November 20, 1901, at Lyons. Watson defends Strang at length, particularly with regard to plural marriage, and decries what he views as the narrow and illogical basis of belief upon which the Reorganized Church has been erected; he also explains the reasons for his own exertions in defense of the faith: "as the Mormons under Mr. Strang, after his death were scattered here and there for a long time without anyone to admonish or warn them against deception and fraud, there have many of them fallen a prey to the abominable influences around them, such as spiritualism, infidelity, atheism, {and sundry Mormon isms} . . . and being ordained to watch over a few branches of the church, I have been under the necessity of writing these controversies to vindicate Mr. Strang's claims and ministry, and to put a stop to their being further duped and swallowed up by these foul delusions."

CtY-C, MH, MoInRC, UHi, WBuC, WHi, Morgan

1905

WINGFIELD WATSON

{70} *Prophetic Controversy No. 6, or "Facts" for the Anti-Mormons Located at Grayson, Kentucky, Being an Answer to the Following Letter of Inquiry.* {Signed:} Wingfield Watson.

{Burlington, Wis.? 1905.} 14 pp. 19.3 × 13.5 cm.

Caption title. In double columns. Watson's letter is dated Lyons, Wis., June 9, 1905, in reply to one by R. B. Neal asking him for facts to substantiate Watson's published statement that Strang was "legally and duly appointed to succeed Joseph Smith, Jr." Watson outlines Strang's claims and answers Neal's questions, telling him that although it is plainly to be seen that Neal, as an anti-Mormon, is bent on crushing the truth, the more Mormonism is opposed, the more it prospers and prevails; men "can do nothing against the truth, but for it." Over Neal's shoulder Watson also addresses himself to Davis H. Bays, whose *Doctrines and Dogmas of Mormonism* he finds "like all other anti-Mormon works, abounding in error, while sometimes telling the truth." This "Controversy," Watson says, was begun soon after the receipt of Neal's letter in June, but by reason of "the pressing demands of a northern dairy farm," he was some months getting it written and printed.

CtY-C, MH, UHi, WBuC, WHi , Morgan

1906

EDWARD T. COUCH

The Everlasting Covenant or Prophets of God Teach Alike{.} By Edward T. Couch of the Church of Jesus Christ of Latter Day Saints.

Boyne City, Charlevoix Co., Mich.: July, 1906. 56 pp. 18.6 × 11.9 cm.

This tract undertakes to show as harmonious the teachings of the Biblical prophets and those of the New Dispensation.

CtY-C, UHi, WBuC, Morgan

{WINGFIELD WATSON}

Non-Mormon Lectures on Polygamy From Non-Mormon Viewpoint{.} *Copied from the Deseret Evening News Saturday, October 13, 1906.*

{Burlington, Wis.? 1906?} 10 pp. 20.1 × 13.9 cm.

Caption title. In double columns. Watson here republishes an address by V.S. Peet in Philadelphia before the Friendship Liberal League "on the question of polygamy from a Gentile viewpoint," neither advocating nor defending the doctrine, "simply confining his expressions as to how noted Presbyterian, Methodist and other divines had done so, surprising many of his hearers, who made up a large and intelligent audience, how leaders of their own sects had contended for that which the Mormon people have relinquished to obey the laws of the country in which they live." In a concluding note Watson says, "After reading over the conclusions and allowances entered upon by foreign Christian missionaries in foreign lands, in behalf of their polygamic converts, we can only conclude that the Reorganized Mormon missionaries and the so-called Christian missionaries of Utah, who would ruthlessly separate the innocent wives of the plurally married men of Utah, are the most unfeeling and brutish of all inhuman brutes, and the most savage and fanatic of all human savages." The social excitement to which Watson alludes was that aroused by the [Reed] Smoot election case; the Strangite elders were not indifferent to the anti-polygamy crusades, since some of them had entered into polygamy under Strang on Beaver Island.

OClWHi, UHi, WBuC, Morgan

WINGFIELD WATSON

3} *Prophetic Controversy No. 7.* {Signed:} Wingfield Watson.

{Burlington, Wis.? 1906?} 9 pp. 20.8 × 13 cm.

Caption title. In double columns. This "Controversy" is another letter to R.B. Neal, dated Lyons, Wis., Dec. 22, 1906, which quite possibly was published early in 1907. Principally,

Watson's is a rejoinder to some remarks on *Prophetic Controversy No.* 6 by Prof. J. B. Grubbs in the anti-Mormon *Sword of Laban.* The argument revolves around Strang's denial of the contention that "Jesus, the anointed, was without human father"—in other words, that he was other than the natural son of Joseph and Mary.

MH, UHi, WBuC, WHi, Morgan

1907

EDWARD T. COUCH

{74} *The Two Bibles or Scholarship and Inspiration Compared*{.} By Edward T. Couch.

Boyne City, Charlevoix Co., Mich.: April, 1907. 71 pp. 22 × 14.9 cm.

Couch contrasts the King James or Authorized Version of the Bible with Joseph Smith's Inspired Revision. Numerous extracts are published in parallel columns—not, Couch says, with a view to finding fault with "the common Bible," but to show the useful information added in the Joseph Smith version, by which the Bible may be read "more understandingly."

CtY-C, MH, OClWHi, UHi, USlC, WBuC, Morgan

WINGFIELD WATSON

{75} *Prophetic Controversy No. 8.* {Signed:} Wingfield Watson, Burlington, Wis., July 20, 1907.

{Burlington, Wis.? 1907.} 7 pp. 21.1 × 14.6 cm.

Caption title. In double columns. This "Controversy" was undertaken at Nauvoo, Ill., on July 16, 1907, and completed at Burlington four days later; it is an open letter to *Liahona,* the organ of the Central States Mission of the Utah church, replying to a comment upon Strang in that periodical. Watson concludes that the writer was either "densely ignorant of the calling, appointment and claims of James J. Strang," or else "designedly trying to keep his readers in the dark" concerning them: "I sincerely doubt whether the great majority of the prophets of God ever gave any more evidence of their calling and appointment than Mr. Strang did of his." Watson cites prophecies by Strang which in his view have been fully borne out, including the pronouncement that Brigham Young "was an imposter, a usurper, and was utterly destitute of the Keys of Mysteries and revelations which belong always to the prophetic office."

MH, UHi, WBuC, WHi, Morgan

WINGFIELD WATSON

Prophetic Controversy No. 9. {Signed:} Wingfield Watson, Burlington, Wis., Sept. 25, 1907.

{Burlington, Wis.? 1907.} 5 pp. w.p. 21.7 × 14.7 cm.

Caption title. In double columns. This "Controversy" is a third letter to R. B. Neal, dated at the beginning July 26, 1907, and at the end September 26, 1907, with an undated postscript tacked on. Watson expresses his indifference to the behavior of Oliver Cowdery or any others after their apostasy, and tells Neal he is wasting his time seeking out "the follies, the disagreements, the nonsense and THE TOMFOOLERIES of some poor broken-down and apostate Mormons," arraying them together, and marshaling their disagreements to cry out that Mormonism is false. The only way by which any creed, Mormon, Jewish, or Gentile, may be judged is by searching the Scriptures in relation to it. Watson explains the varying attitudes he has displayed toward Joseph Smith III over a period of years, culminating in his final rejection of him, and declares that the "great grand facts in the history of Mormonism is that Joseph Smith WAS TO HAVE A SUCCESSOR, and that Mr. Strang came into that successorship, according to the law of heaven, touching the prophetic office, as given in this age, and in the ages of the past." His postscript lists five criteria by which Neal and others may be enabled to see who was and who was not the true successor of Joseph Smith, "according to the law laid down by him, by revelation."

MH, UHi, WBuC, WHi, Morgan

1908

EDWARD T. COUCH

7} *The Prophetic Office*{.} By Edward T. Couch of the Church of Jesus Christ of Latter Day Saints.

Boyne City, Charlevoix Co., Mich.: September, 1908. 67 pp. 18 × 12 cm.

Couch reviews the claims of Brigham Young, Joseph Smith III, and James J. Strang to the prophetic office, finding the matter to boil down to this: "The Utah Saints take a man they call an apostle and elect him to be their president, or what they call a prophet of God. When he dies, his successor is voted in the same way. The Reorganized Church . . . took their president and got a man who called himself an apostle to ordain him to be what they call a prophet of God. James J. Strang, the true successor, was called by the voice of God, appointed through Joseph the Seer, and ordained by an angel. . . . So he is in harmony with the law of God on this question, and the others are not." Other chapters argue that "prophets of God teach alike," and canvass "the marriage question," finding ample Scriptural sanction for plural marriage, whether or not Joseph Smith ever taught it.

CtY-C, MoInRC, OClWHi, UHi, WBuC, Morgan

WINGFIELD WATSON

{78} *Prophetic Controversy No. 10.* {Signed:} Wingfield Watson.

{Burlington, Wis.? 1908.} 10 pp. 21.1 × 14 cm.

Caption title. In double columns. An open letter to E. W. Nunley, dated Burlington, Sept. 3, 1908, this "Controversy" is an extension of the long argument between Watson and the partisans of the Reorganized Church over the question of Strang's authority, here revolving around the question of ordination.

CtY-C, MH, UHi, WBuC, WHi, Morgan

WINGFIELD WATSON

{79} *Prophetic Controversy No. 11.* {Signed:} Wingfield Watson.

{Burlington, Wis.? 1908?} 4 pp. w.p. 20.7 × 13.7 cm.

Caption title. In double columns. Though labeled "No. 11," this is in effect a supplement to No. 10. It must have been printed in rather a small edition, since Watson two years later published another and quite different "Controversy" also numbered "11" {No. 80}. Watson complains to Nunley about his letters, which are "not only ungentlemanly, but exceedingly cramp . . . the most cramp and enigmatical hyerogliphical and hieratic of any that I have yet seen," and disclaims possession of a Urim and Thummim by which to translate them. As the heart of the dispute between them, Watson insists that Nunley point out "the man who was appointed by *revelation through* Joseph, who was to be ordained as Joseph." If this was not Strang, who was it?

WBuC, Morgan

WINGFIELD WATSON

{80} *Prophetic Controversy No. 11.* {Signed:} Burlington, Wis., Aug. 1, 1910, Wingfield Watson.

{Burlington, Wis.? 1910.} 13 pp. 21.2 × 14.2 cm.

Caption title. In double columns. In an open letter to John R. Haldeman, editor of the Hedrickite *Evening and Morning Star,* Watson expresses his sorrow at the sore tax facing the Church of Christ consequent upon the paving of the street east of the temple lot in Independence, after which he asks the "big broad question," what is going to be done with that temple lot? Isn't it about time "that it was put to the use intended for it by Revelation in the early thirties—1831?" With the temple unbuilt, the enemy can cry "failure of prophecy," inasmuch as it had been prophesied "that it would be built before all the generation who were on the earth in 1832 would have passed away." There must be something wrong somewhere, Watson argues, and he finds this wrongness to consist in the rejection of Strang by the several churches. He is critical of the defective revelations of Granville Hedrick but finds "no difference between Hedrickites, Reorganized, or Brighamites. They are all apostates."

MH, MoInRC, UHi, WBuC, WHi, Morgan

WINGFIELD WATSON

Prophetic Controversy No. 12 {Signed:} Burlington, Wis., March 13, 1912, Wingfield Watson.

{Burlington, Wis.? 1912.} 20 pp. 21.2 × 14.5 cm.

Caption title. In double columns. As with the preceding "Controversy," this is an open letter to John R. Haldeman. Watson argues against the thesis that the ancient churches of Christ were apostolic in organization, and that the First Presidency over the Church in these latter days was "a creation of Joseph Smith for his own special benefit and aggrandizement." Watson also devotes attention to the righteousness and Scriptural warrant for plural marriage, with animadversions upon the contrary views held by the Reorganized Church. He comments, too, on the Utah Saints, called by Brigham Young and others the most obedient people who ever lived. "Yet they were driven. 'Why then were they driven?' asked Mr. Strang. 'Was it not because they had followed the wrong leaders?' Just so." The second page of this pamphlet was misprinted, and 15 lines of a reprinted text are tipped in to replace the faulty matter.

MH, UHi, WBuC, WHi, Morgan

1913

EDWARD T. COUCH

2} *The Teachings of Jesus*{.} By Edward T. Couch of the Church of Jesus Christ of Latter Day Saints.

Boyne City, Charlevoix County, Michigan: May, 1913. 44 pp. 22 × 14.7 cm.

The chapter titles serve to summarize the argument: "All the Teachings of Jesus Are to Be Kept Up." "When the Law of Moses Ceased." "Jesus Gave the Law and the Revelations Come Through Him." "All the Lost Scriptures Are to Be Restored." "Only One True Church." "The Gospel of Christ is the Same All Through the World's History." "James J. Strang the Successor to Joseph Smith." "The Voree Plates." "The Book of the Law of the Lord." "Prove All Things." The Voree Plates are reproduced in facsimile on p. {19}, and p. {20} is blank. The chapter on "The Book of the Law of the Lord" is the only general account of this book which has appeared in any Strangite publication; it is not, however, in all respects accurate.

CtY-C, MoInRC, OClWHi, UHi, USlC, WBuC, Morgan

WINGFIELD WATSON

{83} *A Friendly Admonition.* {Signed:} Burlington, Wis., July, 1913, Wingfield Watson.

Nauvoo, Ill.: Rustler Print. {1913.} 7 pp. 20.3×14 cm.

Caption title. In double columns. Having been a believer for some 63 years, and unlikely to live many years longer, Watson puts on record, "by way of admonition," a few lines concerning his experience in the faith of the Latter Day Saints. The result is not an autobiography but a reaffirmation of his belief in the Book of Mormon.

CtY-C, UHi, WBuC, Morgan

WINGFIELD WATSON

{84} *The "One Mighty and Strong{.}"* {Signed:} Wingfield Watson, Burlington, Wis., March, 1915.

{Burlington, Wis.? 1915.} 12 pp. 20.9×14.4 cm.

Caption title. In double columns. Watson disputes a 20-column treatise by G. D. Cole in the *Evening and Morning Star* which argued that Jesus was the "one mighty and strong" who would be sent to set the House of God in order. Watson concludes that this person, not Christ, is unidentifiable as yet, and warns that those "who have despised and condemned and hated James J. Strang, and his appointment, or the revelations or translations given us by him as the word of the Lord, must perish, unless they sorely repent of their wickedness."

OClWHi, UHi, WBuC, Morgan

GEORGE MILLER

{85} *Correspondence of Bishop George Miller{.}*

{Burlington, Wis.? 1916?} 50 pp. 21.7×14.6 cm.

Wrapper title. The caption title is: *Correspondence of Bishop George Miller With The Northern Islander From his first acquaintance with Mormonism up to near the close of his life. Written by himself in the year 1855.* In double columns. There are two apparent issues of this, differing only in the binding and the degree of trim. One binding is square-backed and measures 22.4×15 cm., while the copies not square-backed have the dimensions above described. The wrapper title is the same with both, printed on the same cream-colored paper. For general Mormon history, no other pamphlet which has issued from the Strangite press is comparable in interest with this compilation of the seven letters George Miller contributed to the *Northern Islander.* Severally dated at St. James, Mich., on June 22, 26, 27, 28, July 1, 4, and August 10, 1855, they were published in the *Islander* for August 9, 16, 23, September 6, 13–20, October 11, and 18. Only the last few pages, reciting Miller's coming to Beaver Island in the fall of 1850, are concerned with Strang's church. More broadly, the narrative is Mormon history, as Miller had seen it from the strategic vantage point of the presiding bishop's office, from 1839 to 1849. No other source is so explicit for some of the undercurrents of Mormon history during the last three years in Nauvoo, especially for the developments immediately preceding Joseph Smith's death. Miller left Nauvoo with the migration under Brigham Young, his advance party getting farther west than any other of the main immigration in 1846 before he turned back to winter on the Niobrara River in northern Nebraska. Continual friction had attended his relations with Brigham Young, and the two men came to an open break in the spring of 1847. Miller then made his way south to the Lyman Wight colony in Texas, but was unable to get along with Wight, either. A copy of *The Diamond* having fallen into his hands, he made overtures to Strang which were so well received that he took his family north to Beaver Island. His narrative ends with his arrival there. He half promised that at some future time he would resume his narrative, subsequent events being "fraught with some of the most thrilling incidents of my life." It is unfortunate that he did not live to redeem this promise, for he was one of Strang's most trusted associates, "general-in-chief" of Strang's kingdom, and county sheriff. After Strang was killed, he set out with his family for California but did not long survive his prophet, dying later in 1856 at Marengo, Iowa.

In the absence of an imprint, Miller's *Correspondence* has been regarded of much earlier date than is actually the case; see, e.g., the Clements Library's *100 Rarities in Michigan History*, which supposes it to have been a Beaver Island imprint of 1855. The caption title, with its phrase, "up to near the close of his life," is clear evidence of the incorrectness of such an attribution. The letters seem to have been compiled by Wingfield Watson from his file of the *Northern Islander* at Burlington about 1916. When a copy first came to my attention in 1939, I was told by the owner that it had been published "in Wisconsin in 1917," but more satisfactory evidence comes from the *Journal of History of the Reorganized Church, January*, 1917, Vol. X, pp. 18–38, in which are printed some extracts from the *Correspondence*; the editors express their thanks to the compiler, Wingfield Watson, of Burlington, Wis. This issue of the *Journal of History* was received at the Library of Congress late in December, 1916, hence it may be concluded with reasonable safety that Watson published the pamphlet in that year.

Strangely enough, concurrently with the appearance of the letters in Watson's pamphlet, the originals turned up in the possession of a son in California. With some added material, these were printed by H. W. Mills in an article about the senior and junior Millers, "De Tal Palo Tal Astilla" {A Chip of the Old Block}, in *Annual Publications of the Historical Society of Southern California*, 1917, pp. 86–172, and separately under the title, *A Mormon Bishop and His Son*. The California publication contained an autobiographical sketch of Miller's life before joining the Mormons, which was not published in the *Islander*, and also reproduced a portrait. On the other hand, Mills did not fully succeed in putting the sheets of the narrative in proper order, and a few paragraphs were missing. Consequently each publication, California and Wisconsin, supplements the other.

CtY-C, CU-B, MH, Mi, MiU-C, UHi, Morgan

WINGFIELD WATSON

Prophetic Controversy No. 13. {Signed:} Burlington, Wis., June 27, 1918, Wingfield Watson.

{Burlington, Wis.? 1918.} 14 pp. 21.3 × 14.5 cm.

Caption title. In double columns. This last of Watson's "Controversies" replies to an attack on Strangism by R. S. Salyards in the *Saints' Herald* of June 5, 1918. Watson defends Strang and the Church, and aims a few return blows at the Reorganized Church, which "has been all along from 1860 up to this day 1918 as destitute of any true Priesthood as any one of the sectarian churches." Admitting that the Strangite church has not accomplished much, Watson lays this to "the usurpation of Brigham Young and the false and forbidden revelations and teachings of the Briggses and the Gurleys and the Granville Hedric{k}s, and a lot of others. . . . The plain and simple truth of the whole matter is, that pretty nearly the whole church has been brought under the dominion of satan, by false leaders, and their false doctrines and teachings."

MH, MoInRC, UHi, WBuC, WHi , Morgan

1919

CHURCH OF JESUS CHRIST OF LATTER DAY SAINTS

{87} *The Latter Day Precept.* Kansas City, Mo. Edited by John Flanders. Vol. I, No. 1. August, 1919. 8 pp. 28.3 × 21.7 cm.

The only number of this periodical I have seen is the issue for October, 1919, Vol. I, No. 3, having the pagination 17–24, in the Coe Collection. The date of the first issue is derived from an article on Mormon periodical literature in *Journal of History*, July, 1921, Vol. XIV, p. 289, but this is borne out by the numbering of the issue seen. As a 4-column paper, the *Precept* was published monthly, and sold for 5 cents a copy, 50 cents a year. A complete file is reported to be in the possession of Mr. Chester K. Flanders, Merriam, Kansas, but I have been unable to learn details of it. The *Precept* was still being published in the fall of 1920, for in a letter Wingfield Watson wrote at that time to Dr. Quaife, he expressed misgivings over the future of the paper if the editorial policy were not changed. It probably died before the completion of the second volume.

{JAMES J. STRANG}

{88} *A Few Historical Facts Concerning the Murderous Assault at Pine River Also the Life, Ministry, Ancestry and Childhood of James J. Strang.*

{Kansas City, Mo.? 1920?} 9 pp. 20.8 × 14.4 cm.

In double columns. A reprint of the pamphlet Charles J. Strang printed in 1892 {No. 52}, to which is added the *Daily Northern Islander*'s account, June 20, 1856, of the "Murderous Assault" which gave Strang his death wound; this in turn is followed by some comment on the State and Federal governments which permitted the two prophets, Joseph Smith and James J. Strang, to be murdered with impunity. The only indication in the tract as to time and place of publication is a passing allusion to "the readers of the Precept," from which it may be conjectured that it was published in Kansas City about 1920.

CtY-C, MH, MoInRC, UHi, WBuC, Morgan

WINGFIELD WATSON

The True Gospel. A Comparison of the Primitive, and True Gospel, and the Modern Sectarian interpretation if {sic} *It.* By Wingfield Watson.

{Kansas City, Mo.? 1920?} 8 pp. w.p. 17 × 10.5 cm.

Caption title. This is in reality a folder, 4 pages on a side, measuring 17 × 42.6 cm. The only indication as to time of publication comes from a note at the end: "If you wish to criticise the above article or care for further information on the subject Address The Latter Day Precept 497 Chestnut St Kansas City, Mo." From this it is concluded that the tract was published at Kansas City about 1920. Reprinted in 1948 {No. 102}.

WBuC, Morgan

1926

SAMUEL H. MARTIN

{Tract without title, discussing Divine Authority, Church Organization, Principles and Doctrines of the True Church, Repentance, Baptism, The Laying On of Hands, and The Resurrection of the Dead. Signed at end: Elder S. H. Martin, Route 4, Kansas City, Kansas.}

{Kansas City, Kansas? 1926?} 4 pp. w.p. 23 × 153 cm.

Martin became presiding high priest of the Church in 1923, serving until his own death in 1935. Mr. Lloyd Flanders is of the opinion that this tract was printed late in 1925 or early in 1926. In his introductory paragraph, Martin gives the following as his purpose in writing it: "Inasmuch as so much has been said about the menace of what the world terms Mormonism, (the Church of Jesus Christ of Latter Day Saints) and being an elder in that church, and fully understanding its doctrines and the principles of the gospel taught by it, I feel it my duty to set those principles before the world in order to correct a false impression that has been made by the misrepresentations of some persons who know absolutely nothing about this church, or are wilfully misrepresenting it."

UHi, WBuC, Morgan

1927

JAMES J. STRANG

The Book of the Law of the Lord Consisting of an Inspired Translation of Some of the Most Important Parts of the Law Given to Moses, and a Very Few Additional Commandments, with Brief Notes and References. Printed by Command of the King at the Royal Press, Saint James, A. R. I.

{Kansas City, Mo.: 1927.} viii, 9–80 pp. 20.5 × 12.2 cm.

Sabin has attributed this reprint tentatively to 1930, but in a letter of November 1, 1930, to Dr. George B. Arbaugh, the late Ben T. Short stated that he had had 1,000 copies printed in November, 1927. This is a reprint of the original or pamphlet edition of 1851, made from Wingfield Watson's copy. Although the Church supposes the work to have been faithfully done, it did not officially sanction this reprint, and does not vouch for its accuracy. The title page is preceded by 4 blank leaves on the first of which is pasted a leaf, 19.1 × 13.9 cm., advertising the book. Under the heading "The Book of the Law of the Lord," Ben T. Short states in this advertisement: "We submit this book to be the lost Book of Moses, the book that he wrote and commanded the Levites to place in the ark of the covenant. . . . We submit that this book has been reserved by God for the express purpose of convincing the Jews of the errors of their fathers. We also submit that the Ten Great Commandments contained in this book are the exact substance of the commandments written on the Tables of Stone, and that it contains the Mosaic Economy in perfect order. We further submit that this book was translated by James J. Strang, a Jew, a lineal descendant of David, the king, from a record engraved on metallic plates, made long previous to the Babylonish captivity. We further submit that this book of the Law is the Stick of Judah referred to by the Prophet Ezekiel. . . . Finally we submit that it has been ordained by God to be a means of eventually bringing to pass the fulfillment of the promise unto the Jews when one shall chase a thousand and two shall put ten thousand to flight." The title page is modeled upon that of the original edition, including a reproduction of the same cut, but is not a facsimile or precise copy of it. The verso of the title contains, in addition to the "Testimony" of the seven witnesses, an "Announcement" by Ben T. Short, in which it is explained that the book has been reprinted so that all people who so desire may test the claims made for it, "that it was translated by James J. Strang, by the aid of the Urim and Thumim [*sic*]; that it is the book that Joseph Smith was not suffered to translate, spoken of in the Book of Mormon . . . the book that Moses wrote and commanded the levites to place in the Ark of the Covenant . . . and that it is in exact harmony with the Bible, Book of Mormon, and Book of Doctrine and Covenants, and that it should be accepted as authoritative as the said books. . . ." It was Short's hope to publish at a later date pamphlets in defense of such claims. This hope was never realized.

MH, WBuC, WHi Morgan

{BEN T. SHORT, *ET AL.*}

{92} *Important.* {Signed by:} S. A. Martin, Moroni Flanders, Roy Straton Neal, Lloyd Flanders, John Willis, H. A. Anderson, John Wake, Ben T. Short.

{Kansas City, Mo.? 1928?} Broadside. 20.3 × 10.8 cm.

I am informed by Mr. Lloyd Flanders that Ben T. Short published this broadside upon his own initiative, probably late in 1928 or early in 1929. Short mentioned the broadside, which challenged Frederick M. Smith, President of the Reorganized Church, to a debate over Strang's claims to the Succession, in a letter of about that time to Mr. Flanders, then living at a distance. As the letter was not dated, the precise date of the "throw away" itself is not established, but it may be dated within fairly narrow limits, for one of the elders named, Roy Stranton Neal, was baptized by Mr. Flanders on July 9, 1927, and ordained an elder on May 4, 1928, while a copy of the broadside was given in 1930 by Short to Dr. George B. Arbaugh, to whom I am indebted for the description of it. Some errors in the signatures doubtless were occasioned by Short's difficult handwriting, e.g., S.H., rather than S.A. Martin, H.C. rather than H.A. Anderson, Roy Stranton Neal rather than Roy Straton Neal.

BEN T. SHORT

} *We Should* Pity *That Poor Child.* {Signed:} Ben T. Short.

{Kansas City, Mo.? 192–?} Placard. 28 × 14.4 cm.

Information as to this title, as in the case of No. 92, comes from Dr. Arbaugh. The card contains two hymns, "We Should Pity That Poor Child," and "There Is No-one Who Can Love Like Mother," as also "Ten Infallible Rules" which insure success, health, and happiness. No date appears, but the card was printed before 1930, when Dr. Arbaugh was given his copy.

CHURCH OF JESUS CHRIST OF LATTER DAY SAINTS

4} *Facts for Thinkers.*

{Pueblo, Colo.? 1930?} Broadside. 23 × 15 cm.

This circular advertising various publications of the Church is included in this bibliography only as a borderline entry. The date does not appear, except that it was published after Ben T. Short reprinted *The Book of the Law of the Lord,* and too early, as it would seem, to list any of the concluding entries in the present bibliography (or for that matter, either No. 92 or No. 93). The circular advises concerning the *Book of the Law,* "We can furnish the 'small edition' containing 80 pages, but of the large edition our supply is too limited to promise you a copy," which is of interest as showing how late copies of the 1856 *Book of the Law of the Lord* could still be obtained. The single leaf which comprises this circular is signed: H.C. Anderson, 1636 E. 7th Street, Pueblo, Colo. Mr. Anderson's home was used as a mailing point during the early thirties in connection with missionary activity of the Church in the Western states.

MoInRC

1931

CHESTER K. FLANDERS

95} *Infant Baptism.*

{Kansas City, Kansas: 1931.} 8 pp. 19.4 × 13.5 cm.

Caption title. The principal article contained, "Baptism of Infants," is dated January 28, 1931, and signed "C. K. F.," i.e., Chester K. Flanders. A second article deals with idolatry. This tract was published in the name of "The Latter Day Precept, 1735 Haskell, Kansas City, Kansas," but as appears from other sources and as I am informed by Mr. Lloyd Flanders, the *Precept* had ceased publication a decade earlier.

WBuC, Morgan

{CHESTER K. FLANDERS}

{96} *Modern Christianity*{.} *A Dialogue Between a Baptist and an Infidel.*

{Kansas City, Kansas: Published by Chester K. Flanders. 1933?} 16 pp. 19.3 × 12.8 cm.

Caption title. The tract is dated Kansas City, Kansas, Dec. 31, 1932, hence doubtless appeared early in 1933. Slightly changed, so that it is "supposed to have taken place in 1918 during the prevalence of the 'Flu' epidemic," this is the dialogue published by Wingfield Watson in 1884 {No. 41}.

WBuC, Morgan

JAMES J. STRANG

{97} *The Diamond Being the Law of Prophetic Succession and a Defense of the Calling of James J. Strang as Successor to Joseph Smith and A Full Exposition of the Law of God Touching the Succession of Prophets Holding the Presidency of the True Church. Voree, Wis.,* 1848. {At head of title:} Gospel Tract No. IV. First published by the Church of Jesus Christ of Latter Day Saints at Voree, Wisconsin, 1848{.}

{Pueblo, Colo.? 1934?} 15 pp. 23.1 × 15.3 cm.

Caption title. In double columns. This fourth edition of *The Diamond* is understood to have been printed by John Flanders and associates working out of Pueblo, who advertised "Joseph Smith's Last Revelation" in Western papers and sent copies of *The Diamond* to interested inquirers. The first page contains a paragraph summarizing the contents, with the explanation that it "was published by the prophet James in his day and time and we are only printing it and sending it forth to you, that you might be given an opportunity to hear and to know the truth in regard to this very important matter." References to Doctrine and Covenants [*sic*], which in earlier editions were to the Nauvoo edition, are changed in this printing so that they may be used in connection with the versions of D&C in use among the Reorganized and Utah churches.

WBuC, Morgan

JOHN FLANDERS

{98} *Prophetic Controversy No. 14*{.} *James J. Strang's Memorial to the Nation and An Open Letter to Rudger Clawson, President of the Quorum of Twelve, (Utah) Church of Jesus Christ of Latter Day*

Saints, written in reply to a false and misleading statement against "Strangites" which was published in "Quorum Bulletin," Vol. 1, No. 2, of their 1935 Sunday School Quarterly, on pages 20 and 21. {By John Flanders.}

{Pueblo, Colo.? 1936?} 16 pp. 23.1 × 15.1 cm.

Caption title. In double columns. The Memorial of April 6, 1850 {No. 18} is reprinted on pp. 2–6. The rest of the pamphlet is given over to the open letter challenging Clawson in his dismissal of Strang's claims to the Succession. The date of publication is indicated by a reference on p. 13 to "this date (March 1936)."

MoInRC, WBuC, Morgan

JAMES J. STRANG

)} *The Revelations of James J. Strang.*

{Cheboygan, Mich.: Cheboygan Observer.} 1939. 28 pp. 21.7 × 15 cm.

Cover title. In double columns. This new edition of the revelations, authorized by the Church at its 1939 conference, was seen through the press by Stanley L. Johnston, and I am informed by Mr. Stephen West that it was printed at Cheboygan in an edition of 2,000 copies. The text of the second edition {No. 64} is followed, but with some added "testimonies." The verso of the front cover contains a table of contents, with a paragraph explaining that the revelations "are like the wheels of a motor, which when put in proper relation to the other parts, make a perfect, smooth running machine," wherefore readers are urged to contact an elder of the Church "and get acquainted with the gospel as taught by divine inspiration through Joseph Smith and James J. Strang." Another feature is a kind of preface on the first page pointing out parallels in the careers of the two prophets; this preface is signed: "Church of Jesus Christ of Latter Day Saints Often identified as 'Strangites' 1939."

UHi, WBuC, Morgan

UNITED STATES BUREAU OF THE CENSUS

oo} *Church of Jesus Christ of Latter Day Saints (Strangites).* {In:} *Religious Bodies: 1936,* Volume II Part 2 Denominations K to Z Statistics, History, Doctrine{,} Organization, and Work{.} Prepared under the supervision of Dr. T.F. Murphy Chief Statistician for Religious Statistics{.}

Washington: United States Government Printing Office. 1941. xiv, 799–1695 pp. 23 × 14.7 cm.

The section, "Church of Jesus Christ of Latter Day Saints (Strangites)," appears on pp. 836–839 as the sixth of six denominations treated under the general classification, "Latter Day Saints." The Strangite church had not previously been reported in the census of religious bodies. A statement on "History, Doctrine, and Organization," prepared by Lloyd A. Flanders, occupying pp. 837–839, is accompanied by two statistical tables prepared by the Bureau of the Census. The contribution by Mr. Flanders is the most informative printed source concerning the Church as it exists today.

CSmH, CU-B, CtY, DLC, MH, MoInRC, NN, OClWHi, USlC, WBuC, WHi, Morgan

CHURCH OF JESUS CHRIST OF LATTER DAY SAINTS

{101} *The Gospel Herald.* {Bay City, Mich.} Edited by Stanley L. Johnston. Vol. I, No. 1. April, 1941. 4 pp. 21.6 × 14 cm.

This little 2-column, 4-page periodical, published in the interest of "The True Church of Jesus Christ of Latter Day Saints" by Stanley L. Johnston, was suspended after six issues in consequence of Mr. Johnston's induction into the armed forces. The numbers printed were dated April, September, October, and November, 1941; and January and March, 1942. There is some variation in the vertical dimension of the several issues, which contain doctrinal articles, news notes, and researches by Mr. Johnston into various phases of the history of the Church.

WBuC Complete
Morgan Nov 1941; Jan 1942.

1948

WINGFIELD WATSON

{102} *The True Gospel. A Comparison of primitive, and True Gospel, and The Modern Sectarian Interpretation of it.* By Wingfield Watson.

{Burlington, Wis.: Voree Press. May, 1948.} 8 pp. w.p. 22.2 × 14.2 cm.

In double columns. A reprint of No. 89. I am informed by Mr. West that this was the first issue from the new press of the Church at Voree, and that 2,000 copies were printed.

UHi, WBuC, Morgan

CHURCH OF JESUS CHRIST OF LATTER DAY SAINTS

{103} *Articles of Faith Of The Church of Jesus Christ Of Latter Day Saints.*

{Burlington, Wis.: Voree Press. 1948.} 4 pp. w.p. 15.3 × 11.5 cm.

This leaflet, of which 2,000 copies were printed, contains 13 articles of faith attributed to Joseph Smith and 4 paragraphs of comment unsigned but by Stephen West.

WBuC, Morgan

1949

JAMES J. STRANG

4} *The Book of the Law of the Lord Consisting of An Inspired Translation of some of the most Important Parts of the Law given to Moses, and a very few Additional Commandments, with Notes and References. Printed by Command of the King, at the Royal Press, Saint James, A. R. I.*

Burlington, Wis.: Reprinted at Voree Press. 1948 {i.e., 1949}. 8, {17}–336 pp. 14.6 × 9.5 cm.

This word-for-word, line-for-line, page-for-page reprint of the large edition of *The Book of the Law of the Lord* is by far the most ambitious publication of the present-day Strangite church. An effort undertaken in 1941 to reprint the book failed from causes connected with the war, but a second attempt was successful. Although the title page bears the date 1948, press work was not completed until the following year. The title page is hand-stamped "Copyright 1949 by Voree Press," but by some intricacy of the law this copyright had not been granted at the time this bibliography went to press. The copy used in the reprinting, as observed in No. 31, Note, was one which formerly belonged to Charles J. Strang, bearing his notation that it came from the bindery June 30, 1891; it contains the 8-page preface, with the testimony that is signed by seven witnesses. Except for the imprint, nothing has been added to the present edition, of which 2,000 copies were printed.

DLC, UHi, WBuC, Morgan

1950

JAMES J. STRANG

05} *The Diamond Being the Law of Prophetic Succession and a Defense of the Calling of James J. Strang as Successor to Joseph Smith and A Full Exposition of the Law of God Touching the Succession of Prophets Holding the Presidency of the True Church.* {At head of title:} Gospel Tract No. IV. First published by the Church of Jesus Christ of Latter Day Saints at Voree, Wisconsin, 1848{.}

Burlington, Wis.: Reprint Voree Press. 1950. 19 pp. 21.7 × 14.4 cm.

Caption title. In double columns. This fourth reprint of *The Diamond,* of which 1,000 copies were printed, was the first to carry its own imprint. The text is that of the 1934 edition, but on pp. 17–19 is added "An Extract from Voree Chronicles giving History of Letter of Appointment and note by Wingfield Watson." This is the material printed by Watson in the 1896 edition of his *Open Letter to B. H. Roberts* {No. 61}, divested however of its argumentative asides to W. W. Blair.

UHi, WBuC, Morgan

Dissenting Works

1846

REUBEN MILLER

{1} *James J. Strang, Weighed in the Balance of Truth, and Found Wanting. His claims as first President of the Melchisedek Priesthood Refuted.* By Reuben Miller, Elder of the Church of Jesus Christ of Latter Day Saints.

Burlington, Wis.: September, 1846. 26 pp. 18.3 × 12.8 cm.

Wrapper title. One of Strang's first important converts, Miller was also one of the earliest to leave him. His faith in the prophet's authority was shaken during the summer of 1846, and with this pamphlet he turned his back upon Strang to fellowship Brigham Young again. The first 4 pages are devoted to a personal narrative, then follows a long argument against the validity of Strang's claims. The last few pages contain some details concerning the "Order of the Illuminati" instituted among the Saints by Strang and John C. Bennett, with which Miller was less than favorably impressed. Some rebuttal to this pamphlet appeared in *Voree Herald,* October, 1846, and in *Zion's Reveille,* January 14, February 4, 11, and March 25, 1847. Miller went on to Kanesville in 1848 and to Utah the following year, where he became bishop of Mill Creek Ward in Salt Lake Valley, serving in that capacity until his death in 1882. In addition to the copy located below, a second copy has been turned up by Edward Eberstadt & Sons.

USIC

{CHURCH OF CHRIST (VOREE)}

{2} *Mormon Doings.*

{Elkhorn, Wis.: 1846.} Broadside.

No copy located. Some ten years ago the late Morten A. C. Nicolaysen of Salt Lake City sent Mr. Lloyd A. Flanders a handwritten copy of this broadside, soliciting comment upon it, but I have been unable to learn where Mr. Nicolaysen saw the original. I am able to describe its contents authoritatively by virtue of notes Mr. Flanders preserved.

Mormon Doings proceeded directly out of the antagonisms at Voree of which John C. Bennett was the heart and center. General dislike of Bennett and the secret covenant he and Strang had instituted in the Church led to an attempt, just before Strang's return from the East in October, 1846, to try Bennett on various charges of immorality and official misconduct. The manuscript minutes of that trial, of rather extraordinary character, have never been published, but are now preserved with the Strang MSS, having fallen into Dr. Quaife's hands in 1930. On his return to Voree, Strang brushed these proceedings aside as illegal, but at the cost of an open rebellion among the dissidents. Aaron Smith, Strang's first convert and a member of his First Presidency, turned violently against him, and called a protest meeting on December 7, 1846. An account of that meeting opens the broadside. Those who attended voted to reject the controversial "covenant" as false in its claims and dangerous in its effects. It was further voted to withdraw fellowship from all who adhered to the covenant, "as persons who follow evil and choose darkness, instead of light," and to publish the trial and excommunication of Bennett from "the Church of Christ in Voree," that the world might "behold the man." The meeting also appointed a committee of three to draft resolutions expressing the sentiments of those present, to be reported at a meeting the following evening. The bulk of the broadside is given over to these resolutions, which declare patriotic sentiments in defiance of the tendentious covenant, charge the authorities of the Church with attempting to institute a gag law and with falsifying the published minutes of the October General Conference, declare the intention of sustaining Aaron Smith in the office to which he was called by Joseph Smith's Letter of Appointment, and deplore Strang's tyrannical conduct in cutting off men who had made great sacrifices, toiled and suffered, and were among the best members of the Church. These resolutions are followed by an account of Bennett's trial and excommunication, insisted upon as legal and binding. This in turn is followed by a purported true copy of "the covenant—(so-called) administered by J. C. Bennett under the direction of James J. Strang," attested by Willard Griffith, Collins Pemberton, Isaac Scott, and Allen Waite. The broadside concludes with some remarks upon the covenant and the present exposure of "the arch knavery of James J. Strang and John C. Bennett." Strang is declared, on his return from the East, to have said that the covenant was part and parcel of a revelation from God, though at the same time he said it was no part of the Gospel so that any man dissatisfied could withdraw from it and still remain in the Church. Far from abiding by this principle, Strang was "now charging and expelling the best men in the Church for covenant breaking and heresy," by which the broadside has reference to Aaron Smith, Jared Carter, Collins Pemberton, Duty Griffith, John Gaylord, and Isaac Scott.

Years later, in the *Saints' Herald,* December 29, 1888, Isaac Scott claimed to have got out 2,000 copies of the broadside, credit which was also claimed, at the time of the Temple Lot suit, by Willard Griffith (see *Complainant's Abstract . . . ,* Lamoni, 1893, p. 463). The most noteworthy feature of *Mormon Doings* was the version of the covenant it printed. It has since developed, as Dr. Quaife has written on the authority of Strang's handwritten original, that although the apostates "did not have an exact or complete copy of the covenant . . . it was substantially correct as far as it went." The broadside was replied to in detail in *Zion's Reveille* for November, 1846 (not issued until January), and received considerable attention in succeeding issues. See also Nos. 3 and 4 below.

1847

COLLINS PEMBERTON

3 *Strangism Exposed to the World.*

Chicago: January 5, 1847. Broadside.

No copy known. Virtually all that is known of this broadside is gleaned from the columns of *Zion's Reveille.* It appears that on December 1, 1846, Collins Pemberton published an article against Strang in the Chicago *Morning Mail.* This was replied to by Strang shortly after in the same paper, but meanwhile, according to the *Reveille,* Pemberton had gone to Elkhorn, Wis., and in association with three others had published what the Reveille called "Placard Number 1," evidently the broadside, *Mormon Doings.* This second broadside, "Placard Number 2," as the Reveille referred to it, carried on the wordy warfare, which was at once taken up by the *Reveille* of January 14, 1847. Apparently *Strangism Exposed to the World* contained some numerously signed certificates concerning wrongdoing at Voree. According to the *Reveille,* most of the signatures were forged. A considerable number of the broadsides must have been printed, for one of the letters in the Strang MSS mentions that 25 copies had been sent by the dissenters to the writer's neighborhood alone. Another letter in the Strang MSS, from Daniel P. Botsford at Chicago, dated January 12, 1847, provides information that the dissenters expected soon to have a press in Chicago. In this expectation they were disappointed.

{CHURCH OF CHRIST (VOREE)}

{4} *The New Era, and Herald of Zion's Watchmen.* Voree, {Wis.} Vol. I, No. 1. January, 1847. 4 pp. 44.7 × 29.4 cm.

Of the two issues of the *New Era,* only a tattered copy of the first is known. The prospectus is torn, so that the publisher, if stated, does not appear, but the *New Era* was the organ of the dissenters at Voree, whose short-lived organization seems to have borne the name, "Church of Christ." When the second and last issue, for February, was published, *Zion's Reveille* of February 28, 1847, said that John Gaylord, Isaac Scott, and Robert Maltly (i.e., Malby?) were listed as the editors. The *New Era* was printed on the press of the *Elkhorn Star,* but like the *Voree Herald* in its time, bore the Voree dateline. A 4-column paper, it was to have been published semi-monthly. The first issue contains a long "Proclamation" and many miscellaneous articles against Strang and secret covenants, emanating not only from the schismatics at Voree but from the congregation in Kirtland, Ohio. The principal feature of the unlocated second issue would seem to have been a 7-column article, "On Priesthood." No more issues were published, for the *Gospel Herald,* November 25, 1847, in an article on "anti-Mormon papers," commented that two numbers of the *New Era* were got out in three or four months, since which none had appeared. Again on March 22, 1849, the *Gospel Herald* declared that but two issues of the *New Era* were printed.

MoInRC Jan 1847 {microfilm in DLC}

REUBEN MILLER

{5} *Truth Shall Prevail: A Short Reply to an Article Published in the Voree Herald (Reveille) by J. C. Bennett; and the Wilful Falsehoods of J. J. Strang, Published in the First Number of Zion's Reveille.* By Reuben Miller.

Burlington, W. T.: 1847.

No copy known. The title is derived from a reply by John C. Bennett under date of February 1, 1847, in *Zion's Reveille,* February 4, 1847. From points made in rebuttal, it is seen that the pamphlet consisted of at least 12 pages.

1849

INCREASE McGEE VAN DEUSEN

Visions and Revelations of I. Van Dusen.

{New York: 1849.}

No copy known. The title comes from *The Olive Branch,* January, 1850, Vol. II, p. 111, which says: "We have lately received a small pamphlet of the above title. It is, to say the least of it, a very singular document. It is intended for all who profess to be Mormons, but more particularly for that part of the Church over which James J. Strang presides." *The Olive Branch* prints the four revelations it contains, all very short, and tending to reiterate that James J. Strang and George J. Adams are led by the Devil. The earliest of these is dated October 12, 1849, the last November 23, 1849, both at New York City. From numerous references in the Strang MSS and in the *Gospel Herald,* it is evident that the pamphlet was printed early in December. A letter from Van Deusen himself to Strang among the MSS, written about December 21, reacts vigorously to Strang's blunt request that Van Deusen cease sending him anything through the mails: "God has said you And Adams Are led Purely by the Devil & there are many things revealed of Great importance to the saints (notwithstanding your opinion to the contrary) And by the Grace of God I shall do my duty wether the church will hear or forbear."

1850

INCREASE McGEE VAN DEUSEN

} {Revelations of I. Van Deusen.}

{New York?, 1850.}

Even less is known of this title by Van Deusen than of the preceding one; it is just barely established that such a work appeared. A letter from Samuel Graham to Van Deusen, printed in the *Gospel Herald,* January 24, 1850, mentions taking from the office "a small paper containing your revelations," in which, apparently, Van Deusen said that L. D. Hickey was dead and Strang soon would be. As nothing to this effect appears in Van Deusen's first "budget of revelations," it may be assumed that a second work appeared. This is also the inference to be drawn from a letter by Moore Walker in the Strang MSS, dated New York, February 2, 1850: "Van Deusen has received a nother revelation I heare so that you see that we are not yet left without revelations of at least some kind." Finally, the *Gospel Herald* of

May 30, 1850, sums up Van Deusen: "Professed to be a follower of prophet Strang, but there being the most imminent danger that either the prophet or some of his counselors would commit some heinous sin, he and all that followed him were rejected of God; that is, by Van Dusen. He soon commenced the publication of a series of revelations, and preaching from house to house." This language, "series of revelations," would indicate that Van Deusen got out at least two publications of this character. In later years Van Deusen seems to have been identified for a time with the Kirtland congregation, but I cannot date his residence there. See also No. 10.

Chapter 10

Contractual Writing (1950–1951)

Editor's Introduction

Between 1948 and 1952, while he was nominally hard at work on a manuscript for *The Mormons*, Dale Morgan scratched together a bare living from contractual research and writing. The process began immediately after returning home from his cross-continental trip on the Guggenheim fellowship. In 1948 he was able to land a commission to produce an automobile tour description of Utah for the Mountain West States volume of *The American Guide*, and another to produce data for the *Utah Historical Trails Map* published by the state tourism agency. The next year he worked on a volume of community descriptions (which was never released or completed) for a private publisher, and was paid a small stipend for intense but sporadic work for the Utah State Historical Society as the editor of the *Utah Historical Quarterly*.[1] These small make-work jobs allowed him to exist—barely—but were individually unfulfilling. Practical needs ate into the time needed to work on larger projects. After a year and a half of anxiously marking time in a basement apartment in Salt Lake City, it was clear that he was unlikely to find work there and could not make ends meet on the small means he could scratch together. "The economic thing boils down to this, that I can either make a living freelancing or can write my histories, but not both," he told Charles Kelly bluntly. "If I want to write the latter, a job will have to provide the wherewithal."[2] After making the decision in July 1949 to return

[1] *Utah Historical Trails Map* (Salt Lake City: Utah State Department of Publicity and Industrial Development, ca. 1948); "The Mountain States," *The American Guide*, ed. Henry G. Alsberg (New York: Hastings House, 1949). *Life In America: The West* (Grand Rapids, Mich.: Fideler Co., 1952).

[2] DLM to Charles Kelly, 11 October 1949, Charles Kelly papers, Utah State Historical Society, Salt Lake City.

to Washington, D.C., in September and October Morgan packed file cabinets of transcripts and case upon case of books, stowed much of it in his mother's basement, and returned eastward, sure the capital's enlarged post-war economy would provide easier employment pickings than Salt Lake City. It did not.

For a year he wrangled with the Civil Service Division about professional ratings, living with his sister's young family in Alexandria, Virginia. He covered his living expenses after the move eastward by writing a junior high school geography textbook on the West on commission, but his chief income while again living in the East was to compose attractive and scrupulously accurate catalogue descriptions for manuscript material being sold by Edward Eberstadt & Sons.[3] The Eberstadts, New York book dealers who also traded in historical documents and collections, occupied the pinnacle of the book trade in historic Americana. Much of Morgan's descriptive work for the firm is not credited and cannot be recovered. The Eberstadt commissions put a lot of Mormon- and West-related primary material into Morgan's eager hands, and the process provided an unparalleled opportunity for intensive study essentially on his own terms. The bulk of material had nothing to do with the Mormons, bit several important commissions did. Besides the Milo Quaife collection of Strang material and the Oliver H. Olney papers, both of which went to Yale University, Morgan described important letterbooks by John W. Young and Albert Rockwood, surveyor William H. Emory's papers, and small groups of papers and single documents by the score. These commissions demanded all his attention and furious effort on short schedules. His work certainly appears without attribution in many Eberstadt catalogues between numbers 126 and 168 (1950–1968), including probably but not certainly the entire unnumbered *Utah and the Mormons* (1956). Meanwhile, as he catalogued he also burned midnight oil completing and editing the Rod Korns memorial volume *West from Fort Bridger* and the John Wesley Powell expedition journals for volumes 14, 16–17, and 19 of the *Utah Historical Quarterly*.

It is easy to overstate the importance of Morgan's contribution to history as a sales cataloguer. His intended audience was no larger than the three Eberstadts, William Robertson Coe, and the firm's circle of customers. The importance of these assignments as Latter Day Saint research lay in their intersection with Morgan's contemporary writing priority, *The Mormons*. While he had these papers strewn across his basement apartment and

[3]The lengthy exchange documenting Morgan's commissions as a cataloguer for the Eberstadts is in boxes 7 and 34, Morgan papers.

sister's tiny kitchen, Dale was also occasionally typing out a page or two of conceptual drafts for "the Mormon book" as ideas struck him. Morgan clearly sees Olney and Strang as respectively deluded and deceptive; surviving drafts for *The Mormons* suggest the writer shaped his views about Joseph Smith at the same time and in the same mold. To none of the three men does he ascribe sincerity or belief: they are creatures of their environment. In fact, throughout his career the only historical worlds his human subjects occupy are the circumstances immediately around them. To former chess partner Richards Durham, proselyting as an LDS missionary in South Carolina, Morgan had once asserted "I have never known, save only now in you, a person I could respect who held to the Mormon beliefs."[4] Throughout his writing, individuals tended to be portrayed as either actors or victims. Morgan's presentation of historical subjects casts them chiefly in the role of doers rather than thinkers, emotive feelers, or believers.

The first two works reproduced here introduce calendars of Mormon manuscripts, which Morgan catalogued for the Eberstadts. The individual descriptive abstracts themselves are not included. The Oliver Olney papers were produced while living in Salt Lake City toward the end of 1949. The Milo Quaife collection of James J. Strang papers, a larger collection representing a much more involve process, dates to the middle of 1950. "James J. Strang's 'Letter of Appointment' " was a private study compiled for one of the partners in Edward Eberstadt & Sons and undoubtedly formed the historical basis for Charles Eberstadt's article "A Letter That Founded a Kingdom" about the James Strang "appointment" letter, which had been among the Quaife material.[5]

The Olney Papers
Foreword and Calendar of the Documents
By Dale L. Morgan[1]

From the internal evidence of these papers, it would appear that Oliver H. Olney was born in England. If so, he apparently moved to Connecticut early in his life, and subsequently to Ohio, where he was converted to Mormonism in 1831. He was with the Saints in Ohio and Missouri, and moved with them

[4]DLM to Richards Durham, 4 December 1940.

[5]Charles Eberstadt, "A Letter That Founded a Kingdom," *Autograph Collector's Journal* (October 1950): 3–8, 32.

[1]Dale Morgan, noted authority on the Mormons, is presently engaged on his history of the Saints, which will be published this fall [i.e., 1950].

to Illinois after the expulsion from Missouri. He was married and had seven children, but was a widower at the time he began writing the documents which make up this collection.

From the Mormon annals, it appears that Olney was given a hearing before the High Council in Nauvoo on March 17, 1842, after which they withdrew the hand of fellowship and took his license from him, on charges of having set himself up as a prophet. On April 1, 1842, in an editorial in the *Times and Seasons,* Joseph Smith commented adversely upon Olney among others: "Mr. Olney has also been tried by the high council, and disfellowshipped because he would not have his writings tested by the word of God; evidently proving that he loves darkness rather than light because his deeds are evil."

This denunciation in the Mormon news organ at Nauvoo clearly provoked Olney into beginning the record which principally comprises the Olney Papers. This record is of somewhat mixed value. The bad features are that Olney fancied himself as something of a writer, and elected to write his message in a prose style abstract in character, inclined to word transpositions, and capitalization of words at the beginning of lines. Because of the general fuzziness of his literary inclinations and his concern, moreover, to establish a new dispensation in the place of the fallen church at Nauvoo, he is often hard to read and is repetitious.

On the positive side, this is almost the only contemporary record of life in Nauvoo at the critical period of the Bennett scandal known to exist outside the church archives, and perhaps the only one extant which deals with the events of this period from a critical point of view. Its greatest contributions is that it makes plain that Joseph Smith was ready to abandon Nauvoo and take his church west to the Rockies at this early date. Olney describes the plans as they were discussed on the street in Nauvoo, and in the light of what he says, it may be realized that it was only Joseph's trial at Springfield in January, 1843, which demonstrated the power of habeas corpus to keep him out of the hands of the Missouri courts, that postponed the Mormon migration to the Rockies. Ironically, this reprieve also resulted in Joseph's being murdered before he could take his church west.

Olney likewise provides evidence that the facts about polygamy in Nauvoo had become common gossip before the break between Bennett and the Church, particularly the involvement of the Twelve; and he is a mine of information on the state of public opinion in Nauvoo on a host of other matters which were shaping Mormon society at the time. His record would be much more valuable had he written it as a conventional diary more immediately factual in its purpose, but in any form it is welcome in view of the gap that exists in source material of whatever description.

The corpus of this collection of papers has some further significance as exhibiting the body of the material from which Olney wrote his now-rare pamphlet, *The Absurdities of Mormonism Portrayed,* published in March, 1843, he had early decided upon that title, and these papers include several trial drafts of his introduction and other items he ultimately included in the pamphlet.*

Included in the collection are two letters written by Phoebe M. Wheeler, who as the second of the letters {manuscript No. 46} notes, became Olney's wife in October, 1843. She appears as a person more solidly grounded in reality than her husband, and its would be interesting to know what she made of the pretensions which take up part of the bulk of these papers, that is, Olney's having been set apart by some supernatural beings he called "the Antient of Days" to bring forth a new dispensation. It has been known from Mormon annals (see *History of the Church,* 5: 269–70) that Olney did make such claims, but it is only seen in the light of the papers now discovered that he proceeded seriously to the establishment of a church on the basis of these revelations; the Olney Papers make manifest his intention of making Squaw Grove, Illinois, the place of gathering. The dissenting churches established out of Mormonism during Joseph Smith's own lifetime may be counted on the fingers of one hand, and it is extremely valuable therefore to have these papers at the inner core of one of these schisms.

Apart from a letter by his wife dated in January, 1844, the last document in this collection is dated February 5, 1843. According to the Mormon annals, five days later Olney was tried before the mayor's court in Nauvoo on charges of having stolen goods from the store of Moses Smith on January 23, 1843; he was bound over to the next circuit court for trail, in the sum of $5,000, and for want of bail committed to Carthage jail. Whether this was merely a means of disposing of Olney as an irritant in Nauvoo or whether there was some wrongdoing on Olney's part would require investigation in the court records of Hancock County in Illinois; it is evident from the letter by his wife, however, that he was a free man at the time of their marriage in October following, and that as late as January 24, 1844, they were living in Nauvoo. He and his wife may have gone to St. Louis, where a pamphlet by

*[*The Absurdities of Mormonism Portrayed: A Brief Sketch by Oliver H. Olney, Hancock County, Illinois, March 3d., 1843* (s.l.: s.n.). Flake/Draper 5991. —Ed.]

Olney on the subject of spiritual wifery was published in the fall of 1845.* No copy of that pamphlet is known, but some extracts were printed that fall in the newspapers of St. Louis and Warsaw. Nothing is yet knows of his life after that date.

The Olney Papers, 1842–1843
The Sole Critical Account of Nauvoo Affairs
Disclosing Smith's Plans for Removal to the Rockies

Olney (Oliver H.). The original manuscript documents of Oliver H. Olney constituting the records of Mormon affairs and events at Nauvoo during the critical period 1842–3, as set forth and described in the Morgan calendar hereto attached. The archive consists of 46 separate documents ranging in length from single sheets to sewn manuscript volumes extending in one instance to 88 folio pages. Written mainly in Nauvoo, 1842–1843.

[*Eleven pages of summary descriptions follow, which are not included in this edition*]

The Strang Manuscripts**

The extraordinary documents which make up this collection comprise the most important group of manuscripts pertaining to the history of the Mormons which have ever reached the market, and it is difficult to imagine that a collection comparable in significance will ever come to light. Central to the history of one of the most important of the Mormon factions, the Strang Manuscripts are unique. Only the archives of the Reorganized Church might have afforded a similar collection of documents, and those archives went up in smoke in the Herald Office fire of 1907. The archives of the Church of Jesus Christ of Latter-day Saints at Salt Lake City, with their enormous reach back over a century, are of course in a class by themselves, but it is not to be expected that they will ever be offered for sale nor even, very soon opened to research; and those archives themselves are significantly incomplete in the absence of the present collection. It is clear that no large treatment either of the Mormon Church itself or of the many factions into which it split up after the death of its founder, Joseph Smith, can hereafter be regarded as authoritative without reference to the Strang Manuscripts.

*[*Spiritual Wifery at Nauvoo Exposed: Also a True Account of Transactions In and About Nauvoo* (St. Louis: Published for the Author, 1845). BYU holds a photocopy of the publication discovered after Morgan's day, along with a copy of the *Warsaw Signal*'s reproduction of the text. Flake/Draper 5991a. —Ed.]

**[Morgan papers, Bancroft Library. —Ed.]

James Jesse Strang was born at Scipio, N.Y., March 21, 1813. His childhood, as he records in the never-completed autobiography included in these Manuscripts, was sickly and unhappy, so that he was never afterwards able to look back up its without "a creeping sensation akin to terror." He grew up without much formal education but had an active, impressionable mind which ingested learning rapidly and found play in the neighborhood lyceums and debating societies. A fragment of the diary he kept from his nineteenth to his twenty-fourth year, also in the present collection,* graphically illustrates the qualities which were to make his influence so powerfully felt on the course of Mormon history. He had wide-ranging interests, and immediate sensitivity to the ideas and opinions of his times, a distinct flair for words, a liking for disputation, and above all a hunger for recognition which he united with singular tenacity of will. His diary shows also, in its occasional employment of a cipher he himself worked out, a certain liking for mystification and privacy unto himself which was to recur significantly in his later life.

Strang taught school and read for the law, being admitted to the bar of Chautauqua County in 1836. He did not, however, entertain a very high opinion of the legal profession, as his letter written to A. J. Graham in 1849 makes abundantly clear, and he varied his practice by serving as a village postmaster, temperance lecturer, and editor of a village paper. Finally, in the summer of 1843, he followed his wife's relatives to Wisconsin. Two brothers-in-law were Mormon converts, and under their influence Strang made a visit to Nauvoo early in 1844. He had once been inclined to infidelity and later had been a communicant of the Baptist church, but now he too became a Mormon, being baptized, it is said, by Joseph Smith. Whether the doctrine appealed to him or whether he saw clearly into the dynamism inherent in the new faith and joined the church under the spur of his driving ambition still remains a fundamental enigma; his friends and relatives pondered the question at the time, and sometimes, as in the letter of Wealthy Smith, faced him with it: "What your object could have been in joining them {the Mormons}, I am at a loss to know, unless it was for the sake of gain or (as I have often heard you say) to immortalize your name, for it does not seem possible that you can be a sincere believer."

*[Morgan painstakingly broke the cipher in which Strang recorded part of this diary, correcting his copy of the translation Quaife had published in *The Kingdom of St. James*. The diary was later published as *The Diary of James J. Strang*, ed. Mark Strang (Lansing: Michigan State University Press, 1961). Morgan's own translation was the basis for his review of the book, which follows in the second volume. Morgan's annotated copy of Quaife's book is at Brigham Young University. —Ed.]

The most important single document in the Strang Manuscripts is the letter which launched him upon his career as prophet, seer, and revelator, the "Letter of Appointment" purportedly sent to Strang by Joseph Smith from Nauvoo on June 19, 1844, eight days before the Prophet's death. Upon the question of the authenticity of this letter Strang's integrity as a religious leader and the whole vitality of his claims to lead the Church stand or fall. Under close examination the letter appears to be what the embattled Twelve Apostles branded it when it first began to stir the Church, a forgery. But it assailed Brigham Young and his associates from an unexpected quarter. The fight for the Succession originally had lain between the Twelve and Sidney Rigdon, and in August, 1844, they triumphed over Rigdon by imputing to him personal ambitions which they, collectively, could not hold. "I will tell you who will lead the Church," Brigham Young roared to the Saints, "the Twelve—I at their head!" Effective as this argument had been in disposing of Rigdon, it was totally inadequate in dealing with one of Strang's tenacity and ability. To a Church which long had sung, "The Church without a Prophet is not the Church for me," Strang brought the unequivocal claim that he was the appointed and only Prophet—selected by Joseph Smith himself—to lead them. Strang could find ample precedent in the church law, the *Doctrine and Covenants,* to support his contention that the Twelve were out of their place in "usurping" the rights and duties of the First Presidency, and after a period of preparation, following his initial rebuff in the summer of 1844, he launched a smashing attack upon the position of the Twelve through the columns of the *Voree Herald,* which he began publishing in January, 1846.

The Strang Manuscript fully display the staggering effect of this assault upon the citadels which earlier had fallen almost by default into the hands of the Twelve. Numerous letters in the present collection, written to Strang from every quarter through the spring and summer of 1846, show how deeply disturbed many of the Saints were over the condition in which the Church found itself. Jacob Gibeon spoken eloquently for many of his brethren when he wrote Strang from Philadelphia in June, 1846, that he could not fellowship the Twelve with their false doctrines—"Twelve Heads, ralleing for origan California Taking the gospel from the Gentiles no Proffit to Lead no Sear to disurn the Calamities &c &c."

From the viewpoint of the Twelve, no time could have been more unfortunate for a formidable claimant to the Succession to take them in the flank. They were launching upon their exodus out of Nauvoo, by no means assured of finding a safe haven in the Rockies, the mob spirit growling around them in Illinois, their followers unhappy and unsettled. It was entirely possible that their following would melt away altogether. Only in light of the Strang Manuscripts can the pressures that bore upon Brigham Young as his Camp of Israel moved west across Iowa toward the distant Rockies be fully understood, or the anger and apprehension which warmed his harangues to the Saints the whole length of their journey to Utah.

Moreover, Strang found himself immediate and able lieutenants to carry the Word in person. Reuben Miller, sent by the Twelve to combat him, succumbed to his claims and personality, and as he writes Strang in an important letter of February 15, 1846, republished in the first issue of the *Herald* in pamphlet form, 3,000 copies of which he spread about the countryside. Two disaffected apostles, George J. Adams and John E. Page,* likewise gave in their adherence, and the smoldering feud between the Smith family and Brigham Young was productive of the conversion of William Smith, the Prophet's only surviving brother, who was soon promising to move the whole family, with all their sacred relics, to Strang's gathering place at Voree. Letters from these three men are most revelatory of their character and motives, and must have their influence in any new study of Mormon history.** Quite as important in the collection is the astonishing correspondence between John C. Bennett and Strang. Notorious for his spectacular break with Joseph Smith in the summer of 1842, when he spread about the country the most damaging stories concerning the iniquities of the Saints at Nauvoo, Bennett airily dismissed all this in his letters to Strang. It was, he said, a result of the machinations of the apostles, Willard Richards, Brigham Young, and John Taylor, who "by a system of duplicity, fraud and corruption, succeeded in souring the mind of Joseph and producing an open rupture between us," which compelled him to fight and sustain himself "by recrimination."

Having thus shrugged off the embarrassments of his bad name, Bennett proceeded to shower Strang with ideas, suggestions, publicity notices, and deft flattery, all the while prodding Strang to offer him a potent place in his hierarchy in return for his support. With their double and triple underscorings, their "Private," and "Confidential" annotations, the Bennett letters

*[Adams was an apostle under Strang but not Joseph Smith or Brigham Young; Page was excommunicated by the Nauvoo church in June 1846 after which he became one of Strang's apostles before breaking with him. —Ed.]

**[A subtle reference to his own writing project, being set aside to complete this particular report. —Ed.]

themselves, quite apart from their content, afford a sufficiently illuminating insight into Bennett's character. Ultimately, students of Mormon history will have to write an exhaustive inquiry into Bennett's influence upon that history, from 1840 through 1860, and that study can be made only in the presence of this impressive collection of his letters.

By the summer of 1846 Strang was ready to extend his personal activities to the East. The manuscripts show how ripe was the field for the harvest. The church Sidney Rigdon had founded in opposition to the Twelve was already in process of the utter disintegration which befell it the next year. In city after city—Cincinnati, Kirtland, Pittsburgh, Philadelphia, New York, and Boston—the congregations fell like as many ripe plums into Strang's hand. His tour of the East was virtually a triumphal procession, and ambitious plans were on foot to send missionaries to fight for the control of the English churches and carry the gospel to the virgin terrain of the Continent. By the fall of 1846 Strang had made himself so formidable a rival as to face the Twelve with a fight to the death.

Meanwhile, however, dissension had been brewing at his home stake in Wisconsin. Under Bennett's influence, before his departure Strang had instituted a secret "Order of the Illuminati" into which the elite of the Church were initiated, binding themselves by "a great covenant" not to reveal the mysteries they were taught. Some of the Saints were offended at this "secret combination" in their midst, on the grounds that the *Book of Mormon* enjoined against all such; and others took umbrage at Bennett's autocratic administration and easy morals. By late summer Reuben Miller had broken with Strang's church, publishing a notable pamphlet, *James J. Strang Weighed in the Balance of Truth, and Found Wanting*,† against his former leader, and in October Strang's insurgent brother-in-law, Aaron Smith, sat with a high council in Voree in judgment upon John C. Bennett, the astonishing and illuminating minutes of which constitute one of the most important documents in the Strang manuscripts.

Strang returned to Voree in mid-October to face open insurrection. The "anti-covenant" faction broke away entirely, publishing broadsides against him and commencing a dissenting paper. Letters in the Strang manuscripts exhibit the doubt and dismay of his followers everywhere attending this

†[*James J. Strang Weighed in the Balance of Truth, and Found Wanting. His Claims as First President of the Melchisedek Priesthood Refuted* (Burlington, Wisc. Terr., 1846). Flake/Draper 5406. A comment on the pamphlet will be found in Morgan's *Bibliography of the Church of Jesus Christ of Latter Day Saints (Strangite)*, as well. —Ed.]

onslaught by the "Pseudoes" (pseudo-Mormons), as Strang called the dissenters; and they also exhibit the counter-measures taken by Strang and those who remained loyal. The mails brought Strang other bad news preserved in this collection[:] Lester Brook's sad intelligence of the utter failure of the English mission in consequence of the babbling of his fellow missionary, the celebrated Martin Harris; the rebellion of the Boston branch over the misbehavior of George J. Adams; and many other troubles. Other prophets, too, now were making their appearance, including James C. Brewster, whose circumspect inquiry to Strang early in 1846 is one of the most curious documents in the manuscripts. The Twelve also were taking steps to mend their fences, throwing overboard their earlier contention that none should ever be allowed to stand in Joseph's place and organizing a First Presidency of their own, drawn from the Quorum of the Twelve. It must have been discouraging for Strang to receive such letters as he had from George Walter, an old Missouri Saint. "{C}ant all be right," Walter wrote him laconically, "& I hope that we are not all wrong But I am Sertainly A fraid that there is Sumthing wrong with us all if I was Axacly right I think then I could see where the wrong was but As it is I cannot tell."

Struggling manfully with schism, apostasy, unstable and unreliable aides, and the depressing poverty of his sincerest believers (the rich hung on to their wealth, as one discouraged laborer in the vineyard remarked, as though it were "expence money to Hell"), Strang endeavored with the one hand to build up a large church at Voree, and with the other to find a new gathering place. Beaver Island in Lake Michigan as early as 1846 attracted his attention, but a strange and hitherto neglected letter, unsigned, in the manuscripts, indicates that the talk about Beaver Island may have been intended as dust in the eyes of the public, with Strang's real objective being a gathering place on the islands of the St. Lawrence River. Evidently the St. Lawrence project proved not to be feasible, and finally Strang definitely decided upon Beaver Island as the place of gathering for the faithful.

The second great mission to the East, in the winter of 1849–50, which is so fascinatingly reported in the letters to and from Strang, his principal lieutenants, and the laborers in the ranks, seemingly had as its great objective the stirring up of a wave of migration to Beaver Island, where Strang was making plans to inaugurate a literal Kingdom of God. This was a mission attended by the most turbulent events, for before setting out, Strang took his first plural wife, Elvira Field, and in the guise of a young male secretary, "Charles J.

Douglass," she accompanied him east. Rumors of some sexual irregularity preceded Strang from Beaver Island, and in New York, in September, he had to meet charges brought against him in the branch by one of his apostles, L[orenzo] D. Hickey, and the rambunctious Increase Van Deusen, who for two years had been hawking about the New York streets a celebrated exposé of Brigham Young's Nauvoo temple endowment, and who was not averse to exposing Strang in his turn. The minutes of this conference, in the present collection, show how skillfully and boldly Strang met this first ordeal. During the fall, however, persistent rumors pervaded the Strangite branches in Philadelphia and New York concerning the "physiological peculiarities" of C. J. Douglass. Strang was in no position to admit to the truth and adopted the bold course of denying nothing while standing majestically on his dignity, meantime reproaching his followers in sometimes biting language for their insinuations against his good name. The letters to and from Strang in Baltimore and the leaders of his Philadelphia branch are fascinating to read; and with them are two letters to Strang, written while he was in Washington from "Charles J. Douglass" herself, with much that may be read between the lines.

The correspondence of his missionaries to Strang during this winter of 1849–50, imposing in its proportions, shows how bitterly the battle for converts and whole congregations was still being carried on between Strang's Church and the Twelve, now securely established in Utah. Both Strangites and Brighamites regarded themselves as shepherds in whose keeping were the lambs of God, the antagonist being a wolf ravening among the flock. This struggle between the two major divisions of the original church has not heretofore been seen in proper perspective, the Strangite documents not having been available to students as have those favorable to the Utah Church. The struggle was complicated by the delicacy of the situation of the Utah Saints, who were petitioning Congress to recognize their provisional State of Deseret, and thus were anxious that no applecarts be upset. Thus D. R. Whipple writes Strang from Washington on December 28, 1849, that the day before A. W. Babbitt had come to the Strangite meeting for the first time: "after the meeting was closed he came up and told us who he was . . . he informed us of his being the Delegate from the Seeking to be State of Deseret. He told us that he was once a Member of the Church of the Saints but that now he was not a member of any Church yet felt an attachment to the name of Saint, he also spoke about the Church being devided and invited us to call and see him . . . he speaks of them [the Saints in Utah] not as Bretheren but as his Constituents." And again Whipple writes on January 9, that Babbitt "appears very anxious that we should not say or do any thing calculated in the least to hinder them in obtaining a State Government or him a Seat in Congress we have no disposition to interfere with them unless they attack You or your calling in your absence. Mr. Babbitt also informed Brother Grie{r}son that every thing pertaining to the Authority of the Church would be made perfectly Satisfactory to him."

In a position fraught with so many arresting possibilities, however, Strang could not forbear meddling. A letter from Charles Durkee, then a Wisconsin Congressman, and by interesting coincidence later a governor of Utah, addressed to Strang on January 13, 1850 a note which reveals that Strang had urged upon him the exclusion of slavery from the Territory of Deseret (Brigham Young was making the most energetic effort to keep Deseret out of the dangerous cross-fire between slavery and anti-slavery representatives in Congress, and was not likely to thank Strang for this); and among Strang's own papers in the manuscripts is a draft of a forcible statement written for the press in which he calls the State of Deseret a myth, its constitution drawn up by a mere town meeting in a single settlement of trifling size, its population insufficient to maintain a government in any regular form, and having not only no attachment to the United States but neither moral virtues nor intelligence to conduct an organized government.

Eventually the Deseret delegates failed of their objective, the Territory of Utah being created in its stead. Still another document in the Strang manuscripts is a fantastic sequel to this, a letter of March 7, 1853, by one of Strang's fellow members of the Michigan legislature commending him as a most suitable candidate "for the appointment of Governor of the new Territory of Utah," which bears out the story told in the *New York Times* of September 3, 1882, to the effect that Strang at one time "applied to Robert McClelland, of Michigan, who was then Secretary of the Interior in the cabinet of President Pierce, for an appointment as governor of Utah, promising that his administration should be attended by the uprooting of Brighamite Mormonism in the Salt Lake valley." James J. Strang as governor of Utah, successor to Brigham Young, is a prospect fearful and wonderful to contemplate; in the interests of a more rousing history, it is a pity President Pierce did not improve his opportunity.

The whole richness of this manuscript collection cannot even be suggested in a galloping appraisal of this kind. It may better be appreciated by examining the typed summaries attached to each document in the collection;‡ and appreciated best of all by reading through the documents in their entirety. They are so full of human hope, fear, mistrust, and anger, often sad and as often exalted, that to read them is to be given a fresh understanding of Mormonism, what it brought into the lives of its believers, and what they suffered in the cause, a special ironic perspective being afforded by the remembered fact that Strang was assassinated on Beaver Island in the summer of 1856, so that all this striving came to naught.

The emphasis in this appraisal has rested upon the significance of the Strang Manuscripts in their organic relationship to Mormon history in the large. This is indeed their first and highest importance, the more evident because no use has ever been made of them in such a connection. Heretofore they have been drawn upon only in narrow monographs, the Strangite church considered as a purely local phenomenon in the history of Wisconsin and Michigan. Even the history of the Strangite Church, however, must be reconsidered and rewritten when these documents become fully available to students. Out of the ruins of the Strangite Church have sprung the majority of the other factions which have made so picturesque (and so embattled) the history of the Succession. The founders of the Reorganized Church, Brewster's church, William Smith's church, and numerous others first had been associated with Strang, and their correspondence with him, while they were still numbered among the faithful, is not least interesting among the documents which make up this collection.

In general, the Manuscripts comprise a heavy correspondence incoming to Strang through 1846 and the early months of 1847, a scattering of letters through the rest of 1847 and 1848, another heavy correspondence through 1849 and the early months of 1850, and a relatively small number of letters written after Strang settled permanently at Beaver Island in the summer of 1850. With this voluminous incoming correspondence are drafts of Strang's outgoing correspondence, of roughly the same proportions as between the years though not comparable in bulk, reports of Church conferences, of individual branches, and of the "Associated Order of Enoch" at Voree, letters to Strang and his wife from their relatives in New York and Illinois, documents pertaining to Strang's life before he became a Mormon, especially including his fragmentary diary, and a large miscellany.

Most of the Manuscripts were brought together by Strang's son Charles.

‡[Unlike the unitary calendar for the Olney material, Morgan attached his catalogue descriptions to individual items within the collection. His documentary abstracts are not included in this volume, and in fact are not among his papers. —Ed.]

At the death of the latter they passed to Charles' brother Clement, and from him to Dr. Milo M. Quaife, who drew upon them in writing his *Kingdom of St. James* (New Haven, 1930).* Continual additions were made to the collection of this whole long period before it was finally placed on the market by Dr. Quaife. Some few Strang manuscripts passed through another branch of the family into the hands of the Reorganized Church of Jesus Christ of Latter Day Saints [Community of Christ], which preserves them in its library at Independence, Mo.; and it appears that a number of documents dating from the Beaver Island period are preserved by the present-day Strangite church at its headquarters on the site of old Voree outside Burlington, Wis. Both these collections have only incidental interest as compared with the present group of documents, which quite properly are denominated the Strang Manuscripts.

James J. Strang's "Letter of Appointment"

History of the Document

The account of this famous letter supposedly written by Joseph Smith to James J. Strang from Nauvoo under date of June 18, 1844, which Strang first published in the *Voree Herald*, January 1846, and subsequently in *The Diamond* (1846), the *Prophetic Controversy* (1855?), and elsewhere is as follows:

> "This letter was received at Burlington {Wis.,} by regular course of mail, coming through the distributing office at Chicago, and bears the Nauvoo post-mark of June 19, the day following its date. It arrived at Burlington July 9th, and was immediately taken from the office by C.P. Barnes, Esq., a distinguished lawyer at that place {who also at the time was Strang's law partner —DLM}, who, in consequence of the rumors of the persecution and evil war against the Mormons, and a general anxiety to hear the latest news, immediately carried it to Mr. Strang, with the request to be informed of any news of public interest which it might contain. It therefore became public the same evening."

Strang carried this letter to a Church conference at Florence, Mich., in August, 1844, where he exhibited it in support of his claim to lead the Church. Objection subsequently was made that the letter was postmark was in black ink rather than in red, as an authentic Nauvoo postmark should be, and in denying this Strang declared in his *Prophetic Controversy*:

*[Milo M. Quaife, *The Kingdom of Saint James: A Narrative of the Mormons* (New Haven: Yale Univ. Press, 1930). —Ed.]

"... this letter had been on daily public exhibition something over four weeks at the time of the Conference at Florence.... And it has before and since then been exhibited in all the principal cities and many of the towns and villages from the Mississippi to the Atlantic, and from the Potomac and Ohio to the Canada boundary; and scattered in all that region, a hundred thousand witnesses are ready to bear testimony that the post stamp on my letter of appointment was red, not black.

"The letter, though badly worn, is yet {1855} preserved. Its identity can be proved by ten thousand witnesses. And it remains in my hands, to cry out 'false witness; perjury,' against all who say it has or had a black stamp. Look at it. It will answer for itself that the stamp is red, and not black. Go with me through the seventeen States, through which it has been exhibited ... and witnesses will rise up like an exhalation, in city, town and hamlet, to prove it the identical, original letter, with the same original red stamp on, {which Strang displayed at the Florence conference}."

The letter was preserved, and Strang's son, Charles, wrote concerning it from Lansing, Mich., July 18, 1882, "Some time ago I was permitted to see what purported to be the original letter of appointment...." He pointed out that a postscript to the letter, "P.S.—Write me soon and keep me advised of your progress from time to time," had not been included in any published version of the letter he had seen. (*Saints' Herald*, August 1, 1882.) Shortly after, the letter was again referred to in a story in the Detroit *Evening News*, August 22, 1882, which declared that Charles' brother, Clement, "visited Voree two years ago in search of documents and evidence relative to his father. While there, he succeeded in getting the original letter, with its postscript, written by Smith to Strang in June, 1844. This letter is now in the possession of one of the brothers and can be produced, if necessary, within 24 hours. He got it from one of the original Beaver Island members who had kept it since Strang's death. Its genuineness seems to be established by the red Nauvoo postmark, by its long continuance in the possession of the Beaver island member, by the firm belief of Strang's immediate followers, by the internal evidences of its being a Mormon document, and by its appearances of age." From the fact that the letter passed from Charles to his brother Clement and subsequently with the other Strang MSS passed from Clement to M. M. Quaife, presumably it came into Charles's possession about the time of these published accounts indeed, the *Evening News* story may be read as saying that it was in Charles's hands from about 1880.

When the genuineness of the letter was first impeached, objections centered around the character of the postmark: the cancellation was declared to be in black rather than red ink; and it was held to vary in size from the normal Nauvoo stamp. Objection was also made that no proper entry of the mailing of such a letter could be found in the register of "mails sent" from Nauvoo.

To such objections Strang replied in the most forcible terms that the postmark was and always had been red, as thousands could testify; that the postmark could be measured and found to vary not an iota from the size of the Nauvoo stamp, and that he had "caused the register to be examined, and under date of June 19th, 1844, the proper entry was found of such a letter to the distributing P. O. at Chicago, and the register at Burlington of 'mail received' contains the proper entry from Chicago. In the winter of 1845–6 these facts were publicly proclaimed in the Temple at Nauvoo by Moses Smith, Samuel Shaw, and others, and an examination of the registers called for. The next day crowds were at the P. O. to inspect the register. But, though the register of every other quarter from the establishment of that P. O., was safely there, that particular quarter was nowhere to be found. It has never since been produced."

To these remarks, published in *The Diamond*, Strang added in his *Prophetic Controversy*:

> ". . . the day previous to Moses Smith's speaking in the upper room of the Temple, which Jacob mentions, a large number of gentlemen examined the account of mails sent from the office at Nauvoo, and found that on the 19th of June, the date of the post mark on my letter of appointment, a considerable package of letters were mailed at Nauvoo, sent to the Chicago D. P. O., one of which was paid 18 3/4 cts.
>
> "Moses Smith stated this fact . . . and challenged the examination of the account by all who doubted. I run assured that several hundred went immediately from the Temple to the post office to make the examination, but were denied admission.
>
> "The next day it was found that the account of mails sent for the second quarter of the year, 1844, had been withdrawn from the files of the office, and for two years, at least, they were not returned. I presume they never have been. This fact is sufficiently significant.
>
> "But the evidence of the mailing of the letter could not be suppressed by this means. The account of mails received for distribution at Chicago D. P. O., credited this same package to Nauvoo; and the account of mails distributed charged this paid letter to Burlington, Wisconsin. So instead, the post office records showing that no such letter was sent, they show clearly that it was sent and received."

An additional point brought up by Strang concerned a peculiarity of the postmark or stamp, which "had a dot at the left of the top of the J in 'June,' which ought not to be there." He not only conceded this point but stood upon it:

> "So much stress was laid on the fact of the dot before the J in the mailing stamp, that a more thorough investigation was had than the subject called for, and the result was that every letter that could be found mailed at Nauvoo the 19th of June, had the same dot before the J. Here then sprung up an unlooked for evidence of the genuineness of the letter of appointment, the strongest which the human mind can conceive.
>
> "However corrupt the heart, or skillful the head, how would the forger know that on that on that particular day, for the first time since the office was established, a little splinter would get into the mailing stamp, and mark every letter with one dot which ought not to be there? He could not have known it. It was impossible. Thus the proof that this letter was duly mailed at Nauvoo, the 19th of June, 1844, is astounding; actually overwhelming.
>
> "The single fact of the dot, once the sole ground of impeachment of this letter of appointment, has thus established its genuineness by the most singularly strong combination of facts ever presented in human evidence."

Character of the Document

From the above it is seen that almost the whole controversy which raged around the letter hinged on the question of the postmark. The handwriting itself was never brought in question, either affirmatively or negatively, except as the letter was declared to be a forgery, and there was very little effort toward textual analysis. In his manuscript letter to the branches of the Church in the neighborhood of Ottawa, Ill., January 24, 1846 {in the present collection}, Brigham Young or Orson Hyde in Young's name argued that the letter was "a base and wicked forgery" on the basis of certain features of style and content: "He appeared and moon and stars went out.' This is a lie. 'The Earth dissolved in space.' *false.* The Earth did not, neither will it till the elements melt with fervent heat. He may say that it so appeared to him, but this would only show that a lie appeared to him and not the truth. 'I trod on air, and was borne on the wings of cherubims, I bowed my head to the Earth. After the Earth was dissolved and I stood on air.['] Mr. Strang has high strains of poetry here, but not a word of truth—all contradictory and false."

In the presence of the document itself, it is possible to make a fresh approach. It consists of two leaves, 31.2 × 19.6 cm., which for better preservation have at some time been bound in paper. A blank sheet of paper serves as a front cover, and the fourth page, originally bearing the address and postmark, has been pasted to marbled paper backing from which a circle has been cut to display the disputed postmark. The postmark thus displayed conforms in all respects to Strang's description of it; in red ink it is stamped "Nauvoo Ils. June 19." The red dot before the J, to which Strang made reference, is clearly seen: and there is an additional feature of the cancellation of which Strang made no mentions, the 'l' in "Ils" being upside down. The address has been pasted over, but the brown ink used soaked sufficiently into the paper that it may be made out from the other side by the employment of a mirror; it reads

Mr. James J. Strang
Burlington Racine Co.
Wisconsin

The letter also has the postscript to which Charles Strang referred in 1882.

A striking peculiarity of the document has passed without comment down to the present. The letter is written not in script but in hand print. Dr. Quaife concluded that the body of the letter, which runs to about 2⅔ pages, was in the hand of a clerk and the purported signature, "Joseph Smith," in a different hand. "To detect a forged signature alone," he observed in his *Kingdom of St. James*, "is obviously less easy than to detect an entire forged letter, and closer familiarity with Smith's handwriting than the writer can claim would be requisite to determine the issue in question." This, however, was much too hasty a judgment. Though the signature, "Joseph Smith," is written in ink which stands out more boldly than most of the text of letter, there is no doubt that both are in the same hand. The structure of every letter in the signature, with the single exception of the initial "J" is the same as that of the same letters in the body the letter, and the "J" itself differs only in a preliminary flourish from the lower case "j" employed in writing the name, "James J. Strang."

Another feature of the document is that the two leaves of which it is made up are distinctly different kinds of paper. The second leaf, bearing the signature on one side and the postmark and address on the verso, has a distinct vertical grain which is not found in the first leaf. This opens up the question whether an actual letter was not mailed Strang from Nauvoo on the indicated date, June 19, 1844, written upon a sheet fold to make four pages, with the first and second pages conveying the original letter the third page being left blank. In this event it is convincible that the first and second pages were destroyed, a new sheet supplied in their place, and a letter commenced upon those pages and carried to a conclusion and signed in on what was originally blank third page of the letter. Against this is the fact that the address, to the extent that it can be made out in reverse, and assuming that it was not written over the original address, is hand-printed like the body of the letter and very likely is in the same hand, though there are some differences, e.g., the character of the initial "J" employed for the name "James." The question may be raised whether the postmark has been "feathered" into the document, but it seems conclusive that the paper has the same grain as the leaf as a whole and in other respects appears to be identical with it.

That the entire letter appears in one hand is strongly indicative that it is a forgery. Joseph Smith was much addicted to the practice of dictating to clerks, so that ALS [autographed letter, signed] are uncommon, particularly dating from the turbulent final weeks of his life. Moreover, no document has ever come to light which he wrote in printed characters rather than in script; his characteristic sprawling hand is readily identifiable. It is also to be remarked that no other letter than the one under discussion, hand-printed rather than written in script, is known to have been written during the entire course of Mormon history, down to the death of Joseph Smith—or, indeed, after. The uniqueness of the letter of appointment in that respect makes it all the suspect. From the Nauvoo point of view, there is no reason why an exception should have been made in Strang's case; from Strang's point of view, there is every reason why the letter should have been hand-printed, the danger and difficulty of trying to imitate the hand-writing of Joseph Smith (assuming that a specimen was at hand) or any of his clerks in a letter which must extend to nearly three pages being manifest.

Though it seems entirely evident that no part of the famous letter is in Joseph Smith's own hand, especially the signature, which does not have the slightest resemblance to Joseph's own, only a specialist in disguised handwritings could undertake to establish whether the letter is in Strang's hand. It differs markedly from specimens of his handwriting on the present collection, but the differences between printed characters and script are a complicating factor. It must be recognized that Strang, with his interest in ciphers, three different examples of which occur in the collection, had the patience and ingenuity to have worked out an alphabet, a form to be followed in setting down each printed letter, deliberately different from his own normal handwriting, if he were so moved.

It is not here intended to go farther a field in analyzing the genuineness of the document, the controverted question whether it could have been discussed in councils unknown to the Twelve, and other such questions over which argument has raged. But it is proper to point out in reexamining Strang's account of how the letter came into his hands that he does not say explicitly that it was opened in the presence of others. It was brought to him by his partner from the Burlington post office, and it "became public the same evening."

Although not properly a part of the present discussion, which has an eye primarily to the physical characteristics of the document, it may be noted that its style is much more characteristics of Strang himself than of Joseph Smith. It is difficult to point to anything in Joseph Smith's proved writings having the sound of this passage from the letter: "I beheld a light in the heavens above and streams of bright light illuminated the firmament varied and beautiful as the rainbow, gentle, yet rapid as the fierce lightning. The Almighty came from his throne of rest. He clothed himself with light as with a garment. He appeared and moon and stars went out, the earth dissolved in space. I trod on air and was borne on wings of cherubims. . . ."

In Strang's own diary, however, also in the present collection, passages are found of strikingly similar character, notably his entry of March 20, 1833:

"How strangely beautiful this night. . . . The piercing red flashes of the noiseless and unseasonable lightning in the distant west; the solemn rolling of distant and eternal waters: the beautiful murmur of a pleasant waterfall in an adjacent brook: the more than usual warmth of the season moderated by a pleasant western breeze: the uncouth darkness which mantles the whole face of heaven enveils the throng of the Spirit of Nature, spangled over by the bright radiant stars of a western sky and broken only by the distant flashings of the deep tinged lightning: . . . I was alone: the works of nature and of art surrounded me: . . . I gazed upon them: I turned my eyes to their glimmering lights: they did not dazzle but bedimmed my eyes: I turned from them in unsatisfied silence: the beauty of the scene around me attract attracted my attention: the sun had hid her face beneath the western horizon and the moon was veiled in clouds far over the western waters: . . . beauties appeared at a distance: but like the rainbow they were beyond my reach: but the illusion drew me on: the darkness grew thicker, the sun appeared not, nor did the moon unveil her face, even the light of the stars dazzled my eyes to blindness, so long had I gazed on the shades around me. . . ."

Dale L. Morgan

Title Index

Subject Index

The Editor

Richard L. Saunders has studied and written on Mormonism, bibliography and print culture, Yellowstone National Park, and U.S. civil rights history since 1990. He previously published a biographical study of historian Dale L. Morgan's youth in *Dialogue: A Journal of Mormon Thought* (1995), a Morgan bibliography as *Eloquence from a Silent World* (Caramon Press, 1990), and collected the historian's writing on Native Americans in *Shoshonean Peoples and the Overland Trails* (Logan: Utah State Univ. Press, 2007). He remains at work on a biography of Dale L. Morgan.

Saunders currently holds a faculty appointment as an academic librarian and adjunct professor of history for the University of Tennessee-system campus at Martin, Tennessee. He earned graduate degrees in history and library science from Utah State University and Brigham Young University respectively, and is a doctoral candidate in history at the University of Memphis.

Kingdom in the West Series

The role of the Church of Jesus Christ of Latter-day Saints in the settlement of the American West has been a subject of controversy and fascination for 150 years. Kingdom in the West: The Mormons and the American Frontier explores the story of the Mormon people and their part in the wider history of the American West.

1. *The Pioneer Camp of the Saints: The 1846 and 1847 Mormon Trail Journals of Thomas Bullock,* edited by Will Bagley. 1997.
2. *Forgotten Kingdom: The Mormon Theocracy in the American West, 1847–1896,* by David L. Bigler. 1998.
3. *Scoundrel's Tale: The Samuel Brannan Papers,* edited by Bagley. 1999.
4. *Army of Israel: Mormon Battalion Narratives,* edited by Bigler and Bagley. 2000.
5. *Defending Zion: George Q. Cannon and the Mormon California Newspaper Wars of 1856–1857,* edited by Roger Ekins. 2002.
6. *Fort Limhi: The Mormon Adventure in Oregon Territory, 1855–1858,* edited by Bigler. 2003.
7. *Gold Rush Saints: California Mormons and the Great Rush for Riches,* edited by Kenneth N. Owens. 2004.
8. *On the Way to Somewhere Else: European Sojourners in the Mormon West, 1834–1930,* edited by Michael W. Homer. 2006.
9. *Doing the Works of Abraham: A Documentary History of Mormon Polygamy,* edited by B. Carmon Hardy. 2007.

10–11. *At Sword's Point, A Documentary History of the Utah War, 1857–1858,* edited by William MacKinnon. Two volumes, 2008 and 2013.

12. *Innocent Blood: Essential Narratives of the Mountain Meadows Massacre,* edited by Bigler and Bagley. 2009.
13. *Playing with Shadows: Voices of Dissent in the Mormon West,* edited by Polly Aird, Jeff Nichols, and Will Bagley.

Series subscriptions are welcomed. Manuscript proposals of a documentary nature may also be submitted. Address inquiries to the publisher:

The Arthur H. Clark Company
2800 Venture Drive
Norman, Oklahoma 73069-8218
(405) 325-5609